Historical Perspectives
in Industrial and Organizational
Psychology

Historical Perspectives in Industrial and Organizational Psychology

Editor

Laura L. Koppes
LK Associates
Lexington, Kentucky

Associate Editors

Paul W. Thayer
North Carolina State University

Andrew J. Vinchur
Lafayette College

Eduardo Salas
University of Central Florida

2007

LAWRENCE ERLBAUM ASSOCIATES, PUBLISHERS
Mahwah, New Jersey   London

Series in Applied Psychology

Edwin A. Fleishman, *George Mason University*
Jeanette N. Cleveland, *Pennsylvania State University*
Series Editors

Gregory Bedny and David Meister
The Russian Theory of Activity: Current Applications to Design and Learning

Winston Bennett, David Woehr, and Charles Lance
Performance Measurement: Current Perspectives and Future Challenges

Michael T. Barannick, Eduardo Salas, and Carolyn Prince
Team Performance Assessment and Measurement: Theory, Research, and Applications

Jeanette N. Cleveland, Margaret Stockdale, and Kevin R. Murphy
Women and Men in Organizations: Sex and Gender Issues at Work

Aaron Cohen
Multiple Commitments in the Workplace: An Integrative Approach

Russell Cropanzano
Justice in the Workplace: Approaching Fairness in Human Resource Management, Volume 1

Russell Cropanzano
Justice in the Workplace: From Theory to Practice, Volume 2

David Day, Stephen Zaccaro, and Stanley Halpin
Leader Development for Transforming Organizations

James E. Driskell and Eduardo Salas
Stress and Human Performance

Sidney A. Fine and Steven F. Cronshaw
Functional Job Analysis: A Foundation for Human Resources Management

Sidney A. Fine and Maury Getkate
Benchmark Tasks for Job Analysis: A Guide for Functional Job Analysis (FJA) Scales

J. Kevin Ford, Steve W. J. Kozlowski, Kurt Kraiger, Eduardo Salas, and Mark S. Teachout
Improving Training Effectiveness in Work Organizations

Jerald Greenberg
Organizational Behavior: The State of the Science, Second Edition

Uwe E. Kleinbeck, Hans-Henning Quast, Henk Thierry, and Hartmut Häcker
Work Motivation

Laura L. Koppes
Historical Perspectives in Industrial and Organizational Psychology

Ellen Kossek and Susan Lambert
Work and Life Integration: Organizational, Cultural, and Individual Perspectives

Martin I. Kurke and Ellen M. Scrivner
Police Psychology Into the 21st Century

Joel Lefkowitz
Ethics and Values in Industrial–Organizational Psychology

Manuel London
Job Feedback: Giving, Seeking, and Using Feedback for Performance Improvement

Copyright © 2007 by Lawrence Erlbaum Associates, Inc.

Lawrence Erlbaum Associates, Inc., Publishers
10 Industrial Avenue
Mahwah, New Jersey 07430
www.erlbaum.com

Cover design by Tomai Maridou

Additional cip information may be obtained by contacting the Library of Congress

Koppes, Laura L.
    Historical perspectives in industrial and organizational psychology / edited by
    Laura L. Koppes.
            p. cm.
    Includes bibliographical references and index.

ISBN 0-8058-4439-2 (cloth : alk. paper)

ISBN 0-8058-4440-6 (pbk. : alk. paper)

Books published by Lawrence Erlbaum Associates are printed on acid-free paper,
    and their bindings are chosen for strength and durability.

Printed in the United States of America
10 9 8 7 6 5 4 3 2 1

*This volume is dedicated to all individuals who advance
the science, practice, teaching, and service
of industrial and organizational psychology.*

Contents

Part VI: Reflections and Future

Part VII: Appendix

Series Foreword

Edwin A. Fleishman
George Mason University

Jeanette N. Cleveland
The Pennsylvania State University

Series Editors

There is a compelling need for innovative approaches to the solution of many pressing problems involving human relationships in today's society. Such approaches are more likely to be successful when they are based on sound research and applications. This Series in Applied Psychology offers publications that emphasize state-of-the-art research and its application to important issues of human behavior in a variety of social settings. The objective is to bridge both academic and applied interests.

The field of industrial and organizational (I–O)psychology is a notable example of the interplay of science and its application. This book is a major contribution to our understanding of the individuals, institutions, and events that shaped the development of this field over the past century. It represents the most comprehensive history of the development of industrial and organizational psychology available today. No comparable treatment exists. The Editor, Laura Koppes, has developed a major work that must be read by scientists, educators, practitioners, and others interested in improving our understanding of the world of work

The book is the product of an enormous collaborative effort, spanning several years, during which Dr. Koppes, enlisted leading authorities in the various sub fields of industrial and organizational psychology to write chapters, taking a fresh look at their discipline in tracing its historical perspective and in evaluating those events that had shaped the field as it exists today. Each of these eighteen chapters, written especially for this book, represents a unique and important contribution to the mosaic of activities that constitute the dynamic field we now call I–O psychology. The total effect is to provide an appreciation for the achievements and contributions of those who came before us and their roles in shaping the field, as we know it today.

Laura Koppes is especially well qualified to have initiated and taken on this effort. She was the official historian for the Society of Industrial and Organizational Psychology (SIOP) for five years, and more recently has served as the Editor of *The Industrial–Organizational Psychologist (TIP)*, the official journal of SIOP concerned with contemporary and historical professional issues in the field. As can be seen from her Preface to this volume, she has been able to persuade a wide range of senior colleagues in the field, many of whom have made significant and enduring contributions of their own to the history of I–O psychology, to review and provide comments and suggestions to chapter authors.

The book deals with the history of industrial and organizational psychology from multiple perspectives. The first chapters deal with the beginnings of the field, stemming from its roots in experimental psychology and psychophysics, and focus on its founders and their original ways of bringing their science into practice, developing new methodologies and applying these to the world of work and even to the solution of pressing national problems, such as the need for improved methods for screening of military conscripts for the Army. Also, while the book emphasizes historical development in the United States, it has an international perspective and includes a special chapter on the history of I–O psychology in other countries around the world.

Another important perspective provided throughout the book is the placement of various developments in industrial and organizational psychology within the particular historical societal, political, and cultural context that influenced the need and timeliness of these developments. Although the stress throughout the book includes considerable emphasis on scientific development and programmatic research, the book is full of applications in the world of work and on the practice of I–O psychology. And there is a chapter on the history of educational developments in the field, including evolution of the major university graduate programs and the recent migrations of I–O to other university departments.

The reader will learn about the history of major research centers that were developed within universities, and about the development of other research institutions that had particular impact on the history of I–O psychology and have helped shape the field. These include private research and consulting organizations, governmental research centers and research funding organizations, individuals and research departments within particular companies, and even informal groups of I–O psychologists. The special role of the military in fostering and supporting large scale, multi year research programs of direct relevance to I–O psychology is featured in a separate chapter, as well as in many other chapters in the book.

The field has benefited from the contributions of many related fields, including psychometrics, social psychology, engineering psychology, and consumer psychology. The reader may be surprised that consumer psychology was one of the earliest areas of applications to the world of work made by psychologists to the new field of industrial psychology. The special role of these and other related disciplines in the history of I–O psychology is shown throughout the book. Another feature of this book is the historical treatment of the professionalization of the field through the years: the organizations developed to represent I–O psychology and the changes over time, the relations with other organizations, the contributions of international organizations, the journals founded, the key individuals influential in these developments, and so on.

The useful Appendices in the book provide some special archival information about these and other developments. Additionally, there are extensive reference lists, including many to original and hard-to-locate books, articles, research reports, internal institutional documents and other identified sources of information. The book includes a comprehensive Name Index, not confined only to the many authors with cited publications, but inclusive of individuals who played other important roles in the history of I–O psychology (e.g., developers of consulting firms, founders and early editors of journals, founding university department chairpersons, heads of pioneering government agencies, previously "unsung" heroes who made key decisions to fund major programs, provide a few examples).

The volume editor's Preface describes much of the rationale for her organization of the chapters to cover these diverse topics and issues. A major section of the book is devoted to more intensive treatment of historical developments in areas that have become central to the field as we know it today. These chapters are written by individuals who know their way around in these areas and have been sensitive to historical developments in these sub fields of industrial and organizational psychology. Thus, separate chapters are devoted to historical developments in personnel selection, training, job analysis, performance assessment, motivation, organizational behavior, leadership, and team performance, in addition to the separate, chapters on consumer psychology and the human factors area, which have had a special role in the history of industrial psychology. The final chapter, written by John Campbell after reading all the chapters, provides a look at some unfinished tasks and challenges ahead, and offers some ways we might increase our contributions in the future.

Although the book has unique archival value, the chapter authors have provided their own perspectives on this history, as they were asked to do. These authors had to make choices about what to include and exclude and to decide what was important and what conclusions to reach. Arnold Toynbee, in his monumental *A Study of History,* points out that there is some inherent subjectivity and an evaluative nature in all attempts to write history. This is no less true of a history of industrial and organizational psychology. Some of the perspectives presented in these chapters may challenge different readers and provide a basis for discussion in the classroom and in other forums.

By and large, these authors have brought to life the people, places, and events that have shaped our field over its first hundred years. Today's computerized retrieval systems and databases, regardless of their increasing sophistication, do not fill in much of the texture and flavor of our history. The volume editor and authors have presented us with a lively and fascinating historical review of the many facets of industrial-organizational psychology and provided an indispensable contribution to the literature of this field.

Preface

"How did you become interested in history?" This is a question I've been asked several times. I've also been asked, "Why do you pursue this knowledge?" A colleague once told me that only retired scholars are interested in their discipline's history, and I'm not retired yet! The answers to these questions initially emerged during a "critical incident" that I remember as if it happened yesterday. In 1989, while teaching a brief history of industrial–organizational (I–O) psychology in an introductory course, I wrote on the board, "The Fathers of I–O Psychology," which was information from a standard I–O psychology textbook. I stopped midsentence and stared at those words. I turned to the class and asked if they noticed anything unusual or missing from these words. It was obvious to me! That day, I began a journey to search for our "mothers." I realized then that historical accounts of I–O psychology were incomplete.

I found that I enjoy historical research because I feel like a detective who is continuously searching for clues about the roles of women during the early years of I–O psychology. I perused many sources to find pieces of a larger puzzle and to discover a more complete history of the pioneers. I read at length the literature about women in psychology and about the history of applied psychology. I visited numerous archives and dug through paper collections. Much to my delight, I identified several women who were active contributors to the discipline during those early years. Why conduct this research? Historical research stimulates my intellectual curiosity. But more important, my understanding of I–O psychology is enriched, and I believe that all scholars, scientists, and practitioners benefit from historical investigations, regardless of career position.

I have thought about creating this volume for more than 10 years. I originally planned to collaborate with Jim Austin, an I–O psychologist who studies history, on a similar but different handbook. Whereas Jim chose other endeavors, I continued to believe that a book containing a history of I–O was needed. Until fairly recently, historical treatments of I–O psychology were scarce, and in fact, before this text, there was no one publication containing a collection of historical accounts. I finally decided to become serious about the idea, wrote a book prospectus, and submitted it to publishers. I certainly benefited from learning the history of I–O, and I only hoped that others could learn as well. I wake up at night pinching myself that this idea is now a reality!

This particular project has been interesting and challenging. Each of us has an idea, perception, or opinion about the events, individuals, and developments that constitutes a discipline's history. Although facts may exist, a historical account results from the interpretation of those facts. Thus, only one history does not exist. There were times while preparing this book that I thought I would never experience closure because reviewers continually offered numerous new suggestions of material to include. It really is impossible to include all those suggestions. Consequently, this book does not contain everything you always wanted to know about the history of I–O psychology. The original purpose, however, was not to create an exhaustive, comprehensive, and regimented coverage of I–O psychology history. My vision for this book was to provide creative and scholarly views of selected topics in I–O psychology so that readers may gain a more deep understanding of the discipline. I believe this vision has been realized, and after reading these historical perspectives, you will know why psychologists came to apply psychology to business and the workplace.

The authors of each chapter chose how to tell the stories of their topics. I encouraged them to be innovative and scholarly. Variation exists between the chapters with regard to time periods covered and the format or organizing schemes used. The time frame varies in each chapter because some authors chose to cover a comprehensive time period (e.g., 100 years), whereas others chose more in-depth coverage of a particular time period. Substantive topics emerged at various points, and some topics were part of the early history but then separated from I–O psychology; thus, the ending points in the chapters may not be the same. Each story has a different emphasis, which may or may not be the emphasis you would choose to tell. Furthermore, you may notice contradictions in the interpretations of events and activities. Some reviewers did not favor these inconsistencies; however, I believe the value of diverse historical perspectives is for the reader to learn different approaches for investigating events and developments.

The book's content is structured around substantive topics and not professional areas. It may appear that greater emphasis is placed on science rather than practice. This was not the intent at the outset, and in fact, the goal was to provide a balanced view of science and practice. The authors relied more heavily on science because better and more accessible documentation exists for scientific developments than practice. The authors were asked to consider the context of their topics and developments. Themes about various contextual forces influencing I–O psychology's evolution are apparent throughout the chapters. You also will notice some repetition in the material. Although attempts were made to minimize the duplication, it was necessary, in some cases, to repeat information to provide a background or context for the individual, event, or development. Several reviewers expressed concerns about repeating information; I think it indicates the importance of that particular occurrence in the history of I–O. I conducted a rudimentary content analysis of major developments to determine the extent of the repetition (see Table 0.1). One explanation for the results in Table 0.1 is that these activities occurred during the early years, and many chapters included an early history. Each of these topics is described in later chapters.

This volume is organized into 7 sections. The first section gives historical background information (precursors, individual contributors). The second section provides an overview of the evolution within the United States and outside the United States. Most of the book focuses on American developments; chapters 1, 2, and 4 offer insights about the history of I–O psychology outside the United States. To readers who take exception to the heavy emphasis on I–O psychology in the United States, I apologize. This emphasis is certainly not any indication of importance or value. After reading chapter 4, you will realize the history of I–O psychology is extensive in other countries, which warrants yet another book! The third section focuses on the influences of education, organizations, and the military in I–O history. The fourth section includes topics that prevailed during the early years, and the fifth section contains topics that emerged in later years. The sixth asks certain questions of the historical record in an attempt to

TABLE 0.1
The I–O Developments Described in Four or More Chapters

World War I: Committee on Classification of Personnel*

Münsterberg's 1913 text, Psychology and Industrial Efficiency

The Scott Company

Carnegie Institute of Technology

The Psychological Corporation

Viteles 1932 text, Industrial Psychology

McGregor's text, The Human Side of Enterprise

Army Alpha and Army Beta tests

First I–O PhD, Bruce Moore

Hawthorne Studies

Tavistock Institute

Viteles 1953 text, Motivation and Morale in Industry

*The most frequently mentioned topic.

infer how we might maximize our contributions in the future. Finally, a list of resources and a timeline of major developments primarily in the United States are located in the Appendix.

A history book is never complete. We tried to document to the best of our abilities important historical I–O related events, places, and findings. You may find some omissions, however. Although the chapters include themes and developments in specific content areas, other streams of activities were occurring in the evolution of I–O psychology, including the proliferation of journals and publications, the development of professional associations, the migration of psychologists to business (as well as from academic psychology departments to business departments), the influx of consultants, and the rise in grant research. These historical trends are mentioned throughout the text and may someday warrant their own books, but they are not the focus here. I and the book contributors believe that the historical scholarship presented in the 18 chapters is the beginning and not the end.

This book is directed toward contemporary and aspiring scholars of I–O psychology and related fields (history of psychology, human resource management, organizational behavior, public administration). Both scientists and practitioners will benefit from reading this text. I hope you will gain a deeper understanding and appreciation of I–O psychology. If, after reading any given chapter, you find yourself having a new insight, wanting to know more, or asking questions, then the author has been successful in stimulating your curiosity.

—Laura L. Koppes
Lexington, Kentucky

Acknowledgments

This endeavor is a result of support, encouragement, and insights from friends, family, and colleagues. I am forever grateful for benefiting from these individuals during my lifetime.

I appreciate the leadership provided by the associate editors. They were involved from the outset in formulating the vision of the book. They were responsible for overseeing the development of specific chapters, and they also read the entire text. Paul Thayer's sense of history, diligence in assisting authors, and belief in the importance of this book facilitated the completion of this project. Andy Vinchur provided wonderful insights and valuable feedback to authors and to me. Eduardo Salas supported the idea of this project from the beginning and gave his assistance and guidance throughout the process.

I am also indebted to all the chapter authors who contributed. This book would not exist without their patience and scholarly work. In addition to writing, several authors reviewed other chapters.

I can never thank enough two colleagues who read the first draft of the entire text and provided suggestions for chapters and the book as a whole. My long-time friend and colleague, David Devonis, a historian of psychology, offered detailed constructive feedback for each separate chapter and taught me a lot about writing history. Bill Siegfried, another good friend and colleague, gave numerous ideas to improve the book. In addition, Benjamin Schneider and Mary Tenopyr, at the request of Lawrence Erlbaum Associates (LEA), read the first draft in its entirety and provided constructive suggestions along with William H. Macey, Erich Prien, and Richard T. von Mayrhauser. I also thank Neal Schmitt, who gave tremendous encouragement from the beginning and provided feedback on multiple chapters.

I appreciate the assistance of several colleagues who served as reviewers at the request of myself or the associate editors, including Wally Borman, Clint Bowers, Shawn Burke, John Campbell, Bianco Falbo, Richard Guzzo, Ruth Kanfer, Ed Locke, Kevin Murphy, Frank Schmidt, Jeffrey Schippmann, Mel Sorcher, Scott Tannenbaum, Wayne Viney, Vic Vroom, Mike Zickar, and others mentioned throughout the chapters.

Numerous friends were involved in various stages of development, from the initial idea of conducting historical research to the actual printing of this book. Some taught me how to conduct historical research, others reviewed manuscripts (including references), and all provided moral support. I gratefully thank the following people: Jim Austin, Adrienne Bauer, Karen Budd, Ludy Benjamin, Kelly Carper, Eugene Cech, Pam Collins, Gary Cordner, Leslie Combs, Donald Freedheim, Jude Garnier, E. Alan Hartman, Frank Landy, Rosemary

Hays-Thomas, Susan McFadden, Jane Mitchell, Robert Mitchell, Paul Muchinsky, Anna Onkst, Jerry Palmer, Rose Perrine, Zuzana Pešáková, Wade Pickren, Doris Pierce, Kay Scarborough, Mike Sokal, Tanlee Taulbee, Darrell Van Orsdel, Lee Van Orsdel, Richard von Mayrhauser, and Elizabeth Wachtel.

A large portion of the work was completed while I was living in the Czech Republic as a U.S. Fulbright Scholar. I am grateful for the resources and support given by the University of Hradec Králové, especially from the Dean of the Faculty of Informatics and Management, Josef Hynek, the Department Head of Economics and Management, Ladislav Hájek, and the department secretary, Veronika Jašiková. I also appreciate my Czech family, who were gracious in opening their wonderful home, which provided a warm, comfortable, and inspirational place to live and work: The Vilím Family, Radan, Radana, and Dominik.

I enjoyed collaborating with the LEA Applied Psychology Series coeditors, Ed Fleishman and Jan Cleveland. I first approached Jan about my idea, and she responded with enthusiasm and provided a path to Lawrence Erlbaum Associates. Ed Fleishman has been a wonderful mentor throughout the entire process, giving much time, energy, and thought. He added much value to the scholarship, resulting from his experience and expertise. I especially appreciate the guidance, support, and patience of Lawrence Erlbaum Associates editor Anne Duffy.

Additionally, I would like to thank my mother, Dolores Koppes, and my sister, Kathy Ray, for believing in me and for their love, kindness, and encouragement. I also appreciate the support of my family, Elizabeth and Allison Bryan.

Finally, a special "thank you" goes to my husband, Kim Robert Bryan, who supported the creation and development of this book from beginning to end, through patience, humor, and perspective when they were needed most (as well as reading every word I wrote!).

Thanks to all my friends, family, and colleagues, who were interested, encouraging, and supportive.

About the Contributors

Editor

LAURA L. KOPPES is President of LK Associates, a human resources, organizational development, and leadership consulting firm. Before full-time consulting, she worked in higher education, with the most recent appointment as Associate Vice-President of institutional Effectiveness and Associate Professor of Industrial–Organizational (I–O) Psychology. As a U.S. Fulbright Scholar, she taught and conducted research at the University of Hradec Králové and University of Pardubice in the Czech Republic. Laura established the position of Historian for the Society for Industrial and Organizational Psychology (SIOP) and contributed to the preservation of SIOP's history and I–O psychology through international and national presentations, publications, and other documents. She served as membership chair on the Executive Committee of the Society for the History of Psychology (American Psychological Association Division 26). Her interests include leadership, organizational effectiveness, worklife, motivation, diversity, climate and culture (making great places to work), and history of I–O psychology. She is a member of SIOP and is currently the Editor of *TIP* (*The Industrial–Organizational Psychologist*). She is also a member of the American Psychological Association, American Psychological Society, the International Association for Applied Psychology, and the Society for Human Resources Management. She was recently appointed as Associate Editor of *The Psychologist-Manager Journal*. She earned her BS, MA, and PhD in I–O psychology from The Ohio State University.

Associate Editors

PAUL W. THAYER is Professor Emeritus of Psychology at North Carolina State University, where he was head of the department from 1977 to 1992. Before that, he worked at the Life Insurance Marketing and Research Association for 21 years, rising from training researcher to research vice-president to senior vice-president. He has been a consultant for many arms of federal and state governments and hundreds of companies in the United States and Canada. He is author or coauthor of dozens of articles on selection, training, job design, and related areas, and with McGehee wrote the classic text *Training in Business and Industry*. He is a fellow of the American Association for the Advancement of Science, the American Psychological Society, the American Psychological Association, and the Society for Industrial and Organizational Psychology.

He has held all elective offices of the Society for Industrial and Organizational Psychology, including president, and is recipient of its Distinguished Professional Contributions Award and Distinguished Service Contributions Award. He served 6 years as Treasurer of the American Psychological Society. He was on the editorial board of *Personnel Psychology* from 1967 to 1996 and is currently on its Book Review Board. He is President of the SIOP Foundation and serves on the Technical Advisory Board of ePredix, a consulting firm providing selection services on the net. He claims to be retired.

ANDREW J. VINCHUR is Head of the Psychology Department at Lafayette College. He received his undergraduate degree in psychology from Rutgers and his MS and PhD in industrial–organizational psychology from Memphis State University (now the University of Memphis). His research interests include employee selection, meta-analysis, measurement and prediction, and the history of psychology, especially the early history of industrial psychology.

EDUARDO SALAS is Trustee chair and Professor of Psychology at the University of Central Florida, where he also holds an appointment as program director for Human Systems Integration Research Department at the Institute for Simulation & Training. Previously, he was head of the Training Technology Development Branch of the Naval Air Warfare Center Training Systems Division for 15 years. He has coauthored more than 300 journal articles and book chapters and has coedited 15 books. He is on or has been on the editorial boards of *Journal of Applied Psychology, Personnel Psychology, Military Psychology, Applied Psychology: An International Journal, International Journal of Aviation Psychology, Group Dynamics,* and *Journal of Organizational Behavior* and is the past Editor of *Human Factors* journal. He is the past series editor for SIOP's Professional Practice Book Series and has served in numerous committees throughout the years. Dr. Salas is a fellow of the American Psychological Association (SIOP and Division 21), the Human Factors and Ergonomics Society. He received his PhD (1984) in industrial and organizational psychology from Old Dominion University.

Chapter Authors

MARIE-HÉLÈNE BUDWORTH is an Assistant Professor of Human Resource Management at York University in Toronto. She is a PhD candidate in organizational behavior and human resource management at the Rotman School of Management, University of Toronto, and holds a master's degree in counseling psychology. Her primary research interests are in the areas of motivation and training. Currently, she is working on a project with Aboriginal Canadians, training youth in interview skills to increase their self-efficacy and outcome expectancies. This work is being conducted with Gary P. Latham as part of an SSHRC grant.

C. SHAWN BURKE is a Research Associate at the University of Central Florida, Institute for Simulation and Training. Primary research interests include teams, team leadership, team adaptability, team training and measurement, and team effectiveness. In this vein, Dr. Burke has presented at 49 peer-reviewed conferences and has published 26 articles in scientific journals and books related to these topics. Current projects include investigating team adaptability and its corresponding measurement, issues related to multicultural team performance and the leadership of such teams, and the impact that stress has on team process and performance. Dr. Burke earned her doctorate in industrial and organizational psychology from George Mason University and is a member of the American Psychological Association, the Society for Industrial and Organizational Psychology, and Academy of Management. Dr. Burke serves as an ad hoc reviewer for the *Human Factors* journal and *Quality and Safety in Healthcare.*

JOHN P. CAMPBELL is Professor of Psychology at the University of Minnesota. He received his PhD from Minnesota in 1964. From 1964 to 1966 he was Assistant professor of Psychology at the University of California–Berkeley and has been at Minnesota since 1967. He was elected President of the APA division of industrial–organizational psychology in 1977. From 1974 to 1982 he served as Associate Editor and then Editor of the *Journal of Applied Psychology*. He authored the first *Annual Review of Psychology* chapter on organizational training (1971). From 1970 to 2001, he coauthored books including *Managerial Behavior, Performance and Effectiveness, Measurement Theory for the Behavioral Sciences, What to Study: Generating and Developing Research Questions, Productivity in Organizations,* and *Exploring the Limits of Personnel Selection and Classification.* From 1982 to 1994 he served as principal scientist for Project A. He was awarded the Society for Industrial–Organizational Psychology Distinguished Scientific Contribution Award in 1991. He is currently a consultant to the Occupational Information Network (O*NET) and is serving a 3-year term on the board of directors of APS.

EDITH DAVIDSON (BA, MBA, Jackson State University) is a senior doctoral student in the Department of Marketing and Logistics at the University of Tennessee. Her research interest is focused on audience response to ethnic stereotypes in various forms of marketing communication.

DAVID V. DAY received a BA degree in psychology from Baldwin-Wallace College (Berea, OH) and MA and PhD degrees in industrial–organizational psychology from the University of Akron. He is presently Professor of Psychology and Director of graduate training at the Pennsylvania State University and is also a fellow of the American Psychological Association. Dr. Day has published more than 50 journal articles and book chapters, many pertaining to the topics of personality, leadership, and leadership development. He serves on the editorial board of the *Journal of Applied Psychology, Journal of Management,* and *Personnel Psychology* and is an associate editor of *Leadership Quarterly.* Dr. Day also is the lead editor on a recent book, *Leader Development for Transforming Organizations* (Lawrence Erlbaum Associates, 2004). Beginning July 2006, Dr. Day will be a professor of organizational behavior at the Lee Kong Chian School of Business, Singapore Management University.

RENÉE E. DEROUIN is a doctoral student in the industrial and organizational psychology program at the University of Central Florida. She is the recipient of the Society for Industrial and Organizational Psychology's Robert J. Wherry Award for 2004. Her research interests include training, distance learning, learner control, mentoring, and stereotype threat, and her work appears in the *Journal of Management, Human Resource Management Journal, Research in Personnel and Human Resource Management, Advances in Human Performance and Cognitive Engineering Research,* and the *Handbook of Human Factors and Ergonomics Methods.*

JAMES L. (JIM) FARR received his PhD in industrial and organizational psychology from the University of Maryland. Since 1971 he has been on the faculty of the Pennsylvania State University, where he is currently Professor of Psychology. He has also been a visiting professor at the University of Sheffield, England, the University of Western Australia, and the Chinese University of Hong Kong. His primary research interests are in the areas of performance appraisal and feedback, personnel selection, the older worker, professional updating and obsolescence, and individual innovation in work settings. Dr. Farr is the author or coauthor of more than 70 publications in professional journals and books. He is the current editor of the journal *Human Performance* and has served on the editorial boards of numerous other professional journals. Active in a number of professional organizations, Dr. Farr was president of the Society for Industrial and Organizational Psychology (SIOP) in 1996–1997 and has served in a variety of other positions for SIOP. He has also been a member of the Council of Representatives of the American Psychological Association, serving from 1993 to 1996 and from 2002 through 2004, representing SIOP.

J. KEVIN FORD is a Professor of Psychology at Michigan State University. His major research interests involve improving training effectiveness through efforts to advance our understanding of training needs assessment, design, evaluation, and transfer. Dr. Ford also concentrates on building continuous learning and improvement orientations within organizations. He has published more than 50 articles and chapters. Currently, he serves on the editorial boards of the *Journal of Applied Psychology* and *Human Performance*. He is a coauthor with Dr. Irwin Goldstein of the fourth edition of the textbook *Training in Organizations* and coauthor with Dr. Joel Cutcher-Gershenfeld of the book *Valuable Disconnects in Organizational Learning Systems: Integrating Bold Visions and Harsh Realities*. He is an active consultant with private industry and the public sector on training, leadership, and organizational change issues. He is a fellow of the American Psychological Association and the Society of Industrial and Organizational Psychology. He received his BS in psychology from the University of Maryland and his MA and PhD in psychology from the Ohio State University. Further information about Kevin and his research and consulting activities can be found at http://www.io.psy.msu.edu/jkf.

PAUL A. GADE, a Vietnam-era Air Force veteran, is a Senior Research Psychologist and the Chief of the Organization and Personnel Resources Research Unit at the U.S. Army Research Institute for the Behavioral and Social Sciences. He received his BA in psychology from Hiram College and his MS and PhD in experimental psychology from Ohio University. He is a fellow of the Inter-University Seminar on Armed Forces and Society and the American Psychological Association and past president of the Association's Division of Military Psychology. Dr. Gade has published more than 50 book chapters, journal articles, magazine articles, and technical reports and is an associate editor of the journal *Military Psychology*.

ROBERT E. GIBBY, PhD (Bowling Green State University, 2004), is Manager of Organizational Research for Procter & Gamble in Cincinnati, OH. Dr. Gibby's work and research focus on the cross-cultural development and global delivery of advanced (e.g., computer adaptive) assessments, including biodata, personality, situational judgment, cognitive ability, and interviews. His historical research has focused on understanding the development and use of personality testing in industry from its inception. His work has been published in *Journal of Vocational Behavior* and *Organizational Research Methods*.

SCOTT HIGHHOUSE received his PhD in 1992 from the University of Missouri at St. Louis. He is a Professor and former director of the industrial–organizational area in the Department of Psychology, Bowling Green State University. Scott is associate editor of *Organizational Behavior and Human Decision Processes* and serves on the editorial boards of *Journal of Applied Psychology* and *Journal of Occupational and Organizational Psychology*. He is a member of the Society for Judgment and Decision Making and was named a fellow of the American Psychological Association and Society for Industrial and Organizational Psychology. Scott has published numerous studies on decision making in employment contexts. His research interests include organizational image and attraction, employee recruitment and selection, context effects on judgment and choice, and the history of applied psychology.

JOHN KANTOR, PhD, is an Associate Professor of Psychology at the California School of Organizational Studies at Alliant International University (AIU) in San Diego, California. He has been with United International University since 1992, before the merger of the two founding institutions of AIU. He received a BA (1972) from Alma White College, his MBA (1983) from Wichita State University, and a PhD (1988) in I–O psychology from the California School of Professional Psychology. He has taught organizational behavior, organizational development, performance appraisal, and numerous other courses for graduate and undergraduate students. Before joining USIU, he worked as a research psychologist for the U.S. Navy, developing and administering various organizational surveys as well as serving as consultant on organizational change efforts. He has presented the results of his research at national and international conferences as well as in various publications. His latest interest is identifying causes for unplanned absenteeism. He is a member of APA, SIOP, and Personnel Testing Council of Southern California.

KURT KRAIGER is a Professor of Psychology at Colorado State University. He is also Director of the university's Center for Organizational Excellence. He received his PhD in I–O psychology from The Ohio State University in 1983. He is a fellow in the Society for Industrial–Organizational Psychology. Dr. Kraiger has published and presented more than 100 papers, most on issues of training research and performance measurement. He has edited or coedited two books on training, including *Creating, Implementing, and Managing Effective Training and Development Systems in Organizations.* Dr. Kraiger has also consulted in the areas of training evaluation, needs assessment, and certification with a number of private organizations and government agencies.

SHAROLYN CONVERSE LANE is Assistant Department Head and undergraduate coordinator for the Department of Psychology at North Carolina State University, where she has been a member of the ergonomics faculty since 1988. She received her BA in psychology from the University of Texas at San Antonio (1984) and an MA in general psychology (1986) and a PhD in I–O psychology (1988) from Old Dominion University. She is a member of the editorial board of *Human Factors,* the flagship journal of the Human Factors and Ergonomics Society. Dr. Lane completed her PhD while serving as a NASA Graduate Research Fellow at the NASA Langley Research Center. Her work there focused on the creation and evaluation of flight displays to be used in complex tasks or environments. This interest has led her to the study of human memory organization, concept elicitation, and cognitive modeling. She has collaborated with government and industry on research that compares the difference in memory organization between novices and experts and tracks changes in memory organization as novices become practiced and eventually experts. The information gleaned from these studies has been used to develop intelligent computer systems and computer interfaces and to design programs to train cognitive skills.

GARY P. LATHAM is the Secretary of State Professor of Organizational Effectiveness in the Rotman School of Management at the University of Toronto, past president of the Canadian Psychological Association, and a fellow of the Academy of Management, American Psychological Association, American Psychological Society, Canadian Psychological Association, and Royal Society of Canada. He is the recipient of the Awards for Distinguished Contributions to Psychology as a Profession and as a Science from the Society for Industrial–Organizational Psychology. He is also the recipient of the Distinguished Scholar Practitioner Award from the Academy of Management and the Heneman Career Achievement Award from the Academy of Management Human Resource Division.

PAUL E. LEVY, PhD, is a Professor of Psychology, Chair of the Department of Psychology, and past program chair of the industrial–organizational psychology program at the University of Akron. Dr. Levy received his PhD in I–O psychology from Virginia Tech in 1989 and has been a faculty member at the University of Akron since that time. His consulting and research interests include performance appraisal, feedback, motivation, coaching, and organizational surveys/attitudes. He is the author of one textbook (*Industrial/Organizational Psychology: Understanding the Workplace,* second edition) and more than 40 refereed publications, with many appearing in the top journals in the field such as the *Journal of Applied Psychology, Organizational Behavior and Human Decision Processes*, and *Personnel Psychology*. He has nearly 15 years of consulting and grant-related experience. Dr. Levy has been married to Sylvia Chinn-Levy since 1988 and they have three wonderful young boys: Christopher (12), Sean (9), and Jared (6), who have very little interest in psychology but love playing sports, watching TV, and reading great books.

RODNEY L. LOWMAN currently serves as interim Provost and Vice President for Academic Affairs and a Professor at Alliant International University. He is a fellow of the American Psychological Association in two divisions, I–O psychology (14) and Consulting Psychology (13). Dr. Lowman has been a prolific contributor to the professional literature. The author or editor of seven books and monographs, he has to date published more than 70 publications of a scholarly nature. His books include *Handbook of Organizational Consulting Psychology, Counseling and Psychotherapy of Work Dysfunctions, The Clinical Practice of Career Assessment: Interests, Abilities, and Personality, Pre-Employment Screening: A Guide to Professional Practice,* and *The Ethical Practice of Psychology in Organizations*. Dr. Lowman is past president of the Society of Consulting Psychology. He has served on the American Psychological Association's Committee on Psychological Tests and Assessments and Ethics Committee and as chair of its Board of Professional Practice. He has also served as head of the Education and Training Committee of Division 13 (Consulting Psychology) of APA. He is past president of the Society of Psychologists in Management. He serves on the editorial boards of prestigious scholarly journals and was the editor of *The Psychologist-Manager Journal*. He received his PhD in psychology from Michigan State University, specializing in industrial–organizational and clinical psychology, and completed his clinical psychology internship at the Texas Research Institute of Mental Sciences.

HERBERT H. MEYER is an Emeritus Professor in the Department of Psychology at the University of South Florida. His doctoral degree with a major in industrial and organizational psychology was from the University of Michigan in 1949. He came to the University of South Florida in 1973 to assist in developing a new PhD program in I–O psychology. He directed that program in its first 12 years. Previously, he had worked as a consultant in the Industrial Division of the Psychological Corporation from 1950 to 1953 and as the director of a personnel research program in the corporate office of the General Electric Company from 1953 to 1973. He is a past president of SIOP.

ROBERT PERLOFF is Distinguished Service Professor Emeritus of Business Administration and of Psychology at the Joseph M. Katz Graduate School of Business, University of Pittsburgh, on whose faculty he has served since 1969. He received his PhD in quantitative psychology, under Herbert A. Toops and Robert J. Wherry, at Ohio State University in 1951. His publications and research have been in psychological measurement, consumer behavior, program evaluation, and evaluation research, and more recently general psychology and the history of psychology. He is the founding editor of *TIP*, the newsletter of SIOP. He has served as President (and Treasurer) of the American Psychological Association, American Psychological Foundation, Eastern Psychological Association, Evaluation Research Society, Division of Consumer Psychology of APA, Knowledge Utilization Society, Sigma Xi Chapter of the University of Pittsburgh, and Society of Psychologists in Management (SPIM). He is a member of Psi Chi, Sigma Xi, Beta Gamma Sigma, and Phi Beta Kappa. He is a fellow of the American Association for the Advancement of Science, APA, and APS. In 2000, he received the American Psychological Foundation's Gold Medal Award for Lifetime Achievement in Psychology in the Public Interest. Earlier he received SPIM's Distinguished Psychologist Award, the Distinguished Psychologist Award of the Pennsylvania Psychological Association, and the Greater Pittsburgh Psychological Association Legacy Award.

WADE PICKREN grew up with his 11 siblings in then-rural central Florida, where he roamed the forests and orange groves. He earned his PhD in the history of psychology with a minor in the history of science. He now serves as the American Psychological Association's Historian and Director of Archives. Wade's scholarly interests include the history of post–World War II American psychology, especially the history of psychology and ethnicity.

HEATHER A. PRIEST is currently a PhD candidate enrolled in the Applied Experimental and Human Factors Psychology PhD program at the University of Central Florida. Ms. Priest earned a BA in psychology and an MS in experimental psychology from Mississippi State University. She now works as a graduate research assistant at the Institute for Simulation and Training and has completed an internship at Aptima, Inc., doing research on culture, teams, and communication analysis. Ms. Priest's research interests include teams, training, performance, measurement, teams and technology, distributed teams, and medical human factors. She is currently doing research on teams and stress, leadership and culture, learning technologies, and teams and collaborative technologies. Ms. Priest has also presented at national and international conferences and has publications in numerous journals and books. She is a member of the American Psychological Association and the Human Factors and Ergonomics Society.

DAVID W. SCHUMANN (PhD, social psychology, University of Missouri) holds the William J. Taylor Professorship of Business in the Department of Marketing and Logistics at the University of Tennessee. His research interests center on issues concerning marketing communication with specific focus on belief structures, attitude formation, and persuasion. His work has appeared in numerous scientific journals in the areas of advertising, communications, consumer psychology, marketing, and social psychology. He is a past president of the Society for Consumer Psychology and is a fellow of the American Psychological Association.

DANA E. SIMS is a doctoral student of I–O psychology at the University of Central Florida. She received her master's in I–O psychology from the University of Central Florida in 2003 and is a student affiliate of the American Psychological Association, Society for Industrial Psychology, and Academy of Management. Currently, she works as a graduate research assistant at UCF's Institute for Simulation and Training on topics such as teamwork, team training, mentoring, patient safety, and trust in organizational settings. She has presented and published on these topics in local, national, and international conferences and other outlets. In addition, Ms. Sims has worked on various organizational development projects through internships with the U.S. Marine Corps in Okinawa, Japan and Booz, Allen, Hamilton Inc., in McLean, Virginia.

KEVIN C. STAGL is a doctoral candidate in the industrial and organizational psychology program at the University of Central Florida. Kevin is currently employed as a research assistant at UCF's Institute for Simulation and Training (IST). At IST his theoretical and empirical research addresses the full spectrum of multilevel team effectiveness issues with an emphasis on the promotion of team leadership, distributed team performance, and team adaptation. His research has been featured in dozens of scholarly outlets such as the *Organizational Frontiers Series, International Review of Industrial and Organizational Psychology, International En-*

cyclopedia of Ergonomics and Human Factors, and *Research in Multi-level Issues*. Prior to joining IST, Kevin spent 5 years as a member of an organizational consultancy. In his former role, Kevin worked with a global team of experts to provide clientele with customized human resource decision support strategies, systems, and solutions.

PETER WARR is Emeritus Professor in the Institute of Work Psychology at the University of Sheffield. He was previously director of the Social and Applied Psychology Unit at that university. The recipient of all three awards of the British Psychological Society for distinguished contributions to the development of the discipline, he is carrying out research into employee happiness and effectiveness, personality and work behavior, meeting processes, and aging in work settings.

MARK A. WILSON is an Associate Professor of Psychology and Coordinator of the doctoral program in I–O psychology at NC State University. He received a PhD in I–O psychology from The Ohio State University. While completing the PhD, he worked for Organizational Research and Development, Inc., on a project involving human resource planning, job analysis, managerial selection, performance appraisal, and compensation for a large insurance company under the direction of his advisor Milt Hakel. While working on the project he developed his interest in the integration of human resource systems and his love for fieldwork. In addition, he has always been interested in models of human job performance and research methods. He has consulted and conducted research in with a number of organizations including GlaxoSmithKline, U.S. Army Special Operations Command, the FBI, the Clorox Company, the North Carolina State Highway Patrol, and State Bureau of Investigation. He taught management at both Texas Tech University and Iowa State University. In 1999, he was made an honorary member of the U.S. Army Special Forces.

STEPHEN J. ZACCARO is a Professor of Psychology at George Mason University, Fairfax, Virginia. He has been studying, teaching, and consulting about leadership for about 20 years. He has written more than 90 articles, book chapters, and technical reports on leadership, group dynamics, team performance, and work attitudes. He has written a book titled *The Nature of Executive Leadership: A Conceptual and Empirical Analysis of Success* (2001) and coedited three other books, *Occupational Stress and Organizational Effectiveness* (1987), *The Nature of Organizational Leadership: Understanding the Performance Imperatives Confronting Today's Leaders* (2001), and *Leader Development for Transforming Organizations* (2004). He has also directed funded research projects in the areas of leadership training and development, leader adaptability, and executive leadership, and team performance.

MICHAEL J. ZICKAR, PhD (University of Illinois at Urbana–Champaign, 1997), is an Associate Professor of Industrial–Organizational Psychology at Bowling Green State University (BGSU), in Bowling Green, Ohio. Dr. Zickar's empirical research focuses on developing psychometric tools that help solve organizational staffing and training problems. His historical research has concentrated on the relationship between I–O psychologists and organized labor. His work has been published in *Journal of Applied Psychology, Applied Psychological Measurement, Personnel Psychology,* and *Journal of Vocational Behavior.*

I

The Beginning

This section contains two chapters that prepare the readers with background material for reading the entire volume.

In chapter 1, the authors begin by exploring precursors of industrial psychology. Following a discussion of these precursors and a look at the science of work in Europe, the authors provide an overview of the discipline's evolution. After describing the context for which an applied psychology emerged, the authors describe the period of establishment from 1890 to 1930 by addressing the following: Who was studying work? What were the problems and questions? What methods and techniques were used? These descriptions are based on an analyses of primary resources, historical accounts, and top-tier psychology journals during the early years. The authors then provide an overview of developments from 1930 through today.

The beginning of industrial psychology was a result of a confluence of external factors, and the establishment of the discipline was largely attributable to individual contributors who believed in the value of applying psychology to solve business problems. Therefore, chapter 2 is devoted to giving credit to those individual contributors before 1930. Although the authors recognize a plethora of pioneers throughout the evolution of industrial psychology, they concentrate on the early years to provide background for the other chapters. The chapter's focus is on biographical information; individual contributions are mentioned, but are also located in the later content chapters.

1

Industrial and Organizational Psychology: An Evolving Science and Practice

Laura L. Koppes
LK Associates

Wade Pickren
American Psychological Association

> *"If you would understand anything, observe its beginning and its development."*
> —Aristotle

The history of science, a well-established discipline of scholarly research, has existed for many years. George Sarton's (1927) classic *Introduction to the History of Science* represents that early work. The scholarship initially concentrated on the physical and biological sciences but now includes social and behavioral sciences. The interest in and awareness of the history of social and behavioral sciences can be partially attributed to Kuhn's pieces of 1962 and 1968. In addition, Watson's (1960) call for a history of psychology has elicited much scholarly work from both historians and psychologists. Jaynes (1973) presented an elegant logic for conducting historical research, "to discover the historical structure under the logical surface of science, to understand the present, to be relevant to real questions, to liberate ourselves from the persuasions of the fashions" (p. xi).

According to Wertheimer (1980), knowing and understanding psychology's history are important for several reasons: (a) History sets a current issue of study into a context of ongoing work, (b) knowing about past mistakes may prevent future errors, (c) research ideas may be gathered from the past, (d) history may help with solving current problems, (e) the past helps us see or forecast the future, (f) knowing the discipline's roots makes a scientist a more complete scholar, (g) history gives perspective and keeps current thinking straight, (h) great past ideas may be rediscovered, (i) history assists scientists in focusing on fundamental issues, and (j) the study of history provides a mean for integrating diverse areas and issues. Schultz and Schultz (2000) stated in their seminal history of psychology textbook: "Only by exploring psychology's origins and studying its development can we see clearly the nature of psychology today" (p. 2). We contend that these reasons are applicable to knowing the history of industrial and organizational (I–O) psychology.

Most historical accounts of I–O psychology describe various aspects of the discipline's evolution by identifying and recognizing individuals and events. For example, Morris Viteles

(1932) presented independent investigators whose work comprised the field during the early years. Leonard Ferguson's (1962–1965) series of pamphlets is viewed as a primary source for the early historical developments within the discipline. Other historical scholarship covering portions of the history have been completed and some historical treatments include a contextual analysis of the history (e.g., Baritz, 1960; Benjamin, 1997b; Capshew, 1999; Colarelli, 1998; Ferguson, 1952, 1961; Highhouse, 1999; Hilgard, 1987; Koppes, 1997, 2003; Landy, 1992, 1997; Napoli, 1981; Sokal, 1987; Stagner, 1981; van Strien, 1998). Katzell and Austin (1992) and, more recently, Koppes (2003) provide the most comprehensive historical overviews to include both developments and influences on those developments. To further advance the scholarship in the history of I–O psychology, historical perspectives of selected topics are presented in this volume.

OVERVIEW OF THIS BOOK

As noted in the Preface, the purpose of this volume is not to be a textbook or to provide an exhaustive, comprehensive, and regimented coverage of I–O psychology history. Rather, selected historical perspectives are told through the eyes of I–O psychologists and subject matter experts. Today, I–O psychologists "help develop strategies that build better organizations" and "contribute to an organization's success by improving the performance and well-being of its people" (Society for Industrial and Organizational Psychology, n.d.a). From reading the scholarship in this text, readers will know the answer to the following question: Why did psychologists come to apply psychology to businesses and in the workplace? Scientists, practitioners, teachers, students, and other scholars will gain a deeper understanding of the field's past so they have a fuller comprehension of the present, which enables them to look to the future. Readers will come to appreciate that I–O psychology is an evolving science and practice.

The historical perspectives in this book are structured around substantive topics and not professional areas. It may appear that greater emphasis is placed on science rather than practice. This was not the intent at the outset. The authors relied more heavily on science because better and more accessible documentation exists for scientific developments. In some cases, authors pulled information from other historical treatments; however, this volume is not an attempt to replicate those comprehensive treatments.

The selected historical perspectives of I–O psychology are organized into seven sections. The first section provides background information, including the beginning of I–O history and the roles of individual contributors (chaps. 1 and 2). The second section provides authors' perspectives of I–O in the United States (chap. 3) and in other countries (chap. 4).[1] The third section focuses on the role of education, organizations, and the military in the evolution of the field (chaps. 5–7). The fourth section includes historical perspectives on topics that prevailed during the early years: selection, job analysis, human factors, advertising, training, and performance appraisal (chaps. 8–13). The fifth section examines topics that emerged in later years, including organizational psychology, motivation, leadership, and work teams (chaps. 14–17). The sixth section presents insights and reflections on the past and thoughts for the future (chap. 18). Finally, a list of resources of a historical nature about I–O psychol-

---

[1]Most of the authors throughout this text focus on American developments, although chapters 1, 2, and 4 offer insights about the history of I–O psychology outside the United States. To readers who take exception to the heavy emphasis on the United States, the editor apologizes. This emphasis is certainly not any indication of importance or value. After reading chapter 4, the reader will realize that the history of I–O psychology is extensive in other countries, which warrants another book!

ogy is presented in the appendix, followed by a timeline of major developments primarily in the United States.

The authors had the liberty to decide how to tell the stories of their topics. Thus, variation exists in the time periods covered and the format or organizing schemes used within the chapters. Some authors cover a comprehensive time period (e.g., 100 years), and other authors provide in-depth coverage of a specific time period. The time periods may also differ in each chapter because the substantive topics began at various points in time. In addition, some topics are part of the early history but later separated from I–O psychology, so the ending points in the chapters may not be the same. The reader may also notice some contradictions in the perspectives of historical events and developments. Only one history may not exist because a history results from perception and interpretation of facts. The value of this diversity is that the reader can realize the many approaches to studying history. On the other hand, some repetition occurs across the chapters, with regard to significant events and individuals. Although attempts were made to minimize duplication of material, some information was repeated to provide the context of a specific development in I–O (see Preface). Several authors also provide lessons learned from examining the history of a particular topic.

To better understand a history, authors were asked to consider the context or climate (i.e., political, societal, economic) in which major developments occurred. Variation exists in authors' selection and presentation of contextual influences, however, themes are apparent throughout the chapters. Although the chapters include developments in specific content areas, other streams of activities were occurring throughout the evolution of I–O psychology, such as the explosion of publications, the development of professional associations, civilian efforts in the government sector, the migration of psychologists to business (as well as from academic psychology departments to business departments), and a rise in grant research. These activities are important for understanding history; however, there are no chapters specifically devoted to these and other trends because they are interspersed throughout the text. To begin the volume, this chapter presents a historical overview to give background and to set the stage for subsequent chapters.

PRECURSORS OF I–O PSYCHOLOGY

The establishment of an applied psychology in business organizations, then known as industrial psychology (now known as I–O psychology), did not occur in a vacuum. It evolved from a confluence of precursors and has roots in philosophy, psychology, science, and so forth (Koppes, 2003; Landy & Conte, 2004). Viteles (1932) noted economic (e.g., emphasis on efficiency), social (i.e., societal), and psychological (e.g., experimental psychology, study of individual differences) factors that served as the foundations of industrial psychology. Katzell and Austin (1992) and Koppes (2003) identified several cultural forces that came together at the turn of the 20th century in the United States, such as (a) advances in science, (b) the rise of Darwin's evolutionary theory, (c) the functionalist school of thought in psychology, (d) faith in capitalism and the Protestant work ethic, and (e) the growth of industrialism. Other influences affecting the beginnings of an applied psychology in business include the introduction of mass production, expansion of vertical and horizontal organizations, growth of mega corporations, rise of measurement and statistics, and new engineering developments. This background is complex, and a complete account is beyond the scope of this chapter. Thus, a few important precursors to the establishment of industrial psychology were selected and highlighted. In subsequent chapters, origins and contextual forces that influenced particular major developments are presented.

Philosophy: Humans and Natural Law

In the early modern period (14th and 15th centuries), a new worldview began to take shape. This new view sought to explicate the world in naturalistic terms. Humans were referred to as creatures of nature, as evidenced by the rise of the term *human nature*. All was to be explained in lawful terms. According to Viney and King (2003), naturalism is "the doctrine that scientific procedures and laws are applicable to all phenomena" (p. 171). The term *scientific naturalism* came to be used for this particular worldview by the end of the 19th century. The commercial society, which began in the early modern period, was part of this new view of human nature that arose among European elites. Commercial or economic humans were seen to act in terms of self-interest, and life was construed in terms of the exchange of goods. This development was controversial, of course, and many held that such a view was counter to religious piety and threatened established social hierarchies.

John Locke (1632–1704), the English philosopher, writing in the aftermath of the horrors of the religiously motivated English civil war, placed human thought and action on a nontheological basis meant to provide an orderly foundation for civil society. Locke posited that (a) all knowledge begins with sensory experience and (b) logical thinking guided by sensory experience was superior to religion as a basis for civil society. His emphasis was on human experience and human thought in this world, not on divinely implanted reason or innate moral instinct. As part of his rhetorical strategy, Locke consistently referred to the "mind" rather than the "soul." He further argued that property had its basis in natural law as well and that human affairs, including government and economics, could be understood in terms of the same causal natural laws. Locke was influenced by Francis Bacon (1561–1626), who has been called "a pioneer in the experimental, incremental approach to science" (Boorstin, 1992, p. 566). Consequently, Locke promoted an empirical psychology in which the study of the mind would be freed from the metaphysics of the soul (Durant, 1961). The work of Locke, although intensely debated at the time, helped shift the focus of philosophical and political debate to the natural world and facilitated the rise of a natural philosophy devoted to explaining and guiding human affairs on a naturalistic basis. (For a more in-depth discussion, see Pickren, 2000.)

In the 18th century, Adam Smith (1723–1790), economist and philosopher, wrote, in the natural law tradition, about matters of practical judgment in the material conditions of life. For Smith, and others of his generation, such judgment was part of moral philosophy. The substance of his writings was later called *economics*. For Smith, commercial society was the last step in the progress of civilization. However, he recognized the nature of commercial society and sought to provide moral guidance to men, especially young men, so that there would be a strong connection between personal virtue and the common good. Smith transcended earlier views that wealth was tied to holding workers' wages low by positing that wealth was created by the expenditure of labor (Smith, 1904). Rational self-interest was seen to guide individuals to save, with the money invested, allowing for further extensions of the division of labor. Thus, the social order and economic balance were based on the division of labor and the wealth created by savings. (For a recent discussion of these developments, see Firth, 2002.)

Adam Smith's analysis of the capitalist system of production formed the foundation of economic thought for those who succeeded him, including Karl Marx (1818–1883), a philosopher. As a young radical, Marx was committed to the view that freedom defines what it is to be human. His later socioeconomic analyses were efforts to explicate the struggle for freedom in a capitalist system that actively sought to create a false consciousness of freedom in its workers. In the production mode necessary for the Industrial Revolution, Marx (1867/1887) argued, the worker is alienated from himself because he does not have control over the means of production. Manufactory capitalism depends on the division of labor and the increased efficiency of production that such a division makes possible. At the same time, the church and the state lead the worker to embrace the false view that the exploitation of his labor is part of the natural order of the world. Only if workers owned the means of production and thus owned their identities could this false consciousness be destroyed and true freedom be found. This view helped fuel the tension between workers and owners and continued into the period when industrial psychology emerged.

Measurement and Function: Phrenology as a Useful Metric

With rapid population growth, the spread of the Industrial Revolution across Europe, and the need of nation–states to have greater control over the lives of their citizens, it became even more important to understand one's self and abilities in relation to other individuals. Science, or systematic knowledge, had increasing appeal. Whereas elites discussed these issues in terms of philosophy or physiology, members of the general population developed their own methods for understanding the social order and their place in it. It is in this context that we can understand the role of phrenology and "function" in industrial psychology.

At the end of the 18th century, Franz Josef Gall (1757–1828), anatomist and medical scientist, developed his "craniology" theory as a means to assign functions to definite brain sites. The theory was quickly elaborated, especially in England during the first half of the 19th century. According to Cooter (1984), a number of English pundits perceived that Gall had described the division of mental labor in the same way that Adam Smith had described a division of physical labor. Phrenology evolved from Gall's views and along with its close relative, physiognomy, developed as "sciences of human traits and differences." There was a long and popular tradition of interpreting the world and the actions of people in terms of their physical characteristics: Numerology, palmistry, and even the analysis of the blood or other bodily products were other popular practices.

During the Industrial Revolution it became especially important for factory managers to sort workers into hierarchies based on individual capabilities. For the workers, it was even more important to know where one stood in relationship to other workers. The systematic knowledge generated by phrenology promised greater self-understanding and perhaps competitive advantage in the new order of work. Although phrenological abilities were assumed to be inherited, it was thought that these abilities could be strengthened or weakened by exercise and effort.

The practicality of phrenology made it appealing. Its simplicity and anti-intellectual rejection of academic or highbrow philosophy attracted young workers, especially males, among the lower middle class and working class. At a deeper level, phrenology sought to rationalize the new social/labor structures and relations predicated on the division of labor in this time, thus making those structures and relations seem "natural." The emphasis on "function" at the heart of phrenology corresponded, as well, to the demands of labor functionality. Thus, Gall and his successors revealed the "natural" relation between the "mental" and the "manual" division of labor. Last, phrenology was employed "measurement." Abilities were measurable, not imputed from birth status or social class. All these assumptions legitimized the role of the individual as an entrepreneur of his or her own destiny and heightened awareness of "function."

Acceptance of phrenology in the United States was facilitated by the tenor of Jacksonian America, which emphasized the rise of the "common man." The suggestion that it was possible to change through education and exercise was consistent with the optimistic mood of the time. It favored the American ethos of self-help and self-improvement. Phrenologists' claims attracted paying clients who accepted phrenologists' authority and analyses. Through the mid 19th century, three types of counseling were made available in the United States, commonly dispensed by the itinerant phrenologists in towns and villages. Today, we would call these vocational guidance, marital counseling, and child-rearing advice. The fee for service for identifying abilities and proposing remediation served as a precursor for later applied psychology. Specifically, when turning to application, American psychologists found that they were working with a population prepared for their expertise and services due to the work of phrenologists. Although phrenology was an important precursor, it is no longer considered a valid approach. (For further discussion of phrenology, see Bakan, 1966; Sokal, 2001.)

As stated previously, the concept of "function" was central to phrenology. Later in the 19th century, Charles Darwin's theory of evolution by natural selection enhanced the role of function. Variations in function, Darwin (1809–1882), a scientist, argued, were key to adaptation and species change. Darwin's theory stands as a punctuation mark in the establishment of scientific naturalism as the dominant worldview.

Individual Differences

In his writings, Darwin firmly placed humans in the natural order, thus subject to natural law (Darwin, 1859). But his emphasis on the variability between and among species that underlies natural selection served as a foundation for a science of work (see Bowler, 1996, for more information).

In the hands of Darwin's cousin, Francis Galton (1822–1911), who was the founder of differential psychology, individual differences and their functions were seen as important to understanding and reforming society (see also chap. 3). Although the invidious assertions of Galton's eugenics had different effects in Britain (i.e., positive) and the United States (i.e., negative), eugenics found one expression in the rise of mental testing, especially intelligence testing. The notion that such tests could reveal unseen and underlying abilities and character traits was useful to the emergent field of industrial psychology (for more information on Galton, see Pearson, 1914–1930). Other chapters in this volume further explain individual differences as a precursor.

Experimentation—Energy and Fatigue: A European Science of Work

The establishment of industrial psychology in the United States was predated by a European science of work, which was shaped by physiology, nutrition, and fatigue in the second half of the 19th century. According to Rabinbach (1990), the first and second laws of thermodynamics, that energy can neither be increased nor destroyed and that the transfer of energy from one system to another is accompanied by a decrease in the amount of available energy (entropy), contributed to hopes that a science of work based on the energy present in human labor could be established.

European scientists, as they sought to create a science of work that would help maximize human resources, expanded the notion of energy into the idea of labor power. Scientist Hermann von Helmholtz (1821–1894) articulated the principle of the conservation of energy, giving rise to hopes that the energy present in human labor would prove sufficient to the demands for energy created by the Industrial Revolution. The locus of these hopes was the human body, conceptualized as a motor capable of converting "energy to mechanical work" (Rabinbach, 1990, p. 2). However, the discovery of "entropy" complicated these hopes. In the aftermath of these discoveries, the problem of fatigue became the focus of those who sought to develop a science of work in Europe.

In the 19th century, the laboratory became the primary place to search for truth, and the "experiment" became the primary method for finding truth. Angelo Mosso (1846–1910), a physiologist, approached the problem of fatigue through laboratory experimentation (1891/1906).

With the use of an ergograph, Mosso showed how the contraction time of a muscle grows as the muscle becomes fatigued, with the result that work potential is reduced. In this technique, Mosso borrowed from Wilhelm Wundt's (1832–1920) physiological psychology to graphically show a physiological process that had psychological implications. Wundt, a German psychologist often referred to as the founder of modern psychology, used the experimental method to control observations for objectively studying mind and behavior to distinguish psychology from philosophy in his Leipzeg University laboratory in Germany. (For additional information on Wundt, see Rieber & Robinson, 2001.) Two graduates of Wundt's doctoral program, James McKeen Cattell (1860–1944) and Hugo Münsterberg (1863–1916), relocated to the United States and initiated the application of psychology to solve industry problems. Cattell was first located at the University of Pennsylvania and then Columbia University. Münsterberg headed the psychological laboratories at Harvard University in 1892. (See chap. 2 in this text for more information about these individuals.)

Among those in Europe who pursued the psychological aspects of fatigue was Emil Kraepelin (1856–1926). A psychiatrist who also had trained with Wundt in psychology, Kraepelin examined both physical and mental fatigue. He first worked with schoolchildren measuring fatigability on various cognitive tasks (Kraepelin, 1896). Kraepelin's core construct, however, was work performance and he argued that there were few differences between mental and physical performance. Workers experienced fatigue in similar ways for both types of performance. He interpreted the results in terms of work curves, which showed a decline in production over time. In an explicit assent to the need for division of labor in manufactory capitalism, he then argued that individuals should be marked according to their capacity for work. The worker, specifically the worker's body, was a tool to be harmonized with the demands of industrial processes. Critical to this harmonization was the reduction of fatigue, because fatigue always decreased work performance. Kraepelin believed that his research showed that fatigue could be reduced through practice and training. He also sought to eliminate the subjective aspects of work, such as feelings of tiredness and satisfaction. Where Kraepelin sought to remove these subjective aspects from the study of fatigue, Münsterberg studied them. Beginning in Germany (and later at Harvard), Münsterberg's experimental research on labor, fatigue, and training was focused on improving the output of each worker in industry. He later wrote that work pauses and increases in free time would make workers more efficient and reduce accidents (Münsterberg, 1913).

Kraepelin had acknowledged that each worker's work productivity curves were unique but did not believe that other characteristics of the individual were important. Münsterberg, however, emphasized individual differences and claimed that understanding them was critical to a successful "psychotechnics." Psychotechnics, a term coined by the German psychologist Lewis William Stern (1871–1938, known for developing the concept of intelligence quotient [IQ]), was the scientific way to capture these differences to reduce fatigue, improve efficiency, and match the worker to the best situation. Each worker, Münsterberg wrote (1913), brought to the work situation a unique pattern of fatigability, training, intellectual capacity, attitude, and personality. Perhaps because Münsterberg spent the greater part of his professional life in the United States, he came to emphasize the importance of individual differences.

Although some of Münsterberg's early psychotechnical work was in America, this field developed more rapidly in Germany. There, the approach was to use either standard psychological laboratory apparatus, or modified versions of that apparatus, for various applications. This was in marked contrast to the development in the United States of paper-and-pencil tests for psychological applications (see van Drunen, 1997). The German applications of psychotechnics ranged widely. These included various applications for personnel tasks (van Drunen, 1997), training railroad engineers (see Hacker & Echterhoff, 1997), and selecting streetcar conductors, military drivers, and pilots during the first World War (see Hacker & Echterhoff, 1997; Gundlach, 1997; van Drunen, 1997).

There were clear early indicators that European psychologists were moving toward concerns of utility. They advocated that human relations were a part of all business activity, and were concerned with a broad range of factors that may influence the efficiency of workers. Such factors included methods of work, training, effects of rest periods and working conditions on productivity, monotony and fatigue, and selection (Baritz, 1960; Myers, 1929). Additional information about developments outside the United States can be found in chapter 4.

Shifts in American Society and Culture

As described throughout this volume, at the turn of the 19th and 20th centuries, American society experienced rapid changes including industrialization, immigration, a high birth rate, education reform, and urban growth. Dramatic technological changes, such as the development and widespread use of the telephone, telegraph, and typewriter, sped up communication. The expansion and standardization of railroads increased domestic travel. Furthermore, the Industrial Revolution created a prevailing faith in capitalism, at least among those who benefited from it. Businesses emphasized improving efficiency, increasing productivity, and decreasing costs through standardization and simplification (Koppes, 2003).

To manage such change, the generation of Americans known as Progressives wanted to make the American society a better and safer place to live and work (see also chap. 3 in this text), and to do so, they sought to rationalize society and rebuild the social order. Examples of such rational approaches included the standardization of goods and measures and the creation of new bureaucratic structures (e.g., the U.S. Food and Drug Administration) to ensure orderly change (Haber, 1964). This search for a new social order created a demand for new forms of expertise, that is, specific knowledge-based disciplinary experts such as political scientists, sociologists, or psychologists (Minton, 1988). In short, society turned to science for pragmatic solutions. The study of work was part of the desire to place all life on an orderly and scientific basis. A rational approach for studying work to address prevalent business objectives (i.e, efficiency, productivity, cost) was scientific management.

Scientific Management

The timing was right for industrial engineer Frederick Winslow Taylor's new systematic management approach, known as scientific management, in America because his ideas meshed with the prevalent Progressivism. Taylor, working as a manager, became interested in how to influence workers to be productive. He developed or recommended several procedures for increasing production, including the improvement of work methods and the provision of effective tools (Taylor, 1911). Taylor argued that his approach was "scientific" because he emphasized the use of the scientific method and empirical measurements to evaluate the effects of changes. In addition to Taylor, Frank and Lillian Gilbreth, also known as scientific management experts, used time and motion studies to investigate and design work to improve efficiency. (See chaps. 3, 8, 10, 12, and 15 for more information about scientific management.)

Although American psychologists initially embraced Taylor's ideas, his program eventually came under scrutiny for neglecting human welfare and the worker's well-being (Baritz, 1960; Viteles, 1932). Viteles (1932) even argued that "Taylor contributed little to the theory and procedures of psychology as applied in industry" (p. 16). The primary importance of Taylor's and the Gilbreths' work, however, may have been its programmatic nature and its suggestions of new possibilities for the study of industrial organization and productivity. Taylor and the Gilbreths provided a foundation for the scientific investigation of work behavior and the establishment of a precedent for scientists to enter organizations to carry out such investigations. Their work also provided the basis for the discipline of human factors (now known as ergonomics), which was considered to be part of early industrial psychology. As described in chapter 10, human factors and I–O psychology evolved into related but distinct entities.

The Birth of an Applied Psychology in the United States

From the previous discussion, one can surmise that an applied psychology was a direct legacy of phrenology (with the emphasis on function and measurement) and reflected Americans' demand for a "useful" science, such as psychology (James, 1892), indicative of the Progressive era. The birth of an applied psychology in business organizations in the United States is also linked to the inception of psychology as a scientific discipline at the end of the 19th century, the period described as the flowering of science (Roback, 1952). During this time, the intellectual climate consisted of positivism, materialism, and empiricism. Scholars, including psychologists, became interested in empirically investigating the mind and behavior using experiments and psychometric methods, as opposed to studying humans from a philosophical view (see Coon, 1993). Psychology laboratories were established in universities, and the American Psychological Association (APA) was founded in 1892 to formalize psychology as a discipline (see Pickren & Fowler, 2003).

Furthermore, a shift in the school of thought in psychology was observed during this time. An American functional psychology (functionalism), based on Darwinism and individual differences, was formulated, which challenged the pervading structuralism view in psychology because it emphasized how and why the mind adapts the individual to his or her environment (Angell, 1907) rather than focusing solely on the structure of the mind. This functional perspective provided a foundation for applying psychology, especially for the mental testing movement that took place at the turn of the 20th century, and served as a basis for studying work. Psychologists who preferred this view and applied psychology faced resistance from their contemporaries. According to O'Donnell (1979), E. B. Titchener (1867–1927), for example, proclaimed the distinction between pure and applied psychology illegitimate and "argued that psychology's rush toward technology threatened scientific overreach" (p. 290). (Titchener was a Wundt student and psychologist who helped establish experimental psychology in the United States.) (See chap. 3 for more information about the intellectual climate for the establishment of an industrial psychology; see also Hergenhahn, 1997, or Schultz & Schultz, 2000, for a lengthier discussion of the development of American psychology.)

During this period, institutional pressures to justify psychology departments and resources forced psychologists to popularize their science (Burnham, 1987). Buchner (1910) quoted Lightner Witmer (1867–1956; known as the father of clinical psychology), "The development of an applied psychology assures the future of psychology as a pure science, for in the final analysis the progress of psychology, as of every other science, will be determined by the value and amount of its contributions to the advancement of the human race" (p. 9). According to Camfield (1973), taking psychology beyond academic laboratories and conducting psychological research on practical applications in education, medicine, criminology, business, and industry were expressions of the intense desire of psychologists for social recognition and support.

Summary

The I–O psychology we know today has its roots in philosophy, measurement, the study of individual differences or differential psychology, experimental psychology, scientific management, functionalism, and so forth. Based on this foundation and pulled by the demands and expectations of industry and by an ever-changing society and economy, psychologists firmly established the economic objectives of industrial psychology. Several early psychologists trained in experimental psychology advocated that psychology could improve business and operations and argued that the results of industrial psychology would benefit workers as well as employers. In 1913, Hugo Münsterberg stated, "Our aim is to sketch the outlines of a new psychology which is to intermediate between the modern laboratory psychology and the problems of economics: the psychological experiment is systematically placed at the service of commerce and industry" (Münsterberg, 1913, p. 3). Later, Viteles (1932) stated that "industry can expect a definite return from an investigation and analysis of human behavior" (p. 18).

We turn now to an overview of developments in I–O psychology in the United States, with a focus on the years of establishment, 1885–1930.

DEVELOPMENTS IN I–O PSYCHOLOGY: AN OVERVIEW

Early Years: 1885–1930

The period of 1885–1930 was a time of establishment for today's industrial and organizational psychology (Austin, Scherbaum, & Mahlman, 2002). Thus, to set the stage for understanding the historical perspectives in this book, it is important to portray industrial psychology during this period. Who were the early applied psychologists? What questions and problems were examined? How were questions investigated and problems resolved? For purposes of this chapter, two strategies were used to answer these questions. One strategy was to examine original research, early literature reviews, textbooks, and other accounts of applied psychology history (i.e., Arthur & Benjamin, 1999; Baritz, 1960; Capshew, 1999; Ferguson, 1962–1965; Hilgard, 1987; Katzell & Austin, 1992; Koppes, 1997, 2003; Landy, 1992, 1997; Napoli, 1981; and Shimmin & van Strien, 1998). The second strategy entailed a review of articles published in leading psychology journals of the time as identified by Bruner and Allport (1940),[2,3] and in the *Journal of Applied Psychology* (founded in 1912), *Journal of Personnel Research* (founded in 1922, later known as *Personnel Journal*) and *Industrial Psychology Monthly*.

For each of the articles reviewed, a judgment was made about the relevance of the article to industrial psychology.[4] Some difficulty was experienced initially in determining relevance because there were many articles had potential for application to work. One could argue that any article studying psychological phenomena during this time is relevant. For example, Richardson's (1912 in *Pedagogical Seminary*) article entitled "The Learning Process in the Acquisition of Skill" was a review of the literature on favorable conditions for learning as well as mental conditions for learning attention, effort, and conscious and unconscious processes. The author did not mention the application of these concepts to business settings; however, one could ascertain the relevance of the material for training in organizations.

[2]We thank then graduate assistant and now organizational effectiveness consultant, Adrienne Bauer, and assistant professor Dr. Jerry K. Palmer, at Eastern Kentucky University, for their tremendous help conducting this research.

[3]The leading journals were examined for every fifth year of publication, beginning with articles published in 1887 and ending with 1927. In addition, every issue of the *Journal of Applied Psychology* was reviewed between 1917 and 1930. As the industrial psychology discipline evolved, other outlets for publishing research and applications emerged, including the *Journal of Personnel Research* (later known as *Personnel Journal*) and *Industrial Psychology Monthly*. For this chapter, every issue of the *Journal of Personnel Research* between 1922 ane 1930 was also reviewed. Book reviews, personal notes, letters to the editor, and other incidental material were not included in this analysis.

[4]Interrater agreement was initially 98%; we then discussed the articles for which we disagreed and jointly decided which articles to include in the description.

For purposes of this chapter, theoretical, discursive, or empirical contributions aimed primarily at the direct application of psychological principles to business and industry problems were identified. Of the 3,151 articles reviewed, 298 articles were found to be relevant to industrial psychology (10.6% of the sample articles). Four of 10 leading psychology journals included industrial psychology articles.[5] As expected, the majority of the articles sampled were published in the *Journal of Applied Psychology* (31%) and in the *Journal of Personnel Research* (66%). Table 1.1 shows the number of such articles per journal. This small percentage of articles focusing on industrial psychology topics in the leading psychology journals is understandable given that psychology was relatively new and was undergoing a transition and that industrial psychology as a scientific discipline was in its infancy. It is also true today, however, that a small percentage of articles focusing on I–O psychology are published in mainstream psychology journals.

Who Was Studying Work?

To those who are furthering industrial efficiency and happiness by studying human beings in the spirit and with the methods of science—may their numbers increase! (Laird, 1925, frontspiece)

Several historical accounts credit the start of an industrial psychology in the United States to Hugo Münsterberg. Described in several chapters throughout this text, his book, *Psychology and Industrial Efficiency* (1913), is frequently acknowledged as the most notable work for stimulating research and applications of psychology to business problems. This assertion may mask a more complex and interesting story. The application of psychology to business predated Münsterberg's work, however, by more than 15 years in America (see Walter D. Scott in chap. 2; and Arthur & Benjamin, 1999) and more than 25 years in Europe (see earlier section in this chapter, and Bringmann et al., 1997; Bingham, 1929; de Wolff & Shimmin, 1981; Shimmin & van Strien, 1998). Furthermore, we will demonstrate that numerous contributors were engaged in the science and practice of an applied psychology to business.

Moore and Hartmann (1931) noted that European countries, such as England and Germany, were further advanced in industrial psychology, and that U.S. psychology suffered from a lack

TABLE 1.1

Industrial Psychology Articles in 4 Leading Psychology Journals (1887–1927, every 5th year), in the *Journal of Applied Psychology* (1917–1930, every year), and in the *Journal of Personnel Research* (1922–1930, every year)

Journal	Total No. of Articles Reviewed in Each Journal	Relevant Industrial Psychology Articles, n (%)
Psychological Review	211	3 (1.4)
Pedagogical Seminary	247	2 (0.8)
Psychological Bulletin	449	1 (0.2)
Journal of Educational Psychology	261	4 (1.5)
Journal of Applied Psychology	548	92 (17)
Journal of Personnel Research	288	196 (68)

Note. Leading psychology journals as determined by Bruner and Allport (1940); 4 of 10 journals contained articles relevant to industrial psychology.

[5]Six journals did not contain any industrial psychology articles (*American Journal of Psychology, Journal of Abnormal and Social Psychology, Journal of Comparative Psychology, Journal of Experimental Psychology, Journal of General Psychology, Journal of Social Psychology*).

of centers organized around various research objectives. In England, Germany, Russia, Czecho-Slovakia (now known as the Czech Republic and Slovakia), Italy, and Japan, centers or institutes were established to study work (Bringmann, Lück, Miller, & Early, 1997; de Wolff & Shimmin, 1981; Shimmin & van Strien, 1998; Viteles, 1932). In contrast to industrial psychologists in Europe, industrial psychologists in the United States had to succeed without government sponsorship during the early years. Although several personnel research agencies conducted studies on employment management, industrial relations, and working conditions (Thompson, 1921), no coordinated effort existed. Thus, industrial psychology was not institutionalized but was a result of the work of independent investigators who were full-time teachers and researchers at universities (Viteles, 1932). Viteles (1932), specifically, recognized several individuals as proactive contributors, primarily university professors, to the development of industrial psychology in the United States. They include Walter Dill Scott at Northwestern, Walter Van Dyke Bingham at Carnegie Institute of Technology, Clarence Yoakum and Arthur Kornhauser at Chicago, Albert Poffenberger at Columbia, Harold Burtt at Ohio State University, and Fred Moss at George Washington University.

The authors and their affiliations of industrial psychology–related articles in four leading journals are listed in Table 1.2. Table 1.3 lists the authors with two or more contributions and their affiliations in the *Journal of Applied Psychology,* and Table 1.4 lists the authors with three or more contributions and their affiliations in the *Journal of Personnel Research.* The authors of well-known texts were also considered to be major contributors (e.g., Burtt, 1926; Hollingworth & Poffenberger, 1917; Laird, 1925; Link, 1919; Münsterberg, 1913; Poffenberger, 1928; Scott, 1911a; see Table 1.5).

The prevalence of psychologists housed in academic institutions is apparent by examining authors' affiliations. For the leading psychology journals listed in Table 1.2, the affiliation of one author is unknown and the other authors were in academic settings. In the *Journal of Applied Psychology,* the affiliation of one author was not listed; all the other authors were in academic settings. And in the *Journal of Personnel Research,* the affiliation of one author is not listed, four authors were in industry, and the other nine authors were in academic settings.

TABLE 1.2
Names and Affiliations of Authors of Industrial Psychology Articles in Four Leading Journals (1887–1927, Every Fifth Year)

Journal	Author	Affiliation
Journal of Educational Psychology	B.F. Pittinger	University of Texas
	B. W. Robinson	Bureau of Personnel Research; Carnegie Institute of Technology
	E. K. Strong	Stanford University
	W. F. Book	Indiana University\
Psychological Review	H. L. Hollingworth	Columbia University
	E. L. Thorndike	Columbia University
	D. Starch	University of Wisconsin
	T. E. Ash	Ohio State University
Pedagogical Seminary	H. A. Sprague	State Normal School, Newark, NJ
	C. A. Osborne	No affiliation listed
Psychological Bulletin	A. W. Kornhauser	University of Chicago

Note. Leading psychology journals as determined by Bruner and Allport (1940).

TABLE 1.3
Names and Affiliations of Authors in *Journal of Applied Psychology*
(1917–1930) With Two or More Contributions

Author	Number of Articles	Affiliation
A. T. Poffenberger	7	Columbia University
H. E. Burtt	5	Ohio State University
E. K. Strong, Jr.	5	Stanford University
M. A. Bills[a]	4	Carnegie Institute of Technology; Life Insurance Sales Research
M. Freyd	3	Carnegie Institute of Technology; University of Pennsylvania; Personnel Research Federation
H. D. Kitson	3	Indiana University
A. J. Snow	3	Northwestern University
H. A. Toops	3	Ohio State University
W. V. Bingham	2	Carnegie Institute of Technology
E. O. Bregman[a]	2	Columbia University
J. Crosby Chapman	2	Western Reserve University
D. Fryer	2	New York University
H. C. Link	2	No affiliation listed
H. R. Nixon	2	Columbia University
R. Pintner	2	Ohio State University
M. J. Ream	2	Carnegie Institute of Technology; Mutual Benefit Life Insurance Co.
R. Schultz	2	Columbia University
E. L. Thorndike	2	Columbia University
L. L Thurstone	2	Carnegie Institute of Technology Pennsylvania
M. S. Viteles	2	University of Pennsylvania
C. J. Warden	2	University of Wisconsin

[a]Women psychologists full-time in industry.

Some academic psychologists pursued part-time consulting work to supplement their meager academic salaries, whereas others sought applied work because the number of psychology doctoral graduates rapidly outgrew the number of academic positions. Cattell (1946) estimated that as late as 1917, 16 of the more than 300 members of APA were working primarily in the various applications of psychology. Although individuals were practicing industrial psychology from 1913 through 1917, Napoli (1981) noted that no full-time industrial psychologists were identified then because their work was not labeled "industrial psychology."

After the war and during the 1920s, euphoria and prosperity swept the United States, and the gross national product rose significantly (Cashman, 1989). This resulted in a growth of employment, which provided opportunities for industrial psychologists as full-time employees or consultants in industry (Arthur & Benjamin, 1999; Katzell & Austin, 1992). Companies created personnel departments to centralize hiring and job placement activities. According to Arthur and Benjamin (1999),

TABLE 1.4

Authors and Affiliations in *Journal of Personnel Research* With Three or More Contributions (1922–1930)

Author	Number of Articles	Affiliation
A. W. Kornhauser	9	University of Chicago
M. S. Viteles	7	University of Pennsylvania
M. Freyd	6	University of Pennsylvania; Personnel Research Federation
H. D. Kitson	6	Indiana University; Columbia University
W. H. Woodruff	5	Assistant Personnel Director, NJ; Ingersoll Rand Co.
M. A. Bills[a]	4	Carnegie Institute of Technology; Aetna Life Insurance Co.
D. G. Paterson	4	University of Minnesota
S. M. Shellow[a]	4	Milwaukee Electric Railway & Light Co.
E. K. Strong, Jr.	4	Carnegie Institute of Technology; Stanford University
J. H. Greene	3	Research Bureau for Retail Training, CIT
E. Mayo	3	University of Queensland; University of Pennsylvania
F. J. Meine	3	Chicago (no affiliation listed)
M. Pond[a]	3	Scoville Manufacturing Co.
L. L. Thurstone	3	Personnel Research Federation; Bureau of Public Personnel Administration, Washington, DC.

[a]Women psychologists full-time in industry.

TABLE 1.5

Early Texts on Industrial Psychology

Title of Text	Date	Author
Increasing Human Efficiency in Business	1911	W. D. Scott
Psychology and Industrial Efficiency	1913	H. Münsterberg
Applied Psychology	1917	H. L. Hollingworth & A. T. Poffenberger
Employment Psychology	1919	H. C. Link
The Psychology of Industry	1921	J. Drever
Industrial Psychology and the Production of Wealth	1925	H. D. Harrison
The Psychology of Selecting Men	1925	D. A. Laird
Principles of Employment Psychology	1926	H. E. Burtt
Applied Psychology: Its Principles and Methods	1928	A. T. Poffenberger
Industrial Psychology	1932	M. S. Viteles
Psychology in Business and Industry	1935	J. G. Jenkins

These departments typically included psychologists, either as consultants or full-time employees, and emphasized (1) job analyses to identify the individual components of all jobs, and (2) testing of current and potential employees to make appropriate matches between work skills and job requirements. (p. 101)

Positions in business and industry provided alternatives for women psychologists because of limited opportunities in academe (Koppes, 1997).

Katzell and Austin (1992) estimated that the total number of full-time psychologists in industry was approximately 50 by the end of the 1920s, despite an eventual decline of psychological applications in the latter part of the 1920s (See chap. 8; Hale, 1992; Sokal, 1984). Between 1916 and 1938, the number of APA members in teaching positions increased fivefold, from 233 to 1,299; however, the number of members in applied psychology positions grew from 24 to 694 (Finch & Odoroff, 1939). Table 1.6 contains examples of companies that employed psychologists, part-time or full-time, between 1910 and 1930. In sum, most historical accounts attribute early developments to only a few individuals; however, a plethora of contributors are apparent from reviewing Tables 1.2, 1.3, 1.4, and 1.5 and from reading the chapters throughout this text.

What Questions or Problems Were Investigated?

The psychologist has entered the factory with his apparatus, his tests and his notebook, and has begun to apply to industry the new and highly specialized knowledge of human behaviour and the functioning of the mind of man which the new psychology has made available … this new knowledge will revolutionise man's economic life. It promises to increase production without increas-

TABLE 1.6
Companies That Employed Psychologists, Part-Time or Full-Time, Between 1910 and 1930

Name of Company
Aetna Life Insurance
American Tobacco Company
Boston Elevated Company
Clothcraft Shops of the Joseph and Feiss Company
Kaufman Department Store
Loose-Wiles Biscuit Company
Macy's Department Store
Metropolitan Life
Milwaukee Railway Electric Company
National Lead Company
Procter & Gamble
Scoville Works
U.S. Civil Service Commission
U.S. Rubber Company
Western Electric
Winchester Repeating Arms Company

Note. Sources of this information: Baritz, 1960; Katzell & Austin, 1992; Viteles, 1932, as well as original sources.

ing effort and while decreasing discontent and unhappiness. By so doing it will promote welfare and enrich life not for any section of the people alone, but for the community in general. (Harrison, 1925, pp. 4–6)

In the beginning, industrial psychology was labeled *economic psychology* (Münsterberg, 1914), *business psychology* (Kingsbury, 1923; Münsterberg, 1917), or *employment psychology* (Burtt, 1926; Laird, 1925). The term *industrial psychology* was used infrequently before World War I and became more common after the war (Viteles, 1932).[6] Viteles (1932), perhaps, was the most influential in stimulating the use of the term *industrial psychology*.

Kingsbury (1923) noted that business psychology or psychotechnology is "interested in acquiring facts and principles only in so far as they can be turned directly to account in the solution of practical problems, in industry, selling, teaching, or other fields of human behavior" (p. 5). Laird (1925) defined industrial psychology as "the application of the methods of science to the human side of industry" (p. 10). Poffenberger (1928) further distinguished between vocational psychology, industrial psychology, and business psychology.[7] According to him, vocational psychology entails the selection and guidance of individuals into the appropriate occupations. Industrial psychology includes work activities with regard to all the variables that maximize return for the labor expended. Business psychology consists of psychological problems that result from the distribution of products to the consumer and meeting the consumers' needs, desires, and their satisfaction.

Tables 1.7 and 1.8 list topics found to be related to industrial psychology in 4 leading psychology journals, the *Journal of Applied Psychology,* and in the *Journal of Personnel Research*. Fewer topics were relevant to industrial psychology in the leading psychology journals, and more varied topics were in the *Journal of Personnel Research*. Examples of article titles in *Industrial Psychology Monthly,* which was published primarily for business leaders, include, "Does Leadership or the Machine Determine Production?" "Four Practical Tests of Personality Expression in Business," "Personnel Factors and Turnover of Sales Clerks," "Job Analysis in the Textile Industry," and "Transportation Safety by Selection and Training." Reviewing the contents of important texts of the time also reveals pertinent topics and further defines the discipline in the early years (see Tables 1.9–1.14).

In 1911, Scott described the application of psychology to business in his book *Influencing Men in Business* (1911b). In reference to his book, Scott stated,

> The purpose of the present work is to set forth certain facts and principles of psychology which are established, and which have a most direct and practical bearing upon the problem of influencing men under conditions existing in the business world. Typical examples of definite business problems for psychological solution are such as the following: (a) How may I induce my employees to improve the quantity and quality of their work? (b) How may I induce particular men to enter my employ? (c) How may I sell you my line of goods by personal appeal? (d) How may I induce you to purchase the same line of goods if I confine my selling plan to printed advertising? (pp. 11–12)

Later, Kingsbury (1923) identified two primary topics of industrial psychology: employer–employee relations (selection and maintenance), and psychology of the consumer. Viteles (1926), in a summary of the literature, noted that some research was conducted on fatigue, vo-

---

[6]According to Muchinsky (2003), *industrial psychology* was used for the first time in an article by Bryan (1904). It appears that this was a typographical error, however. Bryan was referring to a quote he had written before (Bryan & Harter, 1899) in which he called for more research in *individual* psychology. Bryan wrote *industrial* psychology instead and apparently did not notice the mistake.

[7]Poffenberger noted, however, that the distinction is an arbitrary one.

TABLE 1.7

Industrial Psychology-Related Topics in Four Early Leading Psychology Journals Listed in Table 1.1, 1887–1927, and in *Journal of Applied Psychology*, 1917–1930 ($N = 102$)

Topic	Number of Articles
Selection/placement	39
Advertising[a]	19
Performance	11
Vocational guidance	11
Ratings/performance evaluation	5
Miscellaneous[b]	4
Vocational tests	3
Classification	2
Training	2
Efficiency	1
Human relations in industry	1
Job analysis	1
Turnover	1
Unemployment	1
Work environment	1

[a]Research investigating psychological phenomena (e.g., recall, attention) were included; research investigating characteristics of advertisements were not included.
[b]These discussion articles review various topics of industrial psychology without emphasis on any particular issue.

cational guidance, training, accidents, monotony, and analysis of methods of work; however, he stated, "The application of psychology in industry in this country has been practically limited to vocational selection and merchandizing, although the possibilities for more extended research are recognized" (pp. 657–658). One of the earliest examples of research was a study with professional telegraphers examining the learning curves of their skills acquisition in sending and receiving Morse code (Bryan & Harter, 1897).

An emphasis on productivity during this period influenced organization leaders to explore ways to advertise, sell, and distribute their goods. As early as 1895, E. W. Scripture, professor of psychology at Yale University, noted in his book *Thinking, Feeling, Doing* (Scripture, 1895) that advertisers could benefit from psychology with regard to attention and memory. In 1901, a young psychologist, W. D. Scott, gave a presentation about the value of psychology for advertising to the Agate Club, a group of business leaders in Chicago, and then published his ideas in a book, *The Theory of Advertising* in 1903 (see also chap. 2). Although advertising was viewed as being part of early industrial psychology, it eventually developed into a separate discipline, now known as consumer psychology. A historical perspective on psychology applied to consumer response is described in chapter 11.

During the late 19th and early 20th centuries, the appearance of capitalism and an emphasis on efficiency forced companies to determine how to hire the most qualified employees. Also, a developing specialization of the labor market required a system in which individual differences in ability could be identified (Minton, 1988). Most authors agree that personnel selection and placement issues "dominated industrial psychology at its inception" (Austin & Villanova, 1992, p. 839; Katzell & Austin, 1992; Koppes, 2003; Kornhauser, 1922; Scott, 1920). Specific

TABLE 1.8
Topics in *Journal of Personnel Research* (1922–1930)

Topic Examined	Number of Appearances in Articles
Selection/placement	52
Training	17
Turnover/absenteeism/attendance/tardiness	15
Vocational tests/predictors	13
Vocational guidance	13
Performance	11
Rating scales/performance evaluation	10
Vocational interests	8
Safety/accidents	7
Industrial psychology as a field	6
Personnel research	6
Boredom/monotony/feelings	3
Job classification	3
Performance/stability	3
Leadership	3
Fatigue	2
Job analysis	2
Job requirements	2
Laws	2
Promotion/transfers	2
Surveys	2
Wages	2
Work environment	2
Benefits	1
Employability	1
Groups	1
Health	1
Orientation	1
Recruiting	1
Termination	1
Validation	1

Note. Some articles covered more than one topic, thus, the total number in this table is greater than the total number of articles reviewed.

issues included job analysis, use of tests and other predictors, and validation (e.g., Freyd, 1923–1924; Kelley, 1919; Kornhauser & Kingsbury, 1924; Link, 1919, 1920). Münsterberg demonstrated the validity of his psychotechnics with the development of an aptitude test for streetcar operators in 1910 (Luck & Bringmann, 1997).

TABLE 1.9
Increasing Human Efficiency in Business (Scott, 1911)

Table of Contents

The possibility of increasing human efficiency

Imitation as a means of increasing human efficiency

Competition as a means of increasing human efficiency

Loyalty as a means of increasing human efficiency

Concentration as a means of increasing human efficiency

Wages as a means of increasing human efficiency

Pleasure as a means of increasing human efficiency

The love of the game and efficiency

Relaxation as a means of increasing human efficiency

The rate of improvement in efficiency

Practice plus theory

Making experience as asset: judgment formation

Capitalizing experience: habit formation

TABLE 1.10
Applied Psychology (Hollingworth & Poffenberger, 1917)

Table of Contents

Efficiency and applied psychology

Influence of heredity upon achievement

Family inheritance

Efficiency and learning

Influence of sex and age on efficiency

Environmental conditions

Work, rest, fatigue and sleep

Drugs and stimulants

Methods of applying psychology in special fields

Psychology and the executive

Psychology in the workshop

Psychology and the market

Psychology and the law

Psychology for the social worker

Psychology and medicine

Psychology and education

The future of applied psychology

TABLE 1.11
Psychology and Industrial Efficiency (Münsterberg, 1913)

Table of Contents

Introduction

1. Applied psychology
2. The demands of practical life
3. Means and ends

I. The best possible man

4. Vocation and fitness
5. Scientific vocational guidance
6. Scientific management
7. The methods of experimental psychology
8. Experiments in the interest of electric railway service
9. Experiments in the interest of ship service
10. Experiments in the interest of telephone service
11. Contributions from men of affairs
12. Individuals and groups

II. The best possible work

13. Learning and training
14. The adjustment of technical to physical conditions
15. The economy of movement
16. Experiments on the problem of monotony
17. Attention and fatigue
18. Physical and social influences on the working power

III. The best possible effect

19. The satisfaction of economic demands
20. Experiments in the effects of advertisements
21. The effect of display
22. Experiments with reference to illegal imitation
23. Buying and selling
24. The future development of economic psychology

As discussed throughout this text, an early endeavor for applying psychology (including selection and placement) occurred when the United States declared war (World War I) on Germany in April 1917. A psychology committee of the National Resource Council was formed to evaluate a psychological examining program for recruits, and the Committee on Classification of Personnel was also created to aid the Army in the selection of officers (von Mayrhauser, 1987). (See chaps. 7 and 8 in this text for more information about the influence of the military on the evolution of I–O psychology.)

After World War I, corporate leaders were primarily concerned with finding the right employee for the job; consequently, research on personnel issues (e.g., selection, placement, fatigue, safety) in organizations flourished during the early to mid-1920s (e.g., Bregman, 1922;

TABLE 1.12
The Psychology of Selecting Men (Laird, 1925)

TABLE 1.13
Principles of Employment Psychology (Burtt, 1926)

TABLE 1.14

Applied Psychology: Its Principles and Methods **(Poffenberger, 1928)**

Table of Contents

Part I: Psychology applied to individual competence
           Efficiency and applied psychology
           The influence of heredity upon achievement
           The influence of family inheritance upon achievement
           Efficiency and learning
           Thinking
           Suggestion
           The influence of age upon efficiency
           The influence of sex upon efficiency
           Work, fatigue, rest, and sleep
           The influence of environmental conditions: I: Ventilation
           The influence of environmental conditions II: Illumination
           The effects of distraction
           The influence of drugs and stimulants

Part II: Psychology applied to occupational activities
           The principles of vocational psychology
           The role of judgment in vocational psychology
           The measurement of general and special capacity
           The measurement of character and interest
           Industrial Psychology: I: Psychological factors in output
           Industrial Psychology: II: Economy of effort
           Industrial Psychology: III: Satisfaction as a product of work
           Business Psychology: I: The nature of the consumer
           Business Psychology: II: The adjustment of advertising and selling methods to the consumer
           Psychology and the law: I: The prevention of crime
           Psychology and the law: II: The determination of guilt
           Psychology and the law: III: Treatment of the offender
           Psychology and medicine: I: The prevention of disease
           Psychology and medicine: II: The diagnosis of disease
           Psychology and medicine: III: The treatment of disease
           Psychology and education

Pond, 1927). An early example of research carried out for these practical purposes was the development of a simulator and a battery of paper-and-pencil tests claiming to measure intelligence of taxicab drivers. In 1925, David Wechsler and The Psychological Corporation (a consulting firm, see chap. 6) were commissioned by the Yellow Cab Company in Pittsburgh to select stable, efficient, and safe taxicab drivers (Wasserman & Maccubbin, 2002). The driving simulator consisted of a dummy card and flash board to assess carefulness and reaction time. The driver reacted with the clutch and foot brake to traffic signal lights of various colors flashing at irregular intervals on a gray board 10 feet from the driver. The test battery consisted of digit-symbol learning, arithmetical reasoning, and picture completion tests. The battery also included a self-administering maze. Approximately 250 adult males were tested from April to June 1925. Wechsler then compared the test scores and the driving records of these participants. The results revealed that drivers who failed on the simulator averaged more than twice the number of accidents than drivers who passed (Wasserman & Maccubbin, 2002). In addition, drivers with fast reaction times were found to have a high number of accidents, however, drivers with the slowest reaction times had the greatest number of accidents. Wechsler also examined the relation between the test battery scores and the earnings of the drivers. Drivers with higher intelligence test scores typically made more money; however, some drivers with very high scores had lower daily revenues because "a man of superior intelligence who takes to cabbing as a profession is likely to have some special limitations" (Wechsler, 1926, p. 28).

A historical perspective on selection is presented in chapter 8 and perspectives on several early topics are provided in other chapters, including job analysis (chap. 9), human factors (chap. 10), advertising and consumer psychology (chap. 11), training (chap. 12), and performance appraisal (chap. 13).

During the 1920s, a widely published research program known as the Hawthorne studies was initiated at the Hawthorne Works of the Bell System's Western Electric Company in Cicero, Illinois. Although the original research purpose focused on the relation between illumination levels and productivity, researchers observed that workers changed their behaviors regardless of the illumination levels. These studies are frequently regarded as the basis for a human relation movement in I–O psychology, which resulted in a shifting of research questions and problems investigated by psychologists in business after 1930. (See chaps. 14 and 15 for more information on these studies; Roethlisberger & Dickson, 1939.)

How Did Psychologists Study Work and Apply Psychology to Business Problems?

It [industrial psychology] is the application of methods of science to the human side of business.... It becomes psychological when one gathers trustworthy data, studies it with the aid of adding machine and slide rule, and finally reaches some practical decision that is scientifically sound and mathematically justified. Whenever the human problems of industry approached in this fashion, one may say here is an example of industrial psychology. (Laird, 1925, p. 10)

As described in chapter 3, psychologists placed a great emphasis on empirical methods and quantification during the early 20th century because they felt compelled to legitimize their science and to address society's skepticism of the profession. As psychology's popularity increased, many individuals not trained in psychology began practicing to gain financial rewards. Consequently, psychologists had to combat society's images of psychology as common sense or as occultism and superstition and society's stereotype of the psychologist as an "absent-minded professor, preoccupied with abstruse manners" (see Burnham, 1987, p. 92). Experimentation was used to invalidate the claims of pseudoscientists (see chap. 3 for more information on pseudoscientists). According to Gillespie (1988), the decision to undertake social scientific research in the workplace during the 1920s was a political process, and "social and behavioral scientists believed that experimentation would guarantee objectivity of their findings and recommendations, and ensure their professional standing on an intellectual and moral plane above that of capitalists and workers" (p. 133; see also Coon, 1993).

The emphasis on empirical methods resulted in developments including various measurement methods (mental tests, observations, case studies, experimental and quasi-experimental studies) and statistics for analyzing individual differences (regression, simple correlation, partial correlation, factor analysis; Cowles, 1989). In the 1920s, the concepts of validity and criterion were introduced, analysis of variance was developed, and the measurement of attitudes was improved by the scaling techniques of L. L. Thurstone in 1927 and later, Rensis Likert in 1932.

On review of industrial psychology-related articles in the psychology journals for this chapter, we identified the following methods: laboratory experiments, quasi-experimental studies, direct observations, archival records, and case studies. Statistical analyses included frequencies, means, standard deviations, percentages, and correlations. (See chaps. 3 and 8 in this text for additional information about the emphasis on quantification; see also Austin, Scherbaum, & Mahlman, 2002)

In addition to research methods and statistics, tools and techniques for solving business problems were developed. The primary focus was on the development of psychological measuring tools or mental tests for assessing individual differences. According to Arthur and Benjamin (1999),

> Most of the early twentieth-century work by business psychologists was centered on mental testing.... Mental tests were used to measure advertising appeals, sales strategies, management styles, consumer behavior, and were also valuable in personnel matters such as worker selection, job analysis, production, and efficiency. (p. 100)

In fact, mental tests were considered to be the field's first technical product (Van De Water, 1997). As described throughout this volume, those psychologists involved with World War I collaborated in developing intelligence tests to be administered in groups for selection and classification purposes. These tests paved the way for large-scale intelligence testing and for later expansion of psychological testing into government, industry, and education.

Other tools and techniques were developed for forward-looking managers and organization leaders who sought the use of psychological applications. Consultants of the Scott Company, an early consulting firm, used techniques such as job standards, performance ratings, and oral trade tests as well as application blanks, standardized letters to former employers, and an interviewer's guide and record blanks. Bingham and his colleagues of the Division of Applied Psychology at Carnegie Institute of Technology (CIT) developed sales training and established procedures for correcting mistakes in sales (Baritz, 1960). The Psychological Corporation, established in 1921, developed and implemented techniques for the advancement and promotion of an applied psychology. Also, in the 1920s, the graphic rating scale for performance appraisal was published.

In sum, when industrial psychology was established, the objective of the discipline was to improve the achievement of organizational goals (i.e., productivity and efficiency) with an emphasis on individual differences. The field was described almost exclusively as a "technology" with a focus on practical issues. Due to the efforts of numerous individuals, the foundation for today's I–O psychology was created through the development of methods and techniques to solve business problems.

1930–1960

During the 1930s, refinements of existing techniques and instruments were emphasized (Katzell & Austin, 1992). The first modern I–O psychology textbook was published by Morris Viteles in 1932, and John G. Jenkins published his book *Psychology in Business and Industry* in 1935 (see Tables 1.15 and 1.16). An emphasis on employee welfare during the Depression led to the development of personnel counseling as a popular organizational intervention for helping employees solve problems (Highhouse, 1999). Following the Hawthorne Studies, work motivation theories were formulated (see chap. 15) and attempts were made to measure job satisfaction (see chaps. 14 and 15). Statistics and other methods continued to be developed, including the introduction of factor analysis. The American Association of Applied Psychology (AAAP) Section D, Industrial and Business Psychology, was established in 1937 as an early professional organization for applied psychologists in industry (Benjamin,1997a).

Psychologists were ready to respond to new challenges associated with World War II. The Army General Classification Test (AGCT) was developed, situational stress tests were created, and the selection and simulation training of pilots to fly warplanes were implemented. The U.S. Office of Strategic Services (OSS) developed the assessment center as a technique for se-

TABLE 1.15
Industrial Psychology (Viteles, 1932)

Table of Contents

Introduction to a study of industrial psychology

The economic foundations of industrial psychology

The social foundations of industrial psychology

The psychological foundations of industrial psychology

The rise and scope of industrial psychology

The nature and distribution of individual differences

The origin of individual differences

Fitting the worker to the job
    Basic factors in vocational selection
    Job analysis
    The interview and allied techniques
    Standardization and administration of psychological tests
    Tests for skilled and semi-skilled workers
    Tests in the transportation industry
    Tests for office occupations, technical and supervisory employees

Maintaining fitness at work
    Safety at work
    Psychological techniques in accident prevention
    Accidents in the transportation industry
    The acquisition of skill
    Training methodsIndustrial fatigue
    The elimination of unnecessary fatigue
    Machines and monotony
    Specificinfluences in monotonous work
    Motives in industry
    The maladjusted worker
    Problems of supervision and management

lecting spies and sabotage agents. One of the first comprehensive applied psychology programs was established, the Aviation Psychology Program directed by John Flanagan (see chap. 7). World War II was a turning point for leadership research (see chap. 16).

After World War II, the economy provided for prosperity, affluence, education, and a heightened awareness of the good life. As described throughout this volume, psychological applications and research opportunities proliferated, especially in commercial testing. The focus was on both fitting people for the job and fitting the job for people. Other developments occurred in areas of job analysis and job evaluation, salaries and wages, placement, promotions, training, performance appraisal, job satisfaction and morale, counseling and guidance, labor relations, industrial hygiene, accidents and safety, equipment design, and quality circles. The forced choice rating system for evaluating performance was introduced during the 1940s. Work motivation theories were further developed and leadership research ensued, such as the Ohio State Leadership studies (see chaps. 6 and 16). Psychological research organizations were created (e.g., American Institutes for Research), consulting firms were established (e.g., Richardson, Bellows, Henry, & Company), and research groups were formed in private corporations (e.g., AT&T, General Electric, Standard Oil of New Jersey). Universities also organized research centers to investigate aspects of work. The economic and political division of

TABLE 1.16
Psychology in Business and Industry (Jenkins, 1935)

Table of Contents

Introduction of psychotechnology

    Psychotechnology and the arts of practice

    Psychotechnology as a field of psychology

Psychological problems in industrial selection

    Short cuts to prediction

    Selection by means of personal estimates

    Selection by tests

Psychological problems in industrial production

    Effects of narcotics

    Effects of method of work

    Effects of conditions of work

Psychological problems in personnel

    Problems of individual differences

    Problems of human motivation

Psychological problems in industrial distribution

    The primary problem of advertising

    Accessory problems in advertising

    Psychotechnology in selling

Psychological problems in market research

    Problems and principles of market research

    Instruments and techniques of market research

    Measuring the results of advertising

the world along capitalistic–communist lines, the emergence of the Soviet Union as a super-power, and the threat of nuclear war increased military spending. Consequently, military research centers were established (e.g., the Navy Personnel Research and Development Center, NPRDC; see chap. 7). The development of numerous graduate programs helped legitimize industrial psychology as a discipline during this period (see chap. 5).

In 1945, the AAAP merged with the American Psychological Association (APA) to form APA Division 14, Industrial and Business Psychology (Benjamin, 1997b). Several division members and others began meeting separately in a group called Psychologists Full-Time in Industry to discuss pertinent topics. Additional informal groups were established in the 1950s, such as the Dearborn Conference Group and the No-Name Group, with the purpose of facilitating communication and interaction to advance the science and practice of I–O psychology (see chap. 6).

By the end of the 1940s, the discipline of I–O psychology had significantly evolved. Viteles admitted that he had to revise the title of his seminal 1932 book in 1953 to *Motivation and Morale in Industry* because of numerous developments in the field, including more complex theories of motivation and attention to emotions and attitudes. Edwin E. Ghiselli and C. W. Brown published a major text, titled *Personnel and Industrial Psychology* in 1948, which became the key reference in industrial psychology training and education. Modern cognitive psychology began in the 1950s, which provided a foundation for significant developments in years to come. In 1959, McCollom found at least 1,000 psychologists who were employed full-time industry in the United States (McCollom, 1959).

1960s and 1970s

Unrest surfaced in America's society because of changes in values, enhanced attention to discriminatory and unfair practices, the Vietnam War, baby boomers in the workforce, and international and foreign competition (Koppes, 2003). In the 1950s, the civil rights movement had begun when the separate-but-equal doctrine in education was struck down in the case of *Brown v. Board of Education* (1954). This movement led to the Civil Rights Act (CRA) of 1964, Title VII, which prohibits discrimination in employment because of race, color, religion, sex, or national origin. As noted throughout the chapters, this and other legislation (e.g., Age Discrimination in Employment Act of 1967) significantly influenced I–O developments in fair employment practices and test validation (e.g., see chaps. 8 and 9).

American society observed the emergence of a new generation of employees who questioned the authority of organizations and consequently created interest in democracy and autonomy in the workplace. A flagging productivity in conjunction with these shifting societal views forced American companies to rethink their methods of interacting with and managing employees. An emphasis was placed on how the organization could best serve the individual. Organizations evolved from highly bureaucratic authoritarian structures to open systems, using such methods as total quality management, teamwork, and employee participation. Research was stimulated in areas of communication, conflict management, socialization, organizational climate and culture, and group/team development and maturation (see chap. 17). Interventions for facilitating organizational change and development (OD) were created during this time (see chap. 14). The education and training of I–O psychology became legitimized with the development of guidelines for doctoral training in 1965 (see chap. 5).

In 1962, *business* had been dropped from the name of APA Division 14, which became the Division of Industrial Psychology. In 1973, the name changed again because of the evolving nature of the discipline. *Organizational* was added and the division became labeled as APA Division 14, Industrial and Organizational Psychology. A one-volume *Handbook of Industrial and Organizational Psychology* was published in 1976 (Dunnette, 1976).

1980s and Beyond

Sluggish productivity, threats to economic well-being, and increased competition heightened concerns about productivity and quality in the United States during the 1980s. With the fall of communism and the passage of the North American Free Trade Act, a global and diverse workforce became commonplace (Landy & Conte, 2004). Organizational changes included restructuring, mergers, and acquisitions. Earnest attention was given to utility analysis, and a renewed interest in organization development improved relations between organizations and employees. In 1990, the Americans with Disabilities Act (ADA) emphasized the importance of identifying essential job functions and physical requirements and redesigning jobs to accommodate employees. The ADA is considered to be one of the most significant pieces of legislation to influence the work of I–O psychologists since the CRA of 1964 (Koppes, 2003).

To achieve some independence from the APA, the APA Division 14 incorporated as the Society for Industrial and Organizational Psychology (SIOP) in 1982 (Hakel, 1979). Since 1945, the organization has experienced changes in structure, membership, and activities, primarily due to the growth of the discipline and the membership. Membership has grown from 130 members (fellows and associates) in 1945 to 3,627 professional members (fellows, members, associates, international affiliates) and 2,901 student members in 2005 (David Nershi, executive director, SIOP, personal communication, July 6, 2005). One obvious development was the shift from being totally managed by volunteers to being staffed with professionals (Koppes, 2000). SIOP has developed several awards to recognize significant contributors to the discipline (Koppes, 1999) and established the SIOP Foundation to secure the financial future of I–O psychology. Table 1.17 lists the presidents of SIOP since its founding as APA Division 14 (Society for Industrial and Organizational Psychology, n.d.b). In 1988, some SIOP members were instrumental in creating a new psychology organization known as the American Psychological Society (APS), which was established to advance and promote the science of psychology. Numerous SIOP members elect to join APS rather than APA. Benjamin (1997a, 1997b) provided a more complete historical account of the development of professional organizations in I–O psychology.

As previously described, the *Journal of Applied Psychology* and the *Journal of Personnel Research* were the primary outlets for publishing research and practice. Over the years, additional journals were established. Most recently, the top I–O journals were considered to be *Journal of Applied Psychology, Personnel Psychology, Academy of Management Journal, Academy of Management Review, Organizational Behavior and Human Decision Processes, Administrative Science Quarterly, Journal of Management, Journal of Organizational Behavior, Organizational Research Methods,* and *Journal of Vocational Behavior* (Oliver, Blair, Gorman, & Woehr, 2005; Zickar & Highhouse, 2001).

A number of developments in I–O psychology have occurred since the 1980s, many of which are presented in subsequent chapters (e.g., cognitive perspective of performance appraisals, organizational justice theory, computerized adaptive testing, and the O*NET to replace the *Dictionary of Occupational Titles*). Also during this time, the second edition of the four-volume *Handbook of Industrial and Organizational Psychology* (Dunnette & Hough, 1990–1992) was published and an *Encyclopedia of Industrial and Organizational Psychology* was recently developed (Rogelberg, 2006).

CONCLUSION

By 1930, American and European psychologists had developed the basic infrastructure for applications in business and industry. Methodologies borrowed from experimental psychologists and mental testers had given legitimacy to the nascent field of industrial psychology. Psychologists and corporate leaders benefited from the marriage of science and utility. The groundwork had been laid for greater concern with employees' place in the workplace.

Unlike the beginnings of the broad perspective of the science of work in Europe, I–O psychology in the United States evolved from a simple, narrowly defined technical field focused on individual issues for accomplishing organizational objectives (i.e., selection, advertising) to a complex, broad scientific and applied discipline emphasizing individual and organizational issues for achieving both individual and organizational goals. Today, the objective is to improve both organizational goals/efficiency and individual goals/efficiency by theorizing, researching, and applying psychology in the workplace, with consideration for individual and organizational factors. As demonstrated throughout this text, these developments are the result of confluences of dynamic external (socioeconomic, business, legal, military, technology, psychology) and internal forces (individuals, theories, scientific investigations, applications). The constant key challenge within the discipline is to maintain an identity as a

TABLE 1.17
Past Presidents of APA–Division 14 and SIOP

Date	Name	Date	Name
1945–46	Bruce V. Moore	1976–77	Paul W. Thayer
1946–47	John G. Jenkins	1977–78	John P. Campbell
1947–48	George K. Bennett	1978–79	C. Paul Sparks
1948–49	Floyd L. Ruch	1979–80	Mary L. Tenopyr
1949–50	Carroll L. Shartle	1980–81	Victor H. Vroom
1950–51	Jack W. Dunlap	1981–82	Arthur C. MacKinney
1951–52	Marion A. Bills	1982–83	Richard J. Campbell
1952–53	J. L. Otis	1983–84	Milton D. Hakel
1953–54	Harold A. Edgerton	1984–85	Benjamin Schneider
1954–55	Edwin E. Ghiselli	1985–86	Irwin L. Goldstein
1955–56	Leonard W. Ferguson	1986–87	Sheldon Zedeck
1956–57	Edwin R. Henry	1987–88	Daniel R. Ilgen
1957–58	Charles H. Lawshe, Jr.	1988–89	Ann Howard
1958–59	Joseph Tiffin	1989–90	Neal W. Schmitt
1959–60	Erwin K. Taylor	1990–91	Frank J. Landy
1960–61	Raymond A. Katzell	1991–92	Richard J. Klimoski
1961–62	Orlo L. Crissey	1992–93	Wayne F. Cascio
1962–63	William McGehee	1993–94	Paul R. Sackett
1963–64	S. Rains Wallace	1994–95	Walter C. Borman
1964–65	Brent N. Baxter	1995–96	Michael A. Campion
1965–66	Ross Stagner	1996–97	James L. Farr
1966–67	Marvin D. Dunnette	1997–98	Kevin R. Murphy
1967–68	Philip Ash	1998–99	Elaine D. Pulakos
1968–69	Stanley E. Seashore	1999–00	Angelo S. DeNisi
1969–70	William A. Owens	2000–01	Nancy Tippins
1970–71	Herbert H. Meyer	2001–02	William H. Macey
1971–72	Douglas W. Bray	2002–2003	Ann Marie Ryan
1972–73	Robert M.Guion	2003–2004	Michael Burke
1973–74	Edwin A. Fleishman	2004–2005	Fritz Drasgow
1974–75	Donald L. Grant	2005–2006	Leaetta Hough
1975–76	Lyman W. Porter	2006–2007	Jeffrey J. McHenry

rigorous scientific discipline while at the same time providing a growing range of professional services and applications.

ACKNOWLEDGMENTS

In addition to the Associate Editors and the Series Editor Edwin A. Fleishman, we thank the following individuals for their intensive review of this chapter: Kim Bryan, David Devonis, Bill Seigfried, and Wayne Viney.

REFERENCES

Angell, J. R. (1907). The province of functional psychology. *Psychological Review, 14,* 61–91.

Arthur, W., Jr., & Benjamin, L. T., Jr. (1999). Psychology applied to business. In A. M. Stec & D. A. Bernstein (Eds.), *Psychology: Fields of application* (pp. 98–115). Boston: Houghton Mifflin.

Austin J. T., Scherbaum, C. A., & Mahlman, R. A. (2002). History of research methods in industrial and organizational psychology: Measurement, design, analysis. In S. G. Rogelberg (Ed.), *Handbook of research in industrial and organizational psychology* (pp. 3–33). Oxford, England: Blackwell.

Austin, J. T., & Villanova, P. (1992). The criterion problem: 1917–1992. *Journal of Applied Psychology, 77,* 836–874.

Bakan, D. (1966). The influence of phrenology on American psychology. *Journal of the History of the Behavioral Sciences, 2,* 200–220.

Baritz, L. (1960). *The servants of power: A history of the use of social science in American industry.* Middletown, CT: Wesleyan University Press.

Benjamin, L. T., Jr. (1997a). Organized industrial psychology before division 14: The ACP and the AAAP (1930–1945). *Journal of Applied Psychology, 82,* 459–466.

Benjamin, L. T., Jr. (1997b). A history of Division 14 (Society for Industrial and Organizational Psychology). In D. A. Dewsbury (Ed.), *Unification through division: Histories of the divisions of the American Psychological Association* (Vol. 2, pp. 101–126). Washington, DC: American Psychological Association.

Bingham, W. V. (1929). Industrial psychology in the United States: An appraisal. *Annals of Business Economics and Science of Labour, 3,* 398–408.

Boorstin, D. J. (1992). *The creators: A history of the heroes of the imagination.* New York: Random House.

Bowler, P. J. (1996). *Charles Darwin: The man and his influence.* Cambridge, England: Cambridge University Press.

Bregman, E. O. (1922). A scientific plan for sizing up employees. *System,* 696–763.

Bringmann, W. G., Lück, H. E., Miller, R., & Early, C. E. (Eds.). (1997). *A pictorial history of psychology.* Carol Stream, IL: Quintessence.

Brown v. Board of Education. (1954). 347 U.S. 483.

Bruner, J. S., & Allport, G. W. (1940). Fifty years of change in American psychology. *Psychological Bulletin, 37,* 757–776.

Bryan, W. L. (1904). Theory and practice. *Psychological Review, 11,* 71–82.

Bryan, W. L., & Harter, N. (1897). Studies in the physiology and psychology of the telegraphic language. *Psychological Review, 4,* 27–53.

Bryan, W. L., & Harter, N. (1899). Studies of the telegraphic language. *Psychological Review, 6,* 345–375.

Buchner, E. F. (1910). Psychological progress in 1909. *Psychological Bulletin, 7,* 1–16.

Burnham, J. C. (1987). *How superstition won and science lost: Popularizing science and health in the United States.* New Brunswick, NJ: Rutgers University Press.

Burtt, H. E. (1926). *Principles of employment psychology.* New York: Harper.

Camfield, T. (1973). The professionalization of American psychology, 1870–1917. *Journal of the History of Behavioral Sciences, 9,* 66–75.

Capshew, J. H. (1999). *Psychologists on the march: Science, practice, and professional identity in America, 1929–1969.* New York: Cambridge University Press.

Cashman, S. D. (1989). *America in the twenties and thirties.* New York: New York University Press.

Cattell, J. M. (1946). Retrospect: Psychology as a profession. *Journal of Consulting Psychology, 10,* 289–291.

Colarelli, S. M. (1998). Psychological interventions in organizations: An evolutionary perspective. *American Psychologist, 53,* 1044–1056.

Coon, D. J. (1993). Standardizing the subject: Experimental psychologists, introspection, and the quest for a techno-scientific ideal. *Technology and Culture, 34*(4), 757–783.

Cooter, R. (1984). *The cultural meaning of popular science: Phrenology and the organization of consent in nineteenth-century Britain.* New York: Cambridge University Press.

Cowles, M. (1989). *Statistics in psychology: An historical perspective.* Hillsdale, NJ: Lawrence Erlbaum Associates.

Darwin, C. (1859). *On the origins of species by means of natural selection.* London: John Murray.

de Wolff, C. J., & Shimmin, S. (1981). Work psychology in Europe: The development of a profession. In C. J. de Wolff, S. Shimmin, & M. De Montmollin (Eds.), *Conflicts and contradictions: Work psychologists in Europe.* New York: Academic Press.

Drever, J. (1921). *The psychology of industry.* New York: Dutton.

Dunnette, M. D. (Ed.). (1976). *Handbook of industrial and organizational psychology.* Chicago: Rand McNally.

Dunnette, M. D., & Hough, L. (Eds.). (1990–1992). *Handbook of industrial and organizational psychology* (2nd ed., Vols. 1–3). Palo Alto, CA: Consulting Psychologists Press.

Durant, W. A. (1961). *The age of reason begins*. New York: Simon & Schuster.

Ferguson, L. (1952). A look across the years, 1920–1950. In L. L. Thurstone (Ed.), *Applications of psychology: Essays to honor Walter V. Bingham* (pp. 1–17). New York: Harper.

Ferguson, L. W. (1961). The development of industrial psychology. In B. von Haller Gilmer (Ed.), *Industrial psychology* (pp. 18–37). New York: McGraw-Hill.

Ferguson, L. W. (1962–1965). *The heritage of industrial psychology* [14 pamphlets]. Hartford, CT: Finlay Press.

Finch, F. H., & Odoroff, M. E. (1939). Employment trends in applied psychology. *Journal of Consulting Psychology, 3,* 118–122.

Firth, A. (2002). Moral supervision and autonomous social order: Wages and consumption in 18th century economic thought. *History of the Human Sciences, 15,* 39–57.

Freyd, M. (1923–1924). Measurement in vocational selection: An outline of research procedure. *Journal of Personnel Research, 2,* 215–249, 268–284, 377–385.

Ghiselli, E. E., & Brown, C. W. (1948). *Personnel and industrial psychology*. New York: McGraw-Hill.

Gillespie, R. (1988). The Hawthorne experiments and the politics of experimentation. In J. G. Morawski (Ed.), *The rise of experimentation in American psychology* (pp. 114–137). New Haven: Yale University Press.

Gundlach, H. U. K. (1997). The mobile psychologist: Psychology and the railroads. In W. G. Bringmann, H. E. Luck, R. Miller, & C. E. Early (Eds.), *A pictorial history of psychology* (pp. 506–509). Chicago: Quintessence.

Haber, S. (1964). *Efficiency and uplift: Scientific management in the progressive era 1890–1920*. Chicago: University of Chicago Press.

Hacker, H., & Echterhoff, W. (1997). Traffic psychology. In W. G. Bringmann, H. E. Luck, R. Miller, & C. E. Early (Eds.), *A pictorial history of psychology* (pp. 503–505). Chicago: Quintessence.

Hakel, M. (1979). Proposal to incorporate as the Society for Industrial and Organizational Psychology. *Industrial-Organizational Psychologist, 16*(4), 4–5.

Hale, M. (1992). History of employment testing. In A. Widgor & W. R. Garner (Eds.), *Ability testing: Uses, consequences, and controversies* (pp. 3–38). Washington, DC: National Academy Press.

Harrison, H. D. (1925). *Industrial psychology and the production of wealth*. New York: Dodd, Mead.

Hergenhahn, B. R. (1997). *An introduction to the history of psychology* (3rd ed.). Pacific Grove, CA: Brooks/Cole.

Highhouse, S. (1999). The brief history of personnel counseling in industrial-organizational psychology. *Journal of Vocational Behavior, 55,* 318–336.

Hilgard, E. R. (1987). *Psychology in America: A historical survey*. New York: Harcourt Brace Jovanovich.

Hollingworth, H. L., & Poffenberger, A. T. (1917). *Applied psychology*. New York: Appleton.

James, W. (1892). *Psychology: Briefer course*. New York: Henry Holt.

Jaynes, J. (1973). Introductions: The study of the history of psychology. In M. Hengle, J. Jaynes, & J. J. Sullivan (Eds.), *Historical conceptions of psychology* (pp. ix–xii). New York: Springer.

Jenkins, J. G. (1935). *Psychology in business and industry*. New York: Wiley.

Katzell, R. A., & Austin, J. T. (1992). From then to now: The development of industrial-organizational psychology in the United States. *Journal of Applied Psychology, 77,* 803–835.

Kelley, T. L. (1919). Principles underlying the classification of men. *Journal of Applied Psychology, 3,* 50–67.

Kingsbury, F. A. (1923). Applying psychology to business. *Annals of the American Academy of Political and Social Sciences, 110,* 2–12.

Koppes, L. L. (1997). American female pioneers of industrial and organizational psychology during the early years. *Journal of Applied Psychology, 82*(4), 500–515.

Koppes, L. L. (1999). Ideals of science: Persons behind the SIOP awards. *Industrial-Organizational Psychologist, 36*(4), 75–86.

Koppes, L. L. (2000). A history of the SIOP administrative office. *Industrial-Organizational Psychologist, 38*(2), 48–54.

Koppes, L. L. (2003). Industrial-organizational psychology. In I. B. Weiner (General Ed.) & D. K. Freedheim (Vol. Ed.), *Comprehensive handbook of psychology: Vol. 1. History of psychology* (pp. 367–389). New York: Wiley.

Kornhauser, A. W. (1922). The psychology of vocational selection. *Psychological Bulletin, 19,* 192–229.

Kornhauser, A. W., & Kingsbury, F. A. (1924). *Psychological tests in business*. Chicago: University of Chicago Press.

Kraepelin, E. (1896). A measure of mental capacity. *Appleton's Popular Science Monthly, 49,* 756–763.

Kuhn, T. S. (1962). *The structure of scientific revolutions*. Chicago: Chicago University Press.

Kuhn, T. S. (1968). The history of science. In D. Sills (Ed.), *The international encyclopedia of the social sciences, Vol. 14* (pp. 74–83). New York: Macmillan and Free Press.

Laird, D. A. (1925). *The psychology of selecting men*. New York: McGraw-Hill.

Landy, F. J. (1992). Hugo Münsterberg: Victim or visionary? *Journal of Applied Psychology, 77,* 787–802.

Landy, F. J. (1997). Early influences on the development of industrial and organizational psychology. *Journal of Applied Psychology, 82,* 467–477.

Landy, F. J., & Conte, J. M. (2004). *Work in the 21st century: An introduction to industrial and organizational psychology.* New York: McGraw-Hill.

Link, H. C. (1919). *Employment psychology.* New York: Macmillan.

Link, H. C. (1920). The applications of psychology to industry. *Psychological Bulletin, 17,* 335–346.

Luck, H., & Bringmann, W. G. (1997). Hugo Münsterberg: Pioneer of applied psychology. In W. G. Bringmann, H. E. Luck, R. Miller, & C. E. Early (Eds.), *A pictorial history of psychology* (pp. 471–475). Chicago: Quintessence.

Marx, K. (1887). *Das Kapital* (S. Moore & E. Aveling, Trans.). Moscow, USSR: Progress Publishers. (Original work published 1867)

McCollom, I. N. (1959). Psychologists in industry in the United States. *American Psychologist, 14,* 704–708.

Minton, H. L. (1988). Charting life history: Lewis M. Terman's study of the gifted. In J. G. Morawski (Ed.), *The rise of experimentation in American psychology* (pp. 138–162). New Haven and London: Yale University Press.

Moore, B. V., & Hartmann, G. W. (Eds.). (1931). *Readings in industrial psychology.* New York: Appleton-Century.

Mosso, A. (1906). *Fatigue* (M. Drummond & W. B. Drummond, Trans.). London: Allen & Unwin. (Original work published 1891)

Muchinsky, P. (2003). *Psychology applied to work* (7th ed.). Belmont, CA: Wadsworth/Thomson Learning.

Münsterberg, H. (1913). *Psychology and industrial efficiency.* Boston: Houghton Mifflin.

Münsterberg, H. (1914). *Psychology: General and applied.* New York and London: Appleton.

Münsterberg, H. (1917). *Business psychology.* Chicago: La Salle Extension University.

Myers, C. S. (1929). *Industrial psychology.* New York: Holt.

Napoli, D. S. (1981). *Architects of adjustment: The history of the psychological profession in the United States.* Port Washington, NY: Kennibat Press.

O'Donnell, J. M. (1979). The crisis of experimentalism in the 1920's. *American Psychologist, 34*(4), 289–295.

Oliver, J., Blair, C. A., Gorman, C. A., & Woehr, D. J. (2005). Research productivity of I–O psychology doctoral programs in North America. *Industrial-Organizational Psychologist, 43*(1), 55–63.

Pearson, K. (1914–1930). *The life, letters, and labours of Francis Galton* (Vols. 1–3). London: Cambridge University Press.

Pickren, W. E. (2000). European psychology. In G. B. Ferngren (Ed.), *The history of science and religion in the western tradition* (pp. 495–501). New York: Garland Publishing.

Pickren, W. E., & Fowler, R. D. (2003). A history of psychological organizations. In I. B. Weiner (General Ed.) & D. K. Freedheim (Vol. Ed.), *Comprehensive handbook of psychology: Vol. 1. History of psychology* (pp. 535–554). New York: Wiley.

Poffenberger, A. T. (1928). *Applied psychology: Its principles and methods.* New York: Appleton.

Pond, M. (1927). Selective placement of metalworkers. *Journal of Personnel Research, 5,* 345–368, 405–417, 452–466.

Rabinbach, A. (1990). *The human motor: Energy, fatigue, and the origins of modernity.* Berkeley: University of California Press.

Richardson, R. F. (1912). The learning process in the acquisition of skill. *Pedagogical Seminary, 14,* 376–394.

Rieber, R. W., & Robinson, D. K. (2001). *Wilhelm Wundt in history: The making of a scientific psychology.* New York: Plenum.

Roback, A. A. (1952). *A history of American psychology.* New York: Collier-Macmillan.

Roethlisberger, F. J., & Dickson, W. J. (1939). *Management and the worker: An account of a research program conducted by the Western Electric Company, Hawthorne Works, Chicago.* Cambridge, MA: Harvard University Press.

Rogelberg, S. (Ed.) (2006). *Encyclopedia of industrial and organizational psychology.* Thousand Oaks, CA: Sage.

Sarton, G. (1927). *Introduction to the history of science.* Baltimore, MD: Williams & Wilkins.

Schultz, D. P., & Schultz, S. E. (2000). *A history of modern psychology.* New York: Harcourt College Publishers.

Scott, W. D. (1911a). *Increasing human efficiency in business.* New York: Macmillan.

Scott, W. D. (1911b). *Influencing men in business.* New York: The Ronald Press Company.

Scott, W. D. (1920). Changes in some of our conceptions and practices of personnel. *Psychological Review, 27,* 81–94.

Scripture, E. W. (1895). *Thinking, feeling, doing.* New York: Chautauqua-Century Press.

Shimmin, S., & van Strien, P. J. (1998). History of the psychology of work and organization. In P. J. D. Drenth, H. Thierry, & C. J. de Wolff (Eds.), *Handbook of work and organizational psychology (2nd ed.): Vol. 1. Introduction to work and organizational psychology.* East Sussex, England: Psychology Press.

Smith, A. (1904). *An inquiry into the nature and causes of the wealth of nations* (5th ed.). London: Metheren.

Society for Industrial and Organizational Psychology. (n.d.a). *Building better organizations: Industrial-organizational psychology in the workplace.* Retrieved June 30, 2005, from http://www.siop.org/visibilitybrochure/memberbrochure.htm

Society for Industrial and Organizational Psychology. (n.d.b). *SIOP past presidents.* Retrieved July 6, 2005, from http://www.siop.org/Presidents/PastPres.htm.

Sokal, M. M. (1984). James McKeen Cattell and American psychology in the 1920s. In J. Brozek (Ed.), *Explorations in the history of psychology in the United States* (pp. 273–323). Lewisburg, PA: Bucknell University Press.

Sokal, M. M. (1987). *Psychological testing and American society 1890–1930.* London: Rutgers University Press.

Sokal, M. M. (2001). Practical phrenology as psychological counseling in the 19th-century United States. In C. D. Green, M. Shore, & T. Teo (Eds.), *The transformation of psychology: Influences of 19th-century philosophy, technology, and natural science* (pp. 21–44). Washington, DC: American Psychological Association.

Stagner, R. (1981). Training and experiences of some distinguished industrial psychologists. *American Psychologist, 36,* 497–505.

Taylor, F. W. (1911). *The principles of scientific management.* New York: Harper & Row.

Thompson, J. D. (1921). *Personnel research agencies* (Bureau of Labor Statistics Bulletin No. 299). Washington, DC: U.S. Government Printing Office.

Van De Water, T. J. (1997). Psychology's entrepreneurs and the marketing of industrial psychology. *Journal of Applied Psychology, 82,* 486–499.

van Drunen, P. (1997). Psychotechnics. In W. G. Bringmann, H. E. Luck, R. Miller, & C. E. Early (Eds.), *A pictorial history of psychology* (pp. 480–484). Chicago: Quintessence.

van Strien, P. J. (1998). Early applied psychology between essentialism and pragmatism: The dynamics of theory, tools, and clients. *History of Psychology, 1,* 208–234.

Viney, W., & King, D. B. (2003). *A history of psychology: Ideas and context* (3rd ed.). Boston: Allyn & Bacon.

Viteles, M. S. (1926). Psychology in industry. *Psychological Bulletin, 23,* 631–680.

Viteles, M. S. (1932). *Industrial psychology.* New York: Norton.

Viteles, M. S. (1953). *Motivation and morale in industry.* New York: Norton.

von Mayrhauser, R. T. (1987). The manager, the medic, and the mediator: The clash of professional psychological styles and the wartime origins of group mental testing. In M. M. Sokal (Ed.), *Psychological testing and American society 1890–1930* (pp. 128–155). New Brunswick, NJ: Rutgers University Press.

Wasserman, J. D., & Maccubbin, E. M. (2002, August). *David Wechsler at the Psychological Corporation 1925–1927: Chorus girls and taxicab drivers.* Paper presentation at the Annual Convention of the American Psychological Association, Chicago, IL.

Watson, R. I. (1960). The history of psychology: A neglected area. *American Psychologist, 15,* 251–255.

Wechsler, D. (1926). Tests for taxicab drivers. *Journal of Personnel Research, 5,* 24–30.

Wertheimer, M. (1980). Historical research—why? In J. Brozek & L. J. Pongratz (Eds.), *Historiography of modern psychology: Aims, resources, approaches* (pp. 3–23). Toronto: Hogrefe.

Zickar, M. J., & Highhouse, S. (2001). Measuring prestige of journals in industrial-organizational psychology. *Industrial-Organizational Psychologist, 38*(4), 29–36.

2

Early Contributors to the Science and Practice of Industrial Psychology

Andrew J. Vinchur
Lafayette College

Laura L. Koppes
LK Associates

In historical treatments of the early years of industrial psychology, a number of names consistently appear: Hugo Münsterberg, Walter Dill Scott, and Walter Van Dyke Bingham chief among them. These pioneers were certainly central to the fledgling field that evolved into present day industrial–organizational psychology (I–O). As indicated in chapter 1, however, many other men and women contributed, in ways large and small, to the development of industrial psychology in the early years. The purpose of this chapter is to identify some of these individuals and to present their contributions.

Viteles (1932) saw the growth of industrial psychology in the United States as primarily due to university psychologists who, while maintaining their university affiliations, applied the new psychology to business situations. Ferguson (1961) disagreed. He saw the growth of industrial psychology as due not so much to university professors branching out as to interested businesspeople seeking out these professors to help them solve practical business problems. For example, Ferguson noted that businessmen Edward A. Woods and Winslow Russell contacted Bingham, and Griffin M. Lovelace approached Edward Strong, Jr., in the area of sales (as we will see later, other examples occurred in Switzerland, where Ivan Bally, the shoe manufacturer, approached Jules Suter of the University of Zürich [Heller, 1929–1930], and in England, where businessman H. J. Welch and psychologist C. S. Myers jointly founded the National Institute of Industrial Psychology [Burt, 1947]).

Both Ferguson's and Viteles' views have merit. In the early part of the 20th century, some stigma was attached to applied psychology by mainstream experimental psychologists. By maintaining their university positions and the prestige associated with their involvement in a scientific enterprise, these professors with an interest in applying psychology had a secure base from which to operate. For a variety of reasons (including, at times, monetary considerations), these academics were interested in branching out and applying the new psychology to the world of business. It is equally true, however, that in the progressive climate of the times, the impetus for action often came from the business side, because business leaders saw psychology as a means of increasing efficiency. The creation of new opportunities for psychologists was another consideration. Psychologists, particularly women psychologists, who had difficulty securing academic positions often found opportunity in applied psychology. As we shall see, meaningful contributions came from both those maintaining their academic affiliations and those whose careers were spent entirely in industry.

Writing this chapter presented us with a classic "personnel selection" dilemma: There are far too many qualified candidates than we could include in this brief chapter. We did not have to worry about false positives; we are confident that the individuals included made meaningful contributions to the new discipline of industrial psychology. Space constraints, however, did not permit as complete a treatment as we would ideally hope for: Some men and women are mentioned only briefly, some are discussed in other chapters of this volume, and some await future historical publications to detail their contributions. In this limited space we concentrated on the positive highlights of individual careers. We examine certain industrial psychologists who we believe made a significant contribution to the field before 1930.

Some of the individuals examined are well known, and others less so. Some women and men worked primarily in academia, and others in industry or consulting. Some contributors worked in the United States, and others abroad. Criteria for inclusion were not number of publications, number of citations, or other quantitative measures but our own subjective evaluation of each individual's contributions and impact on the emerging field of industrial psychology. We make no attempt to rank or rate those contributions or contributors (to the possible chagrin of James McKeen Cattell, one of our contributors and a great believer in such rankings). In writing this chapter we intentionally sacrificed depth for breadth to increase the number of individuals covered. We hope that interested readers will go beyond the brief sketches found here to other sources, especially original sources, to learn more about the careers and lives of these early pioneers. More information about these contributors, their work, and the relevant time periods can also be found throughout this volume.

The chapter is organized as follows: First we discuss Scott and Münsterberg; then Bingham and individuals associated with the groundbreaking program at the Carnegie Institute of Technology are covered. Next, psychologists associated with Cattell and Columbia University are discussed, followed by other prominent academic–practitioners, such as Morris Viteles and Donald Paterson. Early contributors who worked for the most part outside of academia are covered next. We close with brief sketches of contributors from outside the United States.

SCOTT AND MÜNSTERBERG

The first installment of Leonard Ferguson's (1962–1965) series of *Heritage of Industrial Psychology* is titled "Walter Dill Scott: First Industrial Psychologist." This leaves little doubt as to whom Ferguson viewed as the founder of the discipline. Although Ferguson was certainly aware of the individuals doing applied work before Scott, he based this judgment on Scott's impact. Ferguson did note the important contributions of Münsterberg, but believed that Münsterberg's untimely death lessened both the impact and follow-through of his pioneering work. Ferguson also pointed out that when Scott reviewed H. Münsterberg's 1913 text, Scott was in his 12th year as an industrial psychologist (vs. 2 or 3 for Münsterberg). Although identifying the "founder" of any field is likely to be contentious given the varying criteria for founding and multiple candidates for the honor (and we will make no attempt to do so in the chapter), Scott's contributions to industrial psychology were certainly noteworthy enough to support Ferguson's nomination.

Walter Dill Scott was born in Cookesville, Illinois, on May 1, 1869. He received his AB degree from Northwestern University in 1895. While at Northwestern he studied psychology with George Albert Coe. Choosing psychology over missionary work, Scott, on the advice of

Coe, did his postgraduate work under Wilhelm Wundt at the University of Leipzig in Germany, earning his doctorate in 1900 (Ferguson, 1962–1965).

Scott returned to America and took the position of instructor at Northwestern, rising to the rank of professor in 1907. In 1901, Thomas L. Balmer, advertising manager for *The Delineator, The Designer,* and *New Idea Woman's Magazine,* asked Scott (after unsuccessfully contacting Münsterberg, E. L. Thorndike at Columbia, and George A. Coe at Northwestern) to give a talk on how psychology might be useful in advertising. Initially reluctant, Scott delivered the talk at the Agate Club in Chicago. An audience member, John Lee Mahin, offered to start a magazine if Scott would contribute articles to it. Scott agreed, and his career as an industrial psychologist was underway. Scott was prolific; by 1915 he had produced six books and 101 articles (Ferguson, 1962–1965). During this period Scott also attempted some of the earliest efforts at group intelligence assessment (von Mayrhauser, 1989). In 1916, Scott took a leave of absence from Northwestern University to join the applied psychology program at the Carnegie Institute of Technology (also referred to as Carnegie Tech). There, in addition to directing the Bureau of Salesmanship Research, Scott became the first person to receive the title "professor of applied psychology" (Prien, 1991). He pioneered the development of selection devices such as application blanks, interview ratings, and various tests (Ferguson, 1962–1965).

As part of the contingent of psychologists who met in 1917 to decide how they could best assist the war effort, Scott clashed with Robert Yerkes, the American Psychological Association (APA) president (see Ferguson, 1962–1965, and von Mayrhauser, 1987, for details). Scott saw Yerkes as more concerned with furthering the interests of psychology than contributing to the war effort. While Yerkes concentrated on the development of group intelligence tests (the Army Alpha and Beta), Scott went his own way, eventually directing the Committee on Classification of Personnel in the Army. The committee adapted procedures used at Carnegie Tech, developed new procedures (e.g., trade tests), and used these procedures to place recruits. In recognition of Scott's efforts, he was the only psychologist awarded the Distinguished Service Medal.

Scott was elected APA president in 1919. Following the war, Scott, with Robert Clothier, L. B. Hopkins, Beardsley Ruml, Joseph W. Hayes, and Stanley B. Mathewson, organized the Scott Company in 1919, the first personnel consulting organization (see chap. 6). Although the company lasted only a few years (the recession of 1921–1922 took its toll), it was a successful and innovative organization. Ferguson (n.d.) listed 11 types of services offered, including preparation of technical manuals and books such as Scott and Clothier's influential book, *Personnel Management* (1923). In 1920, Scott was appointed president of his alma mater, Northwestern University, where he served with great success until his retirement in 1939 (Jacobson, 1951). Walter Dill Scott died in September of 1955.

Scott's legacy in industrial psychology is secure. His pioneering work in advertising, his seminal work in selection before and during his time at Carnegie Tech, and in particular his work in World War I all contributed greatly to the science and practice of industrial psychology. Whether or not we designate him the "first" industrial psychologist, Scott was a pioneer in the field. (See chap. 11 in this text for more information about Scott.)

Despite recent attention to the career and life of Hugo Münsterberg (e.g., Benjamin, 2000; Hale, 1980; Landy, 1992, 1997; Spillmann & Spillmann, 1993), for much of the 20th century there was relatively little interest in Münsterberg. At the time of his death, however, he was perhaps America's best known psychologist (Hale, 1980). This relative neglect is both unfortunate and undeserved, because Münsterberg (in addition to possessing a colorful personality) made major contributions to applied psychology. In addition to industrial psychology, he did pioneering work in forensic, clinical, and educational psychology.

The details of Münsterberg's life and career are well documented (e.g., Hale, 1980; his daughter, M. Münsterberg, 1922). Briefly, Münsterberg was born in Danzig, Germany on June 1, 1863. He earned his doctorate at Leipzig in 1885 under Wundt and completed an MD degree 2 years later at the University of Heidelberg. Münsterberg taught at the University of Freiburg, where he developed the psychology laboratory and something of an international reputation. William James, an admirer, brought Münsterberg to Harvard in 1892 to oversee that university's psychology laboratory. Although Münsterberg had many misgivings and still hoped for an appointment at a prestigious German university, he went to Harvard on a trial basis and eventually accepted a permanent position. Münsterberg was elected president of APA in 1898.

Although Münsterberg is now identified as a pioneer in applied psychology, like a number of his experimentally minded colleagues he was once quite hostile toward the application of psychology (Benjamin, 2000). But by the early 1900s he had reversed his position completely. In 1910–1911, Münsterberg taught what he claimed was the first course in applied psychology (Hale, 1980). Benjamin (2000) noted that between 1906 and 1916 Münsterberg published 20 books, for the most part on applied psychology. Although Münsterberg was by any standard extremely prolific, Landy (1997) pointed out that Münsterberg did tend toward redundancy in some of his works.

Münsterberg's initial publication in industrial psychology was a 1909 article in *McClure's Magazine* discussing possible applications of psychology to business. The consulting opportunities that followed became part of *Psychology and Industrial Efficiency* (Benjamin, 2000), the most relevant Münsterberg publication for industrial psychology (H. Münsterberg, 1913). This text set the initial agenda for what was then commonly called business or economic psychology. Münsterberg divided the book into three major sections: The first, The Best Possible Man, emphasized vocational guidance and selection and included summaries of Münsterberg's own investigations in selecting street car motormen, ship officers, and telephone switchboard operators. Hale (1980) noted that Münsterberg was among the first to use selection tests in industry. The second section, The Best Possible Work, included the topics of training, monotony, attention, and fatigue. There was also a discussion on physical and social influences on work (which includes a rather lengthy discussion of the effects of alcohol). Finally, the third section, The Best Possible Effect, covers topics such as advertising, buying, and selling. (See chap. 1 of this volume for a table of contents.) Although Münsterberg did cite some work other than his own (e.g., Scott, Weber, Hollingworth), he seemed most concerned with his own vision for applied psychology, a vision that would be very influential in the years to follow. The final years of Münsterberg's life were not happy ones. Reviled by both his colleagues and the general public for his support of Germany in World War I, he was under a great deal of stress. Arriving to teach a class at Radcliffe College in December of 1916, his graduate student, Harold Burtt, noted that Münsterberg looked exhausted. A few minutes into the lecture Münsterberg was dead of a cerebral hemorrhage at the age of 53 (Bjork, 1983).

BINGHAM AND HIS CARNEGIE TECH ASSOCIATES

Walter Van Dyke Bingham is probably best known for organizing and directing the groundbreaking applied psychology program at Carnegie Tech. Even if this were his only contribution, Bingham would merit a place of prominence in the history of industrial psychology. As we shall see, however, he made many other contributions throughout his long career. Bingham was born October 20, 1880, in Swan Lake City, Iowa. He attended the University of Kansas his freshman year and then transferred to Beloit College (AB, 1901), where he came under the influence of Guy Tawney, a Wundt PhD. Bingham did his graduate work at the University of Chicago at a time of great intellectual excitement over the new functionalism in psychology (see chaps. 1 and 3 for a description of functionalism). He worked with James Angell and was John B. Watson's student assistant. Before completing his doctorate at Chicago in 1908, Bingham took time to travel to Europe, where he met Kurt Koffka, Wolfgang Köhler, Hans Rupp, and Carl Stumpf in Berlin and Charles Spearman, Cyril Burt, and future pioneering industrial psychologist C. S. Myers in England (Bingham, 1952). Bingham then went on to Harvard, where he became acquainted with Münsterberg and completed his philosophy minor under William James and the other prominent Harvard philosophers (Ferguson, 1962–1965). Bingham first taught at Columbia where he was E. L. Thorndike's assistant, working with Thorndike on his differential research and the development of mental tests (Edwin A. Fleishman, personal communication, May 15, 2005) and later at Dartmouth in 1910.

By 1915, when he accepted the offer of A. A. Hamerschlag to found a new type of program at the Carnegie Tech, Bingham had a unique background in psychology (Ferguson, 1962–1965). He had been exposed to functionalism and behaviorism at Chicago; the Gestalt psychology of Kafka, Köhler, and Stumpf in Berlin; the beginnings of an applied psychology with Münsterberg at Harvard; and the influence of Cattell, Thorndike, and Robert Woodworth at Columbia. Bingham accepted Hamerschlag's invitation to direct the program, and the Division of Applied Psychology was born. The interested reader is referred to Ferguson (1962–1965) for a detailed treatment of Bingham's beginnings at Carnegie Tech. Space does not permit detailing the accomplishments of the Carnegie Tech program, which, despite its success, closed in 1924. The staff and students associated with the program read like a virtual "who's who" of early industrial psychology. We meet many of these individuals later in this chapter. (See chap. 6 in this volume for information about the Carnegie Tech program.)

Many of the members of the Carnegie Tech programs contributed to the World War I effort, including Bingham, who served as the executive secretary of the Committee on Classification of Personnel in the Army. Bingham also had an important role as conduit between Scott and Yerkes, who, as previously mentioned, did not agree on how psychology could be of most use in the war effort. Following the armistice, Bingham returned to his Carnegie Tech program. When that program was terminated, he moved to New York to direct the Personnel Research Federation, edit the *Journal of Personnel Research* (later *Personnel Journal*), and engage in private practice. During World War II, Bingham served as chief psychologist for the Adjutant General.

In addition to his many administrative and editing roles (not by any means all detailed here), Bingham produced a significant amount of scholarship, more than 200 books and papers (Zusne, 1984). Some notable books are *Procedures in Employment Psychology* (1926, with Max Freyd), *How to Interview* (1931, with Bruce Moore), and *Aptitudes and Aptitude Testing* (1937).

Bingham's contributions to the development of industrial psychology were substantial. In addition to his pioneering work at the Carnegie Tech, his efforts on behalf of psychology in two world wars, and his published works, Bingham acted as an influential advocate for industrial psychology. Unlike Scott, who virtually left the discipline in 1920 when he became president of Northwestern, or Münsterberg, whose untimely death cut short his potential contributions, Bingham was able to use this influence over the course of a long and productive life.

Many of the women and men associated with Bingham's short-lived program at Carnegie Tech had an impact on the development of industrial psychology. Walter Dill Scott is the best known example. James B. Miner and Edward K. Strong, Jr., both associated with the program, are discussed later in this chapter. Other staff members and students who contributed at Carnegie Tech and elsewhere include the following individuals.

Clarence Stone Yoakum (1879–1945) had three distinct career phases (Pillsbury, 1946). He conducted research into animal learning processes and human fatigue as a graduate student under James R. Angell at the University of Chicago (Yoakum received his PhD in 1908) and as professor and chair of the psychology department at the University of Texas. Next, his applied work in World War I led him to an interest in industrial psychology. And finally, there was his administrative career beginning in 1927, when he became director of the Bureau of University Research at the University of Michigan, followed by 1 year (1929–1930) as dean of the college of liberal arts at Northwestern University. Yoakum then returned to Michigan as vice-president of the university and dean of the graduate school (Bingham, 1946).

His second career phase is most relevant to this chapter. Commissioned as an Army first lieutenant under Yerkes, Yoakum rose to the rank of major and field supervisor for all mental testing (Bingham, 1946). In a 3-month period, Yoakum and his team (C. C. Brigham, M. V. Cobb, E. S. Jones, L. M. Terman, and G. M. Whipple) revised an earlier test (group examination a) into the Army Alpha in 1918. The test was eventually administered to more than 1½ million Army soldiers and officers in World War I. With Yerkes, Yoakum published *Army Mental Tests* (1920), a summary of the army's testing program.

In 1919 Yoakum accepted an appointment as professor of applied psychology and director of the Bureau of Personnel Research at Carnegie Tech. Bingham had considered him, as well as Harold Burtt and H. D. Kitson, when the program began, but none of the three were part of the original group (Ferguson, 1962–1965). Although Yoakum did adapt the Alpha for industrial use, he did not view it as a stand-alone method of selection. Yoakum also explored nonintellectual predictors such as past accomplishment records, personality factors, and interests. As Bingham (1946) noted, the last factor proved fruitful. The dissertations of Yoakum's students Max Freyd, Grace Manson, Bruce Moore, and M. J. Ream inspired E. K. Strong, Jr., to develop his well-known vocational interest inventory (Strong [1927] credits Yoakum, Freyd, J. B. Miner, and his Stanford graduate student Karl Cowdery as influences). Yoakum (with Kenagy) published *Selection and Training of Salesmen* (1925). Following the 1924 demise of the Division of Applied Psychology at Carnegie Tech, Yoakum went to the University of Michigan as professor of personnel management and then to his career in administration.

Arthur W. Kornhauser (1896–1990) made important contributions to at least four areas of industrial psychology: psychological testing and selection, employee attitude surveying, labor unions, and worker mental health (Zickar, 2003). Born in Steubenville, Ohio, he earned his BS from the University of Pittsburgh, his MA from Bingham's Carnegie Tech program in 1919, and his PhD from the University of Chicago in 1926. Kornhauser spent a brief period in the army in World War I, where he worked on trade tests under W. D. Scott; he then spent 1919–1920 continuing that work for the Scott Company. He began his academic career at the University of Chicago in 1921 and remained there until 1943 (he also worked part-time in the Chicago office of the Psychological Corporation from 1935 to 1943). In 1947, Kornhauser accepted a position at Wayne State University, where he remained until his retirement in 1962.

Kornhauser's work and philosophy on testing is summarized in *Psychological Tests in Business* (1924), a book he coauthored with Forrest A. Kingbury. Kingsbury, who received his PhD from Chicago (1920), was a colleague of Kornhauser's at Chicago. This book is noteworthy for a number of reasons. Test construction, validation, and selection procedures were carefully explained and relevant even by today's standards. Unlike Münsterberg, for example, Kornhauser was very cautious in his recommendations and careful not to oversell the usefulness of tests. His later work on employee welfare is also foreshadowed in this text. Kornhauser's interests, however, were broader than testing and selection. As early as 1923 he published an article on employee motivation (Kornhauser, 1923). Kornhauser (with Agnes A. Sharp) is credited with the earliest well-developed attitude survey (Kornhauser & Sharp, 1931–1932) at the Kimberly–Clark Corporation (Baritz, 1960). His interest and concern for the worker resulted in *Mental Health of the Industrial Worker* (1965) published after his retirement. Zickar (2003) stated that one of Kornhauser's most important contributions was to the psychology of the relations between labor and management. He was one of only a handful of the early industrial psychologists whose concern for unions (and the worker) took precedent over concern for management. (See chap. 3 for a discussion on I–O and labor unions.)

Louis Leon Thurstone (1887–1955) is remembered today for his many contributions to measurement theory, factor analysis, intelligence testing, and scaling. His early career, however, was spent doing applied work in testing, selection, and vocational guidance. Thurstone received a master of engineering degree from Cornell in 1912, worked briefly for Thomas Edison, and then accepted an instructorship from the University of Minnesota, where he studied psychology with H. Woodrow and J. B. Miner. He continued his psychology studies at the University of Chicago and earned his PhD in 1917 under J. Angell (Beardsley Ruml was a fellow student). While Thurstone was still a graduate student in 1915, he was chosen by Bingham to be an assistant in the Department of Psychology in the new Division of Psychology. Thurstone rose steadily through the ranks to a full professorship and chairmanship of the psychology department. During the first World War he worked on trade tests for the army. In 1923, Thurstone went to Washington to work on civil service personnel methods in the Institute for Government Research. He returned to teaching at the University of Chicago in 1924 (and married Thelma Gwinn, who had received her master's degree at Carnegie Tech in 1923). Thurstone was elected president of APA in 1933. He remained at Chicago until 1952, when he moved to the University of North Carolina (biographical information from Adkins, 1964; Ferguson, 1962–1965; Jones, 1998; Thurstone, 1952) as the first director of the Psychometric Center there (Edwin A. Fleishman, personal communication, May 15, 2005). Thurstone did early pioneering work in test construction and selection. His later innovations in factor analysis (e.g., Thurstone, 1935; 1947) and scaling had a major impact on I–O psychology.

Other staff at Carnegie Tech included Guy Montrose Whipple (1876–1941), who received his AB degree from Brown in 1897 and his PhD (under E. B. Titchener) at Cornell University in 1900. Whipple was a member of the original advisory committee (with Raymond Dodge and F. L. Wells) for the Division of Applied Psychology (Ferguson, 1962–1965). Whipple followed Scott as acting director of the Bureau of Salesmanship Research and also was professor of applied psychology. During the war Whipple worked on the Army Alpha. Beardsley Ruml (1894–1960) served as an instructor at Carnegie Tech and was then one of the founding members of the Scott Company. He was also an officer in the Personnel Research Federation. Ruml received his BS from Dartmouth (1915) and PhD from the University of Chicago (1917). At age 27 he was appointed director of the Laura Spelman Rockefeller Memorial. Ruml was also a professor at the University of Chicago, chairman of the Federal Reserve Bank of New York, chairman of R. H. Macy, and creator of the pay-as-you-go federal income tax plan (NY Times, 4-19-60).

After working in several brief academic positions, Marion A. Bills (1890–1970) was hired by Bingham as a research assistant for the Bureau of Personnel Research, a component of the Division of Applied Psychology. Bills became the associate director and consulted with businesses on selection, training, and supervision (1919–1923). She received a bachelor's degree in 1908 from the University of Michigan and her PhD in 1917 from Bryn Mawr College, where she studied with Clarence E. Ferree, a student of Titchener and a widely published researcher on visual perception (Austin & Waung, 1994). In 1924 and 1925, while working for the Life Insurance Research Bureau (later known as the Life Insurance Marketing and Research Association [LIMRA]), Bills conducted research on what she labeled as "permanency" (now known as retention; Bills, 1923, 1925, 1926–1927a, 1926–1927b, 1928). In 1926, Bills joined the Aetna Life Insurance Company as an assistant secretary, where she continued to use scientific research methods to understand and resolve business personnel problems. For example, she developed a unique wage incentive system for clerical positions, devised a job classification method, instituted a job evaluation program, and served as a consultant to top management (Austin & Waung, 1994). Bills' long-term research on selection and retention of clerical and sales personnel for the life insurance industry is considered as one of the first congenial collaborations between business individuals and psychologists (Ferguson, 1952). Her studies were regarded as being at the forefront of selection research. Bills was on the original committee that structured Division 14 of the APA (now known as the Society for Industrial and Organizational Psychology [SIOP]) and served as the seventh president of the division, the first woman, and one of three women to be elected in 50 years (Koppes, 1997; Koppes & Bauer, in press). It's important to note that Bills' job title, assistant secretary, did not accurately reflect the authority and responsibility of her position. She joined Aetna under the circumstances that she would also be a voting officer.

Students in the Carnegie Tech program included Max Freyd, who received his BA (1918) and MS (1920) degrees from the University of Washington and his PhD from Carnegie Tech in 1922. Following his graduation he taught at the University of Pennsylvania for 1 year and then worked with J. B. Watson conducting marketing, merchandising, and advertising research for the J. Walter Thompson Company. This was followed by employment at the Personnel Research Federation (1925-1928) and the Retail Research Association. In 1936, Freyd headed the research section for the Personnel Division of the Social Security Board and later headed the development of personnel manuals for the Civil Service Commission. Freyd retired in 1946 (biographical information from Freyd, 1951). Freyd's publications were primarily in personnel selection and measurement of interests (e.g., Freyd, 1922–1923). Freyd was involved in the development of the graphic rating scale (Freyd, 1923) and, with Bingham, wrote *Procedures in Employment Psychology* (1926). Guion (1976), in his chapter on recruiting, selection, and job placement in the first edition of the *Handbook of Industrial and Organizational Psychology*, demonstrated how Freyd's prescriptions remain relevant and called Freyd's 1923–1924 article *Measurement in Vocational Selection* "marvelously up to date" (p. 783).

Another student was Grace Manson (1893–1967), who received her AB from Goucher College in Baltimore in 1915, an AM degree in 1919 from Columbia University, and her PhD in 1923 from Carnegie Tech. She was the head of the Psychology Department at Salem College from 1919 to 1921 and an instructor and investigator for Carnegie Tech from 1923 to 1924. She went to the University of Michigan as an investigator for the National Research Council on Human Migrations (1924–1926) and as a research associate for the Bureau of Business Research (1926–1931) in the School of Business Administration, where she worked with C. S. Yoakum. The purpose of the bureau was to conduct research on various business issues such as unemployment, occupational interests, and earnings.

While at the Bureau of Business Research, Manson conducted numerous studies (Cook & Manson, 1925–1926; Manson, 1925a, 1925b, 1925–1926a) on selection techniques, application blanks, rating scales, occupations of women, and the relation of personal history data to success in department stores and in insurance companies. She gathered data on the occupations and earnings of 14,000 women and developed an Occupational Test for Women to measure vocational interests (Elliott & Manson, 1930). Manson also published a bibliography, frequently cited by her contemporaries, on psychological tests and other measures used in industry in the *Journal of Personnel Research* (1925–1926b).

Bruce V. Moore (1891–1977) received his AB (1914) and MS (1917) from Indiana University. Although initially headed to Columbia and E. L. Thorndike to complete his doctorate, Moore instead accepted an invitation from R. M. Yerkes to help in the World War I effort in the area of psychological testing. This experience contributed to his decision to enroll in the Division of Applied Psychology in 1919 (Farr & Tesluk, 1997). Moore was the first of only four to receive doctorates from the program (Merrill Ream, Max Freyd, and Grace Manson are the others [Ferguson, n.d.]). This is generally acknowledged as the first U.S. PhD granted from an industrial psychology program. For his dissertation, Moore developed an inventory of occupational interests as an aid in the selection of engineers in the Westinghouse Electric Company. Subsequently, with Moore's approval, E. K. Strong, Jr., further developed this inventory for use in the selection of life insurance salesmen. This was the genesis for the eventual development of the widely used Strong Vocational Interest Blank (Farr & Tesluk, 1997). Moore joined the faculty at what was then Pennsylvania State College in 1920 and remained until his retirement in 1952, serving as department head for much of that time. Moore was elected first president of APA Division 14 (Industrial and Business Psychology, known today as SIOP).

In addition to the individuals mentioned, others contributed to the Carnegie Tech program as faculty, staff, or students. A partial list includes L. Dewey Anderson, Eugene Benge, W. W. Charters, Glen Cleeton, David Craig, Thelma Gwinn Thurstone, C. F. Hansen, Dwight and Newman Hoopingarner, H. G. Kenagy, Franklyn Meine, Merrill Ream, and Edward S. Robinson (Ferguson, n.d.; 1962–1965 described additional contributors).

CATTELL AND COLUMBIA UNIVERSITY

James McKeen Cattell's contributions to industrial psychology were more subtle and indirect than the contributions of others discussed in this chapter. Unlike, for example, Scott, Münsterberg, or Bingham, Cattell conducted no research in selection, training, or any other substantive area of industrial psychology. His own experimental research output, although productive early in his career, virtually halted after 1900 as he diverted his considerable energy to teaching, editing, and promoting psychology (although not necessarily applied psychology). Yet Cattell's role in the origin and growth of industrial psychology is an important one.

Born in Easton, Pennsylvania, in 1860, Cattell received his undergraduate degree from Lafayette College, where his father William was president from 1863 through 1883. At Lafayette, the renowned philologist Francis March greatly influenced Cattell. March's emphasis on Baconian inductive principles can be found in Cattell's work in psychology (Sokal, 1987). While in Europe to study philosophy, Cattell was impressed by both Wundt and Lotze. Returning to America, Cattell spent a year at Johns Hopkins with G. Stanley Hall before returning to Leipzig and Wundt. Cattell received his PhD under Wundt in 1886. While at Leipzig, Cattell developed a strong interest in the variability of human performance (Woodworth, 1944).

Returning to the United States in 1887, Cattell lectured at Bryn Mawr and the University of Pennsylvania (Boring, 1950). Intending to study neurology, he next journeyed to Cambridge University, where he came under the influence of Francis Galton (Cattell wrote that his career was shaped by three men named Francis: Bacon, March, and Galton [Sokal, 1987]). Galton inspired Cattell to use the experimental procedures he developed at Leipzig to collect quantitative measurements of psychological individual difference characteristics (Sokal, 1987).

For detailed information on Cattell's career, the interested reader should consult Sokal (1971, 1981, 1984, 1987, 1995). To briefly summarize, Cattell was a professor of psychology at the University of Pennsylvania from 1888 to 1891, where he influenced Lightner Witmer, who, as we will see, influenced Morris Viteles. After establishing the psychology laboratory at Penn, Cattell moved to Columbia University, where he headed the psychology program. Cattell remained at Columbia until 1917, when he was dismissed for his pacifist opposition to World War I, his persistent antagonism toward the university president, or some combination of both (see Summerscales, 1970). Cattell then devoted much of time and effort to editorial duties, a pursuit he had been active in since he and Mark Baldwin cofounded the *Psychological Review* in 1894. Cattell also purchased and revived the journal *Science* and became a leader in the American Association for the Advancement of Science (Coon & Sprenger, 1998). In 1921, he founded the Psychological Corporation, the oldest consulting company still operating today, for the promotion of applied psychology (Cattell, 1923). (See chap. 6 for more detailed information.)

Although Cattell was an important pioneer in psychology, what can we say about his contribution to industrial psychology? There was the direct impact of the Psychological Corporation, which after a shaky start was put on firm financial footing by Bingham, Paul Achilles, and others. Cattell's early studies on testing were an important influence, despite the failure of his anthropometric tests to predict meaningful criteria (see Sokal, 1987). He championed individual differences, quantification, and objectivity; these values continue to have an impact on the field (F. L. Wells, 1944, repeated a remark attributed to Titchener, perhaps apocryphal, that "Cattell's god is Probable Error"). And finally, doctoral students educated in the Columbia program during and shortly after Cattell's tenure made important contributions to industrial psychology, for example, E. L. Thorndike (PhD 1898), James B. Miner (PhD 1903), Harry Hollingworth (PhD 1909), Edward K. Strong, Jr. (PhD 1911), Albert Poffenberger (PhD 1912), Herbert W. Rogers (PhD 1921), Herbert Toops (PhD 1921), Elsie Oschrin Bregman (PhD 1922), Paul Achilles (PhD 1923), Sadie Shellow (PhD 1923), and Richard Uhrbock (PhD 1928).

Regarding Thorndike, Bingham (1952), who served as an instructor and Edward L. Thorndike's (1874–1949) assistant at Columbia from 1908 to 1910, described Thorndike as a "dynamo." With a bibliography of more than 450 articles and books (Zusne, 1984) over a wide range of interests, Thorndike certainly fit that label. Best known for his pioneering contributions to animal and human learning (e.g., the "law of effect" and "law of exercise"), early work in measurement (*Introduction to a Theory of Mental Measurement,* 1904), and educational psychology, Thorndike earned ABs from Wesleyan (1895) and Harvard (1896) and his MA (1897) and PhD (with Cattell) at Columbia in 1898. He taught at Columbia from 1899 to 1940. Among Thorndike's many honors were presidencies of both the APA (1912) and the American Association for the Advancement of Science (1934). Thorndike did find the time to make contributions specific to industrial psychology in the areas of selection (particularly in World War I; Ferguson, 1962–1965), testing, and vocational guidance (see R. L. Thorndike, 1991).

J. B. Miner (1873–1943) earned three degrees, a BS (1897), LLB (1899), and SM (1901) at the University of Minnesota (Harlow Gale, a pioneer in applying psychology to advertising, was the psychologist on the faculty at this time; Ferguson, 1962–1965). Miner attended Columbia University as a university fellow under Cattell and obtained his PhD in 1903. After short teaching stints at the universities of Illinois and Iowa, he returned to the University of Minnesota until Bingham brought him to the new program at Carnegie Institute of Technology. Miner brought a strong quantitative background to Carnegie Tech (he published an annual review of correlation for a number of years in *Psychological Bulletin*). Miner was initially an assistant professor of psychology and education in the Department of Training for Teachers. Miner had an interest in assessing vocational interests and eventually influenced Strong (Ferguson, n.d.). He became executive secretary and acting director of the Research Bureau for Retail Training as well as a consultant to the Bureau of Salesmanship Research. Miner went to the University of Kentucky in 1921, where he organized the psychological clinic and Personnel Research Bureau. He remained at Kentucky until his death (White, 1943).

Harry Levi Hollingworth (1880–1956) was a reluctant applied psychologist. His first major consulting project began in 1911, when despite his awareness of the stigma attached to applied research he agreed to study the behavioral effects of caffeine for the Coca-Cola Company (Hollingworth, 1911). The fee for this research allowed Hollingworth to supplement his meager Columbia University salary and enabled his wife Leta to complete her doctoral studies

(Benjamin, Rogers, & Rosenbaum, 1991). Following the completion of the Coca-Cola study, Hollingworth was inundated with consulting opportunities. From 1914 though 1917 he completed some 40 reports of consultant investigations, most involving marketing and advertising (Benjamin, 1996).

Hollingworth received his AB from the University of Nebraska in 1906 and his PhD from Columbia in 1909. He published *Vocational Psychology* in 1916, closely followed in 1917 by *Applied Psychology* with A. Poffenberger. Despite his many contributions to industrial psychology and his successful consulting career, Hollingworth was blunt regarding his motivation. In an unpublished autobiography, he stated that although he is considered a pioneer in applied psychology, he never had any genuine interest in the area (Benjamin, 1996). Although Hollingworth preferred theoretical work and lamented that he could never shake the applied psychologist label, reluctant or not he contributed to applied psychology in substantial ways.

Edward K. Strong, Jr. (1884–1963) is best remembered today for his work in the measurement of vocational interests. Involved in applied work from the beginning of his career (the topic of his 1911 dissertation under Cattell concerned the relative merits of advertisements, a topic suggested by Hollingworth; Hansen, 1987), Strong spent 3 years after graduation at Columbia working in advertising and marketing. After a period at the George Peabody College for Teachers, he served on the Committee for Classification of Personnel in World War I (Darley, 1964). In 1919, following his military service, Strong became a member of the faculty at the Carnegie Institute of Technology; in 1923 he went to Stanford University and remained until his retirement in 1949.

Although others preceded Strong in vocational interest research (e.g., Carnegie Tech students Bruce Moore, Max Freyd, Grace Manson, and M. J. Ream), it was Strong (initially with his student Karl Cowdery) who saw the potential in it and maintained a lifelong research program on the topic. The Strong Vocational Interest Blank, first published in 1927, remains his primary and most important contribution (see also chap. 11 in this text).

Herbert Anderson Toops (1895–1972) spent the bulk of his professional career at Ohio State (1923–1965). After completing his BA and MA at Ohio State, Toops completed his PhD in 1921 under E. L. Thorndike at Columbia. The topic of his dissertation was trade tests (work samples; Austin, 1992), a topic he had also researched in the Army in World War I (Ferguson, 1962–1965). Both a teacher and mentor, Toops also contributed to industrial psychology in the areas of testing and statistics (Austin, 1992).

Elsie Oschrin Bregman (1896–1969) earned a BA from Barnard College in 1918 and a PhD from Columbia University in 1922. She worked in various fields including measurement of intelligence, counseling, vocational guidance, and personnel selection. She did pioneer work in applied psychology while at R. H. Macy Company, New York, from 1919 to 1921, one of several businesses that hired psychologists to examine their personnel processes after World War I (Sokal, 1981). She began her career there, where she initiated psychological research and procedures for employee recruitment, selection, training, and management and for adjustment of sales and clerical positions (e.g., Bregman, 1921; Oschrin, 1918). In addition to working as a research assistant and instructor at Teachers College, Columbia University, from 1923 to 1934 Bregman worked for the Psychological Corporation. Beginning in 1923, Cattell used tactics to save the corporation (Sokal, 1981). One such tactic was hiring Bregman as an associate to develop and publish revisions of the Army Alpha General Intelligence Examinations for use by businesses and educational institutions. The revisions were entitled Bregman Revision of the Army Alpha Examinations for General Intelligence Forms A and B (Bregman, 1926, 1935a) and were sold and administered as a means to generate revenue for the corporation. Unfortunately, there was little net income once royalties and overhead costs were paid (Sokal, 1981). Bregman received royalties (10% of every sale) throughout her lifetime. By receiving these royalties, she is considered to be the only individual to profit from the Psychological Corporation during its early years (Sokal, 1981).

Bregman published 12 scientific papers between 1918 and 1947, three books that she coauthored with Thorndike and others, the revisions of the Army Alpha exams (1926, 1935a), and the well-known Bregman Language Completion Scale in 1935 (Bregman, 1935b) for the Psychological Corp. One noteworthy publication written in 1922 is entitled "Studies in Industrial Psychology," published in the *Archives of Psychology*.

Sadie Myers Shellow earned a bachelor's degree in 1915 from Smith College, a master's degree from Utah University in 1917, and a PhD from Columbia University in 1923. On completion of her doctorate, Shellow was hired by the Milwaukee Electric Railway and Light Company as a psychologist. She continued work begun by Morris Viteles and subsequently collaborated with him on several research projects. In 1935, she joined the Milwaukee Police Department as a personnel consultant, where she advised on selection, placement, and training issues. Specifically, she researched and provided techniques for selection of recruits, sergeants, lieutenants, captains, instructors, patrolmen, detectives, laboratory assistants, and clerks. She created methods for training for promotion, and she developed psychological tests and examined the relationships between these tests (Shellow, 1925–1926, 1926–1927a, 1926–1927b).

Other Columbia PhDs involved in industrial pursuits include Albert Theodore Poffenberger (1885–1977) and Herbert W. Rogers (1890–1964). Poffenberger chaired the psychology department at Columbia University and, with H. L. Hollingworth, wrote the early and influential text *Applied Psychology* (1917). He was elected president of APA in 1935 (see chap. 11). Rogers, who chaired the psychology department at Lafayette College from 1929 until his retirement in 1957, authored one of the first selection validation studies (Rogers, 1917). Although Ferguson (1962–1965) credited Carnegie Tech student Dwight Hoopingarner as the first master's-level psychologist to work full-time in industry, that distinction may belong to Rogers, who worked as an applied psychologist for the Charles Williams Stores in New York in 1916 (Rogers, 1946).

OTHER ACADEMIC–PRACTITIONERS

Harold Ernest Burtt was born in Haverhill, Massachusetts, on April 26, 1890. A senior at Dartmouth College when Bingham joined the faculty, Burtt recalled Bingham's influence as being less from any coursework he may have taken from Bingham than from the correspondence they maintained following Burtt's graduation in 1911. Burtt chose psychology as a career (over classics or mathematics) and, at Bingham's suggestion, went to see Münsterberg at Harvard in the summer of 1912 (Burtt, 1953).

As Burtt noted in a 1953 letter to Leonard Ferguson, instead of becoming Münsterberg's student he was claimed by Herbert S. Langfeld, who "saw me first" and assigned a thesis, which Burtt said he completed for "diplomatic reasons," on factors influencing the arousal of the visual memory image (Burtt, 1953). Burtt did, however, get an opportunity to work with Münsterberg on an applied project involving streetlight illumination and safety.

Following receipt of the PhD from Harvard in 1915, Burtt worked as an instructor at Harvard and at Simmons College and then chaired the Committee on Psychological Problems on Aviation in World War I (Ferguson, 1962–1965). In 1919 he took a position as Instructor at Ohio State University, obtained the rank of professor in 1923, and chaired the department from 1938 until his retirement in 1960 (Thayer & Austin, 1992).

Burtt's contributions to industrial psychology were wide ranging. As noted by Thayer and Austin (1992), Burtt published a number of early, influential textbooks, beginning with *Principles of Employment Psychology* (1926) and continuing with *Psychology and Industrial Effi-*

ciency (1929) and *Applied Psychology* (1948). Burtt was instrumental in the founding of the American Association of Applied Psychology (AAAP) and served as the first president of the Section of Industrial and Business Psychology when AAAP merged with the APA in 1946 (Austin, 1992). He had a large influence through the teaching and mentoring of students. Four of his doctoral students became presidents of the APA's industrial psychology Division 14: Carroll L. Shartle, Edwin A. Fleishman, Donald L. Grant, and Paul W. Thayer (Thayer & Austin, 1992), and one, Frank N. Stanton (PhD 1935) became president of the Columbia Broadcasting System (CBS). Burtt died at the age of 101 on August 15, 1991.

One name missing from Viteles' (1932) list of academic–practitioners important to the early growth of industrial psychology was his own. Morris Simon Viteles was an early exemplar and lifelong advocate of the scientist–practitioner model, successfully juggling careers in academia and industry. Born in Russia on March 21, 1898, Viteles immigrated to England with his family shortly after his birth and then settled in the United States in 1904. Viteles's entire postsecondary education and subsequent academic career were spent at the University of Pennsylvania, where he earned the AB (1918), AM (1919), and PhD (1921) degrees. His academic career at Penn began in 1918 with his appointment as assistant in the Department of Psychology and ended with his retirement as dean of the Graduate School of Education in 1968 (Viteles, 1974). Viteles (1967, 1974) recalled that his major influences at Penn were Lightner Witmer, a Wundt PhD and strong proponent of applied psychology, and Edwin B. Twitmyer, an advocate of rigorous research standards.

Viteles was a pioneer in internationalizing I–O psychology. In 1922 and 1923, Viteles traveled through Europe. He met with Jean Marie Lahy, a psychologist in France, and was impressed by the work of the German psychologists Lipmann, Stern, and Giese (he was less impressed by Moede and Piorkowski's psychotechnical approach). Viteles noted that he was particularly influenced by Myers in London, who viewed pure and applied science as mutually beneficial. Viteles also cited Bingham as one of his major influences, through his encouragement and inclusion of Viteles in meetings of the Personnel Research Federation. In the 1930s, Viteles visited the Soviet Union, where he established relations. He was the first U.S. psychologist elected president of the International Association of Applied Psychology (IAAP; 1958–1968). The only other U.S. presidents of IAAP have been Edwin Fleishman (1974–1982) and Harry Triandis (1990–1994) during the first 70 years of IAAP's existence (Edwin A. Fleishman, personal communication, May 15, 2005).

Viteles maintained long-standing relationships with a number of companies (e.g., Yellow Cab Company of Philadelphia, Philadelphia Electric Company, Bell Telephone), often publishing the results of his investigations (e.g., Viteles, 1925–1926). In 1926, he established the first vocational guidance program based at a university (Thompson, 1998). Viteles pioneered job analysis methods with his job psychograph method (Viteles, 1974). Perhaps his best known accomplishment was the publication of his influential textbook *Industrial Psychology* in 1932. Dubbed the "Bible" by generations of students, the text's comprehensive coverage of industrial psychology both in the United States and abroad was instrumental in defining the field (Thompson, 1998). A follow-up, *Motivation and Morale in Industry*, published in 1953, expanded the field to include the "O" portion of modern I–O psychology. Morris Viteles died at the age of 98 on December 7, 1996.

Donald Gildersleeve Paterson (1892–1961) received his AB and MA (1916) from the Ohio State University. A captain in the army in World War I, Paterson served as chief psychological examiner. He worked for 2 years in the Scott Company, amd then in 1921 he moved to the University of Minnesota, where he spent 39 years, retiring in 1960. Despite never completing the PhD degree, Paterson supervised at least 88 PhD students in his time at Minnesota ("Donald G. Paterson," 1961).

Paterson was instrumental in the founding of the Minnesota Employment Stabilization Research Institute and the University of Minnesota Industrial Relations Center. He was editor of the *Journal of Applied Psychology* for 12 years, and he was the author of more than 300 publications, including authoring or coauthoring *Minnesota Mechanical Ability Tests* (1930) and *Men, Women, and Jobs* (1936).

EARLY PRACTITIONERS

Henry Charles Link had a very successful career as an industrial psychologist outside of academia. Link was born in Buffalo, New York, on August 27, 1889. His undergraduate and graduate education took place at Yale University (PhD 1916). Link was a pioneer in the use of employee selection procedures. His 1919 book *Employment Psychology* outlined an early attempt at criterion-related test validation procedures. Kornhauser and Kingsbury (1924) called this book "probably the best description of sound scientific methods in constructing and standardizing selective tests for use in an industrial establishment" (p. 186). In 1917, Link became director of training and psychological research for the Winchester Repeating Arms Company. Ferguson (1962–1965) claimed that Link was the first PhD psychologist to work full-time as a psychologist in industry. While at Winchester, Link (1918) conducted an innovative study evaluating a series of tests for selecting shell inspectors and gaugers, using job performance (pounds of shells inspected in a day) as an external criterion. In addition to working at Winchester, Link worked for U.S. Rubber, Lord & Taylor, and Gimbel Brothers. While secretary–treasurer of the Psychological Corporation, Link in 1931 developed the *Psychological Barometer,* one of the first market research surveys (von Mayrhauser, n.d.). Link died in January 1952.

Millicent Pond was another psychologist who graduated from Yale and worked at the Winchester Repeating Arms Company. She received an AB in 1910, an AM from Bryn Mawr College in 1911, and a PhD from Yale University in 1925. Pond worked as an employment interviewer at the Winchester. She was also director of employment test research at Scovill Manufacturing Company in Connecticut and then supervisor of employment research. Her responsibilities included selection, placement, and training of factory workers. Pond conducted a series of studies to examine selection and placement of factory workers. She examined the relations between predictors such as intelligence tests, employment tests, and application blanks with criteria, such as foremen's ratings, pay, pay progress, and employees' ability and willingness to stay on the job for at least 6 months (Pond, 1926–1927a; 1926–1927b, 1926–1927c).

In recent years, Lillian Moller Gilbreth (1878–1972) has been acknowledged and recognized as a significant contributor to the evolution of I–O psychology (i.e., Koppes, 1997; Koppes, Landy, & Perkins, 1993; Perloff & Naman, 1996). She received a bachelor's degree in 1900 and a master's degree in English in 1902 from the University of California. She then received a PhD in psychology at Brown University in 1914 for her application of scientific management principles to increasing the efficiency of classroom teachers. Gilbreth may have completed the first dissertation on a topic relevant to industrial psychology.

Gilbreth and her husband, Frank Gilbreth, had their own consulting firm, in which they pioneered observational methods and measurement of work motions in laboratories outside universities. Although the Gilbreths supported Fredrick Taylor's work on scientific management, Lillian Gilbreth, in particular, believed he neglected attention to individual rights and needs in the work setting (Kelly & Kelly, 1990). Gilbreth compensated for Taylor's omission of human aspects by applying psychological principles.

Although she did not publish in applied psychology journals, Gilbreth's writings were at the forefront of many modern ideas of I–O psychology (e.g., Gilbreth, 1925). Her dissertation was published as a book, *The Psychology of Management* (1914), which was considered to be one of the most influential textbooks on industrial relations (Stevens & Gardner, 1982). She presented novel ideas to business leaders of the time by asserting that the laws of psychology support the laws of management. Each chapter represents an underlying idea of scientific management, and within each chapter, she presented elements of the idea that can be subjected to psychological investigation. She integrated throughout the book the importance of human relations in business and the need to consider individual differences and needs.

Following the death of her husband, Gilbreth managed her consulting company, Gilbreth, Inc., for an additional 45 years, and she was an outspoken advocate for applying psychology to business and engineering problems. She has been labeled as the Mother of Scientific Management and the First Lady of Management (Stevens & Gardner, 1982). In addition, she was an innovator; examples of her inventions include the foot-pedal trashcan and shelves inside refrigerator doors (Kelly & Kelly, 1990).

Mary Holmes Stevens Hayes (1884–1962) earned an AB from the University of Wisconsin in 1904, and then went to the University of Chicago and studied under Angell. She received her PhD in experimental psychology in 1910. When Hayes worked for the army from 1917 to 1919, her job title was laboratory technician and civilian expert in the Army Medical School and Surgeon General's Office. After World War I and in 1919, Hayes was asked to join the first consulting firm, the Scott Company, as a consultant. It is clear from examining the Scott Company papers that Hayes was regarded as a professional. She worked with a variety of organizations on a diversity of issues. One particular accomplishment to note is the publication of a book with W. D. Scott (Scott & Hayes, 1921). After the Scott Company dissolved, Hayes worked for a brief time at the U.S. Children's Bureau in the Department of Labor and then went to New York, where she was employed at the Vocational Service for Juniors (1924). During her tenure at the Vocational Service for Juniors, Hayes developed an interest for the problems of youth and subsequently became a recognized expert on guidance and placement. She published several articles in *Personality Journal* and *Occupations*.

Because of Hayes' prior experience with the Children's Bureau and expertise of youth problems, she was hired by the Children's Bureau of the Department of Labor as a general consultant to conduct a youth study requested by the U.S. Congress in 1935. The purpose of this study was to examine the problems of unemployed youth. This study and the program proposed by Hayes laid the groundwork for the New Deal program, the National Youth Administration (NYA), housed within the Works Progress Administration ("N.Y.A. Leader Finds State Progressive," 1939, March 15). The proposed program was to help employ the unemployed, especially those located in depressed areas. As the director of the Division of Guidance and Placement, a division of the NYA, Hayes developed performance appraisal systems, selection techniques, and training programs and made decisions regarding selection, placement, compensation, and training. In 1940, the NYA was reorganized, and the Division of Guidance and Placement was renamed the Division of Youth Personnel. Hayes' tasks were vast and diversified, and all required her to use applied psychology. She shifted her efforts from a focus on the Depression to the war. She made decisions about how to organize the defense and to prepare the youth for defense jobs. Other responsibilities included being a member of the Advisory Group of the Civil Service Commission and a member of a committee appointed by the Secretary of Labor to consider coordination of labor and training facilities of the government (Koppes, 1997).

Although not a psychologist, Mary P. Follett (1868–1933) merits inclusion in this chapter for her anticipation of much of present-day management theory. Educated at Radcliffe College, Follett took the lessons she learned as a community activist and applied them to business. Her lectures and writings on topics such as authority, conflict, power, leadership, and group processes seem remarkably fresh today and continue to influence organization and management theorists (Tonn, 2003). (See also chap. 16 in this text.)

CONTRIBUTORS FROM OUTSIDE THE UNITED STATES[1]

Outside the United States, psychologists were also beginning to apply the new scientific psychology to business and industry. In Switzerland (where Münsterberg had been offered a position at the University of Zürich at the same time as he received an offer from Harvard), Jules Suter, in 1913, introduced Münsterberg's ideas into the Bally shoe factory there. In 1924, Suter established an Institute of Industrial Psychology to conduct research in the areas of selection, vocational guidance, training, and the psychological aspects of labor management, human relations, and leadership (Heller, 1929–1930). Also active was Franziska Baumgarten-Tramer. Baumgarten-Tramer (1886–1970) has been called "one of the earliest and most influential occupational, i.e., industrial, psychologists in the world" (Stevens & Gardner, 1982, p. 212). She was awarded a PhD in 1917 from the University of Berlin. In France, as early as 1905, Jean Marie Lahy was conducting studies on the selection of stenographers (Viteles, 1923) and later working on other problems in selection, scientific management, and vocational guidance (Fryer, 1923–1924). In Russia, Hellerstein, Spielrein (who received his doctorate in Leipzig in 1912), and Kraval were leaders in the scientific study of work (Viteles, 1932), although in the opinion of one observer (Hartmann, 1932), industrial psychology in Russia was hampered by the "constant intrusion of Communist propaganda into purely factual or theoretical material" (p. 354). These "intrusions" proved fatal for I. N. Speilrein, who vanished in one of Stalin's purges (Viteles, 1974).

It was in Germany and Great Britain, however, where industrial psychology was becoming most established (see also chap. 4). Kornhauser (1929–1930) and Viteles (1923) both noted that in Germany (as in the United States), the primary topic of industrial psychology was employee selection. One notable psychologist active in selection research before 1930 was Walter Moede (1888–1958), who founded the Psychotechnical Institute of the Charlottenburg Technische Hochscule (Viteles, 1932) and published a number of texts on industrial psychology (Zusne, 1984). Others of note include M. Atzler, who founded the Institut für Arbeits-Physiologie in Berlin in 1916; C. Piorkowski, who, with Moede, conducted selection research as early as 1916; the psychiatrist E. Kraepelin, who in 1902 worked on learning curves (Viteles, 1932); Walther Poppelreuter (Kornhauser, 1929–1930), who had a number of industrial psychology publications (Zusne, 1984); and Hans Rupp (Geuter, 1992). In addition, Lipmann (1926–1927) mentioned Blumfeld, Bogen, Friedrich, Giese, Hellpach, Klemm, Marbe, Peters, Sachenberg, and Schlesinger (see Lipmann, 1926–1927 and Geuter, 1992, for more information). Two early contributors of particular note are (Louis) William Stern and Otto Lipmann.

William Stern (1871–1938) received his PhD under Herman Ebbinghaus at the University of Berlin in 1893. Best known today for applying his concept of "mental quotient" to intelligence tests, Stern contributed developmental psychology and testing and was one of the founders of differential psychology. By 1900, Stern had anticipated much of Münsterberg's work in applied psychology (Hale, 1980). In a 1903 pamphlet, Stern used the terms *applied psychology* and *psychotechnics* (Zusne, 1984). In 1907, with Otto Lipmann, he cofounded the journal *Zeitschrift für angewandte Psychologie* (Viteles, 1932).

Otto Lipmann, although a generalist, also contributed to industrial psychology through his founding in 1906 and financial support of the Institute of Applied Psychology in Berlin (later Neu-Babelsberg; Stern, 1934). Born in Breslau, March 6, 1880, Lipmann studied with Ebbinghaus and Stern, earning a doctorate at the University of Breslau in 1904. Independently

---

[1]See also the extended treatment in chapter 4.

wealthy, he worked as a private scholar his entire career, publishing in a wide array of areas including psychodiagnostic methods for physicians (Stern, 1934), a psychology outline for jurists, and early work on mental sex differences. Baumgarten (1934) noted that Lipmann concluded that no mental characteristic is exclusive to one sex nor do these mental traits show difference of degree across the sexes. This was cited in the early feminist literature (Baumgarten, 1934). In addition to editing his journal and running his institute, Lipmann worked on selection tests for aviators (the first in Germany), typesetters, industrial apprentices, and telegraphers and was first to acquaint German readers with the principles of vocational guidance (Baumgarten, 1934). Lipmann was an early and trenchant critic of scientific management, arguing for a more individual approach. He saw the aim of the "science of work" of increased production as only a means to the ultimate goal of giving workers a level of economic security and comfort (Hausmann, 1931).

Declining financial fortunes made it necessary for Lipmann to consider a university appointment. In February 1933, the University of Berlin made an offer (Stern, 1934). However, as with so many of Germany's psychologists, the rise of national socialism made it impossible for him to continue professionally. He was prevented from taking the position and was also discharged from editorship of the journal he cofounded (Baumgarten, 1934). Otto Lipmann died October 7, 1933, an apparent suicide (Lamiell, 1996). Stern was dismissed from his position at the University of Hamburg after Hitler came to power in 1933. He was forbidden to use the libraries, offices, or laboratories, and many of his books and papers were destroyed. Stern was able to flee to the United States, where he accepted a position at Duke University. He died on March 27, 1938 (Lamiell, 1996).

Industrial psychology was also well underway in Great Britain. The Industrial Fatigue Board and the National Institute of Industrial Psychology housed investigators involved in industrial research. Psychologists in England involved in industrial work included T. H. Pear, Cyril Burt, G. H. Miles, A. Muscio, Sir Frederick Bartlett, and especially C. S. Myers. In addition, Moore and Hartmann (1931) identified four British women (Ethel Osborne, Winifred Spielman, Hilda Woods, and Ethel May Newbold) as contributing to the industrial psychology literature.

Charles Samuel Myers was born in London on March 13, 1873, and is widely regarded as the most important British psychologist of the first half of the 20th century. He earned his AB (1895), AM (1900), and ScD (1909) from Gonville and Caius College, Cambridge University, as well as an MD from Cambridge in 1901 and then qualified as a doctor in 1902. Myers' career can be viewed as having two major stages. The first stage focused on laboratory experimental psychology and a conventional career in academia at King's College and Cambridge University. At Cambridge, Myers wrote his *Textbook of Experimental Psychology* (1909), which became the standard British textbook on the subject (Burt, 1947). Myers directed the Psychological Laboratory at Cambridge University that opened in 1912 and became a fellow of the Royal Society in 1915.

World War I interrupted his academic life, and like many of his fellow academic psychologists in America, Myers discovered an interest and affinity for applied psychology during his military service (although, as Burt [1947] noted, two of the seven chapters of his *An Introduction to Experimental Psychology* [1911] were concerned with mental tests; perhaps this is evidence of some interest in applied psychology at that early date). As consultant psychologist and psychiatrist in World War I to the British armies in France, Myers' primary concern was treating "shell shock." He did, however, find time to conduct research on the selection of men suited for hydrophone work (detecting enemy submarines; Myers, 1936).

Returning to Cambridge, Myers found the status quo unsupportive of his new interests. In 1918 he gave two lectures on applying psychology. A listener, prominent businessman H. J.

Welch, wondered if Münsterberg's methods could be applied in Great Britain (Burt, 1947). Myers severed his connection to Cambridge (Bartlett, 1946) and with Welch founded the National Institute of Industrial Psychology, incorporated in 1921 (Myers, 1936). The early history of this institute can be found in *Ten Years of Industrial Psychology* (1932) by Welch and Myers. Although the institute began with only two rooms and two staff members, by 1930 50 persons were involved in applied work, teaching, and research in the areas of improving the human factor in factories, employee selection, vocational guidance, productivity, fatigue, and test construction. The institute was supported by grants from firms and individuals and fees for investigations (Viteles, 1947). Myers worked as director of NIIP (1921–1930 and as principal between 1930 and 1938) to strengthen and apply psychology for nearly 20 years.

In addition to directing the institute, Myers published a number of influential textbooks in industrial psychology, including *Industrial Psychology* (1925) and *Industrial Psychology in Great Britain* (1926). Like Lipmann in Germany, Myers was a thoughtful critic of scientific management, debating Lillian Gilbreth in print (Myers, 1923) on the meaning of the phrase "the one best way" of working (Pear, 1947). C. S. Myers died at home on October 12, 1946.

LET US NOT FORGET ...

In 1959, Douglas Fryer wrote a memo to Herbert Toops and Morris Viteles proposing a "Pioneer Day," honoring industrial psychology pioneers, to be held at either the 1960 or 1961 APA conference (in 1958 Fryer helped organize a symposium of "grandfathers" at that year's APA convention; Fryer, 1959, April 15). Attached to the memo was Fryer's list of pioneers, defined as industrial psychologists who would have been more than 60 years of age in 1960. There are 40 names on the list. In this chapter we have presented, briefly or in some detail, just over 40 contributors and mentioned in passing a number of others. There is some overlap between Fryer's list and our coverage (Bills, Burtt, Freyd, Gilbreth, Kornhauser, Moore, Paterson, Poffenberger, Strong, Toops, and Viteles). And although it is true that many of the individuals we presented had died before 1960, there were still many names on the list worthy of inclusion in any chapter of industrial psychology contributors (e.g., Paul Achilles, Harry Hepner, John G. Jenkins, Forrest Kingsbury, Donald Laird, N. R. F. Maier, Marion Richardson, L. J. O'Rourke, Daniel Starch, M. R. Trabue, Richard Uhrbock, and Fryer himself). In addition, there were many names not on that list and not covered in this chapter (e.g., Harlow Gale, Carroll Shartle, Elton Mayo), whose contributions merit inclusion. Some of these contributors appear in later chapters devoted to history of particular areas in I–O. We hope that the brief coverage in this chapter will stimulate future research on these and other deserving contributors.

ACKNOWLEDGMENTS

We would like to thank the following individuals for assisting with the chapter: Paul Thayer, David Devonis, Bianca Falbo, Adrienne Bauer, Edwin Fleishman, the staff at the Archives of the History of American Psychology at the University of Akron, and the Lafayette College Special Collections and College Archives.

REFERENCES

Adkins, D. C. (1964). Louis Leon Thurstone: Creative thinker, dedicated teacher, eminent psychologist. In N. Frederiksen & H. Gulliksen (Eds.), *Contributions to mathematical psychology* (pp. 1–39). New York: Holt.

Austin, J. T. (1992). History of industrial-organizational psychology at Ohio State. *The Industrial-Organizational Psychologist, 29,* 51–59.

Austin, J. T., & Waung, M. P. (1994, April). Dr. Marion A. Bills: Allegan to Aetna. In L. Koppes (Chair), *The founding mothers: Female I-O psychologists in the early years*. Symposium conducted at the Ninth Annual Conference of the Society for Industrial and Organizational Psychology, Inc., Nashville, TN.

Baritz, L. (1960). *The servants of power: A history of the use of social science in American industry*. Middletown, CT: Wesleyan University Press.

Bartlett, F. C. (1946). Dr. Charles S. Myers, C.B.E., F.R.S. *Nature, 158*, 657–658.

Baumgarten, F. (1934). Otto Lipmann—Psychologist. *Personnel Journal, 12*, 324–327.

Beardsley Ruml, 65, tax planner, dead. (1960, April 19). *The New York Times*, pp. 1, 37.

Benjamin, L. T., Jr. (1996). Harry Hollingworth: Portrait of a generalist. In G. A. Kimble, C. A. Boneau, & M. Wertheimer (Eds.), *Portraits of pioneers in psychology: Vol.2* (pp. 119–135). Washington, DC: American Psychological Association & Hillsdale, NJ: Lawrence Erlbaum Associates.

Benjamin, L. T., Jr. (2000). Hugo Münsterberg: Portrait of an applied psychologist. In G. A. Kimble & M. Wertheimer (Eds.), *Portraits of pioneers in psychology: Vol. 4* (pp. 113–129). Washington, DC: American Psychological Association and Mahwah, NJ: Lawrence Erlbaum Associates.

Benjamin, L. T., Jr., Rogers, A., & Rosenbaum, A. (1991). Coca-Cola, caffeine, and mental deficiency: Harry Hollingworth and the Chattanooga trial of 1911. *Journal of the History of the Behavioral Sciences, 27*, 42–55.

Bills, M. A. (1923). Relation of mental alertness score to positions and permanency in the company. *Journal of Applied Psychology, 7*, 154–156.

Bills, M. A. (1925). Social status of the clerical worker and his permanence on the job. *Journal of Applied Psychology, 9*, 424–427.

Bills, M. A. (1926–1927a). Permanence of men and women office workers. *Journal of Personnel Research, 5*, 402–404.

Bills, M. A. (1926–1927b). Stability of office workers and age at employment. *Journal of Personnel Research, 5*, 475–477.

Bills, M. A. (1928). Relative permanency of men and women office workers. *American Management Association, 5*, 207–208.

Bingham, W. V. (1937). *Aptitudes and aptitude testing*. New York: Harper.

Bingham, W. V. (1946). Clarence Stone Yoakum 1879–1945. *American Psychologist, 1*, 26–28.

Bingham, W. V. (1952). Walter Van Dyke Bingham. In E. G. Boring, H. S. Langfeld, H. Werner, & R. M. Yerkes (Eds.), *A history of psychology in autobiography: Vol. 4* (pp. 1–26). New York: Appleton-Century-Crofts.

Bingham, W. V., & Freyd, M. (1926). *Procedures in employment psychology: A manual for developing scientific methods of vocational selection*. New York: McGraw-Hill.

Bingham, W. V., & Moore, B. V. (1931). *How to interview*. Oxford, England: Harpers.

Bjork, D. W. (1983). *The compromised scientist: William James in the development of American psychology*. New York: Columbia University Press.

Boring, E. G. (1950). *A history of experimental psychology* (2nd ed.). New York: Century-Appleton-Crofts.

Bregman, E. O. (1921). A study in industrial psychology—Tests for special abilities. *Journal of Applied Psychology, 5*, 127–151.

Bregman, E. O. (1922). Studies in industrial psychology. *Archives of Psychology, 9*, 1–60.

Bregman, E. O. (1926). *Revision of the Army Alpha Examination: Form A*. New York: The Psychological Corporation.

Bregman, E. O. (1935a). *Revision of the Army Alpha Examination: Form B*. New York: The Psychological Corporation.

Bregman, E. O. (1935b). *Bregman Language Completion Scales, Forms A and B*. New York: The Psychological Corporation.

Burt, C. (1947). Charles Samuel Myers. *Occupational Psychology, 21*, 1–6.

Burtt, H. E. (1926). *Principles of employment psychology*. New York: Harper.

Burtt, H. E. (1929). *Psychology and industrial efficiency*. New York: Appleton.

Burtt, H. E. (1948). *Applied psychology*. New York: Prentice-Hall.

Burtt, H. E. (1953, January 14). Letter to L. W. Ferguson, Ferguson Collection. Carnegie Mellon University Archives, Pittsburgh.

Cattell, J. M. (1923). The Psychological Corporation. *Annals of the Academy of Political and Social Science, 110*, 165–171.

Cook, H. E., & Manson, G. E. (1925–1926). Abilities necessary in effective retail selling and a method for evaluating them. *Journal of Personnel Research, 4*, 74–82.

Coon, D. J., & Sprenger, H. A. (1998). Psychologists in service to science: The American Psychological Association and the American Association for the Advancement of Science. *American Psychologist, 53*, 1253–1269.

Darley, J. G. (1964). Edward Kellogg Strong, Jr. 1884–1963. *Journal of Applied Psychology, 48*, 73–74.

Donald G. Paterson 1892–1961. (1961). *Journal of Applied Psychology, 45*, 352.

Elliot, M., & Manson, G. E. (1930). Earnings of women in business and the professions. *Michigan Business Studies, 3*(1).

Farr, J. L., & Tesluk, P. E. (1997). Bruce V. Moore: First president of Division 14. *Journal of Applied Psychology, 82,* 478–485.

Ferguson, L. W. (n.d.). *A new light on the history of industrial psychology,* Ferguson Collection, Carnegie Mellon University Archives, Pittsburgh.

Ferguson, L. W. (1952). A look across the years 1920–1950. In L. L. Thurstone (Ed.), *Applications of psychology: Essays to honor Walter V. Bingham* (pp. 7–22). New York: Harper.

Ferguson, L. W. (1961). The development of industrial psychology. In B. V. Gilmer (Ed.), *Industrial psychology* (pp. 18–37). New York: McGraw-Hill.

Ferguson, L. W. (1962–1965). *The heritage of industrial psychology* [14 pamphlets]. Hartford, CT: Finlay Press.

Freyd, M. (1922–1923). The measurement of interests in vocational selection. *Journal of Personnel Research, 1,* 319–328.

Freyd, M. (1923). The graphic rating scale. *Journal of Educational Psychology, 14,* 83–102.

Freyd, M. (1923–1924). Measurement in vocational selection: An outline of research and procedure. *Journal of Personnel Research, 2,* 215–249, 268–284, 377–385.

Freyd, M. (1951, March 7). Letter to L. W. Ferguson, Ferguson Collection. Carnegie Mellon University Archives, Pittsburgh.

Fryer, D. (1923–1924). Psychology and industry in France and Great Britain. *Journal of Personnel Research, 2,* 396–402.

Fryer, D. H. (1959, April 15). Memo to H. Toops and M. Viteles, Viteles Papers. Archives of the History of American Psychology, University of Akron, Akron, OH.

Geuter, U. (1992). *The professionalization of psychology in Nazi Germany* (R. J. Holmes, Trans.). Cambridge, England: Cambridge University Press.

Gilbreth, L. M. (1914). *The psychology of management.* New York: Sturgis & Walton.

Gilbreth, L. M. (1925). The present state of industrial psychology. *Mechanical Engineering, 47*(11a), 1039–1042.

Guion, R. M. (1976). Recruiting, selection, and job placement. In M. D. Dunnette (Ed.), *Handbook of industrial and organizational psychology* (pp. 777–827). Chicago: Rand McNally.

Hale, M., Jr. (1980). *Human science and the social order: Hugo Münsterberg and the origins of applied psychology.* Philadelphia: Temple University Press.

Hansen, J. C. (1987). Edward Kellogg Strong, Jr.: First author of the Strong Interest Inventory. *Journal of Counseling and Development, 66,* 119–125.

Hartmann, G. W. (1932). Industrial psychology today in Germany and Russia. *Personnel Journal, 10,* 352–354.

Hausmann, M. F. (1931). Otto Lipmann and industrial psychology in Germany [review of *Grundriss der arbeitswissenschaft und ergebnisse der arbeitswissenschaftlichen statistik*]. *Personnel Journal, 9,* 417–420.

Heller, W. J. (1929–1930). Industrial psychology and its development in Switzerland. *Personnel Journal, 8,* 435–441.

Hollingworth, H. L. (1911). The influence of caffeine on mental and motor efficiency. *Archives of Psychology, 3,* 1–166.

Hollingworth, H. L. (1916). *Vocational psychology: Its problems and methods.* New York: Appleton.

Hollingworth, H. L., & Poffenberger, A. T. (1917). *Applied psychology.* New York: Appleton.

Jacobson, J. Z. (1951). *Scott of Northwestern.* Chicago, IL: Louis Mariano.

Jones, L. V. (1998). L. L. Thurstone's vision of psychology as a quantitative rational science. In G. A. Kimble & M. Wertheimer (Eds.), *Portraits of pioneers in psychology* (Vol. 3, pp. 85–102). Washington, DC: American Psychological Association and Mahwah, NJ: Lawrence Erlbaum Associates.

Kelly, R. M., & Kelly, V. P. (1990). Lillian Moller Gilbreth. In A. N. O'Connell & N. F. Russo (Eds.), *Women in psychology: A bio-bibliographic sourcebook* (pp. 117–124). New York: Greenwood Press.

Kenagy, H. G., & Yoakum, C. S. (1925). *Selection and training of salesmen.* New York: McGraw-Hill.

Koppes, L. L. (1997). American female pioneers of industrial and organizational psychology during the early years. *Journal of Applied Psychology, 82,* 500–515.

Koppes, L. L., & Bauer, A. M. (in press). Marion Almira Bills: Industrial psychology pioneer bridging science and practice. In D. A. Dewsbury, L. T. Benjamin, Jr., & M. Wertheimer (Eds.), *Portraits of pioneers in psychology* (Vol. 6). Washington, DC: American Psychological Association.

Koppes, L. L., Landy, F. J., & Perkins, K. N. (1993). First female applied psychologists. *The Industrial-Organizational Psychologist, 31,* 31–33.

Kornhauser, A. W. (1923). The motives in industry problem. *Annals of the American Academy of Political and Social Science, 110,* 105–116.

Kornhauser, A. W. (1929–1930). Industrial psychology in England, Germany, and the United States. *Personnel Journal, 8,* 421–434.

Kornhauser, A. W. (1965). *Mental health of the industrial worker.* New York: Wiley.

Kornhauser, A. W., & Kingsbury, F. A. (1924). *Psychological tests in business.* Chicago: University of Chicago Press.

Kornhauser, A. W., & Sharp, A. A. (1931–1932). Employee attitudes: Suggestions from a study in a factory. *Personnel Journal, 10,* 393–404.

Lamiell, J. T. (1996). William Stern: More than "the IQ guy." In G. A. Kimble, C. A. Boneau, & M. Wertheimer (Eds.), *Portraits of pioneers in psychology* (Vol. 2, pp. 73–85). Washington, DC: American Psychological Association & Hillsdale, NJ: Lawrence Erlbaum Associates.

Landy, F. J. (1992). Hugo Münsterberg: Victim or visionary? *Journal of Applied Psychology, 77,* 787–802.

Landy, F. J. (1997). Early influences on the development of industrial and organizational psychology. *Journal of Applied Psychology, 82,* 467–477.

Link, H. C. (1918). An experiment in employment psychology. *Psychological Review, 25,* 116–127.

Link, H. C. (1919). *Employment psychology.* New York: Macmillan.

Lipmann, O. (1926–1927). Industrial psychology in Germany. *Journal of Personnel Research, 5,* 97–99.

Manson, G. E. (1925a). Group differences in intelligence tests: The relative difficulty of types of questions. *Journal of Applied Psychology, 9,* 156–175.

Manson, G. E. (1925b). Personality differences in intelligence test performance. *Journal of Applied Psychology, 9,* 230–255.

Manson, G. E. (1925–1926a). What can the application blank tell? Evaluation of items in personal history records of four thousand life insurance salesmen. *Journal of Personnel Research, 4,* 73–99.

Manson, G. E. (1925–1926b). Bibliography on psychological tests and other objective measures in industrial personnel. *Journal of Personnel Research, 4,* 301–328.

Moore, B. V., & Hartmann, G. W. (Eds.). (1931). *Readings in industrial psychology.* New York: Appleton-Century.

Münsterberg, H. (1913). *Psychology and industrial efficiency.* Boston: Houghton Mifflin.

Münsterberg, M. (1922). *Hugo Münsterberg: His life and work.* New York: Appleton.

Myers, C. S. (1909). *A textbook of experimental psychology.* London: Arnold.

Myers, C. S. (1911). *An introduction to experimental psychology.* Cambridge, England: Cambridge University Press.

Myers, C. S. (1923). The efficiency engineer and the industrial psychologist. *Journal of the National Institute of Industrial Psychology, 1,* 168–172.

Myers, C. S. (1925). *Industrial psychology.* New York: People's Institute.

Myers, C. S. (1926). *Industrial psychology in Great Britain.* London: Cape.

Myers, C. S. (1936). Charles Samuel Myers. In C. Murchison (Ed.), *A history of psychology in autobiography* (Vol. 3, pp. 215–230). Worcester, MA: Clark University Press.

N.Y.A. Leader Finds State Progressive. (1939, March 15). *The Courier-Journal,* p. 2.

Oschrin, E. (1918). Vocational tests for retail saleswomen. *Journal of Applied Psychology, 2,* 148–155.

Paterson, D. G. (1936). *Men, women, and jobs: A study in human engineering; a review of the studies of the Committee on Individual Diagnosis and Training.* Minneapolis: University of Minnesota Press.

Paterson, D. G., Elliot, R. M., Anderson, L. D., Toops, H. A., & Heidbreder, E. (1930). *Minnesota Mechanical Ability Tests.* Minneapolis: University of Minnesota Press.

Pear, T. H. (1947). Charles Samuel Myers: 1873–1946. *American Journal of Psychology, 60,* 289–296.

Perloff, R., & Naman, J. L. (1996). Lillian Gilbreth: Tireless advocate for a general psychology. In G. A. Kimble, C. A. Boneau, & M. Wertheimer (Eds.), *Portraits of pioneers in psychology* (Vol. 2, pp. 106–116). Washington, DC: American Psychological Association.

Pillsbury, W. B. (1946). Clarence Stone Yoakum 1879–1945. *Psychological Review, 53,* 195–198.

Pond, M. (1926–1927a). Selective placement of metalworkers: I. Preliminary studies. *Journal of Personnel Research, 5,* 345–368.

Pond, M. (1926–1927b). Selective placement of metalworkers: II. Development of scales for placement. *Journal of Personnel Research, 5,* 405–417.

Pond, M. (1926–1927c). Selective placement of metalworkers: III. Selection of toolmaking apprentices. *Journal of Personnel Research, 5,* 452–466.

Prien, E. P. (1991). The Division of Applied Psychology at Carnegie Institute of Technology. *The Industrial-Organizational Psychologist, 29,* 41–45.

Rogers, H. W. (1917). Psychological tests for stenographers and typewriters. *Journal of Applied Psychology, 1,* 268–274.

Rogers, H. W. (1946, October 14). Biographical information. Lafayette College Archives, Easton, PA.

Scott, W. D., & Clothier, R. C. (1923). *Personnel management.* Chicago: Shaw.

Scott, W. D., & Hayes, M. H. S. (1921). *Science and common sense in working with men.* New York: Ronald.

Shellow, S. M. (1925–1926). Research in selection of motormen in Milwaukee. *Journal of Personnel Research, 4,* 222–237.

Shellow, S. M. (1926–1927a). Selection of motormen: Further data on the value of tests in Milwaukee. *Journal of Personnel Research, 5,* 183–188.

Shellow, S. M. (1926–1927b). An intelligence test for stenographers. *Journal of Personnel Research, 5,* 306–308.

Sokal, M. M. (1971). The unpublished autobiography of James McKeen Cattell. *American Psychologist, 26,* 626–635.

Sokal, M. M. (1981). The origins of the Psychological Corporation. *Journal of the History of the Behavioral Sciences, 17,* 54–67.

Sokal, M. M. (1984). James McKeen Cattell and American psychology in the 1920s. In J. Brozek (Ed.), *Explorations in the history of psychology in the United States* (pp. 273–323). Lewisburg, PA: Bucknell University Press.

Sokal, M. M. (1987). James McKeen Cattell and mental anthropometry: Nineteenth-century science and reform and the origins of psychological testing. In M. M. Sokal (Ed.), *Psychological testing and American society, 1890–1930* (pp. 21–45). New Brunswick, NJ: Rutgers University Press.

Sokal, M. M. (1995). Stargazing: James McKeen Cattell, American men of science, and the reward structure of the American scientific community. In F. Kessel (Ed.), *Psychology, science, and human affairs: Essays in honor of William Bevan* (pp. 64–86). Boulder, CO: Westview.

Spillmann, J., & Spillmann, L. (1993). The rise and fall of Hugo Münsterberg. *Journal of the History of the Behavioral Sciences, 29,* 322–338.

Stern, W. (1934). Otto Lipmann: 1880–1933. *American Journal of Psychology, 46,* 152–154.

Stevens, G., & Gardner, S. (1982). *The women of psychology, Vol. 1: Pioneers and innovators.* Cambridge, MA: Schenkman.

Strong, E. K., Jr. (1927). Vocational interest test. *Educational Record, 8,* 107–121.

Summerscales, W. (1970). *Affirmation and dissent: Columbia's response to the crisis in World War I.* New York: Teachers College Press.

Thayer, P. W., & Austin, J. T. (1992). Harold E. Burtt (1890–1991). *American Psychologist, 47,* 1677.

Thompson, A. S. (1998). Morris S. Viteles. *American Psychologist, 53,* 1153–1154.

Thorndike, E. L. (1904). *Introduction to a theory of mental and social measurement.* New York: Science.

Thorndike, R. L. (1991). Edward L. Thorndike: A professional and personal appreciation. In G. A. Kimble, M. Wertheimer, & C. L. White (Eds.), *Portraits of pioneers in psychology* (pp. 139–151). Washington, DC: American Psychological Association & Hillsdale, NJ: Lawrence Erlbaum Associates.

Thurstone, L. L. (1935). *The vectors of mind: Multiple factor analysis for the isolation of primary traits.* Chicago: University of Chicago Press.

Thurstone, L. L. (1947). *Multiple-factor analysis.* Chicago: University of Chicago Press.

Thurstone, L. L. (1952). L. L. Thurstone. In E. G. Boring, H. S. Langfeld, H. Werner, & R. M. Yerkes (Eds.), *A history of psychology in autobiography* (Vol. 4, pp. 295–321). New York: Russell & Russell.

Tonn, J. C. (2003). *Mary P. Follett: Creating democracy, transforming management.* New Haven, CT: Yale University Press.

Viteles, M. S. (1923). Psychology in business—In England, France, and Germany. *Annals of the American Academy of Political and Social Science, 110,* 207–220.

Viteles, M. S. (1925–1926). Research in the selection of motormen. Part I. Survey of the literature. II. Methods devised for the Milwaukee Electric Railway and Light Company. *Journal of Personnel Research, 4,* 100–115, 173–199.

Viteles, M. S. (1932). *Industrial psychology.* New York: Norton.

Viteles, M. S. (1947). Charles Samuel Myers 1873–1946. *Psychological Review, 54,* 177–181.

Viteles, M. S. (1953). *Motivation and morale in industry.* New York: Norton.

Viteles, M. S. (1967). Morris S. Viteles. In E. G. Boring & G. Lindzey (Eds.), *A history of psychology in autobiography* (Vol. 5, pp. 415–449). New York: Appleton-Century-Crofts.

Viteles, M. S. (1974). Industrial psychology: Reminiscences of an academic moonlighter. In T. S. Krawiec (Ed.), *The psychologists* (Vol. 2, pp. 440–500). New York: Oxford University Press.

von Mayrhauser, R. (n.d.). *Link, Henry Charles.* Unpublished manuscript.

von Mayrhauser, R. (1987). The manager, the medic, and the mediator: The clash of professional psychological styles and the wartime origins of group psychological testing. In M. M. Sokal (Ed.), *Psychological testing and American society, 1890–1930* (pp. 128–157). New Brunswick, NJ: Rutgers University Press.

von Mayrhauser, R. (1989). Making intelligence functional: Walter Dill Scott and applied psychological testing in World War I. *Journal of the History of the Behavioral Sciences, 25,* 60–72.

Welch, H. J., & Myers, C. S. (1932). *Ten years of industrial psychology: An account of the first decade of the National Institute of Industrial Psychology.* Oxford, England: Pitman.

Wells, F. L. (1944). James McKeen Cattell 1860–1944. *American Journal of Psychology, 57,* 270–275

White, M. M. (1943). James Burt Miner 1873–1943. *Psychological Review, 50,* 632–634.

Woodworth, R. S. (1944). James McKeen Cattell 1860–1944. *Psychological Review, 51,* 201–209.

Yoakum, C. S., & Yerkes, R. M. (1920). *Army mental tests.* Oxford, England: Holt.

Zickar, M. J. (2003). Remembering Arthur Kornhauser: Industrial psychology's advocate for worker well-being. *Journal of Applied Psychology, 88,* 363–369.

Zusne, L. (1984). *Biographical dictionary of psychology.* Westport, CT: Greenwood.

II

Historical Overviews

This section contains two chapters to provide readers with overviews of the history of industrial and organizational psychology.

Chapter 3 focuses on a history of I–O psychology in the United States. In addition to discussing external influences, the authors chose to explore four major themes that characterize the development of the discipline: (a) emphasis on productivity and efficiency, (b) emphasis on quantification, (c) focus on selection and differential psychology, and (d) the interplay between science and practice. The authors chose not to provide a chronological description of the past 100 years because this type of historical account is available in print elsewhere.

Chapter 4 contains influences and description of I–O histories in countries outside the United States. Specifically, the author discusses three influences that need to be taken into account when exploring historical patterns: (a) a country's baseline, (b) characteristics of individuals, and (c) extra-domain influences, such as cultural, social, economic, and technological processes and events, including specific geographic or localized factors. To introduce the reader to the numerous developments in other countries, the author chose to organize the histories according to several geographic areas, including Germany, Eastern Europe, Netherlands, France, Belgium, Spain, China, Japan, Australia, Israel, and Canada. In addition, a chronological account of I–O psychology in Great Britain is provided. The chapter concludes with a comparison of a history of I–O psychology within and outside the United States.

3

Four Persistent Themes Throughout the History of I–O Psychology in the United States

Michael J. Zickar
Bowling Green State University

Robert E. Gibby
Procter & Gamble

In this chapter, we focus on the impact of trends and events in American business and industry as well as changes in the general intellectual climate that influenced the development of industrial–organizational (I–O) psychology. Given the nature of this book, we have narrowed our retelling of the I–O psychology story to concentrate on four themes that we believe pervade the history of the field as it has evolved in the United States: concentration on productivity and efficiency, reliance on quantitative methods, a focus on employee selection, and the interplay between science and practice.[1] These four themes are not exhaustive; others might question our selection or may find other themes to consider. However, we believe that these four themes can be reasonably used to better understand the evolution of I–O psychology in the United States.

THE BUSINESS AND POLITICAL CONTEXT

To better understand the development of I–O psychology, it is imperative to understand how external influences contributed to and shaped the field. As described in chapter 1, the beginnings of applied psychology in the United States can be traced back to the first quarter of the 20th century, a period of great political, social, and economic upheaval. This period was marked by continued growth of the transcontinental railways of the late 19th century that had allowed for a national market, the creation of great wealth, increased industrialization, increased urbanization, and the rise of corporations. The industrialization of the American workforce brought about issues of job satisfaction, alienation, and supervision that had been less salient in the previous agricultural, craft-based economy. The middle class was born, and managerial practices were modified because business owners could no longer directly oversee their employees and larger numbers of immigrants were being included into the workforce.

---

[1]Other histories are more comprehensive (e.g., Baritz, 1960; Katzell & Austin, 1992; Koppes, 2003; Landy, 1997; Napoli, 1981) and should be consulted for a more chronological retelling of I–O history.

This period was also marked by the entry of the United States into World War I, in which a large organization (the U.S. military) was forced to deal with a massive influx of organizational members in a short amount of time; allocating those recruits to positions suited to their capabilities required standardized techniques that had not yet been developed. It was against all of these changes that the political climate of the period operated (for general history of the management and economic changes of this era, see Jacoby, 2004; Montgomery, 1987; Zunz, 1990).

As noted in chapter 1, the first quarter of the 20th century has been labeled the "Progressive Era" by numerous historical commentators (e.g., Hofstadter, 1955; Link, 1954). During the Progressive Era, the public turned to populist politicians such as President Theodore Roosevelt and progressive Wisconsinite Robert LaFollette (senator and governor) to reduce social problems, to reduce the power of business monopolies and trusts, and to reduce corruption in government. One of the main targets of the progressives was the world of work. Reformists such as Florence Kelly (Kelly, 1905), future Secretary of Labor Frances Perkins (Perkins, 1934), Cardinal John Ryan (Ryan, 1906), and others worked to reduce the numbers of hours worked per week to a level that would allow for leisure and family activities (Fine, 1953), to eliminate child labor (Nardinelli, 1980), and to guarantee a living wage for the working class (Fusfeld, 1973). The reformers worked mainly by lobbying legislators and by working with social organizations such as the Roman Catholic Church and civic groups such as the Grand Eight-Hour League of Massachusetts. One only has to listen to folk songs of that era to obtain a sense of the tumult and upheaval brought by all of these forces.[2]

In addition to the reformists, labor unions were also influencing the world of work by direct aggressive action such as strikes, boycotts, and even industrial sabotage. Labor leaders such as conservative leader of the American Federation of Labor Samuel Gompers, the socialist party leader Eugene Debs, and communist William Z. Foster were demanding fair compensation and decent working conditions for the laboring classes. Early industrial psychologists would be affected indirectly and directly by all of these groups of individuals.[3] In fact, many of the early industrial psychologists would work with these individuals and consider them important colleagues and constituents. Any attempt to consider and evaluate the history of I–O psychology without consideration of these forces would be unnecessarily incomplete (see Robertson, 2000, for an excellent summary of this era).

THE INTELLECTUAL CLIMATE

In addition to understanding the business and social climate, we must also consider the general intellectual context. The early part of the 20th century was an exciting time for social science in general and psychology specifically. As it was forming its foundation as a separate scientific area of study, psychology was engaged in exciting debates between diverse schools of thought, such as William James' functionalism, Sigmund Freud's psychodynamism, and Wilhelm Wundt and Edward Titchener's structuralism. Those psychologists who would become the first industrial psychologists who received training, not in industrial psychology, but in the basic psychology of these schools, generally with a strong experimental bent. For example, Walter Van Dyke Bingham's first research was in auditory perception, whereas

---

[2]We recommend Pete Seeger's compact disc *American Industrial Ballads* available on the Smithsonian/Folkways record label.

[3]The distinction between *industrial psychology* and *industrial–organizational psychology* is not arbitrary. Although many different terms were used to describe psychologists working on industrial problems (e.g., *applied psychologist, business psychologist, economic psychologist*), this was the most common. The latter term was officially adopted by the American Psychological Association Division 14 in 1973 (see Koppes, 2003, and other chapters in this book for more information).

Walter Dill Scott completed his dissertation on the consideration of impulses under the supervision of Wundt. It would be much later until psychologists were specifically trained to become industrial psychologists (see Katzell & Austin, 1992, and chapter 5 on education and training in this text).

Early applied psychology overlapped nearly as much with more established disciplines outside of psychology as it did with the mother field of basic psychology. Other disciplines were attacking labor and personnel problems with different academic lenses. Industrial engineers such as Frederick Taylor (Taylor, 1911), Harvey Gantt (Gantt, 1919), and Frank Gilbreth (Gilbreth, 1911) developed methods of improving efficiency through work standardization, piecework compensation, and an understanding of timing and motion. Sociologists such as Elton Mayo (Mayo, 1945) and Max Weber (Weber, 1921/1968) were also important because of their focus on human relations in the workplace and the optimal organization of bureaucracies. In addition, labor economists such as John R. Commons, Summer Slichter, Dale Yoder, and Paul Douglas researched important topics such as turnover, staffing, and motivation (see Kaufman, 2000). Finally, a hodgepodge of characters with little or no academic training developed novel techniques of studying behavior in the workplace. For example, Whiting Williams, an executive at Hydraulic Steel, became a labor expert by doffing his executive clothes and observing workers while toiling alongside them in steel mills and coal mines throughout the United States and Europe (Williams, 1920). Self-proclaimed industrial evangelist John Leitch proposed a system of industrial democracy based on the U.S. Constitution and Bill of Rights that would reform the way managers and workers related to each other (Leitch, 1919). Oftentimes, characters from all of the different disciplines coalesced in a generic field of personnel management. Arthur Kornhauser observed, "In contrast, however, to the small amount of work being done by industrial psychologists, are the extraordinarily wide-spread activities of industrial engineers, efficiency experts, and personnel consultants, and the extensive interest in and use of a semi-scientific practical psychology by business managers" (Kornhauser, 1930, p. 423). People who we view today as the early applied psychologists were in contact with these individuals. To understand the early days of applied psychology, we must examine the interaction of psychology with these related disciplines.

WHAT ARE THE FOUR THEMES?

To characterize I–O psychology in the United States, we felt it necessary to focus on several characteristics that distinguish I–O psychology in the United States from I–O psychology as it has evolved in other countries and cultures. In addition, we have sought to come up with four themes to distinguish I–O psychology from other disciplines that have studied similar areas (e.g., industrial sociology, labor economics, and industrial engineering). To begin, I–O psychology as a field has generally focused (with many notable exceptions) on research topics of interest to management, including productivity and efficiency. In addition, the field has been praised and criticized for its heavy reliance on sophisticated quantitative and statistical methods. Related to these first two themes, I–O psychology in the United States has historically had more of a focus on selection than has I–O psychology in other countries. Finally, despite occasional writings to the contrary, I–O psychology in the United States has long had an interplay (viewed by some as a tension) between the goals and methods of science with the demands and practices of the business world. Although a more formal study of the comparison of the development of I–O psychology in the United States compared with other cultures is beyond the scope of this chapter, several differences that seem responsible for the uniqueness of I–O psychology in the United States are the relatively greater strength of labor unions elsewhere, greater governmental control of the employee–employer relationship abroad, and the stronger development of functionalist psychology (and its inherent interest in application) in the United States compared with abroad. (See chap. 4 for I–O psychology in other countries.)

For the rest of the chapter, we focus on each of the four themes and trace the historical roots of each. As can been seen, these characterizations were present even in the nascent periods of I–O psychology in the United States.

Theme 1: Emphasis on Productivity and Efficiency

In the early history of industrial psychology, applied psychologists made a name for themselves in business through marketing and advertising and through work on increasing productivity and efficiency. It was the psychologists who focused on advertising and marketing, however, who first entered the business world. These psychologists were headed by Walter Dill Scott and formed a discipline commonly labeled business psychology. In fact, Scott's initial work in psychology came in the form of his 1903 book on advertising (see also chaps. 2 and 11). Despite this initial interest in advertising and marketing, however, Scott eventually became part of the early movement in industry that was fascinated with worker efficiency. Originally fueled by industrial engineers, such as Frederick W. Taylor, this topic was soon taken up by psychologists. Scott published the first psychologically based book on efficiency, *Increasing Human Efficiency in Business,* in 1911, just before Frederick W. Taylor published his book on the same topic, and Hugo Münsterberg was not far behind with his own version of the topic (1913). The great deal of work being performed in this area by psychologists during the second decade of the 20th century primed applied psychologists for the important roles that they would soon carry in World War I.

In addition to the work by early applied psychologists in advertising and business psychology pursuits, applied psychologists mobilized extensive efforts to cope with problems of large institutions. As mentioned in chapters 1 and 2, this early work climaxed during World War I, during which industrial psychologists organized personnel rating forms used for evaluating officers and determining promotions. In addition, a second group led by Robert Yerkes was involved in developing intelligence tests used to identify the mental capacity of recruits for screening purposes and trade tests used to identify concrete job-related knowledge needed by the military for the successful execution of the war efforts (see Yoakum & Yerkes, 1920). Personality inventories were developed to identify recruits who might be prone to experience paralyzing anxiety under the threat of enemy fire (shell shock). These latter measuring instruments morphed into the Woodworth Personal Data Sheet, which in turn created many other personality instruments that would be used in industry.

After the war, businesspeople began demanding many of the techniques that had been shown to be successful (or at least marketed to be). American industry thrived with the war and expanded to new levels. With that expansion, psychologists were looking to solve many of the problems that had plagued organizations. These problems included turnover, soldiering (i.e., purposively working slowly), strikes, ineffective supervision, and motivating employees to increase efficiency. Labor economist John R. Commons observed that "it is astonishing what easy marks for experts many employers had become in the summer of 1919. From all sides and several vocations these experts were coming in and setting themselves up" (Commons, 1921, p. viii).

Early applied psychologists joined the fray in attempting to solve many of industry's new problems. Independent consulting firms such as the Scott Company, the Industrial Service Corporation, and the Psychological Corporation were formed at this time (see chap. 6 for additional information on organizations). Millicent Pond at Scoville and Marion Bills at Aetna Insurance, to mention only two, were employed full-time by industry. In addition, academics consulted directly with industry. For example, Arthur Kornhauser while employed by the University of Chicago was also a regional director of the Chicago office of the Psychological Corporation. Bingham maintained a consulting relationship with the Edison Company while leading the Carnegie Tech Division of Applied Psychology. Like many of today's I–O psychologists employed in academia, many psychologists supplemented primary income by performing side jobs with other organizations. In any case, these organizations that employed I–O psychologists (in either of the types of relationships) could count on these psychologists to devote their energy to solving problems specific to that organization. (See chap. 2 for detailed information about contributors to I–O psychology before 1930.)

Although applied psychologists were likely to work on organizationally relevant problems, they were less likely to tackle problems of labor organizations. The relation between I–O psychology and organized labor is quite complex (see Baritz, 1960; Gordon & Burt, 1981; Stagner, 1981; Zickar, 2001; Zickar, 2004). For example, Baritz (1960) characterized I–O psychologists as "servants of power" because they tended to work in opposition to organized labor. Although there is some truth to Baritz's thesis, the historical relation between labor and psychology was actually more complicated in that initially the relation was actually strong and positive. Samuel Gompers, the founder and long-time president of the American Federation of Labor, held industrial psychology in high regard. He corresponded with psychologists such as Hugo Münsterberg, James McKeen Cattell, and Bingham. Gompers advised Münsterberg that "the experience of workingmen has made them distrusting of 'investigations,' and intolerant of patronage. However, if you can convince them of your earnestness and sincerity of purpose you may be able to get sufficient material to serve as a basis for analysis" (Gompers, 1913). Gompers was a vice-president in the Personnel Research Federation started by Bingham and on the editorial board of their publication, *Journal of Personnel Research,* until his death in 1924. Interestingly enough, Gompers was also on the board of an organization called the Society of Applied Psychology that promoted correspondence courses on topics such as "Understanding your Mental Machine" and "Talk That Wins Men Over" (Walter Van Dyke Bingham Collection, n.d.). Gompers's successor as president of the AFL, William Green, made presentations to industrial psychologists and industrial engineers on cooperation between labor and management (Green, 192/1976) and labor's interest in efficiency (Green, 1927/1976) at meetings of the Taylor Society. Early labor leaders were clearly intrigued with (but also wary of) the possibilities inherent in industrial psychology.

Early consulting efforts by industrial psychologists were explicitly neutral in their position in the labor–management conflict. W. D. Scott and the Scott Company had a progressive policy in refusing to work with companies with explicit anti-union policies. In fact, the Scott Company brokered a labor truce with the Chicago Wholesale Tailor's Association in Chicago and with Full Fashioned Hosiery Manufacturers Association and the Men and Management's Textile Council, both in Philadelphia. Despite this early progressive side of applied psychology, industrial psychologists soon became allied with management and focused on topics of interest to management.

Management turned to applied psychologists because traditional methods of dealing with employees who agitated for labor unions were made illegal. Progressive New Deal legislation in the 1930s expanded the rights of labor unions to organize by banning many tactics that had previously been used by employers to thwart unionization. For example, the U.S. Supreme Court had previously ruled that "yellow-dog contracts" (contracts that allowed companies to terminate employment of employees who agitated for unions) were legal. The National Labor Relations Act of 1935, often called the Wagner Act, outlawed this and other "unfair labor practices." Management turned to social scientists to strengthen managerial power without explicitly flouting the new legislation.

After passage of the Wagner Act, some companies used personality tests to identify appli-cants who might be likely to agitate for labor unions (see Baritz, 1960; Zickar, 2001). Humm and Wadsworth (1943), in promoting their personality inventory, stated that "now is the time to keep the unemployables, the slackers, and the saboteurs out of the work-shop and factory" (p. 315). Stagner stated, "One [criticism of I–O psychologists] which I think has some justifica-tion is that psychologists have been persuaded to use their selection skills to exclude from em-ployment applicants with prounion sympathies" (1981, p. 504). In addition to screening out pro-union applicants, management also used the techniques of attitude surveys to identify ar-eas of organizations that were ripe for unionization efforts (see Smith, 2003). In 1938, the retail organization Sears, Roebuck, and Company, in assistance with a private consulting company Houser Associates, began surveying employees to determine attitudes toward workplace prac-tices, supervision, and salary (Jacoby, 1986; Worthy, 1984). According to Jacoby, "Sears took a 'firefighting' approach and surveyed units thought to be potential union organizing sites" (p. 621). Once a unit was surveyed, management had the upper hand in countering organizing ef-forts. Both of these strategies (i.e., personality testing and employee attitude surveying) dem-onstrated that industrial psychologists were willing to collaborate with management in direct opposition to labor unions. If an organization was already organized, a survey of morale would help the company in collective bargaining efforts (see "How to Learn Worker Attitudes," 1938).

Throughout the history of industrial psychology, the field has focused on issues of direct concern to management such as productivity, turnover, and organizational commitment. As noted in chapter 1, Viteles (1932) defined the aims of industrial psychology to be maximum ef-ficiency and maximum adjustment or betterment of the individual. Even when psychologists pursued topics that might be more related to worker betterment, such as job satisfaction, labor unionists and leftist managerial critics claimed that psychology ignored the power differences between workers and management and that psychologists emphasized cooperation over con-flict. William Gomberg, a management professor with training in sociology, criticized indus-trial psychologists' general lack of knowledge of labor history and their ignorance of labor–management dynamics: "How are we to regard evangelistic behavioral scientists converted to participative managerial democracy who have failed to understand democracy's most funda-mental tenet? Democracy cannot exist where management is free to give and to take without any countervailing force" (Gomberg, 1973, p. 19). In addition, worker well-being topics were often studied only in relation to other constructs of interest to management. For example, job satisfaction was often studied not as a dependent variable, or for its own sake, but because it was thought to be related to worker efficiency and productivity (see Nord, 1977). Blum (1955) wistfully observed that "efficiency has been overemphasized and often regarded as the sole ob-jective of industrial psychology" (pp. 3–4). With management's financial clout and control over the workplace, psychologists were more likely to study topics such as efficiency that were consistent with management's priorities.

Rarely did I–O psychologists pursue explicitly prolabor research and practice agendas, partly because management had greater financial resources than labor unions (see Zickar, 2004, for other explanations). Two exceptions were Arthur Kornhauser and Ross Stagner, who were perhaps the most persistent critics of I–O psychology's management focus; both pursued many questions of interest to labor unions. Over the years there have been occasional efforts to stimulate cooperation between labor unions and I–O psychologists (e.g., Hammer, 1976; Schmitt, 1982), although such efforts have not resulted in a radical reshifting of the field's em-phasis. In latter years, there have been several I–O psychologists who have pursued research agendas that would benefit labor unions (e.g., union commitment, dual loyalty; see Barling, Fullagar, & Kelloway, 1992; and Hartley, 1992, for summaries of this research). Many of those who have, not surprisingly, have been from countries that have a much larger union presence. Examples are Julian Barling and Kevin Kelloway from Canada and Jean Hartley from Great Britain. In those countries, labor unions are a much stronger part of the cultural and political fabric. For example, the Labour Party in Great Britain has been an exceptionally powerful political party throughout the 20th century. In comparison, labor unions in the United States have generally not pursued independent political parties and have had a relatively low percentage of the workplace unionized. Recent research activity has suggested that I–O psychologists are more willing to embrace topics that are of direct importance to worker well-being and less related to efficiency and productivity. Topics such as work–family conflict (Zedeck, 1992) and occupational health (Quick & Tetrick, 2003) are experiencing resurgences. Perhaps Viteles' dream of an I–O psychology focused equally on efficiency and well-being will someday be realized.

Theme 2: Emphasis on Quantification

Statistical advances played a large part in the early development and creation of a scientific psychology. For example, Francis Galton, while working on how to show the relation between anthropometric data, coined the term "co-relation" (see Galton, 1888). In addition, his disciple, Karl Pearson, worked out the mathematics behind calculating the correlation coefficient and the chi-square distribution. Another important statistical advance incorporated into data analysis techniques during this early period of psychology was the application of analysis of variance (ANOVA) techniques (Fisher, 1926) from agricultural research. A great deal of the early statistical advances took place in Great Britain by researchers working outside or on the fringes of psychology. This trend of borrowing statistical methods from other disciplines continued throughout the first quarter of the 20th century, as applied psychologists worked to incorporate this quantitative methodology into research, including the design of experiments, application, and teaching.

It must be stressed, however, that in the early days of psychology, doctoral students did not specialize in particular content areas to the degree that they do presently. Students took coursework in basic areas, such as sensation and perception, and were trained in the experimental methods of the time. It was not until 1921 that Bruce V. Moore was granted the first official PhD in industrial psychology, by Carnegie Institute of Technology (CIT). Despite this lack of a focused I–O curriculum, several of the early industrial psychologists studied psychometric methods and statistical techniques before moving on to applied work after World War I. For example, Beardsley Ruml, an early member of the Scott Company and an instructor at CIT, conducted research on computing standard deviations as well as on evaluating the statistical properties of mental tests (Ruml, 1916a, 1916b) before moving on to applied psychology and studying trade tests. Herbert Toops, at Ohio State, made many early quantitative contributions (e.g., Toops, 1922) and also studied trade tests (1923) and problems of criteria (1944).

During and after World War I, there was a focus in I–O psychology–related journals to educate both practitioners and researchers in statistical methodology and techniques. Early volumes of the *Journal of Applied Psychology (JAP)* had articles that demonstrated the usefulness of new statistical techniques. An early example of such a tutorial was a series of tables, authored by the Scott Company (1920), that allowed for easier computation of correlation coefficients by the rank difference method. As noted in the article, it was hoped that "industry will also find in these tables a short cut to the determination of many important relationships" (p. 115). In another early *JAP* publication, Toops (1922) provided a detailed account of how to compute intercorrelations of tests on an adding machine. And Edward L. Thorndike (1918) detailed the differences between scientific (statistically oriented) and impressionistic or intuitional methods of combining information about a person to determine his or her fitness for a job. In the article, Thorndike argued for a statistical approach to personnel selection. Such a statistical focus on personnel selection was embraced early on by I–O psychologists and resulted in the wedding of quantitative methodology with selection techniques and personnel testing, a practice that continues to the present.

Besides the early focus on selection testing, another area in industrial psychology that helped further stress the importance of quantitative methods was employee rating systems. During World War I, Scott, who headed the Committee on Classification of Personnel for the Army (see also chaps. 2 and 7), introduced a standardized rating system that was to be used for promotion of candidates for officer training. Employee rating systems were then introduced into organizations for the purposes of promotion, firing, and investigating the quality of foremen (see Humke, 1939, and chap. 13 on performance appraisal in this text). Similar to employee rating programs, employee morale surveys quickly became popular, with David Houser and his consulting firm Houser Associates administering surveys to assess employee morale on a scale that ranged from *hostility* to *enthusiasm* (Houser, 1927). Quantitative methods of analyzing employee opinions were viewed as more useful than the previously anecdotal information gathered from foremen, industrial spies, and people like Whiting Williams who worked jobs for the purposes of learning about what workers thought. As mentioned in the previous section, learning about workers' attitudes was viewed as important in evaluating supervision as well as in preempting unionization.

As mentioned previously, sophisticated methodological techniques quickly found early application within I–O psychology. In addition, early researchers in I–O psychology were instrumental in creating and extending statistical techniques, such as factor analysis, that have been widely used in industry and government programs. Paul Horst, a pioneer in factor analysis, was employed in the Personnel Research Department of Proctor and Gamble, as was George Frederic Kuder, who was responsible for developing important methods for evaluating the reliability of tests (e.g., the Kuder–Richardson formulas for reliability).

It would be difficult to imagine the field without the contributions of psychologists whose primary interests were psychometrics, quantitative methods and theory, and the understanding and measurement of individual differences. The books by Spearman (1927) and by Thurstone (1935, 1947) were particularly influential. J. P. Guilford's book *Psychometric Methods* (1936), Thorndike's *Personnel Selection: Tests and Measurement Techniques* (1949), and books later published on psychological tests by Anastasi (1954) and Cronbach (1949) became staples in the future education of I–O psychologists. The paper by Cronbach and Meehl (1955), "Construct Validity in Psychological Tests," continues to be required reading for I–O psychologists today.

This connection of quantitative methodology and I–O psychology has continued up to the present, and has allowed for the development, fine-tuning, and dissemination of complex statistical techniques within the field (Austin, Scherbaum, & Mahlman, 2002). In fact, I–O psychologists have played an important role in the development and refinement of methodological tools that have found wide use in the social sciences in general. For example, Frank Schmidt and John Hunter implemented techniques for quantitatively synthesizing results from a disparate body of studies, called meta-analysis, in roughly the same time that education researcher Gene Glass (1976) was developing these techniques (Hunter & Schmidt, 1990). In addition, item response theory technique of appropriateness measurement was developed, which has since been used in multiple testing contexts (Drasgow & Hulin, 1990; Lord & Novick, 1968). These examples are just a few I–O psychologists who have carried on traditions begun by their early predecessors.

As evidenced in these examples, early applied psychologists were very interested in statistical functioning and in disseminating this knowledge to others in the field. Part of the reason for this interest had to do with the notion that quantification was seen as a way to be more scientific, described in chapter 1. This was important because many consultants of industry advocated methods that relied on pseudoscience or what Roback referred to as "pseudosophy" (1929, p. 263). Roback (1929) observed that "psychology, alas, seems to have polarized all the cranks, quacks, and faddists" (p. 264). In describing one charlatan who made outlandish claims about the effects that the new applied psychology could have on industrial prosperity, Roback complained, "To think that I had to spend four years toiling in Münsterberg's laboratory, measuring willed reactions on smoked paper, chewing quassia wood in memory experiments, while honorary degrees were being handed out for—for what?" (Roback, 1929, p. 266). One particularly prominent charlatan, character analyst Katherine Blackford, advocated using physical characteristics such as form, proportion, texture, and hair color to judge the fitness of applicants (Blackford & Newcomb, 1914, 1922; see also chap. 8). A survey of companies in the Chicago area found that 9% used the unvalidated, pseudoscientific Blackford system (Kornhauser & Jackson, 1922).

Charlatans were an especial concern for early industrial psychologists because of their popularity and sway over management. One advocate for a scientific psychology lamented the gullibility of managers: "Some business men still continue to consult the stars instead of the psychologists and study the signs of the Zodiac instead of the signs of ability" (Wiggam, 1931, p. 400). Bingham complained that "the typical private employer places too much blind faith in the tests and attaches too much weight to its results" (Bingham, n.d.). Ross Stagner demonstrated that managerial gullibility persisted into the 1950s by administering false descriptions of personalities to managers and demonstrating that an overwhelming majority of them believed the results of this bogus personality test (Stagner, 1959). Applied psychologists' reliance on statistical and scientific methods allowed them to distinguish themselves from the numerous charlatans who offered cheap and easy panaceas for industry's woes. Despite the use of these methods by applied psychologists, however, managerial gullibility still survives to the present day in the form of unvalidated personality tests and methods, including graphology and phrenology, which are still used to select and classify employees in the United States and Europe (see Ben-Shakhar, Bar-Hillel, Bliu, Ben-Abba, & Flug, 1986; see chap. 8 for a discussion of these approaches in the context of selection).

Although I–O psychology embraced quantification early on, a small number of psychologists expressed hesitation and caution in blindly applying statistical methodology to organizational phenomena. For example, Hersey (1932) criticized the "isolation and measurement of the part as contrasted with the whole, illustrated by the development of psychological tests for certain traits and abilities and the study of the effect of single elements in the worker's environment" (p. 4). Hersey and others (see Humphrey, 1925; Tead, 1931) expressed reservations in applying the methodology developed by experimental psychologists, who worked in carefully controlled situations, to the organization in which isolation of causes was often unrealistic given the multiple factors that affected worker behavior. Hersey and others advocated for an industrial psychology based less on psychometric tests and laboratory studies and more on naturalistic observation methods. According to Hersey and others, open-ended interviews would be as important as a research tool as standardized tests. Observation of workers in their natural work setting (and their home life) was as important as controlled studies conducted in laboratories. In modern terms, these psychologists viewed idiographic and ethnographic research as important as nomothetic research.

In the early days of industrial psychology, there were several examples of ethnographic studies conducted by psychologists. For example, Hersey (1932) investigated the effects of emotional adjustment and maladjustment on the productivity of railroad employees by observing their emotional changes over a 1-year period. Hersey made a point to involve his participants in the conduct of the study by discussing stimulus materials and to "observe the workers as much as possible and let them tell him [the observer] their stories rather than always be asking questions" (p. 9).

Although early industrial psychologists were receptive to research that was qualitative, idiographic, and ethnographic, this research fell out of favor with I–O psychologists in the later part of the 20th century. For example, one respondent in a survey complained that "lots of bad journalism gets packaged as social science under the banner of qualitative methods" (Hemingway, 2001, p. 49). Qualitative research in organizations is still being conducted by sociologists (e.g., van Maanen, 1988), organizational behaviorists (e.g., Barker, 1993), and popular writers (e.g., Bowe, Bowe, & Streeter, 2000; Terkel, 1975) but is rarely published by top I–O journals. Research conducted by I–O psychologists tends to be quantitative and nomothetic. At the beginning of 21st Century, several I–O psychologists advocated greater acceptance of qualitative methodology (e.g., Hemingway, 2001; Locke & Golden-Biddle, 2002). It remains to be seen whether their advice will be heeded. The quantitative emphasis is further highlighted in conjunction with Theme 3.

Theme 3: Focus on Selection and Differential Psychology

Consistent with the focus on managerial issues and with heavy quantification, the single most studied topic in industrial psychology in the United States has been employee selection, a focus that can be traced to the initial work of applied psychologists prior to World War I.

The foundation for I–O psychology's entry in the business and research of personnel selection was begun by the work of differential psychologists such as James McKeen Cattell and Edward L. Thorndike. This work can be traced to beginnings made by Sir Francis Galton (see Galton, 1907/1973), who developed an "anthropometric laboratory." This laboratory consisted of techniques to measure factors that Galton thought might be connected with potential human eminence; he measured physical factors such as arm span and strength of squeeze as well as mental abilities such as memory of form (see Galton, 1907/1973; Gillham, 2001). The goals of differential psychology were in direct conflict with experimental psychology as dictated by its founder Wilhelm Wundt. Wundt believed that variation due to individuals should be treated as error and canceled out by averaging across a large number of individuals (see Rieber & Robinson, 2001). Differential psychologists treated individual variation not as error but as the focal point of study. This issue was discussed in Münsterberg's early text (1913) and in Burtt's 1926 text, *Principles of Employment Psychology*.

In his presidential address to the American Psychological Association (APA), Lee Cronbach, himself largely a differential psychologist, argued that psychology as a whole could benefit with better integration of experimental psychology and differential psychology. He called these two areas the "two disciplines of scientific psychology" (Cronbach, 1957). Later examples of research integrating these "two disciplines" are found in Fleishman's programmatic work (e.g., Fleishman, 1972).

The experimental psychology tradition has had a large impact on I–O psychology, although the experimental methods of the laboratory often had to be modified to deal with the practical realities of organizations. The difficulties in using random assignment in organizations led Donald Campbell and colleagues to develop quasi-experimental methods that allowed field researchers to reap some of the scientific benefits of experimental methods without random assignment (Campbell & Stanley, 1966; Cook & Campbell, 1979). Quasi-experimentation has been very influential in training evaluation (Goldstein & Ford, 2002) and workplace intervention evaluation (Hackman, Pearce, & Wolfe, 1978). In addition, the field of social psychology (with its methods mostly dependent on experimental psychology) has had a large impact on the development of I–O psychology. I–O psychology research on group dynamics, job attitudes, and motivation has benefited from basic research conducted in social psychology. Experimental psychology (and its quasi-experimental offshoot) and social psychology could rightfully be considered two of the academic foundations of I–O psychology. In fact, in 1973, the phrase *industrial and organizational psychology* was officially adopted so as to recognize the work being done by applied psychologists more influenced by the social or organizational psychology focus of the field (see chaps. 1, 14, and other chapters throughout this text for more detail on the name change as well as the overall influence of social psychology on I–O). Throughout its history, though, we argue that differential psychology has had the most extensive connection with I–O psychology, largely through its connection with personnel selection. Arthur Kornhauser observed that "to the extent that psychologists have devoted themselves to problems of industry in this country their research has been preponderantly concerned with psychological tests for employment selection" (Kornhauser, 1930, p. 423).

In a survey of American personnel experts, employee selection was ranked as the most important topic of applied psychology (Goode & Trimble, 1939). Academics (presumably applied psychologists) also ranked selection as the most important problem, whereas management ranked selection second behind supervision. Other topics that received much more attention from industrial psychologists in Europe received much lower rankings by their American counterparts (e.g., elimination of fatigue was 17 and reduction of monotonous operations was last at 23). Even though employee selection was viewed as most important, the percentage of companies that used tests in the early days was relatively small. In a survey of 195 organizations, Mathewson (1931) found that only 17% used psychological tests and 27% used trade tests. Paterson (1951) found in a sample of sales organizations, though, that most companies that used selection tests were satisfied with them. Companies that discontinued testing generally did so not out of dissatisfaction with testing but because they received inadequate training and advice in using the tests.

Employee selection was viewed as important in the 1930s and onward because the government was placing restrictions on hiring and firing practices. A student of personnel administration stated that "since management is so definitely limited in the degree of control over labor and wages it is more essential than ever that greater attention be given to the initial selection of applicants" (Quick, 1938). Legislation such as the Wagner Act placed employee selection under the scrutiny of government; companies no longer could hire and fire employees without any oversight. In addition, companies placed a high demand on selection of qualified applicants because some managers believed that hiring the right employees was all that was needed for organizational success. The belief was that the right employee, through hard work and talent, could achieve high performance, regardless of training, mentoring, or any other personnel support.

In addition, civil rights legislation in the 1960s as well as general cultural concern for civil rights led to a heightened scrutiny of employment practices. The Civil Rights Act of 1964 and successive U.S. Supreme Court decisions expressively forbid using hiring devices that resulted in adverse impact against several protected classes (race, national origin, color, religion, or sex) unless the test was shown to be valid for the particular personnel decision for which it was being used. Although these rulings frightened employers from using employment tests (for fear of being sued), these rulings highlighted the importance of using well-developed selection testing practices. I–O psychologists quickly assumed the role of experts in deciding whether particular tests were biased in particular test usages. A large amount of research in the 1960s and 1970s was devoted to developing appropriate methodologies for determining fairness and measurement bias in selection tests (e.g., Cleary, 1968; Cleary & Hilton, 1968; Peterson & Novick, 1976). Current definitions and explanations of these concepts are presented in the *Principles for the Validation and Use of Personnel Selection Procedures* published by the Society for Industrial and Organizational Psychology (2004).

This theme of I–O psychology that developed in reaction to the legislative climate continued with later research in personnel selection being concerned with topics such as banding, validity generalization, certification testing, and race-norming, all of which were topics influenced by the legislative climate. Supreme Court and Federal Court decisions such as *Albermarle v. Moody, Griggs v. Duke Power,* and *Washington v. Davis* (Sharf, 1976) and federal laws such as the Age Discrimination in Employment of 1967, American Disabilities Act of 1990, and the Civil Rights Act of 1991 all placed certain constraints on the practice of employee selection; at the same time, these legal restrictions provided opportunities for I–O psychologists to help employers comply with the regulations (see Gutman, 2000). As Division 14 President Lyman Porter stated, I–O psychologists "are thrust into the midst of significant social issues" (Porter, 1976, p. 3).

Although vocational interest testing and vocational selection are small areas of contemporary I–O psychology (these topics have largely been ceded to counseling psychologists), early industrial psychologists focused on helping individual employees find the best occupation for their skills and interests; essentially this was selection from the employee's perspective, "how to choose the best occupation." Early industrial psychologists, such as Edward Strong, were concerned with this issue and published in journals alongside articles related to personnel selection from the management perspective. Although there was initially a confluence between these groups (see Morrison & Adams, 1991), vocational researchers left I–O psychology to form its own area, which had only some overlap with mainstream I–O psychology. The frequency of articles on vocational interests published in the primary industrial psychology journals (e.g., *Journal of Applied Psychology* and *Personnel Psychology*) diminished substantially, with new journals such as *Journal of Vocational Behavior* taking over as premier outlets for this research.

Despite the relative neglect of vocational interests by current I–O psychologists, early psychologists spent more effort in this area. An excellent example of how industrial psychologists dealt with vocational testing and counseling can be found in Bingham's correspondence. W. Y. Rumsey, a farm manager in Goshen, New York, wrote Bingham describing how he felt that perhaps he had made the wrong career choice: "I have come to ask myself if I am not a square peg in a round hole" (Rumsey, 1922). He approached Bingham about taking a test that might help him choose the right occupation. Another psychologist, Donald Paterson, worked on a more systematic basis to develop programs of vocational counseling, organized a conference in Minnesota around the theme of vocational guidance, and developed a test for vocational interests. Although this work on vocational counseling consumed much of the effort of early I–O psychologists, the field of counseling psychology eventually subsumed this topic to the point that very few I–O psychologists do such work today.

Just as in the early days of I–O psychology, employee selection remains the most popular focus of contemporary I–O psychologists. Sixty-five percent of new I–O graduates in 1976 were engaged in "personnel/industrial" work (Mayfield, 1977); 75% of I–O psychologists in APA were engaged in personnel research in 1960, whereas 72% did the same in 1990 (Jeanneret, 1991). This is in contrast to I–O psychologists in other countries, in which selection has less of an emphasis than other topics. For example, in Europe, topics such as occupational health and stress are relatively more important compared with the United States. Explanations for the relative lack of emphasis on employee selection might be the more constrained regulations guiding employee selection in Europe and the stronger presence of labor unions (which have traditionally been opposed to selection) in Europe.

Throughout I–O psychology's history, the popularity of certain topics has risen and fallen in response to internal and external events. For example, personality was a popular topic of study from the 1930s to the 1950s. However, reviews of the validity of personality tests by Stogdill

(1948) and Ghiselli (1966) suggested that such tests had very low validities in predicting job performance relative to cognitive tests and discouraged their use in selection. Thus, a drought on personality testing lasted until the 1980s, when newer constructs and measurement approaches became available. Other once-popular topics such as consumer psychology, ergonomics, and vocational counseling have largely fallen from the purview of I–O psychology. Despite all of these changes, employee selection always has been the bread-and-butter issue for American I–O psychologists and will likely continue to be in the future. The influence of the early differential psychologists is still being felt (see Ackerman & Humphreys, 1990).

Theme 4: Interplay Between Science and Practice

From its beginnings, I–O psychology and other areas of applied psychology have had to manage a balance between the scientific and applied sides of the discipline (see Hulin, 2001; Latham, 2001; Schoenpflug, 1992). Academics complain that practitioners compromise scientific standards, whereas practitioners complain that academics study insignificant problems in artificial settings that have little relevance to the business setting. Early psychologists, such as Münsterberg and Scott, worked hard to convince their experimental and lab-oriented colleagues of the importance of applying psychological principles to American society in general and more specifically to the business community. For example, Münsterberg opened his seminal 1913 book with a long discussion of why the existing hesitation among American psychologists to apply psychological principles to business had to be overcome. Fortunately, the initial hurdles encountered by Münsterberg, Scott, and other I–O psychologists started to be overcome prior to World War I, as these psychologists began not only to conduct research in industry but also to seek full-time employment as consultants and as in-house personnel within corporations. By the time that World War I was over, the demand for graduates of programs such as Carnegie Tech was higher than the supply. In response to a query from a company looking for a new industrial psychologist, Bingham replied, "Men with any substantial training in psychology are scarce and very much in demand" (Bingham, 1919, p. 1).

The interplay between science and practice can sometimes lead to tension and debate within the discipline. This tension between those focused on asking fundamental questions about human behavior and those interested in solving a particular problem is based partially on the patient, slow, cautious, tentative nature of science versus the business world, in which timing is often just as important as anything else. There was an early recognition even among scientific management practitioners and critics that what might work well in theory might not work well in practice. In the 1910s there was great debate over the merit and effects of scientific management in the workplace. Economist Robert Hoxie investigated several plants that had instituted Taylor-based programs to determine their effectiveness. He lamented that few managers were willing to follow the slow process involved in implementing the Taylor system: "Management usually wants to see quicker returns than can be secured by the slow process of systematic and thoroughgoing reorganization and the expert is usually forced to yield to the demand for immediate results that can be measured in cash terms" (Hoxie, 1915, p. 29). Beardsley Ruml, a practitioner with the Scott Company and steward of some of the Rockefeller social science foundations, lamented basic psychologists' ignorance of the "values of industry." He argued that "the merit of his work, even from the standpoint of science, is judged by his resourcefulness in detecting and eliminating costs and by his far-sightedness in securing and estimating returns" (Ruml, 1922, p. 5). The difficulty of assigning cost–benefit analyses to management has been a continual source of frustration to managers (see Boehm, 1975). In response, I–O psychologists have developed complicated methods for determining the utility of interventions, although such methods of utility analysis are often not well accepted by managers (see

Hazer & Highhouse, 1997; Latham & Whyte, 1994). Demonstrating value of interventions remains a constant concern.

In addition, the rigid standards of scientific practice are often difficult to follow in the field. Garry Myers, developer of the Myers Mental Measure, an early intelligence test, responded to Walter Bingham's query about the validity evidence for the test that was being advertised and promoted by Newson and Company. Myers' response was, "I wonder if you have taken into account the learning time and cost in deriving the correlations you refer to" (Myers, 1922, p. 1). In the rush to market their test, validity evidence would be something that could be collected later. Myers conceded, "Perhaps Newson and Company have been far too optimistic in their ad" (Myers, 1922, p. 1). Although it is unfair to generalize from this single example to all test developers, the Myers example illustrates the pressures experienced by test developers and practitioners in general.

Some psychologists used the term *technician* to refer to those who were engaged in applying psychological techniques and principles to solving human problems. For example, Charles Seashore argued for "psychological technicians" to be placed in organizations to help deal with workers with mental disorders (Seashore, 1912). The word *psychotechnician* or *psychotechnologist* was often used to describe those who used the methodologies of psychology without contributing to its knowledge base (Kornhauser, 1930; Münsterberg, 1913). Seashore (1912) claimed that "the little 'free' research that he can do must be done on his own initiative, or in co-operation with other qualified research men" (p. 474).

The interplay and, in some cases, the tension between scientists and practitioners is not unique to industrial psychology; the discipline of clinical psychology holds a long tradition of managing this tension. In fact, the rift between the research and practice sides of clinical psychology was the topic of a 1949 2-week conference in Boulder, Colorado. Seventy-three psychologists met to discuss a host of topics for clinical psychology, including training for research, private practice, and what would be the focus of core curriculum (see American Psychological Association, 1950). The result of the conference was to create a model within clinical psychology that encouraged training clinical psychologists to be both research-oriented scientists and applied practitioners. The distinction between science and practice, commonly referred to as the Boulder model and made popular by the Boulder conference, has had far-reaching effects throughout all areas of American psychology and has arguably been the model of choice used in I–O psychology graduate training.

We believe that the interplay and, in some cases, tension and debate between the two sides of psychology have been positive forces that have helped temper I–O psychology. Basic researchers are forced to make their research more relevant; practitioners are forced to confront basic scientific issues of reliability, validity, and generalizability that might be ignored otherwise. Gary Latham, who has been both a practitioner and an academic, believes that practitioners can greatly benefit from academic research that explicitly addresses the utility of each scientific contribution (Latham, 2001). Reflections on a tension between practitioners and scientists have occurred several times throughout I–O psychology's history (e.g., Sashkin, 1974). These dialogues and introspections have generally been viewed as helpful even if little consensus has been obtained. We believe that it would be impossible to eliminate satisfactorily a scientist–practitioner debate. Industry leaders values I–O psychologists for their high standards in statistical and experimental methods, although they lament the lack of business knowledge of I–O graduates (see Mayfield, 1977). There have been efforts to incorporate more practical business training into the graduate curriculum; however, an overemphasis on such practical training (and the resulting deemphasis on methodological training) might reduce the distinctiveness of I–O graduates from other types of management consultants (see Kaufman, 1985).

Although managing a balance between science and practice can create tension and a debate, for the most part the interplay between basic research and applied practice has been a success in I–O psychology (Benjamin Schneider, personal communication, April 25, 2004; Mary Tenopyr, personal communication, April 30, 2004), which has resulted in a psychology meaningful to both personnel managers and academics, who are often hidden from the "real world" in universities.

CONCLUSIONS

Scientific practice evolves within a political, social, intellectual, and cultural milieu that places certain incentives as well as certain constraints on the development of that science. A comparison of the development of industrial psychology across different societies would undoubtedly demonstrate this. We argue that within the United States, I–O psychology can be characterized by its alignment with management prerogatives of efficiency and productivity, its emphasis on quantification, its focus on employee selection, and its interplay between science and practice. Although we argue that these four themes pervade the history of I–O psychology, other historians and commentators might have focused on other themes and characterizations.

The success of I–O psychology can be gauged in many different ways. The list of companies that have used I–O psychologists in some capacity would probably parallel very closely the lists of successful companies published by *Fortune* and other sources. Blum (1955, pp. 9–10) listed organizations that employed industrial psychologists; the list reads like a who's who of American industry (e.g., Aetna Life Insurance, Caterpillar Tractor, Chrysler, Columbia Broadcasting System, International Harvester, Marshall Field, & Standard Oil). The list of organizations that currently employ I–O psychologists remains very impressive (e.g., State Farm Insurance, Microsoft, IBM, Proctor & Gamble, Motorola). Efforts by I–O psychologists have certainly resulted in increased productivity, reduced turnover, increased retention, fewer accidents, and more humane working conditions. All of these consequences helped transform the American economy throughout the 20th century.

The business world values I–O psychology so much that business schools employ many I–O psychologists to teach undergraduates and Master's of Business Administration students who go on to be corporate leaders. This is a trend that began in the 1950s (see Blood, 1994). In fact, this trend has worried many I–O psychologists, who fear that lucrative opportunities in business schools will weaken training in I–O psychology (Highhouse & Zickar, 1997; Lawler et al., 1971; Naylor, 1971). The logic is that I–O psychologists who move to business schools are unlikely to train new doctoral students in I–O psychology. There is evidence to suggest that productive researchers are moving from psychology departments to business schools. Highhouse and Zickar (1997) found that the editorial boards of *Journal of Applied Psychology* and *Personnel Psychology* had more business school faculty than psychology departments faculty (the opposite was true just 13 years earlier from their analysis of 1984 data). Faculty in business schools become somewhat isolated because they are less likely to interact with fellow I–O psychologists daily. In addition, business school faculty are encouraged to pursue research outlets that are different from those most valued by fellow I–O psychologists (see Judge, 2003). The migration of faculty from psychology departments to business schools is a sign of managements' confidence in the value of I–O psychology but also a concern for the training of the field.

An indirect sign of I–O psychology's impact on the workplace can be judged by the dramatic change in managerial attitudes toward workers that occurred over the 20th century; part of that change was due to the popularization of psychology in general and part of it was due to writings of I–O psychologists. Indeed, Ordway Tead (1931) claimed that "the greatest value of psychological study in industry has been its effect upon the attitude of executives" (pp. 118–119). Through efforts of I–O psychologists and other social scientists, American managers have become more open to experimentation and more receptive to listening to their employees (although certainly not as much as I–O psychologists would like). Early industrial psychologists helped managers value the worker as an individual human being (as opposed to just another cog in the machinery of the factory). This has helped create the environment in which quality circles, labor–management cooperation, and flat organizations have all been possible. This trend would most likely have occurred without I–O psychology (market pressures and economic forces would have been important), but it is clear that I–O psychology has helped make the workplace more efficient and more humane.

Although industrial psychology has made many large advances, there has always been a sense of frustration lingering among I–O psychologists that they could have more influence with business and government leaders. Back in the inception of the field in the 1920s and 1930s, Kornhauser observed that "relatively few employers have called upon the psychologist for aid. The great majority have remained unaware of the problem or have believed that present methods are 'good enough'" (Kornhauser, 1930, p. 423). Lack of influence with government and the general public can be best gauged by the continual effort of members of I–O psychology associations to create awareness through public relations committees. These committees have attempted to inform the public about the existence of I–O psychology and to demonstrate its potential worth (e.g., Engelhardt, 1975). The results of such efforts are of marginal success. For example, respondents to a Society of Industrial–Organizational Psychology survey reported lowest satisfaction with "promoting I–O to business," which was lowest of all 25 items except for "conference hotel room availability" (Waclawski, Church, & Berr, 2002). In fact, the general public often confuses I–O psychologists with clinical psychologists. One I–O psychologist complained that "mere mention of the word 'psychology' often invokes vague images of Freud, couches, and psychoanalysis, not to mention sex therapy" (Renwick, 1978). This problem of marginalization has existed throughout I–O psychology's history; knowledge of I–O psychology remains fairly low among the general public (see Gasser et al., 1998).

Back in 1922, Bingham replied to a letter by Professor A. J. Snow in which Snow asked Bingham to evaluate his new program of research in industrial psychology. Bingham ended his letter with a sentence that could end almost any contemporary review in I–O psychology: "There is a long, long road ahead of us" (Bingham, 1922). A review of the history of I–O psychology in the United States further reinforces this. Although the accomplishments of the field have been important, the 21st century of work will provide many new challenges to I–O psychologists. Just as psychologists in the early part of the 20th century adapted to a changing workplace brought about by industrialization and urbanization, psychologists in the 21st century must cope with globalization and technology changes. We should be guided by the spirit of some of our predecessors as we attempt to forge our own paths.

REFERENCES

Ackerman, P. L., & Humphreys, L. G. (1990). Individual differences theory in industrial and organizational psychology. In M. D. Dunnette & L. M. Hough (Eds.), *Handbook of industrial and organizational psychology* (Vol. 1, pp. 223–282). Palo Alto, CA: Consulting Psychologists Press.

American Psychological Association. (1950). *Training in clinical psychology.* Oxford, England: Prentice-Hall.

Anastasi, A. (1954). *Psychological testing.* New York: Macmillan.

Austin, J. T., Scherbaum, C. A., & Mahlman, R. A. (2002). History of research methods in industrial and organizational psychology: Measurement, design, analysis. In S. G. Rogelberg (Ed), *Research methods in industrial-organizational psychology* (pp. 3–33). Malden, MA: Blackwell.

Baritz, L. (1960). *The servants of power: A history of the use of social science in American industry.* Middletown, CT: Wesleyan University Press.

Barker, J. (1993). Tightening the iron cage: Concertive control in self-managing teams. *Administrative Science Quarterly, 38,* 408–437.

Barling, J., Fullagar, C., & Kelloway, E. K. (1992). *The union and its members: A psychological approach.* New York: Oxford University Press.

Ben-Shakhar, G., Bar-Hillel, M., Bliu, Y., Ben-Abba, E., & Flug, A. (1986). Can graphology predict occupational success? Two empirical studies and some methodological ruminations. *Journal of Applied Psychology, 71,* 645–653.

Bingham, W. V. (n.d.). Letter to Cody. Walter Van Dyke Bingham Collection, 1880–1952 [1900–1916], Staff and Faculty Papers. Carnegie Mellon University Archives, Pittsburgh.

Bingham, W. V. (1919, July 2). Letter to Wells. Walter Van Dyke Bingham Collection, 1880–1952 [1900–1916], Staff and Faculty Papers. Carnegie Mellon University Archives, Pittsburgh.

Bingham, W. V. (1922, March 18). Letter to Snow. Walter Van Dyke Bingham Collection, 1880–1952 [1900–1916], Staff and Faculty Papers. Carnegie Mellon University Archives, Pittsburgh.

Blackford, K. M. H., & Newcomb, A. (1914). *The job, the men, and the boss.* New York: Doubleday, Page.

Blackford, K. M. H., & Newcomb, A. (1922). *Reading character at sight.* New York: Blackford.

Blood, M. R. (1994). The role of organizational behavior in the business school curriculum. In J. Greenburg (Ed.), *Organizational behavior: The state of the science.* Hillsdale, NJ: Lawrence Erlbaum Associates.

Blum, M. L. (1955). *Industrial psychology and its social foundations.* New York: Harper.

Boehm, G. (1975). Industrial/organizational psychology and its works: From the outside looking in. *Industrial–Organizational Psychologist, 11,* 23.

Bowe, J., Bowe, M., & Streeter, S. (2000). *Gig: Americans talk about their jobs at the turn of the millennium.* New York: Crown.

Burtt, H. E. (1926). *Principles of employment psychology.* New York: Harper.

Campbell, D. T., & Stanley, J. C. (1966). *Experimental and quasi-experimental design for research.* Chicago: Rand McNally.

Cleary, A. T. (1968). Test bias: Prediction of grades of Negro and white students in integrated colleges. *Journal of Educational Measurement, 5,* 115–124.

Cleary, A. T., & Hilton, T. L. (1968). An investigation of item bias. *Educational and Psychological Measurement, 28,* 61–75.

Commons, J. R. (1921). *Industrial government.* New York: Macmillan.

Cook, T. D., & Campbell, D. T. (1979). *Quasi-experimentation design and analysis issues for field settings.* Boston: Houghton Mifflin.

Cronbach, L. J. (1949). *Essentials of psychological testing.* New York: Harper.

Cronbach, L. J. (1957). The two scientific disciplines of psychology. *American Psychologist, 12,* 671–684.

Cronbach, L. J., & Meehl, P. E. (1955). Construct validity in psychological tests. *Psychological Bulletin, 52,* 281–301.

Drasgow, F., & Hulin, C. L. (1990). Item response theory. In M. D. Dunnette & L. M. Hough (Eds.), *Handbook of industrial and organizational psychology* (Vol. 1, pp. 577–636). Palo Alto, CA: Consulting Psychologists Press.

Engelhardt, O. E. (1975). Creating interest in industrial–organizational psychology. *Industrial–Organizational Psychologist, 12,* 10–11.

Fine, S. (1953). The eight-hour day movement in the United States. *Mississippi Valley Historical Review, 40,* 441–462.

Fisher, R. A. (1926). The arrangement of field experiments. *Journal of the Ministry Agriculture of Great Britain, 33,* 505–513.

Fleishman, E. A. (1972). On the relation between abilities, learning, and human performance. *American Psychologist, 27,* 1017–1032.

Fusfeld, D. R. (1973). A living wage. *Annals of the American Academy of Political and Social Science, 409,* 34–41.

Galton, F. (1888, November 15–April 11). Co-relations and their measurement, chiefly from anthropometric data. *Proceedings of the Royal Society of London, 45,* 135–145.

Galton, F. (1973). *Inquiries into human faculty and its development.* New York: AMS Press. (Original work published 1907)

Gantt, H. L. (1919). *Organizing for work.* New York: Harcourt Brace and Howe.

Gasser, M., Whitsett, D., Mosley, N., Sullivan, K., Rogers, K., & Tan, R. (1998). I-O psychology: What's your line. Industrial–Organizational Psychologist, 35, 120–126.

Ghiselli, E. E. (1966). *The validity of occupational aptitude tests.* New York: Wiley.

Gilbreth, F. B. (1911). *Motion study: A method for increasing the efficiency of the workman.* London: Constable.

Gillham, N. W. (2001). *A life of Sir Francis Galton: From African exploration to the birth of eugenics.* New York: Oxford University Press.

Glass, G. V. (1976). Primary, secondary, and meta-analysis of research. *Educational Research, 5,* 3–8.

Goldstein, I. L., & Ford, J. K. (2002). *Training in organizations: Needs assessment, development, and evaluation.* Belmont, CA: Wadsworth.

Gomberg, W. (1973). Job satisfaction: Sorting out the nonsense. *AFL-CIO American Federationist, 80,* 14–19.

Gompers, S. (1913, October 1), Letter to H. Münsterberg. Münsterberg Collection. Boston Public Library Collections, Rare Books Department.

Goode, C. E., & Trimble, O. C. (1939). Industrial uses for applied psychology. *Personnel Journal, 18,* 173–176.

Gordon, M. E., & Burt, R. (1981). A history of industrial psychology's relationship with American unions: Lessons from the past and directions for the future. *International Review of Applied Psychology, 30,* 137–156.

Green, W. (1976). Labor's ideals concerning management. In D. Del Mar & R. D. Collons (Eds.), *Classics in scientific management* (pp. 352–359). Tuscaloosa, AL: University of Alabama Press. (Original work published 1925)

Green, W. (1976). Labor's interest in industrial waste elimination. In D. Del Mar & R. D. Collons (Eds.), *Classics in scientific management* (pp. 360–364). Tuscaloosa, AL: University of Alabama Press. (Original work published 1927)

Guilford, J. P. (1936). *Psychometric methods.* New York: McGraw Hill.

Gutman, A. (2000). *EEO law and personnel practices.* Thousand Oaks, CA: Sage.

Hackman, J. R., Pearce, J. L., & Wolfe, J. C. (1978). Effects of changes in job characteristics on work attitudes and behaviors: A naturally occurring quasi-experiment. *Organizational Behavior and Human Performance, 21,* 289–304.

Hammer, T. H. (1976). Collective bargaining in the public sector. *Industrial–Organizational Psychologist, 13,* 46–47.

Hartley, J. F. (1992). The psychology of industrial relations. *International Review of Industrial and Organizational Psychology, 7,* 201–243.

Hazer, J. T., & Highhouse, S. (1997). Factors influencing managers' reactions to utility analysis: Effects of SD-sub(y) method, information frame, and focal intervention. *Journal of Applied Psychology, 82,* 104–112.

Hemingway, M. A. (2001). Qualitative research in I–O psychology. *The Industrial–Organizational Psychologist, 38,* 45–51.

Hersey, R. B. (1932). *Workers' emotions in shop and home.* Philadelphia: University of Philadelphia Press.

Highhouse, S. E., & Zickar, M. J. (1997). Where has all the psychology gone? *Industrial–Organizational Psychologist, 35,* 82–88.

Hofstadter, R. (1955). *The age of reform: From Bryan to F.D.R.* New York: Vintage Books.

Houser, J. D. (1927). *What the employer thinks: Executive attitudes toward employees.* Cambridge, MA: Harvard University Press.

How to learn worker attitudes. (1938). *Personnel Journal, 16,* 258–264.

Hoxie, R. F. (1915). *Scientific management and labor.* New York: Appleton.

Hulin, C. (2001). Applied psychology and science: Differences between research and practice. *Applied Psychology: An International Review, 50,* 225–234.

Humm, D. G., & Wadsworth, G. W. (1943). Temperament in industry. *Personnel Journal, 21,* 314–322.

Humphrey, G. (1925). Psychology revolts against atomism. *New Republic, 43,* 257–258.

Hunter, J. E., & Schmidt, F. L. (1990). *Methods of meta-analysis: Correcting error and bias in research findings.* Newbury Park, CA: Sage.

Jacoby, S. M. (1986). Employee attitude testing at Sears, Roebuck and Company, 1938–1960. *Business History Review, 60,* 602–632.

Jacoby, S. M. (2004). *Employing bureaucracy: Managers, unions, and the transformation of work in the 20th century* (2nd ed.). Mahwah, NJ: Lawrence Erlbaum Associates.

Jeanneret, P. R. (1991). Growth trends in I–O psychology. *Industrial–Organizational Psychologist, 29,* 47–52.

Judge, T. A. (2003). Marginalizing the *Journal of Applied Psychology. Industrial–Organizational Psychologist, 40,* 56–58.

Katzell, R. A., & Austin, J. T. (1992). From then to now: The development of industrial-organizational psychology in the United States. *Journal of Applied Psychology, 77,* 803–835.

Kaufman, G. G. (1985). What causes trouble: From graduate school to applied settings. *Industrial–Organizational Psychologist, 21,* 24–30.

Kaufman, B. E. (2000). Personnel/human resource management: Its roots as applied economics. *Journal of Political Economy, 32,* 229–256.

Kelly, F. (1905). Child labor legislation and enforcement in New England and the Middle States. *Annals of the American Academy of Political and Social Science, 25,* 66–76.

Koppes, L. L. (2003). Industrial–organizational psychology. In I. Weiner (Series Ed.) & D. K. Freedheim (Vol. Ed.), *Handbook of psychology: Vol. 1: History of psychology* (pp. 367–389). New York: Wiley.

Kornhauser, A. W. (1930). Industrial psychology in England, Germany, and the United States. *Personnel Journal, 8,* 421–434.

Kornhauser, A. W., & Jackson, A. W. (1922). A note on the extent to which systems of character analysis are used in the business world. *Journal of Applied Psychology, 6,* 302.

Landy, F. J. (1997). Early influences on the development of industrial and organizational psychology. *Journal of Applied Psychology, 82,* 467–477.

Latham, G. P. (2001). The reciprocal transfer of learning from journals to practice. *Applied Psychology: An International Review, 50,* 201–211.

Latham, G. P., & Whyte, G. (1994). The futility of utility analysis. *Personnel Psychology, 47,* 31–46.

Lawler, E. E., Cranny, C. J., Campbell, J. P., Schenider, B., MacKinney, A. C., & Vroom, V. H. (1971). The changing role of industrial psychology in university education: A symposium. *Professional Psychology, 2,* 2–22.

Leitch, J. (1919). *Man-to-man: The story of industrial democracy.* New York: B.C. Forbes.

Link, A. S. (1954). *Woodrow Wilson and the progressive era, 1910–1917.* New York: Harper.

Locke, K., & Golden-Biddle, K. (2002). An introduction to qualitative research: Its potential for industrial and organizational psychology. In S. G. Rogelberg (Ed.), *Handbook of research methods in industrial and organizational psychology* (pp. 99–118). Malden, MA: Blackwell.

Lord, F. M., & Novick, M. R. (1968). *Statistical theories of mental test scores.* Reading, MA: Addison-Wesley.

Mathewson, S. B. (1931). A survey of personnel management in 195 concerns. *Personnel Journal, 10,* 225–231.

Mayfield, E. C. (1977). Preparation for work in industry: A survey of employers of recent I–O graduates. *Industrial–Organizational Psychologist, 14,* 29–31.

Mayo, E. G. (1945). *The social problems of an industrial civilization.* Boston: Harvard.

Montgomery, D. (1987). *The fall of the house of labor: The workplace, the state, and American labor activism.* New York: Cambridge University Press.

Morrison, R. F., & Adams, J. (1991). *Contemporary career development issues.* Hillsdale, NJ: Lawrence Erlbaum Associates.

Münsterberg, H. (1913). *Psychology and industrial efficiency.* Boston: Houghton Mifflin.

Myers, G. (1922, May 29). Letter to Bingham. Walter Van Dyke Bingham Collection, 1880–1952 [1900–1916], Staff and Faculty Papers. Carnegie Mellon University Archives, Pittsburgh.

Napoli, D. S. (1981). *Architects of adjustment: The history of the psychological profession in the United States.* Port Washington, NY: Kennikat Press.

Nardinelli, C. (1980). Child labor and the Factory Acts. *Journal of Economic History, 40,* 739–755.

Naylor, J. C. (1971). Hickory, dickory, dock! Let's turn back the clock! *Professional Psychology, 2,* 217–224.

Nord, W. R. (1977). Job satisfaction reconsidered. *American Psychologist, 32,* 1026–1035.

Paterson, D. G. (1951). *A survey of 195 companies on the use of tests in selection salesmen.* Chicago: The Dartnell Corporation.

Perkins, F. (1934). *People at work.* New York: John Day.

Peterson, N. S., & Novick, M. R. (1976). An evaluation of some models for culture-fair selection. *Journal of Educational Measurement, 13,* 3–29.

Porter, L. (1976). Interview with the outgoing president. *Industrial–Organizational Psychologist, 13,* 3–4.

Quick, W. R. (1938). Graduate training in personnel administration. *Personnel Journal, 16,* 290–294.

Quick, J. C., & Tetrick, L. E. (2003). *Handbook of occupational health psychology.* Washington, DC: American Psychological Association.

Renwick, P. A. (1978). A psychologist is a shrink, right? *Industrial–Organizational Psychologist, 15,* 30.

Rieber, R. W., & Robinson, D. K. (Eds.). (2001). *Wilhelm Wundt in history: The making of a scientific psychology.* New York : Kluwer Academic/Plenum.

Roback, A. A. (1929). Quacks. *Forum, 81,* 263–269.

Robertson, D. B. (2000). *Capital, labor, and state: The battle for American labor markets from the Civil War to the New Deal.* Lanham, MD: Rowman & Littlefield.

Ruml, B. (1916a). The measurement of the efficiency of mental tests. *Psychological Review, 23,* 501–507.

Ruml, B. (1916b). On the computation of the standard deviation. *Lancet, 26,* 444–446.

Ruml, B. (1922). *Notes on applied psychology.* Walter Van Dyke Bingham Collection, 1880–1952 [1900–1916], Staff and Faculty Papers, Folder 148. Carnegie Mellon University Archives, Pittsburgh.

Rumsey, W. Y. (1922, June 7). Letter to Bingham. Walter Van Dyke Bingham Collection, 1880–1952 [1900–1916], Staff and Faculty Papers. Carnegie Mellon University Archives, Pittsburgh.

Ryan, J. A. (1906). *A living wage: Its ethical and economic aspects.* New York: Grosset & Dunlap.

Sashkin, M. (1974). The Vail Conference: Challenges to industrial/organizational psychology. *Industrial–Organizational Psychologist, 12,* 41–43.

Schoenpflug, W. (1992). Applied psychology: Newcomer with a long tradition. *Applied Psychology: An International Review, 42,* 5–29.

Schmitt, N. (1982). Unions as potential clients and research sites. *Industrial–Organizational Psychologist, 19,* 15.

Scott, W. D. (1911). *Increasing human efficiency in business.* New York: Macmillan.

Scott Company. (1920). Tables to facilitate the computation of coefficients of correlation by rank differences method. *Journal of Applied Psychology, 4,* 115–125.

Seashore, C. E. (1912). Psychologist vs. consulting psychologist. *Journal of Educational Psychology, 3,* 473–474.

Sharf, J. C. (1976). Washington v. Davis decided by Supreme Court. *The Industrial–Organizational Psychologist, 13,* 13–15.

Smith, F. J. (2003). *Organizational surveys.* Mahwah, NJ: Lawrence Erlbaum Associates.

Society for Industrial and Organizational Psychology. (2004). *Principles for the validation and use of personnel selection procedures.* Bowling Green, OH: Author.

Spearman, C. (1927). *Abilities of man.* New York: Macmillan.

Stagner, R. (1959). The gullibility of personnel managers. *Personnel Psychology, 41,* 226–230.

Stagner, R. (1981). Training and experiences of some distinguished industrial psychologists. *American Psychologist, 36,* 497–505.

Stogdill, R. M. (1948). Personal factors associated with leadership: A survey of the literature. *Journal of Psychology, 25,* 35–71.

Taylor, F. W. (1911). *The principles of scientific management.* New York: Harper.

Tead, O. (1931). Trends in industrial psychology. *Annals of the American Academy, 149,* 110–119.

Terkel, S. (1975). *Working.* New York: Avon.

Thorndike, E. L. (1918). Fundamental theorems in judging men. *Journal of Applied Psychology, 2,* 67–76.

Thorndike, E. L. (1949). *Personnel selection: Tests and measurement techniques.* New York: Wiley.

Thurstone, L. L. (1935). *The vectors of mind.* Chicago: University of Chicago Press.

Thurstone, L. L. (1947). *Multiple factor analysis.* Chicago: University of Chicago Press.

Toops, H. A. (1922). Computing intercorrelations of tests on the adding machine. *Journal of Applied Psychology, 6,* 172–184.

Toops, H. A. (1923). Some fancies and facts about human abilities and their significance for trade education. *Ungraded, 9,* 1–14.

Toops, H. A. (1944). The criterion. *Educational & Psychological Measurement, 4,* 271–29.

van Maanen, J. (1988). *Tales of the field: On writing ethnography.* Chicago: University of Chicago Press.

Viteles, M. S. (1932). *Industrial psychology.* New York: Norton.

Waclawski, J., Church, A. H., & Berr, S. (2002). And the survey says …. The 2002 SIOP member survey results. *Industrial–Organizational Psychologist, 40,* 16–27.

Walter Van Dyke Bingham Collection. (n.d.). Walter Van Dyke Bingham Collection, 1880–1952 [1900–1916], Staff and Faculty Papers. Carnegie Mellon University Archives, Pittsburgh.

Weber, M. (1968). *Economy and society.* G. Roth & C. Wittich (Eds. & Trans.). New York: Bedminster Press. (Original work published 1921)

Wiggam, A. E. (1931). What the scientists are doing in personnel research. *Personnel Journal, 9,* 392–400.

Williams, W. (1920). *What's on the worker's mind by one who put on overalls to find out.* New York: Scribner's.

Worthy, J. C. (1984). *Shaping an American institution: Robert E. Wood and Sears, Roebuck.* Urbana: University of Illinois Press.

Yoakum, C. S., & Yerkes, R. M. (1920). *Army mental tests.* New York: Holt.

Zedeck, S. (Ed.). (1992). *Work, families, and organizations.* San Francisco: Jossey-Bass.

Zickar, M. J. (2001). Using personality inventories to identify thugs and agitators: Applied psychology's contribution to the war against labor. *Journal of Vocational Behavior, 59,* 149–164.

Zickar, M. J. (2004). An analysis of applied psychology's indifference to labor unions in the United States. *Human Relations, 57*(2), 145–167.

Zunz, O. (1990). *Making America corporate, 1870–1920.* Chicago: University of Chicago Press.

4

Some Historical Developments in I–O Psychology Outside the United States

Peter Warr
University of Sheffield

Historical trends can differ from country to country, and national developments in industrial and organizational (I–O) psychology are unlikely to be the same throughout the world. To better understand one's own situation, it is often helpful to view that in the context of others'. To what extent do patterns in a particular country represent a universal trend, and how far are they unusual and situation-specific? Those questions have not been answered comprehensively for the history of any branch of psychology, and their detailed study would require substantial international collaboration beyond the intentions of this book.

However, partial investigations can be made. This chapter will take a twin-track approach, presenting brief accounts across a range of countries and also a more detailed review within a single country, the United Kingdom.[1] Although the existence of a common language encouraged interchange between United Kingdom and the United States, the British pattern remained distinct in many ways. Those two countries' histories will also be compared in terms of the principal U.S. features identified by M. J. Zickar and R. E. Gibby in chapter 3.

INFLUENCES ON HISTORICAL DEVELOPMENT

In seeking to account for historical patterns in a particular domain, such as industrial–organizational psychology, three main kinds of influence might be considered. A first impact derives from a country's baseline: the current state of knowledge, the methods and theories available, and the human and other resources available in the domain. In this way, countries' historical trends in, say, the 1950s were in part a function of their varying conceptual and resource starting points.

Second, progress in any country is partly determined by the characteristics of certain individuals. Some people have a disproportionate impact on development, through their own ideas and through the high and influential status that they acquire in their setting. For example, as noted in chapter 1, Hugo Münsterberg (1863–1916) made major contributions in Germany and in the United States (e.g., see reviews by Greif, 2003, and Landy, 1992), Charles Myers

---

[1]That choice is both pragmatic (information is accessible) and conceptually appropriate in view of the nature of I–O developments in the United Kingdom.

(1873–1946) was singularly important in the United Kingdom, and Edward Webster (1909–1989) substantially influenced developments in Canada. In seeking to understand the history of any country, one needs to examine the role played by particular individuals and the organizations through which they worked.

Third, and most broad, historical progress in any domain is also determined by cultural, social, economic, and technological processes and events unconnected with that domain. Such extradomain influences may occur widely across the world or be specific to a single country. As an instance of extended impact, depressed economic conditions in the 1930s reduced activity in I–O psychology across countries in general. Similarly, recent developments in computing and communication technology have transformed psychological research and interaction throughout the world.

Other extradomain impacts are geographically more specific. Within a particular country, events or processes elsewhere in that country can shape the progress of a scientific discipline. Those localized influences are of two kinds. Some are a reflection of continuing cultural norms and values. For example, a country with a traditional concern for citizen welfare is likely to encourage activities (through legislation, financial provision, professional initiatives, etc.) to improve mental health at work or in unemployment; topics selected for investigation in collectivist countries are likely to differ from those in cultures that are more individualistic. Other extradomain influences of this more localized kind come from specific events in the country rather than from cultural norms. For example, a population imbalance in Britain in the 1950s (with many older workers and few young ones) led to an expansion in that country of research into age and behavior. As outlined later, political upheavals in many other countries have sharply affected the history of the subdiscipline in those countries.[2]

One aspect of this third form of influence is the extent to which a country is open to outside ideas. If a country is generally open to ideas from elsewhere in the world, scientific disciplines in that country tend to incorporate developments from other regions. Recent decades have seen more international travel and the growing use of English as a common scientific language, encouraging greater interchange between countries. In previous years, between-country transfer of I–O psychology has often been from the United States to elsewhere. For example, early American applications of psychometric testing led to many similar programs in European countries; the commencement of Marshall Aid from the United States to Europe in 1948 led to a widespread application of American I–O themes (Shimmin & van Strien, 1998); and a substantial number of European psychologists spent some time in the United States in the 1960s and 1970s, acquiring American preferences for quantitative methods and for particular research topics. On the other hand, transfer in the opposite direction has been more restricted, with American psychology described as "parochial" by Triandis (1994, p. 104). Recent trends toward globalization in many forms might perhaps lead to greater importation into the United States of ideas and findings from other countries.

Broad influences on the development of industrial–organizational psychology are illustrated here through brief accounts of some cultural norms and specific events in several countries. A preliminary contrast is of a surface kind, in terms of labeling. The description *industrial–organizational (I–O) psychology* (adopted by the American Psychological Association in 1973) is now rarely used outside the United States. In Britain, the established reference is to *occupational psychology,* although in its early history the label *industrial* was more generally used. In many countries of continental Europe, reference has traditionally been made to *work psychol-*

---

[2]These broad and narrow influences (worldwide and country specific, respectively) are of course accompanied by an intermediate category, with influence on a scientific domain in a set of countries rather than in all or in one of them. For example, communist takeover in several parts of Eastern Europe was of the intermediate kind.

ogy, and in recent years the wider term *work and organizational psychology* has become common. In Australia and New Zealand, the most common label is merely *organizational.*

These forms of applied psychology were until the 1950s often seen as falling within the field of "psychotechnics" (e.g., Jenkins, 1935). That term emerged in the first decades of the 20th century to cover practical aspects of psychology (e.g., Münsterberg, 1914). With an initial interest in individual differences in real-life situations and a concern for practical applications, the label came to cover mainly industrial psychology and educational psychology (Carpintero & Herrero, 2002).

The International Association of Psychotechnics was founded (at a conference in Geneva) in 1920, with initial members from Belgium, Bulgaria, France, Germany, Greece, Holland, Italy, Spain, Switzerland, United Kingdom, and the United States. Meetings of the International Congress of Psychotechnics were held in several European cities in the 1920s and 1930s. Early in that period, psychotechnic institutes were established in many European countries (some are illustrated later), usually with a strong emphasis on I–O psychology as then practiced but also often with a wider (perhaps educational) remit. The term *psychotechnics* gradually moved out of favor toward the end of the 1930s, and in 1955 the International Association of Psychotechnics became the International Association of Applied Psychology (IAAP).[3]

Since its foundation in the 1920s, the IAAP has been a major historical force in the internationalization of I–O psychology. Through its international congresses held every 4 years in different countries around the world, its journal *Applied Psychology: An International Review,* its stimulation and sponsorship of regional meetings, and its recent programs in developing areas, the association has provided opportunities for scientific and professional communication between psychologists in different parts of the world (see Fleishman, 1979, 1999, and the Appendix in this volume). IAAP was reorganized into a divisional structure, beginning in 1982, during the presidency of Edwin Fleishman. Bernard Bass of the United States was responsible for organizing Division 1 as the Division of Organizational Psychology and served as its first president (Edwin Fleishman, personal communication, July 22, 2005).

SOME WITHIN-COUNTRY INFLUENCES[4]

Across the world there has been a general expansion and consolidation of I–O psychology since its initial years early in the last century. In most countries, acceptance of the discipline as an established profession did not occur until the second half of that century, and later decades have been accompanied by a shift of emphasis from physical working conditions to more psychosocial features and issues at the group or organizational level. In conjunction with broad similarities of those kinds, some divergences arising from specific within-country influences may be identified. Illustrations are as follows.

Some German Developments

As in other countries, initial contributors to German psychology were physiologists, physicists and medical doctors, drawing on their primary expertise when viewing psychological problems. The emergence of psychology as a profession came initially through practical applications, including work in the industrial–organizational domain (Greif, 2003; Sprung & Sprung, 2001).

---

[3]Some aspects of IAAP's history were examined by Carpintero and Herrero (2002) and Fleishman (1979, 1999).

[4]For information about their own and other countries, I am very grateful to Masao Baba, Pol Coetsier, Pieter Drenth, Dov Eden, Miriam Erez, Edwin Fleishman, Michael Frese Siegfried Greif, Mark Griffin, Claude Levy-Leboyer, Michael Knowles, Jose Maria Peiro, Robert Roe, Pat Rowe, Dirk Steiner, and Ronald Taft.

For example, the Institute for Applied Psychology and General Psychological Research was founded near Berlin in 1906 to carry out investigations for industrial companies, government departments, and schools. The Institute for Industrial Psychotechnics (in Berlin from 1918) studied work tasks, carried out job analyses, and developed applications of aptitude tests. The Institute for Vocational and Business Psychology (from 1920, also in Berlin) emphasized vocational guidance and career counseling.

Applied themes of these kinds were accelerated by demands made in World War I (1914–1918), for example, for the creation and application of aptitude tests for military pilots, transport drivers, radio operators, and munitions workers. Those tests were expanded during the 1920s, particularly in the metal industries and transportation services. Viteles (1932) described how a large number of German companies (e.g., the Saxon Railway Company and the General Electric Company of Germany) were by then applying psychometric procedures in employee selection and how government finance supported psychological laboratories in many public organizations. In 1926, there were more than 100 firms applying psychological methods in selection and 22 companies had their own psychological laboratories (Viteles, 1932). Subjects examined included selection, training, time and motion study, analysis of monotony and fatigue, and effects of ventilation. Several industrial psychology journals were founded in the first part of the century, including *Zeitschrift für Angewandte Psychologie* in 1918, *Industrielle Psychotechnik* in 1923, and *Psychotechnische Zeitschrift* in 1926. Psychological aspects of working methods were of particular interest in German engineering schools, creating closer links between those two professions than in most other countries (Kornhauser, 1930; Shimmin & van Strien, 1998).

During the 1930s, Germany expanded economically, linked to the buildup of armaments under National Socialist control. Psychology flourished in that decade (at its outset already an "enormous structure of research and application"; Viteles, 1932, p. 51), but after 1933 (when the National Socialists took over) staffing decisions became increasingly based on ethnic background and political preferences. "The Nazis were against individual psychologists who were Jewish, political opponents, or otherwise out of favor" (Sprung & Sprung, 2001, p. 371). Nearly a third of Germany's leading psychologists lost their jobs for political, racial, or religious reasons, and a substantial number left the country. However, many others remained and psychology as a discipline was encouraged (Geuter, 1992).

Working groups of psychologists were established in railway and other companies, and military psychology was highly valued. Training studies were expanded, and psychometric applications became common. For example, after the introduction of compulsory military service in 1935, hundreds of thousands of psychological tests were administered (Ansbacher, 1941). Of particular importance was the creation of typologies, seeking to define sets of characteristics thought to coexist and distinguish one person from another (Wyatt & Teuber, 1944). The emphasis in selection practice was often "less on technical abilities than on soldierly qualities" (Vernon & Parry, 1949, p. 22), with an emphasis on the qualitative interpretation of temperament and behavioral type (McCollom, 1960; Shimmin & van Strien, 1998).

Those developments were halted around 1943, as military psychology was cut back and the mounting destruction of institutions brought work to a close. The war ended in Europe in 1945, and the country was divided in 1949. The Berlin Wall was erected between the two German states in 1961, and an organizational split between the two sets of psychologists was enforced. Within western Germany, academic I–O psychologists were increasingly influenced by advances in the United States (and they were at that time little involved in practical work; see McCollom, 1960). On the other hand, in eastern Germany, psychologists' training primarily involved inputs from the Soviet Union. Some differences thus ensued prior to reunification in 1990.

In general, German psychologists have been more sympathetic to broad conceptual frameworks (taking a top-down view) than have Americans (whose approach tends to be more bottom-up, in terms of specific findings and small-scale models). This German preference is illustrated by the development of broad "action theories." Those draw on earlier concerns for the analysis of tasks and also from Soviet and Polish thinking (e.g., Frese & Zapf, 1994; Leonova, 1994), viewing the concept of action as integrating otherwise unrelated issues of job performance, stress, errors, skill development, and other processes.

Whereas American I–O psychology has focused more on abilities, motivation, and similar precursors of work behavior, action theory examines knowledge, cognitive understanding, mental strategies, and processes of self-regulation. Given that actions are usually directed at a conscious goal, analysis of the characteristics of goals and the control of goal-related behavior become key topics for investigation (e.g., Hacker, Volpert, & Cranach, 1982). This traditional focus on regulatory processes between an environmental input and behavior has been different in both style and content from most American theorizing.

Some Developments in East European Countries

Countries in eastern parts of Europe have traditions and languages that differ between them, but they may be grouped together here because of their common control by communist authorities for several decades up to about 1990.[5] Prior to communist takeover, developments in I–O psychology were broadly similar to other European countries. For example, in 1920 were established the Central Institute of Labor in Moscow (Russia), the Institute of Psychotechnics in Cracow (Poland), and the Psychotechnic Institute and the Center for Vocational Counseling in Prague (Czechoslovakia). By 1926 there were 11 such institutes in Czechoslovakia, and psychometric testing was widely applied (Podrabsky, 2001); by 1931 the Central Institute of Labor had about 1,000 branches throughout Russia (Viteles, 1932, 1938).

The first shift to communism was in Russia, which became the Soviet Union after a revolution in 1917. Communist rule, first under Lenin and later under Stalin, set up a centralized and all-powerful organization to control lives, businesses, and scientific disciplines. From its early days, the country was kept apart from others, so that international scientific interchange was very limited. Distinguishing between people on the basis of their psychological characteristics conflicted with Marxist ideology and the interests of the communist party, and applied psychological research and practice were banned in 1936 by a special decree of the Soviet government.

There was thus an enforced break from the mid-1930s until the end of the 1950s. Contact with Western psychologists was prohibited, and psychological thinking developed in relative isolation from the west. In subsequent decades, funding was scarce and mainly directed at military, sports, and space research.

Leonova (1994) described a focus on constructs associated with "human functional states" affecting worker efficiency, examined through methods that are physiological, behavioral, and phenomenological. Those constructs emerged from the Russian emphasis in the 1920s on employee fatigue and its reduction and particularly emphasized the integration of different states around a dominant goal orientation rather than their investigation singly (see also Vieteles, 1938).

After World War II, the Soviet Union occupied East Germany and established similar forms of rule there and in other East European countries. These became "satellites," controlled by

---

[5]These countries included Albania, Bulgaria, Croatia, Czechoslovakia, Hungary, Poland, Romania, Russia, and Yugoslavia.

communist decision makers in the Soviet Union. Economic and military agreements enforced links between the satellites, and parallel forms of social organization were required in each case. Communist ideologies shaped each society in similar ways, and committees of the Communist Party set plans for activity in particular sectors of society and industry (Roe, 1995).

Centrally set targets for production and guaranteed jobs protected people from unemployment but also created labor surpluses and organizational inefficiencies. Workers' well-being was to be sustained, and, because workers were considered to own the means of production, management–worker conflicts were supposedly not possible. Almost all workers were employees of the state, and the state controlled their communication, transport, education, welfare systems, and cultural life.

Psychotechnic institutes in satellite countries were soon closed. Teaching of I–O psychology in universities was largely abandoned, and psychologists came under still greater central control. Their activities were scheduled as part of a state's 5-year plans and controlled by the Communist Party. Scientific publications were sometimes required to espouse communist political views, and exposure to material from the West was very limited. Direct personal contact with Western psychologists was extremely rare and happened only after gaining permission from the communist authorities.

Most plans for the employment and allocation of personnel were made by party officials in these countries, so that organizations' own recruitment and selection activities were very limited. Managers were appointed largely in terms of their political acceptability, and the small amount of management training was undertaken along political lines. Applications of personnel psychology were thus restricted. More generally, Roe (1995, p. 301) pointed out that "management practices and working conditions were such that motivation, satisfaction and performance … had limited relevance. The political control of organizations made the study of management issues, organizational design and change virtually impossible." Instead, psychologists' attention in these countries (especially from the 1950s onward) was more directed to engineering psychology, health and safety, and transportation problems. Broad frameworks of action theory (discussed previously), systems theory, and dynamic modeling were important.

An improvement in contacts between Soviet and Western psychologists occurred in 1960, when the American Psychological Association (APA) was able to arrange for eight U.S. psychologists to make separate individual visits to psychologists in Soviet universities and research centers, under APA's auspices (see Bauer, 1962). The group included Otto Klineberg, Neal Miller, Gardner Murphy, Urie Bronfenbrenner, Yvonne Brackbill, Carl Pfaffmann, Harold Scholsberg, and Edwin Fleishman. In respect of industrial psychology, Fleishman (1962, 1963) documented the absence of research in areas such as motivation, group dynamics, leadership, attitude change, and social–industrial psychology. A complete shift had occurred away from the use of psychological tests in selection and placement, because they were seen as artificially perpetuating class differences. Major emphases were on methods of training, studies of the acquisition and transfer of skills, fatigue and monotony, work methods, and structuring of skilled acts and procedures (Fleishman, 1963). Research primarily took place in university-based Laboratories of Labor Psychology, located in Moscow and Leningrad.

In 1976, a National Academy of Sciences Task Force (including psychologists Richard Atkinson, Donald Campbell, Leon Festinger, Edwin Fleishman, and others) returned to Moscow to negotiate an exchange of joint seminars with the Soviet Institute of Psychology. By this time the successful Russian space program had generated considerable research on human performance and engineering psychology, with the social–organizational aspects of I–O psychology still lagging.

During the 1980s, Eastern European countries permitted greater openness and flexibility, which led gradually to economic and political freedom. With the breakup of the Soviet Union, the situation markedly changed, with considerable research, institutional development, and applications of I–O psychology in Russia and other Eastern European countries. Industrial–organizational psychology has become increasingly accepted, but it is clear that its history has been strongly influenced by wider aspects of society. In seeking to understand the development of the subdiscipline, we must find explanatory links to a societal framework.

Some Dutch Developments

Psychology in Holland (otherwise called the Netherlands) took root in the 1920s, with chairs being established in several universities in that period. "That the Netherlands was acting with its usual pragmatism is borne out by the fact that almost all of these appointments included the responsibility to study and practice applied psychology" (Drenth, 2000a, p. 102). However, despite this practical interest, developments unlike those in the United States arose from two aspects of Dutch society.

First, life at the time was strongly influenced by religious concerns and an explicit compartmentalization between Protestant, Roman Catholic, and secular ideologies. Drenth (2000a) described how separate institutions (schools, personnel recruitment offices, universities, etc.) operated for each group, and how scientific concepts of psychology were subject to close religious scrutiny. A second, linked process derived from the academic preeminence of philosophical and conceptual argument. In that respect, empirical procedures of, for example, vocational guidance or staff selection were viewed as excessively simple and mechanical. Instead, a widespread preference was for qualitative analyses, interviews, projective tests, and interpretative observations.

This more qualitative and phenomenological approach dominated I–O (and other aspects of) psychology in Holland up to the late 1950s. As the discipline expanded in the 1960s, new members of university staff saw greater value in quantitative empirical approaches, and academic inputs from the United States became common. Statistical and methodological rigor became more valued. The shift occurred more slowly in practical applications, because consultants and others were less exposed to international influences. Later in the 1960s, critical social movements, based on antiauthority ideologies and opposition to possible misuse of capitalist power, had considerable impact on the organization of universities and many other institutions. Industrial–organizational psychology was widely criticized for its alleged bias against workers, and ethical codes for psychologists were redrafted to emphasize broader societal responsibilities.

Those processes have yielded an I–O psychology that is both similar and dissimilar to that in the United States. On the one hand, many Dutch psychologists display empirical and conceptual approaches similar to those of their American counterparts, and their pragmatic concerns are widely reflected in applied work. On the other hand, within a network of relatively communal European laws and national norms, their activities tend to be less focused on management issues than has been the case in the United States.

Some French Developments

French scientists were early contributors to applied psychology. A Psychological Institute was formed in Paris in 1920, and the International Association of Psychotechnics (later becoming the International Association of Applied Psychology) was based in that city for two decades after its founding in that year (discussed previously). Major contributions to mental testing (initially in educational settings) had previously been made (from 1905) by Binet, Simon, and others. During that period, Toulouse (from a psychiatry department) was one of the first scientists to argue that psychological examination and testing are valuable in assessing people in their daily life.

One of Toulouse's colleagues, Jean Marie Lahy (1872–1944), played a central role in the development of French work psychology. He used an approach centered on both differential psychology and what became called "ergonomics" to study human aptitudes and work conditions. After World War I (1914–1918), during which Lahy and his team were involved in selection and training for the armed forces, developments included the creation of l'Institut d'Orientation Professionnelle (for vocational guidance) and psychological departments in the Paris transportation system, the French railways, and the Peugeot and Renault automotive companies.

In 1920, a Psychological Institute was created at the Sorbonne University, under the leadership of Henri Piéron. The aim of this institute was to train applied psychologists for their roles in clinical, school, and work psychology. Piéron was the first to organize a special program to train school psychologists.

Lahy established the journal *Le Travail Humain* in 1932 and was editor-in-chief until his death. The first International Congress of Psychotechnics was organized by Claparede in 1920, with Lahy elected as the general secretary of the new organization. The 4th and 11th Congresses took place in Paris in 1927 and 1953.

Early French I–O activities were of two principal kinds. First was a concern for personnel issues, accidents, and working conditions. Procedures for staff selection and vocational guidance ("professional orientation") were extended beyond an initial concern with education, especially into railway and other transport systems. For instance, Jean Lahy studied tramway staff from 1908, and driving potential was later examined through performance in a mock-up cabin (Lahy, 1927). In addition to conventional psychometric applications, interpretative evaluations and graphological analyses have also been important. Applied research was restricted during the 1960s and 1970s, associated with student and other opposition to capitalist authorities.

Second, deriving from a strong experimental psychology, studies of sensation, vision, memory, and similar processes were undertaken from the outset. These gave rise in due course to a strong interest in ergonomic issues. The French Ergonomics Society was founded in 1963, with closer links between psychologists and the professions of medicine and physiology than was the case in some other countries (where interaction was more with engineers or industrial managers). As information technology later became widespread, ergonomic studies in France came to place more emphasis on cognitive and social features than previously.

As in other countries, social and organizational studies became common only in the 1970s. A principal concern was for microsocial issues in small groups (interpersonal relationships, conflict, etc.), perhaps in part because of the preponderance in the country of small employing organizations (Lévy-Leboyer & Sperandio, 1987). In addition, sociological (often case study) inputs were common. Social–psychological themes were also important in approaches to staff selection, for example, in the examination of interpersonal processes in interviews or assessment centers.

Some Belgian Developments

Industrial–organizational psychology in Belgium initially became established through guidance centers. For example, the Intercommunal Office for Professional Orientation was opened in Brussels in 1912, and after the end of World War I (1918), handicapped and other veterans were assisted in this way through the Belgian Military Institute. Early procedures were based on tests developed in France, Germany, the United Kingdom, and the United States, with a focus on manual dexterity and the psychomotor skills required in manual jobs. In later years, greater emphasis was given to clinical interpretation of individuals' behavior in group settings than was the case in similar American activities.

Contributions from outside the discipline included work by the Young Christian Workers movement, founded in Brussels in 1925 by a Catholic priest, Joseph Cardijn (1882–1967).[6] Working with poorer young people, that movement opened a network of centers for professional orientation, applying job analyses and tests from within psychology. Procedures applied in those and other centers were increasingly also used by employers for personnel selection.

However, applied psychology in Belgian universities was held back until the 1940s by philosophers' objections to empirical forms of the subject. Some teaching was undertaken under the focused title of "professional orientation and selection," until the term *organizational psychology* became acceptable in the 1960s. That was typically taught in those years only as part of broader courses in psychology as a whole. Developments in personnel selection occurred from the 1950s, for example, in the Belgian Air Force's work to validate tests for pilot selection (Fleishman, 1956).

The country has both French-speaking (southern) and Dutch-speaking (northern) regions, and some influence from those other countries occurred. For example, a stronger emphasis on ergonomic issues was usual in the 1970s and 1980s in French-speaking Belgium, whereas Dutch-speaking psychologists more often examined psychosocial themes of interest in Holland and the United States. However, those internal differences are less strong than previously.

Some Spanish Developments

The impact of societal features on the development of I–O psychology is also illustrated by the pattern in Spain. That country was predominantly agricultural until well into the 20th century, behind most of Europe in industrial development. Progress was impeded by a civil war and a later dictatorship, before a concerted attempt at advancement was made within the European Union.

Early in the century, psychology was imported from other countries "mostly for pragmatic and utilitarian reasons" (Carpintero, 1994, p. 132), initially with help from a small number of pro-European neurologists, physiologists, and medical doctors. By the 1920s, psychotechnic centers had been established in Madrid and Barcelona to examine rehabilitation programs for disabled workers, work efficiency, vocational guidance, and personnel selection. The general concern was for practical rather than theoretical issues.

The Spanish Civil War (1936–1939) interrupted psychological and other activities. Many scientists left the country, and the war was followed by a totalitarian regime led by General F. Franco and supported by the army and the Roman Catholic church. That regime, especially in its early years, exercised tight control over many aspects of society. For example, in the 1940s pressure was sometimes placed on psychologists to use only introspective methods and to build on the writings of Aristotle and St. Thomas Aquinas.

After Franco's death in 1975 and a shift to constitutional monarchy, scientific advances occurred more rapidly, with new I–O centers established and an expansion beyond psychometric and other traditional themes. Of particular importance were the economic and social pressures to change, which derived from Spain's entry into the European Union in 1986 (Peiró & Munduate, 1994). Since then Spanish I–O psychology has become increasingly integrated with that of other countries (Peiró, 2001). As part of that process, the International Association of Applied Psychology held its 1994 Congress in Madrid.

---

[6]The movement expanded into an international organization, providing guidance and developmental assistance for young people.

Some Chinese Developments

Wang (1994) outlined main themes in the history of Chinese industrial–organizational psychology. He described early academic interest in the 1920s, with a small number of books available after translation from other languages. The first Chinese text in industrial psychology was published in 1935. As in other countries, attention was primarily directed at personnel selection and guidance, but studies of improved working conditions were also undertaken. Progress in I–O psychology was greatly influenced by other happenings in the country. A Japanese invasion in 1937 led to a decline in the school and university systems, so that little teaching and research were undertaken. From 1949, after the founding of the People's Republic under Mao, psychology in China was recommenced, strongly influenced by Russian ideas and priorities. I–O projects focused on equipment operation, display systems, health and safety, and technical training. However, those were halted by the Cultural Revolution (1966–1976), associated with which psychology was deemed to be a pseudoscience. During this period, many academics were required to leave their jobs and instead undertake manual work in factory, agricultural, or similar settings.

In 1978, after Mao's death, China launched a program of economic reform, taking steps to become more open to the rest of the world. Psychologists needed to learn about recent developments and new institutions had to be established. In that year, the Chinese Psychological Society set up a national committee of industrial psychology, with two branches: engineering psychology and organizational psychology. In 1981, the society had its Diamond Jubilee Congress in Beijing, celebrating its 60th year, to which representatives of other national societies were invited. During this visit, it was learned that although many Chinese psychologists had received training in Russia, several others had been trained in the United States or United Kingdom. It was clear that I–O psychology had become a priority in the China of 1981 and was being taught in many Chinese universities (Edwin A. Fleishman, personal communication, July 15, 2005). In 1989, the Chinese Ergonomics Society was formed, with divisions of cognitive ergonomics, engineering, and environmental ergonomics.

Wang (1990, 1994) emphasized that applied psychology in China has been closely linked to its social and cultural context, so that it has a distinct approach and style. Particularly important is an emphasis on group processes and group interventions, for instance in terms of collective rewards, power sharing, and group feedback. Second, material and social themes are explicitly considered together, as in combined social and technical change. Third, educational systems and social norms emphasize mutual understanding and processes of social contribution. Such features are reflected in the research questions posed and topics selected for investigation.

Some Japanese Developments

For approximately 250 years before the late 1800s, Japan was closed to any foreign influence. In its early development, Japanese psychology thus needed to learn about progress elsewhere in the world. Important in this opening up was the translation of key books. For instance, works by Taylor, Münsterberg, and Muscio were published in Japanese in 1912, 1915, and 1919, respectively. A number of Japanese psychologists visited Germany, the United Kingdom, and the United States around this time, and publications from those countries continued to influence Japanese I–O psychology in subsequent decades.

Psychotechnical investigations into work performance, hours of work, and fatigue were initiated in telegraph and post offices in 1916, with an expansion of interest after World War I as employing organizations became larger and more complex. The Institute for Science of Labor was founded in 1921 in Kurashiki City, with initial financial support from a textile industrialist but with activities not restricted to that industry. Early investigations mainly concerned working hours, efficiency, and fatigue. Similar projects were undertaken by the Institute for Industrial Efficiency, established in 1921 in Tokyo. Vocational guidance projects became established from about that time (Kirahara, 1959), with a concern for employees' welfare as well as for organizations' efficiency. Teaching in industrial aspects of the subject was first undertaken in 1924 (at Nagoya Commercial College), but I–O issues were not of widespread interest in other academic institutions.

In the 1930s and early 1940s, psychologists' employment in the army and navy led to expanded studies of personnel selection and placement. American tests were adapted, and new instruments developed. Aptitude testing and vocational guidance continued to be important in subsequent decades, accompanied by a concern for fatigue, accidents, human engineering, time and motion study, and transportation issues. The Industrial Fatigue Research Committee of the Japanese Association of Industrial Health was established in 1952, bringing together psychologists, physiologists, and biochemists. Job satisfaction and motivation were studied from the 1940s and 1950s, although organizational issues appear to have been less examined. The Japanese Association of Industrial and Organizational Psychology was established in 1985.

Japanese organizations have long differed from those in Western countries, for example, in terms of career-long employment, collective responsibility, and within-company trade unions (e.g., Triandis, 1994). There has been an emphasis on interpersonal harmony and frequent use of a metaphorical account of organizations as families (Kashima & Callan, 1994). Industrial–organizational psychology has thus adopted a more collective tone than in the United States and some other countries. For instance, selection tests for managerial staff have tended to focus on fitness for membership of the company itself rather than on suitability for a specific job. Group norms of morale and other features have been of particular interest (Kirihara, 1959) and have been stressed in studies of quality control, work performance, leadership, and training. In several universities, research into organizational psychology more generally has been conducted within a framework of group dynamics.

Some Australian Developments

In 1901, the Commonwealth of Australia was created from previously separate colonies in the British Empire. As in several other countries, formal teaching of psychology started in university departments of philosophy. Instruction initially occurred under titles such as "mental and moral philosophy" or "logic and mental philosophy," and the first university position with *psychology* in its title was the Lectureship in Logic, Psychology, and Ethics at the University of Queensland, to which George Elton Mayo (1880–1949) was appointed in 1911 (Griffin, Landy, & Mayocchi, 2002; O'Neil, 1987).

Mayo remained there until 1923, being promoted to professor in 1919. He had a particular interest in interpersonal relationships and their encouragement through supportive management. His impact on industrial–organizational psychology came primarily after he moved to the University of Pennsylvania in 1923, and through his subsequent involvement in the Hawthorne and other investigations.

Early Australian psychology reflected the country's origins in the United Kingdom, and interchange of people and ideas was common between the two countries. For example, the Australian Bernard Muscio (1887–1926) taught experimental psychology at the University of Cambridge, England, between 1914 and 1916, was a lecturer in philosophy at the University of Sydney (1916–1919), became an investigator of the Industrial Research Fatigue Board in London (1919–1922), and returned to Australia as professor of philosophy in Sydney in 1922 (Hearnshaw, 1964; O'Neil, 1987).

Muscio, his colleagues, and successors developed productive links with local employers, expanding industrial psychology in Sydney more than in other parts of the country (Blackburn, 1998; O'Neil, 1987). In 1923, they founded the *Australasian Journal of Psychology and Philosophy,* with a principal aim of using industrial psychology to promote efficiency. The journal reflected international developments in areas such as vocational guidance, employee fatigue, and the application of scientific management. Australia's first Vocational Guidance Bureau (a joint endeavor between the New South Wales education department and local employers) was founded in 1927, assisting school pupils to select a career, both for their own benefit and to increase industrial efficiency. Similar centers were soon created in other states.

Also in 1927, the Australian Institute of Industrial Psychology was established by A. H. Martin, lecturer in psychology at the University of Sydney. This received funding from employing organizations, help from employers as committee members, and accommodation within Sydney's Chamber of Manufacturers. Its work included making physical assessments; biographical, school, and parents' reports; and interviews with children and parents. In addition to the services it offered in vocational guidance, the institute also advised companies on staff selection and industrial problems associated with working conditions, plant layout, and fatigue (Bucklow, 1977; see also Blackburn, 1998).

In both these ways, the institute played a leading role in laying the foundation for the psychological practices adopted by all three armed services in the second World War (1939–1945; Clark, 1958). Initially, the air force emphasis was on pilot selection, but later all three services developed procedures for the selection, placement, and training of recruits generally, as well as counseling individuals before their discharge (Owens, 1977).

In 1940 the Commonwealth Department of Labour and National Service was established, which was responsible for implementing practices relating to labor policy, industrial training and welfare, and postwar rehabilitation (Bucklow, 1977). For example, the Industrial Welfare Division worked to demonstrate the relevance of applied psychology to a wide range of industrial issues (Cook, 1949).

A postwar development was the emergence of industrial psychologists as consultants to industry and commerce. This movement gathered momentum, so that by the beginning of the 1970s one in every four industrial psychologists in Australia was employed in consultancy (Bordow, 1971). Psychological testing has remained of particular interest, but new practices, involving job enrichment, career planning, training at all levels, and the education of trade union officials, have been accompanied by a growing emphasis on organization development and the context in which work practices occur (Taylor & Taft, 1977).

Some Developments in Israel[7]

The first attempt to establish psychology in Israel was in 1930, when a group of German–Jewish psychoanalysts fleeing persecution in Nazi Germany arrived in Israel under the leadership of Sigmund Freud's student, Max Eitingon. In 1933, Eitingon established the Palestine Psychoanalytic Society, which was followed by the Psychoanalytic Institute in 1936. Eitingon, with the help of Freud, who was a governor of the Hebrew University in Jerusalem, attempted to establish a department of psychoanalysis there. However, the governance of the university staunchly opposed the proposal, preferring a more experimental orientation. The university then solicited Kurt Lewin, who visited Israel to establish the psychology department; however, he left for the United States before completing the task. In 1940, Professor Enzo Bonaventura, who had immigrated from Italy, joined the Hebrew University and started to recruit more fac-

---

[7]This section was provided by Miriam Erez, Dov Eden, and Ed Fleishman.

ulty members to Israel to establish the department of psychology. However, in 1948, he was murdered by an Arab mob that attacked a bus ascending to the University's Hadassah Medical Center on Mount Scopus in Jerusalem.

The establishment of the State of Israel in 1948 accelerated the need for psychologists in clinical, educational, vocational, industrial, and military areas. In the first 3 years of the State, the population grew from about 600,000 to 1.7 million. Clinical psychologists were needed for helping the new immigrants and the survivors of the Holocaust; educational psychologists were required in the new school system; vocational psychologists and industrial psychologists helped in developing the new labor force; and military psychologists were needed mainly for selecting soldiers, pilots, and officers and placing them into the Israel Defense Forces.

In 1947, Louis Guttman (1918–1987) founded the behavioral unit of the military, which eventually became the Israel Institute of Applied Social Research (Guttman, L.—Biography, n.d.). Guttman was described as a brilliant innovator who "saw theory in method and method in theory" (Guttman, L.—Biography, n.d., p. 1). His research contributions to the theory and practice of scale and factor analysis, multidimensional scaling analysis, and Facet Theory have made a significant impact on the fields of social psychology, military, and industrial–organizational psychology.

In 1957, the first department of psychology in Israel was founded at Hebrew University under the leadership of Shlomo Kugelmass, an immigrant from the United States who promoted experimental psychology. In the same year, 170 members created the Israel Psychological Association with divisions in clinical psychology, educational psychology, and, later, social and occupational psychology. Subsequently, a fourth division was formed, in rehabilitation psychology. In 1958, Bar-Ilan University also established a department of psychology, and in 1967 departments were founded at Tel-Aviv University and Haifa University.

As a result of continuous warfare and the ever-present need for experts in rehabilitation, the IPA established is fourth division in rehabilitation psychology. By the 1970s, a growing number of psychologists were practicing and conducting research in industrial, military, and other work settings. In 1985, the Technion–Israel Institute of Technology established a graduate program in industrial psychology, which was and remains unique in that it incorporates three areas of concentration: organizational behavior, cognition and decision making, and human factors. At about the same time, Ben-Gurion University also established a program in psychology, although not yet accredited at the time. In 1977, the Knesset, Israel's parliament, passed the Psychologists' Law, mandating the establishment of the Council of Psychologists in the Ministry of Health to enforce the new law's licensing procedures regulating who may practice psychology and a variety of regulations concerning professional practice. In 1986, the International Association of Applied Psychology held its Congress in Jerusalem. More comprehensive reviews of the development of Israeli psychology, including I–O psychology, may be found elsewhere (e.g., Ben-Ari & Amir, 1986; Levinson, 1997).

Some Canadian Developments

Rowe (1992) pointed out that little information is available about the origins of I–O psychology in Canada but that it developed more slowly than in its larger neighbor. (Canada has about 10% of the population of the United States.) English-speaking Canadian psychologists probably did not start industrial–organizational work until about 1928, and French-speaking teaching in the field commenced only in 1958.

As in other countries, early work concerned employee selection and guidance, and issues of training were also of concern (Webster, 1988). The Psychological Institute was established in Quebec in 1936, primarily to provide vocational guidance. This was a nonprofit organization, operating along the lines of the British National Institute of Industrial Psychology (see later). (It was forced to close early in the next decade because of a lack of available staff.)

The slow initial development meant that few colleagues were available across a large country. Many potential members of the profession moved to the United States for their training and professional socialization, and links with American I–O psychology have been strong. Associated with that, Canadian psychologists appear to have had greater impact on U.S. developments than have those from elsewhere.

Contrary to patterns in some other countries, World War II (1939–1945) did not provide a strong impetus to I–O psychology in terms of job analysis, psychometric assessment, or staff placement. The Canadian Army Directorate of Personnel Selection preferred clinical procedures with an emphasis on interviews and qualitative interpretation. Although I–O psychologists had developed tests for military use, those were not used (Webster, 1988).

After the war, the advance of Canadian psychology in general was not initially accompanied by progress in the industrial–organizational domain. For example, government funding was not made available for training in that field, and organizations tended to prefer applicants with an MBA degree to those qualified in I–O psychology. However, from 1952, Edward Webster and his students in Montreal carried out an influential program of research into processes involved in selection interviewing (Webster, 1964). As in other countries, the subdiscipline became more firmly established in the 1970s. For instance, French-speaking courses (initiated in 1958) grew slowly for some 15 years before a period of rapid growth from about 1975 (Bordeleau & Morin, 1988). Cronshaw (1991) provided additional information about these developments.

INDUSTRIAL–ORGANIZATIONAL PSYCHOLOGY IN BRITAIN

The illustrations in the previous section have made it clear that characteristics of and events in particular countries have shaped the national development of I–O psychology. Those brief accounts will next be augmented by a more detailed review in one setting.

Occupational psychology in Britain has been influenced by features that differ somewhat from those in the United States. Earlier patterns were dissimilar in several respects between the two countries. In comparing developments, I illustrate the changing pattern in Britain through separate presentations in three different periods: up to about 1940, between 1940 and about 1980, and after 1980.

British I–O Psychology Up to 1940

A separate scientific discipline of psychology began to emerge in Britain around 1900. The Psychological Society was created in 1901, becoming the British Psychological Society in 1906 (Edgell, 1947; Lovie, 2001). Progress was slow before the second World War, with the total lecturing staff in British departments of psychology in 1939 numbering only about 30 (Hearnshaw, 1964, p. 208). (However, in some universities psychology was also taught in other departments, such as education.) The early advance of psychology in Britain was thus less marked than in either the United States or Germany (Boring, 1929/1950).

There was considerable initial disagreement in British universities whether psychology should be viewed as empirically scientific in the manner of traditional sciences. It was usual for the subject to be seen as falling within arts rather than science faculties. In those faculties, hostility from established philosophers was widespread in the early years. There was extended debate about the proper object of psychological study and about acceptable methods of inquiry, retarding the progress of psychology for many years.

More broadly, adverse economic circumstances in the 1920s and 1930s severely restricted university expansion. Even within established disciplines, resources were very limited, so that the development of new academic fields such as psychology was inevitably given low priority. British university departments, especially in arts faculties, were tiny, and the handful of staff naturally focused on their own core concerns. Limited and sometimes only short-term psychological developments occurred during this period in only about a dozen universities. Most made no provision, or very little, for psychology of any kind.

Nevertheless, as in some countries illustrated previously, "psychology was saved by its applications, educational, industrial and medical. … Psychologists were needed, and the universities had to train them. It was this more than anything else that surmounted the obstructiveness of philosophic sceptics" (Hearnshaw, 1964, p. 211).

Early training in psychology occurred mainly in university departments of education, and industrial aspects were less frequently covered. At certain periods occupational psychology was taught at the Universities of Glasgow and Manchester (Shimmin & Wallis, 1994), but otherwise formal teaching of the subdiscipline in the first part of the century was almost nonexistent. In addition, there were very few active researchers, and almost none of those had academic qualifications in psychology; they came with backgrounds in physiology, medicine, philosophy, education, or other subjects.

Within its small scale, British industrial psychology moved forward considerably in World War I. Three problem areas were of particular concern: "shell shock," later referred to as "war neurosis"; selection for specialized military roles; and the health of munitions workers. Early in the war, up to 5% of front-line casualties were defined as suffering from shell shock, and more than 80,000 cases of shell shock had been examined by 1918 (Bourke, 2001). The problem was initially believed to be the physical result of a nearby shell burst, with harmful consequences for the brain and nervous system. However, psychologically oriented doctors and neurologists came to the view that emotional factors were important and treatable (e.g., Salmon, 1917).

A second psychological development during World War I led to improvements in personnel selection, although applications were restricted to particular groups. Studies were carried out to better measure neuromuscular coordination and vestibular stability in potential pilots and auditory acuity and localization in listeners working to locate submarines. In addition, intelligence tests were applied to several categories of personnel, linked to wider international expansion at the time of psychometric thinking and measurement.

However, it was the third war-time development that had a particularly distinctive impact on British occupational psychology. Linked to a huge demand for weapons and ammunition, many women and men worked long hours (often around 90 a week) on the production of munitions. The negative impact on health was soon obvious, and in 1915 the government formed a Health of Munitions Workers Committee. This carried out extensive field investigations into working conditions and their physiological and psychological consequences for employees, producing findings about hours of work, fatigue, ventilation, lighting, accidents, labor turnover, and other topics as well as exploring empirical procedures that provided the foundations for many later studies.

As a result of this work, the government after the war encouraged the creation of three new organizations: the Industrial Welfare Society (1919, subsequently the Industrial Society and now the Work Foundation, a commercial advisory and consultancy body), the National Institute of Industrial Psychology (1921, discussed later), and the Industrial Fatigue Research Board (1918, renamed the Industrial Health Research Board in 1927).

Given its remit and the shortage of formally trained psychologists, this board was largely staffed and advised by doctors and physiologists. Its first chairman was Sir Charles

Sherrington (1857–1952), renowned for pioneering work on neural functioning and himself a contributor to the initial volume of the *British Journal of Psychology* in 1904. The board was guided and administered by the government's Medical Research Council. In addition to developing new procedures for vocational guidance and selection, it carried out intensive investigations in work settings of hours and conditions, manual dexterity, accidents, sickness absence, labor turnover, lighting, dust and ventilation, posture, psychophysical abilities, and equipment design.

Work by the Industrial Health Research Board (IHRB) was a precursor of later research into the design of jobs. For example, several studies of repetitive work recorded attitudes and work performance under different operating conditions and also after changes had been introduced. The importance of task variety and appropriate workload was repeatedly emphasized (e.g., Wyatt & Ogden, 1924). One investigation recorded levels of neurosis in more than 3,000 engineering employees, examining relations with personal characteristics (age, intelligence, etc.), social backgrounds, and work environments. The observed distribution of neurosis argued clearly that many jobs required "more variety and scope for initiative and interest" (Fraser, 1947, p. 10). That theme (later identified as "job enrichment") is found in many board reports from the 1920s onward.

The Industrial Health Research Board continued in operation until 1959, although after the World War II its work was increasingly taken over by other bodies. It played an important part in establishing patterns of empirical research in British organizations and in identifying key job features that bear on well-being at work. Kornhauser (1930, p. 426) described it as "clearly the most important organization in the world devoting itself to broad scientific studies in the psychology and physiology of industrial work." Nevertheless, its influence outside the subdiscipline itself was somewhat limited. Practical applications were of secondary concern to IHRB investigators, and findings were published through relatively inaccessible government documents, with few attempts at widespread communication to practitioners (Jones, 1989).

IHRB research addressed issues considered to be general across industry, whereas the National Institute of Industrial Psychology (NIIP) mainly investigated problems in individual firms. That institute was founded in 1921 by Charles Myers (1873–1946) and Henry Welch, a businessman with a strong interest in vocational guidance and selection (Bunn, 2001; Myers, 1936/1970; see chap. 2 in this volume, and Viteles, 1947, for more information on Myers). NIIP was a not-for-profit organization that set out to be scientific, impartial, and commercially neutral. Its ambition was "to promote by systematic scientific methods a more effective application of human energy in occupational life and a correspondingly higher standard of comfort and welfare for the workers" (Welch & Myers, 1932). It did "not attempt to draw any distinctive line between psychology and physiology" (Myers, 1925, p. 12), explicitly addressing both mental and physiological processes.[8]

Aided by an influential executive committee of businesspeople, the institute expanded rapidly and during the 1920s was the country's principal employer of psychologists (Bunn, 2001). Myers (1919/1970) argued that in industry and commerce there are four main areas of psychological application: vocational guidance, fatigue and work performance, movement study and the development of skilled behavior, and management issues. The final area was illustrated as concerning payment systems, worker discontent, restricted output, supervision, and "other conditions which affect the efficiency and the happiness of the workers" (1970, p. 4). Those four themes were to be the basis of British work in I–O psychology for many decades.

The institute carried out a large number of empirical investigations in those areas, extending earlier understanding of fatigue and effectiveness and undertaking the groundwork for later

[8]A summary history of NIIP is provided by Frisby (1970).

studies of skilled performance and of organizational issues. The first area (vocational guidance) became of particular importance as a source of income, with a substantial program of individual counseling (led initially by Cyril Burt) as well as the implementation of psychometric assessment in many organizations.

An important member of the NIIP executive committee was Seebohm Rowntree, of the Quaker confectionery company of the same name, who had chaired the Health of Munitions Workers Committee. Seeking an employer's perspective that was both scientific and humanistic, Rowntree enthusiastically applied and advocated current psychological thinking (Bunn, 2001). He created a psychological department in his company (operating between 1922 and 1946), which developed new tests for selection, carried out extensive training, and undertook time and motion studies to understand and improve manual skills. However, this remained at the time an isolated example in Britain of company interest in the topics of this book.

The tensions arising from conflicting aims—academic understanding and commercial gain—became increasingly problematic for NIIP during the late 1930s, as financially successful projects in market research for individual companies aroused jealousy from competitors, including some represented on the institute's executive committee. Winifred Raphael, a former assistant director, recalls that "there were strong divisions of opinion—was the institute wrong to do so much practical work at the request of industrial and commercial firms and trade unions, or should it undertake more research?" (Raphael, 1970, p. 64). When it was recognized that Myers's guiding principle had become compromised (that industrial psychology should be an impartial and commercially neutral enterprise), all commercially sensitive research was henceforth banned from the institute. This was at a time when it was experiencing great financial difficulty, in part because of adverse national developments (bad economic conditions and high unemployment) as well as widespread ignorance by employers of its role and potential. Rowntree and others concluded that multiple changes to NIIP policy and administration were necessary, and Myers was encouraged to retire from the directorship in 1938.

Myers's perspective summarizes much early British thinking in the field. It was linked to his belief that occupational psychology projects must secure "the approval of the employer and the worker alike" (quoted by Bunn, 2001) and in part derived from his medical background, with an unquestioned assumption that the goal is to help people. "The aim of industrial psychology is primarily not to obtain greater output but to give the worker greater ease in his [sic] work. Ease does not mean merely physical ease but also mental ease" (Myers, 1929, p. 14). Linked to this perspective, a major sponsor of early occupational psychology in Britain was the government rather than employers, for instance through the Medical Research Council. Government-financed investigations tended to seek generalizable findings that did not directly benefit one employer over others.

British I–O Psychology Between 1940 and 1980

Despite progress in a few organizations, by 1940 "there was very little public awareness of psychology in any shape or form, and the pioneering examples of military and industrial applications during World War One had long been forgotten" (Shimmin & Wallis, 1994, p. 13). As in other countries illustrated earlier, war once again created opportunities for occupational psychology.

A major expansion occurred in psychometric assessment for the allocation of British military personnel. Psychological procedures had for some years been applied in educational settings, particularly for the identification of cognitive impairment in children, but in the 1930s were rarely used in Britain with adults. At the outset of the conflict, partly in response to the growing technological complexity of warfare, psychologists from the Industrial Health Research Board, NIIP, and other organizations were joined by specialists in education, physiology, and related disciplines to create new psychometric procedures. These had a great impact on training success rates and broader effectiveness in the army, navy, and air force (Shimmin & Wallis, 1994; Thalassis, 2003; Vernon & Parry, 1949).

In addition to the widespread application of psychometric procedures, an important innovation was the War Office Selection Board (WOSB). This was introduced for officer selection in 1942 and later also applied throughout the British civil service as the Civil Service Selection Board (CSSB). The board's procedures were instigated by psychiatrists as well as psychologists and involved the observation of behavior in practical exercises (such as leaderless group discussion) as well as the application of psychometric instruments and interview procedures (e.g., Highhouse, 2002). The WOSB procedures were later developed into widely used assessment center techniques (see also chap. 17).

The Medical Research Council continued to support psychological research and in 1944 established in the University of Cambridge a Unit for Research in Applied Psychology (later renamed as the Applied Psychology Unit, APU). APU built on wartime research at Cambridge to investigate human skill and explored environmental and task variables that might influence skill acquisition and application. Consistent with the traditional medical emphasis, almost half of the initially appointed research workers were graduates in medicine or physiology (Brown, Batts, & McGougan, 1970).

APU research was linked to practical needs, for example, in its early investigation of perceptual vigilance as required in military and industrial inspection tasks, but the unit worked primarily to meet the Medical Research Council's goal of scientific advance. Research contributions over the next decades covered skills and information processing, human–machine interaction, psychomotor coordination, circadian rhythms, sleep deprivation, noise and performance, heat stress, signal detection, acoustic confusions, memory and recall, and a wide range of issues of importance in cognitive psychology. Among the staff of APU following Sir Frederick Bartlett as founding director, Donald Broadbent (1926–1993) is notable for his contributions to both cognitive and occupational psychology. He worked in the unit from 1949 and was director from 1958 to 1974.

The Medical Research Council (MRC) had traditionally operated through the establishment of long-term research centers providing career opportunities to their staff, rather than providing merely short-term grants for universities themselves to appoint researchers for the duration of a project. Until the 1960s, MRC was the government agency with principal responsibility for applied psychology, and the council also established the Industrial Psychology Research Unit (in London between 1947 and 1969) and the Unit for Research in Occupational Aspects of Ageing (in Liverpool between 1955 and 1970).

As in the earlier period, other forms of government involvement played an important role in the development of British I–O psychology. Although very few commercial companies were aware of or interested in the subdiscipline, around the middle of the century it became firmly established in government (including military) departments. A separate professional category of "psychologist" was established in the civil service in 1950. Shimmin and Wallis (1994) reviewed psychologists' early contributions to civil service operations, in the areas of interviewing, training, and human–machine systems and more widely in the then novel field of ergonomics.

That last domain brought together members of overlapping disciplines—anatomists (especially those with an interest in anthropometry), physiologists, and psychologists. The founders (in London in 1949) of the Ergonomics Research Society[9] described their work as "study of the

---

[9]"Research" was omitted from the Society's title in 1977.

relationship between man [sic] and his working environment." Their focus was on the design of equipment and environments to match human capacity, and the society's activities naturally overlapped with I–O psychology. It founded a new journal, *Ergonomics,* in 1957, with the subtitle "Human Factors in Work, Machine Control and Equipment Design."

Occupational psychologists were also active in other government departments, such as the prison service and the Ministry of Labour (which later became the Department of Employment and has been renamed several times in recent years). For example, psychologists in the latter were active in the Youth Employment Service, and they contributed to national careers and occupational guidance schemes that were available without charge to adults through a national network of Occupational Guidance Units between 1966 and 1979. Individual services for disabled people were also enhanced by guidance from psychologists in each of the Industrial (later Employment) Rehabilitation Centres, for example, applying a composite test battery developed by colleagues working on the selection of naval personnel. More generally, research and good practice in job content and employee well-being were encouraged by the Work Research Unit, a section of the Department of Employment staffed by occupational psychologists between 1973 and 1993.

World War II led also to the birth (in 1947) of the Tavistock Institute of Human Relations, an independent, not-for-profit organization. Staffed by psychiatrists, clinical psychologists, social psychologists, sociologists, and anthropologists, the institute emphasized social relationship aspects of psychoanalysis. Although it worked with little direct contact with occupational psychology itself, its influence on that field was considerable (see also chaps. 14 and 17).

Members of the institute developed practical applications of what they termed "object relations theory." Concepts like emotional transference and personal dependence were examined in groups and wider organizations, through action research projects (typically lasting many months), process consultation, "sensitivity training" workshops, and investigations into company culture. Particularly influential was research into self-regulating groups, guided by an overall perspective on "sociotechnical systems theory." This views organizations as consisting of independent technological and social systems operating under joint causation, such that improvements require joint rather than single optimization. The approach formed the basis of research into group-based rather than individual work in several settings, illustrated by Trist and Bamforth's (1951) study in coal mines.

In arguing for a broad form of psychiatrically based social science, the Tavistock Institute did not fit easily within established academic frameworks. To assist dissemination of its ideas, a new journal was formed (*Human Relations,* in 1947) and extensive international networks were developed. The institute is still active today, although its involvement in I–O psychology is not great.[10]

In the period up to the 1970s, occupational psychology was held in low esteem within the British academic community. The number of departments of psychology had increased substantially between 1940 and 1980, but students were rarely taught about the methods and findings of applied research. Very few students looked for careers in the occupational field, and there was almost no interchange between psychologists active in basic research and those whose interests were applied.

The only substantial provider of training in occupational psychology at the time was Birkbeck College of the University of London. In 1951, Alec Rodger introduced there a postgraduate diploma, and the success of this led (in 1962) to the foundation of the country's first and only department of occupational psychology. Teaching was presented around the "FMJ–FJM" framework: fitting the man [sic] to the job, and fitting the job to the man (e.g., Rodger &

---

[10]However, *Human Relations* retains a primary focus on organizational issues.

Cavanagh, 1962). The FMJ component was taught principally in terms of vocational guidance and personnel selection (but also included training), and Rodger's "seven-point plan" specified the key features of an individual to be assessed.[11] The other aspect of occupational psychology, FMJ (of less interest to Rodger), was treated in terms of working conditions, environmental features, and equipment design, in part through the themes and methods of ergonomics.

In general, academic psychology in British universities in the 1960s retained a strong preference for rigorous laboratory experimentation into issues deriving from previous laboratory experiments rather than from the everyday world. Broader societal attitudes at the time also restricted the development of occupational psychology. As part of a general anti-authoritarian tendency and a preference for freedom of expression and action, critical psychologists in Britain and elsewhere drew attention to possible ideological biases in the selection of topics for investigation and to the alleged promanagement preferences of some occupational psychologists. Student protest movements objected vigorously to "the military–industrial complex," linking employment issues to wider political perceptions.[12] The occupational psychology community responded along the lines of Charles Myers: They were seeking to match a concern for management's problems with a desire to help other employees.

I–O psychology in Britain was also unloved by industrial and commercial organizations, with little demand for psychological expertise and few practitioners working in the field (e.g., McCollom, 1960). In the 1970s, it became common for the latter to describe themselves to potential clients as "behavioral scientists" rather than by the suspicion-inducing title "psychologist." At this time, there were very few psychological consultancies operating anywhere in the country.

Recognizing some of these difficulties, the Medical Research Council founded in 1968 another unit to complement the laboratory-based work of the APU. This was the Social and Applied Psychology Unit (SAPU) at the University of Sheffield. The unit's initial terms of reference concerned "applied cognitive studies," which were taken to include research into attitudes, perceptions, and decision making in organizations as well as in laboratory situations making use of newly available online computers (Warr, 1999, 2001).

Research in the Social and Applied Psychology Unit sought to build on two values from earlier investigators. Consistent with the bipartisan hopes illustrated previously, it was usual to set up project steering groups whose members were drawn from both management and other employees. Research questions (within the broader academic constraints set by SAPU) were thus partly determined by participating organizations and their staff, and research reports were made available to employee representatives as well as to managers. This approach (which was of course facilitated by the unit's financial independence from a research site) also had the advantage of encouraging throughout an organization wider commitment to experimental changes, typically proposed on the basis of initial cross-sectional inquiries.

The 1960s and 1970s saw a widespread national concern for the "quality of working life" and "industrial democracy," at a time when people at work were sometimes suggested to be "alienated" from society. Consistent with this possibility, SAPU research soon expanded to explore the nature of well-being at work, the factors related to well-being, and ways to increase well-being (e.g., Warr & Wall, 1975). Early studies of participation in decision making and the redesign of jobs had a concern for interaction at the collective level (e.g., through employee committees or "action-planning groups"), emphasizing the importance of teams rather than the more individualistic perspective usually adopted at the time.

---

[11]The plan derived from an NIIP scheme created by Cyril Burt and applied by Alec Rodger as a previous employee of that Institute.

[12]These critiques and a general opposition to industrial–organizational psychology occurred in many Western countries at this time. See, for instance, Baritz (1960) and Shimmin and van Strien (1998).

The Social and Applied Psychology Unit worked in many private and public organizations up to its closure in 1996, with a research focus that became described in terms of well-being and effectiveness. Studies examined job content, workload, employee participation, organizational climate, management–union relations, absence from work, organizational change, occupational stress and psychotherapeutic procedures, work–role transitions and career development, advanced manufacturing technology, shift work, work-group innovation, and similar topics. In the 1980s, longitudinal investigations established the causal impact on mental health of transitions from employment to unemployment (and back again). Much of the unit's work thus reflected the growing importance to I–O psychology in general of social and organizational issues and processes, expanding beyond an earlier focus on individual differences and working conditions. In addition, a continuing strand of research explored processes of interaction with computers and decision making in industrial, commercial, and health service settings. Central to this was the notion of "cognitive ergonomics," which was concerned with mental processes in people's interactions with computer systems.

The Social and Applied Psychology Unit had the advantage of receiving funds from the Medical Research Council (and later from the Economic and Social Research Council, the Department of Employment, and other government bodies). On the other hand, the National Institute of Industrial Psychology had to finance itself from industrial and commercial sources, and this was difficult in the 1960s. Projects continued in career counseling, personnel selection, and occupational stress, and a large descriptive study of accidents was undertaken. However, financial problems forced the institute to close in 1973.

NIIP's journal, *Occupational Psychology*, had previously carried advisory and descriptive articles aimed at practitioners. It was taken over by the British Psychological Society to become an international journal of research. Its new title from 1975, *Journal of Occupational Psychology*, was in 1992 changed to *Journal of Occupational and Organizational Psychology*, reflecting its wide coverage of the field beyond the more individual emphasis suggested to some by the term *occupational*.

British I–O Psychology After 1980

Throughout the 1940–1980 period, British I–O psychology grew in strength, as part of the general societal acceptance of the discipline as a whole. The following 2 decades saw the subdiscipline become firmly established in universities, government departments, and employing organizations. Contrary to earlier neglect by departments of psychology, occupational studies became widely accepted as of academic as well as practical value, with master's degree courses in more than 20 universities. A large number of psychological consultancy firms have been created in recent years, reflecting the growing demand for psychology in organizations as well as the increasing number of available specialists and their products.

Consolidation of the profession has been accompanied by a national framework of chartership, a procedure with aims similar to professional licensing in other countries. Since 1987, a register of chartered psychologists has listed those who have reached training standards set by the British Psychological Society and are bound by the society's ethical guidelines. Only individuals on this professional register are permitted to call themselves a "chartered psychologist" (or more specifically, where appropriate a "chartered occupational psychologist"[13]). This form of quality control and public protection (also in force for other professions such as "char-

---

[13]The Occupational Psychology Division of the BPS currently has about 10% of the total society membership, although not all psychologists working in the occupational field are members of that division. In 2002, membership of the occupational, clinical, and educational divisions was about 3,100, 4,800, and 1,400, respectively, out of a total membership around 30,000.

tered engineers" and "chartered accountants") has contributed to the increasing respect accorded to psychology in Britain.

It is not easy to discern general trends in any field across very recent years, but it is clear that I–O psychology is, like many other aspects of life, becoming more internationalized. There is increasing interchange of people and ideas between countries, and it appears that national variations in emphasis and approach are becoming reduced. For example, the multicountry European Association of Work and Organizational Psychology (founded in 1991, but informally active for several previous years), with its journal (*European Journal of Work and Organizational Psychology*) and biennial conferences, is encouraging information sharing and mutual learning. In terms of academic publications, it is notable that papers submitted to a British journal are now often refereed by a non-British psychologist. On the practical level, psychological consulting firms are increasingly multinational, with offices in the United Kingdom as well as in the United States, continental Europe, and Australasia.

This cross-national perspective is illustrated by the recent foundation in Britain of new academic journals explicitly intended for a global readership. These include *International Journal of Selection and Assessment* (1993), *International Journal of Training and Development* (1997), *Journal of Organizational Behavior* (founded as *Journal of Occupational Behaviour* in 1980, renamed in 1988), and *Work and Stress* (1987). These, and the three other journals cited earlier, are in spirit and content international as well as British.

I–O PSYCHOLOGY IN THE UNITED STATES AND UNITED KINGDOM

How does this pattern of development in the United Kingdom compare with that in the United States? It is not always possible to identify what is typical in large and varied systems, so that alternatives to the generalities suggested here are undoubtedly present. As pointed out earlier, some international homogenization has occurred in recent years, so the U.K.–U.S. comparison is best made in respect of former periods.

Zickar and Gibby (chap. 3 in this volume) characterize American I–O psychology in terms of four themes. First is an emphasis on topics of interest to management including productivity and efficiency. Such topics have of course also motivated and sustained occupational psychology in Britain, but, as illustrated earlier, there has also been a strong interest in the welfare of working people. In part this arose from the medical background of many influential contributors and in part from the strong involvement of government departments. The latter sought to improve their own operational effectiveness and the welfare of service recipients, rather than aiming to advance party political positions. In addition, the limited interest from company managers and the initial shortage of psychologists selling their wares meant that a management-driven profession was less likely.

Kornhauser (1930) distinguished between "the non-technical, common-sense sort of psychology" and "psychology of the more technical sort." He emphasized that in the 1920s the United States and United Kingdom differed sharply in those respects. American managers had a strong interest in practical possibilities of the first kind, whereas in Britain those were rarely discussed. Conversely, the United Kingdom encouraged generalizable, scientific projects that were not driven by immediate pragmatic need, "with greatly increased emphasis on human values and satisfactions as separable from standards of output and profit" (p. 425).

This U.K.–U.S. difference may also be viewed in relation to a greater British emphasis on the creation and operation of a "welfare state." For example, proposals by Beveridge (1942) laid the foundations for a comprehensive health care system funded through taxation and operated through government agencies, and a somewhat more collectivist view of behavior in society was associated with substantial trade union membership and influence from about that time.[14] Occupational psychologists both were influenced by and contributed to that cultural process.

Second, Zickar and Gibby (chap. 3 in this volume) draw attention to the heavy quantification of U.S. industrial–organizational psychology, with a strong focus on approved statistical methods and techniques. This emphasis has been linked to a widely encouraged desire for I–O psychology to be explicitly scientific. Consistent with a broad tendency toward positivist science, British developments have also been of that kind. However, it seems fair to say that, in evaluating the worth of a psychologist or a psychological project, observers in Britain have tended to emphasize conceptual or practical issues rather more than statistical or methodological sophistication.

U.S. norms about quantification and scientific rigor might be viewed as part of a wider national feature. Observers in many countries believe that North American psychology tends to be more bound by professional fashion than is generally the case elsewhere. In terms of the historical development of I–O psychology, other countries have supported more eclectic perspectives and methods and been more exposed to suggestions from outside the discipline itself.

It might thus be argued that the boundaries of occupational psychology in Britain have been wider and more permeable than those of American I–O psychology. Inputs from psychoanalytic and ergonomic perspectives have been cited previously, and broad expectations may be illustrated by the eight areas of knowledge and experience demanded of any member of the British Psychological Society hoping to become chartered (see previous discussion). Coverage is required in all eight areas: counseling and personal development, design of environments and work, employee relations and motivation, human–machine interaction, organizational development, performance appraisal and career development, personnel selection and assessment, and training.

A broader framework has also been usual in relation to Zickar and Gibby's third theme: a focus on personnel selection. British psychologists have often worked in that area, but from the outset considerable attention has been paid to vocational and career guidance, working conditions, and employee welfare. Attention to those areas has been encouraged by government support and funding as well as by the preferences of many psychologists.

The scientist–practitioner divide (the fourth theme in chap. 3) is likely to exist in any country, given that the discipline seeks to meet two goals that are inevitably in some cases opposed to each other. (Recall the conflicts between research and practice in the National Institute of Industrial Psychology summarized earlier.) The divide was to some extent bypassed in the early years in Britain by a lack of practitioners, but otherwise the two countries' development appears similar in this respect.

A characteristic of British history in this field that extends across Zickar and Gibby's themes 1 and 3 is a long concern for employee well-being. Psychologists from the earliest days sought to discover "the most effective means of avoiding fatigue and boredom" and "the causes of and remedies for irritation, discontent and unrest" and to reduce "needless effort and strain" (Myers, 1929, p. 9; see also chap. 1). Furthermore, well-being has been viewed more widely than through the conventional American concern for job satisfaction. The construct is part of mental health, being both global (concerning life in general) and domain specific (reflecting feelings about, for example, a job); furthermore, aspects of well-being include anxiety, depression, and other feelings beyond merely satisfaction (Warr, 2005).

Some early American I–O psychologists had an interest in mental health, but their primary concern was often to identify emotional maladjustment that might predispose employees to

---

[14]However, trade union membership in Britain declined substantially in the 1980s, linked in part to high levels of unemployment.

join a trade union. For example, psychometric procedures were sometimes developed to screen out such individuals (Zickar, 2003). A strongly promanagement orientation of that kind was not usual among early British psychologists in this field.

Conversely, an important similarity between the two countries has sometimes been described as "Anglo-American empiricism."[15] Throughout its history, British occupational psychology has been marked by a preference for developing and testing focused models in specific domains rather than working within an overarching theoretical framework. A typical approach has been careful observation to examine plausible expectations in a particular setting rather than the exploration of ideas viewed as important because they are part of a more general conceptual scheme. British and American I–O activities tend to be "bottom-up" rather than "top-down" in those senses. The historical foundations of psychology in both countries are thus more positivist and microscopic than in some other countries.

I–O PSYCHOLOGY OUTSIDE THE UNITED STATES: A PARTIAL PERSPECTIVE

The chapter has primarily examined individual countries separately of each other, tending to emphasize the differences between them. In fact, the development of industrial–organizational psychology has been broadly similar in most countries despite some divergence in content and external influences. International overlap appears to be increasing, as available knowledge, personal communications, scientific organizations, and business processes take on a more globalized character.

Consistent with the chapter's opening suggestion that understanding is aided by viewing oneself in the context of others, an overall perspective about European and U.S. developments may be helpful. Some general themes were considered by de Wolff, Shimmin, and de Montmollin (1981), and keynote speakers at the European Congress of Psychology in 1989 were asked to summarize in general terms the key features of European versus American psychology (Drenth, 2000b). Illustrative themes for Europe in distinction from the United States included higher level theories more than microscopic approaches, more idiographic and less nomothetic, more collectively oriented as opposed to individualistic, and less effective in applying knowledge and exploiting valuable implications.

Such assertions, of course, reflect perceptions rather than empirically supported findings, but more detailed examination of historical developments in different countries might usefully explore variations in those respects as a function of the three possible influences on I–O psychology summarized earlier: baseline position, key individuals, and developments outside the discipline.

REFERENCES

Ansbacher, H. L. (1941). German military psychology. *Psychological Bulletin, 38*, 370–392.

Baritz, L. (1960). *The servants of power: A history of the use of social science in American industry*. Middletown, CT: Wesleyan University Press.

Bauer, R. A. (Ed.). (1962). *Some views on Soviet psychology*. Washington, DC: American Psychological Association.

Ben-Ari, R., & Amir, Y. (1986). Psychology in a developing society: The case of Israel. *Annual Review of Psychology, 37*, 17–41.

Beveridge, W. (1942). *Social insurance and allied services*. London: His Majesty's Stationery Office.

Blackburn, K. (1998). The quest for efficiency and the rise of industrial psychology in Australia, 1917–1929. *Labour History, 74*, 122–136.

---

[15]The "Anglo" reference is to England, which is merely one part of the United Kingdom, so that (as in many similar cases) the label is not strictly appropriate.

Bordeleau, Y., & Morin, E. M. (1988). Industrial-organizational psychology in French Canada: Teaching, research and practice [La psychologie industrielle et organisationelle au Canada Français: Enseignment, recherche et pratique]. *Canadian Psychology, 29*, 44–56.

Bordow, A. (1971). The industrial psychologist: His education, employment history and job functions. *Australian Psychologist, 6*, 80–90.

Boring, E. G. (1929). *A history of experimental psychology*. New York: Appleton-Century-Crofts.

Boring, E. G. (1950). *A history of experimental psychology* (2nd ed.). New York: Appleton-Century-Crofts.

Bourke, J. (2001). Psychology at war, 1914–1945. In G. C. Bunn, A. D. Lovie, and G. D. Richards (Eds.), *Psychology in Britain* (pp. 133–149). Leicester, England: BPS Books.

Brown, I. D., Batts, V., & McGougan, C. E. (1970). The Medical Research Council Applied Psychology Unit. *Occupational Psychology, 44*, 267–279.

Bucklow, M. (1977). Applied psychology in Australia—The history. In M. Nixon and R. Taft (Eds.), *Psychology in Australia: Achievements and prospects* (pp. 23–34). Rushcutters Bay, NSW, Australia: Pergamon.

Bunn, G. (2001). Charlie and the chocolate factory. *The Psychologist, 14*, 576–579.

Carpintero, H. (1994). Some historical notes on scientific psychology and its professional development [in Spain]. *Applied Psychology: An International Review, 43*, 131–150.

Carpintero, H., & Herrero, F. (2002). Early applied psychology. *European Psychologist, 7*, 39–52.

Clark, J. F. (1958). Psychology in the public service, business and industry. *Australian Journal of Psychology, 10*, 30–41.

Cook, P. H. (1949). The work of psychologists in Australian industry. *Occupational Psychology, 23*, 38–46.

Cronshaw, S. F. (1991). *Industrial psychology in Canada*. Waterloo, ON: North Waterloo Academic Press.

de Wolff, C. J., Shimmin, S., & de Montmollin, M. (1981). *Conflicts and contradictions: Work psychologists in Europe*. London: Academic Press.

Drenth, P. J. D. (2000a). The development of psychology in the Netherlands. In A. E. Kazdin (Ed.), *Encyclopedia of psychology* (Vol. 5, pp. 409–413). New York: Oxford University Press.

Drenth, P. J. D. (2000b). An interview with Pieter Drenth. *European Psychologist, 5*, 102–106.

Edgell, B. (1947). The British Psychological Society. *British Journal of Psychology, 37*, 113–132.

Fleishman, E. A. (1956). *Report of official visit to European psychological research centers*. San Antonio, TX: Air Force Personnel and Training Research Center.

Fleishman, E. A. (1962). Observations on Soviet educational and industrial psychology. In R. A. Bauer (Ed.), *Some views on Soviet psychology* (pp. 165–187). Washington, DC: American Psychological Association.

Fleishman, E. A. (1963). Some observations on industrial psychology in the Soviet Union. *Personnel Psychology, 16*, 115–125.

Fleishman, E. A. (1979). The new applied psychology: An international perspective. *International Review of Applied Psychology, 28*, 67–74.

Fleishman, E. A. (1999). Applied psychology: An international journey. *American Psychologist, 54*, 1008–1016.

Fraser, R. (1947). *The incidence of neurosis among factory workers* (Rep. 90). London: Industrial Health Research Board.

Frese, M., & Zapf, D. (1994). Action as the core of work psychology: A German approach. In H. C. Triandis, M. D. Dunnette, & L. M. Hough (Eds.), *Handbook of industrial and organizational psychology* (Vol. 4, pp. 271–340). Palo Alto, CA: Consulting Psychologists Press.

Frisby, C. B. (1970). The development of industrial psychology at the NIIP. *Occupational Psychology, 44*, 35–62.

Geuter, U. (1992). *The professionalisation of psychology in Nazi Germany*. Cambridge, England: Cambridge University Press. (Originally published in 1984 in German)

Greif, S. (2003). *Geschichte der Organisationpsychologie* [History of organisational psychology]. In H. Schuler (Ed.), *Lehrbuch Organisationspsychologie* (pp. 21–57). Bern, Switzerland: Huber.

Griffin, M. A., Landy, F. J., & Mayocchi, L. (2002). Australian influences on Elton Mayo: The construct of revery in industrial society. *History of Psychology, 5*, 356–375.

Guttman, L.—Biography (n.d.). Retrieved December 4, 2005, from http://idi.org.il/english/guttman.asp?did=337&tax=1

Hacker, W., Volpert, W., & Cranach, M. (Eds.). (1982). *Cognitive and motivational aspects of action*. Berlin: Deutscher Verlag der Wissenschaften.

Hearnshaw, L. S. (1964). *A short history of British psychology 1840–1940*. London: Methuen.

Highhouse, S. (2002). Assessing the candidate as a whole: A historical and critical analysis of individual psychological assessment for personnel decision making. *Personnel Psychology, 55*, 363–396.

Jenkins, J. G. (1935). *Psychology in business and industry*. New York: Wiley.

Jones, H. (1989). Industrial research under the MRC. In J. Austoker & L. Bryder (Eds.), *Historical perspectives on the role of the MRC* (pp. 137–161). Oxford, England: Oxford University Press.

Kashima, Y., & Callan, V. J. (1994). The Japanese work group. In H. C. Triandis, M. D. Dunnette, & L. M. Hough (Eds.), *Handbook of industrial and organizational psychology* (Vol. 4, pp. 609–646). Palo Alto, CA: Consulting Psychologists Press.

Kirihara, S. H. (1959). Industrial psychology in Japan. *Reports of the Institute for the Science of Labour, 55*, 1–19.

Kornhauser, A. W. (1930). Industrial psychology in England, Germany, and the United States. *Personnel Journal, 8*, 421–434.

Lahy, J. M. (1927). *La sélection psychophysiologique des travailleurs, conducteurs de tramways et d'autobus* [Psychophysiological selection of tram and bus drivers]. Paris: Dunot.

Landy, F. J. (1992). Hugo Münsterberg: Victim or visionary? *Journal of Applied Psychology, 77*, 787–802.

Leonova, A. B. (1994). Industrial and organizational psychology in Russia: The concept of human functional states and applied stress research. In C. L. Cooper & I. T. Robertson (Eds.), *International review of industrial and organizational psychology* (Vol. 9, pp. 183–212). London: Wiley.

Levinson, S. (1997). Psychology in Israel: 40 years for the Israeli Psychological Association. *Psychology* (in Hebrew), *1*, 109–120.

Levy-Leboyer, C., & Sperandio, J.-C. (1987). Work psychology in France: Birth and development [La psychologie du travail en France: Naissance et développement]. In C. Lévy-Leboyer and J.-C. Sperandio (Eds.), *Traité de psychologie du travail* (pp. 9–18). Paris: Presses Universitaires de France.

Lovie, A. D. (2001). Three steps to heaven: How the British Psychological Society attained its place in the sun. In G. C. Bunn, A. D. Lovie, & G. D. Richards (Eds.), *Psychology in Britain* (pp. 95–114). Leicester, England: BPS Books.

McCollom, I. N. (1960). Psychologists in industry in the United Kingdom and Western Germany. *American Psychologist, 15*, 58–64.

Münsterberg, H. (1914). *Grundzüge der psychotechnik* [Foundations of psychotechnics]. Leipzig: Barth.

Myers, C. S. (1919). Psychology and industry. *British Journal of Psychology, 10*, 177–182. Partly reprinted in *Occupational Psychology*, 1970, *44*, 1–4.

Myers, C. S. (1925). *Industrial psychology in Great Britain*. London: Jonathan Cape.

Myers, C. S. (Ed.). (1929). *Industrial psychology*. London: Thornton Butterworth.

Myers, C. S. (1936). Autobiography. In C. A. Murchison (Ed.), *A history of psychology in autobiography* (Vol. 3, pp. 215–230). Worcester, MA: Clark University Press. Reprinted in *Occupational Psychology*, 1970, *44*, 5–13.

O'Neil, W. M. (1987). *A century of psychology in Australia*. Sydney: Sydney University Press.

Owens, A. G. (1977). Psychology in the Armed services. In M. Nixon & R. Taft (Eds.), *Psychology in Australia: Achievements and prospects* (pp. 202–213). Rushcutters Bay, NSW, Australia: Pergamon.

Peiró, J. M. (2001). Historical overview and recent developments of work, organization and personnel psychology in Spain [Perspectiva historica y desarrollos recientes de la psicologia del trabajo y de las organizaciones en España]. *Revista de Psicologia del Trabajo y de las Organizaciones, 17*, 255–271.

Peiró, J. M., & Munduate, L. (1994). Work and organizational psychology in Spain. *Applied Psychology: An International Review, 43*, 231–274.

Podrabsky, J. (2001). Overview of the development of psychology of work and organization in Czechoslovakia. In M. Solc (Ed.), *Fragments of the 80 years of history of psychology of work and organization in the Czech Republic and Slovakia* (pp. 7–18). Prague: Czech Association of Work and Organization Psychologists.

Raphael, W. (1970). NIIP and its staff 1921 to 1961. *Occupational Psychology, 44*, 63–70.

Rodger, A., & Cavanagh, P. (1962). Training occupational psychologists. *Occupational Psychology, 36*, 82–88.

Roe, R. A. (1995). Developments in eastern Europe and work and organizational psychology. In C. L. Cooper & I. T. Robertson (Eds.), *International review of industrial and organizational psychology* (pp. 275–349). Chichester, England: Wiley.

Rowe, P. M. (1992). *Canadian I-O psychology: Living next to an elephant*. Presentation at the Annual Conference of the Society for Industrial and Organizational Psychology, Montreal.

Salmon, T. W. (1917). The care and treatment of mental diseases and war neuroses in the British army. *Mental Hygiene, 1*, 509–547.

Shimmin, S., & van Strien, P. J. (1998). History of the psychology of work and organization. In P. J. D. Drenth, H. Thierry, & C. J. de Wolff (Eds.), *Handbook of work and organizational psychology* (2nd ed., pp. 71–99). Hove, England: Psychology Press.

Shimmin, S., & Wallis, D. (1994). *Fifty years of occupational psychology in Britain*. Leicester, England: British Psychological Society.

Sprung, L., & Sprung, H. (2001). History of modern psychology in Germany in 19th- and 20th-century thought and society. *International Journal of Psychology, 36*, 364–376.

Taylor, K. F., & Taft, R. (1977). Psychology and the Australian zeitgeist. In M. Nixon & R. Taft (Eds.), *Psychology in Australia: Achievements and prospects* (pp. 35–51). Rushcutters Bay, NSW, Australia: Pergamon.

Thalassis, N. (2003). The use of intelligence testing in the recruitment of "other ranks" in the armed forces during the second world war. *History and Philosophy of Psychology, 5,* 17–29.

Triandis, H. C. (1994). Cross-cultural industrial and organizational psychology. In H. C. Triandis, M. D. Dunnette, & L. M. Hough (Eds.), *Handbook of industrial and organizational psychology* (Vol. 4, pp. 103–172). Palo Alto, CA: Consulting Psychologists Press.

Trist, E. L, & Bamforth, K. W. (1951). Some social and psychological consequences of the longwall method of coal-getting. *Human Relations, 4,* 1–38.

Vernon, P. E., & Parry, J. B. (1949). *Personnel selection in the British forces*. London: London University Press.

Viteles, M. S. (1932). *Industrial psychology*. New York: Norton.

Viteles, M. S. (1938). Industrial psychology in Russia. *Occupational Psychology, 12,* 1–19.

Viteles, M. S. (1947). Charles Samuel Myers, 1873–1946. *Psychological Review, 54,* 177–181.

Wang, Z.-M. (1990) Recent developments in ergonomics in China. *Ergonomics, 33,* 853–865.

Wang, Z.-M. (1994) Culture, economic reform, and the role of industrial and organizational psychology in China. In H. C. Triandis, M. D. Dunnette, & L. M. Hough (Eds.), *Handbook of industrial and organizational psychology* (Vol. 4, pp. 689–725). Palo Alto, CA: Consulting Psychologists Press.

Warr, P. B. (1999). *Work, well-being and effectiveness: A history of the MRC/ESRC Social and Applied Psychology Unit*. Sheffield, England: Sheffield Academic Press.

Warr, P. B. (2001). *Psychology in Sheffield: The early years*. Sheffield, England: Sheffield Academic Press.

Warr, P. B. (2005). Work, well-being and mental health. In J. Barling, K. Kelloway, & M. Frone (Eds.), *Handbook of work stress* (pp. 547–573). Thousand Oaks, CA: Sage.

Warr, P. B., & Wall, T. D. (1975). *Work and well-being*. London: Penguin.

Webster, E. C. (1964). *Decision making in the employment interview*. Montreal: McGill University Applied Psychology Center.

Webster, E. C. (1988). I–O psychology in Canada: From birth to Couchiching. *Canadian Psychology, 29,* 4–10.

Welch, H. J., & Myers, C. S. (1932). *Ten years of industrial psychology: An account of the first decade of the National Institute of Industrial Psychology*. London: Pitman.

Wyatt, F., & Teuber, H. L. (1944). German psychology under the Nazi system, 1933–1940. *Psychological Review, 51,* 229–247.

Wyatt, S., & Ogden, D. A. (1924). *On the extent and effects of variety and uniformity in repetitive work* (Rep. 26). London: Industrial Fatigue Research Board.

Zickar, M. J. (2003). Remembering Arthur Kornhauser: Industrial psychology's advocate for worker well-being. *Journal of Applied Psychology, 88,* 363–369.

III

Educational, Organizational, and Military Influences

This section contains three chapters that focus on organizational-level influences. In addition to individual accomplishments described in chapter 2, universities, formal and informal organizations, and the military had an impact on the development of I–O psychology in the United States.

In chapter 5, the development of education and training in the discipline is discussed. The authors examine doctoral level training and mention master's-level training and undergraduate instruction. Furthermore, information about doctoral programs in academic departments other than psychology is presented, and some changes in programs are discussed as well as the content of graduate programs. The authors cover the period from when the first training program was established (1915) through 2000.

In chapter 6, several informal and formal organizations that are important to the evolution of I–O psychology are discussed. As the author notes, it is impossible to cover all organizations in this one chapter, so the author highlights organizations representative of five major categories: (a) academic organizations, with special attention to separate units established in large research-oriented universities; (b) research organizations outside of the military that focused exclusively on research and development; (c) business and industry consulting organizations; (d) governmental organizations; and (e) informal organizations of I–O psychologists. The chapter does not include in chronological order every organization involved with I–O psychology. The reader will not find in the chapter a discussion of work done in business and industry or the development of professional societies. References to previously published accounts are provided for this information.

In chapter 7, contributions of the military to industrial and organizational psychology are described. The authors note important people and events that have shaped military psychological research, which in turn, the science and practice of I–O psychology. Three major periods are included: World War I, World War II, and post–World War II. In the descriptions, the authors present several military organizations and their activities. For post–World War II developments, research summaries are provided for the following topics: selection and classification, learning and skill acquisition, performance conceptualization and measurement, performance enhancement, teams and team training, decision making, leadership, and expertise.

5

A History of I–O Psychology Educational Programs in the United States

Rodney L. Lowman
Alliant International University

John Kantor
Alliant International University

Robert Perloff
University of Pittsburgh

This chapter considers historical developments in doctoral training programs in industrial–organizational (I–O) psychology and closely related fields. We begin the chapter with the formative years, followed by pre–World War II industrial psychology graduate training, post–World War II graduate training in I–O psychology, master's level training, undergraduate instruction, doctoral training, and related training programs in academic departments other than psychology. We then reflect on changes in programs over time. Finally, we examine training content and curricula of graduate programs.

FORMATIVE YEARS

The roots of modern I–O psychology as a discipline began not long after the founding of psychology itself (see, e.g., Poffenberger, 1927; Viteles, 1932). The foundations of I–O psychology sprang mostly from the interests of a few people who were involved in the new field of psychology. They were fueled perhaps by the headiness that accompanies the birth of any new academic discipline, especially one with ambitions as wide as "the study of behavior." From the very beginning of the psychology field, there was much interest in the application of this exciting new, science-based knowledge to practical, real-world problems, especially those of industry and organizations (Benjamin, 1997) (See chaps. 1, 2, and 3 in this text for more detailed information about the formative years.)

The development of graduate training programs in I–O psychology paralleled and followed the development of the field itself. Early on, there were few textbooks in the field and not many journals, and the small number of faculty offering training in the area were largely creating the field as they were teaching and researching it (Katzell & Austin, 1992; Koppes, 2003).

PRE–WORLD WAR II I–O PSYCHOLOGY GRADUATE TRAINING

The early history of graduate training in I–O psychology had rather diverse, but not discon-
nected, roots. Formal training programs in I–O psychology in the modern sense of "programs"
did not really begin until after World War II (Katzell, 1992a). Few programs were actually labeled as industrial psychology (an early label of the field) in the pre–World War II days. If they
were called anything other than doctoral programs in psychology (as most appear to have
been), programs were called "applied psychology," "personnel psychology," or "personnel research." (Labels later used include some versions of "human resource management" or "administrative sciences.") Many would consider the first degree in industrial psychology or its
precursors to have been the one granted to Bruce V. Moore at Carnegie Institute of Technology
in 1921. Some historical researchers, however, believe that Lillian Gilbreth was the first to
complete a dissertation on industrial psychology. Moore, after graduating from Carnegie,
joined the faculty of Pennsylvania State College (now Pennsylvania State University), which is
said (Jacobs & Farr, 1993) to have graduated its first doctoral student in 1930.

Graduate education in psychology generally appears to have been rather informally done
before World War II because most colleges and universities were predominantly focused on
the education of undergraduate students. Students in doctoral programs in any aspect of psychology were few in number. Katzell (1992a) noted that few universities had more than 10 faculty in psychology and that training in psychology was often housed in departments of
philosophy or combined with areas such as education. (In the U.S. South, it is not unusual even
now to find full-fledged psychology departments housed in schools of education.) Therefore,
to understand the early history of graduate training in applied psychology, it is necessary to
identify the universities that, typically with the strong vision of a university administrator or
department head, hired the early applied psychologists who were concerned with industrial applications. Those individual faculty members, often running solo or very small operations,
were the ones who largely trained early PhDs in the precursors to modern I–O psychology programs. For example, applied psychology at Carnegie Institute of Technology (CIT) was tied to
the presence of Walter Van Dyke Bingham, who is generally credited with having established
in 1915 the first applied psychology program (Prien, 1991). (See chaps. 2 and 6 for additional
information about Bingham and CIT.)

Other universities in this era had fledgling faculties in the work applications of psychology.
In 1921, Moore spearheaded the training at Penn State. The University of Chicago had Arthur
Kornhauser, L. L. Thurstone, and Forrest Kingsbury on its early psychology faculty (Zickar,
2003). Harold E. Burtt, who was hired in 1919 (Thayer & Austin, 1992), and Herbert A. Toops,
hired in 1923, developed the first industrial psychology program at Ohio State University
(Austin, 1992). At the University of Minnesota, there was a curious pattern in that the first PhD
in psychology was granted in 1893 but the next one not until 25 years later (Dunnette, 1993).
Dunnette noted that Donald G. Paterson was brought to Minnesota in 1921 by the department
chair, Richard M. Elliott. Although he did not himself own a doctoral degree, Paterson graduated some 300 master's and 88 PhD students, most studying some aspects of industrial psychology. Although the first "official" degree in industrial psychology from Minnesota was not
granted until 1957, many early PhDs in psychology from Minnesota before that date had an
emphasis on applied psychology (Paul Sackett, personal communication, June 3, 2003).

The early training in industrial psychology was not limited to universities in the Midwest.
New York University's training in this area coincided with the hiring of Douglas H. Fryer as an
assistant professor in 1924 and was further stimulated by the hiring in the 1930s of Edwin R.
Henry and, for a brief period, Rensis Likert (Katzell, 1992b). Thomas Harrell (1992) noted that
training in areas related to industrial psychology at Stanford University began with the training

of Arthur S. Otis under Lewis Terman in 1918. With the closure of Carnegie's focus on applied psychology, E. K. Strong moved west and joined the psychology department at Stanford University in 1923. There he extended the early work on vocational interests begun at Carnegie and went on to supervise research in this area, graduating, among others, Cowdery in 1925, with a dissertation in the area of occupational interests. A number of distinguished I–O psychology-related graduates (e.g., Floyd Ruch, Robert Bernreuter) were also trained in psychology at Stanford, whereas others of note graduated from the organizational behavior (OB) doctoral program there.

In the east, I–O psychology training was also taking root. The University of Pennsylvania hired Morris Viteles in 1918, who offered training in this area (Thompson, 1992). George Washington University (GWU), in Washington DC, also trained applied psychologists well before World War II. Thelma Hunt, the first graduate, was considered to be in I–O and was the second person to graduate with a PhD in psychology from GWU. She completed her dissertation in 1927 on social intelligence and then joined the faculty at GWU in 1928. Fred Moss, the first GWU psychology PhD, was considered an industrial psychologist because he later worked with Thelma Hunt to produce the first Medical College Admission Test in 1934 (Lynn Offerman, personal communication, June 11, 2003).

In 1937, Purdue University is said to have begun I–O psychology. The university's president hired F. B. Knight from the University of Iowa to develop a new unit in what was then a department of education that was turning out a very large number of teachers. The new Division of Education and Applied Psychology was staffed in part by Joseph Tiffin (Lawshe & Weiss, 1991). In a similar era, the psychology department at the University of Maryland began its existence as a Department of Psychotechnology in 1938, founded by John G. Jenkins (Ben Schneider, personal communication, June 27, 2003; Jenkins, 1939). The emphasis at Maryland at the start was applied psychology with a strong experimental and quantitative focus. Jenkins soon hired the modern equivalent of two I–O psychologists, Edwin Ghiselli (who was later to play an active role in industrial psychology program at the University of California at Berkeley) and Roger Bellows (who subsequently helped found the Richardson, Bellows, & Henry consulting firm).

Other early programs have less readily confirmable information about their foundations. The origins of the University of Illinois (Champaign–Urbana)'s program, for example, believed to have started in the 1940s, could not be verified. The department of psychology there lists nine graduates in I–O psychology from the 1950s, beginning, apparently, with Edward Ostrander. The program changed directions substantially, however, with the arrival of such faculty as Charles Hulin in 1962 (Charles Hulin, personal communication, July 3, 2003), Fred Fiedler, Harry Triandis, Lee Cronbach, Ledyard Tucher, Raymond B. Cattell, Joseph McGrath, Lloyd Humphreys, Jack Adams, and others.

There were apparently not large numbers of graduates turned out by these early industrial psychology I–O offerings. George Washington University, after graduating Thelma Hunt in 1927, did not graduate another industrially oriented PhD psychologist (Henry Hubbard, whose dissertation was on *the Selection of Public Employees in the United States*) until 1933 (Lynn Offerman, personal communication, June 11, 2003). New York University had only five graduates before World War II (Katzell, 1992b). The University of Chicago produced only a handful of applied psychology graduates pre–World War II (Frederic Wickert, personal communication, June 3, 2003). The emerging field of applied psychology was attracting interest, students, and graduates, but rather slowly.

Because of this diffuse history and the absence of a common nomenclature for the names of the early I–O psychology programs, it is difficult to establish beginning dates for many of the early graduate training programs. A U.S.-based professional association provided us with a list of graduate school programs and founding dates; however, this listed was found to have some inaccuracies. Therefore, we contacted each program in I–O listed June 2003 on the Web site of the Society for Industrial and Organizational Psychology (SIOP) that was offering graduate I–O psychology training. Those programs not listed as offering degrees in psychology and those offering only terminal master's degrees were excluded. Additionally, several universities were contacted that were known from the literature to have had I–O training programs early in the history of the field but were not offering I–O psychology training now. Not all of those universities responded or were able to provide the requested information because, in some cases, the institutional historians died without having the local history memorialized. Many individuals provided histories that were fascinating glimpses of the educational development of a field. The obtained information is summarized in Table 5.1. In the following section, we present a discussion of some of the decade-by-decade trends in the formation of new I–O doctoral training programs. The chapter then considers other types of training in I–O, including undergraduate and master's-level training and training in schools of business rather than in departments of psychology.

POST–WORLD WAR II GRADUATE TRAINING IN I–O PSYCHOLOGY

As noted throughout this book, the two World Wars in the first half of the 20th century contributed to the rapid expansion of I–O psychology deriving from the military's demand for assistance with selection, placement, and training and the perceived success of these efforts. The ranks of many psychology departments were cut back during World War II by the strong demand for I–O psychology services to support the war effort. Following World War II, industry began making extensive use of I–O psychologists after observing the success of I–O psychology in the war effort (see also chaps. 3 and 7).

After World War II, university-based graduate education in psychology, especially in the applied specialties of clinical and I–O psychology, expanded rapidly and extensively. Fueled by Veterans Administration and National Institute of Mental Health monies, clinical psychology programs were rapidly growing (Katzell, 1992a). These efforts were especially directed to helping to meet the needs of returning veterans with psychological problems. Industrial psychology programs were becoming formalized and labeled with that name.[1] (See also chap. 1 for information about the discipline's name changes.)

Post–World War II also saw the specialization of psychology training. Part of this movement toward specializations in psychology stemmed from the fact that government agencies would not make training grants to a psychology department as a whole but only to areas specifically designated as "programs," according to research by Ted Coons (personal communication, July 3, 2003). This financial pressure, Coons opined, resulted in the rapid postwar

---

[1]Regarding the nomenclature, Ilgen (1984) succinctly explained the metamorphosis of industrial psychology into the more current designation, industrial *and* organizational psychology. Ilgen (1984, p. 281) recalled that the Division of Industrial Psychology of APA changed its name to the Division of Industrial and Organizational Psychology (widely known today as I–O psychology) by way of recognizing that industrial psychology "is a field relevant to a wide range or organizations—schools, service organizations, government agencies—and not just industrial organizations." "Industrial psychology" was the designation of preference in psychology departments, because classic industrial psychology was a hybrid of individual differences, testing, and measurement—areas of study that are comfortably ensconced in the traditional psychology department. "Organizational psychology" or OB is the moniker most often found in I–O-related programs in business schools, schools whose coverage of individual behavior transcends—but certainly does not overlook—measurement and testing and is extended into behavioral processes, organizational climate, leadership, organizational development, modeling, coaching, team building, and empowerment. Generally speaking, the historic content and emphases of industrial psychology—mainly individual differences, testing, and measurement—tends to be found in business school curricula known as HR management (Perloff, 2004).

TABLE 5.1

U.S. and Canadian Doctoral Training Programs in Industrial–Organizational Psychology in Psychology Departments1900s to Early 21st Century (in Chronological Order)

Institution	Founding Date and Founders	Names of First Graduates, if Known, and Year of Graduation	Information Source
Carnegie Institute of Technology	1915, Walter Van Dyke Bingham	Bruce V. Moore, 1921	Prien, 1991
Ohio State University	1919, Harold E. Burtt	L.A. Thompson, 1927 (SIOP, 1989, reports 1919 as first graduate but this appears to be in error)	Austin, 1992; Thayer & Austin, 1992; SIOP, 1989
Columbia University	1920, vocational guidance major, Harry D. Kitson	"O"-oriented I–O program, 1981	Thompson, 1991; SIOP, 1989
University of Pennsylvania	1921, hiring of Morris Viteles	Unknown	Thompson, 1992
Pennsylvania State University	1921, Bruce V. Moore	1930	Jacobs & Farr, 1993; SIOP, 1989
George Washington University	1920s	Thelma Hunt, 1927 (SIOP, 1989, lists first graduate as 1948)	Lynn Offerman (personal communication, June 4 & 11, 2003)
New York University	Douglas H. Fryer hired in 1924; formalized as PhD in I–O in 1958 with Ray Katzell as program coordinator	Sidney Roslow, 1935; first graduate of formal I–O program was David Edelstein, 1959	Ted Coons (personal communication, July 3, 2002); Katzell, 1992b
University of Minnesota	1927, hiring of Donald Paterson	First degree in industrial officially recorded as 1957; earlier degrees issued with similar foci; SIOP, 1989 lists 1947 as year of first I–O degree	Paul Sackett (personal communication, June 3, 2003); SIOP, 1989
University of Chicago	1930s	Unknown	Frederic Wickert (personal communication, June 3, 2003)
Purdue University	1937, hiring of F. B. Knight	Unknown	Lawshe & Weiss, 1991
University of Maryland	Founding of Department of Psychotechnology, by John Jenkins in 1938; became a psychology department in 1946 with a major in industrial psychology	Lester Guest, 1943 (became professor at Penn State) (SIOP, 1989, lists year of first graduate as 1939)	Benjamin Schneider (personal communication, June 27, 2003); SIOP, 1989
University of California–Berkeley	1939, Edwin Ghiselli	Robert Gottsdanker, 1941	Shelly Zedeck (personal communication July 22, 2003)
Illinois Institute of Technology	1940s, unknown	1950	SIOP, 1989

(continued)

115

TABLE 5.1   *(continued)*

Institution	Founding Date and Founders	Names of First Graduates, if Known, and Year of Graduation	Information Source
University of Illinois at Urbana–Champaign	1940s (?)	Possibly Edward Ostrander, 1950s	Charles Hulin (personal communication, July 3, 2003)
Michigan State University	Late 1940s	1951	Frederic Wickert (personal communication, June 3, 2003); Neal Schmitt, (personal communication, June 18, 2003); SIOP, 1989
Louisiana State University	1953, Bernard Bass	James Bryant, 1959	Katie Cherry (personal communication, July 14, 2003)
Western Reserve University	Mid 1950s, Jay Otis, Joel Campbell, Ralph Liske, Erich Prien		Erich Prien (personal communication, June 30, 2003); George Albee, (personal communication; July 2, 2003)
Kansas State University	1950s, Donald Trumbo; restarted in 1976 by Frank "Skip" Skaal	William E. Sedlacek —	Ron Downey (personal communication, June 24, 2003)
University of Houston	1950s, Douglas Ross Talcott	1956	Jim Campion (personal communication, June 19, 2003)
Bowling Green State University	1950s, Robert Guion, Patricia Cain Smith, & Joe Cranny	Frank Landy and Sheldon Zedeck, 1969	Michael Zickar (personal communication, July 8, 2003)
Wayne State University	1955, Arthur Kornhauser joined faculty in 1948	Simon Herman, 1960 (or late 1959) (SIOP, 1989, lists 1959 as the year)	Marcus Dickson (personal communication, July 3, 2003); SIOP, 1989
University of Michigan	Founded approximately 1958, Rensis Likert, Daniel Katz, & Stanley Seashore	Unknown, 1957	SIOP, 1989; Robert Kahn (personal communication, July 29, 2003); Wilbert McKeachie (personal communication, August 5, 2003)
Temple University	1960s, Norman Gekoski	Unknown	Donald A. Hantula and Robert Lana (personal communication, October 1, 2003)
University of British Columbia	1960s, reestablished in 1988 by Ralph Hakstian	Dr. Ross Woolley, 1995 (for revised version of the program)	Ralph Hakstian (personal communication, July 2, 2003)
University of Washington	1960s	1971	SIOP, 1989
Colorado State University	1962, Industrial psychology PsyD, Charles O. Neidt (name changed to I–O psychology in 1973)	Dal Hedlund and Charles Kroen, 1967	George Thornton (personal communication, July 8, 2003); Viney & Punches, 1988

Institution	Founding Date and Founders	Names of First Graduates, if Known, and Year of Graduation	Information Source
University of Waterloo (see also University of Guelph)	1964, Pat Rowe	Jim Miller, 1968	Pat Rowe (personal communication, July 16, 2003)
University of Akron	1965, Erich Prien, Howard Maher, & Margaret Smith	1968	SIOP, 1989; Erich Prien (personal communication, June 30, 2003)
University of Tennessee	1965, joint psychology–business school program	1969	Jack Larsen (personal communication, June 30, 2003)
North Carolina State University	1966, PhD in human resource development; 1979, PhD in industrial–organizational & vocational psychology	Pathe Seshaier, Vivekananathan, 1971	SIOP, 1989 Paul Thayer (personal communication, June 25, 2005)
University of Memphis (then, Memphis State University) (specialty in experimental psychology PhD program)	1966, Roland Frye	Paul Green, 1972	William Dwyer (personal communication, June 20, 2003)
Rice University	1069, Bill Howell	Pat Gaudreau, 1975	Robert Dipboye (personal communication, June 22, 2003)
University of Illinois–Chicago	Unknown	1970	SIOP, 1989
University of Nebraska–Omaha	1970s, Clemm (Chips) Kessler	William Campbell, 1979 (SIOP, 1989, lists 1973 as first degree)	Carl Greenberg (personal communication, July 8, 2003
University of South Florida	1972, Herbert Meyer, first Program Director	Paul Spector, 1975	Michael Brannick (personal communication, June 20, 2003)
Hofstra University	Unknown date, applied research & I–O psych PhD	1976	SIOP, 1989
Carlos Albizu University (formerly, Instituto Caribeño de Estudios Posgraduados)	1976, Lucy López-Roig	Juan Sepúlveda, 1981	Miguel E. Martínez Lugo (personal communication, July 3, 2003)
Virginia Tech University	1976, Joe Sgro (as part of applied behavioral science PhD program track); renamed applied psychology program in 1985; became separate separate I–O program in 1985	Earl C. Pence, 1980, first graduate of the I–O track in the applied behavioral science program; Monnie L. Bittle, 1991, first graduate of separate I–O program	Joe Sgro (personal communication, July 23 & 28, 2003); Neil Hauenstein (July 28, 2003)

(continued)

TABLE 5.1 *(continued)*

Institution	Founding Date and Founders	Names of First Graduates, if Known, and Year of Graduation	Information Source
Georgia Tech University	1977	Bill Sauser, 1978 (SIOP, 1989 lists 1971 as year of first graduate)	Ed Loveland (personal communication, July 3, 2003)
Auburn University	1977, William Sauser, Jr.	Unknown	Philip Lewis (personal communication, June 19, 2003)
University of Georgia	1977, formal I–O psychology program; Donald Grant revised measurement & human differences program to applied psychology PhD with I–O and measurement specializations	Pat Pinto, from predecessor program, 1970	Applied Psychology Student Association, (1997); Charles Lance, (personal communication, July 29, 2003); SIOP, 1989
Old Dominion University	1977, Earl Allusi	Jerry W. Hedge, 1982	Terry L. Dickinson (personal communication, June 25, 2003)
University of Missouri–St. Louis	1978, Gary Burger, doctoral program in applied psychology; became I–O psychology approximately 1986	Rebecca Mann, 1982	Gary Burger (personal communications, July 15, 2003)
Georgia State University	Unknown date, PhD in community/organizational with org psychology and personnel psychology tracks	1982	SIOP, 1989
Ohio University	Unknown, James P. Porter	1985	Klare, 1991; SIOP, 1989
George Mason University	1982, PsyD, Lou Buffardi, Jeanne Mellinger, Alan Boneau 1990, PhD, Edwin Fleishman, Lou Buffardi	Evelyn Hendrix (1985) Pia Crandell (1990)	Odin, 2001 Lou Buffardi (personal communication, 2006)
Claremont Graduate University	1981, Barbara Gutek	1987	Paul Thomas (personal communication, June 24, 2003)
Tulane University	1982, Jeff Sulzer	Alan Witt, 1985	Ron Landis (personal communication, June 20, 2003)
CUNY/Baruch College	1982, Joel Lefkowitz	1987	Joel Lefkowitz (personal communication, July 9, 2003); SIOP, 1989
University of Tulsa	1982, Robert Hogan	1983	www.utulsa.edu; SIOP, 1989
Central Michigan University	1983; revision of PsyD in psychology that had training in clinical, school, and "administrative" psychology founded in 1979; PsyD became a PhD in 1993	PsyD—Daniel W. King, 1986; PhD—Matthew J. Zagumny, 1993	Terry Beehr (personal communication, June 23, 2003)

Institution	Founding Date and Founders	Names of First Graduates, if Known, and Year of Graduation	Information Source
Alliant International University (formerly the California School of Professional Psychology), Los Angeles	1983, organizational psychology PhD	Unknown	Nancy Stevens (personal communication, July 1, 2003)
Alliant International University (then, California School of Professional Psychology), San Diego	1983, Richard Sorenson, I–O PhD	Mark Blankenship, 1988	John Kantor (personal communication, June 23, 2003); Nancy Stevens (personal communication, July 7, 2003)
U.S. International University	1983, Morris Spier	Unknown	Herbert Baker (personal communication, June 30, 2003)
University of Connecticut	1983, Jerome Smith	Beane (O'Neill) Rothenberg, 1986	Janet Barnes-Farrell (personal communication, June 27, 2003)
Portland State University	1984, Dean E. Frost	Tenora Grigsby and Cybelle Lyon, 1999	Dean Frost (personal communication, June 30, 2003
De Paul University	Originally a subfield of experimental; stand-alone PhD program started in 1985	Alan Frost, 1987	Jane Halpert (personal communication, July 3, 2003)
Rutgers University Graduate School of Applied and Professional Psychology	1986, program originally called human resources development psychology as part of School Psychology PsyD, then OB in applied psychology program, then organizational psychology PsyD, its current name	Judith Etlinger Klimoff, 1990	Clay Alderfer (personal communication June 23, 2003); Cary Cherniss (personal communication June 24, 2003); Kathy McLean (personal communication June 24, 2003)
University of Southern Mississippi	1986, Ernie Gurman	Richard Paul Thomlinson, 1989	Vince Fortunata (personal communications, July 9 & 16, 2003)
Alliant International University (then, California School of Professional Psychology), San Francisco Bay	1988; organizational psychology PhD	Donna Montgomery, 1993	Nancy Stevens, (personal communication, July 1, 2003)
University of Guelph & University of Waterloo	1990s	Charles (Chuck) Evans, 1994	Steve Cronshaw (personal communication, June 20, 2003)
Wright State University	1993, Herb Colle, Chair of Psychology Department	Russ Beauregard, 2000	Debra Steele Johnson (personal communication, June 23, 2003)

(continued)

TABLE 5.1   *(continued)*

Institution	Founding Date and Founders	Names of First Graduates, if Known, and Year of Graduation	Information Source
Clemson University	1994, Fred Switzer, I–O psychology PhD	Craig Bevier, 1998	Christoper C. Pagano (personal communication, July 8, 2003)
Florida International University	1986, Scott Fraser & others, applied psychology (with I–O and legal concentration); became separate I–O program in 1997	1993, Nadine Medvin; first graduate of separate I–O program; 1997, Sharon Dolfi	Vish C. Viswesvaran (personal communication, July 9, 2003)
University of North Texas	2000, Doug Johnson	No graduates yet	Douglas Johnson (personal communication, June 30, 2003)
Capella University	PhD in psychology with specialization in I–O	Unknown	www.capella.edu

Note. This table is incomplete; however, this is the best information available at the writing of this chapter.

development of specialty programs in areas such as clinical psychology, industrial psychology, and human factors psychology, rather than in psychology as a single or integrated discipline.

The 1950s

Those programs that had begun before World War II mostly expanded after the war, formally becoming doctoral programs and formally labeled as "industrial psychology." New ones were also being added in diverse places around the United States. At the University of Houston, for example, industrial psychology formally began in 1950 when John MacNaughton (a Michigan PhD) was hired to join the psychology department (James Campion, personal communication, June 3, 2003). Michigan State College (now University) began its graduate training in industrial psychology in the late 1940s (Frederic Wickert, personal communication, June 3, 2003) apparently graduating its first doctoral student in 1951 (Neal Schmitt, personal communication, June 18, 2003). By the early 1950s, Teachers College at Columbia University formalized its previous training in vocational guidance with a new title: Vocational Guidance and Personnel Psychology (Thompson, 1991). Donald Super and Albert Thompson were the early leaders in this program. At Kansas State University, Donald Trumbo started an I–O psychology PhD program in the late 1950s (Ron Downey, personal communication, June 24, 2003). There was also a program at the Western Reserve University (now Case Western Reserve University) begun in the mid-1950s with the involvement of Jay Otis, Frederick Herzberg, Joel Campbell, Donald L. Grant, E. K. Taylor, Ralph Liske, and Erich Prien (Erich Prien, personal communication, June 30, 2003; Robert Perloff, personal communication, July 29, 2003). Bernard Bass (another Ohio State PhD), then at Louisiana State University, started a PhD program in industrial psychology program there in 1953 (Katie Cherry, personal communication, July 14, 2003), well in advance of the trend for I–O psychology programs in the American South to develop later.

I–O psychology had been taught at Bowling Green State University in the late 1940s, followed by organization of a graduate program in 1952 by Robert Guion. Doctorates were awarded later. Other faculty members included Patricia Cain Smith and Joe Cranny. The first graduates were Frank Landy and Sheldon Zedeck.

During this period, and into the 1960s, a doctoral program in organizational psychology at the University of Michigan emerged and flowered. This program, founded about 1958 (Seashore, 1978), differed from many of the other training programs. The program sprang from a strong interdepartmental social psychology program and, thus, emphasized the "O" side of I–O. It also developed around applied research programs and staff at the Institute for Social Research (ISR). ISR, founded in 1947 by Rensis Likert and Daniel Katz, was itself one of the pioneering applied research centers funded, from its inception, on "soft money" (research grants with no assurance of renewal; see also chap. 6). The Organizational Studies division was part of ISR early on. Early ISR staff members who also contributed to the doctoral training were Basil Georgopoulos, Gerald Gurin, Robert Kahn, Seymour Lieberman, Floyd Mann, Stanley Seashore, Arnold Tannenbaum, Nancy Morse Samelson, and (for a brief period) Nathan and Eleanor Maccoby (Robert Kahn, personal communication, July 29, 2003). Another important element of ISR related to I–O psychology was the economic behavior (consumer psychology) program developed by George Katona. Although Wilbert McKeachie (personal communication, August 5, 2003) recalls that some students with industrial psychology interests may have graduated in the 1950s with Floyd Mann (e.g., Larry Williams, who graduated in 1956) and others, the idea of separate areas in psychology at Michigan did not become a reality until the size of the faculty doubled after McKeachie became department chair in 1961. McKeachie traces the birth of organizational psychology as a field at Michigan to the publication of the classic book by Katz and Kahn (1966), *The Social Psychology of Organizations*.

The 1960s

During the 1960s a number of new I–O programs began. A new I–O program at University of Akron began in 1965 through the efforts of Erich Prien, Howard Maher, and Margaret Smith (Paul Levy, personal communication, June 19 and 23, 2003 (Erich Prien, personal communication, June 30, 2003). After Prien's departure from the university and with the lessened involvement of Mahrer, Gary Yukl and Kenneth Wexley joined the faculty and further developed the program (Erich Prien, personal communication, June 30, 2003). The University of Tennessee, which had previously had an industrial psychology program that had essentially become moribund, founded in 1965 a new PhD in organizational psychology, jointly run by the Psychology Department and the business school there. Tennessee's business school then employed four I–O psychologists and Jack Larsen as a new assistant professor. These faculty combined efforts with Ted and Louise Cureton, Jerry Whitlock, and others from the psychology department to create a joint program (Jack Larsen, personal communication, June 30, 2003). The Colorado State University program began in 1962 (George Thornton, personal communication, July 8, 2003).

The 1970s

I–O psychology continued to expand, especially into the southern part of the United States, in the 1970s. The I–O psychology program at Rice University was initiated by William Howell when he joined the Rice psychology faculty in 1969. The program expanded when Robert Dipboye joined the faculty in 1978 and Kevin Murphy in 1979 (Robert Dipboye, personal communication, June 22, 2003). The University of South Florida PhD in I–O psychology began in 1972 founded by Frank Sistrunk, Herb Kimmel, and Dave Clement, who initiated the program and hired Herbert Meyer, who was the program's first director (Michael Brannick, personal communication, June 20, 2003). Georgia Institute of Technology eventually succeeded in establishing a psychology program from an undergraduate degree (in 1969) to a PhD, where Ed Loveland had been working on the development of psychology in a science and engineering-dominated institution. (The doctoral training was authorized in 1969 but students were not accepted until the 1970s when enough faculty had been hired to staff the program; Ed Loveland, personal communication, July 3, 2003).

Also founded in the 1970s was the PhD in I–O psychology at Old Dominion University in Norfolk, Virginia, under the directorship of Earl Allusi (Terry Dickinson, personal communication, June 25, 2003) and the I–O psychology track in the Applied Behavioral Science Program at Virginia Tech under the leadership of Joe Sgro (Joe Sgro, personal communication, July 23, 2003). Again in the south, Auburn University began its I–O PhD program in 1977 under the direction of William Sauser, Jr. (Philip Lewis, personal communication, June 19, 2003). Still another program that started as a measurement and human differences psychology program in this era was that at the University of Georgia, which, under the leadership of William Owens and Donald Grant, transitioned to an I–O psychology program in the 1970s (Applied Psychology Student Association, 1997). At North Carolina State University, the MS program in industrial psychology, established by William McGehee in 1948, became a doctoral program in 1966, first as a human resources development program and then, in 1979, a program in industrial–organizational and vocational psychology, shortly after Paul W. Thayer became the department head.

The 1970s also saw the rise in the professional psychology school movement. Although the I–O psychology programs in the United States initially focused on clinical psychology, an I–O psychology program began in Puerto Rico in 1978 at what is now called Carlos Albizu University (formerly *Instituto Caribeño de Estudios Posgraduados;* Miguel E. Martínez Lugo, personal communication, July 3, 2003).

The 1980s

By the 1980s the professional psychology schools began offering doctoral training in I–O psychology. The California School of Professional Psychology (CSPP), founded in San Francisco in 1969 through the efforts of the California Psychological Association (CPA), initially offered only clinical psychology PhD training. Founders of that institution had been concerned about the failure of most clinical psychology doctoral programs to produce sufficient graduates to address the needs of the burgeoning and culturally diverse population that was developing in California. With the support of then Governor Ronald Reagan, at the time embroiled in tangles with the campus disruptions at the University of California at Berkeley, and against the strong objections of doctoral granting institutions in California, CSPP offered doctoral training beginning in 1969 as the nation's first independent graduate school of professional psychology (*System Catalog,* 1997–1998). The training was more oriented to practice and more sensitive to diversity issues (Cummings, 2001). Known since it acquired the U.S. International University as Alliant International University, and now housing six schools and colleges, the school began offering doctoral training in industrial–organizational psychology at its Los Angeles, San Diego, and San Francisco Bay campuses (John Kantor, personal communication, June 23, 2003; *System Catalog,* 1997–1998). CSPP/AIU board members over the years have included I–O psychologists Warren Bennis, Robert Perloff, and Lyman Porter. Also in this period, Rutgers University's Graduate School of Applied and Professional Psychology, a university-based professional school of psychology, began offering training in the precursors to its current PsyD degree in organizational psychology.

Programs based in more traditional academic institutions continued to expand in North America in the 1980s. New I–O psychology doctoral programs or emphases in other doctoral programs began at George Mason University, Fairfax, Virginia, in the early 1980s (Edwin A. Fleishman, personal communication, December 20, 2003); the University of Tulsa (1982; www.utulsa.edu); Claremont (1982; Paul Thomas, personal communication, June 24, 2003); Tulane (1982; Ron Landis, personal communication June 20, 2003); U.S. International University (Herbert Baker, personal communication, June 30, 2003); De Paul University (1985; Jane Halpert, personal communication, July 3, 2003); the University of British Columbia (a revised version of I–O psychology program began in 1988; Ralph Hakstian, personal communication, July 2, 2003); and the University of Connecticut (1983; Janet Barnes-Farrell, personal communication, June 27, 2003). The University of Missouri–St. Louis transitioned an applied psychology PhD program into an I–O psychology program in 1986 (Gary Burger, personal communication, July 15, 2003).

Some programs founded or transitioned in the 1980s emphasized more the organizational side of I–O. At Columbia University, in New York, Warner Burke, who had been hired in 1979, helped transition Columbia University's applied social psychology program in its Teachers' College to a new program in social–organizational psychology (Warner Burke, personal communication, June 19, 2003; Thompson, 1992). Barbara Gutek founded the emphasis in organizational behavior (OB) in a PhD psychology program at Claremont Graduate University in 1981. That program has expanded over the years to include emphases in I–O psychology and program evaluation research (Paul Thomas, personal communication, June 24, 2003).

In the east, also in the 1980s, SUNY Albany began a new I–O psychology PhD program in 1985 with Kathryn Kelly as area head and Dean McFarlin as a new assistant professor (Kevin Williams, personal communication, June 19, 2003). I–O psychology expanded in the state of Michigan with a new PhD at Central Michigan University. That program began not as an I–O psychology-based degree but rather as a multipurpose PsyD (the first doctoral program of any kind offered at that institution; Terry Beehr, personal communication, June 23, 2003). Subsequently, a full-fledged program in I–O psychology emerged from these historical beginnings.

The 1990s

The 1990s saw somewhat less aggressive expansion of new doctoral programs in I–O. A PhD program at Wright State University in I–O and in human factors psychology with students majoring in one area and minoring in the other began (Debra Steele Johnson, personal communication, June 23, 2003). Doctoral I–O psychology programs also began at the University of Oklahoma (Jorge Mendoza, personal communication, October 6, 2003), Clemson University (Christoper C. Pagano, personal communication, July 8, 2003), and Florida International University (Vish C. Viswesvaran, personal communication, July 9, 2003).

Another approach to doctoral training emerged in the 1990s. This approach placed greater emphasis on humanistic values and was exemplified by doctoral training at the Saybrook Institute, which started in the late 1990s (John Adams, personal communication, June 21, 2003). Although not offering training in I–O psychology per se but rather in organizational systems, the curricula often overlapped considerably with I–O psychology. Programs such as Saybrook's have emphasized values such as human dignity, the promotion of self-awareness among its members, and the need for leaders who can function without compromising basic human values (*Saybrook University Catalog,* 2002).

Programs Since 2000

The newest programs in I–O psychology, founded since the new millennium, include those of the University of Central Florida, which started in August 2000 with founding director Eugene Stone-Romero along with faculty members Barbara Fritzsche Clay, Wayne Burroughs, William Wooten, and Eduardo Salas (Barbara Fritzsche Clay, personal communication, June 21, 2003). This program built on the base, however, of a master's of science program in I–O psychology with a more than 30-year history, founded in 1971 by Cabot Jaffee, Fred Frank, and Wayne Burroughs (Jack McGuire, personal communication, June 23, 2003).

The University of North Texas, which for many years offered a terminal master's degree in I–O psychology and which had sought approval for a doctoral program related to I–O psychology in the early 1980s, began a new PhD program in I–O psychology in 2000 (Douglas Johnson, personal communication, June 30, 2003). An on-line university, Capella University, states that it offers a specialization in I–O psychology in a PhD degree program in psychology (www.capella.edu).

MASTER'S-LEVEL TRAINING IN I–O PSYCHOLOGY

The topic of I–O master's-level training began in the 1950s when the executive committee members of Division 14 Industrial and Business of the American Psychological Association (now known as SIOP) discussed the value of this training and explored training and curriculum guidelines. A review of training in I–O psychology at the master's level is beyond the scope and page limitations of this chapter. However, master's-level training in I–O psychology is certainly flourishing in the United States, judging from the number of programs offered (see, e.g., Koppes, 1991; Lowe 1993, 2000). SIOP provides a current listing of master's-level programs in I–O psychology (www.siop.org). So-called "terminal master's programs," those not offering a master's en route to the doctoral degree, cover much of the same territory as the doctoral-level programs but arguably in a more applied manner and in the level of depth that would be appropriate for a 1- to 2-year program rather than a 4-year one. An accrediting body for master's programs is administered by the Masters in Psychology Accreditation Council, or MPAC (www.enamp.org), and a group called the Council of Applied Masters Programs in Psychology, or CAMPP, provides an organizational context for applied psychology master's programs (www.camppsite.org) in I–O and other areas of psychology.

UNDERGRADUATE INSTRUCTION IN I–O PSYCHOLOGY

Faculty members at the pioneering institutions offering I–O psychology were training undergraduates as well as graduate students. In fact, the influence of I–O psychology education on these students was arguably far more extensive than the training of a few doctoral students. Lawshe and Weiss (1991), for example, noted that a book on industrial psychology, first published in 1942, was adopted for use by the U.S. Armed Forces Institute and distributed to thousands of military personnel around the world. Fred Wickert (personal communication, June 3, 2003) noted that Michigan State was able to hire a large contingent of industrial psychologists (including Wickert, Henry Clay Smith, Orwell Crissey, and Carl Frost) because of its large undergraduate enrollments. (Crissey went on to develop I–O psychology training at the General

Motors Institute.) Small sections of 30 students each were established before the administration discovered it could more efficiently teach these students in groups of 400 to 500. At Penn State, undergraduate instruction was a prime mission of the industrial psychology program (Jacobs & Farr, 1993).

DOCTORAL I–O PSYCHOLOGY AND RELATED TRAINING IN ACADEMIC DEPARTMENTS OTHER THAN PSYCHOLOGY

I–O Psychology in Business Schools

Traditionally, I–O psychology programs have resided in psychology departments of colleges and universities. The exceptions include the professional schools and the various departments of business schools. Of course, it has not been uncommon since the early days of the field for psychology faculty to have joint appointments in schools of business. Arthur Kornhauser, for example, had a joint appointment in both business and psychology at the University of Chicago in the 1920s (Zickar, 2003). In the late 1960s and early 1970s, executive committee members of then APA Division 14 expressed concerns about the influx of psychologists teaching in business department programs established in the 1960s (Mary Tenopyr, personal communication, April 30, 2004). While serving as the chair of the SIOP Education and Training Committee, Laura Koppes received several notes from academicians who noted a significant movement of I–O psychologists from psychology departments to business departments. The psychology faculty expressed concerns about the future of I–O psychology programs in their departments, with the implication that these programs would lose their roots (Laura L. Koppes, personal communication, April 5, 2005).

In some instances, degrees are similarly offered jointly between the psychology departments and business schools (e.g., at one point at the University of Tennessee). The programs offered in business schools are not typically labeled "I–O psychology." As of this writing, there were 27 I–O psychology-related programs listed on the SIOP Web site that are offered in business departments and, of those, 18 were PhDs in organizational behavior (OB) and/or human resource management; only one was in I–O psychology (http://siop.org/GTP/atplookup.asp).

We limit our discussions to the schools offering degrees in I–O psychology, OB, or OB in combination with human resource (HR) management. Programs that offer PhDs in management or HR alone are beyond the scope of this chapter, although some programs may include I–O psychology-type courses.

The history of I–O psychology, or OB, in business schools has at least two roots. One of the antecedents was the decline and transformation of industrial relations (IR) programs. Many of the HR researchers were uncomfortable to be associated with the IR programs because of their perceived heavy association in the 1950s and 1960s with unions; thus, they navigated toward the OB/HR fields. In many cases, IR programs were replaced by OB programs that were the outgrowth of the human relations, organization, and administration branches of business school curricula (Wren, 1987). The development of the field of OB also provided an academic home for HR researchers such as Warren Bennis, William F. Whyte, Chris Argyris, and E. Wight Bakke, who appeared to be more identified with OB rather than with the declining IR programs.

A second reason the field of OB began to develop in business schools was the influence of the Gordon and Howell report (Gordon & Howell, 1959; Pierson, 1959). This study decried the relative lack of social sciences content in business schools, whose programs to that point had been viewed as mostly teaching mainly technical skills to business students. The report encouraged business schools to establish closer working relations with other academic departments, including psychology and sociology. The report highlighted the need for curriculum content that would teach managers "people skills" in addition to technical skills, because managers had to deal effectively with people (Blood, 1994). As the result of the report and reactions to it, there was an influx of I–O psychologists, sociologists, and anthropologists into business schools. The various social sciences often found themselves operating under the umbrella term of "Organizational behavior," and sometimes as "behavioral sciences."

The fields of OB and organizational psychology (OP) in the 1960s also helped to transform the field of personnel management into what is known today as HR management (Dunnette & Bass, 1963; Strauss, 1970). The new management philosophy was that if employers considered workers to be resources, then the employers could take advantage of workers' commitment, which in turn would provide workers with employment security, contingent on the profitable survival of the organization. Workers were being looked at as investments rather than as expenses, which prompted many companies to rename their personnel departments as human resource departments (Lewin, 1991). Many of the business schools eventually started to offer PhD degrees in the field of OB and HR management (HRM), which were not much different from the degrees offered by the professors' base discipline, usually I–O (or industrial) psychology.

Overall, few I–O psychology programs in business school have used or retained the title of "I–O psychology." Programs that resemble I–O psychology in content or those that are the outgrowth of programs initially labeled I–O psychology instead tend to be titled OB, HR, and HRM. In addition to the name change, the content became more business oriented. Table 5.2 provides information on schools offering I–O related doctoral degrees, the starting date of the program, and, if known, their founders and first graduates.

I–O Psychology in Industrial and Labor Relations

In the early 1960s, Ned Rosen, Leo Gruenfeld, and Lawrence Williams joined the faculty of the New York State School of Industrial and Labor Relations (NYSSILR) at Cornell University. Rosen, Gruenfeld, Hammer, and Williams (recently deceased) ultimately became the nucleus of the Organizational Behavior Department within the NYSSILR and maintained informal ties with the business school and the industrial psychologists in the psychology department. Initially, this department was formed under the strong influence of William Foote Whyte, a cultural anthropologist/sociologist who had long been a member of the NYSSILR faculty. Under his stewardship, the Organizational Behavior Department grew to 10 members, 6 of whom were sociologists and 4 of whom were psychologists. Rosen, a Purdue industrial psychology PhD, became chairman of the OB Department. The OB Department was unique when formed. It was a multidisciplinary unit created as a result of the Gordon and Howell (1959) report (described earlier in this chapter). The NYSSILR was unique as a host for such a department. It was established in the mid-1940s as a partial response to a large upsurge in industrial strife following World War II. Most of the school's faculty, initially, were economists but included other disciplines such as labor historians, political scientists, some collective bargaining specialists, and various personnel administration and labor relations practitioners (Ned Rosen, personal communication, March 10, 2005).

I–O Psychology in Public Administration Programs

Another location for programs that overlap with I–O psychology has been those universities offering graduate programs in public administration. Graduate programs in public administration (PA) emphasize management training and applications in the public and not-for-profit

TABLE 5.2
Doctoral Training in Industrial Psychology and Related Fields in Business and Other Departments, 1900s to Early 21st Century (in Chronological Order)

Institution	Department, Founders, and First Year	Names of Degree, Year of First Graduation, and Name of First Graduate	Information Source
Stanford University	Business, 1920s	PhD in OB, 1931, Harrison Hoyt	Elissa Hirsh (personal communication, October 7, 2003)
University of Wisconsin–Madison	Management and Human Resources, 1940s	PhD in OB/HR, 1950, unknown	http://siop.org/gtp/gtplookup.asp; SIOP, 1989
Carnegie Mellon University	Business, Herman Simon and Richard Cyert, 1950	PhD in OB/psychology/industrial administration, 1953, William Dill	Mark Fichman and Paul S. Goodman (personal communication, October 3, 2003)
Case Western Reserve University	Management, Jay Otis, Joel Campbell, Ralph Liske, Erich Prien, mid-1950s	PhD in OB	Erich Prien, George Albee (personal communication, October 12, 2003)
Yale University	School of Engineering, Department of Industrial Administration, Tom Holme, Donald Taylor, Edwin Fleishman, E. Wight Bakke, Chris Argyris, 1955	PhD administrative science, 1966, Clayton Alderfer	Edwin Fleishman (personal communication, April 11, 2005); Victor Vroom (personal communication, June 22, 2005)
Baruch College, City University of New York	Management, 1961	PhD in OB/HRM	http://siop.org/gtp/gtplookup.asp
Case Western Reserve University	Management, Herbert Shepard, 1963	PhD in OB, 1964 Wayne Marshall and Miles Martin	Patricia Petty (personal communication, October 1, 2003)
University of Toronto	Management, Martin Evans and Robert House, 1963	PhD in OB/HRM, 1969, Lawrence Wigdor	Robert House (personal communication, October 10, 2003)
University of North Carolina	Business, J. Stacy Adams, Tom Jerdee, and Dannie Moffie, 1964	PhD in OB, 1967, J. D. Richardson	Ben Rosen (personal communication, October 1, 2003)
University of Maryland	Management and Organization, Stephen Carroll, 1964	DBA with OB orientation until 1978, then PhD in OB/HR, 1969, John Ivancevich	Stephen Carroll (personal communication, October 13, 2003)
University of Missouri–Columbia	Management, 1966	PhD in OB/HR	http://siop.org/gtp/gtplookup.asp
University of Illinois at Urbana–Champaign	Institute of Labor and Industrial Relations, 1966	PhD in OB/HR, 1970, John Niland	Peter Feuille (personal communication, October 6, 2003)
State University of New York Buffalo	Management, Joe Alutto, 1968	PhD in OB, 1968, program started by Joe Alutto (not positive); estimated year of first graduate 1972	Donald Ferrin and Fred Dansereau (personal communication, October 3, 2003)

(continued)

TABLE 5.2   *(continued)*

Institution	Department, Founders, and First Year	Names of Degree, Year of First Graduation, and Name of First Graduate	Information Source
Harvard Business School	OB 1985 (has psychology and sociology tracks in connection with other departments)	PhD in OB	Nat Pollack (personal communication, October 3, 2003)
University of Arizona	Management and Policy, 1989	PhD in OB/HRM	http://siop.org/gtp/gtplookup.asp
Michigan State University	Management	PhD in business administration with emphasis OB/HRM and strategy	John A Wagner III (personal communication, October 6, 2003)
Tulane University	Business, Art Brief, 1990	PhD in OB	Arthur Brief (personal communication, October 3, 2003)
State University of New York, Binghamton	Management, Bruce Avolio and Fran Yammarino, 1998	PhD in management with a specialization in OB/Leadership, 1995, John Sosik	Fran Yammarino (personal communication, October 3, 2003)
University of Oklahoma	Psychology and management, Jorge Mendoza and Michael Buckley, 1998	PhD in I–O psychology, 2001, Thomas Mobbs	Jorge Mendoza (personal communication, October 6, 2003)
New Mexico State University	Management	PhD in OB/HR	http://siop.org/gtp/gtplookup.asp

Note.   This table is incomplete; however, this is the best information available at the writing of this chapter. OB = organizational behavior; HR = human resources; SIOP = Society of Industrial–Organizational Psychology; HRM = human resources management; DBA = doctor of business administration.

sectors. They are typically housed either in political science departments or business schools at universities. The earliest PA programs began in the 1940s. The U.S. accrediting body for PA programs, the National Association of Schools of Public Affairs and Administration ([NASPAA] *Standards*, 2005), requires courses in I–O psychology–related areas. Courses typically part of PA graduate programs include organizational theory, OB, organizational development (OD), HRM, HR development, leadership development, team building, decision making, and organizational psychology (OP).

A survey of 30 heads of public administration programs (Kantor & West, 2003) disclosed that I–O psychology–related courses are considered by PA program directors to be essential to well-rounded PA programs. Because the graduates will be running public institutions, the skills learned in these courses are viewed as helping them to become more effective managers. As one of those surveyed by Kantor and West (2003 stated, "The field of organizational theory and behavior is absolutely at the core of management knowledge. No one is well educated to become a manager in either the business or public sectors without this core knowledge" (p. 5).

CHANGES IN PROGRAMS OVER TIME

Wherever they have been housed, I–O psychology programs have not been static over time. Several of the I–O programs have changed their character over time. At the University of Maryland, for example, the post–World War II emphasis was mostly on psychometrics, test and measurements, consumer psychology, and engineering psychology during the 1950s (Edwin Fleishman, personal communication, April 2006). When Jack Barlett and Emil Heerman were hired, the program began covering more diverse aspects of I–O psychology (Benjamin Schneider, personal communication, June 27, 2003).

As the well-established I–O psychology programs grew over time, the numbers of doctoral graduates greatly increased. New York University, for example, produced about 120 PhDs in the period from 1958 through May 2002 (when the I–O and social psychology programs merged; Ted Coons, personal communication, July 3, 2003). Wayne State has graduated around 160 I–O psychologists since the program's inception in 1955. The professional schools of psychology, typically tuition driven and without undergraduate student bases to subsidize their graduate programs, have tended to accept larger classes.

Surviving and Thriving (But Sometimes Not) in Academic Departments

I–O psychology training takes place, of course, in an institutional context. It has often thrived where there was an I–O psychologist at the helm of the psychology department or otherwise influential in the university's administration. For example, Harold Burtt was chair of the psychology department for 22 years at the Ohio State University (Thayer & Austin, 1991), and Robert J. Wherry also served in that role in the 1960s and 1970s (Robert Perloff, personal communication, July 29, 2003). Other department chairs included Thelma Hunt at GWU (Lynn Offerman, personal communication, June 4 and 11, 2003) and Bruce V. Moore at Penn State (Jacobs & Farr, 1993). Ross Stagner helped I–O psychology flourish at Wayne State University. Additional department chairs were John Wakeley (and, more recently, Neal Schmitt) at Michigan State University and Milton Hakel at the University of Houston, departments all at the time (or still) housing generally well-regarded programs in I–O psychology. Paul W. Thayer was the head of the psychology department from 1977 to 1992 at North Carolina State University.

In fact, I–O psychologists seem to have served in academic administrative positions more frequently than would be expected compared with the number of faculty in psychology areas other than I–O. For example, Naylor was chair of the Psychology Department at Purdue beginning in 1968 (Lawshe & Weiss, 1991) and later served as the chair at the Ohio State University (Robert Perloff, personal communication, July 29, 2003), where he disbanded the I–O program. Other academic administrators include Ed Loveland, who was the head of the School of Psychology at Georgia Tech for a number of years (Ed Loveland, personal communication, July 3, 2003). Robert Hogan was chair of the Psychology Department at the University of Tulsa for 15 years. Gerald Barrett was hired as department head of the University of Akron's Psychology Department (Ken Wexley and Paul Levy, personal communication, June 23, 2003). Irv Lane served as chair of the Psychology Department at Louisiana State University for an extended period. Joe Sgro was chair of the Psychology Department at Virginia Tech University (Joe Sgro, personal communication, July 28, 2003). Jack Bartlett was Psychology Department chair at the University of Maryland, followed by Irwin Goldstein. After serving for many years as department chair, Goldstein became dean of the College of Behavioral and Social Sciences and as of this writing has another high-level administrative position in the University of Maryland system. John Campbell is currently the Psychology Department chair at the University of Minnesota. The first author (Rodney Lowman) has served as systemwide dean of the California School of Organizational Studies at Alliant International University and prior to that as a psychology department chair at a university that offered I–O psychology training.

Psychology and other academic departments have not always been a cordial or long-lasting home to I–O psychology programs, however. Of the five earliest programs in I–O psychology listed in Table 5.1, for example, only two currently have I–O psychology doctoral programs. Institutional politics and needs create challenges in sustaining and growing I–O psychology training programs. One explanation is a long-term division between experimental psychologists and applied psychologists. In the middle of the 20th century, the applied programs were being forced out (Mary Tenopyr, personal communication, June 20, 2003). The first program at Carnegie Tech ended in 1924, only a few years after it had begun with such enthusiasm and flourish, when Carnegie's president Arthur Hamerschlag, who had personally courted and nurtured the program often to the resentment of Bingham's colleagues at Carnegie, died (see Prien, 1991).

A fractious period at the University of Iowa had resulted in Joseph Tiffin's relocating to Brooklyn College before joining the faculty at Purdue (Lawshe & Weiss, 1991). Little recognized also is the brief tenure of a fledgling I–O psychology program at Johns Hopkins University started by none other than the famous behaviorist John Watson. When Watson was fired from Johns Hopkins University, the program was scrapped no sooner than it had been begun (DiClemente & Hantula, 2000). Alphonus Chapanis did later develop a human factors program at Hopkins (Robert Perloff, personal communication, July 29, 2003). At Kansas State only one PhD student graduated from that program, and the entire I–O faculty who had been hired left the program in the late 1960s. The program was restarted in the 1970s. (Ron Downey, personal communication, June 24, 2003).

In 1958, with the arrival of a new chair at the University of Pennsylvania, the reorganization of the Department of Psychology caused a shift in emphasis from applied areas to the basic areas of psychology. When Viteles became a dean at Penn in 1963, he presumably was less involved in the day-to-day operations of the psychology department; consequently, the program was eventually phased out (Thompson, 1992). At Yale University, a very psychologically oriented OB doctoral program was established with a distinguished faculty, including in 1956 E. Wight Bakke, Donald W. Taylor, Edwin A. Fleishman, Thomas Holme, and Chris Argyris. Victor Vroom and Richard Hackman joined the program later. This program, one of the first interdisciplinary programs in this field, was based in the Department of Industrial Administration in Yale's School of Engineering. Bakke had a joint appointment in economics, and Fleishman and Taylor had joint appointments in Yale's psychology department. This was perhaps the beginning of trends to move programs out of psychology departments. A later incarnation of this program was abruptly terminated in 1988 when Benno C. Schmidt, Jr., was Yale president and Michael Levine was dean of the Yale School of Organization and Management.

Programs in I–O psychology strongly tied to a particular faculty member also sometimes vanish when that person dies or leaves the program. For example, when Roland Frye at the University of Memphis died in 1992, the I–O emphasis in the university's experimental psychology doctoral program went into a 6-year hiatus (William Dwyer, personal communication, June 20, 2003).

It can therefore be hypothesized that I–O psychology has tended to flourish at institutions in which there were strong and productive faculty present from the outset, where senior administrators or unit directors were in positions of authority, and where the mission of the institution was consistent with the purposes of applied psychology. Concerning the latter point, it can be noted that some of the most prestigious universities, whose missions have never been terribly applied, have rarely been home to long-lasting, widely recognized programs specifically in I–O psychology (see also Colarelli, 2003).

TRAINING CONTENT OF GRADUATE I–O PROGRAMS
AND SIOP EDUCATIONAL TRAINING GUIDELINES

The early graduate training experiences were somewhat customized—there were few courses as we know them today. Jacobs and Farr (1993) noted that even in 1965 there were 11 courses in industrial psychology offered at Penn State, just 4 of which were graduate courses. Students instead seemed to take the small number of courses, work with professors on applied projects, and engage in an intensive, supervised research projects that became, for many, their dissertations.

Even though early on there were few courses in the field, the core content of the emerging field was not strikingly different compared with the current content. The training of early I–O psychologists essentially involved the mastery of psychological principles, tests and measurements, quantitative methods of analysis, perhaps some work in the area of organizational systems, and often practical experience to apply those principles (Viteles, 1932). Content-wise, an I–O psychologist trained in the 1930s using a book like Viteles' *Industrial Psychology* (1932) would find the topics in the modern textbooks not terribly dissimilar and would notice approaches characterized today by a more sophisticated and larger knowledge base than by a new focus of investigation.

Training in I–O psychology from the field's advent emphasized the integration of science and practice, the so-called scientist–practitioner orientation. The initial problems taken on by the fledgling field, including personnel selection, performance evaluation, employee satisfaction, and motivation, were tackled with empiricism and often with the enthusiasm of those who were engaged in the important business of establishing a new field of study (psychology itself and then applied or industrial psychology in particular). I–O psychology, from its inception, was empirically oriented and it did not suffer the divisiveness of, for example, clinical psychology, which struggled for years with nonempirical, theoretical approaches and with battles with psychiatry, compared with those that derive more coherently from research.

Still, there has been variability over the years in the degree to which I–O psychology has considered itself sufficiently rigorous on the scientific side. Conflicts over applied-versus-science emphases and the degree of rigor of the science have sometimes erupted. A particularly virulent statement of the state of graduate education in I–O psychology was made by Naylor (1971), himself an I–O psychology PhD from Purdue, lamenting the allegedly unscientific and rather pedestrian state to which I–O psychology had then fallen. On the other hand, the tension between science and practice in I–O psychology has been seen by others as being a strength of the field. Viteles, then 93, is quoted by Katzell and Austin (1992, p. 826) as saying, "'If it isn't scientific, it's not good practice, and if it isn't practical, it's not good science.'" (See chap. 3 in this text for additional discussion.)

Humanistic Influences in I–O Psychology

Although scientific approaches have dominated I–O psychology training programs from the fields earliest days, there have been other influences as well. The humanistic influences on I–O psychology can be traced back to several pioneers in the field or those whose work in other areas of psychology was applied to the field. These included Kurt Lewin (Adams & Zener, 1935/1959; Lewin, 1951), Carl Rogers (1977), Douglas McGregor, Abraham Maslow (Lowry, 1973; Maslow, 1954), and Rollo May (Greening, 1984). Maslow, for example, argued for looking at "human potential in the workplace" and the idea that workers can embellish field work with expertise and creativity (Maslow, 1954; see also Schneider, Bugental, & Pierson, 2001).

It is largely deriving from the work of such theorists and scholars that the field of organizational development (OD), which is usually a part of I–O psychology training programs, was born. I–O theorists and professors such as Douglas McGregor, Richard Beckhard, Chris Argyris, Edgar Schein, Warren Bennis, and Herbert Shephard approached the field of I–O psychology from concerns relating as least as much as the purely scientific or productivity-focused approach that had been emphasized since the celebrated days of the time-and-motion-oriented studies of Fredrick Taylor (Montuori & Purser, 2001).

McGregor (1960), for example, was a clinician by training who became interested in the applications of his theories to industry (see chaps. 14 and 15 in this text). He is most known for his management theory, in which he postulated two major approaches that managers can use in relating to workers: theory X, an essentially distrusting and autocratic style, and theory Y, a more respecting and engaged approach. His work with Joe Scanlon and Carl Frost resulted in the development of the Scanlon plan, which formalized many of these ideas into a formal OD program (see, e.g., Frost, 1996; Frost, Wakeley & Ruh, 1974). McGregor's approaches and their derivatives are still taught in many I–O programs, but they are more theoretical and heuristic than scientific in their derivation. Later, however, when McGregor was himself a senior administrator, as president of Antioch University, he acknowledged that sometimes an administrative leader does have to make tough-minded "theory X" decisions (Robert Perloff, personal communication, July 29, 2003).

Kurt Lewin (1951) similarly exemplified an approach to psychology that was value focused rather than strictly scientific or empirically derived. His work on groups and changing attitudes is exemplary (see chap. 14). Within I–O psychology, his change and action research models and his force field analysis model of identifying forces for and against change in organizations are still influential.

Humanistic psychology's influence helped the fields of organizational development (OD) and group dynamics become part of I–O psychology. Since at least the 1970s, OD has been included in some form in most I–O psychology training programs. Typically emphasized are ways to help make organizations and the people within them more effective by change efforts based on the principles of widespread participation by employees in influence and decision making related to work activities. This includes such areas as goal setting, team building, action research, determining the best method to achieve a goal, and developing an interpersonally pleasant and safe work environment (Beer, 1980). Critics of humanistic psychological approaches to I–O often objected to the less than objective, sometimes not-well-validated approaches. Others argue that by putting too much emphasis on the needs of workers or solely on the economic realities of organizations, the scientific side of the field may be ill considered (Montuori & Purser, 2001).

SIOP Guidelines for Education and Training in I–O Psychology

As the field developed, its most notable professional organization, SIOP, became involved in the effort to formalize training requirements in I–O psychology. The early efforts were not without controversy and were partly stimulated more by the needs of the larger American Psychological Association (housing SIOP) than by the perceived needs of SIOP.

The first guidelines for training at the doctoral level in I–O psychology were not issued until 1965 (Division of Industrial Psychology, 1965). Naylor (1971) noted that there were at that time both master's-level and doctoral-level guidelines issued by the Education and Training Committee of the then-Division 14 of APA. However, although recommended for approval by the Education and Training Committee for acceptance, the master's-level guidelines were never adopted by the division's governance. The doctoral-level guidelines were adopted, however, and published in the *American Psychologist*. Indeed, the first master's-level guidelines were not promulgated by SIOP until 1994 (http://SIOP.org/guidelines.htm). In contrast, the doctoral standards have been in place for almost 40 years and have been revised over the years. The current version of the doctoral-level I–O psychology standards was published in 1999 (http://SIOP.org/PhDGuidelines98.html). These guidelines (1999) were never intended to be limiting of the scope, growth, or intellectual development of the field. Rather they were aimed at providing a road map to institutions preparing I–O psychologists at the doctoral level, a source of information for doctoral students enrolled in or applying to I–O programs, and information for the consumers of I–O psychology services.

Content in Programs in Psychology Departments Versus Business Schools

There are several differences noted by Perloff (1992, 1994) in the I–O offerings in business schools and in psychology departments. Typically, business school curricula include such traditional business school subjects as accounting, administrative science, economics, finance, HR, marketing, and operations research, whereas most I–O psychology curricula are more extensive in their psychology and quantitative methods coverage and less typically encompass the business areas. The social sciences and social science research methods are more strongly emphasized in training programs based in departments of psychology (Perloff, 1994).

Field Placement and Training in Professional Practice Roles

From the beginning of the I–O field, there were important links between classroom training and practice. The purpose of applied psychology was to make a difference with real-world problems and the environment provided a number of real-world challenges. Late in World War I, for example, psychology was applied to the problems of selection when a group of applied psychologists introduced intelligence testing to personnel selection in the military (e.g., Prien, 1991; see chaps. 1, 3, 7, and 8). Although those who wanted training in such areas may have received relevant training in places like the University of Chicago and the Carnegie Institute of Technology, the connections were more *ad hoc* and the formal disciplines within psychology in the modern sense had not yet been conceived.

During the first half of the 20th century, few I–O psychology programs had formal internship/field placement requirements. If internships existed, they were informally arranged and were not part of the curriculum. However, there was usually an applied component to the early training. The small number of professors in the applied or industrial area in the early graduate programs seem to have worked diligently to help their students acquire appropriate experiences and paid support on research roles and see to it that the early students supported themselves in a variety of activities, usually I–O psychology related.

Thompson (1992) noted, for example, that at the University of Pennsylvania, Professor Viteles involved his student protégés in all aspects of his professional work. Kornhauser, a doctoral graduate of the University of Chicago and a master's graduate of Carnegie, took it as a personal mission to find his applied psychology students at the University of Chicago opportunities to support themselves on work related to industrial applications (Frederic Wickert, personal communication, June 3, 2003). Other graduate students supported themselves with work in a variety of activities sometimes relevant to their study and sometimes not. Thelma Hunt, for example, worked as a test specialist for the U.S. Civil Service Commission during her study at George Washington University (Lynn Offerman, personal communication, June 4, 2003). Not everyone was able to find applied work in his or her chosen field. C. H. Lawshe, in contrast, worked as the principal of the Mechanic Arts School in Evansville, Indiana, while working on his doctoral degree (Russell, 1992).

Professors obtained grants or consulting contracts and students worked with those professors on consulting assignments or research projects for a fee. Students benefited from these experiences by learning research and consulting skills. Because of the nature and length of the consulting contracts, however, there was little uniformity in the practical aspect of education from school to school, or even within schools (Milton Hakel, personal communication, January 27, 2003; Robert F. Morrison, personal communication, January 13, 2003). To help students financially, universities also began offering teaching assistantships to teach undergraduate students or to assist professors in instructional duties. These assistantships did not always offer any practical experience in consulting or research but were a great help for students who were preparing for academic careers and helpful, also, in infusing the training with basic psychological content.

The SIOP Education and Training Committee guidelines recommended field placement training for both master's- and doctoral-level students. For doctoral students, supervised experience was advised to be focused on learning particular skills under the supervision of qualified personnel. The committee recommended up to a year of *in vivo* experience in business and government for those who intended to become practitioners. Both master's and doctoral field experiences involved modeling and observation, through which students may observe professionals delivering consulting services (http://SIOP.org/PhDGuidelines98.html).

A review of current I–O psychology programs suggests that even now there are quite varied levels of internship requirements. A survey of I–O graduate programs (Kantor, Rickes, & Constantino, 2003) found that about half of the universities offering doctoral programs in I–O psychology could, in our judgment, be regarded as primarily emphasizing preparation of students for teaching and research roles. Such programs typically did not require formal internship experience in industry or government agencies. Many of those programs that did have internship requirements allowed their students to fulfill them during the summers or after completing their graduate programs rather than as a formal requirement of the academic program itself.

A related curriculum issue is licensure of I–O psychologists. Should graduate I–O programs be designed to prepare graduates to meet state licensure requirements? The answer to this question is complex and beyond the scope of this chapter. However, this question and the licensure issue are worth noting given the occurrence of extensive debates among members of SIOP over the past several years. Readers are referred to the SIOP Web site for a current SIOP perspective on licensure (www.siop.org).

SUMMARY

This chapter has demonstrated that the roots of I–O psychology educational efforts are almost a century old. Although there were few formalized programs in I–O psychology before World War II, early psychology graduate programs were training psychologists who applied their knowledge to industry and government's needs from the 1920s. As the programs grew in numbers, and became more formalized, they adopted training guidelines at the doctoral level. For the 21st century, an education and training challenge for the discipline of I–O psychology is the shift in I–O PhD programs out of psychology departments to other departments and professional schools in many universities.

By focusing on doctoral education in the United States and Canada, this chapter has underreported the extensiveness of training in I–O, because there are many courses in I–O psychology at the undergraduate level, many master's programs, and also doctoral programs in other countries. As for content of graduate training programs, many of those who studied some version of I–O psychology in the 1920s would find familiar topics in modern curricula. The interplay between science and practice, and the scientific versus humanistic roots of the field, is perhaps now more prevalent, contributing to the continued vibrancy of the field.

ACKNOWLEDGMENTS

We thank the many I–O psychologists across the United States and Canada who contributed to this chapter information about the graduate programs at their universities. Additionally, we thank two anonymous reviewers for valuable comments and suggestions on an earlier draft of this chapter.

REFERENCES

Adams, D. K., & Zener, K. E. (Trans.). (1959). *A dynamic theory of personality: Selected papers*. New York: McGraw-Hill. (Original work published 1935)

Applied Psychology Student Association. (1997). *The UGA applied psychology program directory 1997–98*. Athens: Department of Psychology, The University of Georgia.

Austin, J. T. (1992). History of industrial-organizational psychology at Ohio State. *The Industrial–Organizational Psychologist, 29*, 51–59.

Beer, M. (1980). *Organizational change and development: A systems view*. Santa Monica, CA: Goodyear.

Benjamin, L. (1997). Organized industrial psychology before division 14: The ACP and the AAAP (1930–1945). *Journal of Applied Psychology, 82*, 459–466.

Blood, M. R. (1994). The role of OB in the business school curriculum. In J. Greenberg. (Ed.), *Organizational behavior: The state of the science* (pp. 207–220). Hillsdale, NJ: Lawrence Erlbaum Associates.

Colarelli, S. M. (2003). *No best way: An evolutionary perspective on human resource management*. Westport, CT: Praeger.

Cummings, N. A. (2001). The professional school movement: Empowerment of the clinician in education and training. In R. H. Wright & N. A. Cummings (Eds.), *The practice of psychology: The battle for professionalism* (pp. 70–103). Phoenix: Zeig, Tucker & Theisen.

DiClemente, D. F., & Hantula, D. A. (2000). John Broadus Watson, I–O psychologist. *The Industrial–Organizational Psychologist, 37*(4), 47–55.

Division of Industrial Psychology, Education and Training Committee. (1965). Guidelines for education and training in industrial psychology. *American Psychologist, 20*, 822–831.

Dunnette, M. D. (1993). Applied psychology at Minnesota. *The Industrial–Organizational Psychologist, 31*, 67–76.

Dunnette, M. D., & Bass, B. M. (1963). Behavioral scientists and personnel management. *Industrial Relations, 3*, 115–130.

Frost, C. F. (1996). *Changing forever. The well-kept secret of America's leading companies*. East Lansing, MI: MSU Press.

Frost, C. F., Wakeley, J. H., & Ruh, R. A. (1974). *The Scanlon Plan for organization development: Identity, participation, and equity*. East Lansing, MI: MSU Press.

Gordon, R. A., & Howell, J. E. (1959). *Higher education for business*. New York: Columbia Press.

Greening, T. (Ed.). (1984). *American politics and humanistic psychology: Rollo May, Carl Rogers and other humanistic psychologists*. San Francisco, CA: Saybrook.

Harrell, T. W. (1992). Stanford University's contributions to I–O psychology. *The Industrial–Organizational Psychologist, 30*, 44–49.

Ilgen, D. R. (1984). Industrial psychology. In R. J. Corsini (Ed.), *Encyclopedia of psychology*, (Vol. 2, pp. 201–203). New York: Wiley.

Jacobs, R., & Farr, J. (1993). Industrial and organizational psychology at the Pennsylvania State University. *The Industrial–Organizational Psychologist, 30*, 75–79.

Jenkins, J. G. (1939). A departmental program in Psychotechnology. *Journal of Consulting Psychology, 3*, 54–56.

Kantor, J., Rickes, S., & Constantino, M. (2003). *Internship requirements for I–O psychology programs*. Unpublished document. San Diego: California School of Organizational Studies, San Diego Alliant International University.

Kantor, J., & West, A. (2003). *A survey of public administration programs*. Unpublished document, Alliant International University, California School of Organizational Studies, San Diego.

Katz, R. L., & Kahn, R. (1966). *The social psychology of organizations*. New York: Wiley.

Katzell, R. A. (1992a). History of early I–O doctoral programs. *The Industrial–Organizational Psychologist, 28*, 51.

Katzell, R.A. (1992b). History of I–O psychology at NYU. *The Industrial–Organizational Psychologist, 28,* 61–63.

Katzell, R. A., & Austin, J. T. (1992). From then to now: The development of industrial-organizational psychology in the United States. *Journal of Applied Psychology, 77,* 803–835.

Klare, G. R. (1991). *Memories: Longer and shorter term. A person-oriented history of the psychology department at Ohio University to the year 1990.* Athens: Department of Psychology, Ohio University.

Koppes, L. L. (1991). I–O masters-level training: Reality and legitimacy in search of recognition. *The Industrial–Organizational Psychologist, 29,* 59–67.

Koppes, L. L. (2003). Industrial-organizational psychology. In I. B. Weiner (General Ed.) & D. K. Freedheim (Vol. Ed.), *Comprehensive handbook of psychology: Vol. 1. History of psychology* (pp. 367–389). New York: Wiley.

Lawshe, C. H., & Weiss, H. M. (1991). History of industrial-organizational psychology at Purdue University. *The Industrial–Organizational Psychologist, 28,* 52–57.

Lewin, D. (1991). The contemporary human resource management challenge to industrial relations. In H. C. Katz (Ed.), *The future of industrial relations.* Ithaca, NY: ILR Press.

Lewin, K. (1951). *Field theory in social science.* New York: Harper & Row.

Lowe, R. (1993). Master's programs in industrial–organizational psychology. Current status and call for action. *Professional Psychology, 24,* 27–34.

Lowe, R. (2000). The silent conversation: Talking about the master's degree. *Professional Psychology, 31,* 339–345.

Lowry, R. J. (Ed.). (1973). *Dominance, self-esteem, self-actualization: Germinal papers of A. H. Maslow.* Monterey, CA: Brooks/Cole.

Maslow, A. H. (1954). *Motivation and personality.* New York: Harper & Row.

McGregor, D. (1960). *The human side of the enterprise.* New York: McGraw-Hill.

Montuori, A., & Purser, R. (2001). Humanistic psychology in the workplace. In K. J. Schneider, J. F. Pierson, & J. F. Bugental (Eds.), *The handbook of humanistic psychology* (pp. 635–646). Thousand Oaks, CA: Sage.

National Association of Schools of Public Affairs and Administration. (2005). *Standards.* Retrieved December 7, 2005, from www.naspaa.org/accreditation/seeking/reference/standards.asp

Naylor, J. C. (1971). Hickory, dickory, dock. Let's turn back the clock. *Professional Psychology: Research and Practice, 2,* 217–234.

Odin, E. (2001, November). Past to present: A brief history of GMU's I–O program. *I/ON: The official newsletter of the I–O program.* Retrieved July 15, 2004, from http://www.gmu.edu/org/iopsa

Perloff, R. (1992). The peregrinations of an applied generalist in government, industry, a university psychology department, and a business school. *Professional Psychology: Research and Practice, 23,* 263–268.

Perloff, R. (1994). Playing the hand that's dealt you: My life and times (so far) as a psychologist. In P. A. Keller (Ed.), *Academic paths: Career decisions and experiences of psychologists* (pp. 121–134). Hillsdale, NJ: Lawrence Erlbaum Associates.

Pierson, F. C. (1959). *The education of American businessmen.* New York: McGraw-Hill.

Poffenberger, A. T. (1927). *Principles of applied psychology.* New York: Appleton-Century.

Prien, E. P. (1991). The Division of Applied Psychology at Carnegie Institute of Technology. *The Industrial–Organizational Psychologist, 29,* 41–45.

Rogers, C. R. (1977). *Carl Rogers on personal power.* New York: Delacate.

Russell, C. J. (1992). A conversation with C. H. Lawshe. *The Industrial–Organizational Psychologist, 29,* 65–69.

Saybrook University Catalog. (2002). San Francisco: Saybrook University.

Schneider, K. J., Bugental, J. F. T., & Pierson, J. F. (Eds.) (2001). *The handbook of humanistic psychology.* Thousand Oaks, CA: Sage.

Seashore, S. E. (1978). Autobiography of Stanley E. Seashore. Retrieved July 30, 2004, from http://siop.org/presidents/seashore.htm.

Society of Industrial–Organizational Psychology (SIOP). (1999). *Guidelines for education and training at the doctoral level in industrial and organizational psychology.* Bowling Green, OH: SIOP.

Society for Industrial and Organizational Psychology (SIOP). (1989). *Graduate training programs in industrial/organizational psychology and organizational behavior.* Bowling Green, OH: SIOP.

Strauss, G. (1970). Organizational behavior and personnel relations. *Review of Industrial Relations Research, 1,* 145–206.

System catalog: Alameda, Fresno, Los Angeles, San Diego. (1997–1998). San Francisco: California School of Professional Psychology.

Thayer, P. W., & Austin, J. T. (1992). Harold E. Burtt, 1890–1991. *The Industrial–Organizational Psychologist, 29,* 69–71.

Thompson, A. S. (1991). The evolution of doctoral training in I–O psychology at Teachers College, Columbia University. *The Industrial–Organizational Psychologist, 29,* 35–39.

Thompson, A. S. (1992). Doctoral training in I/O psychology at the University of Pennsylvania: History and characteristics, *The Industrial–Organizational Psychologist, 30,* 15–18.

Viney, W., & Punches, A. (1988). Nature and necessity in the land grant context: History of psychology at Colorado State University. *Journal of History of the Behavioral Sciences, 24,* 64–68.

Viteles, M. S. (1932). *Industrial psychology.* New York: Norton.

Wren. D. (1987). *The evolution of management thought.* (3rd ed.). New York: Wiley.

Zickar, M. J. (2003). Remember Arthur Kornauser: Industrial–organizational psychology's advocate for worker well being. *Journal of Applied Psychology, 88,* 363–369.

6

Influence of Formal and Informal Organizations on the Development of I–O Psychology

Herbert H. Meyer
University of South Florida

Formal groupings or organizations of psychologists have played a major role in the development of industrial and organizational (I–O) psychology in the United States. Such organizations have enhanced progress in applications of psychological research to improve the working life of humans and the efficiency of business and industrial concerns. However, titles identifying such groups with the field of I–O psychology did not begin to appear until the second decade of the 20th century. As noted in Chapters 1 and 2, the earliest applications were associated with individual contributors rather than groups.

Once I–O-oriented psychological research and applications organizations began to appear, their numbers grew exponentially. Today there are more organizations of this kind in academia, industry, consulting, and research than could possibly be described or even listed in a single volume. I describe here only those formal and informal organizations that seem to have had a significant influence on the growth and development of the profession, highlighting especially those established in the first 60 or 70 years of the development of the specialty that has become known as industrial–organizational psychology. In each category of organizations, I consider them in approximately chronological order. This chapter does not trace the development of professional organizations, such as the American Psychological Association (APA), the American Psychological Society (APS), the International Association of Applied Psychology (IAAP), and the Society for Industrial and Organizational Psychology (SIOP). Readers are referred to historical accounts previously published (e.g., Benjamin, 1997a, 1997b).

Academic organized groups are dealt with first. The earliest work that could be identified as industrial psychology was conducted in a few university psychology departments, most notably by Scott at Northwestern and Münsterberg at Harvard. The work of these individuals is covered in chapter 2 of this book. The description of I–O programs in university departments of psychology, in general, is presented in chapter 5, titled "A History of I–O Psychology Educational Programs in the United States." I focus here only on organizations established as separate units with special titles, usually within or associated with departments of psychology in large research-oriented universities.

Second, I describe organizations established outside of academia with a primary focus on applied psychological research and development. These are labeled Research Organizations. Third, under the heading Business and Industry Consulting Organizations, I describe the work of a few organizations that were established to focus exclusively on I–O research and development. Because of the large number of such organizations that have emerged, especially in the last 30 years, I have included only a few as examples that had either significant historical importance or unusual prominence in their contributions to the development of the field. Fourth, under Governmental Organizations, I give examples of some federal agencies whose research has had a particularly significant impact on the history of I–O psychology.

Last, I cover informal groups of I–O psychologists that began to be formed, for the most part, after World War II. These proved to be valuable means for I–O psychologists in industry, government, and research organizations, and to some degree in academia and consulting firms, to exchange ideas and experiences regarding research and development programs, problems encountered in applications, solutions to vexing problems, and the like. Such informal exchanges proved to be invaluable to members of the groups in problem solving on the job, stimulating new research and development programs and applications, and keeping up to date with emerging developments in the field.

ACADEMIC ORGANIZATIONS

As noted in chapter 1, academic psychological laboratories first began to appear in the last half of the 19th century in Europe, most notably in Germany. The most emulated by American psychologists was probably Wundt's laboratory at the University of Leipzig. William James, who had studied with Wundt, is generally credited with having started the first American psychological laboratory, at Harvard University, in about 1880. Soon after, other large research-oriented American universities established similar laboratories, notably at Johns Hopkins, Michigan, Indiana, Princeton, Illinois, Yale, Wisconsin, Clark, Nebraska, and New York, among others. By 1913, there were 47 such laboratories in American universities (Landy, 1992).

In the last 30 or 40 years, the number of academic organizations that would meet our criteria of separate units devoted to I–O related research and development, with separate titles within a university, has proliferated exponentially. Every research-oriented university has a number of such organizations, each defining a significant research program. All of them cannot be covered in this chapter. Therefore, I focus here only a few that have historical significance in having been started before World War II, and in one case organized just after the war but based on research programs founded before or during the war.

Division of Applied Psychology at the Carnegie Institute of Technology

Carnegie Institute of Technology (also known as Carnegie Tech and now Carnegie–Mellon University) was the first university in America to formally designate a separate organization within the Department of Psychology to focus on research and development in industrial psychology, with the establishment of the Division of Applied Psychology in 1915. Walter Van Dyke Bingham, who had established a reputation as an applied psychologist, was appointed to head this new division (see chap. 2 for more information on Bingham). While at Dartmouth, Bingham introduced a program to administer mental tests to college students. This research impressed the president of Carnegie Tech, who asked Bingham to expand this testing to business and government organizations in the newly established Division of Applied Psychology (Benjamin, 2002). Soon after he assumed the role of director of this new division, Bingham was asked by several business leaders in the area to develop a program to train salespeople. He responded by soliciting the financial support of a number of companies to establish a Bureau of Salesmanship Research. Several future leaders in the field of industrial psychology contributed to the research of this bureau, including W. D. Scott, L. L. Thurstone, J. B. Miner, Marion Bills, Max Freyd, Richard Uhrbrock, E. K. Strong, Jr., and Clarence Yoakum (see Landy, 1997). The activities of these individuals are noted throughout this book.

Unfortunately, the Carnegie Division of Applied Psychology had a relatively short life. A new president of the university abolished the division in 1924. Many of the psychologists on the staff became some of the first industrial psychologists to establish psychological research programs in business, industry, and the government. Others became prominent in university departments, starting a few PhD programs in industrial psychology (see Ferguson, 1952, 1962–1965, and chap. 5 in this text).

Occupational Research Center at Purdue University

An applied psychology program was started at Purdue University in 1937 when F. B. Knight from the University of Iowa was hired specifically for that purpose. Like most early practicing applied psychologists of that time, Knight had not been trained as an industrial psychologist. His doctoral degree was in educational psychology. Knight brought Joseph Tiffin, also an Iowa educational psychologist, to Purdue and told him he was now to be an industrial psychologist (Lawshe & Weiss, 1991). The program started in the Department of Education as the Division of Educational and Applied Psychology.

Tiffin took advantage of the industrial contacts of professors in the Vocational Industrial Education Department to initiate research projects in industrial settings. He also began a PhD program to train industrial psychologists. One of his first graduates was Charles H. (Chuck) Lawshe, who joined the industrial program faculty in 1941. In 1945 N. C. Kephart was added to the staff, and in 1947 Ernest J. McCormick joined them. The four of them, Tiffin, Lawshe, Kephart, and McCormick, formed the Occupational Research Center (ORC). The ORC staff expanded in the 1960s with the addition of Robert Perloff, Hugh Brogden, Karl Weick, Jack Jacoby, and Arthur Dudycha to become the most prolific PhD program in the University. The emphasis on industrial psychology diminished after James Naylor became chair of the Psychology Department in 1968, and the ORC was evidently dissolved shortly after.

Ohio State University Personnel Research Board

The Personnel Research Board (PRB), founded and directed by Carroll L. Shartle at Ohio State University, was one of the first interdisciplinary research groups organized to conduct studies of organizational behavior for industry, military, and governmental agencies. Shartle, an early student of Harold Burtt at Ohio State, had been chief of the Worker Analysis Section at the U.S. Department of Labor.

The major program at the PRB, called the Ohio State Leadership Studies, began in 1945, continued through the 1950s, and had a major impact on the field of I–O psychology. These leadership studies were frequently cited in textbooks and had a strong influence on later leadership research and practice. Studies were carried out first with large agricultural cooperatives and then within military, educational, and industrial settings. In 1950, senior staff members included Ralph Stogdill, John Hemphill, Donald Campbell, Andrew Halpin (psychologists), Melvin Seeman (sociologist), and Alvin Coons (economist). At various times, research assistants included Edwin A. Fleishman, B. J. Winer, Jon Bentz, Edwin F. Harris, Ellis Scott, Paul Thayer, and William E. Jaynes. Funding for this program came from a variety of sources, including the Office of Naval Research, Air Force Office of Scientific Research, Rockefeller Foundation, Kellogg Foundation, various farm bureaus, and the International Harvester Company.

Stogdill's (1948) review, showing low and inconsistent relations between measures of personality constructs (then available) and leader effectiveness, argued for a shift to a more functional approach to leadership emphasizing particular behaviors that differentiated the performance of individuals in leadership positions. Hemphill initially developed a Leader Behavior Description Questionnaire providing 100 behaviors scored on 10 dimensions (e.g., initiation, representation, communication, etc.) derived from descriptions of subordinates or others. Halpin and Winer (1957), using the questionnaire with military and educational groups, and Fleishman (1953a) working with industrial supervisors, carried out independent factor analyses of the items and identified two underlying dimensions of leadership: consideration and initiation of structure.

The advance in this work was the finding that these two dimensions were operationally defined in terms of common behaviors that were most diagnostic of each dimension. It was shown that, as measured in the forms subsequently developed, the two dimensions were relatively independent behavior patterns and not opposite poles of a single leadership dimension (as was assumed in the University of Michigan studies at that time). Individuals in leadership positions could and did exert different combinations of these two behavior patterns. Within the Ohio State program, these and other measures were used in a wide variety of settings to examine leader behavior–criterion performance relations.

Of particular historical impact for I–O psychology were the studies carried out by Fleishman and followed up by Edwin Harris under fellowships from the International Harvester Company (Fleishman & Harris, 1962). Fleishman (1953b) developed the Supervisory Behavior Description (SBD) and the Leadership Opinion Questionnaire (LOQ) specifically for industry and used them to study the effects of leadership training on management behavior and leadership attitudes. This was perhaps the first attempt at evaluating leadership training by a before-and-after design, examining managers' behaviors and attitudes before formal attempts at training at a central school, immediately after the training, and again after the managers returned to their truck manufacturing plants. The research involved control and comparison groups over time and involved managers at different organizational levels. The findings showed that the training had a desirable effect on behavior and attitudes immediately after training, but after the trainees returned to the job, their own managers' behaviors and attitudes (the "leadership climate") proved to be the main factor in determining whether the training effect persisted. Follow-up research also showed that the consideration and structure scores of managers predicted the independent measures of turnover, grievances, absences, and performance of their work groups.

The Ohio State leadership studies had a major early impact on the field of I–O psychology. In 1998, the editors of *Personnel Psychology* declared the article by Fleishman and Harris (1962) to be the most frequently cited article in the journal in the 1960s (Hollenbeck, 1998). This research was described in a book by Fleishman, Harris, and Burtt (1955).

University of Michigan Institute for Social Research (ISR)[1]

The University of Michigan Institute for Social Research is probably the largest social science research organization in the world (Cannell & Kahn, 1984). Its origin dates to 1946, when the U.S. Department of Agriculture decided to discontinue its Division of Program Surveys,

---

[1]Three major reference sources were used for the material in this section: Cannell and Kahn (1984), Institute for Social Research (1998), and Frantilla (1998).

which had been created by Rensis Likert in 1939. Likert explored academic sites to continue a survey program and chose the University of Michigan because of its strong social psychology and sociology programs. The university agreed to provide a home for Likert's program provided that all of its projects would be supported by outside financial sources. Thus, the University of Michigan Survey Research Center was established.

In 1948, the Research Center for Group Dynamics, which had been founded by Kurt Lewin at the Massachusetts Institute of Technology (MIT), moved to the University of Michigan after Lewin's death to join with the Survey Research Center to become the Institute for Social Research (ISR). This move from MIT also brought several rising stars in the field to Michigan, including Leon Festinger, Ronald Lippit, John R. P. French, Jr., and Dorwin Cartwright. Soon after, Alvin Zander also joined them. In later years, two additional centers were organized as part of ISR: the Center for Research on Utilization of Scientific Knowledge in 1964 and the Center for Political Studies in 1970.

ISR was not intended to be an I–O organization but rather an interdisciplinary institution covering all the social sciences. However, a major part of the research at ISR focused on organizational behavior. In 1947, Daniel Katz joined the Survey Research Center and partnered with Rensis Likert to launch a program of research on organizational effectiveness. They focused on differences in the way effective and ineffective organizations were managed. Likert became known worldwide for his participative management theory. Likert's 1961 book, *New Patterns of Management,* summarized their programmatic research to that date. Daniel Katz and Robert Kahn collaborated on *The Social Psychology of Organizations* (1966), which also drew heavily on the center's empirical research. The book soon became a classic in the field of social and organizational psychology. The authors proposed "open-system theory" as a framework for integrating organizational research. Likert's follow-up book, *The Human Organization: Its Management and Value* (1967), described how extremes of management styles from authoritarian to participative affect all facets of management to impinge on organizational effectiveness.

The basic operating unit in ISR was established as the "program," a topical area of research. Each program manager always had primary responsibility for securing the grants or other sources of support for that program. In 1953, the Organizational Behavior and Human Relations Program was started by Daniel Katz and Rensis Likert. The research described in the previous paragraph was undertaken in this program. A major project initiated in the 1960s consisted of experimental field studies in 10 organizational sites to demonstrate how management style affects the quality of working life of organizational members. This research was summarized in a book edited by Stanley Seashore, Edward Lawler, Phillip Mirvis, and Cortlandt Cammann titled *Assessing Organizational Change: A Guide to Methods, Measures, and Practices* (1983). These studies further highlighted the value of participative management, not only to improve the working life of organizational members but also to improve the effectiveness of the organization as a whole. It is interesting to note that the ISR research findings on the effects of participative management had little impact on management practices in the United States until about the last 2 decades of the 20th century. This may have been because the Japanese did buy in with their "quality circles" and other participative programs, and they seemed to be out-competing American companies in several industries, notably autos and electronics. (See chaps. 15 and 17 in this volume for more information on participative management.)

Another program in the I–O field was ISR's Mental Health in Industry Program, a joint effort by the Survey Research Center and the Research Center for Group Dynamics, which was the largest ISR program in the 1960s. It focused on the effect of environmental factors on the mental and physical health of organizational members, with special emphasis on social–psychological factors in large organizations. Other I–O related studies focused on the effects of organizational change (Lawler played a major role in this project), factors facilitating creativity and job involvement, role behavior of executives, factors relating to the effectiveness of scientists, the effects of various colleague interaction practices on the efficiency of organizations, the effects of stress in organizational life, and related projects.

ISR has also been active on the international front. As early as the 1950s, Likert established working relationships with several European research organizations. International activity continued through the years with studies and collaborative research with centers in Europe, Africa, Japan, Australia, and others. In the early 1990s Robert Zajonc, then ISR director, initiated a project to form an international network of cooperating and collaborating centers. Such links were established in Europe, South America, Africa, and China and even in some of the developing nations.

It seems amazing that the institute not only survived but grew through the last half of the 20th century. Having to depend entirely on external grants for financial support was not always easy. In a 1965 letter to Likert, who was traveling abroad at the time, Angus Campbell, then administrative head of ISR, wrote, "The University turns us down because they think we are adequately supported by outside funds and the foundations turn us down because they think we are supported by the University" (Institute for Social Research, 1998, p. 14). A favorable financial factor was an agreement with the university that ISR could keep the overhead portion allocated to grants to help support the staff between grants and when the staff had to devote time to grant proposal preparation. The growth of ISR was especially rapid in the last decade of the 20th century. Dollar volume of activity in 2001 was approximately $70,000,000 (Robert Kahn, personal communication November, 2002).

RESEARCH ORGANIZATIONS

As with academic organizations, a number of research organizations outside of academia have been established to conduct research and development projects that have been important in the field of I–O psychology. A great many of these are human resources research units within the armed services. Some of these are described in chapter 7 of this book, "The Military's Contribution to Our Science and Practice: People, Places, and Findings." Included in this chapter are seven research organizations outside of the military, selected because of their size and influence and the fact that they focus exclusively on research and development. Not included are the many consulting firms that conduct a great deal of research and development in carrying out applied projects.

Only one of the organizations described here originated before World War II, the Personnel Research Federation, which was organized in 1921. After World War II, two organizations are included that have become very prominent in the field of applied psychology, AIR and HumRRO. They started with many staff members who had been involved in military research during the war. Other somewhat similar research organizations that developed out of the wartime psychological research programs are not included here, such as the Rand Corporation and Systems Development Corporation, because they seemed to focus primarily on sociological research, human engineering, or research in other disciplines of marginal interest to many I–O psychologists.

Four additional organizations included in this chapter are ARRO, PDRI, the Center for Creative Leadership, and ETS. ARRO is described because many well-known I–O psychologists got their start there, and several important research programs were conducted. PDRI is included because it was started by I–O psychologists to focus exclusively on I–O research projects. The Center for Creative Leadership is included because of its significant research and development work on leadership, a topic of great interest to I–O psychologists. Finally, ETS is described because considerable research and development that evolved there has direct relevance to I–O psychology.

The Personnel Research Federation

In 1921, a number of psychologists who were interested and/or involved in applying psychology to real-world problems formed an association to include membership and financial support from business firms, unions, universities, government agencies, industrial associations, and individual members, to sponsor applied research in work settings. They called their association the Personnel Research Federation. Their stated purpose was expressed as follows: "The Personnel Research Federation exists for the advancement of scientific knowledge about men and women in relation to their occupations" (Bingham, 1928, p. 299). The group started with support from one business firm, five educational institutions, five associations and bureaus, and 26 individual supporters. Robert M. Yerkes of Yale University was selected as the first president and Samuel Gompers of the American Federation of Labor as the first vice-president. In 1924, when Carnegie Tech abandoned the Division of Applied Psychology, Walter Bingham assumed the presidency of the federation.

By 1927, the membership had grown to include nine business firms, 27 universities, six government agencies, eight associations, and 126 individual members. The government agencies involved were the U.S. Public Health Services, Bureau of Mines, Bureau of Labor Statistics, Women's Bureau, Federal Bureau for Vocational Education, and the U.S. Civil Service Commission. Among the supporting companies, all of whom had psychologists on their staffs, were Dennison Manufacturing Co., Scovill Manufacturing Co., Eastman Kodak, Western Electric, White Motor Co., and the Woolworth Co. Some of the associations involved were the YMCA, the National Research Council, the Engineering Federation, and the American Federation of Labor. Some of the supporting universities were Harvard, Penn, Michigan, Chicago, Pittsburgh, Syracuse, Stanford, Yale, and Oberlin.

A small paid staff (four or five psychologists) consulted with the member institutions on projects. (Incidentally, judging from their budget figures, annual salaries of the staff members must have been in the $3,000–$4,000 range.) Most of the research studies were carried out by the university members. A wide variety of topics were covered by the studies sponsored by the federation, including financial incentives, tedium in jobs, restriction of output, job satisfaction, fatigue, the interview, aging workers, output and morale in repetitive work, causes of accidents, mental hygiene in industry, job analysis, careers, working mothers' problems, worker efficiency, employment of the handicapped, employee selection, and the like.

The federation may have been a casualty of the Great Depression. All reference to the federation in the literature seems to have disappeared in the early 1930s. Bingham had published detailed reports of the annual meetings of the federation in the *Personnel Journal*. The last such report covered the 1930 annual meeting.

American Institutes for Research (AIR)

John C. Flanagan, a master planner and organizer, had earned his PhD in psychology at Harvard in 1935. During the next few years he worked for the Cooperative Testing Service in New York, which led to the opportunity to conduct a survey of Army Air Corps officers. Through his contacts in that study, he was recruited to develop an Aviation Psychology Program for the army in 1941 as the army was preparing for World War II. During the war, that program employed more than 150 psychologists, mostly PhDs, and more than 1,400 others with some psychological training as assistants (Most, 1993; see also chaps. 7 and 10 in this text.)

At the end of the war in 1946, Flanagan resigned as a Colonel in the Air Corps and capitalized on his planning and organizing skills to establish the American Institute of Research (later changed to American Institutes for Research or AIR) as a nonprofit organization, headquartered in Pittsburgh, to focus on "the scientific study of human resources and their effective use" and as its goal "developing the individual and increasing his or her satisfaction." (Flanagan, 1984, p. 1272). AIR's board of directors included, at various times, numerous figures known to industrial psychologists, including Paul Horst, Frederick B. Davis, Paul Fitts, Rains Wallace, Edwin Fleishman, Brent Baxter, and Robert Gagné. In the 1960s and 1970s, AIR staff developed financial support from industry, government, and educational institutions and carried out numerous research projects in a number of traditional I–O areas, such as job analysis, test development, performance measurement, training, leadership, team organization, management, and others.

One of the most prodigious research projects for which AIR became very well known was Flanagan's Project Talent conducted for the U.S. Office of Education starting in the early 1960s. This involved the testing and follow-up of more than 400,000 high school students over a 20-year period. Project Talent has provided data for hundreds of studies (Most, 1993). Another major AIR undertaking was a project called PLAN, in which computer programs were developed to score and analyze test patterns for students and then generate individualized objectives for the respective testees for use by their teachers. The computer programs also generated complete records of the respective students' progress in their scheduled programs and sent these records to their teachers along with recommended learning activities (Most, 1993).

In 1963, a second AIR office was established in the Washington, DC, area under the directorship of Edwin Fleishman, who left Yale University to become senior vice-president of AIR. Over the next 12 years that office grew to a staff of 140 with five institutes: Organizational Behavior Research Institute, Communication Research Institute, Human Performance Research Institute, International Research Institute, and Transnational Family Research Institute (Most, 1994). The research carried out in the Washington office of AIR is of particular historical interest to I–O psychology. Examples of programs in this office included Ed Locke's early work on goal setting (Locke & Bryan, 1967), the extensive program on taxonomies of human performance (described by Fleishman & Quaintance, 1984), Harold Van Cott's early work on the effective design of information systems and his revision of the *Human Engineering Guide to Equipment Design* (Van Cott & Kinkade, 1972), and the work by Al Glickman and colleagues on organizational behavior factors in the retention of personnel and top management development and succession (e.g., Glickman, Hahn, Fleishman, & Baxter, 1968). Other projects were concerned with the evaluation of various drugs, stressors, and environmental factors on aspects of human performance; early studies on improving police–community relations (Eisenberg, Fosen, & Glickman, 1973); and some of the first studies on the selection of police and fire personnel using tests of physical performance.

In the international arena, programs in AIR/Washington included methods of adapting transferred personnel to overseas assignments, introduction of technology innovations for developing countries, and cross-cultural research on family planning. During this 12-year period, this office received funding support from more than 80 different governmental and private sector organizations and foundations.

In 1966, Flanagan decided to resign as president of AIR and moved to Palo Alto, California, to build up a third office. Rains Wallace was appointed to the presidency and Flanagan became chairman of the board. However, in 1970, Wallace decided to move to an offered academic position as chairman of the Department of Psychology at Ohio State University. John Flanagan assumed the role of president again. AIR continued to grow in the following years and, with various mergers, developed a diversity of educational, social, and evaluation projects.

Human Resources Research Organization (HumRRO)[2]

HumRRO was established in 1951 as the Human Resources Research Office to conduct research exclusively for the U.S. Army. In 1967 the organization began to do research for other clients as well, so the name was changed to Human Resources Research Organization.

After World War II, the U.S. Army staff considered various means for strengthening research in the behavioral and social sciences, especially in the area of human factors and related research that had proved so valuable to the armed services during World War II. In 1950, Dr. Harry Harlow of the University of Wisconsin, best known for his work in comparative psychology, learning theory, and cortical functioning, was appointed as science advisor for the U.S. Army. He was asked to head a study group to review the Army's human resources research needs. This group decided that a Human Resources Research Office (HumRRO) should be established, preferably in a university setting. George Washington University was awarded the contract to set up this office. Professor Meredith Crawford of Vanderbilt University, who had done considerable consulting work with the Army during World War II, was appointed as its first director.

The first unit formed within HumRRO was established to focus on research dealing with motivation, morale, and leadership. John L. Fanan, who also had served as a consultant to the Army, was appointed director of that division. Soon after, two field research offices were opened at Fort Knox, Kentucky, and Fort Ord, California. A PsyWar Division also began work at headquarters. Subsequently, research units were established at Fort Benning in 1953, Fort Bliss in 1955, and Fort Rucker in 1958. The potential use of atomic bombs prompted a large-scale study of the psychological effects of chemical, biological, and radiological warfare on troops. This was labeled the Desert Rock research.

The other major research projects undertaken during HumRRO's first 16 years, when research was limited exclusively to projects for the Army, included: behavior of soldiers in battle, especially effects of stress; helicopter pilot proficiency; tank gunner performance; training program performance in general; human factors problems with new airplanes, tanks, boats, and other vehicles; effective leadership behavior; and the increasing use of simulators. This last project, use of simulators, proved in research to be valuable for training but very expensive in costs of training devices. Considerable research with alternative simulation approaches proved that less expensive simulations could be just as effective so long as they included the critical requirements for visual, auditory, and motion cues.

Although still associated with George Washington University, in 1963 HumRRO moved off campus to their own headquarters in Alexandria, Virginia. In 1967 the contract with the Army was modified to allow HumRRO to take on non-Army clients. The "O" in HumRRO was changed from "Office" to "Organization." This also meant that HumRRO had to change course and begin to focus on marketing its services to new clients. A further blow to the operation came in 1974 when the Department of Defense (DOD) decided to move its manpower research in-house. A majority of HumRRO's staff members transferred to newly formed DOD research centers. Internal volume of research declined greatly. While continuing to do some research for the military services, HumRRO also took on a variety of new clients, including the Department of Health, Education, and Welfare; Departments of Labor and Transportation; the U.S. Postal Services; and a number of state and local government units. HumRRO's western division

[2]The major reference source of the material in this section was HumRRO (2001).

formed the HumRRO Institute for the Study of Learning. Capitalizing on the extensive training research that had been conducted for the military, a series of development workshops for teachers and educational administrators was established.

In 1976, Dr. Crawford retired and Dr. William A. McClelland, who had been with HumRRO since 1955 as director of the important Training Methods Division, was appointed president. Unfortunately, his tenure as president was short. In 1979 he died from complications arising from heart surgery, and C. William Smith became president. During the 1970s, due to the Army's decision to move most of its research program in-house, HumRRO's staff declined from about 260 in 1970 to 106 in 1980. It has remained at about that level since then. Much of HumRRO's research for the Army proved to be valuable to organizations of all kinds. For example, a publication developed in HumRRO's leadership research program, titled, *Leadership and Exchange in Formal Organizations,* was adapted as a textbook in many large universities. Some of HumRRO's basic research programs also proved to be of interest and value to many organizations other than the Army on such topics as how to make a training film that really works, the relation of intelligence and authoritarianism to behavioral contagion and conformity, structural characteristics of arithmetic problems, separation of production and evaluation in individual problem solving, and others.

Other major nonmilitary studies carried out by HumRRO staff over the last 30 years of the 20th century included a project conducted for the National Science Foundation concerning the use of computers in schools, development of valid structured interview programs for a host of nonmilitary clients, creation of an organization climate survey for a private-sector engineering firm, identification of internal educational needs of employees in a large hardware/software development firm, and development of computer literacy workshops for a large multinational corporation. HumRRO was also the prime contractor for the U.S. Army's Project A, a large-scale research effort to improve the selection and classification of Army enlisted personnel from 1981 to about 1990. HumRRO teamed with AIR and Personnel Decisions Research Institute (PDRI) in carrying out this project.

Due to increasing research opportunities among nonmilitary clients, along with continued grants for research in military agencies, HumRRO became increasingly stable financially and successful in terms of research output in the last decade of the 20th century. As stated in its 2001 report, "In short, HumRRO will survive another 50 years by finding work that is intrinsically interesting, attacking it with integrity, and maintaining our respect for each other and our sense of humor. By doing so we will be able to continue to apply our collective creativity to the wide range of human resources challenges to come" (HumRRO, 2001, p. 174).

Advanced Research Resources Organization (ARRO)[3]

In 1976, after a year as visiting professor in the Graduate School of Administration at the University of California–Irvine, Edwin Fleishman returned to Washington and with Albert Glickman and some others from AIR organized ARRO. Over the next 10 years, a number of psychologists, now well known in I–O psychology, got their start at ARRO. Those whose first post-PhD positions were at ARRO included Joyce Hogan, Michael Mumford, Debby Gebhardt, Veronica Nieva, David Meyers, Kerry Levin, Mark Schemmer, and Merri Ann Cooper. Senior staff during this period included Sidney Fine, Frank Harding, Jerrold Levine, Marilyn Gowing, Arthur Korotkin, and Sam Schiflett.

ARRO projects received support from a variety of federal government agencies, such as the Departments of Labor, Justice, and Transportation, all branches of the Department of Defense,

---

[3]Material for this section was prepared by Edwin A. Fleishman.

Department of Housing and Urban Development, Office of Personnel Management, the Federal Trade Commission, and many state and local governments. Other organizations sponsoring ARRO research included the Edison Electric Institute, AT&T, Exxon, Safeway, Uniroyal, Panhandle Eastern Pipeline, Alabama Power and Light, Pacific Maritime Association, International Union of Operating Engineers, and many others. ARRO staff opened up the area of physical performance as an important aptitude domain for evaluation in the employment situation, especially in response to social changes affecting the employment of women and minorities in physically demanding jobs. This included developing a job analysis methodology for identifying the physical requirements of jobs and linking these to specific tests (see, e.g., Fleishman, 1979; Hogan, Ogden, Gebhardt, & Fleishman, 1980). Another programmatic area at ARRO was the development and evaluation of a taxonomy of team performance functions and their use in assessing team performance in organizational settings (e.g., Cooper, Schiflett, Korotkin, & Fleishman, 1984).

In the late 1970s, the National Science Foundation funded a proposal by ARRO to examine the linkage of research on human performance to national issues of improving productivity. This project resulted in a series of three books: *Human Performance and Productivity*, with Volume 1 subtitled *Human Capability Assessment* (Dunnette & Fleishman, 1982), Volume 2 subtitled *Information Processing and Decision Making* (Howell & Fleishman, 1982), and Volume 3 subtitled *Stress and Performance Effectiveness* (Alluisi & Fleishman, 1982). Other studies at ARRO of interest to I–O psychologists were the large-scale studies on the relations between trainee characteristics, training content, training outcomes, and the measurement of occupational difficulty (Mumford, Weeks, Harding, & Fleishman, 1988). In the area of job analysis, work at ARRO by Fine on functional job analysis and by Fleishman on the identification of ability requirements of jobs led to further refinements and applications of these methods.

Personnel Decisions Research Institute, Inc. (PDRI)[4]

PDRI was an offshoot of a consulting firm, Personnel Decisions Incorporated (PDI), started in 1967 by Marvin Dunnette, Lowell Hellervik, and Wayne Kirchner, a Minnesota I–O graduate who succeeded Dunnette at the 3M Company when Dunnette joined the University of Minnesota faculty. Dunnette was to work part-time as chairman of PDI and Lowell full-time as president. PDI continues today as a very successful consulting firm with offices in seven or eight of the largest cities in the United States and overseas in London, Paris, Brussels, Hong Kong, and Melbourne. In recent years, PDI has become known as Personnel Decisions International.

In 1975, the National Institutes on Drug Abuse (NIDA) wanted to give PDI a large grant to develop personnel selection techniques to predict drug abuse. This project could not be carried out by PDI because NIDA's rules specified that the research organization had to be nonprofit. Thus, because PDI was a for-profit firm and intended to stay that way, Dunnette, Borman, and Leaetta Hough started the nonprofit PDRI to take on that contract. (In later years PDRI became a for-profit company to be able to receive small business set-aside contracts.) PDRI then began work on the 1975 NIDA grant and a job analysis project with George Hollenbeck at Merrill Lynch. In 1976, Norman Peterson and Janis Houston joined the firm. These two were highly important team members for many years.

PDRI has often been involved in large-scale projects. The largest was the U.S. Army's Project A (described previously) and the follow-on Career Forces Project from 1990 to 1994. PDRI was responsible for predictor development and development of the performance rating

---

[4]Material for this section was provided by Walter Borman of PDRI.

scales for several jobs. In addition, PDRI conducted test validation research for several consortia of companies, including 120 insurance companies for the Life Office Management Association and about 60 electric power companies for the Edison Electric Institute. PDRI, along with American Institutes for Research, Management Research Institute, Jeanerette and Associates, and Westat, Inc., also played a major role in the U.S. Department of Labor's Occupational Information Network, the O*NET project (Peterson, Mumford, Borman, Jeanneret, & Fleishman, 1999). The objective of this effort was to replace the Dictionary of Occupational Titles (DOT) with a database of occupational information (e.g., ability, skill, and generalized work activity requirements) intended to describe these requirements for all occupations in the U.S. economy.

PDRI grew over the years so that in the year 2002 it had about 40 employees.[5] Minneapolis was still headquarters, with about 22 employees working there. In 1995, Jerry Hedge, then PDRI's president and chief operating officer, Mary Ann Hanson, and Walter Borman, chief executive officer, started a Tampa, Florida, office. At about the same time, Elaine Pulakos opened a Washington, DC, office. PDRI staff members have been very active in professional affairs, including administrative roles in the Society of I–O Psychology (SIOP) and publishing in the I–O literature. Marvin Dunnette, Walter Borman, and Elaine Pulakos have served as presidents of SIOP.

Center for Creative Leadership[6]

The Center for Creative Leadership is an international, nonprofit, educational institution devoted to leadership research and training. Its mission has been to advance the understanding, practice, and development of leadership for the benefit of society worldwide. It is headquartered in Greensboro, North Carolina, and also has offices and training centers in Colorado Springs, San Diego, Brussels, and Singapore, in addition to a global network of associates licensed to offer selected center programs.

The center was established in 1970 by H. Smith Richardson, who had been largely responsible for building the Vicks Chemical Company from a one-drugstore operation into a major international corporation over a period of about 70 years. Over his long career as a chief executive, he had seen many old enterprises with a successful history decline and often fail due to what appeared to be management's failure to adjust to changed circumstances. Therefore, he decided that the establishment of a leadership research and development center would be a very worthwhile investment for his Smith Richardson Foundation.

By the year 2002, the center had grown to a staff of nearly 500 individuals who conduct research, produce publications, and provide programs and products to leaders and organizations in all sectors of society. More than half the members of the professional staff have advanced degrees in the fields of psychology, sociology, organizational behavior, business education, economics, and communication. This includes nearly 50 with PhDs or EdDs, many of these I–O psychologists. The center is probably best known for its research that produced a variety of Leadership Development Programs. Each year, some 20,000 managers and executives, educators, government leaders, and community service administrators and volunteers attend these programs.

Following are some of the center's notable research and development contributions to learning and practice.

---

[5]In January 2002, PDRI was purchased 100% by ePredix but the identity and operation of PDRI have not changed.

[6]Material for this section was provided by Melodie Jancerak of the Center staff.

Assessment for Development.   Center researchers pioneered and validated 360-degree feedback techniques, revolutionizing the assessment process. Their research and application of this approach have been used not only with individual managers and executives but also to study teams and entire organizations.

Executive Development.   To study how senior executives develop, the center created an entirely new research methodology, biographical action research, using autobiography and 360 assessment to reveal development pathways and opportunities.

Leadership and Creativity.   The center helped to demystify creativity in the workplace by showing that it is not a mysterious process practiced by a few but an activity that can be managed and motivated.

Teams.   The center's research on teams has led to breakthroughs in knowledge about both face-to-face and geographically dispersed teams.

Looking Glass, Inc.   This is an elaborate simulation developed by the center as a research and training tool that creates a realistic context in which managers can be observed. As part of this exercise, participants reveal how they might behave on the job. More than 30,000 managers have tried their hand at running this fictitious glass company.

The center has received many awards and citations. In 2002, *The Financial Times* ranked the center as one of the top 10 nondegree executive education providers worldwide and placed the center first worldwide for customized education training faculty and teaching materials. In 1999, the *Business Week* Executive Education Survey ranked the center as 1 for leadership, 3 for innovation, 3 for customized programs, and 5 in human resources. In 1996, the center was ranked in the top 10 of nondegree executive education programs by *US News and World Report* and as "one of the most respected in the field" by the *New York Times* with reference to leadership courses. In 1993, a survey by the *Wall Street Journal* and *Bricker's International Directory* ranked two of the center's programs, Leadership at the Peak and the Leadership Development Program, as 1 and 2, respectively, among the top leadership courses for executives.

Educational Testing Service (ETS)[7]

The Educational Testing Service (ETS), which opened on January 2, 1948, was founded as a not-for-profit testing and research organization, by the American Council on Education, the College Entrance Examination Board, and the Carnegie Foundation. The initial goal was to create a single organization to improve and administer existing tests, construct new ones, where needed, and provide a broad program of research, mainly to support future educational programs (see ETS Through the Years: A 50th Anniversary Album, 1998). While initially oriented to the field of education, considerable research and development that has evolved at ETS has been of direct relevance to the field of industrial and organizational psychology.

The founding president of ETS was Henry Chauncey, who had been director of the College Board's testing offices. William W. Turnbull was named director of research and development and, 22 years later, succeeded Chauncey as ETS president. The initial staff consisted of 111 employees, mainly from the founding organizations, with 17 existing testing programs, and a budget of $1,750,000. Staff in 1948 included Harold Gulliksen, Ledyard Tucker, and Norman Fredricksen, and a number of others who became well known for their major contributions to areas relevant to I–O psychology.

---

[7]Material for this section was prepared by Edwin A. Fleishman.

ETS's first home was in cramped space rented (and later purchased) from Princeton University at 20 Nassau Street, and an adjacent building in Princeton, New Jersey. Fifty years later ETS has become the world's largest nongovernmental measurement and testing organization with a staff of approximately 3,000 people, which includes 1,200 professionals, 500 with advanced degrees, and more than 200 doctorates. In 1954, anticipating its rapid development, ETS bought a 349-acre nearby farmland site on Rosedale Road, began a phased building program to develop this site into a campus to house its growing staff and increased diversity of activities.

The public is familiar with ETS's administration of the Scholastic Aptitude Test (SAT), the Graduate Record Examinations (GRE), and the American Council of Education's National Teacher Examinations (NTE) over their long history. In the first 6 months of ETS's existence it administered and scored 798,032 tests! In the 1950s, later programs included the Advanced Placement Program, and the Preliminary Scholastic Aptitude Test (PSAT), Graduate Management Admissions Test, Medical College Admission Test, and in the 1950s, the Selective Service College Qualification Test (SSQT). Much of the early work focused on test theory and methodological studies in test construction, item analysis, alternate forms, etc. ETS staff were able to take advantage of the large numbers of subjects available to produce replicated studies with demonstrated generalizability, taking into account a large number of possible moderator and control variables. Furthermore, ETS began this test construction, administration, scoring, and analysis work at the beginning of the computer age, starting with punch card technology, transitioning to magnetic tape and electronic age technologies while keeping up with ongoing programs.

ETS broadened its scope of work into various occupational areas and workplace settings, with the formation, in 1974, of its Center for Occupational and Professional Assessment (COPA), originally under Benjamin Shimberg, and later through its Chauncey Group. The objectives of these centers are "to improve individual and organizational effectiveness and productivity in the workplace," offering a wide range of products and services for job analysis, alternative forms of test development and assessment (e.g., interactive videodiscs, computer based, computer simulations), training, certification, and career guidance. Examples of ETS-developed licensing and certification exams include those for the American Association of Plumbing Engineers, Association for Investment Management, and the American Association of Certified Public Accountants. For the U.S. government, ETS has carried out test development and evaluation projects for the State Department (Foreign Service Officer Examination), the Army (Armed Services Vocational Aptitude Battery), and the Peace Corps (language training).

ETS staff members have contributed major publications that have influenced the development of I–O psychology. An early example is the landmark book by Harold Gulliksen, *Theory of Mental Tests* (Gulliksen, 1950). Ledyard Tucker began his seminal work on developing more objective methods of factor analysis and providing new methodological advances, leading to three-mode factor analysis and interbattery methods of factor analysis (e.g., Tucker, 1955, 1958, 1967). Another major integrative effort was the work of John French on the description of aptitude and achievement tests in terms of rotated factors (French, 1951) and the very much used kit of reference tests of these factors (1951) and its later revision (French, Ekstrom, & Price, 1963).

Among the most influential contributions for I–O psychologists was the early and sustained research of Fred Lord on test and item response theory (IRT) dating back to the 1952s (see, e.g., Lord, 1952, 1980). And during his long career at ETS, Norman Frederiksen made notable contributions to both industrial and organizational psychology. These included pioneering work on job simulations in performance assessment, including "in-basket tests" (Frederiksen, 1965), evaluation of "response sets" in tests as performance predictors (Frederiksen, 1965), development of measures of creativity (Frederiksen & Ward, 1978), and the development of broader conceptions of intelligence (Fredriksen, 1986). It was also at ETS that John Hemphill published his important article "Job Descriptions for Executives" (Hemphill, 1959).

Another important contribution has been the programmatic work of Sam Messick, formerly an ETS vice-president, on different forms of test validity, in different assessment contexts, and the ethical and values implications in the interpretation of validation studies (Messick, 1975, 1980). More recently, ETS has been at the forefront of the use of computers in testing and in the adaptive testing movement (see, e.g., Wainer, 1990) and in efforts to go beyond multiple-choice tests to "constructed response" tests (Wainer & Thissen, 1992). Certainly, ETS has provided advances in measurement science and application that have been of significance to the field of I–O psychology over the last 55 years.

BUSINESS AND INDUSTRY CONSULTING ORGANIZATIONS

In this section I do not include I–O psychological research and development groups formed early in the history of I–O psychology within companies, such as at AT&T, IBM, GM, GE, Sears, P&G, Detroit Edison, Prudential, Standard Oil of New Jersey, and Merrill-Lynch. There are (or have been in many cases) far too many to identify and describe in a single chapter. The same is true with regard to consulting companies. The number of for-profit consulting organizations that have been created in the field of I–O psychology since World War II is too great to be covered in a single chapter. Four such organizations are described here: the Scott Company, which is generally credited with having been the first consulting firm to focus specifically on I–O psychology; the Psychological Corporation, which was formed in 1921, originally as a research and development organization; LIMRA International, which has roots that go back to 1916, and focuses exclusively on research, development, and training for the insurance industry; and Development Dimensions International (DDI), created in 1970 and has become one of the largest I–O consulting firms in the world.

The Scott Company

After the work of psychologists for the armed services during World War I wound down in 1919, Walter Dill Scott decided to start his own consulting firm rather than returning to the Carnegie staff (see also chap. 2). Thus, his was probably the first consulting firm in I–O psychology of the kind that has proliferated exponentially since World War II. He immediately created a staff of 8 or 10 from the group of psychologists he had worked with in the World War I projects and a few from the Carnegie program. This proved to be a very successful venture in the first few years. By 1923 his firm was providing consulting services to some 40 firms (Hilgard, 1987). Some of the big names in applied psychology of the day who worked with his staff on projects were J. B. Watson, Walter Van Dyke Bingham, Robert Yerkes, and E. L. Thorndike (Landy, 1997). In addition, Mary Holmes Stevens Hayes was one of the first women psychologists to be hired as a professional consultant (Koppes, 1997).

One of the major clients of Scott's firm was the U.S. Civil Service Commission. The consultants developed many selection tests, both mental and work sample, for screening candidates for a variety of civil service jobs. Scott also convinced the commission that they should have a psychologist on staff. Therefore, L. J. O'Rourke was hired as director of personnel research for the Civil Service Commission, probably the first psychologist to work for the federal government outside of the military. Other activities are noted throughout this volume.

The Scott Company, although very successful for a few years, disbanded in the early to mid-1920s, when Scott left to become president of Northwestern University, and several members of the firm's staff who were still on board were hired away by client companies. Among the few who might have remained, none assumed leadership of the company.

The Psychological Corporation

As described in chapter 2 of this text, James McKeen Cattell's relationship within Columbia University became so unbearable that in 1917 he was fired. According to a 1951 personal conversation with George Bennett, then president of the Psychological Corporation, Cattell sued Columbia University when he was dismissed from there without adequate justification. He won a $50,000 judgment with which he established the Psychological Corporation. The stated purpose of the corporation was "the advancement of psychology and the promotion of useful applications of psychology" (Viteles, 1932, p. 47).

Cattell promoted the idea to leaders in the field and sold stock to 170 psychologists, mostly academics. All of the money from the stock sale was to be applied to research. The corporation itself did not plan to conduct the research but to act merely as a clearing house between the general public and psychologists in university laboratories, where the research and construction of psychological examinations would be carried out for individual firms. The university laboratories were to pay to the corporation a portion of the fees charged to companies to cover overhead costs. Any surplus would be applied to research on basic problems.

The original board of directors read like a "who's who" in the field of psychology, including Angell of Yale, Bingham of Carnegie, Cattell as president, G. Stanley Hall of Clark, Hollingsworth of Columbia, Judd of Chicago, McDougal of Harvard, Pillsbury of Michigan, Scott of Northwestern, Seashore of Iowa, Terman of Stanford, Thorndike of Columbia as chairman of the board, Tichener of Cornell, Warren of Princeton, J. B. Watson of J. W. Thompson Company, Yerkes of the National Research Council, and Woodworth of Columbia (Cattell, 1923). This type of board composition continued through the 1950s. In fact, some of the same men listed here were still on the board in the early 1950s.

Originally, only the secretary-treasurer of the corporation was on salary. The corporation worked through universities essentially as a holding company for psychologists. State branches were set up, mostly in universities, in Massachusetts, Pennsylvania, Maryland, District of Columbia, Ohio, Michigan, Illinois, Iowa, and California. At that time, there was no plan to employ salaried experts. The corporation did not intend to engage in research and development activities but to sponsor research in existing university psychological laboratories. The corporation itself would only work to increase endowments for research. Its stated mission was to accomplish for psychology what the industrial research laboratories were doing for the sciences relevant to their purposes (Cattell, 1923).

This approach did not prove to be very successful, and in the mid-1920s the board decided to employ staff experts to conduct research and development work. This change began to take place soon after Cattell resigned as president in 1926. A small staff began to develop tests for industry and conduct a little market research. Paul Achilles, who had joined the staff at about that time, proved to be a savior by personally providing at least partial financial support as the corporation floundered financially in the late 1920s and early 1930s. It began to achieve financial stability in the late 1930s with its test sales and market research. By 1937, four divisions had been established: Clinical, Industrial, Marketing and Advertising, and Test. George K. Bennett became president, and through the ensuing years the corporation became increasingly financially secure. In 1970 it was sold to the book publisher Harcourt Brace Jovanovich. In subsequent years its focus shifted primarily to selection test development and sales. In a 2004 publication, the Psychological Corporation announced that its name was officially changed to Psych Corp.

LIMRA International[8]

LIMRA had several predecessor organizations committed to the same or a similar purpose, with name changes along the way. In 1916 a group of life insurance executives established an Association of Life Agency Offices (ALAO). When the Division of Applied Psychology was established at Carnegie Tech in 1915, Walter V. Bingham received a request from executives to start courses in salesmanship. Bingham recruited Walter Dill Scott to establish a Bureau of Salesmanship Research. After World War I, the name of that bureau was changed to the Bureau of Personnel Research. When Scott left Carnegie in 1919 to start his own consulting firm, the bureau became a separate entity focused exclusively on research for the life insurance business, called the Life Insurance Sales Research Bureau (LISRB), and was headquartered in New York City. In 1924 LISRB moved to Hartford, Connecticut. Then in 1946, ALAO and LISRB merged and became the Life Insurance Agency Management Association (LIAMA). In the early 1970s, in recognition of the increased use of the term *marketing* instead of *sales systems* and the key role of research, the name was again changed to the Life Insurance Marketing and Research Association and in 1994 became LIMRA International.

Over the ensuing years, LIMRA's mission expanded to include compilation of statistics for the industry regarding sales, premiums, persistency, and the like. Annual surveys provided benchmarks for various kinds of insurance offered, size of sales force, and research on sales and managerial compensation, marketing costs, and related issues. In recent years, these surveys have expanded to cover all kinds of financial products sold by insurance companies in addition to insurance. At the end of the 20th century, LIMRA also had research offices overseas in several countries, such the United Kingdom, Australia, South Africa, and others. In terms of amount of research generated, LIMRA is probably the largest of the nonprofit trade groups of its kind, with about 12 PhDs and many with master's degrees, statisticians, computer experts, and the like.

Consulting services were also provided to member companies, helping them to interpret data, research findings, and selection and training tools. LIMRA staffed dozens of schools held all over the world for managers, training directors, marketing officers from the home offices of large companies, and presidents of companies. LIMRA also organized and conducted many conferences for various purposes for member company representatives. The research division conducted its own conferences for the many psychologists and other researchers employed by individual companies, to share research and implications of studies carried out by LIMRA and member companies. In addition, LIMRA home office personnel were assigned member companies to visit annually to carry the results of all of the surveys and research to the marketing officers, explaining the relevance of the data to the respective company. Furthermore, the research division had many committees made up of member company officers who conferred with LIMRA staff regarding research and application needs.

In the field of industrial psychology, the LIMRA psychological research group is probably best known for its intensive research and applications work with the use of inventories of biodata for sales staff selection. An early study was conducted in 1932 by Arthur Kornhauser of the University of Chicago. He administered a group of personality and interest inventories containing about 500 items to about 1,000 insurance sales reps whose on-the-job performance was a matter of record. A number of items were found to correlate with sales success. These items were then administered to 300 newly hired agents and proved to be a useful selection tool.

In 1935, Albert Kurtz was hired to develop and validate a briefer inventory that proved in a study of more than 10,000 sales reps to predict success very well. Then in 1938, the best items

---

[8]I am indebted to Paul Thayer, a former senior vice-president of LIMRA, and to James Mitchel of the LIMRA staff for supplying most of the material in this section.

from both the Kornhauser and the Kurtz studies were combined to form the Aptitude Index. It proved to be the best predictor of success of insurance sales reps

A great deal of research over the ensuing years demonstrated that the validity of many biodata items was affected by age of the respondents and that scoring keys had to be updated periodically because of changes in the culture and economy. Researchers also found that the biodata items predicted turnover of sales staff.

Many prominent psychologists have been involved in the LIMRA research group. Rensis Likert was director of research in the late 1930s; Albert Kurtz was a pioneer in the use of biodata inventories for selection and is generally credited with being the first to recognize the need to cross-validate empirically developed scoring keys. Rains Wallace became vice-president of the Research Division in 1947 and Joseph Weitz was director of human relations research under Wallace. When Wallace left in 1966 to become president of AIR, Paul Thayer became vice-president of research and later senior vice-president of LIMRA. LIMRA produced three presidents of APA's Division 14 (now SIOP): Leonard Ferguson (1955), Rains Wallace (1963), and Paul Thayer (1976).

The LIMRA psychological research group also conducted a great deal of research on personnel activities in addition to selection research. Their intensive studies of the selection interview are well known in the field. These researchers also studied how the jobs of agents and sales managers are carried out to optimize performance, how manager selection can be improved, the development of job satisfaction survey instruments, turnover studies, and consumer research. Some of the first studies of the Realistic Job Preview were done at LIMRA. Training research was also a major activity of the group over the years. By the year 2000, the research staff had published more than 50 articles on their research in professional journals. LIMRA has evolved into one of the largest trade groups of its kind in the world. The psychologists on its staff have made many significant contributions to the field of I–O psychology.

Development Dimensions International (DDI)

Development Dimensions International (DDI), a human resources consulting company, began as the vision of Douglas Bray and William C. Byham in 1970 to help organizations use the assessment center method in the selection and development of managers. In addition to consulting services, the firm offered the first behavioral simulations and related assessment center materials, which covered multiple industries and job levels.

True to its entrepreneurial roots, DDI has continuously invested in research and development. As a result it has brought significant innovation to the methodology and instructional design used today for training, selection, and assessment. In the early 1970s, DDI introduced interaction management (IM), which became a commercially available leadership program based on behavior modeling. More than 16 million leaders around the world have been trained using IM, and it has been translated into 21 languages.

This was followed by the introduction of a worldwide application of behavior-based interview training—targeted selection. The system gained immediate popularity because multiple research studies proved its accuracy and it met all Equal Employment Opportunity Commission guidelines. It has been adopted by thousands of successful companies worldwide—8,000 people a day are hired using targeted selection. In the spring of 2002, "Targeted Selection: Access," an online support tool, provided managers and recruiters hiring tools at their fingertips.

Other areas where the consulting firm has designed leading-edge solutions are around performance management and the development and assessment of executives. Most of DDI's new products have been honored to be "Top New Training Products of the Year" by *Human Resources Executive* magazine.

What began in the basement of Byham's home has grown into more than 1,000 experienced professionals in 75 offices in 26 countries. Most of its offices are wholly owned subsidiaries. The client list has matured into a who's who of the world's most successful organizations. They partner with 75% of the Fortune 500 companies. Programs and services have been translated into as many as 21 languages.

Byham, Bray, and their DDI colleagues have authored hundreds of white papers, articles, and books, including some bestsellers such as *Zapp! The Lightening of Empowerment*. Research to explore key human resource issues and to evaluate the effectiveness of its own implementations has also been at the heart of DDI. Many DDI associates participate in various forms of research, and the firm has its own full-time research group—the Center for Applied Behavioral Research (CABER). CABER produces *The Leadership Forecast*, an annual look at key leadership practices, along with studies such as *Recruitment and Selection Practices, Succession Management Practices*, and *The Globalization of HR*. In 2002, DDI and The Conference Board collaborated on a report entitled *Developing Leaders for 2010*. With its continuing innovation, global capabilities, and breadth of experience, DDI probably represents the most significant and successful entrepreneurial enterprise in the history of I–O psychology. The expansion of DDI seems to epitomize the rapid growth of many I–O consulting firms in the last 30 or 40 years.

GOVERNMENTAL ORGANIZATIONS

Throughout this volume, in other chapters, the role of the U.S. government in the historical development of I–O psychology is made clear. This short section, in the context of the present chapter, is mainly an acknowledgment of the impact these various agencies had on the evolution of I–O psychology. In terms of direct influence on so many areas of I–O and other fields of basic and applied psychology, the military services and their personnel and training and human performance research organizations have had a major impact. Much of the influence has been through funding of research to university and private organizations, and much of it has been due to the internal research of military organizations, conducted on a scale and with numbers of subjects not possible in industry or academia. The reader is referred to chapter 7 on the role of the military in I–O psychology as well as chapter 10 on human factors, for much of this history.

Of course, I–O psychologists work in many other government agencies, and, historically, a number of these organizations have made major contributions to the science and applications of I–O psychology. Psychologists in these agencies play several different roles: as advisors/consultants to the agency, as developers and/or evaluators of research proposals for outside contracts to assist in solving human resource problems, as liaisons with contractors working on such contracts, and as members of an internal ongoing research and development organization within the agency. Historically, a number of such governmental research groups of psychologists have made direct major contributions to the field of industrial psychology, have affected the functioning of these agencies, and have contributed significantly to the national welfare.

U.S. Employment Service (U.S.E.S.)[9]

An early example is the occupational research program of the U.S. Employment Service (U.S.E.S.). In 1934, President Franklin Roosevelt authorized the establishment of the U.S.E.S. to examine methods for dealing with the enormous unemployment problem. Issues of transfer-

---

[9]Material for this section was prepared by Edwin A. Fleishman.

ability of skills across occupational areas were to be dealt with. Carroll Shartle headed the staff of the Occupational Research Program (later to be called the Occupational Analysis Section of the U.S.E.S.). This unit produced what became the *Dictionary of Occupational Titles* and other job analysis innovations to rate jobs on such factors as training time required, transferability of skills, and the impact of working conditions (see Primoff & Fine, 1988). Under Shartle, Beatrice Dvorak, an early female psychologist, was chief of the Worker Analysis Section. Ernest McCormick was a staff member from 1935 to 1939, and Sidney Fine and Ernest Primoff joined in 1940.

Another achievement of the U.S.E.S., a division of the Department of Labor, was the development of the General Aptitude Test Battery (GATB), consisting of cognitive, perceptual, and psychomotor ability tests, used since 1947 in occupational counseling by the Department of Labor to test and refer applicants to businesses unwilling or not capable of engaging in test practices. The GATB is still used to match job seekers to requests for job applicants from private and public sector employers through offices located in 1,800 communities around the United States. About 19 million people move through the system annually! Through various historical periods, including later contexts involving issues of racial and gender fairness and validity generalization, the battery has been reevaluated, revalidated, modified, and continuously studied (see Hartigan & Wigdor, 1989; Wigdor & Sackett, 1993). The unprecedented database has been useful to many I–O researchers, including meta-analyses and statistical methodology and utility studies (see, e.g., Schmidt & Hunter, 1977).

United States Civil Service Commission/Personnel Research and Development Center[10]

The Personnel Research Section of the U.S. Civil Service Commission (USCSC) and its current successor, the Personnel Research and Development Center (PRDC) of the Office of Personnel Management (OPM), have been continuously engaged in test development and personnel research for more than 80 years. PRDC is the largest civilian personnel research center, serving 1.8 million federal government employees. The government agency carries out its mission in support of merit principles for fair testing, established originally under the Civil Service Reform Act of 1883. The original mandate called for the "fair testing for public service of relative capacity and fitness for government jobs." Later, in 1978, under the Civil Service Reform Act of 1978, the restated mandate called for the selection of qualified individuals "solely on the basis of relative ability, knowledge, and skills, after fair and open competition." Clearly, this government agency has had a major historical role in contributing to the science and practice of industrial and organizational psychology. We can acknowledge only a few key individuals in this history, along with some representative studies.

In 1926, the annual payroll of the Civil Service exceeded $800,000,000 (Filer & O'Rourke, 1923). The need for methods of selection as a possible means of improving productivity of the workforce became evident even earlier. Thus, in 1917, the Civil Service Commission consulted with E. L. Thorndike and W. D. Scott to determine the applicability of psychological methods for developing tests for applicants for civil service positions. Several preliminary studies were reviewed, including the administration of the Army Alpha to civilian clerical employees in 1919 and an early study by Robert Watson in the Baltimore Post Office. Consequently, in 1922, a Personnel Research Section of the U.S. Civil Service Commission was established with L. J. O'Rourke appointed as its first director, a position he held until 1943.

---

[10]Material for this section was prepared by Lorraine Eyde and Edwin A. Fleishman.

O'Rourke was an important figure in the early history of industrial psychology, responsible for many pioneering innovations relevant to the later development of I–O psychology. He was among the first to call attention to the importance of job analysis as an essential early step in the selection test development process, he defined the critical steps in the test construction and validation process, and he applied these principles and procedures in the large-scale program of the Civil Service Commission (see O'Rourke, 1926). O'Rourke also contributed studies on how to improve the reliability and validity of the selection interview, including studies on the improvements obtained by training and practice (O'Rourke, 1930), and he also demonstrated how multiple criteria of job performance could be applied to test validation. It was fortunate that O'Rourke retained his professional identification and responsibilities as an industrial psychologist and disseminated much of his work in professional journals and in other publications; thus, this work at the U.S. Civil Service Commission founds its way into early industrial psychology textbooks (e.g., Viteles, 1932).

Aside from the continual development, updating, and revisions of selection and promotion procedures for the tremendous variety and range of jobs in the government world of work, a number of innovative contributions have had relevance to the field of I–O psychology at various historical periods. In 1944, Ernest Primoff transferred to USCSC from the Occupational Research Program of the U.S. Employment Office (see previous section). He proposed that USCSC's examinations be based on competencies (which he called "job elements"), with less emphasis on job experience, and he developed a job analysis system (called th Job Element Method) for identifying these elements in jobs through job element ratings and for evaluating applicants on the basis for their demonstrated competencies on these elements (Primoff, 1975). He also developed the J-coefficient, a forerunner of "synthetic validity," a system of weighting these elements to estimate the validity of tests that measured these elements (see Fleishman & Quaintance, 1984; Primoff, 1959; Primoff & Eyde, 1988).

An example of a contribution to I–O psychology was the book published by Dorothy Adkins, then chief of test development at USCSC, titled *Construction and Analysis of Achievement Tests* (Adkins, 1948), based in large measure on the experience and knowledge gained in the extensive program of proficiency and achievement testing that had been developed at the Civil Service Commission. Another example occurred in the 1980s, when Frank Schmidt, as a staff member, was able to capitalize on the huge database available at the USCSC for his work on validity generalization. In his collaborations with other staff, notably Kenneth Perlman and Hannah Rothstein, as well as with John Hunter, landmark studies were carried out and published estimating the "true" validities of ability tests and further refining the methodologies for meta-analysis (see Schmidt & Hunter, 2002). Several other contributions to I–O psychology exist as well (e.g., Colberg, 1984; Colberg, Nester, Reilly, & Northrup, 1991; Eyde et al., 1993; Eyde, Gregory, Muldrow, & Mergen, 1999; Hayes & Reilly, 2002).

During its long history, the personnel research function at the original Civil Service Commission endured a number of reorganizations and name changes. Table A.3 in the Appendix provides a complete chronology of these organizational changes, including the names and terms of the various directors. A major change occurred in 1980 when the name of the USCSC was changed to the Office of Personnel Management, with the Personnel Research and Development Center (PRDC) representing its primary research and development activity. In 1990, PRDC representatives (primarily Kenneth Perlman and Marilyn Gowing) were among 12 members of the Advisory Panel for the Dictionary of Occupational Titles, chartered in 1990 by Elizabeth Dole, Secretary of Labor, to recommend alternative approaches to the *Dictionary of Occupational Titles,* taking into account the current state of the art and national needs. The resulting recommendation was the impetus for the U.S. Department of Labor's support of the contract to develop the O*Net project (Peterson et al., 1999), which was the development of a new national occupational information system.

In the mid-1990s, during the tenure of Marilyn Gowing, PRDC began doing contracted work for other government agencies, and its mission was expanded from developing standardized tests to providing a broad range of human resource research, products, and services. These included individual, organizational, and outcome assessment. Some of these developments are described in a special issue of *Human Resources Management in the Public Sector* (Gowing & Lindholm, 2002).

INFORMAL ORGANIZATIONS OF I–O PSYCHOLOGISTS

As industrial psychology began to explode as a recognized and valuable discipline in the post–World War II years, the number and variety of applications in the field also grew exponentially. Actually, the majority of psychologists working in industry before the war had not been trained as "industrial" psychologists. At that time, there were not more than a half dozen psychology departments in the United States where one could earn a PhD with a specialty in industrial psychology (see also chap. 5). After the war, as the numbers trained in I–O psychology increased greatly, social networks began to form among those psychologists eager to exchange knowledge and experiences. These networks were often in the form of organized groups of those with similar jobs in different companies, groups of industrial psychologists in a regional area, and a few groups for those who were interested in interorganizational collaborative ties, strategic alliances, and joint ventures. It was a great way for individual psychologists to expand their knowledge and skill base. They could get a certain amount of explicit knowledge from textbooks or workshops, but the associations provided by informal groups often enabled them to gain not only explicit knowledge but also the less accessible, but often very valuable, tacit knowledge. In many ways, these informal organizations were very important to the field of I–O psychology in providing strong networks of individual psychologists who gained personally and professionally from their affiliation with such groups.

A few of such groups are described here that were rather well known and that seem to have made a significant contribution to the development of individuals and the amplification of research, development, and applications in the field as a whole. Because of space limitations, we must omit many similar and valuable groups of this kind, especially those organized in recent years. One, for example, that was organized in the 1960s with more eclectic ground rules for membership, the Summit group, has stimulated exchanges between I–O psychologists in academia, industry, consulting, and other types of employment situations for I–O psychologists. Another important organization not discussed here is the International and Assessment Council, formed in the 1990s to deal with selection testing issues.

Psychologists Full Time in Industry

At an APA meeting in 1947, a group of about 15 or 20 psychologists who had full-time jobs in industrial companies met in Marion Bills' (an industrial psychologist) hotel room to discuss a plan to schedule half-day meetings each year at the annual APA conference to exchange experiences, schedule presentations of major projects underway, and the like (Koppes & Bauer, in press)[11] Each year a volunteer in the group would arrange with APA's Conference Committee to schedule a room for such a meeting.

The interest in these annual meetings grew rapidly in the ensuing years as more and more companies employed psychologists as full-time members of their personnel staffs. Activities

---

[11]About 4 years later, Marion Bills became the first female president of APA's Division of Industrial Psychology.

for the group became more structured, with committees formed for planning, record keeping, and correspondence. In fact, in about the late 1950s or early 1960s, the group became too large to be handled on an informal, volunteer basis. For example, although the mailing list was no more than about 100, mailing expenses and the like could be handled by a volunteer member's employer. As it got much larger, this arrangement began to become difficult to justify. Therefore, at about that time, these annual get-togethers at the APA conferences for psychologists employed full-time in industry were phased out. Nevertheless, for the first 10 or 15 postwar years, this group probably did stimulate a wider variety of I–O research and applications activities in industry than would have been the case without the structured exchange these annual meetings provided.

Regional Groups

The Metropolitan New York Association for Applied Psychology, organized in 1939, is generally acknowledged as the first regional informal association for industrial psychologists. Actually, membership in that group was not limited to industrial psychologists but included anyone interested in applied psychology in general. Thus, the membership included clinicians, vocational counselors, school psychologists, and others in applied fields. This organization is probably the only regional association that existed before World War II. Immediately after the war, regional associations began to be formed in many areas of the country. In almost all cases, these associations were limited to those identified as industrial psychologists. Most associations that were formed in those early years are still extant today. In addition, many more were formed in the ensuing years.

In a 1997 article in *The Industrial–Organizational Psychologist (TIP),* 18 regional groups of industrial psychologists were listed. Some were centered in a city, such as Chicago, Houston, or Atlanta; some were centered in a region, such as Central Florida, Puget Sound, or South Florida; and several were statewide, as in Ohio, Michigan, and Texas. In addition, seven additional groups focused just on selection testing matters and 36 on membership in an "organizational development network" (Baker, 1997). In a similar article in a *TIP* 2001 issue, 29 regional groups were identified, a few in foreign countries, in addition to those groups that focused on testing, and the 36 regional organizational development network groups mentioned in the 1997 article (Benitez, 2001). Almost all of these regional groups indicated that they met at least once a year, and the Metro New York Association met monthly during the academic year. In recent years, a standing column in *TIP* highlights regional organizations both within and outside the United States (see Thompson, 2005).

The Dearborn Conference Group

After World War II, when many large companies began to establish personnel research units in their personnel departments, some of the persons involved in that activity became interested in forming an informal association to exchange experiences. At an American Management Association conference in 1950 in Detroit, where personnel research was included as a subtopic, representatives from about a dozen companies held a separate meeting at the Dearborn Inn near Detroit, where they planned a formal meeting to discuss the possibility of organizing such a group. Douglas McGregor, then president of Antioch College, was asked to sponsor the meeting.

This organizing meeting was held on the Antioch campus in Yellow Springs, Ohio, in May 1951. The attendees at the meeting were 14 members of the personnel staffs of companies that had personnel research or related components in their personnel departments. These were mostly large companies, but not all were among the largest in the United States. The companies represented were General Motors, AT&T, Dupont, Ford, US Rubber, Sears, Inland Steel, Esso Standard Oil, Chesapeake & Ohio RR, Detroit Edison, Eli Lilly, Armstrong Cork, and Socony-Vacuum Oil Co. The representatives were mostly personnel executives in those companies. Only three were PhD psychologists: Ralph Bender of Dupont, William Kendall of Chesapeake & Ohio, and John Rapparlie of US Rubber. In the following years, most of those added to the group were PhD psychologists who headed a personnel research unit in their company, some as replacements for the executive representative of the respective company and others from additional companies. In the next 3 or 4 years, additions were Bill McGehee of Fieldcrest Mills, Bob Selover of Prudential, Wendell Wood of International Harvester, Ed Henry of Esso, and Herb Meyer of General Electric. In fact, after about 1960 every new member was an industrial psychologist, so that by about the mid-1980s all active members were PhD psychologists.

The group met twice a year, in the spring and fall. Discussions at the meetings focused not only on company projects of the members but also on general topics and problems relating to human resources management, such as employee productivity, employee morale, union–management relations, compensation policies and practices, management development, working environments, and job enrichment. Usually the designated chair for an upcoming meeting (the role was rotated) scheduled at least one such topic for general discussion, in addition to the exchange of information about current projects in the member companies.

At the early meetings (in the 1950s), McGregor played an important role in these discussions, often summarizing and interpreting the implications of issues raised, as seen by an outsider with a more theoretical orientation than that held by the company-employed members. These discussions often seemed to result in newly initiated research and development activities in the member companies. They sometimes resulted in expository articles in management or personnel journals by one or more members in attendance. A number of members believed that a very intensive discussion at an early meeting of the group on employee productivity and morale problems and related union–management relations issues contributed to McGregor's formulation of his "theory X–Y," delineated subsequently in his classic book, *The Human Side of Enterprise* (McGregor, 1960; see also chaps. 14 and 15). Another lengthy and somewhat heated discussion of problems encountered with performance appraisal policies and programs seemed to have led to McGregor's widely read *Harvard Business Review* article titled "An Uneasy Look at Performance Appraisal" (McGregor, 1957).

Over the years, additional members were added to the Dearborn Conference Group to maintain the active membership at about 17, as some members retired, changed jobs in their respective companies, resigned when they went into consulting or academia, and so forth. The Dearborn Conference Group was the first of the several similar research-oriented groups organized in the 1950s and 1960s—that is, small groups of I–O psychologists, based on personal membership. It has probably been the most active and viable of the groups of this kind in terms of survival. In 2003, it was still meeting semiannually, continuing the tradition of the active exchange of information and experiences that was envisioned by that first group of professionals who decided to organize the Dearborn Conference Group in 1950.

The No-Name Group

About 3 years after the Dearborn Conference Group was up and running, a number of psychologists involved in personnel research in large companies decided to form a similar exchange group with membership limited to I–O psychologists who had responsibility for personnel research in their companies. Robert Finkle, then of the Metropolitan Insurance Company, hosted a small organization meeting in the spring of 1954. Company representatives at that meeting included John Gorsuch of US Steel, Edwin Henry of Standard Oil, Burt Knauft, then of DuPont and soon after of Aetna, Herb Meyer of GE, John Rapparlie of Owens-Illinois, and Grey Worbois of Detroit Edison. This organizing group decided to invite about 10 additional psychologists from large companies that had active personnel research programs and to meet three times a year on a regular basis. The additional persons added at that time were Brent Baxter of Prudential, Jon Bentz of Sears, Douglas Bray of AT&T, Orlo Crissey of GM, Marvin Dunnette of 3M, Harry Laurent of Standard Oil, Walter MacNamara of IBM, Lynn Munger of Singer, and Sy Levy of Pillsbury. Ground rules established were similar to those adopted by the Dearborn Conference Group.

At the first two or three meetings, the name for the group was discussed with little consensus reached. Therefore, the group finally decided to be known merely as the "No-Name Group." Over the following years the composition of the group changed as some members retired, others assumed management positions that no longer dealt with the personnel research function, and a few died. Those members who left industry for academia, such as Marv Dunnette (early), Mike Beer, Don Grant, and Herb Meyer, were not dropped from membership, as was the case for members of the Dearborn Conference Group who made a similar move.

The Mayflower Group[12]

This group is a little different from other informal groups in that instead of being eclectic in their topics of interest in I–O psychology, they focus exclusively on organization surveys. The group organized in 1971 when professionals from large private-sector companies that had active attitude survey programs decided to form a consortium to share their survey experiences and leverage the value of their respective surveys. A first organizing meeting was held in the Mayflower Hotel in Washington, DC, and was attended by representatives from 18 companies.

In 1976 the company representatives incorporated as a nonprofit group to be supported by dues from membership companies. The Mayflower Group membership consists of companies rather than individuals. Each company designates a member and an alternate to represent it, but these can be changed as job assignments change or for other reasons. The membership expanded over the years so that by 1995 it consisted of 42 companies in six of the major "industrial groups" identified by *Fortune* magazine. Ninety-three percent of those companies were in *Fortune's* list of "Most Admired Companies in America," and 25% were ranked number one in their respective "industrial group." Sixteen of the companies also have active international survey programs.

Objectives formulated by the member representatives were to (a) develop "core" survey items that all members could use, (b) maintain norms that all could use, (c) exchange information on practices, and (d) conduct research on attitude measurement. Originally 18 core items were formulated, but this list was expanded to 34 by the mid-1990s. Continuing research is conducted to improve on the core items. Each member company is required to submit survey data on a minimum of 18 of the 34 core items at least biannually, identifying the nature of the organization surveyed. All such data are considered anonymously and confidentially in the normative data submitted to the membership companies. Norms are computed separately for each of the six identified industrial groups.

The membership representatives are highly organized, with a board of governors and many standing and ad hoc committees on such topics as norms, membership, research, programs, and international issues. Meetings of all member company representatives are held semiannually where such topics are discussed as feedback, data display, use of surveys with senior man-

---

[12]The major reference source for the material in this section was Johnson (1996).

agement, and integrating survey results with business objectives and human resources practices. A few of the well-known I–O psychologists who have been active in the Mayflower Group are Alan Kraut, then of IBM; Nancy Tippins, then of Exxon; Tapas Sen of AT&T; Walter Tornow, then of Control Data; and Lise Saari, then of Boeing and now of IBM. All in all, the Mayflower Group is an important group in I–O psychology. It has played a key role in advancing the art and practice of organizational surveys.

The CINCON Group[13]

The CINCON Group was organized during the APA convention held in Cincinnati, Ohio, in 1959, hence the name CINCON. This was an informal group that did not have officers, clear objectives, membership requirements, or dues structure. However, the clear intent was to meet periodically, with an agenda for that meeting to include presenters and mutually arrived at topics. The idea was to have a mix of I–O psychologists, some practicing and doing research industry and others teaching and doing I–O-related research in academic or private research organizations. There was a chair to the extent that someone took responsibility for putting together an agenda, based mainly on the group's desires at the close of a previous meeting, or soliciting a presenter relevant to the discussion. The second important role was to choose, in advance, the restaurant for dinner. Expenses were paid by the participants or their organization. Most but not all the participants were close to the New York or Chicago area, where meetings would alternate. Most meetings were held in hotels and were 1- to 1½-day affairs.

Perhaps the distinguishing feature of this group was the mix of I–O psychologists from universities and industry, with emphases on ongoing or planned current research by participants relevant to the science and practice of I–O psychology. Or those in industry would share a need in their company that might stimulate research questions or reveal problems or unknown relevant research. This group met perhaps three or four times per year. The membership of this group was fairly stable over many years with new members invited from time to time. Active members over much of this history of this group in the 1950s and 1960s included, among others, Joseph Weitz of New York University, Donald Grant of AT&T, Phillip Ash then of Inland Steel, Robert Dugan of State Farm Insurance, Edwin Fleishman then of Yale University, John Rapparlie of Libby Owens Glass, William Mollenkopf of Procter & Gamble, John Hinrichs, Consultant, Virginia Schein of New York University, Robert Finkle of the Metropolitan Insurance Co., and Patricia Dyer of IBM.

The group is notable in the informal history of I–O psychology because of its interchange of ideas between and among practitioners and academics, in the best tradition of the scientist–practitioner model. The group's activities lent support of this model at a crucial state in the history of I–O psychology (Edwin Fleishman, personal communication, August 7, 2005).

SUMMARY

Applied psychology grew very slowly in the early history of psychology. As described in chapters 1 and 3, when psychology as a science first appeared in the last half of the 19th century, it was usually an off-shoot of the philosophy department in universities. However, the early psychologists were generally determined that, unlike philosophy, their field would develop as a pure science, with measurement used as in the physical sciences. Psychologists who became interested in applying psychology to real-world problems often became outcasts in the profes-

---

[13]Material for this section was prepared by Edwin A. Fleishman.

sion. They did not qualify for membership in the American Psychological Association. Some, like Walter Dill Scott, engaged in their applied work surreptitiously. They knew their colleagues would regard such activity with disdain.

As more and more psychologists became interested in applied research and development in the second decade of the 20th century, some organizations devoted to this work began to appear. Nevertheless, publication customs of the time indicate that applied research and development were predominantly individual rather than group endeavors. In the first 5 years of the publication of the *Journal of Personnel Research* (1921–1925), the primary outlet at that time for research that would be described as industrial psychology, 93% of the articles were by a single author. Of the other 7%, almost all were by only two authors. In the first years, the *Journal of Applied Psychology (JAP)* was more eclectic, covering clinical, school, counseling, and consumer topics along with some industrial psychological topics. It also featured many exhortative or expository articles along with research articles. But even in that journal, in its first 5 years (1917–1921), more than 80% of the articles were by a single author. Only three out of a total of 185 articles were by three authors and 30 were by dual authors, in many cases by husband and wife teams. By contrast, in the last 5 years of the 20th century (1996–2000), only 10% of the articles were by a single author. More than half were by three or more authors (see also chap. 1).

Even in the immediate post–World War II years, in the first 5 years of the publication of the then new *Personnel Psychology* (1948–1952), 73% of the articles were by a single author, and only 4 out of a total of 152 articles were by triple authorship. For that same journal in the last 5 years of the 20th century, only 9% of the articles were by a single author, and more than half were by three or more authors.

These figures seem to provide graphic evidence that research and development in I–O psychology have become more of a team rather than an individual activity. This trend has coincided with the exponential growth in numbers of organized groups of I–O psychologists in the last 50 years. Organized groups of I–O psychologists, whether formal or informal, in academic, research, industrial, or even in social settings, have provided stimulation, cross-fertilization, and individual development that have resulted in much greater volume, diversity, and importance of the contributions of I–O psychologists than would have been the case if research and applications in this field had continued to be primarily individual pursuits.

To conclude, this chapter provides an overview of a number of organizations to demonstrate the impact of such organizations on an evolving I–O psychology. However, these selections are not the only organizations important in the history of I–O psychology. As stated earlier, this chapter did not cover the work of individuals and units within business and industrial organizations (e.g., AT&T, Sears), which was central to integrating science and practice. For information prior to 1970 on contributions of these types of organizations, readers are referred to Campbell, Dunnette, Lawler, and Weick (1970). Furthermore, the historical contributions to I–O psychology of a few major government agency programs were described, although it is acknowledged that individuals in many government agencies have had an impact on this field. Many of them are referenced in other chapters throughout the book. Finally, the evolution of I–O psychology consulting firms is an interesting story of adaptation (e.g., Bill Macey and Personnel Research Associates, now Valtera), especially when the role of I–O psychology was reduced in the 1980s and many from internal positions in business organizations started their own firms. This history would help us understand the influx of consultants in the discipline of I–O psychology and the subsequent impact on the science of and practice of I–O psychology (Benjamin Schneider, personal communication, April 25, 2004). Further research on the role of organizational influences in the evolution of I–O psychology is warranted.

REFERENCES

Adkins, D. G. (1948). *The construction and analysis of achievement tests.* Washington, DC: U.S. Government Printing Office.

Alluisi, E. A., & Fleishman, E. A. (Eds.). (1982). *Human performance and productivity: Vol. 3. Stress and performance effectiveness.* Hillsdale, NJ: Lawrence Erlbaum Associates.

Baker, T. G. (1997). Directory of I–O groups. *The Industrial–Organizational Psychologist, 34,* 41–46.

Benetiz, E. (2001). I–O related groups. *The Industrial–Organizational Psychologist, 39*(2), 113–117.

Benjamin, L. T., Jr. (1997a). Organized industrial psychology before Division 14: The ACP and the AAAP (1930–1945). *Journal of Applied Psychology, 82,* 459–466.

Benjamin, L. T., Jr. (1997b). A history of Division 14 (Society for Industrial and Organizational Psychology). In D. A. Dewsbury (Ed.), *Unification through division: Histories of the divisions of the American Psychological Association* (Vol. 2, pp. 101–126). Washington, DC: American Psychological Association.

Benjamin, L. T., Jr. (2002). Hugo Münsterberg: Portrait of an applied psychologist. In G. A. Kimble & M. Wertheimer (Eds.), *Portraits of pioneers in psychology* (Vol. 4). Mahwah, NJ: Lawrence Erlbaum Associates.

Bingham, W. V. (1928). The Personnel Research Federation in 1927: Annual report of the director. *Personnel Journal, 7,* 299–313.

Campbell, J. P., Dunnette, M. D., Lawler, E. E., Jr., & Weick, K. (1970). *Managerial behavior, performance and effectiveness.* New York: McGraw-Hill.

Cannell, C. F., & Kahn, R. L. (1984). Some factors in the origin and development of the Institute for Social Research, the University of Michigan. *American Psychologist, 39,* 1256–1266.

Cattell, J. M. (1923). The Psychological Corporation. *The Annuals of the American Academy of Political and Social Science, 110,* 165–167.

Civil Service Act of 1883, Chapter 27, January 16, 1883.

Civil Service Reform Act of 1978. Public Law 95-454, October 13, 1978.

Colberg, M. (1984). Towards a taxonomy of verbal tests based on logic. *Educational and Psychological Measurement, 44,* 113–120.

Colberg, M., Nester, M. A., Reilly, S. M., & Northrup, L. C. (1991). *The use of illogical biases in the measurement of reasoning abilities.* Paper presented at the IX International Congress of Logic, Methodology, and Philosophy of Science, Uppsala, Sweden.

Cooper, M., Schiflett, S., Korotkin, A. L., & Fleishman, E. A. (1984). *Command and control systems: Techniques for assessing team performance.* Washington, DC: Advanced Research Resources Organization.

Dunnette, M. D., & Fleishman, E. A. (Eds.). (1982). *Human performance and productivity: Vol. 1. Human capability assessment.* Hillsdale, NJ: Lawrence Erlbaum Associates.

Eisenberg, T., Fosen, R. H., & Glickman, A. S. (1973). *Police-community action: A program for change in police community behavior patterns.* New York: Praeger.

ETS through the years: A 50th anniversary album. (1998). Princeton, NJ: Educational Testing Service.

Eyde, L. D., Gregory, D. J., Muldrow, T. M., & Mergen, P. K. (1999, August). *High-performance leaders: A competency model.* (PDRC-99-02). Washington, DC: U.S. Office of Personnel Management, Personnel Resources and Development Center.

Eyde, L. D., Robertson, G. J., Krug, S. E., Moreland, K. L., Robertson, A. G., Shewan, C. M., Harrison, P. L., et al. (1993). *Responsible test use: Case studies for assessing human behavior.* Washington, DC: American Psychological Association.

Ferguson, L. W. (1952). A look across the years 1920–1950. In L. L. Thurstone (Ed.), *Applications of psychology: Essays to honor Walter V. Bingham* (pp. 7–22). New York: Harper.

Ferguson, L. W. (1962–1965). *The heritage of industrial psychology* [14 pamphlets]. Hartford, CT: Finlay.

Filer, H. A., & O'Rourke, L. J. (1923). Progress on civil service tests. *Journal of Personnel Research, 1,* 484–520.

Flanagan, J. C. (1984). The American Institutes for Research. *American Psychologist, 39*(11), 1272–1276.

Fleishman, E. A. (1953a). The description of supervisory behavior. *Journal of Applied Psychology, 37,* 1–6.

Fleishman, E. A. (1953b). Human relations training and supervisory behavior. *Personnel Psychology, 6,* 205–222.

Fleishman, E. A. (1979). Evaluating physical abilities required by jobs. *Personnel Administrator, 21,* 82–90.

Fleishman, E. A., & Harris, E. F. (1962). Patterns of leadership behavior related to employee grievances and turnover. *Personnel Psychology, 15,* 43–56.

Fleishman, E. A., Harris, E. F., & Burtt, H. E. (1955). *Leadership and supervision in industry: An evaluation of a supervisory training program.* Columbus: Bureau of Educational Research, Ohio State University.

Fleishman, E. A., & Quaintance, M. K. (1984). *Taxonomies of human performance: The description of human tasks.* Orlando, FL: Academic Press.

Frantilla, A. (1998). *Social science in the public interest: A fiftieth-year history of the Institute for Social Research*. Ann Arbor: University of Michigan.

Frederiksen, N. (1962). Factors in in-basket performance. *Psychological Monographs, 76*(22, Whole No. 541).

Frederiksen, N. (1965). Response set scores as predictors of performance. *Personnel Psychology, 18*, 225–244.

Frederiksen, N. (1986). Toward a broader conception of human intelligence. *American Psychologist, 41*, 445–452.

Frederiksen, N., & Ward, W. C. (1978). Measures for the study of creativity in scientific problem-solving. *Applied Psychological Measurement, 20*, 1–24.

French, J. W. (1951). The description of aptitude and achievement tests in terms of rotated factors. *Psychometric Monographs, No. 5*.

French, J. W., Ekstrom, R. B., & Price, L. A. (1963). *manual and kit of reference tests for cognitive factors*. Princeton, NJ: Educational Testing Service.

Glickman, A. S., Hahn, C. P., Fleishman, E. A., & Baxter, B. (1968). *Top management development and succession*. New York: Macmillan.

Gowing, M. K., & Lindholm, M. L. (2002). Human resources management in the public sector. *Special Issue: Human Resources Management in the Public Sector, 283*–296.

Gulliksen, H. (1950). *Theory of mental tests*. New York: Wiley.

Halpin, A. W., & Winer, B. J. (1957). A factorial study of the leader behavior descriptions. In R.. M. Stogdill & A. D. Coons (Eds.), *Leader behavior: Its description and measurement*. Columbus: Bureau of Business Research, Ohio State University.

Hartigan, J. A., & Wigdor, A. K. (1989). *Fairness in employee testing: Validity generalization, priority issues, and the General Aptitude Test Battery*. Washington, DC: National Academic Press.

Hayes, T. L., & Reilly, S. M. (2004, April). The criterion-related validity of logic-based measurement tests. In T. L. Hayes (Chair), *The validity of logic-based measurement for selection and promotion*. Symposium conducted at the 17th Annual Conference of the Society for Industrial and Organizational Psychology.

Hemphill, J. K. (1959). Job descriptions for executives. *Harvard Business Review, 37*, 11–22.

Hilgard, E. R. (1987). *Psychology in America: A historical survey*. New York: Harcourt Brace Jovanovich.

Hogan, J. C., Ogden, G. D., Gebhardt, D. C., & Fleishman, E. A. (1980). Reliability and validity of methods for evaluating perceived physical effort. *Journal of Applied Psychology, 65*, 672–679.

Hollenbeck, J. R. (1998). Personnel Psychology's citation leadership articles: The first five decades. *Personnel Psychology, 51*, 817–818.

Howell, W. C., & Fleishman, E. A. (Eds.). (1982). *Human performance and productivity: Vol. 2. Information processing and decision making*. Hillsdale, NJ: Lawrence Erlbaum Associates.

HumRRO. (2001). *HumRRO: The first 50 years*. Alexandria, VA: Author.

Institute for Social Research. (1998). *50 years of social science in the public interest*. Ann Arbor: University of Michigan.

Johnson, R. H. (1996). Life in the consortium: The Mayflower Group. In A. I. Kraut (Ed.), *Organization surveys* (pp. 285–309). San Francisco: Jossey-Bass.

Katz, D., & Kahn, R. L. (1966). *The social psychology of organizations*. New York: Wiley.

Koppes, L. L. (1997). American female pioneers of industrial and organizational psychology during the early years. *Journal of Applied Psychology, 82*, 500–515.

Koppes, L. L., & Bauer, A. M. (in press). Marion Almira Bills: Industrial psychology pioneer bridging science and practice. In D. A. Dewsbury, L. T. Benjamin, Jr., M. Wertheimer (Eds.), *Portraits of pioneers in psychology* (Vol. 6). Washington, DC: American Psychological Association.

Landy, F. J. (1992). Hugo Münsterberg: Victim or visionary? *Journal of Applied Psychology, 77*, 787–802.

Landy, F. J. (1997). Early influences on the development of industrial and organizational psychology. *Journal of Applied Psychology, 82*, 467–477.

Lawshe, C. H., & Weiss, H. M. (1991). History of industrial/organizational psychology at Purdue University. *The Industrial–Organizational Psychologist, 28*, 52–57.

Likert, R. (1961). *New patterns of management*. New York: McGraw-Hill.

Likert, R. (1967). *The human organization: Its management and value*. New York: McGraw-Hill.

Locke, E. A., & Bryan, J. F. (1967). *Goals and intentions as determinants of performance level, task choice, and attitudes*. Final Report to the Office of Naval Research (Contract ONR 4792). Washington, DC: American Institutes for Research.

Lord, F. (1952). A theory of test scores. *Psychometric Monographs, No. 7*.

Lord, F. (1980). *Applications of item response theory to practical testing problems*. Hillsdale, NJ: Lawrence Erlbaum Associates.

McGregor, D. (1957). An uneasy look at performance appraisal. *Harvard Business Review, 35*(3), 89–94.

McGregor, D. (1960). *The human side of enterprise*. New York: McGraw-Hill.

Messick, S. (1975). The standard problem: Methods and values in measurement and evaluation. *American Psychologist, 30,* 955–966.

Messick, S. (1980). Test validity and the ethics of assessment. *American Psychologist, 35,* 10–12.

Most, R. (1993). John C. Flanagan: The power of planning. *The Industrial–Organizational Psychologist, 30,* 44–49.

Most R. (1994). Edwin A. Fleishman: Applying academia. *The Industrial–Organizational Psychologist, 32,* 32–37.

Mumford, M. D., Weeks, J. L., Harding, F. D., & Fleishman, E. A . (1988). Relations between student characteristics, course content, and training outcomes: An integrative modeling effort. *Journal of Applied Psychology, 73,* 443–456.

O'Rourke, L. J. (1926). Saving dollars and energy by personnel research. Part I: Procedure in effecting improvements. *Journal of Personnel Research, 4,* 351–364.

O'Rourke, L. J. (1930). *A new emphasis on federal personnel research and administration.* Washington, DC: U.S. Civil Service Commission.

Peterson, N. G., Mumford, M. D., Borman, W. C., Jeanneret, P. R., & Fleishman, E. A. (Eds.). (1999). An *occupational information system for the 21st century: The development of O*Net.* Washington, DC: American Psychological Association.

Primoff, E. S. (1959). Empirical validations of the J-coefficient. In the development processes for indirect or synthetic validity symposium. *Personnel Psychology, 12,* 413–418.

Primoff, E. S. (1975). *How to prepare and conduct job element examinations.* TS-75-1. Washington, DC: Personnel Research and Development Center, U.S. Civil Service Commission.

Primoff, E. S., & Eyde, L. D. (1988). Job element analysis. In S. Gael (Ed.), *The job analysis handbook for business, industry, and government.* New York: Wiley.

Primoff, E. J., & Fine, S. A. (1988). A history of job analysis. In S. Gael (Ed.), *The job analysis handbook for business, industry, and government.* NY: John Wiley.

Seashore, S., Lawler, E., III, Mirvis, P. H., & Cammann, C. (Eds.). (1983). *Assessing organizational change: A guide to methods, measures, and practices.* New York: Wiley.

Schmidt, F. J., & Hunter, J. E. (1977). Development of a general solution to the problem of validity generalization. *Journal of Applied Psychology, 62,* 529–540.

Schmidt, F. J., & Hunter, J. E. (2002). History, development, evolution, and impact of validity generalization and meta-analysis methods, 1975–2001. In K. R. Murphy (Ed.), *Validity generalization: A critical review.* Mahwah, NJ: Lawrence Erlbaum Associates.

Stogdill, R. M. (1948). Personality factors associated with leadership: A survey of the literature. *Journal of Psychology, 25,* 35–71.

Thompson, L. F. (2005). Spotlight on local I–O organizations. *The Industrial–Organizational Psychologist, 43,* 111–113.

Tucker, L. R. (1955). The objective definition of simple structure in linear factor analysis. *Psychometrika, 29,* 209–225.

Tucker, L. R. (1958). The interbattery method of factor analysis. *Psychometrika, 23,* 111–136.

Tucker, L. R. (1967). Three-mode factor analysis of Parker-Fleishman complex behavior data. *Multivariate Behavioral Research, 2,* 139–151.

Van Cott, H. P., & Kinkade, R. G. (1972). *Human engineering guide to equipment design.* Washington, DC: U.S. Government Printing Office.

Viteles, M. S. (1932). *Industrial psychology.* New York: Norton.

Wainer, H. (Ed.). (1990). *Computerized adaptive testing: A primer.* Hillsdale, NJ: Lawrence Erlbaum Associates.

Wainer, H., & Thissen, D. (1992). *Combining multiple-choice and constructed response test scores* (Program statistics Research, Tech. Rep. 92-93). Princeton, NJ: Educational Testing Service.

Wigdor, A. K., & Sackett, P. R. (1993). Employment testing and public policy: The case of the General Aptitude Battery. In H. Schuler, J. Farr, & M. Smith (Eds.), *Personnel selection and assessment: Organizational and individual perspectives.* Hillsdale, NJ: Lawrence Erlbaum Associates.

7

The Military's Contribution to Our Science and Practice: People, Places, and Findings[1]

Eduardo Salas
University of Central Florida

Renée E. DeRouin
University of Central Florida

Paul A. Gade
U.S. Army Research Institute

There is no question that the military has influenced the science and practice of industrial and organizational (I–O) psychology in the United States. From its financial support of psychological research through grants and contracts to its involvement with applied research in its major military research institutions, the military is continuously adding to our understanding of psychological issues in industry and organizations. Unfortunately, little is known about the some of the significant people and organizations that have shaped I–O psychology in the service of national defense. In fact, only a brief summary of the military's contributions to I–O psychology is provided in several introductory I–O textbooks (e.g., Berry, 1998; Muchinsky, 1990). We highlight selective contributions of the military to I–O psychology over the last 100 years and introduce some of the historical people, places, and findings that led to these advancements.

A complete history of all military research is not possible within the confines of this chapter. However, an attempt is made to refer readers to works that more adequately serve specific research purposes. We also know that the military invests hundreds of millions of dollars in basic and applied psychological research each year (Driskell & Olmstead, 1989) and has supported and influenced fields like social and cognitive psychology. In this chapter, we emphasize those contributions to psychology that have specifically influenced research and practice in the I–O psychology field.

Because much of the I–O psychology-related work in the military is conducted by I–O psychologists who are employed by the different military research and development institutions, we center our discussion primarily on the work of these "in-house" psychologists. We recognize that a significant amount of the research in I–O psychology is carried out by researchers in academic and research organizations who are funded by military grants and contracts. This

---

[1]The views, opinions, and/or findings contained in this article are solely those of the authors and should not be construed as an official Department of the Army or DOD position, policy, or decision, unless so designated by other documentation.

169

chapter provides a brief introduction to some of the major psychological research programs in the Army, Navy, and Air Force and describes how these organizations have contributed to the science and practice of I–O psychology as we know it today.

In 1956, at the first international symposium on military psychology, Arthur Melton stated that "military psychology is clearly extensive with all psychology, except perhaps developmental psychology, and has as its unique characteristics merely the specific contexts of application" (Melton, 1957, p. 740). Given this, we have chosen to focus on a few key areas of the military's contributions to I–O psychology. In particular, we provide examples of the military's role in our understanding of employee selection and classification, job analysis, training, workplace design, motivation, learning and skill acquisition, performance measurement and enhancement, teams and team training, decision making, and leadership. To place each of these contributions within their historical contexts, we describe developments during World War I, during World War II, and the period since World War II. We also describe some of the people and research organizations behind these contributions. We hope that this review of the contributions of the military to I–O psychology will lead to a better appreciation of the military's support of applied psychological research and to a more thorough understanding of the roots of I–O psychology's science and practice.

WORLD WAR I

Selection and Classification

The initial impetus for the development of military psychological research was the need for a valid and effective way of selecting and assigning military personnel to units in World War I. In response to this need, Robert Yerkes, a Harvard professor and president of the American Psychological Association, convinced the U.S. military that standardized intelligence testing would benefit the process of selecting and classifying recruits. As a result of his efforts, psychologists were hired to help develop standardized tests that would balance the cognitive ability of draftees in military units and identify potential soldiers for officer training (Bingham, 1919; Yerkes, 1918, 1919).

The first test that was developed for the selection and classification of military recruits in World War I was the Army Alpha. The Army Alpha was modeled after other intelligence tests in use at the time (Muchinsky, 1990) and included a variety of different subtests, such as Arithmetic Problems, Practical Judgment, Synonyms–Antonyms, Disarranged Sentences, Analogies, and Number Series Completion (Yerkes, 1921). Although the test was successful, psychologists soon determined that many World War I draftees were foreign-born and non-English-speaking, making it difficult to impossible for them to perform well on the English-intense Army Alpha (Muchinsky, 1990). To remedy this, psychologists created the Army Beta, an intelligence test that did not require a strong knowledge of the English language to complete (Caruano, 1999). Like the Army Alpha, the Army Beta measured a variety of cognitive skills, including problem solving and reasoning ability (Sticht & Armstrong, n.d.); however, the Army Beta used pictures and graphics to present information, and administrators pantomimed instructions (Yerkes, 1921).

The psychologists who developed, administered, and scored the Army Alpha and Beta were considered leaders in their respective lines of research. For instance, Yerkes' psychological examiners and statisticians included such renowned psychologists as Louis L. Thurstone (famous for identifying that intelligence is composed of multiple factors), Edward L. Thorndike (known for his studies on the role of reinforcement in learning), and Edward K. Strong (developer of the Strong Vocational Interest Blank; Yerkes, 1918). In addition to Yerkes' large-scale intelligence testing program, another testing program was simultaneously being developed and administered by Walter Dill Scott and Walter V. Bingham, two psychologists who were working cooperatively with the Army to develop placement tests for military recruits. To accomplish their work, Scott and Bingham assisted the Secretary of War, Newton Baker, in the creation of the Committee on Classification of Personnel in 1917 (Kevles, 1968). This committee was established with the purpose of developing methods for selecting and assigning military officers to particular duties and, in accomplishing these tasks, led to the creation of trade knowledge tests and a standardized system for rating officer candidacy for training and commissions (Bingham, 1919).

Although the Army Alpha and Beta were abandoned by the military after World War I, the emphasis on testing for selection and classification was not forgotten (Berry, 1998). The selection and classification work accomplished by psychologists during World War I led the way for the use of selection tests with civilian populations and to the development of standardized ways to assess personnel for different jobs (see also chaps. 1 and 3). These early efforts affected the way in which selection was conducted with these populations in the future and eventually with military personnel in World War II.

Job Analysis

The selection and classification work conducted by the Committee on Classification of Personnel during World War I required that the Army have an adequate understanding of the different jobs and task skills involved in this branch of the military. Therefore, the committee (headed by Scott, Thorndike, and Bingham; see Berry, 1998) worked to develop definitions of the trades and a listing of the personnel specifications required for each occupation. This work resulted in a book, *Army Trade Specifications*, and a set of tables describing occupational needs and soldier skill requirements (Bingham, 1919). The systematic investigation of job requirements conducted by these psychologists may be one of the first instances of job analysis in the history of I–O psychology (see chap. 9 in this text for a history of job analysis). It is interesting to note that the *Journal of Applied Psychology,* which was founded in 1917, includes in its first volume, the article "Practical Relations Between Psychology and the War," by the journal's founding editor, G. Stanley Hall.

WORLD WAR II

Selection and Classification

After the seemingly effective use of psychology in the selection of World War I military personnel, an Emergency Committee in Psychology was sponsored by the National Research Council (NRC; a quasi-governmental agency whose purpose includes the encouragement of scientific research with military applications) to mobilize psychologists, anticipating U.S. entry into World War II (Samelson, 1977). This committee served as the point of contact between the government and the psychological community, providing psychologists with information about opportunities for applied psychological research and practice.

One such opportunity was the administration of aptitude and intelligence tests to conscripts as was done in World War I (Harrell & Churchill, 1941). The Army General Classification Test was developed and administered during this time and helped to support the use of cognitive ability testing in the selection of military personnel (Samelson, 1977). A second opportunity was research on military personnel selection. During World War II, the Civil Aeronautics Authority (CAA) allocated nearly $6,000,000 for the training of 15,000 civilian pilots (Cochrane, 1978). A certain percentage of that money was set aside for research on pilot selection. To oversee this research, the NRC (the recipients of the CAA contract) established the Committee on Selection and Training of Aircraft Pilots (Capshew, 1999). This organization funded research on pilot selection and training from 1940 to 1947 (National Academy of Sciences, 2004).

One psychologist who participated in the research sponsored by the NRC was John C. Flanagan. Flanagan was a Harvard graduate with a PhD in education. Using his knowledge of developing tests and educational programs, Flanagan developed the Aviation Cadet Qualifying Examination, a test for classifying aircrew candidates (Capshew, 1999). This test assessed a candidate's practical knowledge of flying and was implemented shortly after the 1941 attack on Pearl Harbor (Staff, Psychological Branch, Office of the Air Surgeon, 1944). In addition to developing the Aviation Cadet Qualifying Examination, Flanagan was also sponsored to conduct research on the family size of Air Force pilots by the Pioneer Fund. During this time, Air Force pilots were considered, genetically, to be the "cream of the crop" of military personnel (Capshew, 1999). However, they were in danger of not passing on their genes, because most pilots were having few children. To remedy this problem, Flanagan researched ways with which to encourage pilots to have larger families. His findings suggested that educational scholarships for large families would promote pilots to raise more children (Flanagan, 1942); as a result, the Pioneer Fund decided to implement a child-focused scholarship program for Air Force pilots (Capshew, 1999).

The Aviation Psychology Program.[2]   A major example of how psychologists were mobilized by the military to deal effectively with selection issues was the Aviation Psychology Program of the Army Air Forces organized and administered by Flanagan. In the spring of 1941, before the attack on Pearl Harbor in December of that year, it became clear that there was a need to deal immediately with the impending expansion of personnel selection and training problems and a need for new procedures to be developed and validated for pilots and for other aircrew jobs. The primary method of aircrew selection, up to this point, was the use of adaptability ratings by flight surgeons. In May 1941, the chief of the Medical Division of the Air Corps recommended the establishment of a psychological research agency in the Medical Division.

In July 1941, Flanagan, the associate director of the Cooperative Test Service of the Council of Education, was commissioned for duty as a major in the Officers' Reserve Corps and the following day reported for duty in the Medical Division, Office of the Chief of Air Corps (Flanagan, 1948). Between August and September, invitations were written resulting in the commissioning, as majors, of Dr. Robert T. Rock, head of psychology at Fordham University, and Laurance F. Shaffer, head of the Bureau of Measurement at Carnegie Institute of Technology. In the next few months, the pace intensified with commissions given to Arthur W. Melton, chairman of psychology, University of Missouri; Frank A. Geldard, chair of psychology, University of Virginia; J. P. Guilford, professor of psychology, University of California; and Paul Horst, supervisor of selection research, Procter and Gamble Company. Hundreds of officers and enlisted men were recruited, or transferred from within the Army, after a search for those with training in psychology and measurement. By June 1945, the Aviation Psychology Program included about 200 officers, 750 enlisted men, and 500 civilians (Flanagan, 1948).

The program was organized into psychological research units according to their primary research areas. It is impossible to describe each program here, but it is possible to say that the applied problems dealt with the innovation and development of research that could not have been carried out any where else but in the military: methodological issues of differential test batteries, use of new types of tests such as apparatus psychomotor tests and motion picture tests of perception, successive revisions and improvements of test content based on thousands of subjects, development of sophisticated statistical techniques to evaluate the characteristics of mea-

[2]Material for this section was prepared by Edwin A. Fleishman.

sures, development and analyses of performance criteria, and successive refinement of aptitude definitions.

The legacy provided I–O psychology with 19 volumes (called the "Blue Books"; Flanagan, 1948) that can still be found in some libraries and on the shelves of some senior psychologists. Table 7.1 provides a listing of these volume titles and their distinguished authors. Chapter 10 on human factors in this text provides additional information about the impact of this program on human factors research.

Office of Strategic Services.   In addition to the research on aircrew selection, training, and family size, another application of psychology to military operations emerged during

TABLE 7.1
The 19 Volumes Describing the Aviation Psychology Program of the Army Air Forces[a]

Volume	Title and Author (Directors of Each Program)
1	The Aviation Psychology Program in the Army Air Forces. John C. Flanagan, University of Pittsburgh
2	The Classification Program. Philip H. DuBois, Washington University, St. Louis, MO
3	Research Problems and Techniques. Robert L. Thorndike, Teachers College, Columbia University
4	Apparatus Tests. Arthur W. Melton, Ohio State University
5	Printed Classification Tests, Parts I and II. J. P. Guilford, University of Southern California and John I. Lacey, The Samuel S. Fels Research Institute, Yellow Springs, OH
6	The AAF Qualifying Examination. Frederick B. Davis, American Council on Education, Washington, DC
7	Motion Picture Testing and Research. James J. Gibson, Smith College
8	Psychological Research on Pilot Training. Neal E. Miller, Yale University
9	Psychological Research on Bombardier Training. Edward H. Kemp, University of Rochester, and A. Pemberton Johnson, Purdue University
10	Psychological Research on Navigator Training. Launor F. Carter, University of Rochester
11	Psychological Research on Flexible Gunnery Training. R. N. Hobbs, Columbia University
12	Psychological Research on Radar Observer Training. Stuart W. Cook, Commission on Community Interrelations, New York
13	Psychological Research on Flight Engineer Training. John T. Dailey, Psychological Research Project (Pilot)
14	Psychological Research on Problems of Redistribution. Frederic Wickert, Commonwealth Edison Company, Chicago
15	The Psychological Program in AAF Convalescent Hospitals. Sideny W. Bijou, Indiana University
16	Psychological Research on Operational Training in the Continental Air Forces. Meredith P. Crawford, Vanderbilt University; Richard T. Sollenberger, Mt. Holyoke College; Lewis B. Ward, Harvard University; Clarence W. Brown, University of California; Edwin E. Ghiselli, University of California
17	Psychological Research in the Theaters of War. William M. Lepley, Pennsylvania State College
18	Records, Analysis, and Test Procedures. Walter L. Deemer, AAF School of Aviation Medicine, Randolph Field, TX
19	Psychological Research on Equipment Design. Paul Fitts, Aero-Medical Laboratory, Wright Field, OH

World War II. This was the assessment of men and women who would be involved in covert operations. Henry Murray, a psychologist from Harvard, left teaching to join the Army Medical Corps and to engage himself in this opportunity. More specifically, Murray worked to create assessment tools for the selection and classification of military operatives for the Office of Strategic Services (OSS). He studied and modeled methods used by British and German psychologists in his assessments of intelligence agents. For instance, Murray required potential agents to participate in "situational tests" in realistic settings, to interact with German-speaking personnel disguised as enemy soldiers, and to maintain their cover in camp activities at all times. Most of the assessments were done near Washington, DC, at a location called Station S (see Highhouse, 2002). (For an in-depth description of the OSS assessment program, see Murray & MacKinnon, 1946, and Murray & OSS Assessment Staff, 1946). Although some reservations have been expressed about the programs conducted at Station S (see Highhouse, 2002), these programs soon stimulated interest in "situational tests" and assessment centers for applications in civilian organizations, as well as in the military.

The assessment centers of World War II were the predecessors of the assessment centers developed at AT&T, Standard Oil, and the Central Intelligence Agency (Bray & Grant, 1966; Highhouse, 2002; Hoffman, 1992). These assessment centers relied on many of the same methods of data gathering, in particular, the use of multiple exercises and assessors to measure multiple skills. Today, the assessment center method is a popular tool for I–O psychologists and is used most often for candidate selection, placement, and promotion (Thornton, 1992).

Training

Not only were psychologists faced with the challenges of selection and classification during World War II, but they were also faced with the challenge of training military personnel on equipment designed specifically for the war effort. Much of this equipment had never been used before, and its operating procedures were novel to both the psychologists conducting the training and military personnel who would be using it. To establish a systematic research program on psychology's applications to military training and human engineering, the Applied Psychology Panel was developed during this time in the Office of Scientific Research and Development (a federal institution for military research originally under the direction of Vannebar Bush; Griffin, n.d.) (Capshew, 1999). The panel helped to initiate training programs for radio operators, B-29 gunners, and telephone talkers, among others (Capshew, 1999). The programs developed by the panel during World War II represent some of the earliest efforts of psychologists to create standardized training programs for military personnel.

Training research was also a major component of the Army Air Force Psychological Research Program. Specialized field units were set up for training research, development, and evaluation for pilots, bombardiers, gunnery, radar observers, and flight engineers. Table 7.1 provides the directors of the programs.

Workplace Design

In developing complex training and selection tools, psychologists realized that one way to reduce the difficulties of these tools was to first improve the design of the workplace. These psychologists decided to examine the factors influencing work performance in order to provide recommendations for work area and equipment design. One work performance factor that they studied was the noise experienced by aircrew personnel. In this research, different materials were examined for their ability to absorb the sounds associated with airplane flight and the effect of sustained noise on such variables as hearing, vision, and blood pressure.

Surprisingly, the researchers did not find significant effects of persistent loud noise on human performance with the exception of temporary hearing loss. However, they did provide several recommendations to manufacturers of sound-minimizing materials (Capshew, 1999; Rosenweig & Stone, 1948).

Much of this research was conducted at the Harvard Psycho-Acoustic Laboratory under the direction of the NRC's Sound Control Committee. The findings of the Harvard Laboratory led to much advancement in the development of sound-absorbing materials and the way in which airplane design could be improved (Capshew, 1999). The research program of the Harvard Laboratory was a significant contribution to the examination of work environment factors that impede work performance. In addition, it helped to establish, in the minds of psychologists, the importance of improving workplace design instead of focusing entirely on training and selection.

Equipment Design.   The major effort on equipment design during World War II was directed by Paul Fitts at Wright Patterson Air Force base, established within the Air Force Psychology Research Program. This effort is described more fully in chapter 10 on human factors.

Motivation and Morale

A landmark event in military psychology resulting from World War II was the publication of the four volumes of Samuel Stouffer's *The American Soldier* (Stouffer, 1949). In these books, Stouffer (a sociologist) described the contributions of social/psychological data collected during World War II in different military branches and Army units by psychologists and social scientists for the War Department. In addition to covering issues of measurement and prediction, the volumes dealt with job and contextual factors affecting the job satisfaction of soldiers and attitudes toward their officers, unit, and organization; issues of perceived justice and injustice; perceived valence of rewards offered; determinants of salient motives and group cohesiveness; and factors affecting absenteeism, turnover, and morale. The volumes were subtitled *Adjustment During Army Life, Combat and Its Aftermath, Experiments in Mass Communication,* and *Measurement and Prediction.* These works had considerable impact on several I–O psychologists, were often assigned readings for graduate classes, were frequently cited in psychology texts (e.g., Hollander, 1961), and are highly relevant for I–O psychology even today (Edwin A. Fleishman, personal communication, July 10, 2005).

POST–WORLD WAR II DEVELOPMENTS

As can be seen, the military's contributions to I–O psychology during World Wars I and II were primarily focused on selection, with some research on training and equipment design and some research on motivation and communication. Since then, the military has continued to contribute to our understanding of the world of work. All branches of the Armed Forces established major laboratories and centers, carrying out basic and applied research. Only a few of them can be described here. We first present an overview of the development of two of the largest centers and then review some particular programs and findings of special interest to I–O psychologists today.

Army Research Institute for the Behavioral and Social Sciences (ARI)[3]

The Army Research Institute (ARI), headquartered in the Washington, DC, area, has a long and distinguished history conducting and supporting basic and applied research that has had an important impact on the science and practice of I–O psychology. Although the lineage of ARI can

---

[3]Material for this section was prepared by Edwin A. Fleishman.

be traced back to the Army Alpha and Beta tests of World War I, to the Army General Classification Tests (AGCT) during World War II, and to differential classification during the 1950s, its historical organizational forerunner and direct ancestor was the Personnel Research Section (PRS) of the Adjutant General's Office (AGO) located in the Pentagon and established in 1939.

The National Research Council had selected W. Bingham to head a Committee on Classification of Military Personnel and he also assumed the title of chief psychologist of the Army (see Bingham, 1944). This committee, at that time, included Henry Garrett, L. J. O'Rourke, M. W. Richardson, Carrol Shartle, and L. L. Thurstone. They played a key role in recommending the establishment of this PRS at the AGO, merging several Army testing research units. This was done in response to the need for a new general classification test measuring several aptitudes and for improving Army-wide programs. Marion Richardson, known for his contributions to psychometrics, became the first technical director of PRS.

In 1949, the technical director of PRS was Donald Baier, and its senior staff, during various periods, constitute a "who's who" of psychologists known to I–O psychologists for their psychometric, statistical, and methodological contributions. These included Charles Mosier, then editor of *Psychometrika;* Erwin K. Taylor, who founded (with Frederick Kuder) the journal *Personnel Psychology* and was its first editor; Robert S. Wherry, who contributed to factor analyses and the statistics of multiple test batteries (e.g., optimum differential weighting and multiple R shrinkage corrections); and Donald Sisson, inventor of the "forced choice" approach to performance appraisal.

Julius (Jay) Uhlaner, who later became technical director of ARI, joined the staff that year and developed a Vision Research Laboratory to evaluate human performance under the different low-level light conditions found in combat. A number of specialized tests of visual functions (e.g., peripheral vision) were developed. ARI's subsequent development was largely shaped during Uhlaner's tenure as technical director in the 1960s and 1970s, when ARI responded to the rapidly changing needs of the Army. Some of these issues involved the transition to an all-volunteer army, new technologies requiring new types of training, the integration of women into the military, work and family issues, new types of information, command and control systems, and needs for improving the quality of leadership at all levels. At the same time, there was a need to overhaul the existing selection and classification system.

By 1983, ARI employed about 300 professionals, including 190 psychologists and 70 scientific personnel of other disciplines, distributed over its headquarters and 10 field units (Zeidner & Drucker, 1983). Today, about half its annual budget is spent on contracts with universities, industry, and other research and development organizations. The research produced by ARI's in-house staff and contractors is published in professional journals and at meetings of dozens of professional societies. A history of ARI, until 1983, has been written by Joseph Zeidner, who succeeded Uhlaner and Arthur Drucker, a long-time senior executive at ARI (Zeidner & Drucker, 1983).

Air Force Personnel and Training Research Center (AFPTRC)[4]

The Air Force Personnel and Training Research Center was developed in the post-World War II period, in the late 1940s, with its technical director, Arthur W. Melton, under the air training command. (Its original name was the Human Resources Research Center.) Melton, an experimental psychologist, had been a professor at Ohio State and chair of the Psychology Department of the University of Missouri and was one of the key figures in the early organization of the wartime Army Air Force Psychology Research Program. In 1949, the Center was headquartered at Lackland Air Force Base, San Antonio, Texas, along with two of its laboratories.

---

[4]Material for this section was prepared by Edwin A. Fleishman.

These were the Personnel Laboratory (Lloyd G. Humphries, research director) and the Perceptual and Motor Research Laboratory (later renamed the Skill Components Research Laboratory (Robert M. Gagné, research director). A third laboratory, the Crew Research Laboratory (Robert L. French, research director), was located at nearby Randolph Air Force Base. Other units were later established to deal with specific Air Force missions (e.g., pilot training at Panama City, Florida, and navigator training at Mather Air Force Base, California). In the early 1950s, a Training Research Laboratory was established at Chanute Air Force Base, Rantoul, Illinois, and a Maintenance Laboratory at Lowry Air Force Base, Denver, Colorado.

Robert Gagné became a major figure in the history of training research and application. The program of research he directed at AFPTRC made critical advances in the application of learning principles to education and training (Gagné, 1962; see also chap. 12). Campbell (1971) acknowledged Gagné's contributions to the field of instructional systems design (ISD), which emerged from his research on ongoing military training operations. His early Air Force work on forecasting the personnel requirements of man-machine systems predated the Army's MANPRINT program by many years (Gagné, 1955). Another contribution of this program was in providing the rationale and methodology for simulator development (Gagné, 1962). Both Campbell (1971) and Goldstein (1986) acknowledged the debt of I–O psychology to Gagné's work.

Another example of applied research was the work of Christal and his staff in this Air Force program (AFPTRC), especially in the development of CODAP, a computerized system for carrying out large-scale job analyses involving thousands of tasks. In the Crew Research Laboratory, the early work of Roby and Lanzetta on effective team performance is another example (see also chap. 17). The work of Fleishman (1954) and his associates in the AFPTRC Skill Research Lab may be particularly relevant. Where else could this work in identifying and defining the domain of psychomotor abilities have been carried out? During the 5 years he was with the laboratory, he developed a series of interlocking studies involving the construction and administration of hundreds of specially designed psychomotor tests requiring multiple units of complex apparatus and administered to thousands of basic trainee airmen on a daily basis during each study. His follow-up work in the physical ability domain was begun here and continued later (supported by various Department of Defense agencies) and formed the basis of his taxonomy of human abilities (Fleishman, 1975), which has found applications in I–O psychology. There are many examples like these, and some of them are provided in the sections that follow.

These examples illustrate how the military provides opportunities and challenges to the solutions of applied problems through basic research and tests of findings in the real world. The resources provided make it possible to do research on a scale not possible elsewhere. The large number of subjects available and the replications possible make the findings obtained more reliable. Validation in operational settings increases our confidence in the research conclusions.

Selected Research Summaries

Selection and Classification.   The Navy Personnel Research and Development Center (NPRDC) based in San Diego was organized in the 1970s and was one of the largest agencies supporting personnel and organizational research. (It is no longer in existence, and some of its units have been dispersed to other Navy agencies). NPRDC and ARI were pioneers in computerized adaptive testing (CAT), an assessment technique used often by I–O psychologists today (Wainer, 1990). The development and fielding of the CAT version of the Armed Services Vocational Aptitude battery (CAT–ASVAB) by NPRDC paved the way for the practical application of adaptive testing and item response theory (IRT). Abraham Bayroff's early research at ARI on branching tests that was the forerunner of adaptive testing (Bayroff, 1967) went largely unrecognized until the work of James McBride at ARI on adaptive mental testing (McBride,

1979). The advent of the microcomputer made adaptive testing feasible as well as practical and the use of IRT a necessity. The first widespread practical application of CAT was the Army's Computerized Adaptive Screening Test (CAST; Sands & Gade, 1983). The CAST, developed for ARI by NPRDC based on items and testing strategies from their early CAT–ASVAB work, was used in Army recruiting stations to screen applicants for the ASVAB (McBride, 1997; Sands, Gade, & Knapp, 1997). CAST was one of the first CAT tests to show that a CAT test could be equated to paper-and-pencil tests measuring the same construct (Wainer, 1990). The CAST proved a quick (around 5 minutes), valid estimator of the Armed Forces Qualification Test (AFQT, a measure of psychometric g) portion of the ASVAB, correlating .85 with the AFQT, as good as the test–retest reliability of AFQT itself. Furthermore, the Word Knowledge portion of CAST provides valid estimates of AFQT ($r = .81$) and psychometric g ($r = .72$), even when administered over the telephone by trained interviewers (Legree, Fischl, Gade, & Wilson, 1998). (See chap. 8 for a historical perspective of selection and I–O psychology.)

Learning and Skill Acquisition.   Since World War II, AFPTRC and now the Armstrong Laboratory (one of the four Air Force "super" laboratories now comprising the Air Force Research Laboratory) made significant contributions to the areas of learning and skill acquisition. Armstrong itself represents a partnership between several Air Force research laboratories, including the Harry G. Armstrong Aerospace Medical Research Laboratory, the Air Force Human Resources Laboratory, the Air Force Drug Testing Laboratory, the Air Force Occupational and Environmental Health Laboratory, and the United States Air Force School of Aerospace Medicine. The research at Armstrong has led to a better understanding of the nature of intelligence and of the factors that hold the greatest influence on learning and skill acquisition (Federal Laboratory Consortium for Technology Transfer, 1999–2003).

For instance, while at Armstrong and its research partner, the Air Force Human Resources Laboratory, Kyllonen and colleagues developed the idea that general intelligence or g is nothing more than working memory capacity (Kyllonen, 1996; Kyllonen & Christal, 1989, 1990). Intelligence had traditionally been conceptualized as comprising a combination of verbal, numerical, and spatial abilities (Kyllonen, 1996). Kyllonen and colleagues, however, argued that intelligence might be better conceptualized as an integration of processing speed, working memory, declarative knowledge, and procedural knowledge (Kyllonen, 1996). Research suggested that working memory (i.e., the information-processing resource necessary for comprehension, reasoning, and learning; Riding, Grimley, Dahraei, & Banner, 2003) is a particularly important factor to consider in the design of workplace education and training programs. Specifically, because working memory appears to account for much of the variance in g and in declarative and procedural learning, this research suggests that training practitioners may benefit from first assessing the working memory capacity of trainees before designing training programs. In addition, this research has led to a better understanding of cognitive predictors of learning and transfer, separating the domain-specific content (e.g., verbal, quantitative) from processes involved in learning declarative and procedural knowledge. These ideas are consistent with the paradigm shift to cognitive aspects in training evaluation, task analysis, and systems design. In the future, it is likely that there will be a fruitful integration of cognitive psychology, psychometrics, and training interventions to improve learning and skill acquisition (Embretson, 2003) and that military research will have significantly contributed to these efforts (readers are referred to Green, Self, & Ellfritt, 1995, for a more complete review of the research at Armstrong Laboratory).

Performance Conceptualization and Measurement.   Since World War II, the military has also made significant contributions to the conceptualization and measurement of individual and team performance. For instance, the U.S. Air Force Human Resources Laboratory (AFHRL; now part of Armstrong Laboratory described previously) examined the use of interview testing as a criterion for job proficiency (Hedge & Teachout, 1992). AFHRL participated in this research as part of a large-scale validation effort for its selection, classification, and training programs. Analyzing data from 1,491 job incumbents from eight different Air Force specialties (e.g., air traffic control operator, jet engine mechanic, and personnel specialist), Hedge and Teachout found that interview testing as a work sample measure may be useful for research validation purposes but may not necessarily be useful for training needs assessment and certification.

Additionally, ARI supported research by Campbell, McHenry, and Wise (1990) and Pulakos and Borman (1988), who suggested that individual performance is best conceptualized as a multidimensional rather than a unidimensional construct. With regard to military performance, in particular, Campbell et al. (1990) argued that there are five dimensions of individual performance: core technical proficiency, general soldiering proficiency, personal discipline, personal fitness and military bearing, and effort and leadership.

Project A (Campbell, 1990) was an important project, a major effort sponsored by ARI to overhaul the Army's selection and classification system. The research work was carried out by a consortium of firms consisting of the Human Resources Research Organization (HumRRO), the American Institutes for Research (AIR), and the Personnel Decisions Research Institute (PDRI). Project A was a 7-year project that was conducted with the purpose of enhancing the selection and classification process for Army enlisted entry-level positions. One of its aims was to create criterion variables for performance so that existing and newly created selection/classification tools could be evaluated. A 12-hour test battery was created to serve as this criterion variable for performance. The battery consisted of several measures, such as job knowledge tests and job samples, which were derived from extensive task and critical incident analyses. When the selection/classification tools were validated on the battery, McHenry, Hough, Toquam, Hanson, and Ashworth (1990) found that personal discipline and physical and military bearing were best predicted by tools measuring each individual's temperament, or personality. Moreover, effort and leadership were best predicted by tools that measured both an individual's cognitive ability and his or her temperament/personality.

The military's research on performance measurement aids I–O psychologists in their choice of performance appraisal tools and suggests that performance may not be a unidimensional construct as once thought. In addition, the military's research suggests that performance may best be measured through a variety of different assessment tools (e.g., job knowledge tests, job samples) rather than a single rater's assessment. This information may help I–O psychologists in designing performance measures for organizations and may aid in their understanding of performance as a multifaceted concept. (See also chap. 13 for a historical perspective on performance appraisal.)

Performance Enhancement.   During the 15-year period from 1984 to 1999, military psychologists at ARI sponsored a series of studies that were important for the military and for I–O psychology, because they critically examined a variety of popular, "new-age" organizational practices and human performance enhancement and assessment techniques. These "human technologies," as they were called by the Army at the time, captured the attention of a group of influential officers in the late 1970s and into the 1980s. The earliest documentation of the Army's venture into this new-age psychology was a concept paper prepared by then Lieutenant Colonel Jim Channon for Task Force Delta (not to be confused with Delta Force), entitled the "First Earth Battalion" (Channon, 1979). In addition to its spiritual messages, this concept paper was a call to the Army to embrace new-age technologies, such as neurolinguistic programming and super learning programs, as new and enlightened ways to rapidly enhance soldier performance. The influence of Channon and others continued to grow during the early 1980s and attracted the attention of key Army generals, Maxwell Thurman among them. In 1984, General Thurman and other concerned Army generals turned to ARI for guidance on how much trust to place in the human technologies of the true believers.

As it had in both World Wars, the Army turned to the National Research Council (NRC) for help, requesting that the NRC evaluate the legitimacy of these new-age organizational practices and performance-enhancing technologies. In response to this request, the Committee on Techniques for the Enhancement of Human Performance was assembled by the NRC Commission on Behavioral and Social Sciences and Education and held its first meeting in 1985. Two years later it produced its final report that was subsequently published as a book, entitled *Enhancing Human Performance: Issues, Theories, and Techniques* (Druckman & Swets, 1988), the year after the study was completed. The committee was chaired by John Swets and included 13 other well-known psychologists and researchers: Robert Bjork, Thomas Cook, Gerald Davison, Lloyd Humphrys, Ray Hyman, Daniel Landers, Sandra Mobley, Lyman Porter, Michael Posner, Walter Schneider, Jerome Singer, Sally Springer, and Richard Thompson. Robert Bjork and Jerome Singer would subsequently chair the development of three other books in what turned out to be a five-book series spanning nearly 15 years. The committee studied psychological techniques associated with learning, improving motor skills, altered mental states, stress management, and social processes. They also examined paranormal phenomena.

The second study, *In the Mind's Eye: Enhancing Human Performance* (Druckman & Bjork, 1991), chaired by Robert Bjork, had an equally impressive number of leading psychologists on the committee. The agenda of the second study was set by questions left unanswered or partially answered in the first study, new techniques that had become popular since the first study, and additional topics suggested by Army leaders. The work of the committee was divided into three broad categories: training (optimizing long-term retention, modeling expertise, and developing careers), altering mental states (subliminal self-help, meditation, managing pain, and hiding and detecting deception), and performing (optimizing individual performance and enhancing team performance).

The third volume in the NRC human performance enhancement series, *Learning, Remembering, Believing: Enhancing Human Performance* (Druckman & Bjork, 1994), broadened the mission of the committee to include potential innovations from mainstream basic research as well as controversial techniques from scientifically unconventional sources. Areas investigated included subjective self-judgments of proficiency, cooperative learning, shared mental models, tests used as training devices (not assessment tools) during training, and assessment of training in terms of skill transfer effectiveness to the post-training work environment.

The fourth volume in the enhancing human performance series, *Enhancing Organizational Performance* (Druckman, Singer, & Van Cott, 1997), broadened the scope of work further by bringing experts in from a variety of nonpsychology fields dealing with organizational performance issues and by developing a new set of tasks. The committee confirmed the notion that research badly lags practice in organizational psychology. Second, they found little or no research support for many of the management innovations currently in use. These included the ever-popular, at least at the time, total quality management (TQM), downsizing, and reengineering techniques. Finally, there is no silver bullet technique for producing effective organizational change. There was great interest in the report in the federal government and it was used by Congress to evaluate new management techniques (Edgar Johnson, personal communication, 2003). It appears that the report may have been responsible for the eventual diminution of the use of TQM in government.

The topic of the fifth and final report was *The Changing Nature of Work: Implications for Occupational Analysis* (National Research Council, 1999). Unlike other reports in this series, this report was not so much concerned with assessing the veridicality of popular practices as it was with assessing the changing structure and the nature of interpersonal relationships in the workplace. One of the chief recommendations of the report was that work and job structures needed to be integrated better with technological advancements and the changing nature of Army missions. For example, the Army, although reluctant to do so, should consider flatter, less hierarchical organizational structures for its units.

Taken as a whole, these Army-sponsored studies had far reaching implications for military services, for the general population, and for I–O psychology in debunking many popular, but unsubstantiated, programs and organizational practices for enhancing human performance. They saved the Army millions of dollars that might have been wasted in chasing practices that were marginal at best, and they provided psychology with a basis for closing the gap between theory and research and appealing popular organizational practices (Swets & Bjork, 1990). Finally, they set the standard for evaluating future practices purporting to enhance human performance that may captivate civilian and military organizations alike.

Teams and Team Training.   Since World War II, most of the research on teams and team training has been conducted at the Air Force Research Laboratory (AFRL), Naval Air Warfare Center Training Systems Division (NAVAIR TSD), and ARI. AFRL is part of the Air Force Materiel Command, and its current mission is to "develop, demonstrate, evaluate, and transition training technologies and methods to train warfighters to win" (AFRL, 2003). Its research on team training has recently focused on cockpit resource management training (training that encourages collaboration and communication among cockpit crew members) and distributed training technology (e.g., Nullmeyer & Spiker, 2003), two important areas for I–O psychologists.

ARI's research on team training, in contrast, has primarily focused on ways in which team preparation and performance can be improved. For instance, Jean Dyer's (1984) review of team research and team training revealed that factors such as providing teams with feedback about their performance, offering individual-level training before team-based training, and involving the entire team during team training (including leaders) enhance the development and functioning of teams on interdependent tasks. This information is beneficial for I–O psychologists who study the performance of individuals in team-based environments and/or who are employed by organizations to improve the instruction and performance of teams in workplace settings.

The research on teams and team training at NAVAIR TSD can be traced back to the work of Luis de Florez, the former head of the Special Devices Desk in the Engineering Division of the Navy's Bureau of Aeronautics. In the early 1940s, Florez was tasked with creating synthetic devices that would integrate the work of human and machine. As a result of his efforts, the Navy adopted the use of motion pictures in the training programs of aircraft gunners and models of the terrain when planning covert Navy operations during World War II (NAVAIR TSD, n.d.a.).

On October 1, 1993, the organization became the NAVAIR Orlando Training Systems Division, which is one of the many components of the Naval Air Systems Command (NAVAIR TSD, n.d.b.). The current mission of NAVAIR TSD is "to be the principal Navy center for research, development, test and evaluation, acquisition and product support of training systems, to provide inter-service coordination and training systems support for the Army and Air Force, and to perform such other functions and tasks as directed by higher authority" (NAVAIR TSD, n.d.b. para. 1). Research conducted at NAVAIR TSD can be classified under several training areas: (a) team training and performance (Salas, Cannon-Bowers, & Kozlowski, 1997); (b) aviation team training and crew resource management (Bowers, Thornton, Braun, Morgan, & Salas, 1998; Salas, Bowers, & Edens, 2001); (c) training effectiveness (Cannon-Bowers, Salas, Tannenbaum, & Mathieu, 1995); and (d) decision making under stress (Cannon-Bowers & Salas, 1998a); however, it is their research on teams and team training that has significantly affected how teams are structured and the way in which team training is designed and implemented.

NAVAIR TSD has focused its research on defining what a team is, identifying the team member processes involved in effective teamwork, developing team training programs, and evaluating their success (Salas, Bowers, & Cannon-Bowers, 1995; Salas, Cannon-Bowers, Payne, & Smith-Jentsch, 1998). Because of the research at NAVAIR TSD, I–O psychologists now know that teams perform best and make the best decisions when each team member has a clear understanding of his or her roles and responsibilities as well as those of others (e.g., Volpe, Cannon-Bowers, Salas, & Spector, 1996), individual team members demonstrate teamwork behaviors as well as task competence (e.g., Stout, Salas, & Carson, 1994), and team members are taught how to identify problems and develop ways of solving them (i.e., guided team self-correction) (e.g., Smith-Jentsch, Zeisig, Acton, & McPherson, 1998).

Because teams are becoming increasingly critical to success of work organizations (Cannon-Bowers & Salas, 1998b), organizations need to create conditions under which teams function effectively and team training programs that meet the demands of these special work groups. The research conducted at NAVAIR TSD, AFRL, and ARI will assist I–O psychologists in choosing team training techniques and in establishing workplace conditions that foster successful teamwork. (For a more extensive discussion of how military team research has contributed to I–O psychology, see chap. 17.)

Decision Making.   Both the Office of Naval Research (ONR) and the Army Research Laboratory (ARL) have supported research on individual and team decision making (see chap. 17 in this text). For instance, ARL has formed an alliance (i.e., the Advanced Decision Architecture Alliance) with several renowned research and academic institutions to conduct investigations on decision making in organizations. The objective of this alliance is to examine and develop "human-centered, automated support of individual and distributed team information processing and decision-making to achieve information dominance and decision supremacy" (ARL, 2005, para. 1). Likewise, ONR has funded research by such academicians as Herbert Simon, a Nobel laureate famous for his research on decision making in organizations (e.g., Simon & Kadane, 1975), John Hollenbeck, Jason Colquitt, Daniel Ilgen, Jennifer Hedlund, Jeffrey LePine, and Aleksander Ellis (e.g., Hedlund, Ilgen, & Hollenbeck, 1998; Hollenbeck, Ilgen, LePine, Colquitt, & Hedlund, 1998; LePine, Hollenbeck, Ilgen, Colquitt, & Ellis, 2002).

More recently, after an Iranian commercial plane was mistaken to be an enemy aircraft and was shot down by the USS *Vincennes* in July of 1988, ONR sponsored a 7-year research project to determine the way in which decision making could be enhanced in complex situations (Cannon-Bowers & Salas, 1998a). The project was referred to as Tactical Decision Making Under Stress or TADMUS. The goal of TADMUS was to create training standards that would improve the quality of decision making under stress (Collyer & Malecki, 1998). The information acquired from TADMUS suggests that many training programs (e.g., stress exposure training, team coordination training, cross-training, team dimensional training) are available to enrich the decision-making capacity of individuals and high-impact teams (Cannon-Bowers & Salas, 1998a; see also chap. 17). These training programs are useful to I–O psychologists who are working with individuals and teams in high-stress occupations, because these programs provide a way of improving the decision quality of employees whose judgments vastly affect the lives of those around them.

Paul Nelson (2006), a psychologist who served as chief of the U.S. Navy Medical Service Corps, has recently completed a comprehensive review of the historical highlights of human performance research conducted through the various responsible agencies in the Navy. Included are the important programs supported by the Office of Naval Research and the in-house research carried out at the Naval Research Laboratory, the Bureau of Naval Personnel, the Navy Medical Research Institute, the Aviation Psychology Research Laboratory, the Naval Training Devices Center, and many other research centers, whose work has contributed to the substance of I–O psychology over the past 50 years.

Leadership.   In addition to its work on selection and classification and the conceptualization and measurement of individual and team performance, ARI has supported research on leadership, ranging from the well-known situational (Fiedler, 1967) and transformational (Burns, 1978) leadership theories to the executive leadership paradigm (Hooijberg, Bullis, & Hunt, 1999). More recently, ARI supported Bernard Bass (1985, 1996, 1997), an academic researcher, in his efforts to derive a leadership theory more applicable to a variety of leadership settings. In Bass' view, transformational leadership (i.e., leadership that involves motivating employees by meeting their higher level needs; Burns, 1978) and transactional leadership (i.e., leadership that involves motivating subordinates through rewards; Burns, 1978) are not the either–or concepts Burns originally suggested; instead, transformational leadership can be combined with transactional leadership to enhance leader performance. Bass argues that transformational leader attributes (i.e., confidence, dominance, and trust) appeal to the higher order needs and values of those being led and, as a result, add to the more tangible exchange (or transactional) relationship that already exists. Bass' model of leadership has been supported by ARI and has been found to predict leadership in both military (Bass, 1996) and civilian (Barling, Weber, & Kelloway, 1996) environments.

Another area of leadership that ARI has researched is executive leadership (i.e., leadership at the battalion level or above). In 1981, Kimmel reviewed the literature on military leadership and noted that only 22 studies on the topic of executive leadership were conducted between 1938 and 1981 (Kimmel, 1981). Recognizing the need for more research in this area, ARI focused considerable effort on the study of executive leadership through in-house and contract research (e.g., Zaccaro, 1998, 1999). As a result, many theories and models of executive leadership have been examined by ARI. Much of this research was guided by stratified systems theory (i.e., the assumption that "natural hierarchies assert themselves wherever human beings organize themselves to fight or work"; Ross, 1992, p. 46) (Jacques & Clement, 1991) and is primarily nonempirical in nature (e.g., theoretical/conceptual research and literature reviews; Zaccaro, 1999). Recently, Zaccaro (2001) summarized and transitioned his conceptual and empirical work and the work of others on executive leadership, largely sponsored by ARI, to the I–O community.

A recent invited special issue of the journal *Leadership Quarterly* (2000, Vol. 11[1]) was devoted to the ARI-sponsored programs directed under contract by Edwin Fleishman, Michael Mumford, and Stephen Zaccaro, focusing on metacognitive processes and high-level Army leadership. In this series, a highly empirical study showed that computer interactive measures of six metacognitive skills predicted performance of high-level military, officers at the National Defense University (Marshall-Meis, Fleishman, Martin, Zaccaro, Baughman, & McGee, 2000).

Since 1997, several proposed leadership models supported by ARI have posited that certain cognitive, behavioral, and social complexities are required for leaders to be effective in drastically changing situations (Hooijberg et al., 1999; Zaccaro, 1999). For instance, Hooijberg et al. (1999) proposed a model of leadership involving several of these components, such as behavioral complexity, self-monitoring, self-efficacy, systems thinking, and effectiveness. This model incorporates the characteristics of leaders themselves, including their personality, cognitive processing, and goal-setting capabilities. More recently, ARI has turned to Sternberg's theory of successful intelligence to provide a fresh, if somewhat more controversial, approach for gaining insights into leadership processes and leader development (Sternberg et al., 2000). In this pursuit, Sternberg and his associates have developed and validated the Tacit Knowledge of Military Leaders (TKML) Inventory to measure leadership tacit knowledge (i.e., practical, largely unarticulated, procedural knowledge about leadership). They have shown the TKML to measure practical intelligence that is different from g, experience, and personality. ARI and Sternberg are now attempting to use this captured tacit knowledge in various ways to accelerate the leader development process. These and other models of leadership provided by ARI have significantly contributed to our understanding of the characteristics of effective leaders and have provided I–O psychologists with the groundwork for additional debate as well as research on this topic. (See chap. 16 for a historical perspective on leadership and I–O psychology.)

Expertise.   The initial work in expertise can be traced to Fitts' (1964) seminal work on the different stages of learning. Through a grant from the U.S. Air Force Office of Scientific Research (AFOSR; an Air Force military organization whose sole purpose is to fund basic research), Fitts identified three different phases of learning: the cognitive, associative, and autonomous stages. In the cognitive stage, learners understand how to conduct the task, practice performing it, and establish their own cognitive representation of the task. Next, in the associative stage, learners become more familiar with the task and begin to associate certain cues with certain responses. Finally, in the autonomous stage, learners are able to perform the task with fewer and fewer errors until they reach peak performance. When developing expertise, learners progress through each of these stages consecutively until they can perform tasks automatically.

Since Fitts' (1964) initial work on expertise, researchers have modified the stages of learning so that they more accurately reflect the types of knowledge and skills gained during the learning process. For instance, Anderson's (1982) stages of learning consist of the declarative, knowledge compilation, and procedural stages. In Anderson's declarative stage, learners gain a basic knowledge of what is involved in certain tasks and learn the facts about how to perform them. This stage corresponds with Fitts' cognitive stage but more accurately depicts the type of knowledge being gained at this point in the learning process. Anderson's second stage, the knowledge compilation stage, is similar to Fitts' associative stage but is treated as more of a transition between the two main stages (i.e., the declarative and procedural stages). In this knowledge compilation stage, learners convert declarative knowledge into procedural knowledge. In Anderson's third and final stage, the procedural stage, learners understand how to apply the declarative knowledge they have gained, and they are able to speed up task performance. This stage is similar to Fitts' autonomous stage in that learners are eventually able to perform tasks without thinking about them.

This initial foundation in the study of expertise has provided I–O psychologists with an understanding of how individuals learn and of the processes involved in developing domain-specific expertise. I–O psychologists are now using this information to evaluate the stages in which trainees can be categorized during training and to create effectiveness measures for training programs (e.g., Kraiger, Ford, & Salas, 1993). In the future, it is likely that the military's research on expertise will continue to pave the way to a better understanding of expert thinking and thought processes and will contribute to the development of techniques for evaluating training effectiveness. (See chap. 12 in this book for more information on training.)

CONCLUDING REMARKS

The purpose of this chapter was to briefly present some of the important people and events that have shaped military psychological research over the last 100 years and, in turn, the science and practice of I–O psychology. As can be seen throughout the chapter, I–O psychology had roots in the military research of World Wars I and II and in the research that is continuously being conducted at and/or funded by major military research institutions (e.g., AFPTRC, AFOSR, AFRL, ARI, ARL, Armstrong Laboratory, NAVAIR TSD, ONR). Through publishing their findings, military researchers have significantly contributed to our understanding of employee selection and classification, job analysis, training, workplace design, motivation, learning and skill acquisition, performance conceptualization and measurement, performance enhancement, teams and team training, decision making, leadership, and expertise and have given us the opportunity to apply this knowledge to civilian industries and organizations.

The historical interdependence of I–O and military psychology is evidenced in many different ways. In 1945, the first elected president of APA's Division of Military Psychology (Division 19), John G. Jenkins, served at the same time he served as the elected president of APA's Division 14 (Industrial and Business Psychology). Jenkins, who was the chair of the Psychology Department at the University of Maryland from 1939 to 1948, chaired the Committee on the Selection and Training of Military Personnel from the National Research Council and, during World War II, he served as captain responsible for the Navy's Personnel Research Program. Large numbers of I–O psychologists have been employed by military research centers and laboratories.

In addition to supporting psychological research through grants, contracts, and its involvement in applied research, the military also promotes the exchange of research on topics relevant to I–O psychology through a journal and other publications by military research groups and the development of international conferences and scientific conferences and symposia held jointly with other scientific agencies. Most notably, it promotes this exchange through the *Journal of Military Psychology*, which contains articles on selection, training, and performance assessment of direct relevance to the science and practice of I–O psychology. Also noteworthy are the conventions held by the International Military Testing Association (IMTA), the International Applied Military Psychology Symposium (IAMPS), and APA Division 19. The annual conferences held by IMTA, IAMPS, and Division 19 of APA each provide a forum in which behavioral scientists can describe their research on military personnel assessment and on ways to improve the effectiveness of the Armed Forces. More information about them can be obtained from their Web sites (IMTA: www.internationalmta.org; IAMPS: www.iamps.org; Division 19 of APA: http://www.apa.org/divisions/div19).

These conferences have opened up communication of research results between I–O and military psychologists around the world. An early example of the latter was the 1967 NATO Conference on Manpower Research, held in London, where NATO provided the budget and the Office of Naval Research and others mobilized the participants. I–O psychologists making presentations included Harry Triandis, Ed Fleishman, Peter Drenth, Fred Fiedler, Jon Annett, and K. D. Duncan. Since then, these NATO conferences centered on I–O and military research concerns have been held periodically. The Office of Naval Research and the Army Research Institute have maintained offices in London and elsewhere to facilitate interchange of scientific information about human performance between researchers in the United States and scientists in other countries.

Moreover, the military has also contributed to the field of I–O psychology by promoting the benefits of applied psychology to the public. For instance, during World War II, the NRC created a paperback book entitled *Psychology for the Fighting Man*. This book described, in layman's terms, human behavior with regard to such topics as motivation, sensation and perception, social psychology, and personnel selection. Aimed at military and civilian populations alike, *Psychology for the Fighting Man* became a bestseller, with almost 400,000 copies sold before the end of World War II. The popularity of the book helped legitimize the science of applied psychology and brought public attention to the way in which psychology could aid everyday life (Samelson, 1977).

We believe that due to its continued financial support of basic and applied research through grants and contracts and through its own involvement in applied psychological research, the military will continue to be a strong force in the field of I–O psychology in the future. In addition, we believe that I–O psychology will continue to contribute many theories and ideas to military psychological research, forming a reciprocal relationship between the two disciplines.

ACKNOWLEDGMENTS

We thank Damon Bryant for his help on earlier versions of the manuscript and Walter C. Borman and several anonymous reviewers for their guidance in developing this manuscript.

REFERENCES

AFRL. (2003). *Laboratory introduction.* Retrieved May 7, 2004, from http://www.mesa.afmc.af.mil/html/intro.htm

ARL. (2005). *Collaborative technology alliances: Advanced Decision Architectures.* Retrieved July 26, 2005, from http://www.arl.Army.mil/main/researchopportunities/alliances/advanced_decision_architectures_2005a.cfm

Anderson, J. R. (1982). Acquisition of cognitive skill. *Psychological Review, 89,* 369–406.

Barling, J., Weber, T., & Kelloway, E. K. (1996). Effects of transformational leadership training on attitudinal and financial outcomes: A field experiment. *Journal of Applied Psychology, 81,* 827–832.

Bass, B. M. (1985). *Leadership and performance beyond expectations.* New York: The Free Press.

Bass, B. M. (1996). *A new paradigm of leadership: An inquiry into transformational leadership.* Alexandria, VA: U.S. Army Research Institute for the Behavioral and Social Sciences.

Bass, B. M. (1997). *Transformational leadership: Industry, military, and educational impact.* Mahwah, NJ: Lawrence Erlbaum Associates.

Bayroff, A. G. (1967). *An exploratory study of branching tests* (Technical Research Note No. 188). Alexandria, VA: U.S. Army Behavioral Sciences Research Laboratory (NTIS No. AD 655163).

Berry, L. M. (1998). *Psychology at work: An introduction to organizational psychology* (2nd ed.). Boston: McGraw-Hill.

Bingham, W. V. (1919). Army personnel work: With some implications for education and industry. *Journal of Applied Psychology, 3,* 1–12.

Bingham, W. V. (1944). Personnel testing in the Army. *Science, 100,* 275–280.

Bowers, C. A., Thornton, C., Braun, C., Morgan, B. B., Jr., & Salas, E. (1998). Automation, task difficulty, and aircrew performance. *Military Psychology, 10,* 275–274.

Bray, D. W., & Grant, D. L. (1966). The assessment center in the measurement of potential for business management. *Psychological Monographs, 80,* 1–27.

Burns, J. M. (1978). *Leadership.* New York: Harper & Row.

Campbell, J. P. (1971). Personnel training and development. *Annual Review of Psychology, 22,* 565–602.

Campbell, J. P. (1990). An overview of the Army Selection and Classification Project (Project A). *Personnel Psychology, 43,* 231–239.

Campbell, J. P., McHenry, J. J., & Wise, L. L. (1990). Modeling job performance in a population of jobs. *Personnel Psychology, 43,* 313–333.

Cannon-Bowers, J. A., & Salas, E. (1998a). *Making decisions under stress: Implications for individual and team training.* Washington, DC: APA.

Cannon-Bowers, J. A., & Salas, E. (1998b). Team performance and training in complex environments: Recent findings from applied research. *Current Directions in Psychological Science, 7,* 83–87.

Cannon-Bowers, J. A., Salas, E., Tannenbaum, S. I., & Mathieu, J. E. (1995). Toward theoretically-based principles of training effectiveness: A model and initial empirical investigation. *Military Psychology, 7,* 141–164.

Capshew, J. H. (1999). *Psychologists on the march: Science, practice, and professional identity in America, 1929–1969.* Cambridge, England: Cambridge University Press.

Caruano, R. M. (1999). An historical overview of standardized educational testing. Retrieved December 15, 2002, from http://www.gwu.edu/~gjackson/caruano.PDF

Channon, J. B. (1979). *The first earth battalion*. Task Force Delta Concept Paper, Ft. Monroe, VA. (Available from Paul A. Gade, U.S. Army Research Institute, 2511 Jefferson Davis Highway, Arlington, VA 22202-3926)

Cochrane, R. C. (1978). *The National Academy of Sciences: The first hundred years, 1863–1963*. Washington, DC: National Academy of Sciences.

Collyer, S. C., & Malecki, G. S. (1998). Tactical decision making under stress: History and overview. In J. A. Cannon-Bowers & E. Salas (Eds.), *Making decisions under stress: Implications for individual and team training* (pp. 3–15). Washington, DC: American Psychological Association.

Driskell, J. E., & Olmstead, B. (1989). Psychology and the military: Research applications and trends. *American Psychologist, 44,* 43–54.

Druckman, D., & Bjork, R. A. (Eds.) (1991). *In the mind's eye: Enhancing human performance*. Washington, DC: National Academy Press.

Druckman, D., & Bjork, R. A. (Eds.). (1994). *Learning, remembering, believing: Enhancing human performance*. Washington, DC: National Academy Press.

Druckman, D., Singer, J. E., & Van Cott, H. (Eds.). (1997). *Enhancing organizational performance*. Washington, DC: National Academy Press.

Druckman, D., & Swets, J. A. (Eds.). (1988). *Enhancing human performance: Issues, theories, and techniques*. Washington, DC: National Academy Press.

Dyer, J. L. (1984). Team research and team training: A state-of-the-art review. In F. A. Muckler (Ed.), *Human factors review: 1984* (pp. 285–323). Santa Monica, CA: The Human Factors Society.

Embretson, S. E. (2003). *The second century of ability testing: Some predictions and speculations*. Princeton, NJ: Educational Testing Service.

Fiedler, F. E. (1967). *A theory of leadership effectiveness*. New York: McGraw-Hill.

Fitts, P. M. (1964). Perceptual-motor skill learning. In A. W. Melton (Ed.), *Categories of human learning* (pp. 244–385). New York: Academic Press.

Flanagan, J. C. (1942). A study of factors determining family size in a selected professional group. *Genetic Psychology Monographs, 25,* 3–99.

Flanagan, J. C. (1948). *The aviation psychology program in the army air forces* (Rep. No. 1). Washington, DC: U. S. Government Printing Office.

Fleishman, E. A. (1954). Dimensional analysis of psychomotor abilities. *Journal of Experimental Psychology, 48,* 437–454.

Fleishman, E. A. (1975). Toward a taxonomy of human performance. *American Psychologist, 30,* 1127–1149.

Gagné, R. M. (1955). *Methods of forecasting maintenance job requirements*. Symposium on Electronic Maintenance. Washington, DC: U.S. Department of Defense, Assistant Secretary, Research and Development.

Gagné, R. M. (1962). Simulators. In R. Glaser (Ed.), *Training research and education* (pp. 223–246). Pittsburgh: University of Pittsburgh Press.

Goldstein, I. L. (1986). *Training in organizations: Needs assessment, development, and evaluation* (2nd ed.). Monterey, CA: Brooks/Cole.

Green, R. J., Self, H. C., & Ellfritt, T. S. (1995). *50 years of human engineering*. Dayton, OH: Crew System Directorate, Armstrong Laboratory.

Griffin, S. (n.d.). *Internet pioneers: Vannevar Bush*. Retrieved on June 10, 2004, from http://www.ibiblio.org/pioneers/bush.html

Harrell, T. W., & Churchill, R. D. (1941). The classification of military personnel. *Psychological Bulletin, 38,* 331–353.

Hedge, J. W., & Teachout, M. S. (1992). An interview approach to work sample criterion measurement. *Journal of Applied Psychology, 77,* 453–461.

Hedlund, J., Ilgen, D. R., & Hollenbeck, J. R. (1998). Decision accuracy in computer-mediated versus face-to-face decision-making teams. *Organizational Behavior and Human Decision Processes, 76,* 30–47.

Highhouse, S. (2002). Assessing the candidate as a whole: A historical and critical analysis of individual psychology assessment for personnel decision-making. *Personnel Psychology, 55,* 363–396.

Hoffman, L. E. (1992). American psychologists and wartime research on Germany, 1941–1945. *American Psychologist, 47,* 264–273.

Hollander, E. A. (1961). *Principles and methods of social psychology*. London: Oxford University Press.

Hollenbeck, J. R., Ilgen, D. R., LePine, J. A., Colquitt, J. A., & Hedlund, J. (1998). Extending the multilevel theory of team decision making: Effects of feedback and experience in hierarchical teams. *Academy of Management Journal, 41,* 269–282.

Hooijberg, R., Bullis, R. C., & Hunt, J. G. (1999). Behavioral complexity and the development of military leadership for the twenty-first century. In J. G. Hunt, G. E. Dodge, & L. Wong (Eds.), *Out of the box leadership: Transforming the twenty first century Army and other top performing organizations* (pp. 111–130). Stamford, CT: JAI.

Jacques, E., & Clement, S. D. (1991). *Executive leadership: A practical guide to managing complexity*. Arlington, VA: Cason Hall.

Kevles, D. J. (1968). Testing the Army's intelligence: Psychologists and the military in World War I. *Journal of American History, 55,* 565–581.

Kimmel, M. J. (1981). *Senior leadership: An annotated bibliography of the military and nonmilitary literature* (Tech. Rep. No. 532). Alexandria, VA: U.S. Army Research Institute for the Behavioral and Social Sciences (NTIS No. ADA 115890).

Kraiger, K., Ford, J. K., & Salas, E. (1993). Application of cognitive, skill-based, and affective theories of learning outcomes to new methods of training evaluation. *Journal of Applied Psychology, 78,* 311–328.

Kyllonen, P. C. (1996). Is working memory capacity Spearman's *g*? In I. Dennis & P. Tapsfield (Eds.), *Human abilities: Their nature and measurement* (pp. 49–75). Hillsdale, NJ: Lawrence Erlbaum Associates.

Kyllonen, P. C., & Christal, R. E. (1989). Cognitive modeling of learning abilities: A status report of LAMP. In R. F. Dillon & J. W. Pellegrino (Eds.), *Testing: Theoretical and applied perspectives* (pp. 146–173). New York: Praeger.

Kyllonen, P. C., & Christal, R. E. (1990). Reasoning ability is (little more than) working memory capacity?! *Intelligence, 14,* 389–433.

Legree, P. J., Fischl, M. A., Gade, P. A., & Wilson, M. (1998). Testing word knowledge by telephone to estimate general cognitive aptitude using and adaptive test. *Intelligence, 26,* 91–98.

LePine, J. A., Hollenbeck, J. R., Ilgen, D. R., Colquitt, J. A., & Ellis, A. (2002). Gender composition, situational strength, and team decision-making accuracy: A criterion decomposition approach. *Organizational Behavior and Human Decision Processes, 88,* 445–475.

Marshall-Meis, J. C., Fleishman, E. A., Martin, J. A., Zaccaro, S. J., Baughman, W. A., & McGee, M. L. (2000). Development and evaluation of cognitive and metacognitive measures for predicting leadership potential. *Leadership Quarterly, 11,* 135–153.

McBride, J. R. (1979). *Adaptive testing: The state of the art* (Tech. Rep. No. 423). Alexandria, VA: U.S. Army Research Institute for the Behavioral and Social Sciences. (NTIS No. AD A08800/5).

McBride, J. R. (1997). Dissemination of CAT-ASVAB technology. In W. A. Sands, B. K. Waters, & J. R. McBride (Eds.), *Computerized adaptive testing: From inquiry to operation.* (pp. 251–255). Washington, DC: APA.

McHenry, J. J., Hough, L. M., Toquam, J. L., Hanson, M. A., & Ashworth, S. (1990). Project A validity results: The relationship between predictor and criterion domains. *Personnel Psychology, 43,* 335–354.

Melton, A. W. (1957). Military psychology in the United States of America. *American Psychologist, 12,* 740–746.

Muchinsky, P. M. (1990). *Psychology applied to work: An introduction to industrial and organizational psychology* (3rd ed.). Belmont, CA: Wadsworth.

Murray, H. A., & MacKinnon, D. W. (1946). Assessment of OSS personnel. *Journal of Consulting Psychology, 10,* 76–80.

Murray, H. A., & OSS Assessment Staff. (1946). *Assessment of men: Selection of personnel for the Office of Strategic Services*. New York: Rinehart.

National Academy of Sciences. (2004). *Division of Anthropology and Psychology, 1940–1962*. Retrieved on June 9, 2004, from http://www7.nationalacademies.org/archives/Anthropology_and_Psych_1940-1962.html

National Research Council. (1999). *The changing nature of work: Implications for occupational analysis*. Washington, DC: National Academy Press.

NAVAIR TSD. (n.d.a). *NAVAIR Orlando: History.* Retrieved July 28, 2003, from http://www.ntsc.navy.mil/AboutUs/History.cfm

NAVAIR TSD. (n.d.b). *Mission and vision.* Retrieved July 28, 2003, from http://www.ntsc.navy.mil/AboutUs/Mission.cfm

Nelson, P. D. (2006). Human factors research in the naval service: Historical highlights. In A. D. Mangelsdorff (Ed.), *Psychology in the service of national security*. Washington, DC: APA.

Nullmeyer, R. T., & Spiker, V. A. (2003). The importance of crew resource management behaviors in mission performance: Implications for training evaluation. *Military Psychology, 15,* 77–96.

Pulakos, E. D., & Borman, W. C. (Eds.). (1988). *Development and field test of Army-wide rating scales and the rater orientation training program* (Tech. Rep. No. 716). Alexandria, VA: U.S. Army Research Institute for the Behavioral and Social Sciences (NTIS No. ADB 112857).

Riding, R. J., Grimley, M., Dahraei, H., & Banner, G. (2003). Cognitive style, working memory and learning behaviour and attainment in school subjects. *British Journal of Educational Psychology, 73,* 149–169.

Rosenweig, M. R., & Stone, G. (1948). Wartime research in psycho-acoustics. *Review of Educational Research, 18,* 642–654.

Ross, A. (1992, May). The long view of leadership. *Canadian Business, 65,* 46–50.

Salas, E., Bowers, C. A., & Cannon-Bowers, J. A. (1995). Military team research: 10 years of progress. *Military Psychology, 7,* 55–75.

Salas, E., Bowers, C. A., & Edens, E. (Eds.). (2001). *Improving teamwork in organizations: Applications of resource management training.* Mahwah, NJ: Lawrence Erlbaum Associates.

Salas, E., Cannon-Bowers, J. A., & Kozlowski, S. W. J. (1997). The science and practice of training: Current trends and emerging themes. In J. K. Ford & Associates (Eds.), *Improving training effectiveness in work organizations* (pp. 357–368). Hillsdale, NJ: Lawrence Erlbaum Associates.

Salas, E., Cannon-Bowers, J. A., Payne, S. C., & Smith-Jentsch, K. A. (1998). Teams and teamwork in the military. In C. Cronin (Ed.), *Military psychology: An introduction* (pp. 71–87). Old Tappan, NJ: Simon & Schuster.

Samelson, F. (1977). World War I intelligence testing and the development of psychology. *Journal of the History of the Behavioral Sciences, 13,* 274–282.

Sands, W. A., & Gade, P. A. (1983). An application of computerized adaptive testing in U. S. Army recruiting. *Journal of Computer-Based Instruction, 10,* 87–89.

Sands, W. A., Gade, P. A., & Knapp, D. J. (1997). The computerized adaptive screening test. In W. A. Sands, B. K. Waters, & J. R. McBride (Eds.), *Computerized adaptive testing: From inquiry to operation.* (pp. 69–80). Washington, DC: APA.

Simon, H. A., & Kadane, J. B. (1975). Optimal problem-solving search: All-or-none solutions. *Artificial Intelligence, 6,* 235–247.

Smith-Jentsch, K. A., Zeisig, R. L., Acton, B., & McPherson, J. A. (1998). Team dimensional training. In J. A. Cannon-Bowers & E. Salas (Eds.), *Making decisions under stress: Implications for individual and team training* (pp. 271–298). Washington, DC: APA

Staff, Psychological Branch, Office of the Air Surgeon. (1944). The Aviation Cadet Qualifying Examination of the Army Air Forces. *Psychological Bulletin, 41,* 385–394.

Sternberg, R. J., Forsythe, G. B., Hedlund, J., Horvath, J. A., Wagner, R. K., Williams, W. M., et al. (2000). *Practical intelligence in everyday life.* Cambridge, England: Cambridge University Press.

Sticht, T. G., & Armstrong, W. B. (n.d.). *Adult literacy in the United States: A compendium of quantitative data and interpretive comments.* Retrieved July 26, 2003, from http://www.nald.ca/fulltext/adlitUS/cover.htm

Stouffer, S. A. (1949). *The American Soldier: Vol. 1. Adjustment during army life; Vol. 2, Combat and its aftermath; Vol. 3, Experiments in mass communication; Vol. 4, Measurement and prediction.* Princeton, NJ: Princeton University Press.

Stout, R. J., Salas, E., & Carson, R. (1994). Individual task proficiency and team process behavior: What is important for team functioning? *Military Psychology, 6,* 177–192.

Swets, J. A., & Bjork, R. A. (1990). Enhancing human performance: An evaluation of "new age" techniques considered by the U.S. Army. *Psychological Science, 1,* 85–96.

Thornton, G. C., III. (1992). *Assessment centers in human resource management.* Reading, MA: Addison-Wesley.

Volpe, C. E., Cannon-Bowers, J., Salas, E., & Spector, P. E. (1996). The impact of cross-training on team functioning: An empirical investigation. *Human Factors, 38,* 87–100.

Wainer, H. (1990). *Computerized adaptive testing: A primer.* Hillsdale, NJ: Lawrence Erlbaum Associates.

Yerkes, R. M. (1918). Psychology in relation to war. *Psychological Review, 25,* 85–115.

Yerkes, R. M. (1919). Report of the Psychological Committee of the National Research Council. *Psychological Review, 26,* 83–149.

Yerkes, R. M. (1921). *Psychological examining in the United States Army: Memoirs of the National Academy of Sciences* (Vol. XV). Washington, DC: U.S. Government Printing Office.

Zaccaro, S. J. (1998). *Senior leadership: An annotated bibliography of research supported by the Army Research Institute* (Research Note No. 98-11). Alexandria, VA: U.S. Army Research Institute for the Behavioral and Social Sciences (NTIS No. ADA 347087).

Zaccaro, S. J. (1999). Social complexity and the competencies required for effective military leadership. In J. G. Hunt, G. E. Dodge, & L. Wong (Eds.), *Out of the box leadership: Transforming the twenty first century Army and other top performing organizations* (pp. 131–152). Stamford, CT: JAI.

Zaccaro, S. J. (2001). *The nature of executive leadership: A conceptual and empirical analysis of success.* Washington, DC: APA.

Zeidner, J., & Drucker, A. J. (1983). *Behavioral science in the Army: A corporate history of the Army Research Institute.* Alexandria, VA: U.S. Army Research Institute for the Behavioral and Social Sciences.

IV

Early Topics

This section contains six chapters that provide historical perspectives on topics prevalent during the early years of industrial psychology.

As noted in several previous chapters, selection was and continues to be a significant component of the discipline. Chapter 8 includes a historical perspective on selection and covers three time periods: the late 19th century until approximately 1930, from around 1930 to 1963, from approximately 1964 to the present day. Within each period, contextual and climate factors that influenced selection are examined. In addition, techniques and developments in measurement and statistics are explored, along with the efforts of psychologists in selection research and practice during that period. The major emphasis in this chapter is on the origins and early years of psychology and employee selection to approximately 1930.

Chapter 9 contains a historical view of job analysis and is organized into several sections. Prior histories of job analysis are presented along with descriptions of important contributors to the field. A third section discusses the context in which the field of job analysis developed throughout three eras. Each era concludes with a type of work that is illustrative of that era and with important "firsts" in job analysis. Five schools of job analyses are then described, followed by lessons from examining a history of job analysis.

As explained in chapter 10, the discipline of human factors originated from several sources, most notably, I–O psychology. Until World War II, many applied psychologists considered themselves to be both I–O and engineering psychologists. Given that the history of human factors is considered to be part of the history of industrial psychology, especially during the early years, it was decided to include a chapter to cover a history of human factors. As noted in the chapter, during World War II, applied psychologists began to merge their work with the work of engineers, and the discipline of engineering psychology was born and eventually developed into its own entity separate from I–O psychology.

In addition to selection and human factors, one of the first endeavors to apply psychology to solve business problems was in the realm of advertising at the end of the 19th century. Therefore, chapter 11 is included in this book to provide a historical perspective on the discipline known today as "consumer psychology." The authors discuss three distinct schools that emerged (mentalistic, behaviorism, and dynamic psychology), which influenced the applied psychologists of the day.

Chapter 12 describes the expanding role of workplace training within I–O psychology. The authors identify key chapters, books, and other resources on training from approximately 1910 to the present day. They focus on four different eras relevant to managing work. An analysis of the expanding role of training centers on identifying, for each era, what training "looked" like (e.g., what was the focus of training? who was being trained? what were the typical goals of training?), what learning theories and perspectives were dominant, and what advances were made in training research and practice. After examining each era in detail, the authors analyze key trends or themes in training across era.

Chapter 13 traces the development of performance appraisal over five time periods. The authors note that the focus on measurement was operationalized in the work of I–O psychologists, beginning with World War I and continuing through the 1920s. Other time periods include (a) the 1930s: Depression, (b) World War II and the Eisenhower Years, (c) 1960s and 1970s, and (d) 1980s to present. The chapter concludes with lessons learned from examining the evolution of performance appraisal.

8

A History of Psychology
Applied to Employee Selection

Andrew J. Vinchur
Lafayette College

Central to the development of early industrial psychology, employee selection has been a core activity in the field of industrial-organizational (I–O) psychology for close to 100 years. Although selection can be interpreted broadly to include vocational guidance and placement, that is, selecting jobs for individuals (Kornhauser, 1922), the emphasis in this chapter is on the narrower definition, choosing among individuals to fill a particular job. Employee selection, of course, predates the efforts of applied psychologists. Economic organizations have always had procedures in place to determine whom to admit or reject. What the early industrial psychologists[1] brought to selection was a particular approach, relying on the scientific methodology of the new experimental psychology and grounded in the measurement of individual differences, of empirically verifying the efficacy of their efforts. This approach depended on progress in both measurement and statistics and reflected a pragmatic approach much in harmony with the progressive attitudes of the times.

This chapter is divided into three time periods: "Origins and Early Years" covers the late 19th century until approximately 1930; "Depression, World War II, and Postwar Prosperity" examines selection from around 1930 to 1963; and "Civil Rights Era and Beyond" takes us from approximately 1964 to the present day. Within each section, contextual and climate factors from both inside and outside of psychology that influenced efforts to apply psychology to selecting employees are examined. In addition, methods, procedures, and developments in measurement and statistics are explored, along with an overview, in rough chronological order, of the efforts of psychologists in selection research and practice during that period. Research studies and applications that were innovative or illustrative of accepted practice are emphasized. Although the main focus of this chapter is on work done in the United States, many important developments in selection occurred outside of this country. Space considerations preclude covering these developments in the detail they merit, but an attempt is made to highlight some of these efforts in the "Origins and Early Years" section.

The major emphasis in this chapter is on the origins and early years of psychology and employee selection to approximately 1930. It was during this period that the basic philosophy and

---

[1]Labels for psychologists working in business settings included economic psychologists, business psychologists, consulting psychologists, employment psychologists, psycho-technicians, and industrial psychologists. For consistency, the term *industrial psychologist* is used in this chapter.

paradigm underpinning psychologists' efforts in selection research and practice throughout the 20th century developed. This paradigm has been remarkably resilient. Many of the procedures, predictors, and criteria used in this period are similar (albeit less sophisticated) to those in use today. In addition, origins, arbitrary as they may be, of any endeavor are inherently interesting. Coverage of events after 1930 required trading depth for breadth. Any attempt to cover the massive amount of material generated in employee selection research and practice over this more than 70-year time period is bound to be highly selective and incomplete. Trends and landmark contributions are emphasized, with coverage focusing on scientific developments in the United States.

The history of employee selection encompasses a number of topics covered in other chapters in this volume. To avoid duplication, at various points in the narrative the reader will be directed to other chapters for more information. The very important related topics of job analysis and criteria, for example, are covered in chapters 9 and 13 respectively, and are therefore given minimal coverage in this chapter. More information about employee selection as a core activity in I–O psychology, the social-economic context of early I–O psychology, and the impact of the civil rights movement on selection practice can be found in chapters 1 and 3. Chapter 3 also contains a discussion of pseudoscience relevant for selection. Professional and personal information about Cattell, Münsterberg, Scott, Bingham, and many of the early pioneers in selection can be found in chapter 2. Additional information about development in selection outside of the United States appears in chapter 4. Chapter 6 contains information about organizations important to the development of employee selection, such as the applied psychology program at the Carnegie Institute of Technology, the Scott Corporation, and the Personnel Research Federation. The impact of the military on selection research and practice appears in chapter 7.

ORIGINS AND EARLY YEARS TO 1930

Context and Climate

The efforts of the early applied psychologists occurred in a social and economic environment different in many ways from the present day. For example, as the 20th century began, the population of the United States was 76 million with a total workforce of individuals 10 years and older of 24 million. In 1900 the average life expectancy for both sexes was 47 years, child labor was common, and only 19% of working-age females participated in the workforce. The average workweek in manufacturing was 53 hours. America was a nation of farmers, foresters, and producers of primary products. Farmers comprised 38% of the workforce; producers of goods such as mining, manufacturing, and construction comprised 31%; the remaining 31% were in service occupations (Bureau of Labor Statistics, 2001).

Katzell and Austin (1992) identified four cultural forces that came together from the beginning of the 20th century until World War I and resulted in the establishment of industrial–organizational psychology in the United States: (a) advances in science; (b) the rise of Darwin's evolutionary theory and its psychological counterpart functionalism; (c) faith in capitalism and the Protestant work ethic; and (d) the growth of industrialism, which resulted in a society that valued efficiency in organizations and the people in them (see also Koppes, 2003). Influences from World War I to about 1930 included the war itself, the initial prosperity that followed that conflict, the willingness of executives (perhaps influenced by wartime experiences) to employ psychologists, and the emergence and growth of the employment management field. Because both contemporary (e.g., Viteles, 1923) and recent accounts agree that employee selection was the dominant component of early industrial psychology, it would follow that all of these factors influenced the development of employee selection as well.

The beginnings of an experimental psychology, pioneered by individuals such as Wilhelm Wundt and his students in the late 19th century, provided an orientation and a methodology for the early industrial psychologists. Two industrial psychology pioneers who worked on employee selection, Walter Dill Scott and Hugo Münsterberg, obtained their doctorates under Wundt (James McKeen Cattell, another important figure in the history of selection, was also Wundt's student). The early psychologists who worked on selecting employees did so from within a scientific framework, and personnel selection presented an opportunity for the application of the scientific method. Psychologists like Scott (and eventually Münsterberg) differed from mainstream academic psychologists in the early 1900s because they believed this new scientific psychology should be transferred from the laboratory to business settings. Academic psychologists interested in applied work did have misgivings, however. Prominent psychologists like Wundt and Edward B. Titchener of Cornell looked unfavorably on applied work (Baritz, 1960) and even Münsterberg was once quite hostile to application (Benjamin, 2000).

The influence of Darwinism (often clichéd as the survival of the fittest) on personnel selection (selection of the fittest) seems obvious. The functionalist orientation ("What is it for?" rather than the structuralist "What is it?") fit the pragmatic concerns of early industrial psychology. In functionalism the emphasis is on individual differences and their consequences. An additional influence was scientific pragmatism, which based the worth of ideas on their utilitarian consequences and emphasized prediction over understanding (Austin & Villanova, 1992). This orientation can be found in the work of the early industrial psychologists concerned with selection. Freyd (1923–1924), for example, noted that determining the functions measured by a selection test "may be omitted, since the important point to determine is the correlation of the test scores with the criteria of success" (p. 249). Many of the early industrial psychologists were trained in the functionalist strongholds of the University of Chicago (e.g., Walter Van Dyke Bingham, Clarence Yoakum, L. L. Thurstone) and Columbia University (e.g., E. L. Thorndike, Harry Hollingworth, Edward K. Strong, Jr., Herbert A. Toops).

The early 20th century saw a continuation of the rise of industrialization. Economic firms became larger and more difficult to manage. One result of this increased scale directly relevant for employee selection was the decline in influence of the first-level supervisor, the foreman. Traditionally responsible for recruitment and hiring, the foreman saw his role diminish due to at least three factors (Nelson, 1975). The increasingly large size of organizations resulted in the rise of systematic management, which eventually usurped many of the foreman's responsibilities, including hiring. In addition, the perceived plight of the worker resulted in welfare programs and regulations, further inhibiting the foreman's control over rewards and punishments. And finally, the rise of labor unions around World War I and management's attempts to deal with this development further constrained foremen. With large companies increasingly relying on personnel departments to take on the task of employee selection, some type of systematic approach was needed. Scientific employee selection, particularly the use of tests, seemed to fit the bill. Hale (1992) noted that employment testing rose in response to the rapid growth in industrial society, the need to find a way to manage a chaotic labor market, and the desire to make American society more democratic by selection based on merit rather than privilege. Although it is open to question whether the early industrial psychologists had democratizing society as a goal, explicitly and implicitly they worked from a merit-based model of selecting the most qualified person for a particular job.

Not only were mainstream academic psychologists uncertain of the worth of the new applied psychology, but managers were generally quite skeptical as well. Whether due to the perception that psychologists could not agree among themselves, the perceived questionable practical applications of their findings, or managers' beliefs that they were competent to deal with their problems without outside help (Baritz, 1960), managers remained somewhat indifferent to the new applied psychology until the post-World War I period. To be fair, these misunderstandings were often a two-way street. Link (1920), for example, noted that not only have businessmen failed to appreciate refinements in psychological methods, but psychologists have failed to understand industry. He stated that there have been many applications "of psychology *to* industry, but not so many *in* industry" (p. 336, emphasis in the original). Exacerbating the situation was an inability or unwillingness on the part of management to distinguish between psychologists and a host of other purveyors of "expert" advice, particularly in the area of selection. Properly conducted scientific selection was time-consuming and could be expensive. It was always tempting to go for the quick, inexpensive fix.

Part of establishing a niche for industrial psychology was differentiating it from nonscientific forms of practice. A fair amount of journal space was dedicated to railing against and debunking "the promulgators of the innumerable varieties of fake psychology which are being foisted today upon an uncritical public" (Kingsbury, 1923, p. 3). In the area of selection, particular concern was directed at systems of analysis based on estimates of physiological/psychophysiological traits or on estimates of anatomical traits (Dunlap, 1923). Examples include palmistry, phrenology, physiognomy, and graphology. In the area of personnel selection, a particular target was the popular character analysis system of Katherine Blackford, described in chapter 3. Blackford believed that personality traits could be determined by the analysis of physical traits (e.g., shape of the face). Once determined, applicant characteristics could be matched with job requirements (Blackford & Newcomb, 1914). Although Kornhauser (1922) did credit Blackford and Newcomb for elucidating the selection problem from the employer's perspective and emphasizing individual differences (despite the "thoroughly unscientific and misleading character analysis methods included" [p. 79]), industrial psychologists recognized the importance of distinguishing their scientific approach from these other approaches. Dunlap (1923), for example, noted in a review that no factual basis for any anatomical system of character analysis exists (he did, however, hold off judgment regarding graphology). Paterson and Ludgate (1922–1923) found no evidence for Blackford's contention of personality differences between blondes and brunettes. Cleeton and Knight (1924) found zero correlations between physical character judgments and either judgments made by casual observers or by close associates, concluding that the measurements of character analysis do not agree with other measures of character. Psychologists themselves at times engaged in or advocated selection procedures that would be deemed questionable or worse from a present-day perspective. Examples include the judgment of applicant characteristics based on photographs (see Johns & Worcester, 1930) and the use of anatomical characteristics (e.g., Sheldon, 1927–1928). These procedures, like character analysis, were eventually evaluated empirically and found wanting.

The perceived successes of psychology in World War I contributed to an increased demand for psychological services after the war, especially in the areas of selection and testing (employee testing and employee selection were virtually synonymous in the early years). With the resistance of managers diminishing, testing became very popular, and for at least a few years, demand for psychological services in industry was high. By the mid-1920s, however, demand had dropped. Hale (1992) noted that this decline could have been due to an upturn in the economy and subsequent reduction of turnover rates, the failure of the tests to deliver what they promised, and a growing disenchantment with these tests by industrial psychologists. Sokal (1984) characterized industrial psychology in the 1920s as exhibiting a pattern of limited success, overconfidence and overstatement, and retrenchment. As noted previously, however, much of the overselling of easy solutions came from nonpsychologists. Reputable psychologists urged caution in the use of psychological tests (e.g., Kornhauser & Kingsbury, 1924), and many tests were being used by individuals not qualified to properly administer, score, interpret, or determine the validity of these

tests (Sokal, 1984). It is probably the case, as Sokal (1984) noted, that even conscientious, reputable psychologists could not offer immediate solutions to the problems facing business. By the
1920s, however, there were in place generally accepted employee selection procedures by means
of which reputable industrial psychologists could demonstrate the value of their efforts. We now
turn to the development of these procedures.

Measurement

Scientific employee selection depends on the existence of individual differences in abilities,
aptitudes, attitudes, or interests among individuals. In his presidential address to the American Psychological Association in 1919, Walter Dill Scott (1920) called the establishment of
a psychology of individual differences the greatest single achievement of the members of
that body. Whether or not this is true for psychology in general, the existence and accurate
measurement of these differences are essential for prediction of job performance. Although a
comprehensive history of psychological measurement is far beyond the scope of this chapter,
we can pick up the story in the late 1800s and highlight events relevant for the development of
employee selection.

James McKeen Cattell (1890) is generally credited with coining the term *mental test*. His
own work on the measurement of individual differences relied on the use of anthropometric
tests of physiological and sensory abilities. Test accuracy was based on a test's relation to other
tests (von Mayrhauser, 1992). Cattell's hope that his tests would be predictive of academic
ability was dashed when his student Clark Wissler (1901) found generally low and negative
correlations between these tests and academic performance. This was one of the first uses of
correlation for this purpose (von Mayrhauser, 1992).

Rogers (1995) noted that determining what makes a test "good" was a highly social enterprise, the result of a protracted negotiation among the young testing community in the early
1900s. The negotiation began with the vaguely defined notion of *trustworthiness*, the idea that
tests provided a faithful representation of the world, that arose from Jastrow, Baldwin, and
Cattell's (1898) emphasis on cost efficiency and simplicity and progressed through Charles
Spearman's introduction of reliability or freedom from errors of measurement[2] (T. B. Rogers,
1995). Reliability was not enough, however, for a test could be perfectly consistent and still be
untrustworthy, that is, not faithfully measure what it is supposed to measure. Bingham (1923)
stated that up until 1915, psychologists "were wasting time" (p. 292) devising tests and evaluating them based on their approximations to the normal distribution or their correlations with
other tests.

By 1910, the test-criterion method was becoming the standard for establishing test value. This
method used the correlation coefficient to determine the relation between the test, or any predictor, and some other independent measure termed a *criterion* to evaluate the value of a test. The
coefficient of correlation was based on the work of, among others, Francis Galton, Walter
Weldon, and Karl Pearson.[3] F. Y. Edgeworth introduced the term *coefficient of correlation* "in an
impossibly difficult-to-follow paper published in 1892" (Cowles, 2001, p.145). The use of the
correlational test-criterion method became the standard one in personnel selection (the other two
strategies in the familiar validity trio, content and construct validity, were developed formally af-

---

[2]Spearman first used the term *reliability coefficient* as a correlation describing measurement consistency in his 1907
paper with Kreuger; however, the concept was already in development as early as 1904 (cited in DuBois, 1970).

[3]Pearson made a number of important contributions to statistics relevant for employee selection. In addition to the prod-
uct-moment correlation based on the 1846 work of Bravais, Pearson's standard deviation replaced variability measurement
by probable errors. He devised multiple correlation calculating methods, correlation for qualitative data, the correlation ratio, nonlinear regression, biserial correlation, and the chi-square statistic, all before 1909 (Hearnshaw, 1964).

ter 1930, although their roots are evident in this earlier period). One could evaluate the test's *diagnostic value* (test and criterion measured at approximately the same time) or the *prognostic value* (criterion measured some time after test administration; Rogers, 1995).

Scott (1917) described four methods for estimating the diagnostic and prognostic value of a test used in selection. The *firm rank* method involves comparing test rankings with average supervisor rankings for a group of employees who vary in performance. Testing employees of known ability with applicants and seeing if the test can identify these experienced employees is the *ringers* method. The *vocational accomplishments* method, which Scott called the most dependable method, compares test ratings with later vocational accomplishments. The fourth method, *applicants–experts,* compares a group of applicants, the majority of whom are expected to fail, with a group of successful employees. The test has value to the extent that it separates the two groups.

By the early 1920s, the term *validity* was becoming common (the earliest occurrence of the term *validity* in its current usage that T. B. Rogers, 1995, was able to locate was Starch, 1915). Acceptance was encouraged by the Standardization Committee of the National Association of Directors of Educational Research, which recommended in 1921 that the determination of what a test measures should be termed *validity. Reliability* should be reserved for consistency of measurement (T. B. Rogers, 1995). By the mid-1920s, prognostic value was evolving into *predictive validity,* whereas diagnostic value was increasingly termed *concurrent validity.*

Also by the early 1920s, a method was in place that is recognizably the modern criterion-related validation strategy. By way of illustration, we can sketch the selection process as advocated by Freyd (1923–1924), Kornhauser and Kingsbury (1924), and Bingham and Freyd (1926).[4] Freyd (1923–1924) was self-consciously scientific in his orientation, terming the process an "experiment" and the applicants "subjects." He first recommends consulting a cost accountant to determine the department where improved selection can bring about the greatest economic return. Job analysis is the next step, followed by a decision, in consultation with firm executives, to select a criterion of success. Subjects for the study are then selected, and those abilities necessary for success in the occupation are identified. Based on these requirements, measuring instruments (e.g., tests, questionnaires, rating scales) are selected or constructed and administered to the subjects. Next, scores on the measuring instruments are compared with the criterion of vocational success to "summarize the prognostic value of the tests" (p. 272). Successful instruments are combined and their predictive accuracy is compared with existing methods, determining what today we would call *incremental validity.* Finally, the experimenter must see to the proper installation and use of the procedures, continually check their accuracy, and make adjustments accordingly. Bingham and Freyd (1926) added checking the reliability of the measuring instruments to the list. By this point, they were also using the term *validity* to describe the process of determining value.

Kornhauser and Kingsbury's (1924) procedures were similar. Following a job analysis, tests are devised or selected. Tests scores are obtained from either applicants or, less desirably, current employees. Then a measure of ability, the criterion, is obtained from production records, supervisor methods, or length of time on the job. Agreement is determined between test scores and job ability. The new methods are compared with alternative methods. And finally, standards or critical scores are set for acceptance, rejection, or classification.

Freyd (1923–1924) discussed the various methods extant for combining test scores. Methods include adding raw scores, weighting (i.e., weighting to equalize medians or means or weighting according to reliability), expressing scores in standard deviation units, adding percentile standings, and assigning weights based on the size of the correlation. Freyd recommended multiple re-

---

[4]See Guion (1976) for a detailed discussion of Freyd's procedures.

gression analysis as the most accurate technique. He also discussed combinations based on group comparison or critical scores and the profile method. In keeping with his objective orientation, Freyd criticized the profile method for its reliance on individual judgment.

Bingham and Freyd (1926) included a short list of questions to ask before undertaking selection: Is there an actual selection problem in the occupation? Are there more applicants than jobs? Are there an adequate number of employees in a specific job to make conducting a study feasible? Is a valid and reliable criterion available? And finally, can the investigator count on the cooperation of the organization?

Not all industrial psychologists were comfortable with a reliance on the statistical approach. Viteles (1925) argued for the inclusion of a clinical viewpoint, taking Freyd (1923–1924) to task for his emphasis on statistical validity. Viteles in particular was critical of the notions that a "psycho-technician" without extensive training in psychology can adequately interpret test scores and that a single test score was adequate for diagnosis. Arguing that both the statistical and clinical approaches are necessary in selection, Viteles further stated that the statistical method, with its emphasis on the group rather than the individual, failed to give adequate consideration to the interests and well-being of the individual worker. This is in contrast to what Viteles saw as the more humane European approaches of that time.

Freyd (1925), consistent with Thorndike (1918), reiterated the major points of his 1923–1924 article and refuted Viteles point by point. Freyd defended the experimental method, noting that after careful criterion selection, analysis of job requirements, test construction, and successful correlation of test and criterion, the psychologist has verifiable evidence that the procedure is a valid one. By putting selection on a firm scientific basis, the psychologist can provide empirical proof for his or her judgment. Freyd bluntly stated: "The field for the psychologist in industry is experimental research. If other fields seem greener they are a mirage" (p. 352). Freyd questioned the accuracy of psychologists' judgments over the judgments of experienced managers, noted the evidence for unreliability of judgments in general, and claimed that Viteles' concern for the worker is not served by the "unavoidable prejudices" of the clinical method.

In summary, as illustrated by Bingham and Freyd (1926), Freyd (1923–1924), and Kornhauser and Kingsbury (1924), by the late 1920s components of the selection process included conducting a job analysis, selecting a criterion, constructing or selecting a predictor, empirically determining the relation between the predictor and the criterion, and finally, using some type of decision rule to determine whether to accept or reject an applicant.

As Taylor and Russell (1939) noted, Clark Hull (1928) anticipated a concept important in later discussions of selection "utility." Hull distinguished between predicting individual performance and predicting average performance of a group. Given a large number of applicants and a small number of openings, even tests with moderate validities (less than .50) could have considerably more value than is indicated by his own Index of Forecasting Efficiency.[5]

Although the test-criterion method was in use by the end of the first decade of the 20th century, the term *criterion* in its present-day usage as a job standard came later. Austin and Villanova (1992) credited Bingham (1926) as perhaps the first to define the criterion as a measuring stick for determining an employee's relative success or failure. They also credited Burtt (1926) as perhaps the first to use the term *criterion* as a job proficiency index that can be used in evaluating whether a test is predictive of that proficiency. Early on, industrial psychologists recognized the importance of selecting a relevant criterion, the difficulties associated with criterion selection, and potential problems associated with criteria. Both Freyd (1923–1924) and

---

[5]The Index of Forecasting Efficiency is defined as $E = 1 - [1 - r^2]^{1/2}$, where r is the correlation between the predictor and criterion (Hull, 1928).

Kornhauser and Kingsbury (1924) discussed the importance of obtaining relevant criteria. Viteles (1925–1926a) noted that although there is no shortage of authors who discuss the importance of adequate criteria, in practice the majority of selection experiments in the literature use criteria that are inadequate. In particular, Viteles singled out unreliable ratings and rankings that are used even when less subjective production criteria are available. Austin and Villanova (1992) noted that although it was recognized that the job performance is multidimensional, most empirical studies conducted during these early years used one or two criteria. Categorization tended to be crude, generally into only subjective and objective categories.

Overview of Research and Practice to 1930

As early as 1814, the U.S. Army introduced testing for surgeons, followed by Naval Academy and West Point testing of prospective students (see Hale, 1992, and DuBois, 1970, for details of early testing efforts, including early Civil Service Examinations). In 1901, the Italian psychologist Ugo Pizzoli was using tests to select apprentices (Salgado, 2001), and Jean Marie Lahy in France was studying the selection of stenographers by 1905 (Viteles, 1923) and streetcar drivers by 1908 (Fryer & Henry, 1950). Meriam (1906) correlated normal school grades and city examination results with superintendent and principal estimates of teaching efficiency for a sample of elementary school teachers. In April 1912 at the German Congress of Psychology in Berlin, Hugo Münsterberg presented his study on the selection of streetcar drivers (Salgado, 2001). That same year he published the German edition of *Psychology and Industrial Efficiency;* the English-language version appeared in 1913. In the section of the text titled "The Best Possible Man," Münsterberg describes investigations into the selection of not only streetcar motormen but also ship officers and telephone switchboard operators. (See chap. 1 for the table of contents of this text.)

   Münsterberg's first effort in industrial psychology was a 1909 magazine article on the application of psychology to business. This resulted in the consulting opportunities in selection described in his 1913 book (Benjamin, 2000). In his study of motormen, Münsterberg (1913) focused on accident reduction. After determining attention to be the key function in accident reduction, he developed a laboratory test to duplicate the attentional process in motormen. Münsterberg noted that the examination would be valuable if two conditions were met. First, good results would be associated with reliable motormen, bad results with unreliable motormen. And second, the motormen must believe that the mental functions tested in the experiment were similar to the ones used in driving the electric car (an early example of face validity). Münsterberg found that the older, more experienced motormen with fewer accidents made fewer errors on his test. For selecting ship captains, Münsterberg developed a card-sorting task; however, he did not report any results. For the telephone operators, Münsterberg chose a series of tests (e.g., word association, card sorting, digit span) that measured functions he believed necessary for success. The skeptical telephone company embedded some experienced operators among the trainees. Fortunately for Münsterberg, these women stood at the top of the list of scores.

   In 1914, H. C. McComas of Princeton University published his work on the use of a switchboard and a motor coordination test for selecting telephone operators. In October of the next year Walter Dill Scott's investigation on the use of the interview for the selection of salesmen appeared in *Advertising & Selling.* Two other notable early selection studies in the United States were Edward S. Jones' (1917) use of the Woolley-Test series as a predictor of success in telegraphy and Herbert W. Rogers' (1917) investigation of 10 psychological tests for predicting performance of stenographers and typists. Viteles (1932) called these four selection studies by McComas, Scott, Jones, and Rogers the beginnings of industrial psychology in the United

States. The year 1917 also saw Lewis M. Terman's use of an intelligence test and pedagogical tests to predict, among other things, salary of applicants for police and firefighter positions. Flanders (1918) used the Stanford–Binet to try to predict a number of job-related criteria, with disappointing results. In 1918 Elsie Oschrin published the results of various tests for the selection of retail saleswomen.

Although not without faults from a present-day perspective, early selection studies have a trajectory that demonstrates increasing sophistication in technique. There is a progression toward the increased use of correlation in a test-criterion strategy in evaluating the predictors. H W. Rogers (1917) used an early standard score method proposed by Woodworth to transform scores and measured the typing criterion over a six-month period. Henry C. Link's (1918) work at the Winchester Repeating Arms Company provides another example of an innovative study for its time. In 1916 Link evaluated a series of tests for predicting performance of shell inspectors and gaugers (who gauged the head thickness of the shells). Selection of the tests was based on a subjective analysis of the job and included measures of visual acuity, reaction time, accuracy of movement, and steadiness of attention. In choosing a measure of job performance (pounds of shells inspected in a day), Link recognized that simply measuring performance on the day of testing would be unreliable. Instead, he took the average of a 4-week period. In addition, Link examined the stability of the correlations across other groups of employees.

To illustrate the types of predictors and criteria common in the years up until 1930, I analyzed 170 studies conducted from 1906 through 1930.[6] Working from a core of empirical validation studies identified and summarized in Dorcus and Jones (1950), I included domestic and nondomestic studies that used job proficiency as a criterion and identified the sample size and type of job. Although not comprising all of the validation studies conducted through 1930, the sample is large enough to draw some general conclusions about the state of selection research during this time period. The 170 studies contained 284 separate independent samples, with a median sample size per independent sample of 35 (the range was 4–5,002). The median independent sample size of 35 would be considered small by present-day standards. The total number of individuals tested across the studies was 38,767. Of the predictors that could be categorized, 703 could be classified as tests, 23 were biographical data, 13 were grades, and eight were ratings. Table 8.1 categorizes these tests using Kornhauser and Kingsbury's (1924) functional classification approach. Some tests, particularly those long out of print or "homemade" for a particular study, were difficult to classify; thus, results should be considered merely suggestive of trends. Also included in Table 8.1 are summaries of criteria used and the types of jobs assessed.

Tests of simpler mental functions (e.g., memory span, substitution tests, cancellation tests) proved very popular. Together with the more comprehensive tests of general intelligence, they account for more than 50% of the tests used. Other tests of special aptitudes, such as motor tests (e.g., tapping tests) and sensory tests (e.g., visual acuity) were fairly popular. Personality testing was in its infancy; only a little more than 3% of the tests used were tests of character and temperament (only 4 of the 703 tests were tests of vocational interest). On the criterion side, subjective criteria were most often used, with supervisor ratings the most popular. Objective criteria, primarily production and sales criteria, were used less than one-third of the time. Clerical and office jobs, along with manufacturing and factory work, were popular occupations in validation studies. Given the large of proportion of workers involved in manufacturing at the time, this emphasis on manufacturing is not surprising.

---

[6]Validity studies summarized in Dorcus and Jones (1950) were supplemented by four additional studies. The bulk of these studies (147) took place from 1921 through 1930. Two studies were undated. A list of studies included in the analysis is available from the author.

TABLE 8.1
Summary Information From Validity Studies: 1906–1930

Functional Classification of Tests	Frequency	Percent
Test of proficiencies	46	6.6
Educational tests	2	0.3
Trade tests	44	6.3
Tests of aptitudes	635	90.3
General aptitude tests	75	10.6
General intelligence tests	65	9.2
Mechanical aptitude tests	10	1.4
Special aptitude tests	560	79.7
Physical tests	44	6.3
Motor tests	117	16.6
Sensory tests	96	13.7
Special mental functions	303	43.1
Tests of character & temperament	22	3.2
Total	703	100.0
Criteria		
Objective	59	31.9
Production	19	9.9
Sales	14	7.3
Accidents	5	2.6
Salary	4	2.1
Job level	3	1.6
Subjective	126	68.1
Ratings	94	49.0
Ranking	32	16.7
Type of job		
Clerical & office	80	29.5
Manufacturing	69	25.5
Sales	34	12.5
Teaching	23	8.5
Transportation	23	8.5
Service	14	5.2
Construction	10	3.7
Managerial	8	3.0

Note. Some percentages may not add up to 100% due to unclassified entries.

In Germany, as in the United States, the principle concern of industrial psychologists was employee selection (Viteles, 1923). By 1916 Walter Moede and Curt Piorkowski were developing selection methods for army chauffeurs, and in 1917 the Saxon Railway Company in Dresden established a laboratory for the selection of locomotive engineers and other employees. William Stern undertook an investigation of streetcar drivers in 1917 (Viteles, 1925–1926b), and the Greater Berlin Tramways began investigating motorman selection in 1918 (Viteles, 1923). Two other relevant activities in Germany before 1910 were the founding and support of the Institute of Applied Psychology in Berlin in 1906 by Otto Lipmann (Stern, 1934) and the founding of the journal *Zeitschrift für angewandte Psychologie* (Journal for Applied Psychology) by Lipmann and William Stern in 1907 (Viteles, 1932).

As described in previous chapters, the founding of the Division of Applied Psychology at the Carnegie Institute of Technology in 1915 was a watershed event for industrial psychology in general and personnel selection in particular. Under the direction of Walter Van Dyke Bingham, this was the first graduate program in industrial psychology in America.

The men and women who worked and studied at Carnegie Tech made a number of important contributions to the field of personnel selection. In 1916 Scott, assisted by his students, produced *Aids in the Selection of Salesmen* (cited in Ferguson, 1962–1965). Those aids were an application blank, a letter to former employers, interviewer's guides and record blanks, and a series of five tests. The model application blank, or Personal History Record, requested that the applicant supply personal information, such as height and weight, marital status, number of dependents, time lost due to illness over the previous 2 years, educational background, memberships, reasons for making a job change, and, in at least 50 words, why he believed he would be a successful salesman. The Interviewer's Scale (along with the Interviewer's Rating Sheet, later termed the Scott man-to-man rating system; Ferguson, 1961) had the interviewer rate applicants by comparing them with benchmark salesmen. Test Ia measured mental alertness and was modeled after earlier tests used by Scott in industry between 1908 and 1915. Test II was a test of foresight, whereas Test III, based on earlier work by Thorndike, was designed to measure speed and accuracy in understanding instructions. Test IV, adapted from a test by Marion Trabue, was an incomplete sentences test supposedly helpful in making mental diagnoses. Test V, modeled on a test by Edward S. Robinson, was a test of range of interests, similar to general intelligence informational tests (Ferguson, 1962–1965, n.d.). Ferguson (1962–1965) stated that these five tests represented one of the earliest series of tests constructed for wide use in industry and that testing in industry has closely followed the pattern set by these early tests. Scott's ideas about "testing the tests" were discussed earlier in this chapter.

A partial list of staff and students who made important contributions to the development of personnel selection before, during, and after their time at Carnegie Tech includes Marion A. Bills, Max Freyd, Arthur W. Kornhauser, Grace Manson, James B. Miner, Bruce V. Moore, M. J. Ream, Edward K. Strong, Jr., Louis L. Thurstone, Guy Montrose Whipple, and Clarence Stone Yoakum.

When the United States declared war on Germany in 1917, Scott, Bingham, and others left Carnegie Tech to support the war effort. As described in previous chapters, they joined what was to become a large contingent of psychologists involved in the testing of recruits. Scott and American Psychological Association president Robert Yerkes disagreed on the direction of psychology's involvement (Ferguson, 1962–1965). Yerkes and his group, under the aegis of the Surgeon General's Office, went on to develop the Army Alpha and Beta group tests of intellectual ability. These tests were important in the history of selection because they demonstrated that large groups of individuals could be tested, and the perceived success of this testing program did much to facilitate the expansion of testing into industrial situations. On the negative side, the tests were misinterpreted to cast aspersions on the intelligence of various racial and ethnic groups (Katzell & Austin, 1992).

Of more direct application to personnel selection was the work of Scott, Bingham, and their group, who established a program in the Adjutant General's Office. Scott (with the assistance of some of his Carnegie Tech students) adapted the man-to-man scale into the Rating Scale for Selecting Captains and through dogged determination convinced the Army of its potential usefulness. The Rating Scale instructed officers to rate candidates on appearance, military experience, influence over men, regard for authority, vigor, stability, judgment, and total value to the regiment (Ferguson, 1962–1965). The Committee on Classification of Personnel, described in previous chapters, was established in 1917, with Scott as director and Bingham as executive secretary. Bingham (1919) and Strong (1918) provide brief summaries of the accomplishments of that committee. In addition to adapting the rating scales for military use in selecting and rating officers, the committee and its associates developed trade specifications and an index of occupations, tables of occupational needs and personnel specifications for army units, and qualification cards for officers. They also developed and standardized trade tests for skilled workers (about 130,000 men were tested), and they defined the qualifications and duties of more than 500 kinds of officers. In all, more than 970,000 men were placed into technical units (Bingham, 1919), and more than 3 million men were classified and rated on job qualifications (Sokal, 1981). Investigations were conducted on selecting aviators through the use of the Examining Board application blank and on selecting Navy personnel for specialized duties (Strong, 1918). Katzell and Austin (1992) pointed out that this committee's work also laid the foundations for person and job analysis. Although both the Army and Navy discontinued their general testing programs in 1919 (Hale, 1992), the Army did retain a modified version of Scott's classification system.

Another relevant development of the war effort was Robert S. Woodworth's Personal Data Sheet (1919) designed to measure neuroticism for identifying recruits susceptible to shell shock.[7] Although not successful in identification (Hale, 1992), this questionnaire anticipated later personality inventories. Although other personality inventories followed, personality testing for employee selection was uncommon until the 1930s.

Following the signing of the armistice, members of the committee speculated as to whether they might be able to offer the same type of personnel services to private industry that they had for the Army. With Scott as president and Robert C. Clothier as vice-president (the other original members were Louis B. Hopkins, Beardsley Ruml, Joseph W. Hayes, and Stanley B. Mathewson), the Scott Company opened for business in February 1919. The first personnel consulting organization, the company thrived and soon had offices in Dayton, Chicago, Philadelphia, and Springfield, Massachusetts. Among the selection-related services the Scott Company performed for its large client base were the development of a mental alertness test that was basically a revision of the Bureau of Salesmanship Research's Test I, development of a large number of trade tests under Ruml's supervision, and the replacement of the man-to-man scales with graphic rating scales.[8] The Scott Company also organized and staffed entire personnel departments, based on the philosophy, developed by Ruml, of the "worker in his work." The task of the personnel department was not to look for square pegs to fit square holes, implying a division between the worker and the work, but to view the worker and the job as an integral unit; each could change in response to the other (Ferguson, 1961). Although successful,

---

[7]Pioneering British industrial psychologist C. S. Myers apparently coined the term *shell shock* in World War I (Hearnshaw, 1964).

[8]Freyd (1923) claimed that the graphic scale method originated in 1920 at the Scott Company Laboratory.

the Scott Company was in business only a few years, possibly in part due to the recession of 1921–1922 (Ferguson, 1961), or perhaps its very success led to its dismantling, as some of its members left for other opportunities (Katzell & Austin, 1992).

The year 1921 saw the creation of three organizations important in the history of employee selection: the Psychological Corporation, the National Institute of Industrial Psychology, and the Personnel Research Federation. Organized by James McKeen Cattell (who served as its first president), the Psychological Corporation operated as a holding company providing contact among psychologists and between psychologists and the general public. In addition to the home office, branch offices were established in a number of states to engage in preparation of standardized tests, vocational guidance, job analysis, and other applied activities. Keeping with Cattell's orientation, advancing psychology through research was the primary objective of the corporation (Cattell, 1923). The Psychological Corporation initially floundered under Cattell's leadership; however, a reorganization in 1926 under Bingham and Paul S. Achilles eventually brought the corporation a measure of success (Sokal, 1981). In Great Britain, the incorporation of the National Institute of Industrial Psychology also occurred in 1921. Founded by businessman H. J. Welch and the industrial psychologist Charles S. Myers, the institute conducted research and applied work in various areas of industrial psychology, including employee selection (Myers, 1936).

In an attempt to coordinate the hundreds of agencies that were conducting personnel research in the United States, the Personnel Research Federation was organized in 1921. Bingham was elected chairman a year later (Baritz, 1960). One major contribution of the federation was the publication of the *Journal of Personnel Research* (later *Personnel Journal*), an outlet for a great deal of selection research.

Notable studies and practice in employee selection from 1910 to 1930 not previously mentioned include the following. In the area of testing, a number of studies evaluated intelligence or mental alertness (e.g., Bills, 1923; Cowdery, 1922; Otis, 1920; Scudder, 1929; Snow, 1923). Of particular note are Bingham and Davis (1924) and Pond (1926–1927). Bingham and Davis found no relation between a 15-minute group test of intelligence and success in business as estimated by personal history record items. Millicent Pond conducted a series of studies at the Scovill Manufacturing Company, a brass manufacturer. For example, Pond (1926–1927) evaluated the use of intelligence tests (seven of eight based on the Army tests) on the criteria of highest weekly pay, increase in earnings, foreman's ratings, and terminations. Although Pond found low correlations between test scores and criteria, in subsequent studies she did have some success in developing a useful battery of tests (Scovill, 1928). Morris Viteles (1925–1926b) and Sadie Shellow (1925–1926; 1926–1927) revisited Münsterberg's problem of motorman selection and found promising results with the Viteles Motorman Selection Test, a test designed to measure specific abilities needed for car operation.

Regarding the use of interviews, Ferguson (1961) described Scott, Bingham, and Whipple's demonstration of interviewer unreliability at the 1916 World's First Salesmanship Congress in Detroit. Interviewers had low levels of agreement in ranking job candidates. Another early study on the interview also found little agreement among interviewers (Hollingworth, 1922, cited in Eder, Kacmar, & Ferris, 1989).

Personal history data or biographical information was also used as a predictor during this time period. Based on the notion that past behavior is the best predictor of future behavior, Ferguson (1961) attributed the genesis of the standardized application blanks and personal history inventories to businessman Thomas Peters of the Washington Life Insurance Company of Atlanta, who presented his inventory in 1894. Ferguson (n.d.) noted that it was a group of businessmen, not psychologists, "who invented what is truly the granddaddy of all present day standardized personal history and application blanks" (p. 18). He also pointed out that in 1915,

Pittsburgh businessman Edward A. Woods[9] attempted to evaluate personal history items based on their ability to differentiate successful from unsuccessful groups. In addition to Scott's previously mentioned Personal History Blank developed at Carnegie Tech, Goldsmith (1922) examined personal history data with a sample of salespeople and production as a criterion. Also in 1922, Gertrude Cope at the Phoenix Mutual Life Insurance Company found a number of biodata items related to success and failure for a sample of more than 400 agents (Holcombe, 1922; cited in Thayer, 1977). Another notable early study was Manson's (1925–1926) evaluation of the predictive ability of personal history items for a sample of 4,178 insurance agents.

Work on the use of applicant interests was influenced by the early efforts of J. B. Miner and C. S. Yoakum's doctoral students at Carnegie Tech: Max Freyd, Grace Manson, Bruce Moore, and R. J. Ream. Their efforts inspired E. K. Strong, Jr., to pursue the topic with his student Karl Cowdery when Strong moved from Carnegie Tech to Stanford University (Ferguson, n.d.). Freyd (1922) published an early examination of interests (cf. Strong, 1927).

DEPRESSION, WORLD WAR II, AND POSTWAR PROSPERITY: 1930–1963

The 1929 stock market crash in the United States and the subsequent worldwide economic depression and high levels of unemployment further reduced the need for psychologists and their selection expertise. Test use in industry in the early 1930s was low; a 1932 Bureau of Labor Statistics study found that only 14 of the 224 firms surveyed used any type of test (Hale 1992). Given these circumstances, Katzell and Austin (1992) characterized the 1930s as a time of refinement rather than conceptual breakthroughs in selection research. Germany, once a leader in selection research, saw a change in activity due to the rise of the Nazi Party (see Geuter, 1992, for details). The publication of Viteles' *Industrial Psychology* in 1932 marked a maturation point for the field. This text included a comprehensive treatment of selection practice and research, both in the United States and abroad.

Advances in methods in the 1930s included the following. L. L. Thurstone (1931) published his early work on factor analysis, extending and refining earlier efforts in this area. Content validity, initially termed curricular validity, emerged in the early 1930s in response to a need to determine if test items constituted a representative sample of a content domain of interest (T. B. Rogers, 1995). Work on test reliability continued. Kuder and Richardson (1937) added their general method of estimating reliability (K–R 20) to the existing test–retest, alternate forms, and split-half reliability estimates (DuBois, 1970).

Other notable events in the 1930s include the following. In 1930, Richard Uhrbrook established a psychological research department at Procter and Gamble. The Minnesota Employment Research Institute was established in 1931 and went on to develop a number of occupational tests. In 1933, the National Occupational Conference established a program to promote attitude measurement related to work success and commissioned Bingham's 1937 *Aptitudes and Aptitude Testing*. The U.S. Employment Service established a research program in 1934 to validate aptitude tests used in industry and develop trade tests. The report of the worker-analysis section (Stead, Shartle, & Otis, 1940) was a resource for validation studies in the 1940s (Hale, 1992). The U.S. Employment Service also published the first edition of the *Dictionary of Occupational Titles* (DOT) in 1939.

Just as World War I greatly influenced the development of selection procedures, World War II provided a major stimulus for selection research and practice, because the increased need for manpower in both the military and industry put a great strain on personnel systems (Hale,

---

[9]Woods was the businessman who suggested to Bingham that Carnegie Tech's Division of Applied Psychology include instruction in salesmanship, resulting in 1916 in the Bureau of Salesmanship Research (Ferguson, n.d.).

1992). The military's need for effective methods of selection and classification was enormous. For example, the U.S. Army Air Force experienced failure rates of between 40% and 60% for aviators in the decade preceding the war. Although this was not a major problem when the need for aviators was low (a total of 12 cadets were accepted for training in 1937), 5 years later more than 293,000 were accepted for training (Napoli, 1981).

Shortly after an unsuccessful attempt by Walter Dill Scott in 1938 to convince the U.S. Army to use his expertise, Horace B. English was able to persuade the Army's Adjutant General's office that psychologists would be useful in the selection and classification of recruits, among other services. In 1939 work began on a replacement for the old Army Alpha test. The new Army General Classification Test was ready for the first inductees in 1940 (see Harrell, 1992, for a firsthand discussion of the development of this test). A Committee on Classification of Military Personnel was constituted. Chaired by soon-to-become Army Chief Psychologist Walter Van Dyke Bingham, the committee was staffed by civilian testing experts. Many new tests were developed, such as officer classification tests, trade tests, achievement tests, and mechanical and clerical aptitude tests (Napoli, 1981).

Unlike the Army, the Navy did not have a centralized test development program in place at the war's beginning, although in 1940 a new branch of the Medical Corps was established for psychologists and other specialists (Napoli, 1981). In June 1942, the Applied Psychology Panel was established to work on problems of classification and selection. In 1943, five new tests were being used at all naval training stations: general classification, reading, arithmetic reasoning, mechanical knowledge, and mechanical aptitude. By the war's end, more than 250 tests had been produced (Napoli, 1981), including the Cornell Selection Index, a personality index in the tradition of Woodworth's World War I Personal Data Sheet (DuBois, 1970).

Of particular concern to both the Navy and the Army Air Force was the selection of aviators. John C. Flanagan became the Army Air Force's first psychologist and supervised the construction and administration of the Aviation Cadet Qualifying Exam, a general test for selecting all aviation cadets. John G. Jenkins directed the Navy's aviation psychology program (Napoli, 1981).

Based on earlier work conducted first in Germany and then Great Britain, psychologists in the Office of Strategic Services (OSS, a forerunner to the Central Intelligence Agency) developed a program of global assessment for evaluating candidates for sensitive assignments. A number of procedures were employed, such as casual conversations, interviews, personal history, aptitude tests, and, most notably, situational tests. An example of the situational tests used by the OSS was the Construction Test, in which the candidate had 5 minutes to lead two obstinate privates in building a miniature house (see also Highhouse, 2002).

The late 1930s and 1940s saw advances in utility analysis research. Taylor and Russell (1939) developed a series of tables to predict a dichotomous criterion of success or failure. They demonstrated that the usefulness of a validity coefficient depends on the *selection ratio* (number of hires over number of applicants) and the *base rate* (number of currently successful employees). Given a favorable (i.e., low) selection ratio (SR), even tests with relatively modest validities can have utility in increasing the number of successful hires. Later models (e.g., Naylor & Shine, 1965) refined this technique by predicting mean criterion performance rather than a dichotomous criterion.

It was the work of Brogden (1946, 1949; Brogden & Taylor, 1950), however, that is most directly relevant for current utility models. Brogden demonstrated how the economic utility of a predictor is affected by both the SR and the standard deviation of job performance in dollars (SD_y; Schmidt, Hunter, McKenzie, & Muldrow, 1979). In addition, Brogden considered the cost of testing. Brogden noted that the value of a validity coefficient can be interpreted directly as the percentage gain that would be expected if one could select based on the criterion. Therefore, the validity coefficient can be interpreted directly as a measure of selection efficiency. Cronbach and Gleser (1957, 1965) expanded on this work.

By midcentury the established paradigm of what constituted "good practice" in personnel selection was not appreciably different from that proposed by psychologists such as Freyd, Kornhauser, Kingsbury, Link, and Hull in the 1920s and earlier. What Guion (1976) termed, in a nonpejorative way, as the "tenets of orthodoxy" (p. 783) can be summarized as follows: The prediction of job performance is the purpose of selection; job analysis should be the basis of predictor and criterion selection; instruments should be standardized and tests should be empirically validated; and validity is situation-specific in nature. Additional tenets were the use of multiple tests with only one criterion, the preference of tests over nontest predictors such as interviews, the evaluation of individual differences in testing, and the use of tests only to supplement current employment procedures. Psychologists had a relatively successful technology in place for selection, and by the late 1950s they began to shift their focus to other concerns, such as leadership and morale (Guion, 1976).

Porter (1966) singled out Ghiselli (1963) and Dunnette (1963) as two examples of individuals critical of this classical prediction model. Ghiselli's work focused on the use of moderators to sort individuals into homogeneous groups to improve predictive accuracy. Dunnette's model for selection research took into account intervening events between predictor and criterion behavior, including different subgroups of individuals, different types of job behaviors, and different types of job situations.

One of the most influential developments of the 1950s was the assessment center. Based on the global evaluations conducted by the OSS in World War II, the assessment center was introduced into the Bell System as part of the Management Progress Study in 1956 (Bray & Campbell, 1968; Bray & Grant, 1966). Candidates were assessed in groups, by groups of assessors using techniques such as work simulations, biodata, interviews, and various paper-and-pencil tests (see Bray, Campbell, & Grant, 1974). Among the simulations used was the in-basket test (Frederiksen, Saunders, & Wand, 1957). Initial assessment center validation results were promising, and the procedure was adopted throughout the Bell System and by many other major corporations (Hale, 1992). Another multiple assessment procedure, individual assessment, was receiving increased attention by industrial psychologists in the 1940s and 1950s (Prien, Schippmann, & Prien, 2003). In individual assessment the psychologist uses multiple assessment procedures on an individual applicant and makes a hiring recommendation to management. Although popular with practitioners, individual assessment has received little attention from researchers until recently (see Highhouse, 2002, for an historical account).

By the mid-1950s the interview and application blank remained the most popular selection procedures (Kendall, 1956). Wagner (1949) published a review of interview research. He was able to locate only a small number of empirical studies and concluded that low reliability and validity continued to be a problem. Wagner did note, however, that structured interview appeared promising. Biographical data or biodata continued to show considerable predictive validity during the 1950s (Taylor & Nevis, 1961). Test use in industry was also significant, although survey results varied as to the extent of their use. Kendall (1956), for example, discussed the discrepancy between Scott, Clothier, and Spriegel's survey of 628 companies in 1953 and a 1954 National Industrial Conference Board Study of Personnel Practices (NICB) of 515 companies. Scott et al. found that 75% of reporting companies used selection tests, with clerical and stenographic the most popular. The NICB report found that only 32% of firms with hourly workers, and 43% of companies using salaried workers, reported test use (possible reasons for these differences include survey unreliability and different samples; see Hale, 1992).

Hale (1992) noted trends in the increased use of personality tests in the 1930s and 1940s and the increased use of tests for managerial selection in the 1940s and 1950s. Sears Roebuck, for example, began a comprehensive in-house testing program that included intelligence, personality, and interest tests.

The 1950s and 1960s saw a number of articles and books attacking personnel testing. Personality testing in particular was criticized by both outside commentators (e.g., Gross, 1962; Whyte, 1954) and researchers (Guion & Gottier, 1965). Of note is Baritz's (1960) *The Servants of Power*, which included both a history of industrial psychology and an indictment of psychologists' subservience to management. By the early 1960s attacks from the outside seemed to have abated (Dudek, 1963), at least for a time.

Cronbach (1951) added coefficient alpha to the other methods of estimating reliability. Construct validity, the measurement of postulated attributes, was formalized in the 1950s (Cronbach & Meehl, 1955). Campbell and Fiske (1959) published an influential paper on building evidence for the construct validity of measures by use of multitrait–multimethod matrix. Lawshe's (1952) conception of *synthetic validity*, using job analysis to break down jobs into components and then determining validity for the elements, generated a fair amount of interest due to its perceived usefulness for companies that do not hire enough employees to conduct traditional criterion-related validation studies (see Mossholder & Arvey, 1984, for a review).

In 1954, the American Psychological Association, the American Educational Research Association, and the National Council on Measurement Used in Education published their *Technical Recommendations for Psychological Tests and Diagnostic Techniques*. Although the genesis of this document was primarily due to problems in clinical work and education (Guion, 1976), it did formalize the familiar four aspects of validity: predictive, concurrent, content, and construct.

In the 1940s and 1950s, evaluation of criteria became a focus. Of particular note are Thorndike's (1949) classification of criteria into ultimate, intermediate, and immediate levels and Wherry's model of the rating process (published some 30 years later: Wherry & Bartlett, 1982). Terms such as criterion *deficiency, contamination,* and *relevance* were becoming common (Austin & Villanova, 1992). Flanagan (1954) published his work on the use of examples of successful and unsuccessful job performance, the critical-incident technique. The criterion problem continued as a concern. As Wallace and Weitz (1955) succinctly noted in a review, "The criterion problem continues to lead all other topics in lip service and trail most in terms of work reported" (p. 218).

Other selection-related developments during the 1950s and early 1960s include the publication of Fryer and Henry's (1950) *Handbook of Applied Psychology* and Meehl's (1954) book documenting the superiority of statistical over clinical methods of prediction. In 1955 the journal *Personnel Psychology* established the Validity Information Exchange to facilitate reporting of validation studies. The early 1960s saw the beginning of E. A. Fleishman's long-term investigation of motor abilities necessary for performance and the development of a taxonomy of these abilities (see Fleishman, 1988).

CIVIL RIGHTS AND BEYOND: 1964 TO THE PRESENT

The emergence of the Civil Rights Movement in the 1950s and subsequent legislation in the 1960s had a profound effect on how individuals were selected for employment. Title VII of the Civil Rights Act of 1964 and subsequent interpretive Supreme Court decisions in the 1970s (e.g., *Griggs vs. Duke Power, Albermarle v. Moody, Washington vs. Davis*) greatly influenced the practice of personnel selection. Psychologists involved in selection now had to comply with the dictates of this civil rights legislation as interpreted by the courts. Section 703(h) of Title VII of the Civil Rights Act of 1964 does allow the use of professionally developed ability tests "provided that such test, its administration or action upon the results is not designed, intended, or used to discriminate because of race, color, religion, sex, or national origin" (Bureau of National Affairs, 1973, p. 26). The key phrase is "or used." Inadvertent as well as intentional discrimination could be considered illegal.

Following a number of guidelines produced by various individual federal agencies, the Equal Employment Opportunity Commission, the Departments of Labor and Justice, and the Civil Service Commission issued the joint *Uniform Guidelines on Employee Selection Procedures* in 1978. These guidelines apply to any employment decision where selection procedures are used. Selection procedures are broadly defined to include not only paper-and-pencil tests but also interviews, biodata, and other procedures. Once "adverse impact" on a protected group is demonstrated by the plaintiff, the defendant must demonstrate the "job-relatedness" of the challenged selection procedure. This would generally involve evidence from a properly conducted validation study.

The Civil Rights Act of 1964 and other legal developments prompted a great deal of research into issues such as test fairness, differential validity for protected minority groups, and alternatives to test use. Definitions and models of bias were constructed and debated. Examples include Guion's (1976) definition of the existence of unfair discrimination when individuals with equal probabilities of job success have unequal probabilities of being hired, and various regression models of test fairness (see Arvey & Faley, 1988). Along with the research, however, was an increasing awareness that many of the problems of test fairness could not be solved by methodological advances alone; social factors and conceptions of justice and fairness would come into play. Questions of differential validity, however, were largely put to rest by the validity generalization procedures discussed subsequently.

Two of the most influential methodological developments of the last quarter of the 20th century were Schmitt and Hunter's work on validity generalization and meta-analysis. Validity generalization (VG) offered a direct challenge to the long-accepted doctrine of the situation-specific nature of validity. Schmidt and Hunter (1977) were able to convincingly demonstrate that the apparent variability among validity coefficients for specific predictor-criterion combinations was primarily due to statistical artifacts, such as unreliability of measures, restriction of range, and, most important, sampling error due to small sample sizes. Once validity coefficients are corrected for these artifacts, the apparent variability across studies often disappears, demonstrating the generalizability of the relationship. Their research also demonstrated that the search for moderator variables, popular in the 1960s (Guion & Gibson, 1988), is likely to be unproductive. Although not without controversy (Landy, 2003), VG provided a compelling explanation for vexing problem of situational specificity of validity coefficients.

Hunter and Schmidt (1990; Hunter, Schmidt, & Jackson, 1982) used the logic of their VG procedures to further develop a method of meta-analysis (see chaps. 3 and 18). Conceived as an alternative to the venerable qualitative literature review, their meta-analytic procedures correct for statistical artifacts across studies, allowing researchers to draw strong conclusions about the nature of relations between combinations of predictors and criteria for various occupations. Although not the only meta-analytic procedure developed, the Schmidt and Hunter procedure has proven very influential in personnel selection, as evidenced by the increasing number of meta-analyses published in the last 2 decades of the 20th century. Related to their work on VG and meta-analysis was Schmidt and Hunter's strong criticism of the null hypothesis testing model for conducting research (Schmidt, 1992, 1996).

Work on utility analysis continued to advance on what came to be termed the Brogden–Cronbach–Gleser model. One particular problem with this model is the difficulty in estimating

SD_y, the standard deviation of job performance in dollars. Various procedures were developed for this purpose, and a lively debate ensued regarding the relevant merits and problems with these techniques (see Boudreau, 1991).

There was increasing recognition of the unitary nature of validity, with the familiar criterion, content, and construct validities viewed as strategies for building evidence for this unitary concept that has to do with the meaningfulness, appropriateness, and usefulness of test score inferences (see Guion, 1976). There was also an increased interest in content-related validity (now sometimes known as content-oriented test development) and conceptualizations of construct validity.

Austin and Villanova (1992) noted a shift in the 1960s and 1970s from attention to output measures and personal traits to behavior measures. They suggested that the 1980s were a time of "renaissance" for criteria research, with a large number of books appearing and a shift toward (and criticism of) a cognitive approach. Of particular note was the theoretical work on job performance by J. P. Campbell and his associates (see Campbell, 1990a)

In a review, Hakel (1986) noted advances in selection since the early 1960s to the mid-1980s. Selection was no longer primarily a technology lacking underlying theory, and innovations like structural equation modeling and item response theory were instrumental in better understanding the role of constructs. Schmitt and Robertson (1990) also reported that the major trend in selection research at the time of their review was toward better understanding of constructs being measured. Biodata researchers, for example, began to go beyond a primarily empirical approach toward a theoretical understanding of their instruments. Stokes (1994) cited a 1966 conference chaired by Henry as a major turning point. Of particular note is the longitudinal work of W. A. Owens (e.g., 1976) in subgrouping individuals based on their personal item history responses (Fleishman, 1988; Stokes & Cooper, 2004).

A number of relevant professional standards and revisions were published after 1960, including various editions of the *Standards for Educational and Psychological Tests and Manuals* (American Psychological Association, 1966; American Psychological Association, American Education Research Association, & National Council on Measurement in Education, 1974; American Educational Research Association, American Psychological Association, & National Council on Measurement in Education, 1985, 1999) and *Principles for the Validation and Use of Personnel Selection Procedures* (Division of Industrial–Organizational Psychology, American Psychological Association, 1975, 1980; Society for Industrial and Organizational Psychology, 1987, 2003). Tenopyr and Oeltjen (1982) reported seven major discrepancies between the 1980 *Principles* and the *Uniform Guidelines*, for example, unlike the *Principles,* the *Guidelines* make little provision for validity generalization and require alternatives when a procedure has been found to have adverse impact.

As mentioned, in the last decades of the 20th century, meta-analysis became standard practice in personnel selection research. Increasingly, the validities of various predictors were evaluated through the use of this procedure. Although it is impossible to list all the relevant meta-analyses here, the results of these quantitative reviews, which are not without criticism, have had a widespread influence on the judged validity of various predictors. Cognitive ability tests, for example, following a period of concerns about unfair discrimination, have been shown to be valid predictors across many jobs (Guion & Gibson, 1988).

Personality testing exhibited new life with the advent of meta-analysis and advances in personality theory. As noted, personality testing was subject to a number of attacks from outside the field in the 1950s and early 1960s. In addition, Guion and Gottier (1965) published a review that found personality research seriously flawed. They concluded that personality measures should not be used as instruments of decision. Although they did not recommend that personality measures or research be abandoned (see Guion, 1967, 1991), the general consensus in the profession was that personality tests were not useful predictors. This belief began to change in the late 1980s as the Five-Factor Model (Digman, 1990; Goldberg, 1993) and variations of that model gained acceptance and meta-analyses (e.g., Barrick & Mount, 1991) provided validation evidence, especially for the Conscientiousness factor. Also important was the new emphasis on contextual, nontask dimensions of performance and the perceived usefulness of personality factors to predict these criteria (see Borman & Motowidlo, 1993).

Interviews, long lamented for their questionable reliability and validity, were found through meta-analysis to have respectable validity, particularly in the structured format (e.g., Weisner & Cronshaw, 1988). Meta-analysis also confirmed the long history of respectable validity for predictors such as biodata (see Rothstein, 2003, for a summary of meta-analytic results for various predictors). Schmidt and Hunter (1998) summarized 85 years of research on the validity and utility of 19 selection procedures. Good predictors of job performance included general mental ability, work samples, interviews (structured were better than unstructured), peer ratings, job knowledge tests, the personality dimension conscientiousness, and integrity tests (which are a good measure of conscientiousness). Poor predictors of job performance included years of education, interests, graphology, and age. Schmidt and Hunter also discussed the sizable economic value to the organization of using valid selection procedures. Because meta-analysis is a relatively recent development, it is difficult to put its overall impact in perspective. Its impact on present-day research and practice, however, is undisputable.

One recent large-scale study bears mention, the Army Selection and Classification Project (Project A). The purpose of Project A was to develop an improved selection and classification system for all 276 entry-level positions in the U.S. Army. Conducted by a consortium of research organizations and the Army Research Institute, this 7-year effort was built around the Armed Services Vocational Aptitude Battery (ASVAB) and involved generating needed predictor measures, criterion variables, and validation evidence (Campbell, 1990b). Details of this large-scale project can be found in a special issue of *Personnel Psychology* (1990) and is also described in chapter 7 in this volume.

Finally, many fine books on aspects of personnel selection were published since 1964, too many to list here. Of special note, however, is the work of Guion, including his 1965 book on personnel testing; his chapters on personnel selection in Dunnette's (1976) first edition of the *Handbook of Industrial and Organizational Psychology* and in Dunnette and Hough's (1990) second edition of the *Handbook*; and his 1998 book *Assessment, Measurement, and Prediction for Personnel Decisions*.

CONCLUSION

As is inevitable in trying to cover such a large amount of material, the major difficulty in writing this chapter was not deciding what to include but what to leave out. Drafts would balloon far beyond the allotted page limits, necessitating the painful process of shortening explanations, eliminating detail and nuance, and cutting material out. What is left is *a* history, not *the* history of psychology applied to selection. Any historical account is selective and based on a particular viewpoint. Another history would most certainly emphasize other landmarks, trends, influences, research, and practice. The chapter emphasis is on positive developments in research and measurement, although criticisms are occasionally noted. This is not to minimize abuses, bad practice, and controversies. They have occurred and continue to occur. For example, the tension between researchers and practitioners, although not discussed here, has been a continuing problem in employee selection (see chap. 3 in this volume).

In reviewing more than 100 years of research and practice in employee selection, we can discern a number of trends and draw some general conclusions. First is the durability not only of the basic criterion-related paradigm for determining validity but also of many of the techniques, predictors, and criteria used by the early psychologists. The procedures, predictors, and criteria presented by Freyd, Kornhauser and Kingsbury, Link, Scott, and the other pioneers are still, despite all of the advances and increased sophistication in methods, the backbone of selection research and practice. Their concerns, such as the "criterion problem" and the need to differentiate scientifically sound from unsound practice, are still a matter of concern today. This is not to suggest that there have not been advances. There have been a number of profound changes. There is, however, a consistency underlying selection practice and research that would make much present-day practice recognizable to the early pioneers in the field.

As noted, there have been changes, a number of which have been driven by outside events. The two World Wars and civil rights legislation are examples of events that precipitated major changes in selection research and practice. Improvements and innovations in methodology, such as the development of correlation, VG, and meta-analytic procedures, have opened new avenues of research and called into question some established beliefs. One notable relatively recent trend has been the increasing emphasis on theory, a shift from the practical question of Will this work? to Why does this work?

It is interesting to look over the last 100 years and note the cyclical nature of much of the research and practice. Concepts come, go, and return; predictors fall in and out of favor; procedures are abandoned and rediscovered. General cognitive ability tests are popular, then they fall out of favor due to concerns regarding unfair discrimination, and then they enjoy a comeback due to their demonstrated validity via VG research. Personality testing increased in popularity in the 1930s and 1940s, came under attack in the 1950s, was all but abandoned in the 1960s, and is now enjoying something of a renaissance due to a combination of advances in test theory and meta-analytic confirmation of their usefulness. After a long period of concerns about reliability and validity, the interview is now perceived as a potentially reliable and valid part of the selection process. Moderator variables, popular in the 1960s and 1970s, then seen as rare and elusive in the 1980s and early 1990s, are enjoying a mild return to favor.

Although the preceding paragraph gives the impression that industrial–organizational psychologists are continually reinventing the wheel, that interpretation is unwarranted. Despite missteps, real progress in employee selection has been made. Although that progress has sometime been dramatic, for the most part it involved slow, steady improvement due to methodological advances, more thoughtful conceptualizations of constructs and problems, and a fidelity to sound empirical investigations and the scientist–practitioner model.

ACKNOWLEDGMENTS

I thank Bianca Falbo, Jeffery Schippmann, Neal Schmitt, Paul Thayer, Michael Zickar, and an anonymous historian for helpful comments on earlier drafts of this chapter. All errors are my own.

REFERENCES

American Educational Research Association, American Psychological Association, & National Council on Measurement in Education. (1985). *Standards for educational and psychological testing.* Washington, DC: American Psychological Association.

American Educational Research Association, American Psychological Association, & National Council on Measurement in Education. (1999). *Standards for educational and psychological testing.* Washington, DC: American Educational Research Association.

American Psychological Association. (1966). *Standards for educational and psychological tests and manuals.* Washington, DC: APA.

American Psychological Association, American Educational Research Association, & National Council on Measurement Used in Education (joint committee). (1954). Technical recommendations for psychological tests and diagnostic techniques. *Psychological Bulletin, 51,* 201–238.

American Psychological Association, American Educational Research Association, & National Council on Measurement in Education. (1974). *Standards for educational and psychological tests.* Washington, DC: APA.

Arvey, R. D., & Faley, R. H. (1988). *Fairness in selecting employees* (2nd ed.). Reading, MA: Addison-Wesley.

Austin, J. T., & Villanova, P. (1992). The criterion problem: 1917–1992. *Journal of Applied Psychology, 77,* 836–874.

Baritz, L. (1960). *The servants of power: A history of the use of social science in American industry.* Middletown, CT: Wesleyan University Press.

Barrick, M. R., & Mount, M. K. (1991). The Big Five personality dimensions and job performance. *Personnel Psychology, 44,* 1–26.

Benjamin, L. T., Jr. (2000). Hugo Münsterberg: Portrait of an applied psychologist. In G. A. Kimble & M. Wertheimer (Eds.), *Portraits of pioneers in psychology* (Vol. 4, pp. 113–129). Washington, DC: American Psychological Association and Mahwah, NJ: Lawrence Erlbaum Associates.

Bills, M. A. (1923). Relation of mental alertness test score to positions and permanency in company. *Journal of Applied Psychology, 7,* 154–156.

Bingham, W. V. (1919). Army personnel work. With some implications for education and industry. *Journal of Applied Psychology, 3,* 1–12.

Bingham, W. V. (1923). On the possibility of an applied psychology. *Psychological Review, 30,* 289–305.

Bingham, W. V. (1926). Measures of occupational success. *Harvard Business Review, 5,* 1–10.

Bingham, W. V. (1937). *Aptitudes and aptitude testing.* New York: Harper.

Bingham, W. V., & Davis, W. T. (1924). Intelligence test scores and business success. *Journal of Applied Psychology, 8,* 1–22.

Bingham, W. V., & Freyd, M. (1926). *Procedures in employment psychology: A manual for developing scientific methods of vocational selection.* New York: McGraw-Hill.

Blackford, K. M. H., & Newcomb, A. (1914). *The job, the man, the boss.* Garden City, NY: Doubleday, Page.

Borman, W. C., & Motowidlo, S. J. (1993). Expanding the criterion domain to include elements of contextual performance. In N. Schmitt, W. C. Borman, & Associates, *Personnel selection in organizations* (pp. 71–98). San Francisco, CA: Jossey-Bass.

Boudreau, J. W. (1991). Utility analysis for decisions in human resource management. In M. D. Dunnette & L. M. Hough (Eds.), *Handbook of industrial and organizational psychology* (2nd ed., Vol. 2, pp. 621–745). Palo Alto, CA: Consulting Psychologists Press.

Bray, D. W., & Campbell, R. J. (1968). Selection of salesmen by means of an assessment center. *Journal of Applied Psychology, 52,* 36–41.

Bray, D. W., & Grant, D. L. (1966). The assessment center in the measurement of potential for business management. *Psychological Monographs: General and Applied, 80.*

Bray, D. W., Campbell, R. J., & Grant, D. L. (1974). *Formative years in business: A long-term AT&T study of managerial lives.* New York: Wiley.

Brogden, H. E. (1946). On the interpretation of the correlation coefficient as a measure of predictive efficiency. *Journal of Educational Psychology, 37,* 64–76.

Brogden, H. E. (1949). When testing pays. *Personnel Psychology, 2,* 171–183.

Brogden, H. E., & Taylor, E. K. (1950). The dollar criterion: Applying the cost accounting concept to criterion construction. *Personnel Psychology, 3,* 133–154.

Bureau of Labor Statistics. (2001). *Report on the American workforce 2001.* Retrieved November 2003, from the Department of Labor Web site. www.bls.gov/opub/rtaw/pdf/rtaw2oo1.pdf

Bureau of National Affairs. (1973). *ABCs of the Equal Employment Opportunity Act.* Washington, DC: Author.

Burtt, H. (1926). *Principles of employment psychology.* New York: Harper.

Campbell, D. T., & Fiske, D. W. (1959). Convergent and discriminant validation by the multitrait-multimethod matrix. *Psychological Bulletin, 56,* 81–105.

Campbell, J. P. (1990a). Modeling the performance prediction problem in industrial and organizational psychology. In M. D. Dunnette & L. M. Hough (Eds.), *Handbook of industrial and organizational psychology* (2nd ed., Vol. 1, pp. 687–732). Palo Alto, CA: Consulting Psychologists Press.

Campbell, J. P. (1990b). An overview of the Army Selection and Classification Project (Project A). *Personnel Psychology, 43,* 231–239.

Cattell, J. M. (1890). Mental tests and measurements. *Mind, 15,* 373–381. Reprinted in *James McKeen Cattell: Man of science. Vol. 1: Psychological Research* (1947). Lancaster, PA: Science Press.

Cattell, J. M. (1923). The Psychological Corporation. *Annals of the Academy of Political and Social Science, 110,* 165–171.

Cleeton, G. U., & Knight, F. B. (1924). Validity of character judgments based on external criteria. *Journal of Applied Psychology, 8,* 215–231.

Cowdery, K. M. (1922). Measures of general intelligence as indices of success in trade learning. *Journal of Applied Psychology, 6,* 311–330.

Cowles, M. (2001). *Statistics in psychology: An historical perspective* (2nd ed.). Mahwah, NJ: Lawrence Erlbaum Associates.

Cronbach, L. J. (1951). Coefficient alpha and the internal structure of tests. *Psychometrika, 6,* 671–684.

Cronbach, L. J., & Gleser, G. C. (1957). *Psychological tests and personnel decisions.* Urbana: University of Illinois Press.

Cronbach, L. J., & Gleser, G. C. (1965). *Psychological tests and personnel decisions.* (2nd ed.). Urbana: University of Illinois Press.

Cronbach, L. J., & Meehl, P. E. (1955). Construct validity in psychological tests. *Psychological Bulletin, 52,* 281–302.

Digman, J. M. (1990). Personality structure: Emergence of the five-factor model. *Annual Review of Psychology, 41,* 417–440.

Division of Industrial–Organizational Psychology, American Psychological Association. (1975). *Principles for the validation and use of personnel selection procedures.* Dayton, OH: Industrial–Organizational Psychologist.

Division of Industrial–Organizational Psychology, American Psychological Association. (1980). *Principles for the validation and use of personnel selection procedures* (2nd ed.). Berkeley, CA: Industrial–Organizational Psychologist.

Dorcus, R. M., & Jones, M. H. (1950). *Handbook of employee selection.* New York: McGraw-Hill.

DuBois, P. H. (1970). *A history of psychological testing.* Boston: Allyn & Bacon.

Dudek, E. E. (1963). Personnel selection. In P. R. Farnsworth, O. McNemar, & Q. McNemar (Eds.), *Annual review of psychology* (pp. 261–284). Palo Alto, CA: Annual Reviews.

Dunlap, K. (1923). Fact and fable in character analysis. *Annals of the Academy of Political and Social Science, 110,* 74–80.

Dunnette, M. D. (1963). A modified model for test validation and selection research. *Journal of Applied Psychology, 47,* 317–323.

Dunnette, M. D. (Ed.). (1976). *Handbook of industrial and organizational psychology.* Chicago: Rand McNally.

Dunnette, M. D., & Hough, L. M. (Eds.). (1990). *Handbook of industrial and organizational psychology* (2nd ed., Vol. 1). Palo Alto, CA: Consulting Psychologists Press.

Eder, R. W., Kacmar, K. M., & Ferris, G. R. (1989). Employment interview research: History and synthesis. In R. W. Eder & G. R. Ferris (Eds.), *The employment interview: Theory, research, and practice* (pp. 17–31), Newbury Park, CA: Sage.

Equal Employment Opportunity Commission, Civil Service Commission, Department of Labor, & Department of Justice. (1978). Uniform guidelines on employee selection procedures. *Federal Register, 43,* 38290–38313.

Ferguson, L. W. (n.d.). *A new light on the history of industrial psychology.* Unpublished manuscript, Ferguson Collection, Carnegie Mellon University.

Ferguson, L. W. (1961). The development of industrial psychology. In B. V. Gilmer (Ed.), *Industrial psychology* (pp. 18–37). New York: McGraw-Hill.

Ferguson, L. W. (1962–1965). *The heritage of industrial psychology* [14 pamphlets]. Hartford, CT: Finlay Press.

Flanagan, J. C. (1954). The critical incident technique. *Psychological Bulletin, 51,* 327–358.

Flanders, J. K. (1918). Mental tests of a group of employed men showing correlations with estimates furnished by the employer. *Journal of Applied Psychology, 2,* 197–206.

Fleishman, E. A. (1988). Some new frontiers in personnel selection research. *Personnel Psychology, 41,* 679–701.

Frederiksen, N., Saunders, D. R., & Wand, B. (1957). The in-basket test. *Psychological Monographs: General and Applied, 70.*

Freyd, M. (1922). A method for the study of vocational interests. *Journal of Applied Psychology, 6,* 243–253.

Freyd, M. (1923). The graphic rating scale. *Journal of Educational Psychology, 14,* 83–102.

Freyd, M. (1923–1924). Measurement in vocational selection. *Journal of Personnel Research, 1,* 215–249, 268–284, 377–385.

Freyd, M. (1925). The statistical viewpoint in vocational selection. *Journal of Applied Psychology, 9,* 349–356.

Fryer, D. H., & Henry, E. R. (Eds.). (1950). *Handbook of applied psychology* (2 vols.). New York: Rinehart.

Geuter, U. (1992). *The professionalization of psychology in Nazi Germany* (R. J. Holmes, Trans.). Cambridge, England: Cambridge University Press.

Ghiselli, E. E. (1963). Moderating effects and differential reliability and validity. *Journal of Applied Psychology, 47,* 81–86.

Goldberg, L. R. (1993). The structure of phenotypic personality traits. *American Psychologist, 48,* 26–34.

Goldsmith, D. B. (1922). The use of the personal history blank as a salesmanship test. *Journal of Applied Psychology, 6,* 149–155.

Gross, M. L. (1962). *The brain watchers.* New York: Random House.

Guion, R. M. (1965). *Personnel testing.* New York: McGraw-Hill.

Guion, R. M. (1967). Personnel selection. In P. R. Farnsworth, O. McNemar, & Q. McNemar (Eds.), *Annual review of psychology* (pp. 191–216). Palo Alto, CA: Annual Reviews.

Guion, R. M. (1976). Recruiting, selection, and job placement. In M. D. Dunnette (Ed.), *Handbook of industrial and organizational psychology* (pp. 777–828). Chicago: Rand McNally.

Guion, R. M. (1991). Personnel assessment, selection, and placement. In M. D. Dunnette & L. M. Hough (Eds.), *Handbook of industrial and organizational psychology* (2nd ed., Vol. 2, pp. 327–397). Palo Alto, CA: Consulting Psychologists Press.

Guion, R. M. (1998). *Assessment, measurement, and prediction for personnel decisions.* Mahwah, NJ: Lawrence Erlbaum Associates.

Guion, R. M., & Gibson, W. M. (1988). Personnel selection and placement. In M. R. Rosenzweig & L. W. Porter (Eds.), *Annual review of psychology* (pp. 349–374). Palo Alto, CA: Annual Reviews.

Guion, R. M., & Gottier, R. F. (1965). Validity of personality measures in personnel selection. *Personnel Psychology, 18,* 135–164.

Hakel, M. D. (1986). Personnel selection and placement. In M. R. Rosenzweig & L. W. Porter (Eds.), *Annual review of psychology* (pp. 351–380). Palo Alto, CA: Annual Reviews.

Hale, M. (1992). History of employment testing. In A. Widgor & W. R. Garner (Eds.), *Ability testing: Uses, consequences, and controversies* (pp. 3–38). Washington, DC: National Academy Press.

Harrell, T. W. (1992). Some history of the Army General Classification Test. *Journal of Applied Psychology, 77,* 875–878.

Hearnshaw, L. S. (1964). *A short history of British Psychology: 1840–1940.* Westport, CT: Greenwood Press.

Highhouse, S. (2002). Assessing the candidate as a whole: A historical and critical analysis of individual psychological assessment for personnel decision making. *Personnel Psychology, 55,* 363–396.

Hull, C. L. (1928). *Aptitude testing.* Yonkers-on-Hudson, NY: World Book.

Hunter, J. E., & Schmidt, F. L. (1990). *Methods of meta-analysis: Correcting error and bias in research findings.* Newbury Park, CA: Sage.

Hunter, J. E., Schmidt, F. L., & Jackson, G. B. (1982). *Meta-analysis: Cumulating research findings across studies.* Beverly Hills, CA: Sage.

Jastrow, J., Baldwin, J. M., & Cattell, J. M. (1898). Physical and mental tests. *Psychological Review, 5,* 172–179.

Johns, W. B., & Worcester, D. A. (1930). The value of the photograph in the selection of teachers. *Journal of Applied Psychology, 14,* 54–62.

Jones, E. S. (1917). The Wooley-Test series applied to the detection of ability in telegraphy. *Journal of Educational Psychology, 8,* 27–34.

Katzell, R. A., & Austin, J. T. (1992). From then to now: The development of industrial–organizational psychology in the United States. *Journal of Applied Psychology, 77,* 803–835.

Kendall, W. E. (1956). Industrial psychology. In P. R. Farnsworth & Q. McNemar (Eds.), *Annual review of psychology* (pp. 197–232). Stanford, CA: Annual Reviews.

Kingsbury, F. A. (1923). Applying psychology to business. *Annals of the American Academy of Political and Social Science, 110,* 2–12.

Koppes, L. L. (2003). Industrial–organizational psychology. In I. B. Weiner (General Ed.) & D. K. Freedheim (Vol. Ed.), *Comprehensive handbook of psychology: Vol. 1. History of psychology* (pp. 367–389). New York: Wiley.

Kornhauser, A. W. (1922). The psychology of vocational selection. *Psychological Bulletin, 19,* 192–229.

Kornhauser, A. W., & Kingsbury, F. A. (1924). *Psychological tests in business.* Chicago: University of Chicago Press.

Kuder, G. F., & Richardson, M. W. (1937). The theory of estimation of test reliability. *Psychometrika, 2,* 151–166.

Landy, F. J. (2003). Validity generalization: Then and now. In K. R. Murphy (Ed.), *Validity generalization: A critical review* (pp. 155–195). Mahwah, NJ: Lawrence Erlbaum Associates.

Lawshe, C. H. (1952). Employee selection. *Personnel Psychology, 5,* 31–34.

Link, H. C. (1918). An experiment in employment psychology. *Psychological Review, 25,* 116–127.

Link, H. C. (1920). The applications of psychology to industry. *Psychological Bulletin, 17,* 335–346.

Manson, G. E. (1925–1926). What can the application blank tell? Evaluation of items in personal history records of four thousand life insurance salesmen. *Journal of Personnel Research, 4,* 73–99.

McComas, H. C. (1914). Some tests for efficiency in telephone operators. *Journal of Philosophy, Psychology, and Scientific Methods, 11,* 293–294.

Meehl, P. E. (1954). *Clinical vs. statistical prediction.* Minneapolis: University of Minnesota Press.

Meriam, J. L. (1906). *Normal school education and efficiency in teaching.* Teachers College Contributions to Education, 152, Columbia University, New York.

Mossholder, K. W., & Arvey, R. D. (1984). Synthetic validity: A conceptual and comparative review. *Journal of Applied Psychology, 69,* 322–333.

Münsterberg, H. (1913). *Psychology and industrial efficiency.* Boston: Houghton Mifflin.

Myers, C. S. (1936). Charles Samuel Myers. In C. Murchinson (Ed.), *A history of psychology in autobiography* (Vol. 3, pp. 215–230). Worcester, MA: Clark University Press.

Napoli, D. S. (1981). *Architects of adjustment: The history of the psychological profession in the United States.* Port Washington, NY: Kennibat Press.

Naylor, J. C., & Shine, L. C. (1965). A table for determining the increase in mean criterion score obtained by using a selection device. *Journal of Industrial Psychology, 3,* 33–42.

Nelson, D. (1975). *Managers and workers: Origins of the new factory system in the United States 1880–1920.* Madison: University of Wisconsin Press.

Oschrin, E. (1918). Vocational tests for retail saleswomen. *Journal of Applied Psychology, 2,* 148–155.

Otis, A. S. (1920). The selection of mill workers by mental tests. *Journal of Applied Psychology, 4,* 339–341.

Owens, W. A. (1976). Background data. In M. D. Dunnette (Ed.), *Handbook of industrial and organizational psychology* (pp. 609–644). Chicago: Rand McNally.

Paterson, D. G., & Ludgate, K. E. (1922–1923). Blond and brunette traits: A quantitative study. *Journal of Personnel Research, 1,* 122–127.

Pond, M. (1926–1927). Selective placement of metal workers I. Preliminary studies. II. Development of Scales for placement. III. Selection of toolmaking apprentices. *Journal of Personnel Research, 5,* 345–368, 405–417, 452–466.

Porter, L. W. (1966). Personnel management. In P. R. Farnsworth, O. McNemar, & Q. McNemar (Eds.), *Annual review of psychology* (pp. 395–422). Palo Alto, CA: Annual Reviews.

Prien, E. P., Schippmann, J. S., & Prien, K. O. (2003). *Individual assessment: As practiced in industry and consulting.* Mahwah, NJ: Lawrence Erlbaum Associates.

Project A: The U.S. Army Selection and Classification Project (Special issue). (1990). *Personnel Psychology, 43.*

Rogers, H. W. (1917). Psychological tests for stenographers and typewriters. *Journal of Applied Psychology, 1,* 268–274.

Rogers, T. B. (1995). *The psychological testing enterprise: An introduction.* Pacific Grove, CA: Brooks/Cole.

Rothstein, H. R. (2003). Progress is our most important product: Contributions of validity generalization and meta-analysis to the development and communication of knowledge in I/O psychology. In K. R. Murphy (Ed.), *Validity generalization: A critical review* (pp. 115–154). Mahwah, NJ: Lawrence Erlbaum Associates.

Salgado, J. F. (2001). Some landmarks of 100 years of scientific personnel selection at the beginning of the new century. *International Journal of Selection and Assessment, 9,* 3–8.

Schmidt, F. L. (1992). What do data really mean: Research findings, meta-analysis, and cumulative knowledge in psychology. *American Psychologist, 47,* 1173–1181.

Schmidt, F. L. (1996). Statistical significance testing and cumulative knowledge in psychology: Implications for training of researchers. *Psychological Methods, 1,* 115–129.

Schmidt, F. L., & Hunter, J. E. (1977). Development of a general solution to the problem of validity generalization. *Journal of Applied Psychology, 62,* 529–540.

Schmidt, F. L., & Hunter, J. E. (1998). The validity and utility of selection methods in personnel psychology: Practical and theoretical implications of 85 years of research findings. *Psychological Bulletin, 124,* 262–274.

Schmidt, F. L., Hunter, J. E., McKenzie, R. C., & Muldrow, T. W. (1979). Impact of valid selection procedures on workforce productivity. *Journal of Applied Psychology, 64,* 609–626.

Schmitt, N., & Robertson, I. (1990). Personnel selection. In M. R. Rosenzweig & L. W. Porter (Eds.), *Annual review of psychology* (pp. 289–319). Palo Alto, CA: Annual Reviews.

Scott, W. D. (1915, October). The scientific selection of salesmen. *Advertising & Selling, 5–6,* 94–96.

Scott, W. D. (1917). A fourth method of checking results in vocational selection. *Journal of Applied Psychology, 1,* 61–66.

Scott, W. D. (1920). Changes in some of our conceptions and practices of personnel. *Psychological Review, 27,* 81–94.

Scovill Manufacturing Company Employment Tests. (1928). *Personnel Journal, 7,* 143–145.

Scudder, K. J. (1929). The predictive value of general intelligence tests in the selection of junior accountants and bookkeepers. *Journal of Applied Psychology, 13,* 1–8.

Sheldon, W. H. (1927–1928). Social traits and morphologic types. *Personnel Journal, 6,* 47–55.

Shellow, S. M. (1925–1926). Research in selection of motormen in Milwaukee. *Journal of Personnel Research, 4,* 222–237.

Shellow, S. M. (1926–27). Selection of motormen: Further data on value of tests in Milwaukee. *Journal of Personnel Research, 5,* 183–188.

Snow, A. J. (1923). Labor turnover and mental alertness test scores. *Journal of Applied Psychology, 7,* 285–290.

Society for Industrial and Organizational Psychology. (1987). *Principles for the validation and use of personnel selection procedures* (3rd ed.). College Park, MD: Author.

Society for Industrial and Organizational Psychology. (2003). *Principles for the validation and use of personnel selection procedures* (4th ed.). Bowling Green, OH: Author.

Sokal, M. M. (1981). The origins of the Psychological Corporation. *Journal of the History of the Behavioral Sciences, 17,* 54–67.

Sokal, M. M. (1984). James McKeen Cattell and American psychology in the 1920s. In J. Brozek (Ed.), *Explorations in the history of psychology in the United States* (pp. 273–323). Lewisburg, PA: Bucknell University Press.

Starch, D. (1915). The measurement of efficiency in reading. *Journal of Educational Psychology, 6,* 1–24.

Stead, W. H., Shartle, C. L., & Otis, J. L. (1940). *Occupational counseling techniques.* New York: American Book.

Stern, W. (1934). Otto Lipmann: 1880–1933. *American Journal of Psychology, 46,* 152–154.

Stokes, G. S. (1994). Introduction and history. In G. S. Stokes, M. D. Mumford, & W. A. Owens (Eds.), *Biodata handbook: Theory, research, and use of biographical information in selection and performance prediction* (pp. xv–xvii). Palo Alto, CA: CPP.

Stokes, G. S., & Cooper, L. A. (2004). Biodata. In J. C. Thomas (Vol. Ed.), *Comprehensive handbook of psychological assessment: Vol. 4. Industrial and organizational assessment* (pp. 243–268). Hoboken, NJ: Wiley.

Strong, E. K., Jr. (1918). Work on the Committee on Classification of Personnel. *Journal of Applied Psychology, 2,* 130–139.

Strong, E. K., Jr. (1927). Vocational guidance of executives. *Journal of Applied Psychology, 11,* 331–347.

Taylor, E. K., & Nevis, E. C. (1961). Personnel selection. In P. R. Farnsworth, O. McNemar, & Q. McNemar (Eds.), *Annual review of psychology* (pp. 389–412). Palo Alto, CA: Annual Reviews.

Taylor, H. C., & Russell, J. T. (1939). The relationship of validity coefficients to the practical effectiveness of tests in selection. *Journal of Applied Psychology, 23,* 565–578.

Tenopyr, M. L., & Oeltjen, P. D. (1982). Personnel selection and classification. In M. R. Rosenzweig & L. W. Porter (Eds.), *Annual review of psychology* (pp. 581–618). Palo Alto, CA: Annual Reviews.

Terman, L. M. (1917). A trial of mental and pedagogical tests in a civil service examination for policemen and firemen. *Journal of Applied Psychology, 1,* 17–29.

Thayer, P. W. (1977). "Somethings old, somethings new." *Personnel Psychology, 30,* 513–524.

Thorndike, E. L. (1918). Fundamental theorems in judging men. *Journal of Applied Psychology, 2,* 67–76.

Thorndike, R. L. (1949). *Personnel selection: Test and measurement techniques.* New York: Wiley.

Thurstone, L. L. (1931). Multiple factor analysis. *Psychological Review, 38,* 406–427.

U.S. Employment Service. (1939). *Dictionary of occupational titles.* Washington, DC: Government Printing Office.

Viteles, M. S. (1923). Psychology in business—In England, France, and Germany. *Annals of the American Academy of Political and Social Science, 110,* 207–220.

Viteles, M. S. (1925). The clinical viewpoint in vocational selection. *Journal of Applied Psychology, 9,* 131–138.

Viteles, M. S. (1925–1926a). Standards of accomplishment: Criteria of vocational selection. *Journal of Personnel Research, 4,* 483–486.

Viteles, M. S. (1925–1926b). Research in the selection of motormen. Part I. Survey of the literature. II. Methods devised for the Milwaukee Electric Railway and Light Company. *Journal of Personnel Research, 4,* 100–115, 173–199.

Viteles, M. S. (1932). *Industrial psychology.* New York: Norton.

von Mayrhauser, R. (1992). The mental testing community and validity: A prehistory. *American Psychologist, 47,* 244–253.

Wagner, R. (1949). The employment interview: A critical summary. *Personnel Psychology, 2,* 17–46.

Wallace, S. R., & Weitz, J. (1955). Industrial psychology. In C. P. Stone & Q. McNemar (Eds.), *Annual review of psychology* (pp. 217–250). Stanford, CA: Annual Reviews.

Weisner, W. H., & Cronshaw, S. F. (1988). A meta-analytic investigation of the impact of interview format and degree of structure on the validity of the employment interview. *Journal of Occupational Psychology, 61,* 275–290.

Wherry, R. J., & Bartlett, C. J. (1982). The control of bias in ratings: A theory of rating. *Personnel Psychology, 35,* 521–551.

Whyte, W. H. (1954, September). The fallacies of "personality" testing. *Fortune,* pp. 117–121. Reprinted in A. LaFarge (Ed.), *The essential William H. Whyte* (pp. 43–66), New York: Fordham University Press.

Wissler, C. (1901). The correlation of mental and physical tests. *Psychological Review, 3,* 1–63.

Woodworth, R. S. (1919). Examination of emotional fitness for warfare. *Psychological Bulletin, 16,* 59–60.

9

A History of Job Analysis

Mark A. Wilson
North Carolina State University

Job analysis is the process of collecting, organizing, analyzing and documenting information about work. Because job analysis is a largely descriptive process, different approaches to job analysis are not so much in contention with each other as they are focusing on different aspects of the same problem. The field of job analysis is especially important because it is the precursor to many other areas of industrial–organizational (I–O) psychology. Job analysis often serves as a first step that cannot be ignored even though the investigator's primary interests may be in other areas of I–O psychology. The purpose of this chapter is to provide an understanding of a history of job analysis by reviewing previous histories, establishing a context for the development of the field, organizing the various approaches to job analysis into a series of schools of thought, and looking back over the last 100 years to come to a series of conclusions about the field.

This chapter is organized into five sections. I begin with a brief section where I speculate on ancient job analysis just for fun. The second section discusses the histories of job analysis that have been offered over the years. It is an attempt to honor past historians and point the reader to other views and approaches to the history of job analysis. The second section concludes by presenting the important contributors to the field in a tabular format. The third section describes the context in which the field of job analysis developed. The discussion of context is then broken into three eras of roughly 20 to 40 years each where I examine how legal, economic, and organizational forces shaped job analysis thinking. These forces have caused the formation or expansion of a number of job analysis schools of thought. I conclude the discussion of the context of each era by picking a type of work that is illustrative of that era and citing important achievements in job analysis, which I call "firsts." The fourth section describes five schools of job analysis that have emerged. Some might not recognize the names for some of the schools because they are my labels. However, even if readers disagree with my terms, perhaps they may gain a greater understanding of job analysis by thinking about my attempt to categorize it. In the final section I come to some conclusions and provide a summary. It is here that I go out on a limb and provide a list of the lessons from history for job analysis. Once we have reviewed how we got to this point, we will stop to take stock and consider what it all means for today. I also recognize the contributions of key individuals by proposing a pantheon of job analysis contributors. These individuals are my picks for the job analysts who have had the most impact on the field. I admit at the outset that I have great admiration and respect for those who have struggled with job analysis issues over the past 100 years. I also admit that I have enjoyed the freedom that comes with interpreting the impact of past events on the field, but it is an inherently subjective task unrestrained by the empirical methods we rely on in normal science and practice.

THE FIRST JOB ANALYSIS

Although I choose to start the history of job analysis around 1900 because of my reading of an early job analysis historian (Uhrbrock, 1922), I was fortunate to be present at a meeting where a persuasive case was made that the field of job analysis is much older. Jimmy Mitchell made a presentation where he argued that the first documented use of job analysis was the Chinese Imperial Court in 1115 BC (Mitchell, Bennett, & Strickland, 1999). This ancient job analysis involved a six-factor model including writing, arithmetic, music, archery, horsemanship, ceremonies, and rites. While I was watching Discovery Channel late one night it dawned on me that Mitchell might be wrong. Apparently archeologists have discovered vast settlements near the pyramids where thousands of workers are believed to have lived and worked. The complexity and scale of building these monuments were such that numerous "jobs" were most likely generated on a vast scale. To describe the construction of the pyramids as the first large-scale labor-intensive organization is no great insight. But given the time it took to construct them, it is not too wild a conjecture to imagine that the workers needed to document their activities. Could it be that somewhere buried in the sand there are scrolls of job descriptions with detailed task lists of how to build the pyramids? We may never know because the great fire at Alexandria may have forever destroyed any evidence of any ancient job analysis documents. While we await an Indiana Jones of job analysis history to come along, I am going to defer to Jimmy Mitchell and argue that the first job analysis took place in 1115 BC.

A HISTORY OF JOB ANALYSIS HISTORIES

I wanted to give credit where credit is due, and credit is certainly due to those who came before me and took up the task of writing the history of job analysis. Although some of these histories are easily accessible, others are hard to find. They also vary considerably in both their approach to the topic and their scope. Indeed, one of the greatest influences on writing this chapter was the desire to take a different approach in an attempt to build on what had already been done. But my attempt at a different approach is not motivated out of a lack of appreciation of previous histories. If you do not like what I have to say about the history of job analysis, you are in luck. There are several other histories you can turn to for relief.

The first history of job analysis was written in 1922 (Uhrbrock, 1922) and describes the early beginning of job analysis. This history is significant because it links the need for job analysis to changes in organizational structure (i.e., the development of centralized human resource functions) and recognizes that defining work in an organization is as much about power as it is about description. The need for job analysis was initially linked to the desire to develop accurate job specifications for the purposes of selection interviewing. Uhrbrock recognized the role of job analysis in setting performance standards and increasing organizational efficiency and functioning. Interestingly, he also introduced the much less well known (and by today's standards sexist) term of "man analysis" to describe the determination of whether the individual had the necessary attributes to perform the job. Later he provided more detail on the early practice of job analysis in industry as part of a journal issue containing many early classic job analysis articles (Uhrbrock, 1934).

The next histories appear over 60 years later in *The Job Analysis Handbook for Business, Industry, and Government* (Gael, 1988).[1] There are two chapters, one general history (Primoff &

---

[1]This handbook is by far the most comprehensive and authoritative discussion of job analysis ever assembled.

Fine, 1988) and one devoted to military job analysis (Mitchell, 1988). Given the central role that the military has played in both the science and practice of job analysis, its special treatment is entirely appropriate. Both histories are organized chronologically, but Primoff and Fine began with five issues as a touchstone to examine various approaches to job analysis. Another difference is that Primoff and Fine devoted considerable space to detailing the contributions and backgrounds of key individuals in the field, whereas Mitchell launched straight into his chronology organized around major military conflicts while still noting the contributions of key individuals.

These earlier histories disagree as to the ancient origins of job analysis. Thus, Primoff and Fine looked to Socrates in the 5th century BC defining what was required for a just state, whereas Mitchell cited the Chinese emperor's military needs in 1115 BC to design content valid examinations for entry into the service. Primoff and Fine described a number of early organizations influential in the development of job analysis and specific approaches to job analysis, concluding with the increasing importance of job analysis in legal disputes and the call for greater attention to common taxonomies. Mitchell described the unique contributions of each of the military services to job analysis, the halting efforts toward a more integrated approach, and the movement toward comparative analysis and evaluation of job analysis techniques. After reading both of these chapters, one can appreciate how interlinked the history of job analysis is with the history of military research and practice and I–O psychology.

Mitchell and Driskill (1996) updated the job analysis handbook chapter on the history of military job analysis with a greater emphasis on specific job analysis techniques developed in military research. What is unique to this history is the emphasis on the "theory of job analysis." The job analysis literature is not completely devoid of theory. Moving from McCormick's stimulus-organism-response (S-O-R) theory of work (McCormick, 1979) to an implied early theory of performance based on critical incidents and beyond, they detailed the implications of job analysis choices on our understanding of job performance models. The article ends with their description of the promise of a job component approach in integrating various types of job information and a call for a unified theory of work.

A more recent history of job analysis details the contributions of a number of individuals in the 20th century. The history is titled "Introduction to a New Journal" and describes the founding of a Web-based journal (*Ergometrika*) devoted to job analysis research (Cunningham, 2000). It begins by describing the origins of the term *ergometrics* (Cunningham, 1971). The bulk of the introduction is a history of job analysis that is composed of brief biographical notes on 19 contributors to the field. The biographical notes include information about where the contributors worked, their important publications, and, when appropriate, descriptions of methodology employed. Anyone interested in the highly varied careers of contributors to job analysis would be well advised to read the introduction. It can be found on the Web (www.ergometrika.org/volume1/ergometrika-article.htm). Among other impressions one gets from a reading of these brief biographies is an understanding of how many of the early greats of job analysis were true scientist–practitioners. Cunningham's introduction ends with a brief discussion of some of the contextual factors that have shaped job analysis over the years and his call for a multidisciplinary approach to job analysis.

Important Contributors to Job Analysis

Because Cunningham so recently provided biographical sketches of many of the important contributors to the field, I have developed Table 9.1 based on his work. Table 9.1 provides a list of the original 19 contributors along with a description of their contribution and an important publication when appropriate. Cunningham limited his list to important contributors of the 20th century. I have taken the liberty of adding more recent contributors to the list.

TABLE 9.1
Timeline of Job Analysis Contributors

Contributor	Important Contribution
Beginnings: job analysis in the industrial age (1903–1940)	
Frederick W. Taylor	Developed time and motion study of work called scientific management (Taylor, 1911).
Frank B. Gilbreth & Lillian E. Gilbreth	Developed the "therblig" as a unit of measurement in motion study (Gilbreth & Gilbreth, 1917).
Hugo Münsterberg	Developed systematic methods for estimating job requirements (Münsterberg, 1913).
Walter Van Dyke Bingham	Early advocate of job analysis for use in selection and performance appraisal (Bingham, 1939).
Walter Dill Scott	Co-directed establishment of job specifications for Army officers and enlisted specialties.
Morris S. Viteles	Developed the job psychograph (Viteles, 1923).
The golden era: job analysis in the organizational age (1941–1980)	
Carroll L. Shartle	Oversaw the development of the first *Dictionary of Occupational Titles* and codeveloped the work analysis forms (Shartle & Stogdill, 1957).
John C. Flanagan	Developed the critical incident technique of job analysis (Flanagan, 1949).
Ernest J. McCormick	Pioneered the structured job analysis based on generic worker-oriented descriptors culminating in the Position Analysis Questionnaire (McCormick, Jeanneret, & Mecham, 1972).
Sidney A. Fine	Developed the functional job analysis method (Fine, 1955).
Ernest S. Primoff	Developed the job element method for systematically determining job requirements using j-coefficients (Primoff, 1957).
John L. Holland	Pioneered vocational psychology resulting in the Self-Directed Search (Holland, 1970).
Edwin A. Fleishman	Pioneered and operationalized ability-oriented job analysis and developed a taxonomy of cognitive, psychomotor, physical, and sensory–perceptual abilities (Fleishman, 1975).
Raymond E. Christal	Developed the task inventory method of job analysis and the Comprehensive Occupational Data Analysis Program (Christal, 1974).
Donald G. Paterson, Rene V. Dawis & Lloyd H. Lofquist	Pioneered and developed a number of measures concerning occupational trait requirements (Dawis & Lofquist, 1983; Paterson, Gerken & Hahn, 1941).
Sidney Gael	Directed the development of the Work Performance Survey System (Gael, 1977).
At a crossroads: job analysis in the information age (1981–2003)	
P. Richard Jeanneret	Popularized the structured job analysis based on generic worker-oriented descriptors in the work place using the Position Analysis Questionnaire.
Edward L. Levine	Pioneered comparative job analysis procedures and popularized job analysis (Levine, 1983).
Robert J. Harvey	Developed the Common Metric Questionnaire (Harvey, 1991a).
Jimmy L. Mitchell	Founded the Institute for Job and Occupation Analysis, founded *Ergometrika,* and served as a historian to job analysis in the United States military (Mitchell, 1988).
Joseph W. Cunningham	Developed the Occupation Analysis Inventory and the General Work Inventory (Cunningham, Boese, Neeb, Pass, 1983).

Note. The information from the first two time periods in the table is abstracted from Cunningham (2000).

Whereas Table 9.1 is meant to quickly summarize the important contributors to job analysis over the last 100 years, I wanted to provide some justification for the additions I have made to Cunningham's original list. These individuals have had their greatest impact in the late 20th and very early 21st centuries. I am fully aware that as one gets closer to the present, an objective telling of history becomes more and more difficult. However, given the infrequency with which these histories tend to be written, I have chosen to highlight what I believe to be the important work of some of my contemporaries.

I have chosen to add five additional individuals as important contributors to the field. I discuss them in no particular order. P. Richard Jeanneret has devoted much of his career to popularizing McCormick's generalist approach to job analysis through PAQ Services and Jeanneret and Associates. The Position Analysis Questionnaire (PAQ) remains one of the most comprehensively developed and researched generic job analysis instrument in use today largely because of Jeanneret's and his associates' efforts (see more information about PAQ later in this chapter). Edward L. Levine has made significant and numerous contributions to both the science and practice of job analysis. He authored a highly accessible and humorous (all too rare in the job analysis literature) book to introduce people to the practice of job analysis (Levine, 1983) and coauthored what will become a standard reference in the field for years to come (Brannick & Levine, 2002). Levine and his associates have made a number of important scientific contributions to the field. Robert J. Harvey (Harvey, 1991b) had the unenviable task of following Ernest J. McCormick (McCormick, 1976) in writing the job analysis chapter for the second *Handbook of Industrial and Organizational Psychology*. The chapter waded fearlessly into the morass of job analysis terminology and tried to clearly separate job analysis activities focused on describing work from the various inferences that are made from examining job analysis data about incumbent attribute requirements. Harvey and his associates have developed a generic job analysis instrument (i.e., the Common Metric Questionnaire; Harvey 1991a) and have focused on applying psychometric rigor to the field of job analysis research.

Jimmy L. Mitchell has written and spoken more about the history of job analysis than any other author. He founded and personally funded the Institute for Job and Occupational Analysis (IJOA) and was the founding editor-in-chief of the online journal *Ergometrika*. Although he spent much of his career in the military, he did much to transfer job analysis knowledge gained there to other public and private organizations through IJOA-sponsored seminars and workshops. Finally, Joseph W. Cunningham, a cofounder of *Ergometrika* in 2000, devoted his career to the study and development of job and occupational taxonomic structures. Author of the Occupation Analysis Inventory (OAI) and the General Work Inventory (GWI), Cunningham and his associates have explored numerous taxonomic issues and provided the most comprehensive inventory of generalized work behaviors (GWB). (Descriptions about these inventories are presented later in this chapter.) Occupying the space between job tasks and more generic work dimensions, GWBs may provide the key to a truly comprehensive generalized theory of work.

CONTEXTUAL FORCES THAT SHAPED JOB ANALYSIS

The setting in which job analysis ideas developed has not been a frequent or lengthy topic of discussion in prior histories. A number of events have shaped the history of job analysis that are not always well understood. Such events are legal, economic, or organizational in nature. I have listed what I think are the top events that have shaped the history of job analysis for each of three eras. The first two eras are roughly 40 years each (1903–1940 and 1941–1980) and the third is a little over 20 years (1981–2003). The first two eras are dominated by conflict and the aftermath of conflict (i.e., World Wars). The third era is dominated by substantial technological and economic change. The list of events discussed here is not meant to be exhaustive but rather to provide key contextual information in the development of the field. As these events have taken place, practitioners and researchers in job analysis have struggled to respond. Some events have had rather obvious effects on the history of job analysis, whereas others are more open to interpretation.

Beginnings: Job Analysis in the Industrial Age (1903–1940)

The first era of job analysis development is one of massive and fundamental economic, legal, and organizational change, as noted in previous chapters. With innovations such as the assembly line, which enabled mass production and rapid economic expansion, the scale and nature of work life in organizations was dramatically altered for many. It was during this period, which included World War I and the Great Depression, that modern job analysis originated. Legal, economic and organizational events of this era shaped the early thinking about job analysis. (See also chaps. 1 and 3 in this text.)

Events.   The two most important legal developments during this era were the passage of the National Labor Relations Act 1935 and the Fair Labor Standards Act of 1938. As is well known, the first law gave workers the right to collective bargaining; the second law specified what jobs were exempt versus those that were not exempt from working hour requirements and overtime rules based on specific work activities.[2] Collective bargaining can be termed as "the job analyst retirement act" because ever more detailed job descriptions were needed as part of these collective bargaining agreements. The second law forever divided work into "labor" and "management" categories with not always positive results. Although these laws were passed toward the end of the era, it is fair to say that the entire time period was one where considerable conflict resulted from disputes over who got to define and alter work descriptions.

Unemployment and rapid economic expansion were the major economic events of this era. The dark side of the initial industrial age economy (from the employee's perspective) was unemployment. With the advent of unemployment insurance in 1935, governments became interested in understanding jobs and labor markets in order to return people to the labor markets and minimize unemployment costs. Although this effort began in this era, it reached its height in the next. But it was during this era that unemployment spawned a great interest in the understanding of occupations, occupational trends, and interests, in order to smooth transitions for workers from one industry to the next. The positive side of the industrial age was rapid economic growth, which generated more numerous and varied types of work. Growth has driven job analysts toward more standardized and centralized methods to deal with the increasing complexity and change associated with large new corporate organizations that emerged during the era. Detailed knowledge of the process of production or service became necessary to control quality, solve production problems, and reduce costs.

How did these legal and economic events affect organizations? Small organizations often have far less need for detailed documents containing job information (because everyone knows everyone else), but they lack the scale to compete when their product or service is reduced to a commodity. In industry after industry, initially small organizations expanded through cycles of innovation, rapid growth, standardization, and consolidation. With greater size, organizations become increasingly concerned with standardizing processes to maintain quality. Job information that was once part of the organization's collective memory becomes more complex when

---

[2]Indeed, as this chapter is being finished U.S. Congress is again debating who should receive overtime pay and who should not.

spread over multiple locations and buffered by increasing layers of management. Growth also tends to bring greater specialization, increasing the number and different types of work performed in the organization. Finally, staffs emerge who are often at odds with general managers over how detailed and documented job information should be. It was during this era that the Committee on Classification of Personnel in the Army played an important role in early standardization of job-related information (Uhrbrock, 1922). As described in previous chapters, World War I required for the first time a massive selection and job classification effort of often poorly educated draftees from rural backgrounds. The procedures used for job specification and classification in the Army quickly made their way into the private sector after World War I.

To close my discussion of events during the initial era, I wanted to cite the most important job of the time period, which is clearly manufacturing work. Whether the work was feeding and off-bearing, assembling, or packing and shipping, work in manufacturing was intensely studied and grew enormously during this era. Although the absolute number of manufacturing jobs would not peak until later, it was during this time period when the work was new that such work was conceptualized and designed.

Firsts.   The first form for recording job analysis data was produced in 1914 at Dennison Manufacturing Company by P. J. Reilly (Uhrbrock, 1922). The form included job numbers, length of training period, and age, height, and weight notations along with a narrative description of the duties that were required. A considerable amount of time passed before the first standardized job analysis instrument was developed. The job psychograph was a graphic profile resulting from a number of trait ratings developed by Morris Viteles (Viteles, 1923). The U.S. Employment Service initially used the psychograph as a prototype for the Worker Characteristics Form (Shartle, 1952; Stead & Shartle, 1940). This monumental government effort was the result of C. L. Shartle convincing the government that private sector jobs needed to be classified for potential military use (E. A. Fleishman, personal communication, May 2005). As the era came to a close, the first *Dictionary of Occupational Titles* (DOT) was published in 1939 by the U.S. Department of Labor, providing the first narrative description and categorization of thousands of jobs in the U.S. economy. Publication of the DOT signaled the beginning of a new approach to job analysis that would greatly expand in the next era.

The Golden Era: Job Analysis in the Organizational Age (1941–1980)

The next era was again dominated by military conflict, economic growth, and concern for unemployment. However, it is during this period that what has come to be known as "globalization" was accelerated with dramatic effects on organizations and work. This era is golden because most of the schools of job analysis emerged during this time period and previous schools went through a significant expansion. Nearly everything we know as modern job analysis was designed and implemented during this era.

Events.   Of the various federal laws that have affected job analysis during this period, the Equal Pay Act of 1963 and the Civil Rights Act of 1964 (Title VII) have had the most impact. The Equal Pay Act identified four compensable factors (skill, effort, responsibility, working conditions) on which jobs must be compared to determine their worth. This was an important act because it specified the use of common rational job dimensions to determine job worth without saying a whole lot about what these dimensions were or how to measure them. As we will see in the next section, two entire schools of job analysis have developed around the identification and use of job dimensions. Title VII of the Civil Rights Act was interpreted to require that nearly all employment-related decisions need to be job related (especially the key areas of selection and promotion). The completion of a job analysis is a key step in demonstrating job relatedness of personnel decisions.

This requirement placed nearly every aspect of the collection and documentation of job information under scrutiny. It also encouraged the use of more detailed job analysis data and much more documentation of the job analysis process. Documents and procedures that had largely been for internal use were now central to nearly every discrimination-related dispute. The ideas represented in these laws had the effect of pulling the field of job analysis into two distinctly different directions: (a) job analysis with greater documentation and job descriptions with great specificity, and (b) more general job dimensions to be applied to all work regardless of the specific job activities.

At first glance, the legislation discussed here would seem to drive home the importance of job analysis to organizations. Indeed, the initial reaction of many organizations to these events was to increase the specificity of their job analysis and place more emphasis on documentation. The problem with more detailed information is that it tends to have a shorter shelf life for many jobs. Having out-of-date information may be worse than having none or more general information. Over time, organizations have tended to drift away from maintaining highly specific and well-documented job information until they are challenged to defend their personnel actions. One reason has been the desire to reduce costs and increase job flexibility in an increasingly competitive global market place. It was generally believed that another drawback to increased specificity was the perception that job structure and organizations became less flexible when jobs were specifically defined. Although it can be argued that it is the use of the information rather than its specificity that leads to rigidity, highly detailed job analysis has often been criticized as an indicator of "organizational ossification." When various pieces of legislation are examined in terms of the specificity they imply, they are quite different. Whereas the Civil Rights Act has been interpreted as requiring very specific job analysis information, the Equal Pay Act (enacted in the same era) specifies only four very general dimensions on which to determine and compare the value of work for pay purposes. What cannot be denied is that increasing government interest in how work information is used to make decisions has led to greater emphasis on both the documentation and the evaluation of job information.

An economic factor affecting job analysis during this era was the beginning of globalization of markets with the signing of the first General Agreement on Trade and Tariffs in 1947. Globalization has led to increased competition based on price, resulting in both lower margins and often shorter product life cycles. As profit margins shrink, organizations become less and less interested in conducting detailed and expensive job analysis studies. As the rate of innovation and competition increases, the timeliness of job analysis information often decreases. These factors hold especially true when labor costs are a significant portion of total costs. To remain competitive, work needed to be "redesigned." This redesign often gave the worker more discretion to increase product or service quality and work efficiency. Greater organizational efficiency was often obtained by reducing the complexity and number of people in business decision making through processes referred to as "delayering" and "flattening." It was during this era that American-based organizations worried that Japanese corporations had gained insurmountable leads in manufacturing efficiency and product quality. This concern led to considerable experimentation in work and organizational design at the production level of the organization in an effort to obtain "lean production."

How did these economic and social events affect organizations? As noted in previous chapters, World War II resulted in even greater needs for specialized selection and classification systems to stand up a more mechanized and complex military. The genesis of complex global corporations was the logistical, managerial, and human resource challenges confronted during the war. Eventually globalization caused organizations to emphasize the process improvement applications of job analysis information. With the exception of process improvement, organizations have reacted to these changes in emphasis with greater concerns about the immediate and hidden costs of job analysis. In an effort to control these costs, some organizations have decided to "outsource" human resource functions and much of their workforce through employee leasing arrangements. By focusing on "core functions," where the organization has unique competence, and jettisoning activities that others could do better, the enterprise hopes to maintain or increase competitive advantage.

To close my discussion of the events of this period, I wanted to name my pick for the most important job during the era. It was during this era that "management" as a job became increasingly important and influential in work life. As organizations grew in complexity and faced new and more complex environments, the job of manager evolved from supervisor to strategist. Considerable effort was devoted to understanding the work and the attributes it required of individuals during this period (Baehr, Lonergan, & Hunt, 1978; Hemphill, 1959). Organizational staffs were developed with ever more specialized forms of managers dealing with more layered organizations as the era progressed. However, as the era came to an end, the nature and structure of management were becoming increasingly pressured to produce more with less.

Firsts.   The first empirically derived job dimensions resulted from the work of Ernest McCormick and his students, whereas the first rational job dimensions resulted from the work of Sid Fine. The first taxonomy of human attributes was also proposed (Fleishman, 1975). The first chapter on job analysis in an introductory psychology textbook was published (Gagné & Fleishman, 1959). The first comprehensive review of the research literature (Prien & Ronan, 1971) and the first comprehensive book on job analysis (McCormick, 1979) were published.[3] The first handbook of I–O psychology chapter devoted to job analysis was published (McCormick, 1976) during this era along with the first handbook for analyzing jobs (U.S. Department of Labor, 1971). This time period saw the first extensive application of computer technology to job analysis (e.g. Comprehensive Occupational Data Analysis Program [CODAP] and PAQ).

At a Crossroads: Job Analysis in the Information Age (1981–2003)

During the final period of this history, the field of job analysis began to struggle with a number of issues. Legal, economic, and organizational changes in this era provided new and in some ways much more fundamental challenges to the field. One issue was how to respond to a drastically changing workplace with limited resources to devote to job analysis. Another issue was what to make of the newest school of job analysis thought that focuses on evaluating the quality of job analysis. The reason job analysis is described as being at a crossroads is because it is during this time period that disputes developed over how closely job analysis should be evaluated, how and whether it should be used, and how detailed it should be. What is at stake is no less than the relevance of the field in modern times and whether it has made the transition to a science of work.

Events.   By far the most important legal event of this era was the passage of the Americans with Disabilities Act of 1990 (ADA). The ADA requires that employers examine their jobs to determine "essential functions" as the basis of determining eligibility for work by disabled applicants. The notion that jobs are composed of core or essential functions, along with a

---

[3]To be fair the first job analysis book published in this era was by Fine and Wiley (1971), but it was limited to a discussion of functional job analysis topics (see also Lichtner, 1921, and Fryklund, 1942).

number of other often elective activities, recognizes the important role of the individual worker in defining work and is a nod to the increasing difficulty in defining a "job" in modern organizations. The idea that only essential parts of a job need be considered when making important decisions about that work and that "reasonable accommodation" including job redesign may be required to come into compliance with the law presents several challenges for job analysts. A debate continues as to how "specific" these essential functions need to be and what "reasonable accommodation" might involve, but they clearly imply the requirement for more detail than do the job dimensions cited in the Equal Pay Act. The Americans with Disabilities Act falls somewhere in between the Civil Rights Act and the Equal Pay Act in the level of specificity assumed to be needed to comply with the law and recognizes some fluidity in how jobs are designed and evolve. If one accepts the views of work implied by these laws, it implies that a certain amount of unreliability in responses to job analysis questionnaires is to be expected from individuals holding the same job.

The economic events of this era included increased globalization of markets, growth of the information-oriented economy, and an unprecedented technology upgrade cycle. These developments have led to dramatic improvements in worker productivity. Although globalization began in the previous era, it continued to grow during an era that saw the end of the Cold War and the birth and growth of the Internet. Whereas initial globalization consisted of trade in manufactured goods, this era saw increased world trade for service and labor. High-speed communication enabled the decentralization of administrative and service functions of organizations, which resulted in "telecommuting" and more flexible work schedules. As the year 2000 approached, many organizations chose to replace, rather than reprogram, computer systems to address the "Y2K" problem. Many of these new systems were not replacements of previous systems. Rather, they were powerful work information integration tools driven by sophisticated enterprise software having far greater capabilities. Struggling to implement these systems along with the loss of pricing power led many organizations to rethink what acceptable levels of worker productivity should be in a global market place, with far fewer barriers to trade.

Organizations responded to these legislative and economic events with changes in their structure, procedures, and performance. One of the most consistent trends has been the flattening of organizational structure. Organizations have pursued leaner structures to control costs, increase flexibility, and increase communication internally and with customers. This development has led to more variable and increased responsibilities for those left behind. The rapid rate of change has increasingly meant that the famous "other duties as assigned" component of many workers' jobs has increased as a percentage of their job. With fewer specialized staff members to provide the necessary job information, the task is often left to fewer and fewer overcommitted generalists.

Another change has been the increasing use of process and information technology to improve existing operations. Technology has enabled many workers to achieve more with less and has often added significant mental demands to traditional physical labor. While adding new knowledge elements to work, it has also added greater needs for skills in coordination and communication from workers who formally were supervised. Indeed, this trend has often blurred the line between exempt and nonexempt positions. As more work has evolved to contain a significant and specialized knowledge component that is only superficially supervised, organizations have sought to understand the general competencies of individuals who can do well in these new, more uncertain environments.

The changes in structure and technology have led to the development of high-performance organizations that place extensive emphasis on defining, monitoring, and constantly improving organizational performance. High-performance organizations have been characterized as attacking both the cost and the quality aspects of production to generate higher quality products and services at lower costs. For some workers, this approach has included stock options and more varied pay linked to various measures of organizational performance. For other workers, it has meant higher levels of unemployment, job insecurity, and uncertainty. Interest in fostering high performance has driven organizations to focus less on what is done and more on determining desirable work outcomes and behaviors.

To some extent, organizational changes in structure, process/technology, and performance have caused the field of job analysis to come full circle. The earliest histories of job analysis point out that there was little need for formal job analysis documents because the organizations were small and decision makers often had direct contact with and knowledge about the work being performed. Through the processes of outsourcing and delayering, many organizations have become more like their predecessors at the beginning of the Industrial Age with only core functions remaining to be documented and little perceived need of formal job analysis documents for their functioning. The drive for high performance has to date focused more on the characteristics of the worker rather than on direct organizational involvement in the design of the work. In an increasingly cost-conscious environment, where every organizational activity must be justified, job analysis was no exception.

So what type of job best captures the spirit of this era? It is certainly not the manufacturing work or the managers of previous eras. The number of both these jobs has declined during this time period. An argument could be made that research and development workers are the key contributors in an economy based on the development and exchange of information. However, I believe the call center worker is the job that best typifies this era. Call center jobs include exchanging information about technical help, medical claims, customer service, or telemarketing. These jobs have each played a significant role in the information economy.

Firsts.   It was during this time period that the first attempts were made at developing and implementing integrated human resource systems based on multipurpose job analysis databases (Drauden, 1988; Hakel, 1984). Both Gael (1983) and Fine and Cronshaw (1999) published books concerning how to use task analysis and functional job analysis, respectively, to integrate human resource systems. The first handbook of job analysis was published (Gael, 1988). Perhaps the most important job analysis effort of the era involved the DOT, which underwent an ambitious revision and expansion during this era to become the occupational information network (O*Net; Peterson, Mumford, Borman, Jeanneret, & Fleishman, 1999; Peterson et al., 2001). Fleishman and Reilly (1992) produced the first handbook of human abilities that linked human attributes, job tasks, and commercially available selection tests. Given the increasing mental load on many workers, it is no surprise that the first work on cognitive task and work analysis was documented in a book (Vicente, 1999).

JOB ANALYSIS SCHOOLS OF THOUGHT

In response to the events described in the previous section, a number of schools of thought in job analysis have emerged. These various schools that have emerged should be viewed not as competing schools but as layers in a conceptual archeological dig into the past. Each school clearly reflects the state of affairs at the time it emerged, and these schools are best understood from the legal, economic, and organizational frameworks of their time. The various schools have also responded to events in subsequent eras with varying degrees of success. For example, if employment discrimination is an important legal issue of the time, then job analysis techniques are likely to be more specific and heavily documented. If organizations face increasing competition, they will limit overhead costs associated with collecting job information and process improvement. Although the various schools emerged in different eras, they are all very relevant today.

As I present each school, I have cited what I believe to be the summative or seminal article associated with it, which is often but not always a good way to date the schools. In nearly all cases I have attached names to these schools that are not widely used or even accepted in some cases. The names I have chosen are my attempt to emphasize the school's place in the development of job analysis and to emphasize each school's central driving principle. However, I take full responsibility for creating and assigning the hard work of others into "schools" of my own choosing. Space does not permit an adequate treatment of all the contributions to each school, so I apologize in advance to those who feel someone or something has been left our or not given enough attention.

Elemental Molecularists

The first and oldest school of job analysis is the elemental molecularists. As the name should imply, they focus on breaking work down into very detailed and specific units for study and use by others. Molecularists can be subdivided into camps based on the detail associated with their observations. The founder of the most highly detailed molecularist camp was Fredrick Taylor (Taylor, 1911), with considerable practical assistance by the Gilbreths (Gilbreth & Gilbreth, 1917). This approach sought to break work tasks down into elemental units of motion with the goal of reducing inefficiencies and promoting a standardized approach to work design. Often referred to as scientific management, this approach operated on the fundamental insight that human work could be designed in much the same way early industrial machines were being designed at the beginning of the 20th century. Indeed, this interest in the relations between humans, machines, and systems evolved into an important area of psychology with a rich history of its own (i.e., see chap. 10 on human factors in this text).

The primary benefit of this approach was to reduce the effort needed to the absolute minimum for demanding physical labor and to drastically increase the efficiency of the production process. Although initially analyzing physical labor, ergonomists have turned to studying work "from the neck up" in response to changes in work control systems and the increasing importance of knowledge work in the emerging information economy. The level of detail and painstaking effort associated with the approach is hard to exaggerate. A production process subjected to scientific management could result in hundreds and even thousands of elements or individual motions that needed to be timed and recorded. With a focus on efficiency and the engineering of work, this school provides the highly specific job information necessary to design and staff organizations of growing complexity. It is no exaggeration to say that this first branch of molecularists was the key element in mass production manufacturing based on assembly lines.

Task Analytic Molecularists

Job analysts who focus on job tasks (i.e., task analysis) form the second camp of *task analytic molecularists*. Although no one individual is associated with founding this school, no one has contributed more to the science and practice of task analysis than Raymond E. Christal (Christal, 1974). Task analysts break work down into a series of statements with a specific action, an object, and often an intended result or outcome. A job can be composed of 100 or more individual tasks that are often scaled by incumbents as to their difficulty, importance, significance, criticality, or time spent relative to other tasks in long lists referred to as task inventories. Although the task approach to job analysis probably started on the back of a supervisor's envelope (Uhrbrock, 1922), task inventories have been used extensively in both the private sector and the military for training evaluation and design, selection, and performance appraisal development. They gained popularity because of the specificity and utility of task analysis in training development and evaluation.

The fundamental insight of this approach is that collecting job information expressed in the language of the worker and in considerable detail is an unavoidable task for some human resource purposes that are heavy in face validity. Having completed a number of task-oriented job analysis studies, I can attest to the power and insight of the task-oriented approach. Because of my detailed task knowledge of various jobs, I have been offered production supervisor positions and had it assumed that I was an undercover police officer ("No one but another law enforcement officer knows that much about what I do."). The primary benefit of this approach was to closely link training programs and performance evaluation to actual job activities, resulting in a more rationalized human resource system. The benefit is often gained at considerable costs, with job incumbents rating hundreds of tasks as many as three or four times in job inventories that took numerous analysts to develop and score.

The approach was particularly well suited for the military and its need to train large numbers of individuals in more varied kinds of work for World War II. After the war, this approach reached its zenith in private industry at Control Data Corporation (Turnow & Pinto, 1976). Ideally suited for convincing judges that human resource practices based on it were job related, task-oriented job analysis became the gold standard of legal defensibility during this era. However, although task analysis was useful for many purposes, the advantages of the task analysis approach (i.e., language of the worker, highly detailed and specific) were also the source of problems. It could easily become large, unwieldy, and expensive. The manageability of task data was greatly enhanced with the development of the Comprehensive Occupational Data Analysis Program (CODAP) by the United State Air Force (Christal, 1974). It is no accident that the majority of task-oriented research and development were conducted by the relatively deep pockets of the military. CODAP clearly demonstrated that vast amounts of task data could be manipulated to better understand work and design better training. The high level of detail made the information hard to integrate across jobs and organizations, however. Thus, an important issue was determining how to retain some of the benefits of the approach while providing a more integrated job information system at lower costs.

Functionalists[4]

The *functionalist school* of job analysis is the first to imagine an integrated job information system with some data that may be useful for nearly any purpose for which job information may be collected. By focusing on the various functions for which job information is used, a functional job analysis produces highly detailed job schedules with numerous types of job information in varying levels of detail. The founder of the functionalist movement is Sidney A. Fine (Fine, 1955). Functional job analysis has had its most extensive application in the federal government at the U.S. Department of Labor in the fourth edition of the *Dictionary of Occupational Titles* (U.S. Department of Labor, 1977).

Contributions of the functional approach include a concern with describing the work environment and the requirements that work places on the individual (worker attributes). Functional job analysis is perhaps best known for the popularization and amazing utility of three rational work dimensions (i.e., data, people, things). Thousands of jobs have received data,

---

[4]This is not to be confused with the Functionalist school of thought in psychology around early 20th century and discussed in several chapters throughout the text.

people, and things ratings by occupational analysts using rating scales with highly detailed activity based anchors for each dimension.[5] To this day, anyone seeking job information could do far worse than to find a Department of Labor job schedule for the work they are seeking to understand. The fundamental insight of functionalism is that no one level of specificity of job information data is sufficient to serve all the needs of human resource decisions. Perhaps the greatest benefit of this approach was that it was free of charge to anyone who cared to examine it. A second important benefit was that this type of information allowed direct comparisons between highly dissimilar types of work on a common and easily understood set of variables. The need for highly trained analysts and extensive observations and interviews made this an expensive but highly useful approach to collecting job information.

Generalists

Out of a frustration with the high costs and effort associated with both the molecular and functional approach to job analysis, the *generalist* approach was born. The idea was that for many purposes, such highly detailed information was not necessary and the investment required to collect it was a significant deterrent to job analysis in many organizations. Generalists sought to develop a single common metric for the measurement and comparison of all work based on a simple and straightforward stimulus-organism-response (S-O-R) theory of work. The theory was that work occurred within a social and physical context and could be broken down into input, process, and output components. Ernest J. McCormick and his students are the founders of the generalist approach to job analysis (McCormick, Jeanneret, & Mecham, 1972). They designed the 194-item Position Analysis Questionnaire (PAQ) to be a one-stop all-encompassing job analysis instrument normed on a large sample of jobs meant to mirror the entire workforce in the United States. The normative sample allowed the development of the first empirically derived job dimensions meant to mirror all work. It is perhaps no accident that one of the early and most popular applications of the PAQ was job evaluation. With an elegant policy-capturing approach based on a normative sample of the labor market of 1970, the PAQ is capable of generating predicted wages with various adjustments for any new job with a PAQ profile. The same type of policy-capturing approach was also used to enable PAQ profile prediction of needed worker attributes and potentially valid tests for use in selection of candidates for the job. As with CODAP, the new functionality resulted from using new computer technology in previously unimagined ways.

The fundamental insight of the generalists is that no field of study can move forward without a common language to describe what is being studied. Once this common language was developed, it enabled policy-capturing research (i.e. job component validity) to be conducted where data on abilities, interests, value, and prestige (to name a few) could be studied for a small, carefully chosen subset of jobs and then used to develop equations to predict the same information for any other job knowing only PAQ responses (McCormick, 1959). The significance of the scientific achievement for job analysis research that the PAQ represents can not be exaggerated and has not, I think, been fully recognized or appreciated by the field of I–O psychology. Although a primary benefit of the generalist approach is enabling job component validity[6] (i.e., establishing validity for a specific domain of the job), the price in terms of the generality of the PAQ items is very large. The reading level of the PAQ is said to be postgradu-

---

[5]R. J. Harvey reports that the second order factor analysis of the Common Metric Questionnaire is a three-factor solution closely resembling data, people and things (personal communication, April 2000).

[6]For more information on job component validity and other types of validity, the reader is referred to the *Principles for the Validation and Use of Personnel Selection Procedures*, 4th ed. (Society for Industrial and Organizational Psychology, 2004).

ate school and is clearly intended to be used by well-trained analysts.[7] Much of the data a PAQ job analysis generates would be unrecognizable to the job incumbent. When one is lecturing on job analysis, the famous study revealing that a patrol officer is the closest match in PAQ profile job similarity to the position of homemaker is a never-fail discussion starter (Arvey & Begalla, 1975). It illustrates the point that two very different kinds of work from a task standpoint can be quite similar when classified on a common set of job dimensions.

Taxonomists

Taxonomists have taken a broader view of work in an attempt to obtain a greater understanding of occupations and the demands they place on workers. As with the molecularists, the taxonomists can be divided into two camps. Edwin A. Fleishman and his colleagues have developed a comprehensive taxonomy of human attributes. This taxonomy is important because it includes task-anchored rating scales to measure attributes' relevance to work and a series of tests to measure their presence in workers (Fleishman, 1975; Fleishman & Mumford, 1991; Fleishman & Quaintance, 1984). Fleishman's taxonomy of human attributes, developed through programmatic experimental–correlational studies over many years, is the only generally accepted common language to describe human attributes and represents a significant advance in our understanding of the demands that work places on workers. The idea is that a reliable profile of the cognitive, perceptual, motor, and physical demands that work places on the worker would be invaluable in selecting workers. Ability rating scales that provide the data for the attribute profile have been anchored with empirically derived common work tasks to indicate the high, moderate, and low levels of each attribute (Fleishman, 1992; Fleishman & Reilly, 1992). Cunningham (1996, p. 252) stated, "The Fleishman Job Analysis Survey (F-JAS) is the most rigorously developed and widely used of the ability-requirements inventories."

The second camp of taxonomists seeks to generate variables to categorize occupations rather than human attributes. The idea is that much like any other field of study, we must first agree on what it is that we are studying. Although emerging from the generalist (empirically derived job dimensions) and functionalist (rationally derived job dimensions) perspectives described previously, the second camp has emerged as an underappreciated separate school that focused solely on job analysis as a taxonomic scientific activity. J. W. Cunningham and his colleagues through the development of the Occupation Analysis Inventory (OAI) and the General Work Inventory (GWI) are the founders of an empirical approach to occupational classification (Cunningham, Boese, Neeb, & Pass, 1983). Both of these inventories are job analysis instruments that are designed to provide more detailed information about work for taxonomic purposes. Recognizing that the generalist approach provided too little detail and the molecularists and functionalists provided too much information for occupational classification, these researchers invented generalized work behaviors (GWBs)[8] that lie somewhere between job duties and job dimensions as important job descriptors. By including more items about what gets done in their inventories, they were able to derive job dimensions for occupational classification from a much more detailed but still manageable list of items.

The primary insight of the taxonomists is that the practice of I–O psychology must be based on a commonly accepted language about work and work requirements. The benefit of this approach is that once completed (assuming it gains acceptance), it never has to be redone and only infrequently revised. Jobs may change, but the taxonomic variables to describe them are

[7]Harvey (1991a) produced the Common Metric Questionnaire with a reading level more appropriate for job incumbents.

[8]Cunningham reports that he originally called these variables "work elements" (personal communication, July 2004).

likely to remain the same. The difficulty and cost of this approach cannot be exaggerated. Historically, only the federal government and the military have had the resources and the motivation to sponsor such research involving multiple organizations and hundreds of jobs even though the job analysis procedures used can be administered in a single organization at relatively low cost in terms of time and resources.

Ergometricians

The final and newest school of job analysis is devoted not to understanding work so much as evaluating and better understanding the quality of other job analysis schools' data and methods. The term *ergometrics* was first coined by J. W. Cunningham (Cunningam, 1971) to describe work (*erg*) measurement (*metrics*). I am using the term *ergometricians* much more specifically than Cunningham to refer to those who apply psychological measurement principles to job analysis data. Ergometricians are concerned with psychometric evaluation of job analysis data rather than simply work measurement. Robert J. Harvey has led the development of this school along with me (Harvey & Wilson, 2000). Fredrick P. Morgeson and Michael A. Campion have led another important branch of this same school focusing on moderator variables that may affect job analysis results (Morgeson & Campion, 1997, 2000). As with all evaluation-oriented research movements, the ergometric approach has not always been received with great enthusiasm. This school has sought to develop and apply a number of metrics for evaluating job analysis data and methods. To date, the focus has been on the reliability and validity of job analysis data along with some examination of the relation between rational and empirically derived job dimensions and moderator variables. The primary benefit of this approach has been to stimulate research to improve the psychometric characteristics of job analysis data.

A contribution of the ergometricians is to systematically evaluate the quality of job analysis data and energize the discussion of appropriate methods to evaluate job analysis methods and research. A central tenet of this school is that job analysis is a scientific endeavor that needs to be held to the highest scientific standards because of its foundational nature (i.e., primary input) in so many other areas of industrial and organizational psychology. Surprisingly, not everyone agrees with this approach. Some argue that the consequences of the use of job analysis data are more important than the quality of the data itself (Sanchez & Levine, 2000). Others argue that job analysis is more of an art than a science and presumably should not be held to the same high standards as the rest of the field (Sackett & Laczo, 2003).

CONCLUSIONS

I conclude this chapter by answering the questions, "What have we learned from the history of job analysis?" and "Who are the most important contributors to job analysis?" To answer the first question I discuss what I believe are the lessons of job analysis history. To answer the second question I elevate four contributors who have had the most impact on the field over the last 100 years into the pantheon of job analysis contributors.

Some Lessons of Job Analysis History

I believe there are seven lessons that emerge from an examination of the history of job analysis. I am fully aware that not everyone will agree with these lessons, indeed, the very idea of lessons of history is probably better suited for sparking debate than gaining consensus. However, I feel the responsibility to point out what I believe are lessons in the desire to at least remove the argument of ignorance of their existence by those who follow.

Lesson 1: Change the Name.   The first lesson of history is that it is probably time to change the name of the field. Although I have a personal affection for the term *job analysis,* critics have succeeded in linking it to inflexible and out-of-date organizational practices (Carson & Stewart, 1996). Although it is often how job information is used that is really being attacked, the entire field is sometimes associated with old and inefficient ways of doing business. Perhaps Fredrick Taylor was right in using the term *work analysis* (Cunningham, 2000). It would certainly help shift the focus that critics have from individual incumbent activities and move it back on the need to understand entire work processes, regardless of how they are subdivided and who gets the assignment.

Lesson 2: Purpose Drives Job Analysis.   Job analysis can be conducted for several purposes with vastly different information requirements. Purpose drives all the subsequent decisions that need to be made in conducting a job analysis. The Holy Grail for some in job analysis has been the multipurpose job analysis resulting in integrated job information systems, but most job analysis data are collected for only one purpose. Some of the confusion about this issue has resulted from whether job analysis data collected for one purpose is suitable for others. The desire to extend the application of job analysis data beyond its original purpose comes from the high costs often associated with doing job analysis. Few job analysts have not heard the phrase "we already have a job analysis" only to learn that the existing information is inadequate for the purpose at hand. After costs, the second fault line has been defensibility of job analysis results. Defensibility has often been about appearance and documentation because it is first to be discovered, debated, and submitted into evidence in human resource–related legal disputes. As we have seen, the desire to limit costs while at the same time producing a defensible product has led to innovation in the history of job analysis. Indeed, job analysis techniques have been developed for highly specific purposes such as the design of attribute-oriented selection tests (Fleishman & Reilly, 1992; Lopez, Kesselman, & Lopez, 1981).

Lesson 3: Get the Terms Straight.   There continues to be considerable confusion over common job analysis terms. One person's "job" is another person's "task." Validity in job analysis research has meant everything from reliability to utility. Imagine if biologists were still arguing over the definition of a cell. Although it is not uncommon in academic circles to have disputes over what various terms mean, it is particularly troublesome when the field is a source of the primary data for so many other areas of industrial and organizational psychology. Table 9.2 provides a list of common terms for job analysis specificity, mode, source and evaluation.

When we consider specificity, it is important to determine the level of specificity needed while keeping in mind purpose, cost, and defensibility. With more detail comes more cost but often greater defensibility. More specific information can sometimes be aggregated when more generalized information is necessary, but the reverse is generally not true.[9] One common problem in determining specificity has been lack of agreement about what some commonly used terms in job analysis actually mean. Tasks in one study look more like the duties in another. Newer terms like *competency* can involve several different types of information of varying specificity. Fleishman, Costanza, and Marshall-Mies (1999) discussed the confusion caused by lists of "competencies" that often contain a mixture of knowledge, skill, ability, motivation, belief, value, and interest descriptors. More specific descriptors are often in the imprecise language of the world of work, whereas more general descriptors involve language only a psychologist could love or understand. It has also been argued that individual (worker) attrib-

---

[9]When I say the reverse is "generally not true," I am thinking of synthetic or job component validity as a technique that can derive more specific information from more general (McCormick, 1959).

TABLE 9.2
Important Terms in the Job Analysis Process

1. Specificity	2. Mode	3. Source	4. Evaluation
Work:	Interview	Incumbents	Acceptability
Occupational groups	Observation	Supervisor	Timeliness
Occupation	Survey	Analyst	Utility
Job		Peers	Reliability
Position		Trainers	Validity
Job dimension[a]			
Duty			
Task			
Element			
Worker:			
Attributes/abilities			
Knowledge			
Skills			

[a]Job dimensions can be rationally or empirically derived.

utes do not belong in a list of "job analysis" descriptors (Harvey, 1991b). Others argue that what the work demands of an individual (worker-oriented job analysis) is no less job analysis than what the work actually involves (work-oriented job analysis; McCormick, 1976). I include both here organized by work and worker subcategories.

Decisions concerning the mode of collection often revolve around the level of involvement that the participating organization desires. Surveys are a highly efficient way to provide maximum participation but can be costly and time consuming to develop and administer. Interviews provide more focused information with considerably less intrusion but are prone to potential interviewee distortion and lack the immediacy of observations. Observations whether in physics or psychology run the risk of altering what you are trying to understand. Each mode has distinct advantages and has varied in popularity over the history of job analysis.

Decisions concerning source of job information have been far more controversial. Providing more generalized information about work has often been left to job analysts, whereas highly specific job information usually requires the direct involvement of incumbents, their supervisors, or coworkers. Problems have arisen when sources do not agree. It is fair to say most job analysis techniques involve a mixture of methods. In the event that there has been disagreement over method, it has been over the extent to which it should be customized to fit a particular organization, purpose, or level of specificity of job descriptors. Evaluating the results obtained from various methods has also generated some controversy.

There are at least two perspectives on the importance of evaluation in job analysis. One camp has relentlessly pursued the measurement characteristics of various kinds of job analysis data that report less than impressive reliability and validity results (Harvey & Wilson, 2000). This camp believes that job analysis data should be held to the same high standards of reliability and validity as other areas of I–O psychology (e.g., selection research). Another camp has emphasized that "acceptance" by the users and "utility" are more important given the foundational nature of the data being examined (Sanchez & Levine, 2000). Attempts to increase the reliability and validity of job analysis data have often come at the cost of reducing acceptability of the results. In general, the less specific the job analysis descriptors, the more likely the results will at least be reliable (Dierdorff & Wilson, 2003). Although less detailed data are likely to have a longer shelf life, they may be less applicable to many human resource functions requiring job analytic data.

It does not matter which of the various approaches to job analysis may be preferred; they all have to stake out where they stand on the various choices represented in Table 9.2. As I said at the beginning of this chapter, the various schools I have described are not so much in conflict as they are looking at different things, with different methods, motivation, and purpose. Problems arise when data from the molecularist, functionalist, or generalist schools are used for less relevant purposes and collected using less traditional methods to save costs. This brings us to the next lesson of job analysis history.

Lesson 4: Job Analysis Is Expensive.   The fourth lesson of history is that the costs of good job analysis are large and ongoing for most organizations. One of the reasons I think there has been so much confusion in the use of various job analysis terms has been to hide the true costs of job analysis by changing the name of what is being done ("We're not doing task analysis; we are process reengineering"). The costs of collecting job information can be spread across many budgets by linking job analysis with some personnel activity that has an outcome the organization values. Additional costs can be hidden by decentralizing the job analysis process across several locations. Decentralization can lead to both redundant and conflicting approaches to the type of job information collected and how it is used and evaluated. The expense associated with job analysis will probably always be significant. However, avoiding job analysis leads to even higher costs associated with litigation and flawed failure-prone work systems.

Lesson 5: Defining Work Is an Important Organizational Power.   Defining work is a struggle for power in the organization. I wish I could personally take credit for this insight, but the point was acknowledged in the first history of job analysis. Having the authority to determine what workers do in an organization and write it down is not something that managers give up willingly. It is only when decision makers see the added value of good job analysis information, or they are forced by some outside event, that they are willing to share this power with job analysts. But it bears repeating that job analysis in practice is as much about political issues in many organizations as it is about technical or descriptive ones. Although a common language for describing work may be of great long-term value to the organization, any process that gets between line managers and the decisions they want to make about work is going to draw a lot of criticism.

Lesson 6: Work Knowledge Drives Organizational Performance.   Although this chapter has focused on job analysis in the past, a fundamental lesson is that a detailed understanding of the work processes of the organization is necessary to achieve high performance in the digital information age. The third dimension of organizational structure beyond organizational functions and levels of authority is work process knowledge. Being able to access an expansive world of work knowledge involving not only work process but also social, political, technical, and competitive work contexts may be the key to sustainable high performance. Organizations that ignore this third dimension can never truly be adaptive learning organizations of the future. Organizations that figure out how to collect and provide this information to important decision makers in increasingly flat organizations may gain considerable competitive advantage through higher and more sustainable performance cycles. The insight of this lesson has recently been driven home by the publication of a book summarizing the concept of strategic job modeling (Schippmann, 1999).

Lesson 7: Amateurs Do Most Job Analysis.   The final lesson of job analysis history is that a lot of job analysis has been done and probably will continue to be done by people who do not know what they are doing. All too frequently one need look no further than an organization's job analysis information if one is looking for ways to improve an organization. This is often the case because job analysis is perceived as a means to an end that is best dispatched with quickly. Perhaps job analysts bear part of the burden for not doing a better job of marketing and educating decision makers on the importance of good job information.

Members of the Pantheon of Job Analysis Contributors

When I review Table 9.1 and think about who has made significant and lasting contributions to the field of job analysis, four individuals stand out as deserving special recognition. All made their contributions during what I have called the golden age of job analysis and all have made founding and lasting contributions to one of the first four schools presented in this chapter. Raymond E. Christal elevated the initial school of job analysis thought (molecularist) by the use of computer technology and an untiring focus on the application of task analysis to a number of real organizational problems. Sidney A. Fine embodied the functionalist school of thought and demonstrated extraordinary insight into the nature of work dimensionality. Ernest J. McCormick led a generalist school of job analysis to the first comprehensive and empirically based derivation of work dimensions. Finally, Edwin A. Fleishman provided fundamental insight into the nature of human attributes through both the development and operationalization of a taxonomic structure of human attributes.[10]

SUMMARY

The history of job analysis over the last 100 years (1903–2004) was one of great optimism and achievement. I was lucky to be able to report in this chapter great strides in the study and documentation of what people do at work. The effective use by organizations and appreciation of what has been achieved are another matter. No one could have said it any better than my friend and colleague of many years, Bill Cunningham: "Job analysis is the Rodney Dangerfield of I–O psychology" (Cunningham, 1989).[11] For those outside the field this statement usually provokes a smile, but for those of us (probably the majority of those still reading) who call ourselves job analysts, it is more likely to first provoke a knowing wince before the smile. The field does not deserve this reputation, and I believe it is based on a series of misperceptions about what job analysis is, how it developed, and how it should be evaluated. The hope is that this chapter may help spark new discussions of a very old I–O topic by looking back to speculate on how we have arrived at the current state of affairs and come to a new and better understanding.

This chapter has detailed several previous histories of job analysis and important job analysis contributors. It has also devoted considerable attention to the various contextual factors that helped shape thinking in job analysis. The chapter has organized this field into five schools of thought to provide a descriptive framework for job analysis activities. Seven lessons from history were proposed that dealt with everything from the name of the field to who does most job analysis. Finally, four individuals from the past 100 years were elevated to the pantheon of job analysis contributors.

---

[10]I would argue that Fleishman's contribution to job analysis transcends the field and that the derivation and operationalization of taxonomic structure of human attributes are profoundly important contributions to all of psychology.

[11]For those of you unfamiliar with Rodney's famous line it went something like, "I get no respect!"

REFERENCES

Arvey, R. D., & Begalla, M. E. (1975). Analyzing the homemaker job using the Position Analysis Questionnaire (PAQ). *Journal of Applied Psychology, 60,* 513–517.

Baehr, M. E., Lonergan, W. G., & Hunt, B. A. (1978). *Managerial and professional job functions inventory.* Park Ridge, IL: London House.

Bingham, W. V. (1939). Halo, invalid and valid. *Journal of Applied Psychology, 23,* 221–228.

Brannick, M. T., & Levine, E. L. (2002). *Job analysis: Methods, research, and applications for human resource management in the new millennium.* Thousand Oaks, CA: Sage.

Carson, K. P., & Stewart, G. L. (1996). Job analysis and the sociotechnical approach to quality: A critical examination. *Journal of Quality Management, 1,* 49–65.

Christal, R. E. (1974). *The United States Air Force occupational research project* (Rep. No. AFHRL-TR-73-75). Lackland AFB, TX: Occupational Research Division (DTIC No. AD-774 574).

Cunningham, J. W. (1971). *"Ergometrics": A systematic approach to some educational Problems* (Rep. No. 2 of the Ergometric Research and Development Series, under Grant No. OEG-2-7-070348-2698 with the Office of Education, U.S. Department of Health, Education, and Welfare). Raleigh: North Carolina State University, Center for Occupational Education. (ERIC Document Reproduction Service No. ED 067 443; also abstracted in JSAS *Catalog of Selected Documents in Psychology,* 1974, 4, 144–145, Ms. No. 804).

Cunningham, J. W. (1989, August). *Discussion.* In R. J. Harvey (Chair), *Applied measurement issues in job analysis.* Symposium presented at the annual meeting of the American Psychological Association, New Orleans.

Cunningham, J. W. (1996). Generic job descriptors: A likely direction in occupational analysis. *Military Psychology, 8,* 247–262.

*Cunningham, J. W. (2000). Introduction to a new journal. *Ergometrika, 1,* 1–23.

Cunningham, J. W., Boese, R. R., Neeb, R. W., & Pass, J. J. (1983). Systematically derived work dimensions: Factor analyses of the Occupation Analysis Inventory. *Journal of Applied Psychology, 68,* 232–252.

Dawis, R. V., & Lofquist, L. H. (1983). *A psychological theory of work adjustment.* Minneapolis: University of Minnesota Press.

Dierdorff, E. C., & Wilson, M. A. (2003). A meta-analysis of job analysis reliability. *Journal of Applied Psychology, 88,* 635–646.

Drauden, G. M. (1988). Task inventory analysis in industry and the public sector. In S. Gael (Ed.), *The job analysis handbook for business, industry and government* (Vol. 2, pp. 1051–1071). New York: Wiley.

Fine, S. A. (1955). A structure of worker functions. *Personnel and Guidance Journal, 34,* 66–73.

Fine, S. A., & Cronshaw, S. F. (1999). *Functional job analysis: A foundation for human resource management.* Mahwah, NJ: Lawrence Erlbaum Associates.

Fine, S. A., & Wiley, W. W. (1971). *An introduction to functional job analysis.* Washington, DC: The Upjohn Institute.

Flanagan, J. C. (1949). Critical requirements: A new approach to employee evaluation. *Personnel Psychology, 2,* 419–425.

Fleishman, E. A. (1975). Toward a taxonomy of human performance. *American Psychologist, 30,* 1127–1149.

Fleishman, E. A. (1992). *The Fleishman-Job Analysis Survey (F-JAS).* Palo Alto, CA: Consulting Psychologist Press.

Fleishman, E. A., Costanza, D. P., & Marshall-Mies, J. (1999). Abilities. In N. G Peterson, M. D. Mumford, W. C. Borman, P. R. Jeanneret, & E. A. Fleishman (Eds.), *An occupational information system for the 21st Century: The development of O*Net* (pp. 175–195). Washington, DC: American Psychological Association.

Fleishman, E. A., & Mumford, M. D. (1991). Evaluating classifications of job behavior: A construct validation of the ability requirement scales. *Personnel Psychology, 44,* 523–575.

Fleishman, E. A., & Reilly, M. E. (1992). *Handbook of human abilities: Definitions, measurements, and job task requirements.* Palo Alto, CA: Consulting Psychologist Press.

Fleishman, E. A., & Quaintance, M. K. (1984). *Taxonomies of human performance: The description of human tasks.* Orlando, FL: Academic Press

Fryklund, V. C. (1942). *Trade and job analysis.* Milwaukee: Bruce Pub. Co.

Gael, S. (1977). Development of job task inventories and their use in job analysis research. JSAS *Catalog of Selected Documents in Psychology, 7,* 25.

Gael, S. (1983). *Job Analysis: A guide to assessing work activities.* San Francisco: Jossey-Bass.

Gael, S. (1988). *The job analysis handbook for business, industry, and government.* New York: Wiley.

Gagné, R. M., & Fleishman, E. A. (1959). *Psychology and human performance: An introduction to psychology.* New York: Holt, Rinehart & Winston.

Gilbreth, F. B., & Gilbreth, L. M. (1917). *Applied motion study: A collection of papers on the efficient method to industrial preparedness.* New York: Macmillan.

Hakel, M. D. (1984, August). *What in the world are we doing?* Division 14 of the American Psychological Association Presidential Address at the Annual Conference of the American Psychological Association, Toronto, ON, Canada.

Harvey, R. J. (1991a). *The Common Metric Questionnaire (CMQ): A job analysis system.* San Antonio, TX: Psychological Corporation.

Harvey, R. J. (1991b). Job analysis. In M. D. Dunnette & L. M. Hough (Eds.), *Handbook of industrial and organizational psychology* (2nd ed., Vol. 2, pp. 71–164). Palo Alto, CA: Consulting Psychologists Press.

Harvey, R. J., & Wilson, M. A. (2000). Yes Virginia, there *is* an objective reality in job analysis. *Journal of Organizational Behavior, 21,* 829–854.

Hemphill, J. K. (1959). Job descriptions for executives. *Harvard Business Review, 37,* 55–67.

Holland, J. L. (1970). *The self-directed search for career planning.* Palo Alto, CA: Consulting Psychologists Press.

Levine, E. L. (1983). *Everything you always wanted to know about job analysis.* Tampa, FL: Mariner.

Lichtner, W. O. (1921). *Time study and job analysis as applied to standardization of methods and operations.* New York: Ronald Press.

Lopez, F. M., Kesselman, G. A., & Lopez, F. E. (1981). An empirical test of a trait-oriented job analysis technique. *Personnel Psychology, 34,* 479–502.

McCormick, E. J. (1959). The development of processes for indirect or synthetic validity: III. Application of job analysis to indirect validity (A symposium). *Personnel Psychology, 12,* 402–413.

McCormick, E. J. (1976). Job and task analysis. In M. D. Dunnette (Ed.), *Handbook of industrial and organizational psychology* (pp. 651–696). Chicago: Rand McNally.

McCormick, E. J. (1979). *Job analysis: Methods and applications.* New York: AMACOM.

McCormick, E. J., Jeanneret, P. R., & Mecham, R. C. (1972). A study of job characteristics and job dimensions as based on the Position Analysis Questionnaire (PAQ). *Journal of Applied Psychology, 56,* 347–368.

*Mitchell, J. L. (1988). History of job analysis in military organizations. In S. Gael (Ed.), *The job analysis handbook for business, industry and government* (Vol. 1, pp. 30–36). New York: Wiley.

Mitchell, J. L., Bennett, W., & Strickland, W. J. (1999, April). *Critical job analysis: Issues and advances.* Paper presented at the Future of Job Analysis Symposium, San Antonio, TX.

*Mitchell, J. L., & Driskill, W. E. (1996). Military job analysis: A historical perspective. *Military Psychology, 8,* 119–142.

Morgeson, F. P., & Campion, M. A. (1997). Social and cognitive sources of potential inaccuracy in job analysis. *Journal of Applied Psychology, 82,* 627–655.

Morgeson, F. P., & Campion, M. A. (2000). Accuracy in job analysis: Toward an inference-based model. *Journal of Organizational Behavior, 21,* 819–827.

Münsterberg, H. (1913). *Psychology and industrial efficiency.* Boston: Houghton Mifflin.

Paterson, D. G., Gerken, C. D'A., & Hahn, M. E. (1941). *The Minnesota Occupational Rating Scales and Counseling Profile.* Chicago: Science Research Associates.

Peterson, N. G., Mumford, M. D., Borman, W. C., Jeanneret, P. R., & Fleishman, E. A. (1999). *An occupational information system for the 21st century: The development of O*Net.* Washington, DC: American Psychological Association.

Peterson, N. G., Mumford, M. D., Borman, W. C., Jeanneret, P. R., Fleishman, E. A., Levin, K. Y., et al. (2001). Understanding work using the occupational information network (O*NET). *Personnel Psychology, 54,* 451–492.

Prien, E. P., & Ronan, W. W. (1971). Job analysis: Review of research findings. *Personnel Psychology, 24,* 371–396.

Primoff, E. S. (1957). The J-coefficient approach to jobs and tests. *Personnel Administration, 20,* 34–40.

*Primoff, E. S., & Fine S. A. (1988). A history of job analysis. In S. Gael (Ed.), *The job analysis handbook for business, industry and government* (Vol. 1, pp. 14–29). New York: Wiley.

Sackett, P. R., & Laczo, R. M. (2003). Job and work analysis. In W. C. Borman, D. R. Ilgen, & R. J. Klimoski (Eds.), *Handbook of psychology* (Vol. 12, pp. 21–38). Hoboken, NJ: Wiley.

Sanchez, J. I., & Levine, E. L. (2000). Accuracy or consequential validity: Which is the better standard for job analysis data? *Journal of Organizational Behavior, 21,* 809–819.

Schippmann, J. S. (1999). *Strategic job modeling.* Mahwah, NJ: Lawrence Erlbaum Associates.

Shartle, C. L. (1952). *Occupational Information* (2nd ed.). New York: Prentice-Hall.

Shartle, C. L., & Stogdill, R. M. (1957). *Work analysis forms.* Columbus: Bureau of Business Research, The Ohio State University.

Society for Industrial and Organizational Psychology. (2004). *Principles for the validation and use of personnel selection techniques* (4th ed.). Bowling Green, OH: Author.

Stead, W. H., & Shartle, C. L. (1940). *Occupational counseling techniques.* New York: American.

Taylor, F. W. (1911). *The principles of scientific management.* New York: Harper.

Turnow, W. W., & Pinto, P. R. (1976). The development of a managerial taxonomy: A system for describing, classifying, and evaluating executive positions. *Journal of Applied Psychology, 61,* 410–418.

*Uhrbrock, R. S. (1922). The history of job analysis. *Administration, 3,* 164–168.

Uhrbrock, R. S. (1934). Job analysis in industry. *Occupations, 12*(10), 69–74.

U. S. Department of Labor. (1971). *Handbook for analyzing jobs.* Washington, DC: U.S. Government Printing Office.

U.S. Department of Labor. (1977). *Dictionary of occupational titles* (4th ed.). Washington, DC: U.S. Government Printing Office.

Vicente, K. J. (1999). *Cognitive work analysis.* Mahwah, NJ: Lawrence Erlbaum Associates.

Viteles, M. S. (1923). Job specifications and diagnostic tests of job competency designed for the auditing division of a street railway company. *Psychological Clinic, 14,* 83–105.

*Indicates that this reference includes a prior history of job analysis.

10

A Historical View of Human Factors in the United States

Sharolyn Converse Lane
North Carolina State University

The field of human factors was stimulated by the need to apply knowledge of human physical capabilities and limitations to the evaluation and design of products and environments that reduced human error and enhanced worker productivity and satisfaction. Human factors today originated from several sources, most notably, experimental psychology and industrial–organizational (I–O) psychology. Until the years of World War II, many applied psychologists considered themselves to be both I–O and engineering psychologists (Roscoe, 1997). During World War II, applied psychologists began to merge their work with the work of engineers, and the discipline of engineering psychology, a forerunner of human factors, was born. The fact that human factors and I–O psychology were once interest areas of the same discipline is reflected by the research areas that are still common to both groups (e.g. training, effects of stress, organizational psychology, team performance). Today, the two disciplines are considered to be distinct entities. This is due, in large part, to the fact that the study of human factors has become a multidisciplinary endeavor that has been influenced not only by psychology but also by engineering, design, physiology, and computer science. Regardless of the influence of other disciplines on human factors, I–O psychologists and human factors professionals continue to pursue many common research interests. It well may be that the distinction between the two disciplines has limited the dissemination of knowledge between the two groups to the detriment of all.

This chapter reviews the common antecedents of I–O psychology and human factors, including experimental and applied psychology and scientific management. The events that stimulated the growth of applied psychology and resulted in the emergence of human factors as a distinct discipline are considered. Later, influences on the development of human factors are described, and examples of human factors success stories are given. A discussion of the growing trend within the human factors community to consider topics that have long been of interest to I–O psychologists is provided. Lessons learned by human factors professionals over the last 6 decades are considered. Finally, areas of common interests that help integrate these fields are discussed.

COMMON ANCESTORS OF I–O PSYCHOLOGY AND HUMAN FACTORS

Experimental Psychology

The history of both I–O psychology and human factors can be traced back to Wundt's development of experimental psychology. As noted in other chapters in this text, pioneers of applied psychology such as Cattell, Münsterberg, and Hall studied with Wundt in Leipzig (Hergenhahn, 1992). However, on their return to the United States, the students of Wundt, as well as other psychologists, practiced a psychology that bore little resemblance to the psychology practiced in Wundt's laboratory (Hunt, 1993; Schultz & Schultz, 2000). The United States wanted a psychology that was "usable" (Hall, 1912, p. 414), and the psychology of Wundt did not promise this. The combination of the interest in a practical psychology and Darwin's theory of evolution combined to create fertile ground for the development of Functionalism (Schultz & Schultz, 2000).

Functionalism

James Rowland Angell was a strong champion of functionalism who set the stage for the development of I–O psychology and human factors when he stated that psychology should study the functions of consciousness and how these cognitive functions allowed the individual to adjust to the environment (Angell, 1907). Harvey Carr further refined functionalism by defining the processes of mental activity (e.g., perception, memory, judgment, and will; Carr, 1925), and he stimulated interest in applied psychology by promoting it as a means to provide psychological services to industry and to other aspects of the community (Schultz & Schultz, 2000). The concept of adapting psychology to meet the needs of business and industry was, of course, essential to the development of I–O psychology (as discussed in other chapters) and human factors.

James McK. Cattell was greatly interested in Galton's use of anthropometrical and psychophysical measures to measure IQ. Although Cattell's efforts to use anthropometrics and psychophysics to test IQ were not immediately successful, Cattell's work did stimulate interest in the study of anthropometrics. In turn, anthropometry became one of the earliest disciplines of human factors research and became the basis of early efforts (circa World War I) to reduce errors by designing equipment that could be seen, understood, and controlled more easily and accurately (Hunt, 1993).

In the early years of the 20th Century, John B. Watson explored topics that are of interest to human factors such as perceptual–motor abilities and response time (RT) to extreme environments (Cohen, 1979). Watson was also one of the early promoters of the combination of laboratory and field research that is the hallmark of modern I–O psychology and human factors (Buckley, 1982). The unexpected findings of the famous Hawthorne studies of 1924 highlighted the need to consider the physical aspects of tasks (e.g., lighting) to most successfully enhance worker satisfaction and productivity as well as generated interest in worker motivation (Alluisi, 1994; Hunt, 1993). (See chap. 14 in this text for more information on the Hawthorne studies.)

The work of Hugo Münsterberg was instrumental not only to the development of I–O psychology but also to the creation of human factors. In his book *Psychology and Industrial Efficiency* (Münsterberg, 1913), Münsterberg not only addressed issues of interest to modern I–O psychology as described in previous chapters but also addressed issues that concern modern human factors professionals, such as economy of movement, a forerunner of time and motion studies; design of displays; effects of fatigue and monotony on performance; learning and training; and scientific management.

Scientific Management

As noted throughout this text, scientific management was created to reduce errors and improve the efficiency of work methods by training workers to adapt themselves to the demands of new mechanized systems (Helander, 1997). The management technique supplanted traditional management practices with techniques based on analysis of task components and empirical evidence of task completion times. Tasks are divided into their smallest elements, and performance times are recorded on a stopwatch. The total task time is then determined (Taylor, 1911). Although Münsterberg discussed scientific management, the field can be traced to the work of Adam Smith (circa 1770), who attempted to increase production efficiency by establishing standard times for various tasks involved in the manufacturing process. Despite Smith's work, it was not until the spread of mechanized production that occurred at the early 1900s that scientific management was widely adopted in the United States.

Frederick Taylor is most often considered the "father of scientific management," due, in large part, to his book *The Principles of Scientific Management* (Taylor, 1911), a book that had a great effect on management practices. Taylor, an industrial engineer, tested the use of scientific management at the Midvale and Bethlehem Steel plants in 1883 and reported that he had increased production by 300% (Frederick Winslow Taylor, n. d.). The news of Taylor's success soon spread to other industries whose management teams began to adopt scientific management in their production lines. A notable example of this was Henry Ford's mechanized production methods for the production of Model T cars that were adopted in 1913 (Roscoe, 1997).

Scientific management has always been controversial. Taylor's timing of tasks to 1/100 of a second was resented by workers and criticized by their friends (Roscoe, 1997). However, despite these criticisms, industrialists wanted to produce goods more rapidly, and the onset of World War I increased the demands for rapid production. Thus, scientific management continued to prosper (Helander, 1997; Kanigel, 1997). The continued prosperity of scientific management was aided by the efforts of Frank and Lillian Gilbreth, who are notable for introducing greater concern for the worker into the scientific management system. Frank Gilbreth was a building contractor, and Lillian Gilbreth received a PhD in psychology in 1915. The Gilbreths believed that elimination of worker fatigue and injuries was a managerial responsibility, and they wanted to create a scientific way of doing this (Gilbreth & Gilbreth, 1917). The Gilbreths developed the time and motion study, a technique that measured the direction of movements as well as the speed. This advancement allowed the Gilbreths to identify the least fatiguing and most efficient task performance method and to reduce the number of steps required to perform industrial tasks (Neibel, 1972). Today, time and motion studies are still used by human factors professionals to design efficient and comfortable work stations.

WORLD WAR I

Prior to World War I, interest in work psychology was mainly the domain of private industry (Chapanis, 1999). However, during World War I, systems such as airplanes and tanks became increasingly complex and operator errors began to increase. These errors, their potentially catastrophic consequences, and the need to conserve wartime resources generated military interest in identifying the pressures imposed on operators by new systems and determining whether humans were capable of meeting these demands (Roscoe, 1992). Soon, psychologists and engineers were recruited by the military to determine how errors could be reduced. This work resulted in the creation of new displays and controls as well as research on the effects of environmental factors such as high altitude and extreme gravity on pilot error. The success of these psychologists and engineers stimulated the development of the modern field of aviation psychology (Koonce, 1984).

An important contributor to aviation psychology was Raymond Dodge, who began his career as professor of experimental psychology in 1902 at Wesleyan University. Dodge was interested in both psychology and engineering, and much of his work focused on the study of vision, especially visual fixation and eye movements (Dodge, 1900, 1907, 1921). Dodge left Wesleyan to go to Yale in 1925, where he explored topics such as the effects of alcohol on performance (Dodge & Benedict, 1925), vestibular function, reaction time, visual perception, and personnel selection. Dodge's work formed the basis for the modern human factors method of link analysis (a system of tracking eye movements), and link analysis was instrumental in developing models of visual scanning that formed the theoretical basis for the design of display placement and arrangement.

The study of anthropometry was further developed by applied psychologists during World War I. Anthropometry was used to create standard clothing sizes for soldiers and to create military equipment that fit the dimensions of the average soldier (Roscoe, 1994). Early anthropometrics data were based totally on the body dimensions of males in the military. This tradition continued until the early 1960s, when studies of anthropometrics data began to be collected from women. Examples of these later anthropometrics studies that included measurement of female dimensions include the Health Examination Survey (1960–1962), in which body dimensions of 3,581 females were recorded (Gordon & Miller, 1974), and the collection of anthropometric data from 423 women trainees at the American Airlines Stewardess Training Center (Snow, Reynolds, & Allgood, 1975).

YEARS BETWEEN WORLD WAR I AND WORLD WAR II

The relatively short involvement of the United States in World War I did not provide time for applied psychologists to demonstrate that human-centered design was a superior alternative to the traditional method of adapting humans to the task. As a result, the development of human factors slowed somewhat after World War I (Moroney, 1995; Sloan, 1994). One exception to this trend was work in aviation psychology. Following World War I, the first two aeromedical research laboratories were established: at Brooks Air Force Base, Texas, and Wright Field in Ohio (Chapanis, 1999). Researchers in these laboratories tested the quality of pilot performance, recorded human performance at environmental extremes, and determined the effect of aircraft design on crew performance (Dempsey, 1985). In 1939, the National Research Council Committee on Aviation Psychology was established under the chairmanship of Jack Jenkins of the University of Maryland. The council sponsored a wide range of aviation psychology research at prominent universities, including the research of Williams, Macmillan, and Jenkins (1946), who were the first to record physiological responses in flight.

Psychology began to be applied to the automotive industry by researchers at the Ohio State University in 1927, probably as a result of the increasing popularity of the automobile (Moroney, 1995). The work at Ohio State included behavioral studies of accidents, perceptual aspects of driving (Forbes, 1939), human responses to traffic signs, effects of velocity on driving performance, and social characteristics of traffic law violators (Weimer, 1995). Automotive research was also conducted in the interwar years by Walter R. Miles of the Yale University School of Medicine. Miles was interested in eye movements, night and color vision, and dark adaptation (Miles, 1925, 1928). Miles' work was not only used to solve the problem of dark adaptation for pilots (by using red lighting in ready rooms for pilots who flew night missions) but also to study the effect of aging, poor vision, night driving, and alcohol use on driver performance (Miles, 1931). Miles invented an instrument that he called the Harger Drunkometer to study the effects of alcohol on operator performance in planes and cars (Popplestone & McPherson, 1994). He was also interested in the effects of adverse environmental conditions on human performance, and his data have been used extensively in the study of human performance in extreme environments (Chapanis, 1999).

WORLD WAR II

The advent of World War II involved psychologists in war work and began the divergence of I–O psychology and human factors, which was originally called human engineering. Whereas many I–O psychologists were concerned with the testing, screening, and classification of recruits, others were concerned with adapting knowledge of human abilities and limitations to the design of military equipment that could be used rapidly and accurately. This later focus created a new subspecialty within I–O psychology that was first called engineering psychology but was later to be known as human engineering, human factors, or ergonomics (Schultz & Schultz, 2000).

At the beginning of World War II, industrialists and engineers believed that the speed and accuracy of performance could be enhanced by practice, but that once asymptote had been achieved, there was no additional remedy for the remaining human errors (Chapanis, 1999). This attitude was soon challenged when new types of complex systems such as high-performance jet aircraft, radar, and sonar were developed, and operators were expected to learn to use these systems rapidly and accurately without extended training sessions (Sloan, 1994). Reports of pilot and other types of error increased at an alarming rate (Meister, 1999), indicating that a new method of enhancing the accuracy and safety of human work had to be found and that a design philosophy that considered human capabilities and limitations was needed (Chapanis, Garner, & Morgan, 1949).

Early in the war, the military brought together psychologists, engineers, physicians, and other experts to design military systems that would improve the accuracy of human performance (Sloan, 1994). (See also chap. 7 in this text.) Most of the psychologists were experimental psychologists who had little experience with applied projects and were forced to adapt their research rapidly and without specialized training (Chapanis 1999; Roscoe, 1997). At first, the experimental psychologists tried to use the experimental methods taught in graduate school, but they soon discovered that this approach was insufficient for solving the real-world problems as rapidly as the war effort demanded (Sloan, 1994). Slowly the psychologists learned to adapt a less theoretical and more practical approach. Although this was awkward for many psychologists at first, many wanted to continue their applied work when the war was over (Roscoe, 1997). Many of these psychologists enjoyed working with professionals from other disciplines, especially engineering, and began to refer to themselves as engineering psychologists to distinguish themselves from other I–O psychologists (Alluisi, 1994; Chapanis, 1999).

Aviation psychology research accelerated during World War II. In 1940, the Applied Psychology Panel (APP) of the National Defense Research Committee was created by the Army (see Koonce, 1984; Meister, 1991). In 1941, John C. Flanagan, the associate director of the Cooperative Test Service of the American Council in Education, was commissioned in the Army and began developing the Army Aviation Psychology Program, with specialized Psychological Research Units formed around the country (Flanagan, 1947). In 1945, a unit was developed in the AeroMedical Laboratory at Wright Field in Dayton, Ohio, to conduct research on the applications of fundamental psychological principles to equipment design (Flanagan, 1947). Lt. Col. Paul M. Fitts was transferred from Headquarters Army Air Forces to be chief of this unit. This program is described in the volume *Psychological Research in Equipment Design* edited by Fitts (1947b) and represents a landmark in the history of human factors research and application. Examples of topics covered include display and control problems, human limitations, analysis of human motor abilities, influence of environmental conditions, effective designs of tables and instruments, coding and arrangements of control knobs, effects of anoxia on visual performance, and many others. Those contributing to this program included many who became leaders in the field of human factors, including Walter Grether, Launor Carter, A. C. Williams, and Melvin Warrick, among others.

A major figure in the development of engineering psychology was Alphonse Chapanis (1917–2002), who along with Paul Fitts is often acknowledged as a founding father of the discipline. In 1943, as a lieutenant in the U.S. Army Air Corp, he was the first research psychologist at the AeroMedical Medical Laboratory at Wright Field, Ohio, where he researched user interface problems with aviation equipment and developed solutions (see Krueger, 2004). His applied experimental research included research on night vision and dark adaptation issues and design factors on aviation accidents. This work contributed the foundation for later human engineering developments at Wright Field (Krueger, 2004). Other military research focused on topics such as dark adaptation, night vision, and human discriminability. Findings from this research served as the basis for the development of advanced sonar devices and radar screens (National Research Council, 1949).

During this period, aviation psychology research was also conducted at prominent universities. A notable example of this was the aviation psychology program at Harvard, where S. S. Stevens, J. C. R. Licklider, Karl Kryter, and George Miller addressed speech articulation problems reported by aircraft crews by conducting articulation tests of standard interphone speech taken at varying altitudes in a B-17 bomber (Licklider & Kryter, 1944; Licklider & Miller, 1951). Another Harvard researcher was Ross McFarland, whose research concerned dark adaptation, the effects of adverse environments on human performance, pilot stress and fatigue, transportation safety, circadian rhythms, and the effects of these factors on air crew performance. At the Ohio State University, Samuel Renshaw developed the "Renshaw Recognition System," a training program for naval aviators, gunners, and spotters that increased the speed of differentiation between friendly and unfriendly craft. To create this system, Renshaw created the tachistoscope, a device used by human factors professionals to present experimental stimuli at increasing rates of speed until the advent of computer research. Renshaw used the tachistoscope to present pictures of enemy battleships and aircraft arriving from many angles at speeds of 1/100 of a second until observers could recognize them rapidly (Chapanis, 1999; Flanagan, 1947).

POST–WORLD WAR II

There was ample opportunity for engineering psychologists to continue their work after World War II because the number of deaths in training and combat remained unacceptably high in the Korean and Cold Wars. This motivated the Army, Air Force, Navy, and Bureau of Ships to create human engineering research laboratories, and many psychologists who had helped with the war effort joined these laboratories (Helander, 1997; Meister, 1991). The work in these laboratories immediately following World War II included the development of military human engineering guidelines (Military Standards), the use of which is still required for all work funded by the Department of Defense. At Wright Field, the Air Force Psychology Branch was continued under the direction of Paul Fitts, who was assisted by Walter Grether, Richard Jones, Julien Christensen, Robert Gagné, John Milton, and William Jenkins (Fitts, 1947a). The psychology branch exists today as The Paul M. Fitts Human Engineering Laboratory. In 1947, members of the laboratory published a series of 19 papers describing the wartime work of engineering psychologists (Pew, 1994). Two of Paul Fitts' reports (Fitts, 1947b, 1951b) were of particular importance because Fitts outlined a long-range plan for human engineering research in the post–World War II era. Fitts remained at the laboratory until 1949 when he returned to civilian life and accepted a position at Ohio State University.

At the end of World War II, the Navy opened the Naval Research Laboratory in Washington, DC, under the direction of Franklin V. Taylor, who was assisted by Henry Birmingham, an electrical engineer. The members of the laboratory are perhaps best known for their 1954 report, "A Human Engineering Approach to the Design of Man-Operated Continuous Control System" (Roscoe, 1994). The Naval Electronics Laboratory opened in 1946 at San Diego under the direction of Arnold Small, who was assisted by Max Lund and Wesley Woodson (Alluisi, 1994). It was from this setting that Woodson published his 1954 book, *Human Engineering Guide for Equipment Designers,* a book that became a standard guide for human factors specialists. Revisions of this work are still in use.

Research that had been ongoing at universities during the war continued after the armistice. The three most important university laboratories were headed by Alex Williams at Illinois, Paul Fitts at Ohio State, and Alphonse Chapanis at Johns Hopkins (Roscoe, 1994; Sloan, 1994). Flight training work was conducted at the University of Illinois Aviation Psychology Laboratory under a contract with the Department of Defense, a contract that was renewed for 20 years (Alluisi, 1994). Subsequent directors have included Ralph Flexman, Jack Adams, and Henry Taylor.

At Ohio State, Paul Fitts developed Fitts' law by measuring the length and width (precision) of movements to accurately predict movement time (Paul Fitts, n.d.). Fitts' law has stood the test of time and is still used to create efficient controls and work stations. Fitts also published two influential papers, "Human Engineering for an Effective Air-Navigation and Traffic Control System" (Fitts, 1951a) and *The USAF Human Factor Engineering Mission as Related to the Qualitative Superiority of Future Weapon Systems* (Fitts, Flood, Garman, & Williams, 1957). These works were based on simulator studies of pilot training and studies of air traffic control systems (e.g., Johnson, Williams, & Roscoe, 1951) and studies of display design (Williams & Roscoe, 1949).

In the late 1940s and early 1950s, Alphonse Chapanis and Clifford Morgan of Johns Hopkins University studied systems theory, an approach that had become increasingly popular during the war years (Chapanis, 1999; Sloan, 1994). Systems theory proposed that design and evaluation were best served by performing two types of analysis: a molecular analysis of the system in question and a second analysis that evaluates the functioning of a system as a whole (Chapanis, 1999; Meister, 1991). The initial contract to perform systems theory research was awarded to Chapanis and Morgan at Johns Hopkins in the spring of 1945 by the Bureau of Ships. Their studies used time and motion studies of personnel working in simulated combat information centers (Chapanis, 1999). According to Sloan (1994), the Systems Research Laboratory at Johns Hopkins was perhaps the most prolific human factors laboratory of the early postwar years.

The work on systems theory created a climate in which human factors requirements were included in government contracts with industry, thereby introducing systems research into the industrial sector (Christiansen, 1962). In turn, engineering psychologists began to adapt their work to problems of private industry (Meister, 1999). At Johns Hopkins, the Communications Research Laboratory was opened to conduct communication research that was responsible for the development of the current telephone keyboard configurations (Chapanis, 1999). The engineering psychologists at Johns Hopkins soon developed new research areas such as the design of teleconferencing systems and created improved oil exploration techniques and displays, stove tops, and phone mail. Chapanis also began a relationship with IBM that helped to introduce the principles of engineering psychology to the computer industry and resulted in the creation of modern full-screen interfaces that replaced the awkward line-entry systems of the 1980s (Meister, 1999).

After World War II, members of industry began to hire engineering psychologists and engineers to collect anthropometric and biomechanical data to design jobs and equipment that would not exceed physical capabilities, to increase safety, and to reduce the costs of workers' compensation claims (Dempsey, 1985). To identify potentially injurious tasks, physiological measures were taken to determine the maximum loads that could be manipulated and forces that could be absorbed by the human body without injury (Christensen, 1962). The success of these programs in reducing work injuries encouraged continued government and industry interest in biomechanics and created opportunities for biomechanics experts to open private consulting firms (Roscoe, 1994). Jack Dunlap established one of the first biomechanics consulting firms in 1946 when he opened a biomechanics division at the Psychological Corporation in New York (Orlansky, 1994). (See chap. 6 for additional information about the Psychological Corporation.) In the 1960s, specialists in anthropometrics and biomechanics created the work standards of the Occupational Safety and Health Administration (OSHA) that are currently used in industrial settings to reduce the risk of on-the-job injuries.

THE NEXT GENERATION OF HUMAN FACTORS PROFESSIONALS

University Programs

The human engineering research at universities attracted graduate students, which meant that courses in human engineering were needed. Formal courses began to appear in the late 1940s, accompanied by human engineering texts (Chapanis, 1999; Chapanis, Garner, Morgan, & Sanford, 1947; Meister, 1991). Major university research programs, supported by military contracts, got underway at Johns Hopkins, Harvard, Tufts, Ohio State, Rochester, Maryland, Washington, Holyoke, and California (Berkeley; see Grether, 1968). Among the first human factors texts were *Applied Experimental Psychology: Human Factors in Engineering Design* (Chapanis et al., 1949), which had a major impact in defining the field, and the first edition of the *Human Engineering Guide to Equipment Design* (Morgan, Cook, Chapanis, & Lund, 1963), which updated many of the areas and broadened the scope beyond Fitts' original volume for the Air Force (Fitts, 1947a). The guide was subsequently updated and revised (see Van Cott & Kinkade, 1972).

University programs continued to expand. Arthur Melton moved to the University of Michigan to found the Human Performance Laboratory there and was succeeded by Paul Fitts. After Fitts' untimely death, he was succeeded by Richard Pew. The graduates of the new programs were the first generation of engineering psychologists who were not trained to be exclusively experimental psychologists and who expected to integrate their work with the work of professionals from other disciplines. As graduate students obtained their degrees, they began to be hired not only by the military or by universities but by industry as well.

Programs in Industry

The next generation of human factors specialists were instrumental in adapting aviation psychology to private industry (Koonce, 1984). In 1952, Stanley Roscoe, a student of Paul Fitts, was hired by Hughes Aircraft Company, where he organized research on cockpit design and became the manager of the Display Systems Department (Roscoe, 1997). Gerald Slocum, a graduate of UCLA, was hired by Hughes Aircraft in 1953 and later became vice-president of the firm (Koonce, 1984; Meister, 1991). The first engineering psychologist hired by Douglas Aircraft in 1955 was Harry Wolbers (Meister, 1999). Five students of Alex Williams—Dora Dougherty, Scott Hasler, Fred Muckler, Douglass Nicklas, and Thomas Payne—were the first aviation psychologists hired by the Martin Company in the mid-1950s (Meister, 1991). At Boeing, Conrad Kraft, a student of Samuel Renshaw, performed research on the problems of nighttime landings during which pilots sometimes attempted to land their aircraft short of the runway due to the "black hole illusion," a term coined by Kraft. The black hole illusion can occur during a final approach on a night with no stars or moonlight. The nearly total lack of illumination makes the horizon invisible and hides important visual cues that help pilots orient themselves to the earth. Due to the lack of visual cues, a visual illusion of a high-altitude final approach is created, causing the pilot to lower the approach slope and land short of the runway. Kraft's work on the perceptual characteristics of aircraft landing was used to design displays that would combat the illusion (Chapanis et al., 1949; Roscoe 1997). Some later examples of groups associated with private industry include those at Bell Telephone Laboratories, at IBM's Product Development Laboratory, and at Bolt, Baranach, and Newman (BBN), in Cambridge, Massachusetts.

Private Firms

A number of private companies, organized in the post–World War II period, specialized in human factors research. Examples include Dunlap and Associates, founded by Jack Dunlap, and Personnel Research Associates (PRA),[1] founded by Harry J. Older, who had served as head of the Aviation Psychology Branch, Bureau of Medicine and Surgery, Department of the Navy during the war. PRA, early in it is history, included on its staff Dean Havron, James Parker, and Harold (Smoke) Price. PRA was eventually merged into Essex Corporation, which carried out systems research relevant to military operations.

Role of the Office of Naval Research[2]

Much of the basic research in human factors in industry, private research firms, and universities has been supported by funding from government agencies, especially military agencies organized after World War II. Although all branches of the Armed Forces have such agencies, the Office of Naval Research (ONR), especially, has been instrumental in developing and sustaining pioneering programs that have had an impact on this field. Darley (1957) described the origins of ONR, its mission, and its success in advancing psychological science during the first decade of its life. The field of human factors would be considerably diminished were it not for decisions made by a handful of psychologists in the Engineering Psychology Program of ONR's Psychological Sciences Division in Washington, DC. The heads of these programs had considerable discretion in choosing those ideas and proposals they believed had merit for future development. These "unsung heroes" in engineering psychology at ONR included, at various times, Max Lund, Martin Talcott, Wallace Sinaiko, James W. Miller, Gerald Milaki, Donald Woodward, Marshall Farr, and Nancy Shippman (see Nelson, 2006).

In the early 1950s, the Office of Naval Research also set up a European Liaison Office in London, England, to report on scientific developments in Europe in various scientific fields, including psychology. Prominent U.S. psychologists served successive terms as psychological science liaison officers for 1- or 2-year periods, visiting psychological departments and programs in various European countries and distributing reports on their observations to a U.S. audience. The first such appointment of colleagues in the United States was Henry Imus, a distinguished visual perception psychologist, followed in 1955 by Lee Cronbach and subsequently by Alphonse Chapanis, Jack Adams, John Lanzetta, Wally Sinaiko, and others of this stature. It is noteworthy that most, but not all, of these liaison officers over the years were identified with engineering psychology. These liaison officers also set up contacts between U.S.

---

[1]Not to be confused with Personnel Research Associates in Chicago (now known as Valtera), founded much later by William Macey, an I–O psychologist.

[2]Material for this sections was provided by Edwin A. Fleishman; see also Nelson (2006)

psychologists visiting European colleagues. (For an early example, see Fleishman, 1956). This function of ONR had an enormous impact on the world community of psychologists, especially those in human factors and related areas.

CREATION OF PROFESSIONAL SOCIETIES

American Psychological Association (APA): Division 21

In the years following World War II, most engineering psychologists were members of Division 14 (Industrial and Business Psychology) and/or Division 19 (Military Psychology) of the American Psychological Association (APA). According to Parsons (1999), the focus of these psychologists in this field was on "psychological factors in the design of equipment and man-machine systems." This stimulated a desire to create a new division within APA that focused on these issues. Walter Grether (1968), one of the founders of this field, described the founding of APA Division 21 in 1957, which was then called the Society of Engineering Psychology. The organizing committee included Karl Kryter (Chair), Harry J. Older, and Franklin V. Taylor. The division's first president was Paul Fitts (see Chapanis, 1999; Parsons, 1999).

After a number of debates about its name (described by Parsons, 1999), and as emphases in the field changed and evolved, the division is known, since 1983, as the Division of Applied Experimental and Engineering Psychology. A 1976 by-laws revision had changed the phraseology of its objective to include "to promote research, applications, and evaluations of psychological principles related human behavior to the characteristics, design, and use of environment systems within which human beings work and live" (see Parsons, 1999, p. 45).

The period between 1956 and 1965 was a time of growth for the new division, but membership decreased somewhat after 1965. This was due, in part, to the development of special interest groups for human factors professionals that addressed particular professional interest areas more specifically than did Division 21. Many human factors professionals began to attend the meetings of these groups, rather than the meetings of the APA. However, in recent years, psychologists who specialize in human factors have been returning to Division 21, and the division is now witnessing a period of growth and revitalization (Chapanis, 1999). Although no data have been collected to determine why more human factors professionals are returning to Division 21, the renewed interest may likely have been stimulated, in part, by the fact that the multidisciplinary nature of the Human Factors and Ergonomics Society is believed by some psychologists to have somewhat eroded the scientific base of that organization.

Division 21's pioneers recognized the infeasibility of publishing a technical journal in competition with *Human Factors,* the official journal of the Human Factors Society. However, since 1995, APA began publishing the *Journal of Experimental Psychology: Applied* that goes to each Division 21 member. The division does publish a newsletter on professional, scientific, and organizational matters of interest to division members.

The history of engineering psychology can also be seen in its scientific and professional leadership. Table 10.1 lists Division 21 presidents since its founding in 1957.

In 1962, the division established the Franklin V. Taylor Award for "outstanding contributions to the field of applied experimental psychology." The history of these awards is presented in Table 10.2 (from Parsons, 1999).

According to Parsons (1999), six Fellows of Division 21 have received APA's Distinguished Scientific Award for the Applications of Psychology: Conrad Kraft (1973), Alphonse Chapanis (1978), Edwin Fleishman (1980), Robert Glaser (1987), Herschel Lefkowitz (1993), and Ward Edwards (1996).

TABLE 10.1
APA Division 21 Presidents

Officer	Year	Officer	Year
P. M. Fitts	1957–1958	H. P. Van Cott	1982–1983
F. M. Taylor	1958–1959	R. C. Williges	1983–1984
A. Chapanis	1959–1960	W. C. Howell	1984–1985
W. F. Grether	1960–1961	R. W. Pew	1985–1986
J. C. R. Licklider	1961–1962	N. S. Anderson	1986–1987
J. M. Christensen	1962–1963	M. H. Strub	1987–1988
L. C. Mead	1963–1964	H. L. Taylor	1988–1989
H. J. Older	1964–1965	J. J. O'Hare	1989–1990
W. C. Biel	1965–1966	R. S. Kennedy	1990–1991
K. D. Kryter	1966–1967	E. R. Dusek	1991–1992
A. W. Melton	1967–1968	F. T. Eggemeier	1992–1993
N. H. Mackworth	1968–1969	J. M. Koonce	1993–1994
J. Orlansky	1969–1970	B. B. Morgan, Jr.	1994–1995
J. A. Adams	1970–1971	A. D. Fisk	1995–1996
R. A. McFarland	1971–1972	A. Schmidt-Nielsen	1996–1997
E. T. Klemmer	1972–1973	W. A. Rogers	1997–1998
E. A. Alluisi	1973–1974	C. A. Bowers	1998–1999
G. E. Briggs	1974	J. R. Callan	1999–2000
H. M. Parsons	1975–1976	R.W. Swezey	2000–2001
H. W. Sinaiko	1976–1977	G.P. Krueger	2001–2002
E. A. Fleishman	1977–1978	D. J. Schroeder	2002–2003
J. W. Senders	1978–1979	D. Griffith	2003–2004
R. M. Chambers	1979–1980	D. Boehm-Davis	2004–2005
M. A. Tolcott	1980–1981	G. Shapiro	2005–2006
F. A. Muckler	1981–1982		

Note. Adapted from Parsons (1999). Now called the *Division of Applied Experimental and Engineering Psychology.*

Of interest to I–O psychologists is the overlap in members of Division 14 (now known as the Society for Industrial and Organizational Psychology) with Division 21. In 1997, 17.6% of Division 21 members were also members of Division 14. Ernest McCormick, William Howell, Robert Glaser, and Edwin Fleishman are recognized contributors to I–O psychology as well as to human factors. For example, William Howell, who has authored a text in I–O psychology, was editor of the *Human Factors* journal. And Howell and Irv Goldstein, a past president of SIOP, co-authored the text *Engineering Psychology: Current Perspectives in Research* (Howell & Goldstein, 1971). Fleishman appears to be the only psychologist that has been elected president of both APA Division 14 (1973–1974) and Division 21 (1977–1978).

TABLE 10.2
APA Division 21 Franklin V. Taylor Award Recipients

Recipient	Year	Recipient	Year
A. C. Williams, Jr.	1962	D. Meister	1984
P. M. Fitts	1963	H. L. Snyder	1985
A. Chapanis	1964	H. P. Van Cott	1986
W. F. Grether	1965	R. M. Chambers	1987
J. C. R. Licklider	1966	M. A. Tolcott	1988
E. J. McCormick	1967	R. C. Williges	1989
N. H. Mackworth	1968	J. A. Thorpe	1990
R. A. McFarland	1969	R. S. Nickerson	1991
J. M. Christensen	1970	H. M. Parsons	1992
E. A. Alluisi	1971	C. D. Wickens	1993
W. H. Teichner	1972	H. L. Taylor	1994
K. D. Kryter	1973	No Award	1995
E. A. Fleishman	1974	R. S. Kennedy	1996
G. E. Briggs	1975	B. B. Morgan, Jr.	1997
S. N. Roscoe	1976	R. Glaser	1998
J. A. Adams	1977	A. Dan Fisk	1999
W. Edwards	1978	E. Salas	2000
W. C. Howell	1979	P. A. Hancock	2001
H. R. Jex	1980	W. A. Rogers	2002
R. W. Pew	1981	D. A. Boehm-Davis	2003
R. R. Mackie	1982	R. Parasuraman	2004
J. Orlansky	1983	D. A. Norman	2005

Note. Adapted from Parsons (1999).

The Human Factors and Ergonomics Society (HFES)

By the mid-1950s, interdisciplinary groups of human factors professionals, including nonpsychologists, began to meet in small local groups to discuss research and to share ideas. As the local societies began to proliferate, psychologists, engineers, work physiologists, specialists in biomechanics, and others involved in systems design and related areas began to recognize a need to create a forum for sharing information derived from local society meetings. As a result, a joint committee representing the Aero Medical Engineering Association of Los Angeles and the Human Engineering Society of San Diego was formed in 1955 to plan for a national society of human factors professionals. The committee members included Arnold Small (Chair), Donald Conover, Donald Hanifan, Stanley Lippert, Laurence Morehouse, John Poppin, and Wesley Woodson, a group of professionals that were involved in human factors work in industry, universities, and government (HFES History, n.d.). The committee held their first joint meeting in 1956 at Laguna Beach, California, to create the concept of the new society and develop detailed plans for its formation, including creation of the proposed society's name, Human

Factors Society of America (later the Human Factors Society and, as of 1992, the Human Factors and Ergonomics Society). The plans were approved at a joint meeting of the proposed members of the new society with attendees of the fifth Annual Human Engineering Conference that was held in conjunction with the Fifth Annual Human Engineering Conference sponsored by the Office of Naval Research. This meeting was held at the Pompeian Room of the Mayo Hotel in Tulsa, Oklahoma, in 1957 (Chapanis, 1999).

The first 1-day meeting of the Human Factors Society (HFS) was attended by a group of approximately 90 human factors professionals. Within 3 months, there were more than 200 members of the new society. In 1959, the Human Factors Society meeting was extended to 2 days, and by 1959 the meetings consumed 5 days (Roscoe, 1997). Following the first meeting, the original founding committee was joined by Paul Fitts, Jesse Orlansky, and Max Lund. Membership of the HFS increased rapidly. By 1962 the HFS claimed more than 1,000 members, and the current membership exceeds 5,200 (HFES History, n.d.).

In 1964, the HFS opened its national office in Santa Monica, California (Chapanis, 1999). Two early tasks of the HFS were to create technical groups and methods of disseminating professional information. Two groups claim to be the first technical groups, the San Diego Human Engineering Society and the Aero Medical Engineering Association of Los Angeles. In either case, the number of technical groups is now above 20 (HFES, n.d.). The HFS began publishing its first journal, *Human Factors,* in 1958. That same year, the *Human Factors Society Bulletin*, a more casual method of disseminating information about the activities of human factors professionals, was first published. Publication of proceedings of annual meetings began in 1972, and, in 1993, a new journal, *Ergonomics in Design*, was created to provide a forum for the report of successful projects that were conducted in industrial settings.

THE COGNITIVE ERA

During and immediately after World War II, human factors professionals in the United States continued to use the mechanistic "black box" approach that ignored the importance of cognition and followed the principles of behaviorism (Dempsey, 1985; Hunt, 1993). However, as early as the 1920s, the mechanistic view of the passive mind had been challenged by advances in logic, neuroscience, and psycholinguistics, and European psychologists began to explore cognitive processes (Dempsey,1985). The work done at the Applied Psychology Unit (APU) of Cambridge University, England, was in the forefront of applied cognitive research. The unit first functioned under the directorship of Sir Frederick Bartlett, who was later succeeded by Donald Broadbent. Other prominent researchers at this laboratory were Kenneth Craik, W. E. Hick, and Norman Mackworth (Meister, 1991). The APU papers were soon read by scientists in the United States who began to consider the importance of cognitive research (History of the MRC-CBU, n.d.).

The work of George Miller, a professor of psychology at Harvard, and later at MIT, challenged the theory of behaviorism that pervaded psychology in the United States in the 1950s. At first, Miller conducted studies in speech and communication that were based on the mechanistic viewpoint of the behaviorists. However, the results of his studies demonstrated the importance of cognitive function to human performance (Miller, 1953). In 1956, Miller published his seminal paper, "The Magical Number Seven, Plus or Minus Two: Some Limits on Our Capacity for Processing Information" (Miller, 1956). This paper generated interest in the study of cognition and in the quantification of information processing, which was the basis of information theory (Roscoe, 1994), and led to the exploration of task-based knowledge, decision making, and expertise (Hunt, 1993). Miller's study, along with the book on human communication theory by Shannon and Weaver (1949), Noam Chomsky's review of B. F. Skinner's book on verbal learning (Skinner, 1957), and Newell's and Simon's efforts to simulate cognitive function on computers, is generally considered to be one of the main forces behind the cognitive revolution of the 1950s (Hergenhahn, 1992; Hunt, 1993). Of course, some human factors specialists did not shift their focus to cognitive issues, and two groups began to emerge in the human factors discipline, a group of professionals who focused mainly on physical aspects of work and a group that focused on cognitive issues as well.

One of the major contributions of the cognitively oriented human factors professionals was the development of valid measures of cognitive workload during the 1980s. The work of Diane Damos (Damos & Bloem, 1985) and her colleagues at NASA–Ames resulted in the creation of the (arguably) most reliable and valid measure of mental workload, the NASA Task Load Index (TLX). The NASA–TLX scale evaluates workload by comparing three types of task demand (temporal, mental, physical), records of participants' estimates of the quality of their own performance, and estimates of effort and fatigue. The NASA–TLX has been used successfully for a variety of purposes including job and system design and comparison of system prototypes to determine which exerts the lowest mental workload (Wickens, Gordon, & Liu, 1998).

More recently, human factors professionals have been instrumental in creating designer-oriented human factors guidelines at the request of the Federal Highway Administration (FHWA). Due to the concern with rapidly increasing amount of information that drivers can access, the FHWA sponsored a 6-year program aimed at developing guidelines to assist designers of in-vehicle information displays by encouraging them to consider the potential for driver distraction. The outcome of this project was the *Human Factors Design Guidelines for Advanced Traveler Information Systems and Commercial Vehicle Operations* (Campbell & Kantowitz, 1997). The draft guidelines were distributed for review to 30 designers and engineers from automotive manufacturers and suppliers. The response from industry was overwhelmingly positive.

HUMAN–COMPUTER INTERACTION

The complexity of computer systems could be overcome, at first, only by experts, but consideration of how to make computers accessible to a wider audience began in the 1960s when computer research laboratories began to appear at universities. The interest in adapting human factors principles to computer systems was the basis for a new human factors interest area, human–computer interaction (HCI). Two of the most notable early HCI laboratories were the Stanford Research Institute and the MIT Media Laboratory (Card, 1996; Meyers, 1998). Industry began to open HCI laboratories, as well, when new computer systems were not well received because of the difficulty of learning to use them. The most notable early industry laboratories included those at Xerox, IBM, AT&T, and Bell Laboratories (Bond, 1970).

One of the leaders of the new HCI field was J. C. M. Licklider, who began his career as an experimental psychologist at MIT. In 1960, Licklider wrote one of the first important papers about HCI, "Man–Computer Symbiosis," in which he discussed the development of computer assistants that could graphically display results, create new solutions from old information, and perform simulation modeling (Waldrop, 2001). In 1965, Licklider published an influential book, *Libraries of the Future*, in which he discussed computerized libraries that were based on a powerful network of computers (Licklider, 1965). Licklider and Welden Clark also published a paper, "On-Line Computer Communication," in which they discussed the internet concept (J. C. R. Licklider, n.d.). Later, Licklider was instrumental in developing the first computer network for the Department of Defense (Waldrop, 2001). Another early proponent of HCI was Ben Schneiderman, who received his PhD in computer science from the State University of New York at Stony Brook. In 1976, Schneiderman accepted a position at the University of

Maryland where, in 1982, he founded the Human–Computer Interaction Laboratory (Schneiderman, 1987). The work published by researchers at this laboratory stimulated further interest in HCI. In turn, the increased interest led to the creation of one the earliest HCI professional societies, the Software Psychology Society, in 1976.

The problem of computer usability increased during the 1980s, when personal computers became available to a wider population (Gasen, Perlman, & Attaya-Kelo, 1994). By the 1980s, HCI researchers were joined by designers and specialists in anthropometry and biomechanics. Unfortunately, the nature of the interaction between the various contributing groups has been selective compatibility rather than a true integration of knowledge from each discipline. For example, computer scientists and psychologists work together in a partial truce of the age-old conflict, but psychologists rarely integrate their work with the work of specialists in anthropometrics and biomechanics (Hewett et al., 1992).

During the 1990s, several factors strengthened the need for HCI research and development. These factors included the creation of local area networks, development of laptop computers, and the geometric growth of World Wide Web users. These new technologies resulted in the development of smaller interfaces, information filtering, and navigation tools to be used in large information spaces (Hewitt et al., 1992). Due to increasing complexity of computers of all types, the need for HCI professionals continues to grow, and increasing numbers of HCI courses are being offered (Gasen et al., 1994; Mantei & Smelcer, 1984). In the mid-1990s, the HCI community began to divide into specialist areas, a trend reflected by conferences and journals that focus on special topics (Pemberton, 1996). The specialization of HCI is likely to continue, and the existing collaboration between university and industrial HCI experts is likely to increase (Meyers, 1998),

SCOPE OF THE HUMAN FACTORS FIELD

It is somewhat difficult to identify the scope of human factors because the field is expanding rapidly, with new technical groups being added every few years. However, the general scope of human factors is reflected by its technical groups that include aerospace systems, aging, cognitive engineering and decision making, communications, computer systems, consumer products, education, environmental design, forensic professional, industrial ergonomics, internet, medical systems and rehabilitation, perception and performance, safety, surface transportation, system development, test and evaluation, virtual environments macroergonomics, individual differences in performance, and training.

Many of these technical groups focus on interests shared by I–O psychologists and human factors specialists (e.g., training, aging, decision making, communications, individual differences, education, and macroergonomics). During the late 1980s, some human factors professionals began to realize that analyzing and correcting problems at the work station level did not totally alleviate problems of inaccuracy and inefficient performance (Hendrick, 1995, 2001). This led to the development of a new subdiscipline of human factors known as macroergonomics, which, perhaps, reflects the common interests of human factors and I–O psychology most vividly. Macroergonomics is a top-down sociotechnical systems approach to the design of organizations, work systems, and jobs. The central focus is on optimizing work system design by considering technological, social, task element, and environmental variables (Keidel, 1994). The macroergonomics design approach begins with analysis of sociotechnical variables and then uses these data to design a work system's structure and processes. In consideration of the sociotechnical variables, workers' professional and psychosocial characteristics are evaluated so that design can be based on this information. According to Hendrick (2001), macroergonomics is the third generation of human factors, the first generation being characterized by concern with the human–machine interface, the second with user interfaces, and the third with human–organization, environment–machine interface technology.

ACCREDITATION

During the mid-1980s, concern began to arise that not all people who called themselves human factors professionals were qualified, and interest grew in creating a certification board. Although the idea was controversial, a committee composed of members of the Department of Defense, Human Factors and Ergonomics Society, International Ergonomics Association, NATO, and the National Academy of Science National Research Council was commissioned to identify the knowledge, skills, and abilities needed by human factors professionals (History of BCPE, n.d.). The findings of these reviews were categorized and used to compare the skills needed by human factors professionals with the skills provided by popular human factors texts. In 1990, the Board of Certification in Professional Ergonomics (BCPE) was created, and members of the board used job/task analysis to develop requirements for BCPE certification and to create credentialing criteria for human factors graduate programs. Certification was initiated in 1992.

LESSONS AND SUMMARY

Professional and Application Issues

Today, HFES is represented by 60 local chapters throughout the United States, Canada, and Europe (Moroney, 1995), and the field is continuing to grow at an impressive rate. Although many success stories are reported in the literature, human factors professionals have also learned from their mistakes (e.g., Olsen & Teasley, 1996; Stout, Slosser, & Hays, 2000). One of the earliest lessons was that human factors professionals must balance their focus on efficiency with consideration of safety and job satisfaction. The central focus on efficiency of the first half of the 20th century led to worker injury, dissatisfaction, and rebellion. Another lesson is that human factors professionals must concern themselves with cognitive as well as physical functioning. When systems developed beyond their primitive beginnings and became more complex, it became apparent that effective human factors design must consider cognitive aspects of tasks and abandon the timeworn black-box approach (Meister, 1999).

One of the most painful lessons learned was that research and design must often consider the entire population, rather than only a specific interest group. This fact was extremely salient when the debacle with air bags occurred. The physical data used to design air bags was based on anthropometrics and biomechanics data derived from average adult males, but no consideration was given to the dimensions of children and small people. Although air bags saved many lives, by 1996 they also resulted in the deaths of 87 children and small individuals in accidents that would have been survivable had the air bag not been engaged. In November 1996, the National Health and Transportation Safety Administration issued a ruling that required auto manufacturers to provide warning labels advising air bag users of the danger to small individuals and directing parents to either use the newly available air-bag cutoff switches or, preferably, place children in the rear seat of the car (Campbell & Kantowitz, 1997).

One important fact has been learned by members of private industry as well as by human factors professionals. Unlike industry officials in Europe and Asia, members of industry in the United States remained relatively tepid about human factors design until the dawn of the personal computer. During this period, graduates of human factors programs worked diligently to expand the application base of human factors to include new industrial applications (Sloan,

1994). Slowly, the successes of HCI professionals led the leaders of other industries to accept the credibility of human factors design. In recent years, human factors professionals have succeeded in designing less error-prone medical devices such as heart rate monitors and more easily read and opened prescription bottles. Other human factors experts are involved in designing for disabled and aged persons.

The diversity of the disciplines involved in human factors has increased the arena of human factors applications greatly. However, there is some concern that this diversity may disrupt the solidarity of human factors professionals. Today, increasing numbers of professionals are attending specialized conferences rather than larger national meetings, and many are reading specialized journals rather than major human factors publications (IEA History, n.d.), a trend that some fear could foreshadow the splintering of the human factors profession. However, this trend may be a corollary of the division of psychology into separate disciplines that occurred when it became clear that no one school of psychology could explain the wide array of psychological concerns (Hunt, 1993). Despite this division, psychology continues to exist as a profession and the future of human factors may well mirror this process.

The Science of Human Performance

Why has this chapter about human factors/engineering psychology been included in a book concerned with historical perspectives in industrial and organizational psychology? One reason, of course, involves their common roots in the history of industrial psychology. As earlier chapters in the book document, the field of industrial psychology had its genesis in experimental psychology. Its early texts examined ways in which scientific methods and findings could be turned to applications in the world of work. Topics such as measuring and reducing fatigue, improving legibility of displays, and evaluating environmental effects on behavior were considered alongside topics of personnel selection, training, applications to marketing, performance appraisal, and so forth. Later textbooks in industrial psychology continued to include chapters on "human engineering." The I–O field expanded to include motivational, social, and organizational issues and an increasing sophistication in the measurement of individual differences. At the same time, energized by the successes during World War II and the postwar boom of experiments on and applications of human engineering, with specialized texts and educational programs, a split was inevitable. Yet, there is a common core of interests, methods, and objectives that can be rationalized. Henry McIlvaine Parsons (1912–2004), a past president (1975–1976), and Franklin Taylor, awardee, of Division 21, recently framed the issue in terms of future objectives of the division. They stated,

> Although the division's current name does not include the particular aspect of behavior toward which its members' research is directed, this can be summarized as human performance, initially perceptual–motor performance, in more recent years also cognitive performance. The major criterion of performance has been effectiveness, indicated in human capabilities and limitations related to operating or maintaining equipment and assessed largely in temporal (e.g., latency) or accuracy (e.g., error or accident probability) measures. The objectives of Division 21 members have been to investigate these aspects of human performance not only in general but also in association with proposed or actual designs or devices, environments, or systems with which their users interact, currently or prospectively. What are those users' capabilities and interactions in such situations? How well do they match a particular design's requirements—and vice versa? Especially challenging have been questions concerning whether some technological process or procedures should be performed by a human or be automated, or by both in some special combination. A great range of human behavior has been and continues to be investigated under these objectives, of both general and particular significance. (Parsons, 1999, p. 48)

Parsons' statement underscores the common goal of the fields of human factors and industrial and organizational psychology as the understanding of human performance in the work place. There are some illustrations in our recent history of research, applications, and education that have attempted to unify these fields or, at least, emphasize their common interests.

For example, the journal *Human Performance* was founded by I–O psychologist Frank Landy to bridge these joint interests. Another historical note is the early textbook *Psychology and Human Performance: An Introduction to Psychology* (Gagné & Fleishman, 1959). This text was written specifically for students in schools of engineering or business, taking their first course in psychology (Gagné & Fleishman, 1959), and it stressed the continuity of basic psychology with relevance to human performance in the world of work.

Another example of a program linking engineering and I–O psychology is the programmatic work on taxonomic issues in psychology carried out by Fleishman and his colleagues over many years. Initiated in 1976 with sponsorship of Department of Defense's Advanced Research Projects Agency, this work was summarized in the book by Fleishman and Quaintance (1984). The work examined tasks as central constructs in psychology and evaluated alternative methods for describing tasks. One objective was to improve generalizations obtained in laboratory settings to field settings; another was to provide standardization in methods for defining job requirements. A point here is that publications resulting from this program have been published in the journals *Human Factors* and *Human Performance* as well as in the *Journal of Applied Psychology, Personnel Psychology,* and applications have been found in both fields. The new U.S. Occupational Information System (O*Net) to replace the U.S. Department of Labor's *Dictionary of Occupational Titles* is based, in part, on this system (see Fleishman, 1992; Peterson, Mumford, Borman, Jeanneret, & Fleishman, 1999). And a recent publication (Fleishman & Buffardi, 1998) relevant to human factors concerns has shown that error probabilities in tasks performed in nuclear power plants can be predicted from measures based on an ability requirements taxonomy.

A final illustration came from a project sponsored by the National Science Foundation, where the objective was to bring together existing research on human performance with issues of improving productivity in the workplace. This project brought together prominent industrial and organizational psychologists and human factors/engineering psychology and resulted in three volumes: *Human Performance and Productivity, Vol. 1: Human Capability Assessment* (Dunnette & Fleishman, 1982), *Human Performance and Productivity, Vol. 2: Information Processing and Decision Making* (Howell & Fleishman, 1982), and *Human Performance and Productivity, Vol. 3: Stress and Performance Effectiveness* (Allusi & Fleishman, 1982). It was clear that this effort would have been incomplete without the joint efforts across the fields of I–O psychology and human factors.

To conclude, a history of I–O psychology and human factors shows that research, application, and professional development in both these fields are inextricably linked and both fields are the better for it.

ACKNOWLEDGMENTS

I thank the anonymous reviewers and the editor for their helpful comments on an earlier draft of this chapter. Special thanks go to Dr. Edwin Fleishman for his comments, suggestions and information.

REFERENCES

Alluisi, E. A. (1994). Roots and rooters. In H. L. Taylor (Ed.), *Division 21 members who made distinguished contributions to engineering psychology.* Washington, DC: Division 21 of the American Psychological Association.

Allusi, E. A., & Fleishman, E. A. (Eds.) (1982). *Human performance and productivity, Vol. 3: Stress and performance effectiveness.* Mahwah, NJ: Lawrence Erlbaum Associates.

Angell, J. R. (1907). The province of functional psychology. *Psychological Review, 14,* 61–91.

Baecker, R. M., Grudin, J., Buxton, W. A., & Greenberg, S. (1995) *Human–computer interaction: Toward the year 2000* (2nd ed.). San Mateo, CA: Morgan Kaufmann.

Bond, N. A., Jr. (1970). Some persistent myths about military electronics maintenance. *Human Factors, 12,* 241–252.

Buckley, K. W. (1982). The selling of a psychologist: John Broadus Watson and the application of behavioral techniques to advertising. *Journal of the History of the Behavioral Sciences, 18,* 207–221.

Campbell, J., & Kantowitz, B. (1997). Design guidelines for advanced traveler information systems (ATIS): The user requirements analysis. *Proceedings of the Human Factors and Ergonomists Society 41st Annual Meeting, 2,* 954–958.

Card, S. K. (1996). Pioneers and settlers: Methods used in successful user interface design. In M. Rudisill (Ed.), *Human–computer interface design: Success stories, emerging methods, and real world context* (pp. 122–169). San Francisco: Morgan Kaufmann.

Carr, H. A. (1925). *Psychology.* New York: Longmans, Green.

Chapanis, A. (1999). *The Chapanis chronicles.* Santa Barbara, CA: Aegean.

Chapanis, A., Garner, W. R., & Morgan, C. T. (1949). *Applied experimental psychology.* New York: Wiley.

Chapanis, A., Garner, W. R., Morgan, C. T., & Sanford, F. H. (1947). *Lectures on men and machines: An introduction to human engineering.* Baltimore: Systems Research Laboratory.

Christensen, J. M. (1962). The evolutions of the systems approach in human factors. *Human Factors, 5,* 7–16.

Cohen, D. (1979). *J. B. Watson: The founder of behaviorism.* London, England: Routledge & Kegan Paul.

Damos, D. L., & Bloem, K. A. (1985). Type a behavior pattern, multiple-task performance, and subjective estimation of mental workload. *Bulletin of the Psychonomic Society, 23*(1). 53–56.

Darley, J. G. (1957). Psychology and the Office of Naval Research: A decade of development. *American Psychologist, 12,* 305–323.

Dempsey, C. A. (1985). *Fifty years research on man in flight.* Dayton, OH: Wright-Patterson Air Force Base.

Dodge, R. W. (1900). Visual perception during eye movements. *Psychological Review, 7,* 454–465.

Dodge, R. W. (1907). An experimental study of visual fixation. *Psychological Monographs, 8,* 1–95.

Dodge, R. W. (1921). A mirror-recorder for photographing the compensatory movements of closed eyes. *Journal of Experimental Psychology, 4,* 165–174.

Dodge, R. W., & Benedict, F. G. (1925). *Psychological effects of alcohol: An experimental investigation of the effects of moderate doses of ethyl alcohol on a related group of neuro-muscular processes in man.* (Carnegie Institution of Washington, Publication 232). Washington, DC: Carnegie Institution of Washington.

Dunnette, M. D., & Fleishman, E. A. (Eds.). (1982). *Human performance and productivity. Vol. 1: Human capability assessment.* Hillsdale, NJ: Lawrence Erlbaum Associates.

Fitts, P. (n.d.). Retrieved January 10, 2003, at http:// www.Yorku.ca?mack/RN-Fitts_bib.htm

Fitts, P. M. (1947a). Psychological research on equipment design in the AAF. *American Psychologist, 2,* 93–98.

Fitts, P. M. (1947b). *Psychological research on equipment design* (Rep. No. 19, Army Air Force Aviation Psychology Program Research Reports). Washington, DC: U.S. Government Printing Office.

Fitts, P. M. (1951a). Human engineering for an effective air-navigation and traffic-control system. In S. S. Stevens (Ed.), *The handbook of experimental psychology* (pp. 1–261). New York: Wiley.

Fitts, P. M. (1951b). Engineering psychology and equipment design. In S. S. Stevens (Ed.), *Handbook of experimental psychology* (pp. 1287–1340). New York: Wiley.

Fitts, P. M., Flood, M. M., Garman, R. A., & Williams, A. C., Jr. (1957). *The USAF human factor engineering mission as related to the qualitative superiority of future man-machine weapons systems.* Washington, DC: U.S. Air Force Scientific Advisory Board Working Group on Human Factor Engineering Social Science Panel.

Flanagan, J. C. (Ed.). (1947). *The aviation psychology program in the Army Air Force* (Res. Rep. 1). Washington, DC: U.S. Army Air Forces Aviation Psychology Program.

Fleishman, E. A. (1956). *Report of official visits to psychological centers in England, France, Belgium, Netherlands, Sweden, Denmark, and Norway.* San Antonio, TX: Air Force Personnel and Training Research Center.

Fleishman, E. A. (1992). *Fleishman's Job Analysis Survey (F-JAS).* Potomac, MD: Management Research Institute.

Fleishman, E. A., & Buffardi, L. C. (1998). Predicting human error probabilities from the ability requirements of jobs in nuclear power plants. In J. Misumi, B. Wilpert, & R. Miller (Eds.), *Nuclear safety: A human factors perspective* (pp. 221–242). London: Taylor & Francis.

Fleishman, E. A., & Quaintance, M. K. (1984). *Taxonomies of human performance: The description of human tasks.* Orlando, FL: Academic Press.

Forbes, T. W. (1938). The normal automobile driver as a traffic problem. *Journal of General Psychology, 20,* 472–474.

Gagné, R. M., & Fleishman, E.A. (1959). *Psychology and human performance: An introduction to psychology.* New York: Holt.

Gasen, J. B., Perlman, G., & Attaya-Kelo, M. (1994). Update on the HCI education survey. *SIGCHI Bulletin, 26*(2), 8–11.

Gilbreth, L., & Gilbreth, F. (1917). *Applied motion study.* New York: Sturgis & Walton.

Gordon, T., & Miller, H. (1974). *Cycle I of the Health Examination Survey: Sample and response, United States, 1960–1962.* (Public Service Publication No. 1000-Series 11, No. 1). Washington, DC: U.S. Government Printing Office.

Grether, W. F. (1968). Engineering psychology in the United States. *American Psychologist, 23,* 743–751.

Hall, G. S. (1912). *Founders of modern psychology.* New York: Appleton.

Helander, M. (1997). The human factors profession. In (G. Salvendy (Ed.), *Handbook of human factors and ergonomics* (pp. 3–16). New York: Wiley.

Hendrick, H. W. (1995). Future directions in macroergonomics. *Ergonomics, 38,* 1617–1624.

Hendrick, H. W. (2001). Macroergonomics. A better approach to work system design. *HFES Potomac Chapter Newsletter, 36*(5), 2–4.

Hendrick, H. W., & Kleiner, B. M. (2001). *Macroergonomics: An introduction to work system design.* Santa Monica, CA : Human Factors and Ergonomics Society.

Hergenhahn, B. R. (1992). *An introduction to the history of psychology.* Belmont, CA: Wadsworth.

Hewett, T. T., Baecker, R., Card, S., Carey, T., Gasen, J., Mantei, M., et al. (1992). *ACM SIGCHI curricula for human-computer interaction.* New York: ACM

HFES History. (n.d.). Retrieved May 15, 2002, from http://hfes.org/About/History.html.

History of BCPE.. (n.d.). Retrieved January 10, 2002 from http://www.bcpe.org/newsletters/detail.asp?RecordID=82)

History of the MRC-CBU. (n.d.). Retrieved December 12, 2005, from http://www.mrc-cbu.ac.uk/contact-history.shtml

Howell, W. C., & Fleishman, E. A. (Eds.). (1982). *Human performance and productivity, Vol. 2: Information processing and decision making.* Mahwah, NJ: Lawrence Erlbaum Associates.

Howell, W. C., & Goldstein, I. L. (1971). *Engineering psychology: Current perspectives in research.* New York: Appleton-Century-Crofts.

Hunt, M. (1993). *The story of psychology.* New York: Doubleday.

IEA History (n.d.). Retrieved February 22, 2003, from http://www.iea.cc/about/history.cfm

Johnson, B. E., Williams, A. C., Jr., & Roscoe, S. N. (1951). *A simulator for studying human factors in air traffic control systems* (Rep. 11). Washington, DC: National Research Council Committee on Aviation Psychology.

Kanigel, R. (1997). *The one best way: Frederick Taylor and the enigma of efficiency.* New York: Viking.

Keidel, R. W. (1994). Rethinking organizational design. *Academy of Management Executive, 8*(4), 12–30.

Koonce, J. F. (1984). A brief history of aviation psychology. *Human Factors, 26,* 499–508.

Krueger, A. P. (2004). Alphonse Chapanis (1917–2002). *Ergonomics, 26,* 8–11.

Licklider, J. C. R. (n.d.). Retrieved February 18, 2003, from http://livinginernet.com/?i/ii_Licklider.htm

Licklider, J. C. R. (1965). *Libraries of the Future.* Cambridge, MA: The MIT Press.

Licklider, J. C. R., & Kryter, K. D. (1944). *Articulation tests of standard and modified interphones conducted during flight at 5000 and 35,000 feet* (OSRD Rep. 1976). Cambridge, MA: Harvard University, Psycho-Acoustic Laboratory.

Licklider, J. C. R., & Miller, G. A. (1951). The perception of speech. In S. S. Stevens (Ed.), *Handbook of experimental psychology* (pp. 1040–1074). New York: Wiley.

Mantei, M., & Smelcer, P. (1984). Guidelines for reading the human-computer interaction survey results. *SIGCHI Bulletin, 16*(2), 9–43.

Meister, D. (1991). *The psychology of systems design.* Amsterdam: Elsevier.

Meister, D. (1999). *The history of human factors.* Mahwah, NJ: Lawrence Erlbaum Associates.

Meyers, B. A. (1998). A brief history of human computer interaction technology. *ACM Interactions, 5*(2), 44–54.

Miles, W. R. (1925). Photographic recording of eye movements in the reading of Chinese in vertical and horizontal axes: Method and preliminary results. *Journal of Experimental Psychology, 8,* 344–362.

Miles, W. R. (1928). The peep-hole method of observing eye movements in reading. *Journal of General Psychology, 1,* 373–374.

Miles, W. R. (1931). Measurement of certain human abilities throughout lifespan. *Proceedings of the National Academy of Science, 17,* 627–633.

Miller, G. A. (1953). Information theory and the study of speech. In B. McMillan (Ed.), *Current trends in information theory* (pp. 119–139). Pittsburgh: University of Pittsburgh Press.

Miller, G. A. (1956). The magical number seven, plus or minus two: Some limits on our capacity for processing information. *Psychological Review, 63,* 81–97.

Morgan, C. T., Cook, J. S., Chapanis, A., & Lund, M. W. (Eds.). (1963). *Human engineering guide to equipment design.* New York: McGraw-Hill.

Moroney W. F. (1995). The evolution of human engineering: A selected review. In J. Weimer (Ed.), *Research techniques in human engineering* (pp. 1–19). Englewood Cliffs, NJ: Prentice-Hall.

Münsterberg, H. (1913). *Psychology and industrial efficiency*. Boston: Houghton Mifflin.

National Research Council. (1949). *A survey report on human factors in undersea warfare*. Washington, DC: Author.

Neibel, B. W. (1972). *Motion and time study*. Homewood, IL: Irwin.

Nelson, P. D. (2006). Human factors research in the naval service: Historical highlights. In A. D. Mangelsdorff (Ed.), *Psychology in the service of national security*. Washington, DC: American Psychological Association.

Olsen, J. S., & Teasley, S. (1996). Groupware in the wild: Lessons learned from a year of virtual collocation. In *Proceedings of the 1996 ACM Conference on Computer Supported Cognitive Work* (pp. 419–427). New York: ACM Press.

Orlansky, J. (1994). Jack W. Dunlap, 1902–1977. In H. L. Taylor (Ed.), *Division 21 members who made distinguished contributions to engineering psychology* (pp. 15–18). Washington, DC: Division 21 of the American Psychological Association.

Parsons, H. M. (1999). A history of Division 21 (Applied Experimental and Engineering Psychology). In D. A. Dewsbury (Ed.), *Unification through division: History of divisions of the American Psychological Association, Vol. III* (pp. 43–76). Washington, DC: American Psychological Association.

Pemberton, S. (1996). SIGCHI: The Later Years: Interviews with past chairs. *SIGCHI Bulletin*(1), 1–10.

Peterson, N. G., Mumford, M. D., Borman, W. C., Jeanneret, P. R., & Fleishman, E. (Eds.), (1999). *An information system for the 21st century: The development of the O*Net*. Washington, DC: American Psychological Association.

Pew, R. W. (1994). Paul Morris Fitts, 1912–1965. In H. L. Taylor (Ed.), *Division 21 members who made distinguished contributions to engineering psychology* (pp. 21–25). Washington, DC: Division 21 of the American Psychological Association.

Popplestone, J., & McPherson, M. W. (1994). *An illustrated history of American psychology*. Akron, OH: University of Akron Press.

Roscoe, S. N. (1992). From the roots to the branches of cockpit design: Problems, principles, products. *Human Factors Society Bulletin, 35*(12), 1–2.

Roscoe, S. N. (1994). Alexander Coxe Williams, Jr., 1914–1962. In H. L. Taylor (Ed.), *Division 21 members who made distinguished contributions to engineering psychology* (pp. 8–11). Washington, DC: Division 21 of the American Psychological Association.

Roscoe, S. N. (1997). The adolescence of engineering psychology. In S. M. Casey (Ed.), *Human factors history monograph series, 1* (pp. 1–9). Santa Monica, CA: The Human Factors Society.

Schultz, D. P., & Schultz, S. E. (2000). *A history of modern psychology* (8th ed.). New York: Harcourt Brace Jovanovich.

Shannon, C. E., & Weaver, W. (1949). *The mathematical theory of communications*. Urbana: University of Illinois Press.

Schneiderman, B. (1987). *Designing the user interface*. Reading, MA: Addison-Wesley.

Skinner, B. F. (1957). *Verbal learning*. New York: Appleton-Century-Crofts.

Sloan, G. D. (1994, October). *Human factors and premises liability*. Paper presented at the WSTLA Legal Educational Seminars, Seattle, WA.

Snow, C. C., & Snyder, R. G. (1965). *Anthropometry of air traffic control trainees* (No. AM 65-26; DTIC No. AD 689 810). Oklahoma City, OK: Federal Aviation Agency.

Snow, C. C., Reynolds, H. M., & Allgood, M. A. (1975). *Anthropometry of airline stewardesses* (No. FAA-AM-75-2; DTIC No. AD-A012 965). Washington, DC: Office of Aviation Medicine, Federal Aviation Administration.

Stout, R., Slosser, S., & Hays, R. T. (2000). *Sample lessons learned from advanced distributed learning efforts*. Retrieved February 8, 2003 from http://www.jointadlcolab.org/Stout_LessonsLearnedDoc.doc

Taylor, F. W. (n. d.). *Frederick Taylor, early management consultant*. Retrieved August 13, 2002, from http://www.cftech.com/BrainBank/TRIVIABITS/FredWTaylor.html

Taylor, F. W. (1911). *Principles of scientific management*. New York: Harper.

Van Cott, H. P., & Kinkade, R. G. (Eds.) (1972). *Human engineering guide to equipment design* (Rev. ed.). Washington, DC: U.S. Printing Office.

Waldrop, M. M. (2001). *The dream machine: J. C. R. Licklider and the revolution that made computing personal*. New York: Viking.

Wickens, C. D., Gordon, S. E., & Liu, Y. (1998). *An introduction to human engineering*. New York: Longman.

Weimer, J. (1995). *Research techniques in human engineering*. Englewood Cliffs, NJ: Prentice-Hall

Williams, A. C., Jr., & Roscoe, S. N. (1949). *Evaluation of aircraft instrument displays for use with the omni-directional radio range* (Rep. 84). Washington, DC: Civil Aeronautics Administration, Division of Research.

Williams, A. C., Jr., Macmillan, J. W., & Jenkins, J. G. (1946). *Preliminary experimental investigation of "tension" as a determinant of performance in flight training* (Rep. 54, Publication Bulletin L 503 25). Washington, DC: Civil Aeronautics Administration, Division of Research.

11

Early Influences of Applied Psychologists on Consumer Response: 1895–1925

David W. Schumann
University of Tennessee–Knoxville

Edith Davidson
University of Tennessee–Knoxville

This chapter explores the first 30 years of contributions of early applied psychologists as they initiated the scientific field of consumer psychology. Their story is intriguing. They began by working in relative silence, some splitting from the purist motivations of their doctoral mentors. Moreover, they confronted each other over disagreements regarding approaches to how consumer response should be studied. These disagreements reflected larger theoretical splits occurring in psychological academy at the time. Three distinct schools had emerged: mentalistic, behaviorism, and dynamic psychology. This chapter explores these schools as they influenced the applied psychologists of the day. This chapter owes much to the earlier work of David Kuna (see Kuna, 1976), the historian who thoroughly researched these early schools in psychology, their influence on the scientific study of advertising, and the lives and work of the early applied psychologists.

This story must be told in light of two important contexts. First, these early pioneers in consumer psychology were greatly influenced by their early training and the theories of such giants in experimental psychology as Wundt, James, and Titchener representing the mentalist approach; Watson and Thorndike representing the behavioral or mechanistic approach; and Freud and McDougall touting theories of dynamic psychology. These early "applied" psychologists often had to hide their interest in scientific advertising from some of these same giants who believed that the field of psychology had to mature before applications to the business world could be espoused. Second, and just as important, the work of these applied psychologists reflected the state of business, and particularly advertising, at the turn of the century. These psychologists were initially viewed by the professional advertising world as interfering and, frankly, irrelevant. All this was significantly altered during the early decades of the 20th century.

The labels "consumer psychology" and "industrial and organizational psychology" did not exist during this period of time. Rather, work that explored the application of psychological principles to business activity was known simply as "applied psychology" and the proponents were "applied psychologists." The first contributions occurred within what was termed "scientific advertising," followed closely by the scientific study of personal selling. As is referred to again in the conclusion of this chapter, the labels of consumer and industrial–organizational

(I–O) psychology emerged later in the century as their advocates lobbied for divisional membership in the American Psychological Association (APA; eventually to become Divisions 14 and 23 of APA). Early labels of I–O psychology are presented in Chapter 1 in this volume.

We begin this chapter by providing a brief review of both the practitioner and academic environments as they existed during this period. This is followed by a 30 year overview of the theoretical discussion and related research regarding these early schools of psychological thought and how these schools influenced the study of the consumer's psychological response to promotional stimuli (advertising and personal selling). The first 30 years are a very important period, because the thinking and research endeavors are clearly reflected in today's research in consumer psychology. We end with a discussion of how consumer psychology emerged from the shadow of I–O psychology and became recognized as its own separate discipline.

HISTORICAL CONTEXT LEADING TO THE ADVENT
OF CONSUMER PSYCHOLOGY

Our 30-year period of the study of consumer psychology begins in the last decade of the 19th century. The study of consumer psychology emerged from specific interest in advertising and how advertising influenced people. By the latter half of the 19th century, the advertising industry was well established in the United States. Its growth as an industry paralleled the industrial growth of this country. In the United States, the first organized advertising came to exist during colonial times and was enhanced through the advent of urban newspapers. As the country expanded there was an obvious need to extend the reach of advertising. As noted in other chapters throughout this text, from 1850–1900, transportation and technology brought on a "new industrial age." An explosion in manufacturing productivity led to new factories, increased volume, greater diversity in consumer products, and the need for new markets (Oliver, 1956). Advertising became the critical vehicle for achieving growth. As new markets emerged reflecting new populations centers, so did the concept and practice of national advertising with the advent of large circulation magazines like *Atlantic Monthly, Colliers, Cosmopolitan, Harper's Monthly, Ladies Home Journal, McClure's,* and the *Saturday Evening Post* (Kuna, 1976).

The second half of the 1800s saw the advent and growth of the advertising agent, the advertising copywriter, and subsequently the advertising agency. A newfound need for professionalism resulted in numerous ad clubs, associations, trade journals, and codes of ethics (Wiebe, 1967). During this time period, two schools of advertising emerged (arguably reflecting, but not to be confused with, the schools in psychology and economics). The first school was based on a rational view of people, the potential consumers who carefully paid attention to promotional messages before making product choices. The purpose of advertising was simply to inform the public that the item was available and what it could be used for. The public was viewed as skeptical and mostly incapable of being persuaded to act against their better judgment. This rational perspective followed classic economic theory that people are self-interested and naturally desire to maximize profits while valuing their time. Thus the emphasis was on reasonable price and basic selling points. If one considers that ad agencies were composed of creative individuals all adhering to this "rational man" perspective, the notion of a scientific view of advertising posed an obvious contradiction.

Although the rational school was dominant during the 1890s and 1900s, by 1910 it was supplanted by the nonrational perspective. Followers deemed it likely that the emotions of the public could be manipulated and that people could actually be persuaded to purchase goods. This school was much more open and receptive to a psychological approach to understanding audience response to advertising. Also contributing to the nonrational school was psychology's new emphasis on the unconscious and motivational states (e.g., Freud, 1924/1969) as well as on the mechanistic reinforcement of behavior (e.g., Watson, 1913).

EARLY ROOTS OF THE STUDY OF CONSUMER PSYCHOLOGY

As is the case with most all of experimental psychology, one must go back to Germany in the latter part of the 19th century to understand the roots of what was ultimately to become consumer psychology. These roots began in the laboratory of Wilhelm Wundt (1832–1920) in Leipzig in 1879, described in previous chapters. Of significant relevance to the study of consumer psychological response was Wundt's focus on the topic of attention and his influence on a subset of students who would go on to become, much to Wundt's displeasure, the first applied, I–O psychologists in America. Wundt (as did James and Titchener) believed that psychology needed to first prove its worth and evolve as a pure science before it could adequately respond to problems of the applied world (Kuna, 1976).

During this same period of time, William James (1842–1910), trained as a philosopher, was bringing to light the new science of psychology in his laboratory at Harvard University. James promoted a mentalistic perspective for this new science. In his seminal book entitled *The Principles of Psychology,* he defined psychology as the "science of mental life, both of its phenomena and their conditions" and, like Wundt, professed that this young science needed to rely on introspective observation (James, 1890/1950).

The focus on this mentalistic approach to attention continued with Wundt's students, Edward Bradford Titchener (1867–1927) at Cornell and Hugo Münsterberg (1863–1916), the German transplant, at Harvard. Whereas Titchener believed applied psychology was premature at best, Münsterberg became an important voice in the promotion of applied psychology, as noted throughout this entire text. Although he did little in the way of contributing to knowledge regarding consumer-related psychological topics, his promotion of applied psychology in business settings, in the face of the purists, provided significant professional support for those psychologists scientifically investigating applied business topics. Other students of Wundt's who reinforced the mentalistic focus but turned their interests toward the study of advertising included Edward Wheeler Scripture at Yale, Harlow Gale at the University of Minnesota, and Walter Dill Scott at Northwestern University.

The most dominant belief of the mentalists was ideomotor action. James (1890/1950) defined it this way:

> That every representation of a movement awakens in some degree the actual movement which is its object; and awakens it in a maximal degree whenever it is not kept from so doing by an antagonistic representation present simultaneously to the mind. (p. 526)

James viewed ideomotor action as immediate, that the representations of the movement in the mind remain for a matter of seconds (or less; James 1890/1950). In the early part of the new century, the mentalistic approach had two challenges: behaviorism and dynamic psychology. The two pioneering advocates for behaviorism in America were Edward Lee Thorndike (1874–1949) and John Broadus Watson (1878–1958). Each attempted to discredit the mentalistic approach (as well as the functional approach) by advocating for mechanistic view of behavior.

Dynamic psychology, reflecting the dynamic nature of human behavior, prescribed that people were better understood through instinctive, unconscious, biologically driven actions (Watson & Evans, 1981). The two leading proponents were Sigmund Freud (1856–1939) and William McDougall (1881–1938). Freud was first formally introduced to American psychology in 1909 during his famous visit to Clark University at the invitation of G. Stanley Hall. Dynamic psychologists viewed the conscious state as less important and less reliable than the unconscious state. McDougall (1912) was the first to propose that rather than being a study of consciousness, psychology was more accurately the study of behavior. He focused on the notion of innate instincts that drive humans (and animals) toward goals. Both Freud and McDougall believed that tension reduction was at the root of all motivation and behavior. Their perspectives were reflected in the nonrational school of advertising emerging at the same time (Kuna, 1976). Their theories were obviously antithetical to both the mentalistic and the mechanistic perspectives. This established interesting conflicts and debates, among both "pure" psychologists as well as those psychologists seeking to focus on applied settings.

As will become apparent, each of these explanatory perspectives on psychology, mentalism, behaviorism, and dynamic psychology had its adherents in scientific advertising. Exploring each of these three perspectives in turn, what follows next is a review of the thoughts and research of the early applied psychology pioneers who were motivated to understand consumer responses (i.e., response to advertising or personal selling).

CONSUMER PSYCHOLOGY'S ADHERENTS
OF THE MENTALISTIC PERSPECTIVE

E. W. Scripture and Harlow Gale

Although Edward Wheeler Scripture (1864–1943) and Harlow Gale (1862–1945) are not considered by some to be true forefathers of consumer psychology (see Benjamin, 2004), they appear to be the first psychologists interested in consumer-related issues, specifically consumer response to advertising (Gale, 1896; Scripture, 1895). As such, their work is part of the history of consumer psychology. In perhaps the first discussion of psychology as it pertains to advertising, Scripture (1895), implicitly using Wundt's notion of involuntary attention, denoted several psychological "laws" as they relate to advertising. For example, Scripture noted that "bigness" and the intensity of a sensation regulate attention to commercial promotion, noting the effectiveness of signage and lighting in stores and theaters. Scripture also considered feeling and expectations, proposing that "the degree of attention paid to an object depends on the intensity of the feeling aroused" and that the level of our expectations would determine the amount of attention paid to an object (Kuna, 1976). Here Scripture hinted at the notion of incongruity as attracting attention (e.g., putting notices upside down). Although Scripture discussed these psychological issues related to advertising and business, he left it up to others to do the scientific investigation.

Picking up Scripture's call for greater scientific investigation was Harlow Gale. Gale's undergraduate and graduate years were spent at Yale University, where he was exposed to the physiological psychology of George Ladd and the philosophical psychology of Noah Porter. It is likely that this exposure predisposed Gale toward the study of applied psychology (Kuna, 1976). Gale later traveled to Germany to study at Wundt's Institute for Experimental Psychology in Leipzig.

In 1894, Gale returned to the University of Minnesota as an instructor in psychology. It was there that Gale would spend the remainder of his brief and tumultuous academic career. He began a psychological laboratory at Minnesota and became the first person to do experiments in advertising psychology. Gale conducted what many argue to be the first actual scientific studies of advertising and consumer behavior. He began with a qualitative survey mailed to advertising professionals in which he posed a series of open-ended questions designed to provide practitioner opinions about the best means to attract attention and induce purchasing through advertising. The survey required significant effort and resulted in only a 10% response return. Gale then followed the survey with a series of experiments, using the tachistoscope procedure first learned from Wundt. The attentional issues he examined included relevant versus irrelevant materials (words and advertising "cuts" or representative images), large versus small style of type, the side of the page first attended to, exposure levels, and colors used in advertising. As he moved from one study to another, he discovered potential confounds and attempted to correct for them in subsequent studies. Perhaps of interest at the time, but not surprising today, he found that gender moderated some of his effects.

As Kuna (1976) reflected, Gale was the first to suggest that buying behavior was not as rational and conscious as classical economic theory would suggest. Indeed, Gale provided a mentalist perspective, suggesting that although there was evidence for an unconscious process, it was explained through involuntary attention and impulsive action, all within the law of ideomotor action. Gale's work drew on this law of ideomotor action, in particular the concept of suggestion, as an explanation for the unconscious effects of advertising. Gale replicated his studies in 1900 as did E. K. Strong, Jr. (1911 as cited in Kuna, 1976). His results, although first interpreted by other mentalists as consistent, eventually found a home with the dynamic theorists, suggesting a basic, unconscious, instinctive response.

Gale may have been the first to use the order-of-merit technique in determining the importance of message arguments. Gale would ask respondents to rank order brands based on the information provided in advertisements. E. K. Strong, Jr., first attributed this technique to James McKeen Cattell (Strong, 1911) but later reversed himself, giving credit for the method to Gale (Strong, 1938; see also Kuna, 1979). This method was widely used by subsequent researchers in advertising and business studies (but challenged by Adams, 1915).

Gale confined his work to conducting studies within his classroom and was not willing to establish relationships with members of the advertising industry. His primary interest in undertaking research in advertising psychology was to provide his students with a firsthand practical experience of the science of psychology. Throughout his life, perhaps as a function of socialist leanings, Gale (1896) was very critical of advertising, as the following quote recognizes:

> A vast amount of ingenuity and capital seem misspent in many of the modern schemes of advertising which appeal chiefly to novelty, curiosity, cheapness and excitement. (p. 69)

Gale's socialist political philosophy and controversial teaching practices ultimately resulted in his dismissal from the university in 1903 and the end of his academic career (Kuna, 1976). Gale's work was cited substantively by all of the major figures in advertising psychology through 1916.

Walter Dill Scott

At the turn of the century, the emphasis in psychology was transitioning from a mentalistic perspective, an ideational–cognitive explanation for unconscious phenomena, to the more dynamic notions of instinct and emotion. No more is this transition evidenced than in the long career of Walter Dill Scott (1869–1955). (See chap. 2 in this text for more information on Scott.)

In 1901, advertisers seeking help in applying psychology to advertising approached Scott while he was working as an instructor of psychology and pedagogy at Northwestern University. Although initially reluctant to delve into the "dirty" work of application, Scott saw this as an opportunity to test some of his theories and acquiesced. John Mahin, a prominent figure in advertising, offered to start a journal to publish Scott's articles and others on the scientific study of advertising. Scott published 33 columns over an 8-year span in *Mahin's Magazine*. These columns provided the foundation for Scott's first two books: *The Theory of Advertising* (Scott, 1903) and *Psychology of Advertising* (Scott, 1908). It was in the latter work that Scott brought the terms *psychology* and *advertising* together in a major publication. Both books held that affecting involuntary attention and using suggestion were the primary methods of advertising. His thoughts on suggestion in basic psychology became invited articles in the *Psychological Bulletin* (1910–1916). Scott believed that humans were susceptible to suggestion and that the force of suggestion could lead to action. Effective advertising, according to Scott, should suggest a course of action in a manner that ruled out other contrary actions.

Scott's efforts in the area of psychology and advertising earned him recognition among academicians and practitioners. He is credited with building the bridge for industrial and organizational psychologists between basic theory and applied research. His publications provided the foundation for a communications model to guide advertisers in their quest for understanding the minds and emotions of consumers. His reputation among academicians arose despite Scott's lack of efforts to sell his ideas on advertising psychology to his fellow psychologists— he never published his advertising-related studies in academic journals or presented this work at academic conferences. Scott confined his writings in psychological journals and presented at academic conferences on more traditional topics. However, he lectured to students on business and advertising psychology at Northwestern and as a guest lecturer. A student at one such guest lecture was Daniel Starch. As we shall soon see, influenced by Scott, Starch was to become a major influence in applied psychology.

Daniel Starch

Starch was educated at the University of Iowa and studied under Carl Seashore, who was a student of Scripture's at Yale. Seashore was a strict experimentalist and shared his value for objectivity with Starch. Starch spent most of his relatively short academic life at the University of Wisconsin (1908–1919) and at Harvard (1920–1926). Early in his career he became interested in measuring the effects of advertising on human behavior.

From 1908 until his eventual exit from academia, Starch published numerous studies on advertising. In 1910, he published a small volume entitled *Principles of Advertising—A Systematic Syllabus* (Starch, 1910). This book reflected the studies and principles he taught in his advertising psychology course. Starch divided the focus of this book into two parts: attracting attention and securing action. Although primarily focusing on the attention-oriented topics of Scott, Starch did add the notion of primacy and recency of advertisements as attracting more attention in the mind of the consumer. In 1914, he published *Advertising, Its Principles, Practice and Technique* (Starch, 1914), which established him as a leader in the new field. It not only addressed the psychology of advertising but went further to address other nonpsychological topics like advertising strategy and ethics. The book was again organized around attention and securing response. Several laws of attention were presented to include the laws of intensity, counterattraction, and contrast. In securing a response, Starch focused on argumentation and suggestion. It was under the latter that Starch introduced the strategy of stimulating consumer interest, which he later labeled "appeals" (e.g., Starch, 1923). Interest was an extension of attention, a kind of involuntary prolonged attention to an object. It was assumed that a reader of an ad would be more likely to attend and respond if the stimuli presented in it reflected the reader's interests. Starch suggested that illustrations could be used to stimulate interests. It is interesting to note the similarity of this topic with a more recent, often-studied consumer phenomenon, "involvement." Starch's book became a standard for the advertising practitioner. For every topic, Starch went to significant lengths to support his contentions with empirical evidence from his own studies or the work of other psychologists or practitioners.

In 1926, Starch became the director for the research program of the American Association of Advertising Agencies while still in academia. In 1932 Starch left academia completely and started Daniel Starch & Staff, a marketing research company providing subscribing companies with data on the effectiveness of their ads. Starch became well known for his methodological innovations, including the Starch Recognition Procedure in 1922, which measured consumer reading habits, and the Buyometer in 1948, which isolated the influence of magazine advertising on sales (Kuna, 1976). He retired in 1968. Part of his research efforts included experimentation with the recognition method (previously applied by Walter Dill Scott and Edward Strong under laboratory conditions). Among other projects, Starch also worked on qualitative studies on newspaper and magazine circulation and studies on duplication in circulation in popular media. He published several volumes devoted to analyses of several million inquiries received from magazine and newspaper advertisements. In recognition of his achievements, the American Marketing Association bestowed the Converse Award on him in 1953. Starch continued his pursuits in marketing research as late as 1973, working on measuring the correlation between the perception of advertising messages and the use and purchase of the brand or product advertised. Starch is credited with bringing about widespread adoption of copy research among advertisers.

One could say that Starch followed in the footsteps of Walter Dill Scott, carrying on the mentalist tradition. Like Scott, Starch never published his applied research in an academic journal. During his time in academia, he chose to reinforce his reputation as an experimental psychologist, publishing on traditional topics including a series of review articles for *Psychological Bulletin* (1911–1916) on the topic of auditory space.

In concluding this section reviewing the early pioneers of the mentalist school, we note that after a decrease in the subject of "attention" caused by the counter forces of behaviorism and instinct theories in psychology, consumer psychologists eventually returned to the mentalist approach in the 1970s with the significant focus on the study of consumer information processing and decision making. This focus is still prevalent in the work of many consumer scholars today.

EMERGENCE OF BEHAVIORISM AND DYNAMIC APPROACHES IN CONSUMER PSYCHOLOGY

Behaviorism in Advertising Research

Although the mentalistic approach was prevalent at the turn of the century, it was not without challenges. The notions of behaviorism were formally introduced to the psychology discipline in 1913. Thorndike's (1913) classic paper rejected ideomotor action and promoted new laws of habit, effect, and exercise, Watson released his treatise on behaviorism (1913), and Hollingworth's (1913) book reflected aspects of this new wave of thought. James McKeen Cattell (1860–1944) had earlier challenged the claim that introspection was the most valid methodology for the study of psychology. His focus was on reducing qualitative responses into quantitative data. As an example, his version of the order-of-merit method was strictly objective, requiring subjects to order stimuli on some criterion (Kuna, 1976, 1979). Cattell welcomed new faculty and students to Columbia in the early 1900s, especially those who had interests in applied psychology. Indeed, over time he recruited a remarkable group of faculty to include Robert Sessions Woodworth (1869-1962), Edward Lee Thorndike (1874–1949), Harry Levi Hollingworth (1880–1956), Edward Kellogg Strong, Jr. (1884–1963), and Albert T. Poffenberger (1885–1977).

Harry L. Hollingworth

Harry Levi Hollingworth emerged from his Nebraskan roots to pursue his graduate study under Cattell and Woodworth at Columbia. After completion of his studies, he began employment at Barnard College at Columbia University in 1909 and remained there until his retirement in 1946, serving for a period of time as the department head. Early on, the Advertising Men's League of New York City recognized his work. An association was formed that funded much of Hollingworth's studies as well as the fellowship of an aspiring student, E. K. Strong, Jr. Mainstream psychology was going through a transition from the focus on will, attention, apperception, and decision processes to observable behavioral responses.

Under the influence of his mentors, Cattell, Thorndike, and Robert Woodworth, Hollingworth first became immersed in behaviorism perspectives. Thorndike (1911) had introduced laws of effect (i.e., the role of "satisfiers" and "annoyers" as reinforcing and inhibiting behavior) and exercise (i.e., connection of a response to a situation). In applying these laws to advertising, Hollingworth believed that, rather than merely whether an ad attracted someone's attention, the true measure of the effectiveness of an ad is the actual purchase behavior. Hollingworth held that research conducted by advertisers was by its very nature flawed, because it didn't control for numerous extraneous variables (seasonal sales, competitor actions, amount of media, etc.). As a test, Hollingworth had advertisers send him ads to test in his lab. Interestingly, his lab tests involving the ads were highly correlated with the actual sales figures related to each ad.

In several studies, Hollingworth (e.g., 1911) examined the same variables considered by Gale and Scott (e.g., images, wording, size, color, position, type style) but considered the variance of the response rather than introspection. As his studies progressed, he considered individual differences such as gender and socioeconomic differences. In some cases his results contradicted the results of Gale and Scott. Hollingworth even constructed a panel of New York City residents, the first systematic effort to track consumption behavior (Kuna, 1976). In 1913, *Advertising and Selling: Principles of Appeals and Responses* was published (Hollingworth, 1913). This was the first systematic presentation of a behavioral approach to advertising. Building on his earlier work, his next book on the topic, *Advertising: Its Principles and Practice* (Tipper, Hollingworth, Hotchkiss, & Parsons, 1915) captured four principle functions of advertising: secure attention, hold attention, establish associations, and influence conduct by making associations dynamic. Hollingworth's objectivity in his empirical methods clearly influenced other younger applied psychologists. One of these was Edward K. Strong, Jr.

Edward K. Strong, Jr.

Strong's dissertation, *The Relative Merit of Advertisements* (Strong, 1911), was the first of its type in American psychology and represented a major breakthrough for using the order-of-merit method in an applied area of psychology (advertising research). Strong and Hollingworth took a more "molar" view of behaviorism, with a focus on complex stimuli as opposed to discrete stimuli. Rather than being preoccupied with people's thoughts, they measured what they believed were surrogates for behavioral response to advertising stimuli. They used the order-of-merit method as well as a refined recognition test that Strong (1914) developed in a reaction to the traditional mentalist recall measures. Strong believed that recognition was the best surrogate for actual purchase behavior and tested the influence of several presentation variables to include size and frequency and repetition intervals (e.g., Strong, 1912, 1913, 1914). He was one of the first applied psychologists to openly express his interests in applied psychology within academic circles. His ideas were published in mainstream psychological publications, including the *Journal of Philosophy, Psychology and Scientific Methods, Psychological Bulletin,* and *Psychological Review*.

John Broadus Watson

Before we leave behaviorism for dynamic psychology, it is important to reflect on the contribution to consumer psychology of John Broadus Watson. His treatise on behaviorism in 1913 earned him great acclaim as a psychologist, because he informed the world that psychology should be able to predict and control behavior. His studies would demonstrate the influence of association and conditioning on behavioral response (e.g. Watson & Raynor, 1920). He loudly and passionately disclaimed any reason for a mentalist perspective. He became the chair of the psychology department at Johns Hopkins University, was editor of the *Psychological Review*, and served as a president of the American Psychological Association in 1915. However, a scandal led to his termination and exit from academic life and a transition into a career in advertising. Stanley Resor, the "dean of American advertising," hired Watson to work at J. Walter Thompson in New York. Watson quickly found leverage for success in his psychological expertise. The business world embraced him, and his leadership and philosophy resulted in numerous successful campaigns. Resor showcased Watson in such a way that it legitimized the role of psychologists working in advertising.

Dynamic Psychology's Influence on Advertising Research

To understand how dynamicism eventually evolved from mentalistic and behavioralistic approaches, one needs to consider the influence Freud had at the time. Although Freud's psychology did not take hold immediately after his talk at Clark University, elements of the past now could be explained. Although Gale, Scott, and Starch all brought forth such notions of the unconscious as instincts, emotions, and interests, they continued to offer explanations consistent with a mentalistic outlook. Thorndike (1911) explained instinct and motivation as an inherited response tendency, adhering to a behavioral explanation where the catalyst for the response was a stimulus, not a condition of the being. It was McDougall who took direct aim in differentiating his purposive psychology from Watsonian behavioral psychology, as reflected in the following passage:

> The two principal alternative routes are (1) that of mechanistic science, which interprets all its processes as mechanical sequences of cause and effect, and (2) that of the sciences of mind, for which purposive striving is a fundamental category, which regard the process of purposive striving as radically different form mechanical sequence. (1923, p. vii)

Enter Robert S. Woodworth, a colleague of Thorndike and Hollingworth at Columbia. Woodworth is credited with putting *organism* in the stimulus-organism-response (S-O-R) model and thus finding a home for the contribution of motivation and instinct to human behavior. In his book *Dynamic Psychology* (Woodworth, 1918), Woodworth attempted to bring together (and even expand) the work of Freud and McDougall with mainstream psychology. It is important to note that the term *psychodynamic* often used to describe Freud and his adherents' theories, is not viewed as the same as *dynamic psychology*. Although both referred to notions of the unconscious mind, the former term typically includes identification of certain emotional conflicts and the resolution of these conflicts with specific defense mechanisms. Dynamic psychology's focus was on the influence of basic motivational drives on behavior. McDougall spoke of "drives" as strong and persistent stimulation, as initiating goal-directed actions through selective excitation of response mechanisms related to particular goals (e.g., consumption behaviors). Hollingworth and Strong, as colleagues of Woodworth, were naturally exposed to his thinking and his ideas regarding drives and organism responses, even his early ideas on psychoanalysis. Indeed, Hollingworth earlier had occasion to meet Jung and be exposed to Freud's ideas.

Although Hollingworth and Strong were reticent to adopt the dynamic approach, Hollingworth challenged business leaders to better understand the role of motives, interests, and instincts (Kuna, 1976). In Hollingworth's multiple-authored book, *Advertising: Its Principles and Practice* (Tipper et al., 1915), he provided a listing of a hierarchy of human needs (e.g., comfort, play, sociability, competition, shyness, revenge, pride) as representative of the individual, not a specific stimulus. He also revised his functions of advertising from his previous book to now include tabulating the fundamental needs of men and women, analyzing the satisfying power of the commodity in terms of the consumer's needs, establishing the association between need and commodity, and making the association dynamic. This was a remarkable change. Strong too experienced this transformation, and by 1925 his thinking culminated in his book *The Psychology of Selling and Advertising* (Strong, 1925).

Although Strong provided leadership in the adoption of the dynamic approach to applied psychology, his eventual fame came from a different applied focus. Although he continued to conduct research in advertising, he also served on the Committee on Classification of Personnel during World War I, described in previous chapters. In 1923, he published the Strong Vocational Interest Blank (SVIB), which became the most widely used career interest inventory in publication, a revision of which is still used today to help individuals understand their natural work propensities.

The influence of the work of Hollingworth and Strong on other I–O psychologists was considerable. Another Columbia colleague, Joseph V. Breitwieser (1915), made extensive reference to the work of both Hollingworth and Strong in his textbook *Psychological Advertising* (Breitwieser, 1915). Their work to adopt the order-of-merit method resulted in subsequent usage by many investigators. By 1923, Starch had conducted at least 34 studies using the method. It is interesting to note they each had different motivations for applied psychology, Hollingworth for the money through association with advertising practitioners, and Strong for the promotion and usefulness of applied psychology to better understand the practice of business (Poffenberger, 1957).

OTHER MAJOR CONTRIBUTORS OF THIS ERA

From 1915 to 1925, there was an explosion of applied research on several topics involving consumer response. Whereas the study of the consumer to this point primarily focused on response to advertising, over the next 15 years it spread to include personal selling and buying. The next generation of major contributors included Henry Foster Adams (1882–1973) from the University of Michigan, Harry Dexter Kitson (1886–1959) from Indiana University, and Albert T. Poffenberger, who took Woodworth's position at Columbia University.

In his book entitled *Advertising and Its Mental Laws* (1916a), Adams appears to be carrying on the mentalist tradition by specifically citing the work of those we've previously discussed: Gale, Scott, Hollingworth, Strong, and Starch. However, Adams himself conducted numerous empirical studies. Adams believed in testing factors in isolation applying a "mathematical exactness" in examining various elements found in advertising. Although he respected their contributions, Adams was especially critical of Hollingworth and Strong's use of the order-of-merit method (Adams, 1915). In *Advertising and Its Mental Laws* he repeated his criticism but also devoted one chapter on the use of statistical tools to examine response to advertising (correlation and variance) and another on experimentation in advertising.

One important contribution from Adams' book was his ordering of certain advertising stimulus factors, because he perceived them related to key response variables. Table 11.1 lists these factors. Much of what we study today in advertising relationships concerns these same response factors (e.g., attention, memory, association, perception including aesthetics) as influenced by many of the same advertising elements (e.g., repetition, novelty, interests or as we term it today "involvement," primacy and recency, vividness, type of appeal, context effects).

TABLE 11.1
Summary of Adam's Response and Stimulus factors

Response Factor	Stimulus Factor
Attention	Parts of the page, attention value of color, size, shape, repetition, novelty, pictures, interests, size of type, kind of type, borders
Association	How associations are formed, effect of recency, frequency, primacy and vividness as principles of connection, relative strength of forward and backward associations
Memory	Size, frequency of insertion, position, type of appeal, memorability of different things in the ad
Perception	Effect of surroundings on the same page and opposite page, effect of previous ads for the product, reading and legibility, sizes and kinds of type
Aesthetics	Color preference, color harmony, proportion

Many of these elements are carefully examined today by practitioners in eliciting consumer response to advertising, promotion and packaging (e.g., concept tests of color, size, shape, font, proportion, reading, and legibility).

In *Advertising and Its Mental Laws*, Adams (1916a) also considered the effectiveness of different media. He concluded the book with chapters on fusion (a nod to behaviorism) and action. The book, for the most part, was still a tribute to the mentalistic approach. His concluding chapter dealt with the empirical findings related to gender differences. He noted that women paid attention more to size and personal appeals and observed events whereas men attended more to successive presentations, pictures, industrial-job relatedness, and recommendations of authorities. Of peculiar interest, he found that memory tests contradicted the attention effects. For example, women had better memory with successive presentations and pictures, whereas men had better memory based on size of ad and for trade names.

These comprehensive books by Adams (1915) and also Starch (1914), each promoting the importance of the empirical results to date, set the tone for much work to follow. In a short period of time following these books, numerous studies were reported. For example, Adams (1916b), still maintaining the mentalist approach, went on to study the relative memory for duplication and variation and sizes of ads (1917), as well as the effect of order of presentation (1920). Others, notably Heller and Brown (1916) in their study on memory for streetcar signage, Laslett (1918) in a study of relevance of illustrations, Hotchkiss and Franken (as cited in Poffenberger, 1925) in their study of attention factors, and Turner (1922) in his examination of testimonials used in advertising, continued the mentalist tradition. However, a number of applied researchers were beginning to use more objective measures reflecting a clear leaning toward the behavioral approach. Perhaps the most prolific was Albert Poffenberger, who examined face types (Poffenberger & Franken, 1923), return of coupon resulting from advertising (Poffenberger, 1923a), belief consistency with advertisement (1923b), and the value of lines used in advertising (Poffenberger & Barrows, 1924).

As previously noted, at this time psychologists began to consider other aspects of consumer behavior. For example, Geissler (1917) pointed out that consumers needed to be approached in more ways than just advertising and began to study processing that occurred in consideration of purchase. Heller (1919) studied the impact of package labels on purchasing, whereas Kitson (1923) authored a conceptual article examining the consumer's role in market strategy. Laird (1923) compared demographic and socioeconomic differences in the selection of toothpaste, and Hotchkiss and Franken (1923) considered the importance of brand familiarity.

Henry Dexter Kitson helped set the stage for this focus on other aspects of the consumer in his book titled The *Mind of the Buyer,* published in 1921b. His first chapter examines the "stream of thought" in a sale, prescribing six stages in a sale: attention, interest, desire, confidence, decision and action, and satisfaction. The book clearly takes an eclectic approach, citing researchers and theorists from all three schools of psychology: mentalist, behaviorist, and dynamic. Kitson contributed to the study of advertising as well, especially with his studies regarding illustrations within advertising (1921a) and more specifically the use of color (Kitson, 1922a), various art forms (1922b), package illustrations (Kitson & Campbell, 1924), and illustrations containing people (Kitson & Allen, 1925). This strong focus on illustration is one of the first examples of programmatic research.

To complete this historical review of the first 30 years of consumer psychology, one must return to the work of Albert T. Poffenberger (1885–1977) to close this period of time. Poffenberger studied at Columbia under Cattell and Woodworth, which reflects his lifelong interest in physiological psychology and objective response. His dissertation was titled *Reaction Time to Retinal Stimulation* (Wentzel, 1979). He never lost this interest and continued in this vein through much of his career. However, his strongest interest was in the area of applied psychology (see 1921 edition of *American Men in Science*).

After conducting a number of studies, Poffenberger published the book entitled *Psychology in Advertising* in 1925 (Poffenberger, 1925). This imposing tome is a remarkable recapitulation of all the work up to that time. Aside from a thorough review of traditional subjects like memory and attention and some focus on methodology, statistics, measurement, and appeal, Poffenberger provided new reviews in comprehension, "feeling tone," attitude, human desires, and individual and group differences among others. Although this book formally ends this historical review, it is important to note that shortly after this book, Poffenberger published *Applied Psychology: Its Principles and Methods* (1927). Here he defined applied psychology as "every situation in which human behavior is involved and where economy of human energy is of practical importance." In the section on advertising and selling, he explores the desires, habits, and logic of the consumer and reviews the state of psychology as it has been applied to advertising and selling strategies to date. Poffenberger contributed heavily to the service of the discipline, culminating in his election to the presidency of the APA in 1934. From 1943 to 1944, he served as president of the American Association of Applied Psychology. In this position he successfully spearheaded a campaign for the dissolution of the organization to join forces with the APA.

CONCLUSION: HOW CONSUMER PSYCHOLOGY HAS EVOLVED

This review sought to bring out two points of emphasis regarding the roots of consumer psychology. First, consumer psychology has evolved as the larger domain of general psychology has evolved. This is evident in the transition of schools of thought, from the early mentalist approach of Wundt and his students to a rejection of mentalism in favor of behavioral and dynamic approaches. These three schools are all important in the investigation of consumer behavior as we research it today. The second point of emphasis is that these early psychologists built off of each other's work and that much of what they studied are topics that we're still engrossed with today and expect to be for many years to come.

Whereas the first three decades saw a pioneering effort to examine consumer behavior from a psychological perspective, the next three decades built on the work of these early contributors. Applied psychologists continued to investigate a number of topics related to consumer response, primarily the response to varied advertising stimuli and, secondarily, to personal selling. Advertising response studies explored topics to include memory (recall and recognition), attitude (defined very broadly), preference, evoked emotion, perception (visual vs. audio stimuli), and technical factors like the amount of color used in an ad, typefaces, amount of copy, ad positioning, and the impact of other ads in the advertising context. The subsequent decades were also characterized by advances in methods of inquiry to include attitude assessment, captured eye movement, qualitative interviewing with quantitative analysis, split-run copy, and even galvanic skin response.

Forming Associations

It's hard to know what psychological discipline "owned" consumer psychology in the first 60 years. In developing the sketches of the pioneers described above, we thought it was apparent that they viewed themselves as "applied" psychologists. The words *industrial* and *organizational* rarely appeared. However, because of the broader interests of individuals like Münsterberg, Scott, Strong, and Poffenberger, who as a group moved far beyond a singular focus on advertising and selling response, the study of the consumer was brought into the larger framework of the study of business. Thus consumer psychology for many years was labeled a part of industrial and organizational psychology (APA Division 14, now known as the Society for Industrial and Organizational Psychology). The reader is referred to several early industrial psychology texts that included advertising (e.g., Burtt, 1948; Hepner, 1931; Jenkins, 1935), as well as more recent texts (e.g., Fleishman & Bass, 1974).

In the 1950s, an informal group of applied psychologists known as the "headshrinkers" came into existence in Chicago. The group consisted of applied psychologists primarily working for advertising agencies, polling companies, and marketing research firms. They met on a regular basis and before long they included academics in their meetings. In 1959, they approached the APA Council of Representatives with a proposal for a new APA Division of Consumer Psychology. This proposal was met with mixed reactions, and action was postponed until an inquiry into the role of Division 14 was considered. Some of the leadership in Division 14 resisted this movement and attempted to discuss a widening of the scope of their division. Moreover, a motion was proposed and voted down to further study the divisional structure of APA. Over the objections of Division 14, the APA Council on September 6, 1960, approved the formation of the Division of Consumer Psychology. The proposal won by a one-vote margin. Today, with a membership of more than 600 and a sponsored research journal, the *Journal of Consumer Psychology*, the Society for Consumer Psychology symbolizes the independence of this growing discipline.

Today, consumer psychologists continue to investigate intriguing questions regarding consumer psychological response, both in academia and in the world of practice. Many of the questions investigated today stem directly from the work of these early pioneers that dates back to the turn of the 19th century. No matter the means by which consumer psychologists associate with each other today, history will always be indebted to these early "applied psychologists" who sought to understand the psychology of the consumer.

REFERENCES

Adams, H. F. (1915). The adequacy of the laboratory test in advertising. *Psychological Review, 22,* 402–422.

Adams, H. F. (1916a). *Advertising and its mental laws.* New York: Macmillan.

Adams, H. F. (1916b). The relative memory values of duplication and variation in advertising. *Journal of Philosophy, Psychology and Scientific Methods, 18,* 141–152.

Adams, H. F. (1917). The memory value of mixed sizes of advertising. *Journal of Experimental Psychology, 2,* 448–465.

Adams, H. F. (1920). The effect of climax and anti-climax order of presentation on memory. *Journal of Applied Psychology, 4,* 330–338.

Benjamin, L. T., Jr. (2004). Science for sale: Psychology's earliest adventures in American advertising. In J. Williams, W. Lee, & C. Haugtvedt (Eds.), *Diversity in advertising* (pp. 21–39). Mahwah, NJ: Lawrence Erlbaum Associates.

Breitwieser, J. V. (1915). *Psychological advertising.* Colorado Springs, CO: Apex.

Burtt, H. E. (1948). *Applied psychology.* New York: Prentice-Hall.

Fleishman, E. A., & Bass, A. R. (1974). *Studies in personnel and industrial psychology* (3rd ed.). Homewood, IL: Dorsey Press.

Freud, S. (1969). *A general introduction to psychoanalysis.* New York: Pocket Books. (Original work published 1924)

Gale, H. (1896). On the psychology of advertising. In H. Gale (Ed.), *Psychological studies* (pp. 39–69). Minneapolis: Author.

Geissler, L. R. (1917). Association-reactions applied to ideas of commercial brands of familiar articles. *Journal of Applied Psychology, 1,* 275–290.

Heller, W. S. (1919). Analysis of package labels. *University of California Publications in Psychology, 3*(2), 61–72.

Heller, W. S., & Brown, W. (1916). Memory and association in the case of street-car advertising cards. *University of California Publications in Psychology, 2*(4), 267–275.

Hepner, H. W. (1931). *Psychology applied to life and work.* New York: Macmillan.

Hollingworth, H. H. (1911). Experimental studies in judgment: Judgments of the comic. *Psychological Review, 8,* 132–156.

Hollingworth, H. H. (1913). *Advertising and selling: Principles of appeals and responses.* New York: Appleton.

Hotchkiss, G. B., & Franken, R. B. (1923). *The leadership of advertised brands.* New York: Doubleday, Page.

James, W. (1950). *The principles of psychology* (2 volumes). New York: Dover. (Original work published 1890)

Jenkins, J. G. (1935). *Psychology in business and industry: An introduction to psychotechnology.* New York: Wiley.

Kitson, H. D. (1921a). Minor studies in the psychology of advertising from the psychological laboratory of Indiana University. *Journal of Applied Psychology, 5,* 5–13.

Kitson, H. D. (1921b). *The mind of the buyer: The psychology of selling.* New York: Macmillan.

Kitson, H. D. (1922a). Color in magazine advertising. *Journal of Applied Psychology, 6,* 64–66.

Kitson, H. D. (1922b). Minor studies in the psychology of advertising—Development of art forms in magazine advertising. *Journal of Applied Psychology, 6,* 59–64.

Kitson, H. D. (1923). Understanding the consumer's mind. *Annals of the American Academy of Political and Social Science, 110,* 131–138.

Kitson, H. D., & Allen, I. (1925). Pictures of people in magazine advertising. *Journal of Applied Psychology, 9,* 367–370.

Kitson, H. D., & Campbell, J. J. (1924). The package as a feature in magazine advertising. *Journal of Applied Psychology, 8,* 444–445.

Kuna, D. P. (1976). *The psychology of advertising, 1896–1916.* Unpublished doctoral dissertation, University of New Hampshire.

Kuna, D. P. (1979). Early advertising applications of the Gale-Cattell order-of-merit method. *Journal of History in Behavioral Science, 15,* 38–46.

Laird, D. A. (1923). The basis of toothpaste sales in representative communities. *Journal of Applied Psychology, 2,* 173–177.

Laslett, H. R. (1918). The value of relevancy in advertisement illustrations. *Journal of Applied Psychology, 2,* 270–279.

McDougall, W. (1912). *Psychology, the study of behaviour.* New York: Holt.

McDougall, W. (1923). *Outline of psychology.* New York: Scribner.

Oliver, J. W. (1956). *History of American technology.* New York: Ronald Press.

Poffenberger, A. T. (1923a). The return coupon as a measure of advertising efficiency. *Journal of Applied Psychology, 7,* 202–208.

Poffenberger, A. T. (1923b). The conditions of belief in advertising. *Journal of Applied Psychology, 7,* 1–9.

Poffenberger, A. T. (1925). *Psychology in advertising.* Chicago & New York: Shaw.

Poffenberger, A. T. (1927). *Applied psychology: Its principles and methods.* New York: Appleton.

Poffenberger, A. T. (1957). Henry Levi Hollingworth: 1880–1956. *American Journal of Psychology, 70,* 138.

Poffenberger, A. T., & Barrows, B. E. (1924). The feeling value of lines. *Journal of Applied Psychology, 8,* 187–205.

Poffenberger, A. T., & Franken, R. B. (1923). A study of the appropriateness of type faces. *Journal of Applied Psychology, 7,* 312–329.

Scripture, E. W. (1895). *Thinking, felling, doing.* New York: Flood & Vincent.

Scott, W. D. (1903). *Theory of advertising.* Boston: Small, Maynard.

Scott, W. D. (1908). *The psychology of advertising.* Boston: Small, Maynard.

Scott, W. D. (invited articles 1910–1916). Suggestion. *Psychological Bulletin, 7*(November 1910): 369–372; *8*(September 1911): 309–311; *9*(July 1912): 269–271; *10*(July 1913): 269–270; *11*(July 1914): 250–252; *12*(June 1915): 225–226; *13*(July 1916): 266–268.

Starch, D. (1910). *Principles of advertising: A systematic syllabus.* Madison, WI: University Cooperative.

Starch, D. (invited articles 1911–1916). Auditory space. *Psychological Bulletin, 8* (July 1911): 232–233; *9* (July 1912): 254–255; *12* (June 1915): 213–214; *13* (July 1916): 264–265.

Starch, D. (1914). *Advertising: Its principles, practice and technique.* New York: Appleton.

Starch, D. (1923). *Principles of advertising.* Chicago: Shaw.

Strong, E. K., Jr. (1911). The relative merit of advertisements. In *Columbia contributions to philosophy and psychology* (Vol. 19, pp. 4–5). New York: Science Press.

Strong, E. K., Jr. (1912). The effect of length of series upon recognition memory. *Psychological Review, 19,* 447–462.

Strong, E. K., Jr. (1913). The effect of time-interval upon recognition memory. *Psychological Review, 20,* 339–372.

Strong, E. K., Jr. (1914). The effect of size of advertisements and frequency of their presentation. *Psychological Review, 2,* 136–152.

Strong, E. K., Jr. (1925). *The psychology of selling and advertising.* New York: McGraw-Hill.

Strong, E. K., Jr. (1938). *Psychological aspects of business.* New York: McGraw-Hill.

Thorndike, E. L. (1911). *Animal intelligence.* New York: Macmillan.

Thorndike, E. L. (1913). Ideo-motor action. *Psychological Review, 20,* 91–106.

Tipper, H., Hollingworth, H. L., Hotchkiss, G. B., & Parsons, F. A. (1915). *The principles of advertising.* New York: Ronald Press.

Turner, E. M. (1922). The testimonial as an advertising appeal. *Journal of Applied Psychology, 6,* 192–197.

Watson, J. B. (1913). Psychology as the behaviorist views it. *Psychological Review, 10,* 158–177.

Watson, J. B., & Raynor, R. (1920). Conditioned emotional reactions. *Journal of Experimental Psychology, 3,* 1–14.

Watson, R. I., & Evans, R. B. (1981). *The great psychologists: A history of psychological thought* (5th ed.). New York: Harper Collins.

Wentzel, B. M. (1979). Albert T. Poffenberger (1885–1977). *American Psychologist, 34*(1), 88–90.

Wiebe, R. H. (1967). *The search for order, 1877–1920.* New York: Hill & Wang.

Woodworth, R. S. (1918). *Dynamic psychology.* New York: Columbia University Press.

12

The Expanding Role of Workplace Training: Themes and Trends Influencing Training Research and Practice

Kurt Kraiger
Colorado State University

J. Kevin Ford
Michigan State University

Workplace training is a systematic approach to learning and development to improve individual, team, and organizational effectiveness (Goldstein & Ford, 2002). Industrial–organizational (I–O) psychologists have discussed the importance of training from the earliest works by Münsterberg (1910, 1913). Since that time, I–O psychologists have played various roles relevant to improving the quality and effectiveness of training, including research on learning and transfer, development of methods of training measurement, enhancement of methods for training design and delivery, and positioning of the training function within organizations (Ford, 2000). Training research has focused on theoretical perspectives of what is meant by learning and transfer as well as research on the factors that affect learning during training and the transfer of training to the job. As to training practice, I–O psychologists have developed systematic processes for conducting pretraining needs analysis and posttraining evaluation of training as well as advanced new methods for training design and delivery.

This chapter describes the expanding role of workplace training within I–O psychology. For this task, we identified key chapters, books, and other resources on training from approximately 1910 to the present day. In particular, we focused on changes to the understanding and practice of training across four different eras relevant to managing work: (a) the scientific management era (circa 1900–1930); (b) the human relations era (circa 1930–1960), (c) the participative management era (circa 1960–1990), and (d) the strategic learning era (circa 1990 to present). We contend that these time periods represent not only fundamentally different perspectives of organizing work but also different perspectives on what is meant by learning and development.

Our approach for examining the expanding role of training centered on identifying, for each era, what training "looked" like (e.g., what was the focus of training? who was being trained? what were the typical goals of training?), what learning theories and perspectives were dominant, and what advances were made in training research and practice. After examining each era in detail, we provide an analysis of key trends or themes in training across eras. This analysis leads to a discussion of both potential triggers for advances and innovations in training theory and of the influence of I–O psychology on research and practice in training.

THE SCIENTIFIC MANAGEMENT ERA (1900–1930)

The move from craft to mass production led to major changes in the design and control of work (Morgan, 1997). As noted in previous chapters, between about 1900 and 1930, technological advancements (e.g., the assembly line and the proliferation of simple machines) and principles of scientific management merged to create a vision of workplace efficiency (Taylor, 1911). Supervisors were expected to closely supervise the work to ensure that work standards were maintained and train the worker to follow the prescribed way in which work was to be done. To oversimplify, machines existed to simplify and standardize work, and workers existed to supplement what machines could not do on their own (see chap. 10 in this text).

An examination of early works in I–O psychology by Münsterberg (1913), Myers (1925), Burtt (1929), and Viteles (1932) highlighted the importance of efficiency in the workplace as evidenced through their emphasis on job design, work conditions, and selection procedures:

> If the psychologists succeed in fundamentally improving the conditions of labor, the increased efficiency of the individual will promote such an enriched and vivified economic life that ultimately an increase in the number of laborers needed will result. (Münsterberg, 1913, p. 144)

The focus on efficiency was also the dominant force evident in descriptions of what was being trained and how training was being conducted in the workplace. During the same time period, experimental psychologists held a similar view of human learners. Edward Thorndike had completed his dissertation on animal learning in 1898, initiating the study of stimulus–response associations that became known as behaviorism. Beginning primarily with Thorndike, and continuing through the works of Watson, Hull, Spence, and others, psychologists used both animal and human subjects to study stimulus–response bonds that shape behavior (see Leahey, 2002, for a review). The notion that behavior may be shaped by the careful arrangement of learning conditions and reinforcements designed to elicit the correct sequence of desired behaviors closely parallels the view of early I–O psychologists regarding the role and methods of training.

What Did Training Look Like?

During the 1800s, much of job training was accomplished by one of two means—formal apprenticeship in craft jobs such as carpentry or plumbing and vocational training in either technical schools or institutes. By 1886, various forms of manual training schools had been established in Philadelphia, New York, Baltimore, Cincinnati, Cleveland, Toledo, Chicago, and Omaha (Steinmetz, 1967). By the turn of the century, larger businesses such as Westinghouse, General Electric, and International Harvester were developing "factory schools" to conduct job-specific training on site. Another innovation was vestibule training in which machinery and work sites were created in a training room near the production floor, enabling highly skilled operators or supervisors to train small groups of workers in somewhat controlled conditions (Smith, 1942). In each instance, training "looked" like the job; whether one-on-one or in small groups, the focus of training was demonstrating procedures for safe, efficient work. Training preceded one step at a time, demonstrating and explaining until the step was done correctly (McCord, 1976).

World War I created the need for immediate training of 500,000 workers for almost 100 trade jobs (Steinmetz, 1967). To provide standardization in training, the head of the educational and training section of the Emergency Fleet Corporation of the United States Shipping Board (Charles R. "Skipper" Allen) promoted a four-step method of job instruction: show, tell, do, check (Steinmetz, 1967). By the end of World War I, several principles of on-the-job training were established: (a) Training should be done by supervisors, (b) training should be done on the job, (c) job responsibilities should be established prior to instruction, and (d) supervisors should be instructed how to train (McCord, 1976). Thus, in a relatively short time, much of the responsibility for job training moved from off-site vocational training programs to the purview of knowledgeable supervisors.

Training content expanded as well. Viteles (1932) divided his treatment of training into two types—general training and job training. General training consisted of instruction in plant policies, academic subjects related to work, plant organization, and other topics that were broadly cultural or developmental in character. The purpose of "job training" was to promote trade mastery (from short programs to apprenticeship programs of many years). The Viteles book and other textbooks of this era focused almost exclusively on this second type of training—job training for mastery.

The objectives of job training were twofold: to speed skill acquisition in newcomer and experienced workers and to ensure standardization of performance given stringent work requirements. Research on learning could assist in attaining those objectives. As noted by Münsterberg (1913),

> Every form of economic labor in the workshop and in the factory, in the field and in the mine, in the store and in the office, must first be learned. How far do the experiments of the psychologist offer suggestions for securing the most economic method of learning practical activities? (pp. 144–145)

According to Münsterberg, the important role of training was the standardization of activities across workers, combined with finding methods for improved efficiency. He contended that there must be methods of teaching "muscular work" that are economically more advantageous than the typical approach of leaving this to chance. The most typical instructional approach at that time was learning from other more experienced people, what would later be referred to as "on-the-job training." The challenge, though, was that each experienced worker might have different ways of doing the work. Thus, there was a perceived need for not only optimizing but also standardizing instruction. For example, Myers (1925) noted,

> Who can doubt the importance of determining such undeniably wasteful methods of movement and of preventing the novice from falling into such bad habits of work? Yet how little provision is made of training the worker scientifically, i.e. systematically! In the case of sport, e.g. ... in riding, skating or golfing, few of us would dispense with the instruction of a professional expert. But in the case of industrial work, the novice has in by far the majority of cases to pick up his methods as best he can, perhaps learning from a worker of experience who may, nevertheless, have acquired bad habits of movement, or from one who, if he as acquired good ones, may be quite useless as an instructor. (p. 100)

As one example, Myers (1925) detailed a training program for chocolate factory workers. Researchers photographed the movements of an electric glowlamp attached to the worker's hand to show new and experienced workers that an easier, rhythmic action required much less effort and fatigue and increased output. After 3 months of training in these principles, the workers were producing on average 88% more than workers using the old method in the original room.

What Learning Theories and Perspectives Are Applied?

Early I–O textbooks typically had one chapter on training or learning at the workplace (Burtt, 1929, is the exception with two chapters). For example, as noted by McGehee (1949), Viteles (1932) devoted only 7% of his textbook on training, in contrast to 34% on selection and 19% on issues of fatigue. Nevertheless, these early authors showed an appreciation for learning theory and held a very optimistic outlook on how learning principles from basic research could be applied directly to improving training practices. For example, Burtt (1929) believed that psychology and education had much to offer for improving training, going so far as to note that

> it is logical to apply the general principles which we have found in these fields to the industrial situation. A workman learning to operate a riveting machine is subject to the same fundamental psychological laws as an animal learning to escape from a problem box or a child learning the multiplication table. (p. 15)

Viteles (1932) focused more on the importance of practice in the acquisition of skill and used the learning or practice curve as an example of how practice can lead to the systematic acquisition of skill. He provided examples of practice curves—some from what he called the "classic" experiment by Bryan and Harter in 1897 on improvement in telegraphy over 32-week period. He discussed why learning plateaus occur; one line of reasoning is that the plateau is inherent in the learning process, whereas another point of view is that it represents a temporary failure in attention and effort.

What Key Advances Were Made in Training Research and Practice?

The key advance to training research and practice is evident in this statement by Viteles (1932):

> Training is among the principal factors in increasing efficiency and improving individual adjustment in industry. A well-organized training program, based on a sound analysis of the job and applying well-established learning principles, enables the worker to employ the most effective methods in the performance of his task. Systematic instruction speeds the rate of acquisition of skills and thereby reduces the time required for training. (p. 393)

Thus, the progress during this era was on systematically examining performance on the job and conducting empirical testing of how much efficiency is gained through by training compared with trial-and-error learning. Many studies are cited to show how quickly systematically trained workers can achieve high levels of performance over other workers. Learning curves were seen as a critical way of highlighting changes in performance over time after training. Myers (1925) discussed the systematic training and evaluation of workers packing chocolates into boxes. The researchers found no differences between trained workers and the best untrained workers in time for folding sheets and weighing, but there were time savings for filling trays (47 minutes for trained to 62 minutes for untrained), packing boxes, cording, ribboning, and wrapping. Overall, the untrained group of five took 324 minutes to do all these steps on average and the trained group did it in 256 minutes—21% greater efficiency. The evaluation not only showed an overall effect for training but, due to the categorization of tasks, was able to pinpoint in which part of the operation the greatest gain in efficiency would occur due to the training and where the time interval would be the same for the two groups.

In addition, there are hints and encouragement for research to advance the field of training. Myers (1925) noted that in training, the mental differences of workers are so great that different methods of instruction must be used. Myers contended that such important individual mental differences are a special concern of industrial psychology. So, although we have no empirical data reported here, we do have some of the first notions of aptitude—treatment interactions in training and the need for adaptable trainers.

Viteles (1932) contended that training could benefit from incorporating more psychological principles of learning into the development of skills. In discussing a study of motormen in the electric railway industry, he referred to the interference of habits on the acquisition of new skills and discussed what would later be called automaticity, noting that the experienced motorman can operate the streetcar "without the intervention of consciousness."

HUMAN RELATIONS ERA (1930–1960)

The human relations era stretched from the early 1930s until the late 1950s. The beginning of the 1930s was marked by the Great Depression. Emphasis on industrial training waned, because drawing from the large numbers of unemployed workers provided an easy alternative to improving the skills of inefficient workers. On the other hand, federal legislation during this period generated funding for public training in handicrafts such as leatherwork, weaving, and chair caning (Steinmetz, 1967).

Within organizations, this era was marked by a growing appreciation for the importance of worker attitudes and motivation as well as for the changing role of the supervisor and the increasing complexity of work. We think of the Hawthorne studies of the 1930s (Roethlisberger & Dickson, 1939) as a catalyst for highlighting the critical nature of worker attitudes. (See also chap. 14 in this text.) However, the link between recognition for good work and incentives to perform well in the future was already being discussed (Lee, 1932; Miles, 1932), whereas Viteles (1932) was calling for interventions to be evaluated not only on the criterion of economic return but in terms of their impact on worker attitudes and morale.

Regardless of the trigger, it is clear that workers' psychological states were becoming increasingly important to both I–O researchers and industry leaders. At the same time, the supervisor's role was changing. The growing popularity of personnel management (see Scott, Clother, Mathewson, & Spriegel, 1941, as well as a summary by Gillespie, 1988) shifted much of the responsibility for hiring and placing workers away from supervisors. Jobs were becoming increasingly complex, and supervisors were no longer expected to know everything about the jobs of their subordinates (Tiffin, 1942). World War II was also a significant force in redefining the supervisory role as large numbers of young men were drafted into the armed forces. As work in the defense industries expanded, the jobs of both laborers and supervisors were often filled by individuals new to those roles (Steinmetz, 1967). Because these new supervisors often lacked technical knowledge of jobs below them, they required new methods for influencing and motivating workers.

The International Harvester Company was one of the first industrial companies to recognize this need and established a central school in Chicago to train supervisors from their plants in "human relations" and organizational skills. This program was described by Fleishman, Harris, and Burtt (1955). The effects of this training program on the leader behavior and attitudes of supervisors were evaluated immediately after training and at various intervals after the supervisors returned from the training to their plants (Fleishman, 1953). The results showed that positive results may be obtained immediately after training, but these effects are significantly influenced by the "leadership climate" in the plants to which these supervisors returned.

Whereas the changing role of the supervisor and the emerging professionalism of the personnel function characterized the beginning of this era, the end was marked with new theories of the multidimensional roles of management (e.g., Argyris, 1957; McGregor, 1960; Simon, 1957). These changes had implications for both training content and the emergence of training specialists.

In other areas of psychology, behavioral learning paradigms still dominated. Although in his day Edward Tolman was not as influential as contemporaries such as Clark Hull and Kenneth Spence, he did play an influential role in the development of cognitive behaviorism (Leahey, 2002), a predecessor of modern cognitive psychology. Tolman used terms such as *latent learning* and *cognitive maps* to describe the learning behavior of rats in the absence of a reward (Hothersall, 1995). By the 1950s, even the writings of B. F. Skinner recognized the importance of mental activity. Although Skinner believed in stimulus–response bonds like his behaviorist predecessors, he also accepted mental (verbal) representations of the environment as a potential shaper of human behavior (Skinner, 1957). Thus, in both organizational practices and the study of behavior, writers and theorists were increasingly accepting of the influence that human thoughts, actions, and attitudes had on resulting performance.

What Did Training Look Like?

The emerging appreciation of the importance of worker attitudes can be seen by contrasting two definitions of training. Tiffin (1942) defined training as "the process by which, through some form of instruction, the necessary responses for correctly performing a job are developed" (p. 185). Five years later, Ghiselli and Brown (1948) defined training as "a means of adjusting the worker in the working environment in such a way as to bring about the greatest returns to both the worker and the organization" (p. 308). Ghiselli and Brown (1948) discussed "adjustment" issues extensively, suggesting the need to consider both work-related and personal barriers to successful performance.

Both Tiffin (1942) and Ghiselli and Brown (1948) questioned the utility of traditional on-the-job instruction, noting the increasing complexity of work and questioning the ability of the supervisor to do all necessary training. Tiffin (1942) wrote about training coming of age, particularly in the formalization or recognition of the role of training expert:

> Just as scientific management has found that experts should supplement the work of foreman in making job analyses and setting rates, so also management is finding that the use of experts in training is advantageous as a supplement to the work of foreman. (p. 185)

The training expert was an individual who worked with personnel and had the responsibility for analyzing the job (by reviewing job descriptions, conducting time-and-motion studies, or observing the job first hand), planning training programs, preparing course outlines, selecting and preparing trainers, and publicizing training internally (Planty, McCord, & Efferson, 1948). Rarely were these responsibilities handled by or assisted by I–O psychologists. A work analysis of industrial psychologists in this era (Canter, 1948) ranked "education and training" as one of the least performed functions. Persons responsible for the training function were often found within the company, but Steinmetz (1967) noted that the initial process of selecting training directors was often "crude, arbitrary, and fortuitous." Nonetheless, as early as 1944, the first national conference of training directors was held in Columbus, Ohio. In addition, the American Society of Training Directors (ASTD) was formed in 1945, growing out of informal meetings of training directors in the petroleum industry earlier in the decade. The first ASTD convention was held in Chicago and attended by 56 of the 200 members of the new society. Thomas Keaty, of Esso Standard in Baton Rouge, had earlier lobbied for the need for a national society of training directors and was elected as ASTD's first president (Steinmetz, 1967). The society's name was changed to the American Society of Training and Development in 1959.

The emergence of training as a profession was slow but had significant consequences. A review by McGehee (1949) cited results from a 1946 survey of the National Industrial Conference Board, showing that only 29% of the companies responding to the survey had a separate training function. Even then, most of the training was conducted by foremen or experienced workers without the assistance of a formal training function. However, the shift in responsibility for training from the supervisor to the training department had several profound consequences, including the emergence of new training methods (other than show-and-tell) and the increased importance for training measurement to link training content to job requirements and to show that training had an impact on job performance.

On-the-job training remained a predominant training method, but off-the-job training was becoming increasingly popular, especially for supervisors. Tiffin (1942) suggested job rotation as a new training method (particularly for college graduates, characterized as book smart but lacking in vocational skills). Tiffin noted the effects of increasing job complexity, increased technology, and the passage of labor laws as factors complicating the role of supervisor, necessitating the need for more training. Although supervisors could once be characterized as a "bull of the woods" (Tiffin's words), solely responsible for hiring, firing, compensation, and discipline, the new supervisor had to have a thorough knowledge of the law and an awareness of psychology so as to understand the "desires and wishes of his men."

By 1960, there was considerably more variability in training methods. There was increasing interest in human relations training. Innovative training methods were being introduced that bore less resemblance to the actual job, including case studies, role plays (Maier, 1952), sensitivity training (see Highhouse, 2002), television and films, and simulators (Miller, 1953). Drawn from his 1954 American Psychological Association (APA) Division 14 (Industrial and Business Psychology) presidential address, Edgerton provided a tongue-in-cheek classification of "schools of learning theory" that paints a picture of what much of training looked like at the time. These included the following:

> a. *Chart and flannel board school*—charts, plain, simple, complex or gaudy—MOTTO: "No training can penetrate deeper than the retina without an impenetrable chart." …
>
> c. *Training aids and gadgets*—Those are the people who are trying to get the message across that cutaways, simulators, mock ups, and the like are the high speed vehicles for training. "If you can't see it, how can you learn it?" …
>
> e. In some instances, the *Case Method* holds the center of the stage. This seems to be the property of legal, executive, and clinical psychologist training. "If you can't case it, you can't take it with you."
>
> f. *The role playing school*—requires that we try to show how someone else might act when their shoes pinch our corns. (pp. 19–20)

What Learning Theories and Perspectives Are Applied?

Textbook authors of this era dedicated considerable space to basic learning research. For example, in contrast to the total of 2 pages devoted to training methods and training evaluation, Ghiselli and Brown (1948) invested 20 pages on learning theory, 2 pages on motivation to learn, 2½ pages on transfer, and 2 more pages on motivation and learning.

Consistent with the growing appreciation for human attitudes and cognitive activity, applied learning theory expanded beyond learning curves and learning plateaus to include issues of motivating trainees through incentives, goals, and the perceived relevance of training; providing knowledge of results; linking new tasks to well-learned tasks; providing contextual or experience-based instruction over rote learning; teaching general problem-solving skills to aid transfer; practicing new skills to the point of automaticity and reduced mental effort; practicing goal-directed learning; tying reinforcements to the perceptions (preferences) of the learner; using spaced practice rather than massed practice; and offering either whole or part learning based on the nature of the task. A classic article by Gagné (1962) summarized a number of learning principles appropriate for improving the efficiency of military training, including overlearning tasks to improve retention or transfer and ensuring an identical match between elements of training and conditions of practice in the transfer setting. Paul Thayer (personal communication, April 13, 2003) recalled that during the 1950s and 1960s, most of the applied learning research was being conducted by the military. Gagné was responsible for much of this work in his role as technical director of the Technical Training Research Laboratory of the Air Force Personnel and Training Research Center in Illinois, where he and his staff conducted numerous studies of human learning and performance (see also chap. 7). Gagné's contributions to training were foreshadowed by his 1932 valedictorian speech in high school in which he proclaimed that the science of psychology should be used to relieve the burdens of human life (obituaries: Gagné, Robert; *The Chatanoogan.com,* April 29, 2002).

Early authors of this era continued to see strong relevance to industrial training for research conducted in other areas of psychology. However, whereas Tiffin (1942), Viteles (1932), and others had implicitly assumed that instructional principles demonstrated in animal, experimental, or classroom laboratories would work equally well on the shop floor, Ghiselli and Brown (1948) were more tempered in their approach:

> For the most part it is safe to assume that the reports of classroom and laboratory findings on factors influencing learning and retention are true.... however ... there are many factors in the school not to be found in the factory. The only rational solution is to consider the given specific situation for which training is needed in industry and to learn to what extent it agrees, in terms of important causal conditions, with specific classroom and laboratory situations that have been studied. (p. 306)

By the end of this era, the perceived link between basic learning research and industrial training was seen as more tenuous. McGehee and Thayer (1961) noted a growing split between learning practitioners (including teachers, foremen, and trainers) and learning theorists who "are concerned with the nature of learning ... and the variables that facilitate and retard learning ... though the use of the standard methods of science" (p. 127). The authors lamented that communication between the two groups was rare and suggested that although practitioners must share in the blame, the fault lay primarily with the learning theorists. McGehee (1958) suggested that this split occurred in part because of the use of sterile experimental contexts that bore little resemblance to real-world settings and in part due to the use of a language that was esoteric and mathematical. Consequently, McGehee and Thayer suggested that although modern learning theory may provide useful insights for building better training programs, industrial psychologists must be careful in applying learning principles given their source. McGehee and Thayer's book was the first true I–O book devoted to training. Their contributions are highlighted here in recognition of this fact, to highlight their contributions to training systems, and because it marks a transition between eras of training research.

At the time, Thayer and McGehee were both working in industry managing and doing research on training, Thayer for the Life Insurance Agency Management Association and McGehee for Fieldcrest Mills in North Carolina. They had met in 1953 when Thayer was still in graduate school at Ohio State and, at the suggestion of Harold Burtt, traveled to North Carolina to work with McGehee on a consumer panel (Thayer, 2002).

The idea for collaborating on the book came at an APA convention about 4 years later when Thayer introduced McGehee to a book editor who was seeking someone to write a text on industrial psychology. McGehee didn't feel qualified to write such a book but agreed to write a book on training if Thayer agreed to co-author it (Thayer, 2002). One of their motivations of writing it was the desire to inspire more research on learning and training because they believed at the time there was virtually no research on learning conducted in applied settings (Paul Thayer, personal communication, April 13, 2003).

What Key Advances Were Made in Training Research and Practice?

The emergence of formalized off-the-job training led to more defined roles for trainers and training specialists (i.e., instructional designers). Through the formation of the Training Within Industry (TWI) group of the War Production Board of the U.S. government, a series of 10-hour training programs in job instruction, job relations, job methods, and job safety were given to more than 2 million supervisors and training officers during the war years (Steinmetz, 1967). It is interesting to note that F. J. Roethlisberger, who had collaborated on the Hawthorne studies, was responsible for the initial planning of the job relations training provided to supervisors.

Perhaps as a consequence of the shifting of responsibility for training away from the supervisor and toward the training specialist, this era also saw a growing recognition of the need for training measurement needs assessment and training evaluation. When the supervisor was conducting on-the-job training, there was little need for needs assessment or evaluation. The training content was the job (known by the supervisor) and training was completed when the work was satisfactory. Mahler and Monroe (1952) published one of the first books on needs assessment and noted that at the time, only 10% of surveyed companies reported the use of systematic procedures for determining training needs. As others assumed responsibility for the design and conduct of training, the need to ensure the relevance and impact of training grew. Additionally, there is evidence of tension between the training specialist and the organization regarding this requirement, evident when Tiffin discussed the value of evaluation: "Management need no longer accept a training program on faith or because of someone's flowery statements about the presumed value of the program" (p. 193).

When McGehee and Thayer began work on their book, McGehee held the opinion that organizations too quickly jumped to conclusions about the need for training (Paul Thayer, personal communication, April 13, 2003). This opinion was formed in part by an experience of McGehee and Thayer that they published 20 years later (Thayer & McGehee, 1977). Accordingly, both authors felt the need to specify more formal methods for understanding jobs and their relation to organizational objectives. McGehee and Thayer (1961) formally outlined a three-step needs assessment process that is very similar to modern approaches:

> 1) organizational analysis—determining where within the organization training emphasis can and should be placed. 2) operations analysis—determining what should be the contents of training in terms of what an employee must do to perform a task, job, or assignment in an effective way. 3) man analysis—determining what skills, knowledge, or attitudes an individual employee must develop if he is to perform the tasks which constitute his job in the organization. (p. 25)

McGehee and Thayer thus saw strategic advantages in aligning training goals with organizational objectives, prioritizing performance problems within the organization, and ensuring that the organizational climate (i.e., worker attitudes) was sufficiently positive to encourage productive behavior.

Treatment of training evaluation over this era follows a similar path. Neither Tiffin (1942) nor Ghiselli and Brown (1948) devoted much space to training evaluation. Perhaps because training activities so closely mirrored job activities, there was an assumption that training works. Ghiselli and Brown stated that although performance improvement was not always seen immediately, it would be found "in almost every situation involving worker performance" (p. 304). In contrast, McGehee and Thayer (1961) argued that it is important to show that training does work. They cited an earlier paper by Wallace and Twichell (1953), who noted the lack of experimental evidence "that training ... produces any improvement in workers' performance at all" (p. 25). Writers of this era noted many obstacles to doing evaluation research including lack of statistical skills and research knowledge by training personnel, ethical issues in withholding training from the control group, morale problems for those not trained, and management's lack of support for controlled studies that interfered with work (McGehee, 1949; McGehee & Thayer, 1961; Wallace & Twichell, 1953).

By the end of the 1950s, instructional designers such as Robert Mager would reflect the influence of the behaviorist movement in psychology by insisting that training outcomes be quantified in terms of observable, behavioral change. However, in 1948, Ghiselli and Brown were not so bound. Consistent with the spirit of the human relations movement, these authors believed that the impact of training

> is not always manifest at the moment of termination of the formal instruction. The subtle effects resulting from changes in attitudes, motives, and interests sometime appear only after several months. (p. 304)

Ghiselli and Brown listed possible criteria culled from industry reports that included increased job satisfaction or morale, increased interest in work, reduction in sick time, improved safety records, greater productivity, and reduced variation in output. Tiffin (1942) discussed the development of multiple-choice tests to assess supervisor's knowledge of company policy after training.

McGehee and Thayer discussed criteria but also emphasized the importance of experimental design and sound measures for demonstrating that training worked. McGehee and Thayer suggested that the goal of evaluation is twofold: determining whether training produced desired changes in behavior and determining whether these changes have an impact on organizational goals. They also advocated cost–benefit analyses, including return-on-investment estimates or comparisons to the cost effectiveness of alternative procedures. They did not cite a contemporary paper by Donald Kirkpatrick (1959), who from his position as the president of the American Society of Training and Development recommended measuring "trainee reactions" as one of four steps of training evaluation.

PARTICIPATIVE MANAGEMENT ERA (1960–1990)

Leadership research during the 1950s identified a specific set of effective leader behaviors such as consideration and structure that characterized managerial activity (Fleishman, 1953; Stodgill, 1974; Stodgill & Coons, 1957; see also chap. 16 in this text). Fiedler (1964) then proposed a contingency model of leadership, suggesting that the most effective leader behaviors were contingent on situational favorableness (to the leader). Fiedler suggested that several different leadership styles could be effective; one of these styles he termed *participative*. The 1960s also saw growing application of Drucker's (1954) management by objectives, in which managers and subordinates negotiated performance objectives for subordinates, as well as publication of Katz and Kahn's (1966) classic text describing organizational behavior embedded in open sociotechnical systems. As the formal power of leaders became more distributed, there was a greater emphasis on employee empowerment and upward communication. The

1970s and 1980s saw widespread adoption of a number of participatory management techniques popularized in Scandinavia and Japan, including quality circles, self-directed work teams, total quality management, and continuous process improvement.

Within the field of learning, instrumental conditioning models were being transformed by the incorporation of cognitive elements. For example, Bandura (1977, 1982) described an important modification to behavioral learning theory in which he proposed that thinking beings learn not only through direct reinforcement and punishment but also vicariously through observations of reinforcement and punishment of others. Bandura's theory was applied relatively quickly to training methods by A. P. Goldstein and Sorcher (1974) and Decker and Nathan (1985). In addition, social cognitive theories began to emphasize the role of self-efficacy in self-regulated behavior. Self-efficacy is defined as judgments of how well one can execute courses of action required to deal with prospective situations (e.g., see Bandura, 1977, 1982). These judgments could affect the motivation to learn or the belief that one could master a particular task.

The fields of cognitive psychology and computer science evolved rapidly during this era. Developments in cognitive psychology were heavily influenced by new models of the mind as an information processor (Anderson, 1982; Broadbent, 1958; Neisser, 1967). These models documented how the human mind acts on perception and information by filtering, organizing, and distorting information during the actions of perception, memory storage, and retrieval. Two decades later, Howell and Cooke (1989) wrote an influential chapter summarizing these models and emphasizing their importance for understanding learning during workplace training practices.

Learning theory thus moved from postulating how thought mediated stimulus-response relations to the study of an internal world that seemingly acted on its own but influenced decision making, behavior, and performance. In the field of computer science, scientists originally sought to create computer programs that emulated human intelligence (Turing, 1950) but ended up positioning the computer as a metaphor for how humans think and learn. For example, to create a computer program that plays chess, programmers sought to distinguish cognitive processes that distinguished expert players from novices (Chase & Simon, 1973). The focus on expert/novice differences highlighted the willingness of experimental/cognitive psychologists to go outside the laboratory to study problems within more complex task situations (Glaser & Resnick, 1972). Later, Kraiger and Ford (Ford & Kraiger, 1995; Kraiger, Ford & Salas, 1993) characterized training as a process of transforming novices to trained experts.

What Did Training Look Like?

While the cognitive revolution was brewing in psychology, training writing during this era continued to have a decidedly behavioral feel. In their 1966 book, Bass and Vaughn suggested

> since the primary objective of training is to bring about certain desired changes in behavior as efficiently as possible, and since the essence of learning is change in behavior, the importance of an understanding of the principles of learning to any training endeavor becomes obvious. (p. 4)

Training could be optimized, they suggested, by focusing on four components in the learning process: (a) the drive that energizes the individual to respond, (b) the stimulus that cues the response, (c) the response elicited, and (d) the reinforcers that increase the likelihood that the individual will make the same response again if the same stimulus and drive reoccur.

By the mid 1970s, it was evident that the concept of systems thinking was becoming incorporated into training research. I. L. Goldstein (1974) defined training and education as "the systematic acquisition of skills, rules, concepts, or attitudes that results in improved performance in another environment" (p. 3). Goldstein introduced to I–O psychology an instructional systems design (ISD) model based on systems thinking from an engineering and human factors perspective (Irvin Goldstein, personal communication, May 9, 2003). Goldstein had received little training in I–O psychology as a graduate student, and his first academic job was at the Aviation Psychology Lab at Ohio State under Bill Howell (I. L. Goldstein, 2002). When Goldstein moved to Maryland, the department chair encouraged him to follow his interest in training systems, resulting in his 1974 book and the ISD model.

Goldstein used the ISD model as a way to understand what training is all about. In a way, the formal ISD model sought to explicate all of the steps that were once executed solely by the supervisor but were now shared by multiple persons (i.e., analysts, designers, and trainers). The model included conducting needs assessment, developing objectives, designing the program, and evaluating the program with a feedback loop back to needs assessment. A similar model was introduced in the human performance improvement field by a former student of Skinner's, Thomas Gilbert (Gilbert, 1978).

Influenced by systems theories of organizations (e.g., Berrien, 1976; Katz & Kahn, 1966), Hinrichs (1976) expanded the notion of an ISD model to include three levels of analysis with each level within a systems framework of inputs, throughputs, outputs, and feedback loops. For example, the individual trainee was discussed as a key throughput and the training department as the suprasystem within which learning, altered behavior, personal growth, and an increased sense of competence might result for the individual trainees.

Training methods continued to diversify and now included on-the-job training, orientation training, apprenticeship training, job rotation, coaching, off-the-job training, sensitivity training, behavior modification, vestibule training, lectures, films, television, business games, in-baskets, case study, role playing, simulation, discussion, and team training. Training was seen as an important aspect of development for all levels and functions in the organization to improve individual effectiveness.

However, training researchers and theorists became increasingly less interested in specific training methods. That is, although there were more and more training methods available, few of these methods were either theory based or supported with research. It must be noted, though, that one of the best designed and executed training evaluation studies was conducted on applied learning and found impressive gains for those trained in those methods over a control group (Latham & Saari, 1979).

In the prior era, we saw a shift in responsibility for training away from the supervisor and toward the training professional. Accordingly, I–O psychologists became even less interested in training methods and instead focused on assessment and design functions in advance of training and transfer and evaluation methods after training. This focus is reflected in the title of Goldstein's 1974 book, *Training: Program Development and Evaluation*. The focus on assessment was also stressed by J. P. Campbell (1988). He noted the need to focus more attention to what is to be learned or accomplished in training. He noted that this issue "takes precedence over the traditional questions addressed by research in learning such as whether massed versus distributed practice is more effective" (p. 188). He argued for the need for a paradigm shift from reviewing research results by training methods to training objectives (J. P. Campbell, 1989).

One research area seen as having great potential for enhancing training effectiveness was aptitude–treatment interactions that take both individual differences and learning situations into account (J. P. Campbell, 1971; Cronbach, 1967). Research examined the effects of matching alternative modes of instruction to different characteristics of the individual so that each person uses the most appropriate learning procedure. Although the potential for aptitude–treatment interactions has not been fully realized, J. P. Campbell and Kuncel (2002) recently stressed that there are always relevant individual differences and variety in training programs that make aptitude–treatment interactions relevant to any training effort.

What Learning Theories and Perspectives Are Applied?

Writers of this era continued to see learning theory as relevant to training, but there were relatively few new insights during this era. Bass and Vaughn (1966) reviewed research on classical conditioning and instrumental conditioning and concluded that knowledge of results is the single most important source of reinforcement for the human learner. Bass and Vaughn were also interested in higher order learning and discussed the importance of understanding in learning, modeling, and perceptual organization.

I. L. Goldstein (1974) provided similar prescriptions for structuring the learning environment, drawing on research from classical and instrumental conditioning. Like McGehee and Thayer (1961), he was critical of the applicability of this research to modern issues in training. Goldstein noted that his learning chapter should be "devoted to a review of the learning principles that have been developed in the last 100 years. However … there is a wide gulf separating learning theories and principles from what is actually needed to improve performance" (p. 92). Goldstein believed that learning theories have focused on highly specific lab studies, making generalization very difficult: "The trainer is left with data that do not seem particularly relevant to his needs, and theoretical interpretations which could provide the link do not exist" (p. 93). In addition, learning theory at that time had avoided more complex types of learning such as problem solving and concept learning that are more directly relevant to training. In writing his second edition to the training book (I. L. Goldstein, 1986), Goldstein noted that his goal was to show that progress in the field as training research was leading to new models of training effectiveness that were going beyond basic issues in learning theory (Irvin Goldstein, personal communication, May 9, 2003).

What Key Advances Were Made in Training Research and Practice?

Within this era, the primary advancements centered on the institutionalization of methods for needs assessment and training evaluation. In the case of needs assessment, this institutionalization resulted from the endorsement of the first formal models for needs assessment advanced by McGehee and Thayer (1961). A similar process was proposed by Bass and Vaughn (1966), I. L. Goldstein (1974, 1980, 1986), and Wexley and Latham (1981), with "operations analysis" renamed "job analysis." In addition, the focus on understanding what to train (operations analysis) is evident in the move from a purely task-based approach in I. L. Goldstein's first edition (1974) to specifying knowledge, skill, and ability (KSAs) needed for effective performance in the second edition of 1986. Key advances included the development of the functional job analysis approach (Fine, 1978) and the application of multimethod job analysis (task, KSA, and linking tasks to KSAs) to training by Prien and others (e.g., I. L. Goldstein, Macy & Prien, 1981; Prien, 1977).

In the ISD model, Goldstein refined McGehee and Thayer's organizational analysis through a focus on goals, resources, and the environment. Influenced by the philosophy of behaviorally based instructional designers like Robert Mager, Goldstein linked the needs assessment process to the setting of training objectives. Goldstein's treatment of job analysis reads very much as if it might have come from a book on staffing or selection, evidence that as a whole, the field was focused on solidifying the idea that training could be systematic rather than thinking innovatively about training support methods.

Regarding training evaluation, there were several important changes from prior approaches. First, evidence of training impact changed. As late as 1961, there was no mention in the I–O literature of measuring trainees' perceptions of training as a method for evaluating training programs. Between 1959 and 1960, Donald Kirkpatrick published four papers outlining what is now called the four levels of training evaluation. The four levels consist of measuring trainee reactions (attitudes toward the program), trainee learning, changes in behavior, and changes in performance. One of the first references to Kirkpatrick's four levels in the I–O literature was a mention by Bass and Vaughn (1966) as a structure for evaluating training. Thayer (Paul Thayer, personal communication, April 13, 2003) recalled that the presentation of Kirkpatrick's model in the Bass and Vaughn book was the first time that he and many other I–O psychologists were exposed to the four levels. One of the first research papers to measure trainee reactions was an evaluation of a leadership training course at Bell Telephone (Stroud, 1959). Kirkpatrick (1967) claimed that the Management Institute at the University of Wisconsin had measured trainee reactions since the early 1950s, although data were never published. A 1968 review by Castellano and Kirkpatrick indicated that measuring trainee reactions had become the predominant form of evaluating training, outnumbering other methods by at least three to one. Surveys of industry practice 30 years later revealed similar ratios (Twitchell, Holton, & Trott, 2001; Van Buren, 2001).

The second major change was an emphasis on training evaluation design. Noting the difficulty in conducting training evaluation, Bass and Vaughn (1966) proposed three general principles of evaluation: (a) Evaluation should be planned at the same time as the training program and should constitute an integral part of the total program from beginning to end, (b) evaluations should follow the most rigorous experimental design possible, and (c) evaluation should be carried out at several levels and at several times. I. L. Goldstein (1974) devoted most of a second chapter on the complexities of evaluation, types of evaluation (formative, summative), and extensive treatment of internal and external validity issues based on the work of D. T. Campbell and Stanley (1963).

Consistent with his ISD model, Goldstein's book (1974) presented both the needs assessment chapter and the two evaluation chapters before chapters on learning and training methods. This treatment had a subtle but influential effect on training research for the next 15 years. By ordering topics this way, Goldstein made the case that what are important to the role of the I–O psychologist are decisions about what to train, what to evaluate, and how well training works. The lack of clarity in the ISD model on training design and, particularly, training delivery gives the vague feeling that those topics are left to unspecified others.

There was also a growing awareness of the importance of understanding learning outcomes arising from both training and training transfer. For example, Goldstein (1974) separated "learning" into two chapters—one on the basic issues of learning and one on the transfer of training to the job. This shows the increased interest in enhancing the potential for training to actually have an impact on individual effectiveness back on the job. The concept of transfer climate was discussed as a key factor, and studies appeared identifying some of the factors that determine the support for transfer (e.g., see Baumgartel & Jeanpeiere, 1972; Liefer & Newstrom, 1980).

By the end of this era, there was growing optimism about the future of training research. Changes in attitudes toward training research are highlighted by two quotes by John Campbell. In 1971 he made one of the stronger statements about a field of inquiry when he stated that the field of training is "voluminous, non-empirical, non-theoretical, poorly written, and dull" (p. 565). In a follow-up paper in 1988, Campbell commented that "contrary to my somewhat negative view some eighteen years ago, the field of training and development has entered an exciting age and promises to become even more intense in the future" (p. 208). Other researchers (e.g., Goldstein & Gessner, 1988; Latham, 1988) echoed that sentiment that training research and theory had progressed during the past 15 to 20 years. Advances in cognitive and educational psychology (especially regarding learning processes) provided the foundation for a rapid expansion of training research and practice in the 1990s and beyond. An I–O Frontiers Series book on training by I. L. Goldstein and his associates (1989) ushered in this new and exciting era by integrating new areas of research such as levels of analysis, cognitive models of the adult learner, advances in experimental design, and timely issues such as aging and the learning process. J. P. Campbell (1989) wrote the concluding chapter in Goldstein's book and offered an agenda for training theory and research: "The breaking down of barriers between I–O psychology and instructional psychology is in our future and will enhance the intrinsic value of training and development as a place to investigate human behavior" (p. 485).

STRATEGIC LEARNING ERA (1990–PRESENT)

The last era in training and development is the current one, beginning about 1990. Work in public and private organizations is becoming more knowledge driven. Here, knowledge refers to the combination of information, experience, understanding, and problem-solving skills that can be applied to decisions or situations (Hansen, Nohria, & Tierney, 1999). In modern contexts, competitive advantages are gained not only by technology, capital, or geography but also by an organization's capacity to distinguish its knowledge base from competitors (e.g., Stewart, 1997).

Because internal and external environments change, it is important that the organization have built-in capabilities to detect change, anticipate trends, and adapt internally. Creating mechanisms that maximize the organization's ability to learn over time should result in performance advantages in competitive markets (Senge, 1990). We call this period the strategic learning era, named for the coupling of knowledge management and organizational initiatives that promote system-wide learning behaviors, thus enabling long-term adaptive capacity (cf. Kuwada, 1998; Thomas, Sussman, & Henderson, 2001).

During a period of extensive organizational restructuring and downsizing in the late 1980s, a number of organizations undertook programs of job reengineering. The objective of re-engineering programs was to identify core functions of corporate jobs and determine both job redundancies and more efficient methods for accomplishing work (Hammer, 1995). Although the re-engineering phase was short-lived, it led to an appreciation of the differences between fundamental business processes and traditional jobs within organizations. It became possible to plan for (i.e., select) and develop (i.e., train) critical competencies rather relying solely on selecting and training for specific job knowledge and skills.

Nonaka and Takeuchi (1995) introduced the concept of a knowledge company and the need for organizations to identify and document their intellectual capital—information about customers, business processes, markets and brands, and individual effectiveness—that differentiated successful from less successful companies. Knowledge management became an organizational strategy for the use of technology and formal knowledge elicitation methods to best capture worker knowledge and organize it in a way that facilitates individual, team, and organizational performance (Hedlund, 1994).

At about the same time, other writers promoted the virtues of learning organizations (e.g., Argyris & Schön, 1978; Senge, 1990). A learning organization is one that has an enhanced capacity to learn, adapt, or change (Gephart, Marsick, Van Buren, & Spiro, 1996). It does so by promoting a continuous learning environment, encouraging workers to share knowledge, encouraging flexibility and experimentation on the job, and maintaining a learning culture (Tannenbaum, 1997).

Together, these new approaches to knowledge and learning were seen as essential for improving quality, fostering continuous improvement, and achieving innovation in products or services. Rather than rely on inputs from top leadership or knowledge experts, organizations recognized that the potential for improving organizational effectiveness was vastly increased when knowledge at every level was focused on the goals of quality, innovation, and continuous improvement (Cuther-Gershefeld & Ford, 2005).

There are several important implications of these trends for training and development. One is that both knowledge management and organizational learning initiatives lead to greater depth and breadth to training initiatives (e.g., cross-functional training, problem-solving training). Additionally, they promote a strategic view of training as a key lever for organizational change that in turn led training specialists to reidentify themselves as performance consultants. These trends also shift much of the responsibility for training and development from the organization to the individual learner. Finally, these initiatives have promoted a philosophical perspective that separates knowledge requirements and competencies from the organizational members who might hold them. That is, there is an emerging understanding that it is important for long-term organizational success to preserve certain know-how and to maintain certain core competencies. Maintaining these core competencies in the face of membership changes is a major challenge.

Regarding theories of cognition and learning, this era has been marked by a philosophical debate between objectivist and constructivist perspectives. Consistent with traditional learning theories, objectivists believe that core knowledge can be defined (through learning objectives) and that the goal of instruction is to facilitate the learning of this core knowledge (e.g., that all trainees can identify the difference between a useful and nonuseful goal). Constructivists believe that learners actively construct knowledge by integrating new information and experiences into existing knowledge structures, revising and reinterpreting the older knowledge to reconcile it with the new (Jonassen, 1991). Although there may be learning objectives in a constructivist-based approach, such objectives would center on facilitating learning to learn (Cognition and Technology Group at Vanderbilt, 1992). Knowledge is seen as subjective, in the sense that two persons hearing the same lecture may take different meanings from the same content, or the same content may mean something different to a person each time it is encountered. Applied to instruction, constructivism focuses attention on the learner rather than to content. There are several important implications for training of a constructivist approach including: (a) Instruction must be concerned with the experiences and contexts that increase learners' motivation and readiness to learn, (b) instruction must be structured so that it can be easily understood by the learner, and (c) learning is a social activity—although learning is a personal and unique experience, it often occurs in (and is facilitated by) social contexts (Bruner, 1990). Consistent with constructivist theory, studies of on-the-job learning suggest that learning can be facilitated by expert guidance on how to problem solve or reason in ill-defined situations (Bell & Kozlowski, 2002); active reflection on trial-and-error (Hart-Landesberg, Braunger, & Reder, 1992); or workers' engagement in work-related activities, both guided by experts and with interaction with other learners (Billett, 1993, 1994).

On the one hand, constructivism and strategic learning appear orthogonal. Knowledge management, embedded in strategic learning, seeks to elicit and codify knowledge, making expertise available to all within the organization. At the same time, constructivism preaches that learning is a uniquely individual process—what is knowledge to one may not be meaningful to another. On the other hand, when placed side by side, the two build a compelling vision of individualized learning in which workers can go to a centralized knowledge bank and access information from systems or other workers as they are motivated and ready to learn. In some ways this resembles the vision that drives modern computer-based, just-in-time training.

What Did Training Look Like?

Definitions of training during this era look much as they did in the prior era, though with a greater emphasis on the acquisition of knowledge and skills (components of workers necessary to do jobs). Human resource practitioners began to discuss competencies as the fundamental building blocks of jobs and training programs. Competencies are clusters of knowledge, skills, and abilities that differentiate high versus low performance in a job (Noe, 2002). Competencies are also closely related to business objectives and tend to generalize within an organization but not within job families (Schippmann et al., 2000). Although training for competencies might resemble training for job-specific knowledge or skills, the idea of training for competencies implies the need to target worker competencies or talent pools that transcend individual positions (Boudreau & Ramstad, 2003). Again, we see an emphasis on both long-term organizational adaptation and looser linkages between training activities and specific job demands.

Although instructor-led training remained the predominant form of training (Van Buren, 2001), other forms of training became increasingly popular. One such form is the corporate university. The curriculum of a corporate university not only covers core competencies and professional development skills but also conveys a sense of corporate culture (Meister, 1998). The corporate university is often carried out with the cooperation of a local academic institution, in a sense a modern day version of vocational training programs of the late 1800s (Steinmetz, 1967).

Another increasingly popular form of training consists of variations of a more general class of training called technology-delivered instruction (TDI). TDI methods include distance learning, single-station or networked computer-based training, and Web-based instruction (or learning). Although recent surveys show that TDI accounts for less than 15% of all corporate training, many studies and analyses predict increasing prevalence of TDI in the future (Brennan & Anderson, 2001; Van Buren, 2001). There are several perceived benefits to computer-based training including greater standardization, increased flexibility in scheduling or training content, or reduced costs related to trainer and travel fees. Although cumulative research evidence shows that TDI environments have only a modest impact on learning (Brown, 2001; Kulik & Kulik, 1991; Russell, 1999), there is hope that the combination of greater potential for content customization and enhanced motivation through high learner control can result in more learning in trainees (Brown & Ford, 2002). Customization may be an increasingly critical advantage of TDI because it enables learners to manage more complex and fast-changing job demands.

What Learning Theories and Principles Are Applied?

During the strategic learning era there has been the widespread adoption of modern theory of learning and skill acquisition. The cognitive revolution moved to the training field. A chapter by Howell and Cooke (1989) introduced cognitive theory to the field of training research. They provided an integrated overview to information processing models and learning. A chapter in the I–O handbook by Lord and Maher (1991) provided a more general discussion of potential linkages between cognitive theory and several traditional I–O topics including training. Several years later, Ford and Kraiger (1995) analyzed the implications of cognitive theory for needs assessment, training design, and transfer of training. The analysis challenged many common assumptions in the training literature. For example, needs analysis typically involves interviewing subject matter experts regarding potential training content, but Ford and Kraiger noted that the research on expert/novice differences suggests that experts access task information in ways that may be fundamentally inaccessible to novices.

Finally, Kraiger et al. (1993) directly applied cognitive theory to the delineation of learning outcomes in training. Kraiger et al. criticized past evaluation models (such as Kirkpatrick's) for assuming that learning was unidimensional and discussed how learning may have affective, cognitive, or skill-based components. Kraiger et al. provided both a taxonomy of learning outcomes and suggestions for applications of emerging evaluation methodologies to training.

During this era, training researchers became increasingly interested in how trainees approach and respond to learning during training. For example, research has shown that most individuals enter learning situations with either a mastery or a performance goal orientation. Trainees with a performance orientation are more concerned with public evaluation of their performance and may undermine knowledge or skill acquisition by focusing on immediate performance (perhaps by using pretraining skills). Trainees with a mastery orientation are more focused on acquiring new knowledge or skills and may be more receptive to feedback, trying new behaviors, or persisting in the learning of difficult tasks (e.g., see Fisher & Ford, 1998; Ford, Smith, Weissbein, Gully, & Salas, 1998).

What Key Advances Were Made in Training Research and Practice?

There were a number of advancements in the areas of training theory and training research. Several influential articles in the late 1980s inspired new paradigms or streams of research that have helped to transform the training literature. One was a review article by Noe (1986), in which he proposed a model of training effectiveness. The model suggests that trainee learning and subsequent performance are affected by organizational and attitudinal variables both before and after training. For example, both supervisory support for training (organizational) and trainees' motivation to learn or self-efficacy (attitudinal) might affect trainees' knowledge acquisition during training and attempts to transfer learning after training. Additional training effectiveness models have suggested that variables other than training design or trainer effectiveness could affect trainee learning and provided a backdrop for a number of studies linking the individual and the organization to training (e.g., see Cannon-Bowers, Salas, Tannenbaum, & Mathieu, 1995).

A second influential article was a model of transfer of training developed by Baldwin and Ford (1988). Baldwin and Ford provided a conceptual definition of transfer and identified the trainee characteristics, training design, and work environment factors that can affect knowledge and skill acquisition and training transfer. Throughout this chapter, we have said little about changes in perspectives on transfer over time, but they are considerable. Through at least the 1930s, much of training was done one-on-one at the job site. At that time industrial psychologists borrowed liberally from research studies on animal behavior or verbal learning. In classic experimental research, transfer of training refers to the ease or speed at which new information is learned given prior learning. For example, does learning lists of pairs of nonsense words facilitate the learning of lists of pairs of everyday words? Industrial psychologists at this time faced very similar transfer problems; for example, does learning how to execute tasks on one machine aid the learning of new tasks on a similar machine? Factors thought to increase transfer were principally characteristics of the learning process such as identical elements and over-learning.

We also saw how between 1940 and 1960, much of training moved from the work site to the seminar room, training content was derived through elementary form of needs assessment, and training was often facilitated by a "training expert" who may or may not have once held the job. Accordingly, there was a subtle shift in the meaning of transfer in that it came to mean the extent to which what is learned in training is applied on the job. However, by 1960, very little research on learning (and transfer) was being conducted by training researchers, and traditional learning researchers continued to study a different (task-to-task) phenomenon.

Thus, Baldwin and Ford's (1988) article provided an initial framework to conduct research on transfer from the perspective of applied training. Since then, researchers have shown not only that is posttraining transfer influenced by learning during training but that it is also affected by both attitudinal and organizational variables outside of training. Factors thought to increase this form of transfer were characteristics of learners and the organization. For example, level of transfer may be positively affected by trainees' intentions to transfer (Foxon, 1993) or trainees' self-efficacy (e.g., Ford et al., 1998; Gist, Stevens, & Bavetta, 1991). Other work suggests that organizational variables such as posttraining opportunities to perform trained tasks (e.g., Ford, Quiñones, Sego, & Sorra, 1992; Quiñones, Ford, Sego, & Smith, 1996) and the level of supervisor support or transfer climate can facilitate or hinder training transfer (e.g., Rouiller & Goldstein, 1993; Tracey, Tannenbaum, & Kavanagh, 1995).

SYNTHESIS AND INTEGRATION

This final section takes the basic data across the four eras to develop a better understanding of the expanding role of training. We first summarize key forces and innovations in training from each era. Second, we examine the relation between prevailing forces and training innovation, we evaluate the role I–O psychology has played in increasing our understanding of learning as well as the factors that affect training effectiveness. Finally, we discuss some of the current key challenges facing training research and practice.

Where Have We Been? An Analysis of Key Trends and Themes

We divided the history of training and development into four eras and examined innovations in the theory and practice of training given the predominant management philosophies and theories of learning of that time. We view these two factors as key forces driving the expanding role of training research and practice. The key trends and themes that we have discussed are summarized in Table 12.1.

The evolution of management and organizational effectiveness models has changed expectations for what training should accomplish. Thus, training has evolved from a supervisory requirement to ensure efficient work processes to a mandate to increase organizational flexibility and capability. The increasing sophistication of learning models has expanded our understanding of how (and what) individuals learn and how they should best be instructed. Accordingly, the range of potential learning outcomes and viable instructional strategies has broadened over time.

More specifically, in the initial era, we saw a relatively narrow view of training's role, in part because industrial psychologists of the era viewed work design and selection as the primary strategies for shaping the workforce and enhancing productivity. Nevertheless, psychological theory and research contributed greatly to the appreciation of learning in the workplace. Early application of stimulus-response and reinforcement approaches to workplace learning was invaluable for improving training efficiency. Learning principles developed in animal learning and education psychology were applied (e.g., identical elements) to improve training practice (over trial and error). Training itself was a very straightforward process because jobs were relatively simple. The objective of training was rapid acquisition by frontline employees of simple responses that could be maintained over time. Training was accomplished by identifying the most efficient steps necessary to perform the job and having the worker learn to perform those steps, in sequence, under the watchful eye of the foreman or an experienced worker. Training evaluation was not necessary because training was completed only when the worker could perform the job correctly or more efficiently than he or she had done before.

TABLE 12.1
Key Trends and Themes Across Eras

Era	What Did Training Look Like?	What Are the Dominant Learning Theories?	What Advances Were Made in Research and Practice?
Scientific management (1900–1930)	Job mastery through improving the speed of skill acquisition and training to specified work standards Supervisors as trainers (show, tell, do, check) of shop floor workers with a focus on improving work efficiency	Functionalism (how the human mind adapts to survive in its environment) and objectivist (core knowledge can be defined and trained) perspectives Stimulus–response theory and the impact of stimuli, response, and consequences on shaping behavior	Systematically examining job requirements and conducting empirical testing of how much efficiency is gained with systematic training over trial-and-error learning Directly applying principles of learning (e.g., learning curves) from research to work settings
Humanistic (1930–1960)	Continued emphasis on job training for the shop floor but more off-the-job training for supervisory personnel Emerging role of the training expert within personnel management	Cognitive behaviorism and issues of latent learning and cognitive maps of how thought mediates stimulus–response relations More of a split between learning theorists and learning practitioners	Recognition of need for more formalized methods of training measurement—needs assessment and evaluation with a focus on training objectives Increase in the use of innovative training methods such as case studies, role plays, and simulators
Participative (1960–1990)	Increased emphasis on managerial training such as situational leadership Some movement to more self-directed learning such as programmed instruction and computer-assisted instruction	Social–cognitive and information processing perspectives with the use of computers as a metaphor for how humans think and learn Perceived gap between traditional learning principles and training practice	Systems thinking and standardization of procedures within an instructional systems design training model Focus on issues of transfer of training, aptitude treatment interactions, and the method of behavioral modeling
Strategic (1990–present)	Greater depth and breadth of training options for all employees organized around developing core competencies Increase in self-directed learning activities such as CD-ROM and Web-based training Linking training to broader issue of individual, team, and organizational development	Constructivist perspective and the focus on the learner • Learners actively construct knowledge such that learning is a personal and unique experience • Learning is a social activity as it occurs in and is facilitated by social contexts	Emphasis on cognitive theory and information-processing models and learning Concepts of organizational learning, knowledge management, and intellectual capital Technology-delivered instruction and focus on learner control

The human relations era began with a strong concern for worker attitudes and motivation. Within learning theory, there was also a growing appreciation for both latent learning and links between mental representations of tasks and observed behavior. Psychologists began to think of the human mind as a critical mediator between environmental stimuli and individual behavior. These forces led to gradual recognition of the importance of attitudes, motivation, and emotions as determinants of individual knowledge and skill acquisition and subsequent performance on the job. Training became less about showing workers how to do the job and more about preparing them mentally and emotionally for the tasks they would need to perform. Growth in the labor movement and development of human relations theory created changes in the role of the first-line supervisor. Jobs themselves became more complex and specialized, and supervisors became less knowledgeable than their workers. Together, these forces affected the perceived role of training in organizations. Training methods as well as the population served by training became more diversified. In addition, although much of employee training was still done on the shop floor, by the end of this era, more and more training—especially for supervisors—was in the classroom. Accordingly, there emerged an understanding that training needed to be connected to the job through needs assessment before training and evaluation after training. Responsibility for designing, conducting, and evaluating training fell less to the supervisor and more to the training specialist. Training was becoming a profession. By the end of the era, there was a growing perception that classic learning research was not necessarily relevant to training workers.

During the third (participative management) era there were fewer innovations regarding training methods or learning outcomes but substantial changes at the level of training systems. Management and organizational theory began emphasizing the importance of systems thinking and the role of behavior within complex sociotechnical systems. Within training, the ISD model emerged to characterize a training system, linking the training function to broader organizational systems at both the needs assessment and evaluation phases. Advancements in training were based less on specific instructional methods than on methods for linking training content to organizational reality. Because training was no longer done primarily on the job, by the supervisor, I–O psychologists and other training professional explored ways of showing that training content was relevant and that training worked. Thematics in learning theories shifted dramatically from behaviorally based reinforcement models to cognitively based information processing models. This cognitive revolution led to a greater appreciation (by the modern era) for the mental processes and motivational factors that precede problem solving and skill acquisition and the need for training to consider those mental and motivational variables processes in needs assessment, design, and in evaluation. For the first time, however, we see a tremendous lag between learning theory and application in training.

The lack of progress during the third era was replaced with a flurry of research activity during the current learning strategy era. In their annual review chapter, Salas and Cannon-Bowers (2001) described the 1990s as the "decade of progress." Cognitive theories of learning from the 1970s and 1980s provided a number of insights for training researchers about how and what workers learn. There continued to be work on connecting training to the organizational context in the form of theory and research on training effectiveness and new models for transfer of training and learning outcomes. In addition, advancements in our understanding of levels of analysis led to a greater appreciation for differences between individual skill development and team development issues (e.g., see Kozlowski, Brown, Weissbein, Cannon-Bowers, Salas, 2002; Kozlowski & Salas, 1997). The emergence of the knowledge economy is both leading to the separation of knowledge requirements from job responsibilities and increasing the perceived need to retain and develop human capital. The focus on organizational learning and people as the source of competitiveness placed even greater emphasis on how training could drive change and become more connected to the strategic direction of the firm. In the late 1990s, organizations became increasingly interested in technology-distributed instruction, using the Internet to distribute knowledge to their workforces. The challenge for training practitioners and researchers will be to apply what is known about human learning to maximize learning given advancements in technology and methods of training delivery. The opportunity this provides is the increasing interest in viewing learners as active participants in their own learning process and examining both formal and informal influences on individual learning.

What Have We Learned?: Role of I–O Psychology in Training Research and Practice

The description of each era highlights the changing and expanding role of training and development. Our analysis of the underlying forces and resulting innovations across the eras leads to three observations about the role of I–O psychology in the area of training research and practice. In some instances, these observations are based directly on analysis of trends and innovations (e.g., the lag between innovations in learning theory and application to training is increasing), and in some instances they are based on analysis of what is not seen (e.g., lack of research and discussion on methods of needs assessment). For each observation, we offer a recommendation for training researchers of today and the future.

Training Specific Theory.   In the first 100 years of our field, there have been few theories of learning and behavioral change rooted in the I–O training literature. There are likely multiple reasons for this. Initially, there may not have been a perceived need for work-specific learning theories. Early I–O psychologists expressed considerable confidence in applying research from other psychological disciplines directly to the problems of employee learning. When McGehee and Thayer prepared to write their 1961 book, they conducted a thorough review of the training literature for research on learning but found very few studies or theories (Paul Thayer, personal communication, April 13, 2003). In addition, there is a clear trend of an increasing lag between innovations in cognitive–instructional theory and applications in training. Perhaps the emphasis on instructional systems and reliance on increasingly outdated behavioral learning models provided less fertile ground for training-specific theories of learning. Finally, the focus of more recent research has been on either organizational context (e.g., transfer climate) or individual differences (e.g., motivation to learn) and their impact on training effectiveness. Collectively, latter-day training theorists are more interested in these linkages than the learning process itself.

Although as a field we have contributed little to general learning theory, we have the potential to contribute to an emerging adult-based, context-oriented theory of learning by explicating the way situational and personal variables affect learning behavior in instructional and work contexts. Not only are these variables less often studied in other disciplines, but they also best reflect our own identity. Ultimately, we are not experimentalists but applied psychologists. More specifically, we have a rich history of appreciating individual differences and understanding human behavior in organizational settings. Accordingly, we recommend that training researchers interested in contributing to general theory continue to study individual differences and organizational variables as contextual variables affecting learning in training and transfer. We believe that I–O psychology's most significant contributions are likely to come from research and theories that address issues such as how motivation affects a willingness to learn, how perceptions of training relevancy affect motivation to transfer, or how the probability of transfer is affected by individual perceptions of transfer climate.

Acceptance of Orthodoxy.   Our second observation is that I–O psychologists, at times, have been too willing to accept orthodoxy in the place of reasonable analysis, research evidence, or innovative thought. An early example of this is the readiness of early writers to apply studies of schoolhouse or animal learning to applied training problems. A more recent example is the "theory" of training evaluation. Through 1960, direct observation of job performance was the primary means for evaluating training, with some reliance on written tests for mental components of training. The behavioral emphasis of the 1950s had practitioners wondering how to show what training accomplishes, leading Kirkpatrick to publish a process that had worked for him. It was not offered as a theoretical or researched-based model. Despite the emergence of modern cognitive theory in the 1960s and 1970s, it has only been in the last decade that there has been focused criticism on the framework (Alliger & Janak, 1989; Alliger, Tannenbaum, Bennett, Traver, & Shortland, 1997; Holton, 1996). We are hard-pressed to think of another model or taxonomy in I–O that has been so widely accepted for so long with no theoretical basis.

Similarly, there has been little theoretical attention paid to McGehee and Thayer's (1961) three-step approach of needs assessment (see Ostroff & Ford, 1989, for an exception). Although we do not quibble with the importance of examining organizational, job, and personal factors before designing training, we also note that there is limited theoretical rationale underlying this approach, few practical recommendations as to the order of these steps, and no advice on how to integrate the information from each step to make decisions about training (see also Ford & Kraiger, 1995). We suspect too that, if polled, training experts would show considerable variety in defining the goals and steps in a person and organizational analysis. Our point here is not to criticize either the needs assessment and evaluation frameworks that have become common practice but to note that researchers and practitioners in the training field have tended to accept models such as these for too long without either understanding their conceptual underpinnings or testing them through programmatic research. We recommend that training researchers continually and critically evaluate assumptions that underlie theoretical and empirical models of needs assessment, training design, transfer of training, training evaluation, and so forth.

Lag Between Innovation and Application.   Our third conclusion is that the lag between innovations in learning theory and application to training appears to be increasing. In the 1920s, writers in I–O were well aware of the recent research strides in experimental psychology and readily provided suggestions for incorporating this research into training design. Behaviorally based principles of behavior modification from the 1940s and 1950s were translated into principles of organizational behavior modification and behaviorally based training in the 1950s and 1960s. However, information-processing theories of the late 1960s, as well as the expert–novice research beginning in the early 1970s, did not find its way into mainstream training theory until the early to middle 1990s. We do not yet know when notions of constructivism in instructional design from the late 1980s and early 1990s will reach the training community. There is some indication that research in I–O on training may become more focused on the dynamic learner within context (e.g., see Ford & Oswald, 2002, for a review). Yet, the implications of a constructivist perspective for understanding trainee learning have not been applied to training.

Clearly, there is greater specialization in psychology today than there was 80 years ago. Because researchers are more narrowly trained, there is a tendency to choose increasingly narrower research topics. However, we believe that innovation in the field of training and development will come much more quickly if I–O psychologists can continue to read broadly, integrate research developments from other disciplines into our own, and provide value added by considering the practical implications of that work. Therefore, we recommend that training researchers make every effort to stay up to date in advancements related to learning in other fields of psychology including cognitive psychology, instructional/educational psychology, human factors, and social psychology.

What Challenges Lie Ahead? Final Observations

Over time, the nature of work has changed, resulting in changes in the role, content, and methods of training. As jobs have become more cognitively based and as accountability for work outcomes has become more diffused, responsibility for defining and executing training has shifted from supervisors to training professionals to the workers themselves.

Looking into the near future, we expect to see more training systems providing more rapid transitions from problem identification to needs assessment to training design and delivery. Expert systems integrated into computer-based work stations already have the capability of diagnosing repeatable and correctable errors, and the jump to having such systems recommend remedial training is a small one. Efforts such as standards for sharable content object reference models (SCORM) offer the promise for rapid training design through redeploying previously used training content internal or external to the organization. Whether learning and performance will be better or worse in such situations is an empirical question that should be answered. There will be new research questions regarding the motivation and capabilities of workers to learn in such settings. Furthermore, if problem identification, training design, and training delivery become increasingly automated, then there will necessarily be another step in the evolution of the training professional. Rapid development may enable the transition from basing front-end analysis on individual or job needs to considering organizational goals, and they may be advanced through training and development.

Although the acceleration of expert systems and TDI suggest that the greatest changes in the training field may come in training methods, the perceived value of training in organizations in the future may well come from rethinking training content. Specifically, more thought should be given to how create meaningful learning objectives that are not obviously tied to any one job. Although the benefits of competency modeling over traditional job analyses are debatable (Shippman et al., 2000), centering training on core knowledge, key competencies, or talent pools may represent a competitive advantage to the organization and strategic benefits to training functions within those organizations. Additionally, there needs to be a shift from training of closed skills to open skills (Yelon & Ford, 1999). Closed skills are relatively simple to learn and are appropriate for jobs that are heavily supervised and for which there is a set procedure to follow. Open skills are more difficult to learn and the direct application to the job is not obvious. With open skills, trainees are expected to find ways to personalize the concepts and techniques presented in training, and individuals must be motivated to find opportunities to use the skill on the job. As training content becomes less connected to specific jobs, traditional training principles such as teaching precise procedures, building in high fidelity, and having prescriptive procedural checklists will give way to the need to teach general principles, relate skills to personal goals, show trainees how to modify procedures to fit different situations, and encourage customization of training to the job. Finally, as more and more responsibility will fall to workers to manage their own training, more consideration should be given to skills such as receiving feedback, self-monitoring, and self-regulation.

Historically, one consistency in the training function has been the questions that must be answered in planning training: What and who should be trained? Who should conduct the training? How should training be conducted? In addition, it is in the best interest of both the organization and the training function to consider an additional question—How effectively does training address issues of strategic importance to the organization? These questions will persist and continue to drive training practice and training research.

History has taught us that the role of research on training is to inform how those questions should be asked and answered. The role of training practice is to facilitate better decision making about training (answering the questions), given an understanding of how people learn and organizations function. We foresee continual change in training methods and training content, but we see training maintaining a critical role in facilitating organizational effectiveness.

REFERENCES

Anderson, J. R. (1982). Acquisition of cognitive skill. *Psychological Review, 89,* 369–406.

Argyris, C. (1957). *Personality and organization.* New York: Harper.

Argyris, C., & Schön, D. (1978). *Organizational learning.* Reading, MA: Addison-Wesley.

Alliger, G. M., & Janek, E. A. (1989). Kirkpatrick's levels of training criteria: Thirty years later. *Personnel Psychology, 42,* 331–342.

Alliger, G. M., Tannenbaum, S. I., Bennett, W., Traver, H., & Shortland, A. (1997). A meta-analysis on the relations among training criteria. *Personnel Psychology, 50,* 341–358.

Baldwin, T. T., & Ford, J. K. (1988). Transfer of training: A review and directions for future research. *Personnel Psychology, 41,* 63–105.

Baumgartel, H., & Jeanpeiere, F. (1972). Applying new knowledge in the back home setting: A study of Indian managers' adoptive efforts. *Journal of Applied Behavioral Science, 8,* 674–694.

Bandura, A. (1977). Self-efficacy: Toward a unifying theory of behavioral change. *Psychological Review, 84,* 191–215.

Bandura, A. (1982). Self-efficacy mechanism in human agency. *American Psychologist, 37,* 122–147.

Bass, B. M., & Vaughn, J. A. (1966). *Training in industry: The management of learning.* Belmont, CA: Brooks/Cole.

Bell, B. S., & Kozlowski, S. W. J. (2002). Adaptive guidance: Enhancing self-regulation, knowledge, and performance in technology-based training. *Personnel Psychology, 55,* 267–306.

Berrien, F. K. (1976). A general systems approach to organizations. In M. D. Dunnette (Ed.), *Handbook of industrial and organizational psychology* (pp. 41–62). Chicago: Rand McNally College.

Billett, S. (1993). What's in a setting? Learning in the workplace. *Australian Journal of Adult and Community Education, 33,* 4–14.

Billett, S. (1994). Situated learning: A workplace experience. *Australian Journal of Adult and Community Education, 33,* 112–130.

Boudreau, J. W., & Ramstad, P. M. (2003). Strategic I/O psychology and utility analysis. In W. Borman, R. Klimoski, & D. Ilgen (Eds.), *Handbook of psychology: Vol. 12. Industrial and organizational psychology* (pp. 193–221). New York: Wiley.

Brennan, M., & Anderson, C. (2001). *The U.S. corporate elearning market forecast and analysis, 2000–2005.* Framingham, MA: IDC.

Broadbent, D. E. (1958). *Perception and communication.* Elmsford, NY: Pergamon.

Brown, K. (2001). Using computers to deliver training: Which employees learn and why? *Personnel Psychology, 54,* 271–295.

Brown, K., & Ford, J. K. (2002). Using computer technology in training: Building an infrastructure of active learning. In K. Kraiger (Ed.), *Creating, implementing, and managing effective training and development* (pp. 192–233). San Francisco: Jossey-Bass.

Bruner, J. (1990). *Acts of meaning.* Cambridge, MA: Harvard University Press.

Burtt, H. E. (1929). *Psychology and industrial efficiency.* New York: Appleton.

Campbell, J. P. (1971). Personnel training and development. *Annual Review of Psychology, 22,* 565–602.

Campbell, D. T., & Stanley, J. C. (1963). Experimental and quasi-experimental designs for research on teaching. In N. L. Gage (Ed.), *Handbook of research on teaching* (pp. 171–246). Chicago: Rand McNally.

Campbell, J. P. (1988). Training design for performance improvement. In. J. P. Campbell, R. J. Campbell, & Associates (Eds.), *Productivity in organizations* (pp. 177–215). San Francisco: Jossey-Bass

Campbell, J. P. (1989). An agenda for theory and research. In I.. L. Goldstein & Associates (Eds.), *Training and development in organizations* (pp. 457–468). San Francisco: Jossey-Bass.

Campbell, J. P., & Kuncel, N. R. (2002). Individual and team training. In N. Anderson, D. S. Ones, H. K. Sinangil, & C. Viswesvaran (Eds.), *Handbook of industrial, work, and organizational psychology* (pp. 278–312). Thousand Oaks, CA: Sage.

Cannon-Bowers, J. A., Salas, E., Tannenbaum, S. I., & Mathieu, J. E. (1995). Toward theoretically based principles of training effectiveness: A model and initial empirical investigations. *Military Psychology, 7,* 141–164.

Canter, R. R., Jr. (1948). Psychologists in industry. *Personnel Psychology, 1,* 145–161.

Chase, W. G., & Simon, H. A. (1973). Perception in chess. *Cognitive Psychology, 1,* 55–81

Cognition and Technology Group at Vanderbilt. (1992). Some thoughts about constructivism and instructional design. In T. J. Duffy & D. H. Jonassen (Eds.), *Constructivism and the technology of instruction: A conversation* (pp. 115–119). Hillsdale, NJ: Lawrence Erlbaum Associates.

Cronbach, L. J. (1967). How can instruction be adapted to individual differences? In R. M. Gagné (Ed.), *Learning and individual differences* (pp. 123–144). Columbus, OH: Merrill.

Cuther-Gershefeld, J., & Ford, J. K. (2005). *Valuable disconnects.* New York: Oxford University Press.

Decker, P. J., & Nathan, B. (1985). *Behavior modeling training: Principles and applications.* New York: Praeger Scientific.

Drucker, P. (1954). *The practice of management.* New York: Harper.

Edgerton, H. A. (1955). Some needs in training research. *Personnel Psychology, 8,* 19–25.

Fiedler, F. E. (1964). A contingency model of leadership effectiveness. In L. Berkowitz (Ed.), *Advances in experimental social psychology, 1* (pp. 41–63). Orlando, FL: Academic Press.

Fine, S. A. (1978). *Contribution of the job element and functional job analysis approaches to content validity.* Paper presented at the International Personnel Management Assessment Council Annual Conference, Atlanta, GA.

Fisher, S. L., & Ford, J. K. (1998). Differential effects of learner effort and goal orientation on two learner outcomes. *Personnel Psychology, 51,* 397–420.

Fleishman, E. A. (1953). Leadership climate, human relations training, and supervisory behavior. *Personnel Psychology 6,* 205–222.

Fleishman, E. A., Harris, E. F., & Burtt, H. E. (1955). *Leadership and supervision in industry: An evaluation of a supervisory training program.* Columbus, OH: Bureau of Educational Research.

Ford, J. K. (2001). Employee training and development. In *American Psychological Association encyclopedia of psychology* (pp. 183–191). New York: Oxford University Press.

Ford, J. K., & Kraiger, K. (1995). The application of cognitive constructs and principles to the instructional systems of model training: Implications for needs assessment, design, and transfer. In C. L. Cooper & I. T. Robertson (Eds.), *International review of industrial and organizational psychology* (Vol. 10, pp. 1–48). Chichester, England: Wiley.

Ford, J. K., & Oswald, F. (2002). Understanding the dynamic learner: Linking personality traits, learning situations, and individual behavior. In M. Mount & A. M. Ryan (Eds.), *Personality and work* (pp. 229–261). San Francisco: Jossey-Bass.

Ford, J. K., Quiñones, M. A., Sego, D. J., & Sorra, J. S. (1992). Factors affecting the opportunity to perform trained tasks on the job. *Personnel Psychology, 45,* 511–527.

Ford, J. K., Smith, E. M., Weissbein, D. A., Gully, S. M., & Salas, E. (1998). Relationships of goal orientation, metacognitive activity, and practice strategies with learning outcomes and transfer. *Journal of Applied Psychology, 83,* 218–233.

Foxon, M. J. (1993). A process approach to the transfer of training: Part 1. The impact of motivation and supervisor support on transfer maintenance. *Australian Journal of Educational Technology, 9,* 130–143.

Gagné, R. M. (1962). Military training and principles of learning. *American Psychologist, 17,* 83–91.

Gephart, M. A., Marsick, V. J., Van Buren, M. E., & Spiro, M. S. (1996). Learning organizations come alive. *Training and Development, 50,* 56–66.

Ghiselli, E. E., & Brown, C. W. (1948). *Personnel and industrial psychology.* New York: McGraw-Hill.

Gilbert, T. F. (1978). *Human competence: Engineering worthy performance.* New York: McGraw-Hill.

Gillespie, R. (1988). The Hawthorne experiments and the politics of experimentation. In J. G. Morawski (Ed.), *The rise of experimentation in American psychology* (pp. 114–137). New Haven: Yale University Press.

Gist, M. E., Stevens, C. K. & Bavetta, A. G. (1991). Effects of self-efficacy and post-training intervention on the acquisition and maintenance of complex interpersonal skills. *Personnel Psychology, 44,* 837–861.

Glaser, R., & Resnick, L. (1972). Instructional psychology. *Annual Review of Psychology, 23,* 181–276.

Goldstein, A. P., & Sorcher, M. (1974). *Changing supervisor behavior.* New York: Pergamon.

Goldstein, I. L. (1974). *Training: Program development and evaluation.* Monterey, CA: Brooks/Cole.

Goldstein, I. L. (1980). Training in work organizations. *Annual Review of Psychology, 31,* 229–272.

Goldstein, I. L. (1986). *Training in organizations: Needs assessment, development and evaluation* (2nd ed.). Belmont, CA: Brooks/Cole.

Goldstein, I. L. (2002). *Irwin L. Goldstein: SIOP president 1985–1986.* Retrieved December 19, 2005, from http://siop.org/Presidents/Goldstein.htm

Goldstein, I. L., & Associates (1989). *Training and development in organizations.* San Francisco: Jossey-Bass.

Goldstein, I. L., & Ford, J. K. (2002). *Training in organizations* (4th ed.). Belmont, CA: Wadsworth Thompson Learning.

Goldstein, I. L., & Gessner (1988). Training and development in work organizations. In C. L. Cooper & I. Roberstson (Eds.), *International review of industrial and organizational psychology* (pp. 43–72). London: Wiley.

Goldstein, I. L., Macy, W. H., & Prien, E. P. (1981). Needs assessment approaches for training development. In H. Meltzer & W. R. Nord (Eds.), *Making organizations humane and productive* (pp. 131–165). New York: Wiley.

Hammer, M. F. (1995). *The reengineering revolution.* New York: Harperbusiness.

Hansen, M. T., Nohria, N., & Tierney, T. (1999). What's your strategy for managing knowledge. *Harvard Business Review, 77,* 106–116.

Hart-Landesberg, S., Braunger, J., & Reder, S. (1992). *Learning the ropes: The social construction of work-based learning* (ED 363 726). Berkeley, CA: National Center for Research in Vocational Education.

Hedlund, G. (1994). A model of knowledge management and the N-form corporation. *Strategic Management Journal, 15,* 73–90.

Highhouse, S. (2002). A history of the t-group and its early applications in management development. *Group Dynamics: Theory, Research, and Practice, 6,* 277–290.

Hinrichs, J. R. (1976). Personnel training. In M. D. Dunnette (Ed.), *Handbook of industrial and organizational psychology* (pp. 829–860). Chicago: Rand McNally College.

Holton, E. F., III. (1996). The flawed four level evaluation model. *Human Resource Development Quarterly, 7,* 5–21.

Hothersall, D. (1995). *History of psychology.* Boston: McGraw-Hill.

Howell, W. C., & Cooke, N. J. (1989). Training the human information processor: A review of cognitive models. In I. L. Goldstein & Associates (Eds.), *Training and development in organizations* (pp. 121–182). San Francisco: Jossey-Bass.

Jonassen, D. H. (1991). Objectism vs. constructivism: Do we need a new philosophical paradigm shift? *Educational Technology: Research & Development, 39*(3), 5–14.

Katz, D., & Kahn, R. L. (1966). *The social psychology of organizations.* New York: Wiley.

Kirkpatrick, D. L. (1959). Techniques for evaluating training programs. *Journal of ASTD, 13*(11), 3–9.

Kirkpatrick, D. L. (1967). Evaluation of training. In R. L. Craig & L. R. Bittel (Eds.), *Training and development handbook* (pp. 87–112). New York: McGraw-Hill.

Kozlowski, S. W. J., Brown, K. G., Weissbein, D. A., Cannon-Bowers, J. A., & Salas, E. (2002). A multilevel approach to training effectiveness: Enhancing horizontal and vertical transfer. In K. J. Klein & S. W. J. Kozlowski (Eds.), *Multilevel theory, research, and methods in organizations* (pp. 157–210). San Francisco: Jossey-Bass.

Kozlowski, S. W. J., & Salas, E. (1997). An organizational systems approach for the implementation and transfer of training. In J. K. Ford & Associates (Eds.), *Improving training effectiveness in work organizations* (pp. 291–322). Mahwah, NJ: Lawrence Erlbaum Associates..

Kraiger, K., Ford, J. K., & Salas, E. (1993). Application of cognitive, skill-based, and affective theories of learning outcomes to new methods of training evaluation. *Journal of Applied Psychology, 78,* 311–328.

Kulik, C. C., & Kulik, J. A. (1991). Effectiveness of computer-based instruction: An updated analysis. *Computers in Human Behavior, 7,* 75–94.

Kuwada, K. (1998). Strategic learning: The continuous side of discontinuous strategic change. *Organizational Science, 2,* 719–736.

Latham, G. P. (1988). Human resource training and development. *Annual Review of Psychology, 39,* 545–582.

Latham, G. P., & Saari, L. (1979). The application of social learning theory to training supervisors through behavioral role modeling. *Journal of Applied Psychology, 64,* 239–246.

Leahey, T. H. (2002). Cognition and learning. In I. Weiner (Series Ed.) & D. K. Freedheim (Vol. Ed.), *Handbook of psychology: Vol. 1: History of psychology* (pp. 109–133). New York: Wiley.

Lee, C. A. (1932). Some notes on incentives in industry. *The Human Factor, VI,* 180–186.

Liefer, M. S., & Newstrom, J. W. (1980, August). Solving the transfer of training problems. *Training and Development Journal,* pp. 42–46.

Lord, R. G., & Maher, K. J. (1991). Cognitive theory in industrial/organizational psychology. In M. D. Dunnette & L. M. Hough (Eds.), *Handbook of industrial and organizational psychology* (2nd ed., Vol. 2, pp. 1–62). Palo Alto, CA: Consulting Psychologists Press.

Mahler, W. R., & Monroe, W. H. (1952). *How industry determines the need for and effectiveness of training.* New York: Psychological Corporation.

Maier, N. R. F. (1952). *Principles of human relations.* New York: Wiley.

McCord, B. (1976). Job instruction. In R. L. Craig & L. R. Bittel (Eds.), *Training and development handbook* (2nd ed., pp. 32.3–32.34). New York: McGraw-Hill.

McGehee, W. (1949). Training in industry. In W. Dennis (Ed.), *Current trends in industrial psychology* (pp. 84–114). Pittsburgh: University of Pittsburgh Press.

McGehee, W. (1958). Are we using what we know about training? Learning theory and training. *Personnel Psychology, 11,* 1–12.

McGehee, W., & Thayer, P. (1961). *Training in business and industry*. New York: McGraw-Hill.

McGregor, D. (1960). *The human side of enterprise*. New York: Wiley.

Meister, J. (1998). Ten steps to creating a corporate university. *Training and Development, 52*(11), 38–43.

Miles, G. H. (1932). Effectiveness of labour incentives. *The Human Factor, VI*, 53–58.

Miller, R. B. (1953). *Handbook of training and training equipment design*. Pittsburgh: The American Institute of Research.

Morgan, G. (1997). *Images of organizations* (2nd ed.). Thousand Oaks, CA: Sage.

Münsterberg, H. (1910). *Psychology and the teacher*. New York: Appleton.

Münsterberg, H. (1913). *Psychology and industrial efficiency*. Boston: Houghton Mifflin.

Myers, C. S. (1925). *Industrial psychology*. New York: The People's Institute Publishing Company.

Neisser, U. (1967). *Cognitive psychology*. New York: Appleton-Century-Crofts.

Noe, R. A. (1986). Trainees' attributes and attitudes: Neglected influences on training effectiveness. *Academy of Management Review, 11*, 736–749.

Noe, R. A. (2002). *Employee training and development* (2nd ed.). Boston: McGraw-Hill.

Nonaka, I., & Takeuchi, H. (1995). *The knowledge-creating company*. New York: Oxford University Press.

Obituaries: Gagné, Robert (2002, April 29). *The Chatanoogan.com*. Retrieved December 16, 2005, from http://www.chattanoogan.com/articles/article_2123.asp

Ostroff, C., & Ford, J. K. (1989). Assessing training needs: Critical levels of analysis. In I. L. Goldstein & Associates (Eds.), *Training and development in organizations* (pp. 25–62). San Francisco: Jossey-Bass.

Planty, C. G., McCord, W. S., & Efferson, C. A. (1948). *Training employees and managers*. New York: Ronald Press.

Prien, E. P. (1977). The function of job analysis in content validation. *Personnel Psychology, 30*, 501–504.

Quiñones, M. A., Ford, J. K., Sego, D. J., & Smith, E. M. (1996). The effects of individual and transfer environment characteristics on the opportunity to perform trained tasks. *Training Research Journal, 1*, 29–48.

Roethlisberger, F. J., & Dickson, W. J. (1939). *Management and the worker*. Cambridge, MA: Harvard University, Graduate School of Business Administration.

Rouiller, J. Z., & Goldstein, I. L. (1993). The relationship between organizational transfer climate and positive transfer of training. *Human Resource Development Quarterly, 4*, 377–390.

Russell, T. L. (1999). *No significant difference phenomenon*. Raleigh: North Carolina State University.

Salas, E., & Cannon-Bowers, J. (2001). The science of training: A decade of progress. *Annual Review of Psychology, 52*, 471–499.

Schippmann, J. S., Ash, R. A., Battista, M., Carr, L., Eyde, L. D., Hesketh, B., et al. (2000). The practice of competency modeling. *Personnel Psychology, 53*, 703–740.

Scott, W. D., Clother, R. C., Mathewson, S. B., & Spriegel, W. R. (1941). *Personnel management: Principles, practices, and point of view*. New York: McGraw-Hill.

Senge, P. M. (1990). *The fifth discipline: The art and practice of the learning organization*. New York: Doubleday.

Simon, H. A. (1957). *Administrative behavior* (2nd ed.). New York: Macmillan.

Skinner, B. F. (1957). *Verbal behavior*. New York: Appleton-Century-Crofts.

Smith, L. J. (1942). Vestibule training for today's needs. In A. E. Dodd & J. O. Rice (Eds.), *How to train workers for war industries* (pp. 59–67). New-York: Harper.

Steinmetz, C. S. (1967). The evolution of training. In R. L. Craig & L. R. Bittel (Eds.), *Training and development handbook* (pp. 1–15). New York: McGraw-Hill.

Stewart, T. (1997). *Intellectual capital: The new wealth of organizations*. New York: Currency.

Stogdill, R. M. (1974). *Handbook of leadership*. New York: Free Press

Stogdill, R. M., & Coons, A. E. (1957). *Leader behavior: Its description and measurement*. Columbus: Ohio State University, Bureau of Business Research.

Stroud, P. V. (1959). Evaluating a human relations training program. *Personnel 36*(11), 52–60.

Tannenbaum, S. I. (1997). Enhancing continuous learning: Diagnostic findings from multiple companies. *Human Resource Management, 36*, 437–452.

Taylor, F. W. (1911). *Principles of scientific management*. New York: Harper.

Thayer, P. W. (2002). *Paul Thayer: SIOP president 1976–1977*. Retrieved December 19, 2005, from http://siop.org/Presidents/Thayer.htm

Thayer, P. W., & McGehee, W. (1977). On the effectiveness of not holding a formal training course. *Personnel Psychology, 30*, 455–456.

Thomas, J. B., Sussman, S. W., & Henderson, J. C. (2001). Understanding "strategic learning": Linking organizational learning, knowledge management, and sensemaking. *Organizational Science, 12*, 331–345.

Tiffin, J. (1942). *Industrial psychology*. New York: Prentice-Hall.

Tracey, J. B., Tannenbaum, S. I., & Kavanagh, M. J. (1995). Applying trained skills on the job: The importance of work environment. *Journal of Applied Psychology, 80,* 239–252.

Turing, A. M. (1950). Computing machinery and intelligence. *Mind, 59,* 433–460.

Twitchell, S., Holton, E. F., III, & Trott, J. R., Jr. (2001). Technical training evaluation practices in the United States. *Performance Improvement Quarterly, 13*(3), 84–109.

Van Buren, M. E., (2001). *State of the industry: Report 2001.* Washington, DC: American Society for Training and Development.

Viteles, M.S. (1932). *Industrial psychology.* New York: Norton.

Wallace, S. R., Jr., & Twichell, C. M. (1953). An evaluation of a training course for life insurance agents. *Personnel Psychology, 6,* 25–43.

Wexley, K. N., & Latham, G. P. (1981). *Developing and training human resources in organizations.* Glenview, IL: Scott, Foresman.

Yelon, S. L., & Ford, J. K. (1999). Pursuing a multidimensional view of transfer. *Performance Improvement Quarterly, 12,* 58–78.

13

Performance Appraisal

James L. Farr
Pennsylvania State University

Paul E. Levy
University of Akron

> *Man never gets away from measurement during his stay on earth. At birth he is mea-sured to ascertain his weight, and at death he is measured to determine his length. After death two dates are carved on his tombstone to indicate the span of his life. Measures permeate and influence all of his activities. Progress in any line depends largely on abil-ity to measure exactly.* (F. A. Moss, 1927)

The quote by F. A. Moss in 1927 suggests how important measurement is in the lives of human beings. This belief in the importance of measurement in our daily lives provided the foundation for most of the early work in performance ratings and appraisal. This focus on measurement was operationalized in the work of I–O psychologists. It's interesting to note that this point was more recently discussed at length in the work of Folger and his colleagues, who argued that performance appraisal developed from what they called "a test metaphor," which views perfor-mance appraisal as a straightforward measurement issue and ignores many of the other contex-tual issues that have attracted research attention in more recent years (Folger, Konovsky, & Cropanzano, 1992).

Performance evaluations of individual employees are obtained for several organizational purposes. These include research (e.g., to serve as a criterion measure for validating predictor tests or evaluating the effectiveness of a training program), administrative use (e.g., as input to personnel decisions such as retention, promotion, salary increases, or placement), and the de-velopment and motivation of employees (e.g., assignment to training programs, error correc-tion, role clarification, and goal accomplishment; Landy & Farr, 1983). Murphy and Cleveland (1995) noted that ratings are also used for legal purposes (e.g., documentation of fairness and validity of personnel decisions) and political purposes (e.g., efforts of individual raters to en-hance or protect their self-interests and interests of their employees through the performance evaluation process and system). Historically, application and research related to these pur-poses have emerged in a chronological sequence roughly ordered as listed here (DeVries, Mor-rison, Shullman, & Gerlach, 1986; Murphy & Cleveland, 1995). That is, the initial uses of performance ratings were as criteria for validating predictors of job success and as input for personnel decisions. These purposes place great weight on the accuracy of the performance

ratings, reinforcing the "test metaphor'" described by Folger et al. (1992). Subsequent research on performance appraisal has focused on the influence of the context in which ratings
are obtained. We now turn in more detail to the emergence of performance ratings within industrial psychology near the beginning of World War I.

RATING JOB PERFORMANCE: WORLD WAR I
AND THE ROARING TWENTIES

As indicated in other chapters, Katzell and Austin (1992) identified several societal forces
operating before World War I that influenced the development of I–O psychology. First, the
general growth of science during this period led to empirical studies of the psychology of human behavior, including work performance. In addition, great faith in capitalism was a predominant view during the very early 20th century and was accompanied by a demand for
efficiency. Finally, the capitalist system played a role in the rapid growth of industrialization
that required well-trained, competent, and motivated employees. These forces were integral
to the development of the field of I–O psychology and, we argue, began to lay the groundwork for the development of performance appraisal. However, before World War I, very little
work in the area of performance appraisal was conducted—the impetus to widespread use of
performance appraisal was the outbreak of World War I, which played a large role in the historical development of the I–O field in general (see chaps. 3, 7, and 8, this text) and the development of performance appraisal in particular. Consistent with the opening quote by Moss,
and driven by the forces described by Katzell and Austin (see also Koppes, 2003), the early
work on performance appraisal focused on issues of measurement.

As with just about everything that has developed within the field of I–O psychology, performance appraisal can be traced back to the work of those early pioneers involved in the exciting activities taking place at Carnegie Institute of Technology (CIT; also known as
Carnegie Tech) in Pittsburgh, which was described in chapters 2 and 6. Our story begins with
the hiring of Walter Dill Scott as the first American professor of applied psychology and director of the Bureau of Salesmanship Research in the Division of Applied Psychology at Carnegie Tech, in June 1916. He focused for the first year or so on the selection of salespeople
and noted that there were no established measures of the degree to which applicants possessed many of the traits essential for successful salesmanship. Thus, Scott developed a rating scale in January 1917 to be used in hiring interviews to assess candidates' qualifications
for sales positions, but rating scale instruments were soon used for selection in other occupations and also adapted to be used for the performance evaluation of incumbent employees
(Scott, Clothier, & Spriegel, 1949). (See chap. 8 in this text for additional information on selection.) As noted earlier in this text, war was declared in April 1917, and many of the pioneers of I–O psychology used their skills and intelligence to serve the United States through
military service.

Described in previous chapters, Scott and Bingham served on the Committee on Classification of Personnel under the Adjutant General's Office (AGO) under the Secretary of War.
As well as devising the early "personnel files" for military personnel, this group further developed the "man-to-man" and graphic rating scales that Scott was working on before the
war. These appear to be the first formal mechanisms used in the evaluation of individual performance in the U.S. Army and soon were used frequently in the private sector. The bulk of
the work in the area of performance appraisal during the next 15 years focused on rating
scales (a focus that would reemerge in the middle to late part of the 20th century, only to be
dissuaded in 1980 by Landy and Farr), and it is a discussion of these scales and this work that
we turn to next.

Scott's Man-to-Man Scale

Scott developed the Man-to-Man Rating Scale while at Carnegie Tech and then modified it for use in rating the efficiency of army officers (Paterson, 1922) during World War I. What is interesting about this scale is that each rater was instructed to develop his or her own scale units by thinking about different people he or she had known who possessed different degrees of the relevant trait. In other words, each rater would use his or her own personal experiences with other people to anchor the various scale points. Raters would be asked to fill in names for each anchor of the scale for each trait and then use those anchors in evaluating the target employee. A scale measuring leadership (taken from Poffenberger, 1942) might look like the example in Fig. 13.1 after the rater filled in names to create his or her comparison anchors.

A rating given an employee on this scale is in relation to his or her standing among these men. Thus, if a current employee was rated a 10, this would suggest that his or her leadership skills fell between the levels of leadership possessed by Paul Figg and James Brown. This approach was believed to be superior to the other existing approaches at the time, which simply asked raters to assign a number (e.g., 1 to 5), letter (*A* to *E*), or word (*excellent* to *poor*) to each ratee for each trait or dimension. At a minimum, the Man-to-Man Rating Scale provided a concrete standard developed by the rater against which each employee could be rated (Paterson, 1923).

In May 1917, Scott developed a modified version of the Man-to-Man Rating Scale designed for use in making decisions regarding the promotion of Army first lieutenants to the rank of captain (Ferguson, 1962–1965). By June 1917, Scott had begun a personal campaign to win acceptance for his rating scale, which he believed would be "the greatest contribution [that] psychologists could make" (Ferguson, 1962–1965, p. 125) to the war effort, even exceeding that of the Army Alpha and Beta intelligence tests. Gaining acceptance was not an easy process, but Scott was tenacious in his efforts, presenting himself and his rating scale to numerous Army officers and War Department officials during July and early August 1917 (Ferguson, 1962–1965). Scott's perseverance won out, and the use of the Man-to-Man Rating Scale was approved by the Army War College on August 5 for use in the selection of candidates for Officers' Training Camps. By the end of World War I, more than 180,000 Army officers had been evaluated on Scott's rating scale (Ferguson, 1962–1965). In January 1918, the use of the Man-to-Man Rating Scale was extended to the evaluation of all commissioned officers. General John (Black Jack) Pershing, commander of the American Expeditionary Forces (A.E.F.) in Europe, ordered that all officers in the A.E.F. were to be rated quarterly beginning April 15, 1918. Finally, in August 1918, the merit ranking for promotion of officers in all ranks was based solely on their ratings on the Man-to-Man Rating Scale. Scott's dream was certainly realized!

Although the Man-to-Man Rating Scale provided a concrete set of comparison standards for a given rater, there were other problems with this approach. First, Rugg (1921) and Kingsbury (1926-1927) reported that it didn't work very well because raters were reluctant to put in

Leadership	Descriptor	Name	Score
Initiative, force, self-reliance, decisiveness, tact, ability to inspire men and to command their obedience, loyalty, and cooperation	Highest	Robert Smith	15
	High	James Brown	12
	Middle	Paul Figg	9
	Low	Samuel Hip	6
	Lowest	Donald Trat	3

FIG. 13.1. Scott's Man-to-Man Scale: example.

the necessary time to construct a reasonable master scale or didn't even bother creating the master scale and just assigned numbers to ratees. As described by Paterson (1923), "The method proved to be too time-consuming, cumbersome, and difficult to understand for the average rating executive" (p. 87). Second, because each rater develops his or her own master scale, scales may differ considerably from each other resulting in ratings that are not all comparable. For instance, the same employee could represent a 12 on one rater's master scale and a 6 on someone else's. This would result in rating scales for the two raters that were not equivalent. As Poffenberger (1942) stated, "To measure human qualities with such devices would be like measuring length with a yard stick on which the numbers were jumbled into a random order" (p. 268). He still noted, as did others, that the scale is solid in principle and could be very useful in those situations where the raters would develop similar master scales. Despite these rather serious criticisms, the Man-to-Man Rating Scale was a popular approach to the measurement of human performance. It was widely implemented in the U.S. Army, as we have noted here, and it was used by organizations in the private sector as well. Its popularity was largely a function of it being a scientifically developed approach among very few alternatives—there weren't many other options, but let's consider a few.

Specific Instance Scale

One modification of the Man-to-Man Rating Scale is what Poffenberger (1942) called the Specific Instance Scale, in which rather than raters choosing which people pose as the scale anchors, the scale anchors were developed external to the raters—that is, by the scale developers themselves. These anchors were instances of behaviors that were exhibited by "the best" electrician, "a good" electrician, "an average" electrician, and "a poor" electrician. It seems obvious that this scale was a very early forerunner of the Behaviorally Anchored Rating Scale (BARS) which was developed in the 1960s and is discussed later in this chapter.

Descriptive-Term Scale

Poffenberger (1942) suggested that the most popular type of scale used during this era was the Descriptive-Term Scale, where descriptive phrases or general adjectives were used as anchors rather than the specific behaviors of the previous scale. For instance, a scale measuring the performance appraisal dimension of "promptness" might look like the example in Fig. 13.2.

These scales were generally easy to develop, which was important for the 1920s, when technology helpful to developing scales and implementing them in organizations was quite limited. Rugg (1921) created a hybrid of the Descriptive-Term Scale and the Specific-Instance Scale in which he used the behavioral or specific instance approach in developing questions (e.g., Is he loyal to the administration and other teachers?) that were then answered along a scale anchored by descriptive terms (e.g., *low, average, high*). The performance appraisal rating for a particular dimension would be a combination of the answers to all of the related questions.

Graphic Rating Scale

In many ways the rating scale that has had the greatest impact on the development of the performance appraisal field in the first 100 years is the Graphic Rating Scale, which was initially de-

Work frequently late	Work usually on time	Work always done promptly

FIG.13.2.   Descriptive-Term Scale: example

veloped at the Scott Company (an early consulting firm; see chap. 6). However, according to Donald Paterson (1922), it was Beardsley Ruml (an employee at the Scott Company) who really was the leader of this effort. Ruml went on to become the treasurer of R. H. Macy and a member of FDR's "brain trust" (Katzell & Austin, 1992). While at the Scott Company, Ruml and others such as Donald Paterson and, presumably, Walter Dill Scott himself became involved in the development of the graphic rating scale to use for performance assessment. According to Paterson (1922), there were two essential features to the Scott graphic rating scale: The rater is freed from direct quantitative terms in making his or her ratings, and the rater can make as fine a discrimination as he or she desires. The rater simply makes a check mark along the line defining a particular trait, behavior, or quality. The anchors are short descriptive adjectives, but the rater is instructed that his check mark does not need to correspond directly to any anchor and can be between anchors—this allows for as fine a discrimination as one desires. The performance score is arrived at through the use of a stencil divided into 10 divisions and then placed over the scale. The score corresponds to where on the stencil the checkmark falls. If it falls in the 4th division, then the score would be a 4. This approach provides for more gradations in scores because raters aren't limited to the typical whole numbers such as 1 to 5. An example of part of a graphic rating scale for clerical workers from Burtt's (1926) early text follows in Fig. 13.3.

An interesting wrinkle that was included in the graphic rating scales of the 1920s was that the actual ratings as described in Fig. 13.3 were never used in that raw score form—they were normatively scored. For instance, the top 10% of each rater's scores were all given the same final rating, A, regardless of what the face value of the score was. The next 20% of each rater's scores were given a B rating, and so on. The purpose was to use these relative ratings so that the error associated with a particular rater rating too high (leniency) or too low (severity) could be controlled (Paterson, 1922). Obviously, the emphasis on this normative approach to scoring makes it clear that the early pioneers were aware and concerned about those very rater biases that became the chief focus of the performance appraisal research in the second half of the 20th century. Paterson reported data from the 1920s indicating that the graphic rating scales were quite reliable (as assessed by both test–retest and interrater reliability indices), simple and practical to use, as well as anecdotal evidence of the favorable reactions of both raters and ratees.

It's also interesting to note that the normative scoring idea, which was quite central to these early versions of graphic rating scales, disappeared from later versions of this approach. Instead, the concerns of leniency, severity, and central tendency were dealt with historically in various ways such as the use of forced distributions, which became very popular later in the 20th century. In this approach, raters are prevented from making these rating errors by being forced to rate certain portions of their subordinates at a particular level (e.g., 10% rated as promotable, 25% rated as exceeds expectations, etc.); however, other problems stem from this approach when the true distribution of performance does not match the mandated distribution.

Appearance: neatness of person and dress	Appropriate	Neat	Ordinary	Passable	Slovenly
Ability to learn: ease of learning new methods	Very quick	Catches on easily		Needs repeated instruction	
Accuracy: quality of work; freedom from errors	No errors	Very careful	Few errors	Careless	Many errors

FIG. 13.3.   Graphic Rating Scale: example.

THE 1930s: DEPRESSION

Although a number of texts related to industrial psychology and personnel management were published in the second half of the 1920s and the 1930s (e.g., Bingham & Freyd, 1926; Burtt, 1926; Hepner, 1930; Hull, 1928; Jenkins, 1935; B. V. Moore & Hartman, 1931; H. Moore, 1939; Poffenberger, 1927, 1942; Viteles, 1932, 1934; see chap. 1), across this 15-year period the discussion about rating scales changed little in most of these volumes. The various rating methods discussed here were the primary topics in most of the relevant chapters, along with discussions of concerns about rating errors (e.g., leniency, severity, halo) and unreliability. The predominant purpose of the ratings was to measure accurately the job performance of employees so that predictor tests could be validated and personnel decisions could be made. As noted by Katzell and Austin (1992), this period was characterized more by refinement of existing procedures and instruments than the development of new approaches, perhaps related to the economic conditions that likely severely limited the resources for such developments.

Some exceptions to the status quo should be noted. Hepner (1930) included in his discussion of the value of using systematic performance ratings in work organizations several factors not commonly seen in the 1930s. He noted that raters could learn about their ability to judge others by comparing their ratings to other performance indexes and to ratings of the same individuals made by other raters and, thus, to gain greater insight about the quality of one's judgments. Perhaps more prescient was Hepner's point that employees could learn from ratings about "the particular qualities he should develop or eliminate" (p. 232). Hepner also wrote, "Few employees know their own strong and weak characteristics. They do not improve themselves, because the management does not tell them, what to do to improve or how to do it" (p. 232). Clearly, Hepner was describing a feedback and development purpose for the ratings. Although this appears prosaic in the early 21st century, other industrial psychologists were not generally urging the use of ratings for developmental purposes in 1930. In a set of general principles that Hepner listed for using and making ratings, he listed several prescriptive statements about performance appraisal and feedback that seem sound today. These include that ratings should be obtained in an organization after management has adequately described to employees their purposes and that one of the purposes should be to provide ratings to the employees to assist them in development. In addition, Hepner emphasized that ratings should be used in a timely fashion, soon after they are obtained, in "a friendly discussion with each employee" (p. 245) that emphasizes the employee's strong points and plans a specific "program for the utilization of the positive qualities of each employee" (p. 245). The points raised by Hepner are clearly missing from Paterson's rating principles (see Table 13.1).

Why was Hepner's approach to ratings different from the authors of other industrial psychology texts of the time? The preface to his book provides some clues. Hepner noted that his book was intended for those planning to be managers and owners of business organizations and that his book would focus on how psychology could be used to address the everyday problems that they would face in their careers. He further noted that the contents of existing books were "too abstruse and far removed from the human problems of the shop, the office, the market" (p. vii). He further decried the gap between the academic writers and their business audience, one still not successfully bridged in the ratings literature (cf. Banks & Murphy, 1985).

Certainly, Hepner (1930) was one of the first industrial psychologists to discuss the potential advantages that might result from performance feedback to employees based on ratings, but a few others also had similar ideas. Herbert Moore (1939) noted the use of ratings in promotion as a means of promoting the perceived justice of the decisions (presumably to the unsuccessful candidates) when contrasted to the traditional approach of using "the unguided

TABLE 13.1
Paterson's 12 Principles of Psychological Ratings (1923)

1. Supervisors should file "estimates" of subordinates' performance continually.
2. "Estimates" should be based on unambiguously defined qualities.
3. Qualities to be judged should be defined objectively.
4. Each quality should be unidimensional.
5. Ratings should be confined to past or present accomplishments.
6. The list of qualities to be rated must be directly rated to the work to be performed.
7. The method of recording ratings should be easy to use and understand.
8. Estimates should be expressed in a uniform way by all raters.
9. A statistical method for correcting for ratings that are "too high" or "too low" should be used.
10. The use of ratings should be limited to those made by raters proven to be capable of accurately judging human qualities.
11. Each rater should rate all employees on the first quality and then all employees on the second quality, and so on.
12. As many raters as possible should be used, and an average of all ratings should be used in the final evaluation of an employee.

judgment of one or more (company) officers" (p. 228). Moore was certainly foreshadowing the organizational justice literature that emerged about 50 years later.

In addition, Humke (1938–1939) argued for using a rating system for employee development and identifying individual training needs. Humke also argued that to get the full use of employee ratings, they should be used as an index of employee morale to identify the departments or divisions in which there are serious performance problems. But, he argued, the biggest returns come from a personal audit at the individual level in which ratings are actually used as a diagnostic tool to target particular employees for training, dismissal, and promotion. Although Humke did not explicitly mention using the ratings as a basis for coaching the employee, that seems to be the gist of his thinking. He argued that "this introduces a phase of personnel work that is as yet not fully recognized in industry" (p. 294). Also, he argued that we should be measuring "ability to advance" and not just performance—having these ratings provides the "reserve power of the company" in that it tells the company who is standing in the wings ready to move up and take on more responsibility. Humke further noted that if an organization is not committed to using ratings, then they should not be obtained. Finally, stressing the importance of the feedback use, Humke stated, "A foreman who cannot sit down in quiet with an employee to talk over a weakness is not qualified to handle men in action under the strain of modern production" (p. 295).

WORLD WAR II AND THE EISENHOWER YEARS

The large increase in the overall size of the U.S. Army before and soon after the United States' entry into World War II necessitated a related increase in the number of general officers to command units. When the Army turned to the existing efficiency reports (semiannual performance ratings) to find about 150 top candidates for the rank of brigadier general, it was found that the efficiency reports provided no basis for the decisions: Of the 4,000 officers who were in the candidate pool, about 2,000 had received ratings of "superior and best" (Sisson, 1948, p. 367). With no differentiation on the basis of the performance ratings, the promotion authorities had to resort (apparently reluctantly) to using their personal knowledge of the candidates (Sisson, 1948).

Sisson (1948) noted that the existing efficiency report was "fairly typical and quite respectable" (p. 367) and "would even compare favorably with the run-of-the-mill systems currently in use in business and industry" (p. 367). As Sisson briefly described it, it was a 5-point, adjectival-anchored, graphic rating scale with 10 traits and performance dimensions that were rated. It appears that Scott's Man-to-Man Rating Scale, adopted in World War I, had been dropped early in the 1920s, perhaps a victim of its cumbersomeness and other problems noted by Paterson (1923). Sisson (1948) simply noted that the origin of the efficiency report and its reporting procedure had been "lost in history" (p. 365), but it can be inferred that such were in place no later than the mid-1920s and used until July 1947, when replaced by a new procedure based on a forced-choice evaluation method.

The new forced-choice rating procedure was developed for a single primary purpose: to provide a sound basis for personnel actions (Sisson, 1948). The highly skewed, lenient ratings, although they apparently did identify a "very small number of outstandingly poor officers" (Sisson, 1948, p. 367), were not useful for promotion decisions, and the normal pressures for high ratings led to political and game-playing activities (cf. Kozlowski, Chao, & Morrison, 1998; Longenecker, Sims, & Gioia, 1987).

From a measurement perspective (or the test metaphor), raters were a source of error in the old efficiency reports because they could easily control the ratings they gave to the officers. The new forced-choice ratings eliminated much of that rater control over the rating outcomes by disguising the scoring procedure that transformed the rater's judgments into the ratee's final rating. For a number of sets of four performance statements, the rater had to choose in each set the one statement that best described the officer being rated and the statement that least well described the individual. Each set contained two favorably worded and two negatively worded statements. One of each pair of comparable favorability distinguished between good and poor officers but the other did not, as determined during an extensive item scaling procedure. When selected by the raters as descriptive of the ratee, only the discriminating (valid) items were scored. Thus, the rater merely trying to say something nice about an officer would be as likely to select nondiscriminating items as the valid ones, but the final rating would not be enhanced by the selection of nonvalid descriptors. The forced-choice rating procedure was evaluated as successful (Sisson, 1948) because it did change the overall distribution of ratings when compared with the prior graphic-rating scale procedure, resulting in more officers being rated at both ends of the distribution. Industry and researchers both became interested in forced-choice ratings in the 1950s and 1960s, and these decades saw numerous related publications in both academic and practitioner journals. However, raters have traditionally viewed these with contempt because they felt like they are rating blindly, not knowing which dimensions are really important, and thus perceived a loss of control over the rating process.

The forced-choice rating procedure was not the only contribution that the U.S. Army made to industrial psychology and performance ratings following World War II. The Personnel Research Section, Adjutant General's Office, Department of the Army also funded a ground-breaking foray into the theory of ratings by Robert Wherry. Wherry began with an annotated bibliography drawn from the 1930 to 1950 published literature related to ratings, judgment and decision making, and psychological measurement (Wherry, 1950), culminating in a formal mathematical model that attempted to specify the factors that would affect the accuracy of a performance rating, excluding conscious bias attempts (Wherry, 1952). Wherry (1952) noted that his theory of ratings was influenced heavily by classical mental test theory (Gulliksen, 1950), Helson's (1947) adaptation theory of psychophysical response, and Bartlett's (1932) theory of memory that was among the earliest treatments of cognitive schema, selective memory, and constructive aspects of memory. To summarize his theory very briefly, Wherry viewed the accuracy of a performance rating (usually representing a judgment made about performance over some relatively long time period) to be a function of the actual performance events of the ratee, the rater's observation of those performance events, and the rater's recall of those observations. Accuracy as a focal variable places Wherry in the test metaphor tradition, but he included a host of psychological, situational, and procedural variables as factors that might reliably affect the accuracy of the rating (for details of the theory, see Wherry, 1983; Wherry & Bartlett, 1982). It is clear today that Wherry's theory of rating should have had a strong and widespread impact on research and practice concerning performance ratings, and it is equally clear (if not more so) that it did not until 3 decades after it was written. Its relative lack of impact, at least in contrast to what might have been, was due primarily to Wherry not being overly concerned about publishing his work widely. Although known to Wherry's graduate students at Ohio State University and their students, the theory was available only as a U.S. Army technical report (and as increasingly illegible photocopies of that) until the early 1980s when, ironically, it was published in two slightly different versions. The publication of one version (Wherry & Bartlett, 1982) was encouraged by C. J. Bartlett, one of Wherry's graduate students from the mid-1950s, who became Wherry's co-author as he edited the technical report into a format better suited for a scholarly journal, *Personnel Psychology*. The other version (Wherry, 1983) was published as an invited appendix to Landy and Farr's (1983) work measurement book. This version was closer in form to the original technical report. It should also be noted that "family ties" were still needed for it to appear: Farr was C. J. Bartlett's student and, thus, Wherry's academic "grandson." A search we performed in October 2003 using the Social Science Citation Index Web site revealed more than 100 citations to the several versions of Wherry's theory of ratings (i.e., the original technical reports and the two 1980s publications), suggesting a tardy but nonetheless important impact on performance appraisal researchers.

In contrast to the "test metaphor" tradition of the Army forced-choice rating scale and Wherry's theory of ratings, the 1950s also saw the rapid emergence of other perspectives about performance ratings and appraisal. Although most industrial psychology researchers and practitioners pre-1950 were primarily or exclusively concerned about how to achieve accurate performance ratings to be used to inform personnel decisions and to validate selection instruments, a minority like Hepner (1930) and Humke (1938–1939) also were concerned with using ratings to inform the ratees how their job performance was evaluated by managers and how they might improve that performance. By the 1950s, organizational practice appears to have advanced decidedly beyond industrial psychological research in the area of managers conducting performance review discussions with their employees, especially when those subordinate employees were themselves managers. Perhaps the rise of large organizations with many layers of management resulted in many managers who were well educated, achievement oriented, and not well informed about their own job performance. In any event, Douglas McGregor (1957) could write that the three primary purposes of formal performance appraisal plans were that they (a) provided systematic judgments to support personnel decisions; (b) informed subordinates about how they were doing in the eyes of the boss and suggested changes in knowledge, behavior, and attitudes that needed to be made; and (c) served as a basis for the superior to coach and counsel the subordinate. Quite a change from the test metaphor!

Furthermore, by 1957, McGregor was uneasy with what he could describe as "the conventional performance appraisal plan which requires the manager to pass judgment on the personal worth of employees" (p. 89). He offered an alternative appraisal plan more consistent with his theory Y (of work motivation) that he suggested in the classic *The Human Side of Enterprise* (1960; described in numerous other chapters in this text) in which the primary responsibility for establishing performance goals and appraising progress toward them was placed on the employee. McGregor (1957, 1960) noted that managers disliked so much making such judgments about others, especially when they also had to communicate them directly, that active resistance and avoidance of the appraisal process were as likely outcomes in most organizations as were completed appraisal sessions. The controversy brewing in organizations about performance appraisal suggested by McGregor's writings would become more evident in the 1960s.

1960s AND 1970s

The end of the 1950s was characterized by two generally separate literatures being created: one still focused on issues of measurement, accuracy, and rating format, and a second being concerned with how these ratings actually affected the lives and careers of people in work organizations. This separation would continue in large part in the 1960s, but, consistent with the renaming of the field as industrial–organizational psychology in the early 1970s, the two literatures began to speak to each other in ways that have continued to increase into the present. But, let's go back to the 1960s to pick up our story.

Following on the heels of Wherry's (1952) work was a very clear focus on performance measurement and, more particularly, the development of scales used to rate performance. Performance appraisal of the 1960s was more clearly defined by a refinement of rating scales. Before this time performance rating was largely focused on the description of employees in terms of traits and qualities. You might recall the earlier discussion of Scott's Man-to-Man Rating Scale and others, most of which focused on rating employees along descriptive traits. Soon, however, raters became quite uncomfortable doing these kinds of ratings and were looking for some other approach. The general approach that emerged in the late 1950s and 1960s was one in which an attempt was made to rate employees on behavioral dimensions.

The pioneering work of Smith and Kendall (1963), resulting in the development of the Behaviorally Anchored Rating Scales (BARS), led this movement toward behavioral measurement. As Guion (1998) noted, one should not only characterize BARS as a "rating format" because this format was only a part of a whole rating system that was intended to be an integrated entity. An important aspect was the participation in all phases of scale development by representative raters so that the dimensions, anchors, and language would be meaningful to the raters. This participative feature fit well with the management theories that were emerging at the same time (e.g., Likert, 1961; McGregor, 1960). The use of raters as "partners" in the rating enterprise is radically different than the forced-choice rating system, which attempts to disguise the nature of the scoring process to see if the raters could be "tricked" into being accurate. Thus, we see in Smith and Kendall (1963) the beginning of a less complete focus on the test metaphor than earlier approaches to performance rating scales had evidenced.

Although BARS is the best known of the behavioral measures, many others have been developed over time such as the Mixed Standard Scale (Blanz & Ghiselli, 1972), Behavioral Expectation Scales (BES; Smith & Kendall, 1963), Behavioral Observation Scales (BOS; Latham & Wexley, 1977), Behavioral Discrimination Scales (BDS; Kane & Lawler, 1979), and Behavior Summary Scales (BSS; Borman, 1979). Although research has not supported the markedly increased accuracy or validity that were predicted to come with these behavioral approaches (Murphy & Cleveland, 1995), one advantage that they have in contrast with the trait-focused scales of earlier eras has been that performance feedback can be more directly provided to the employee using behavioral rating scales. Using rating scales as a source of performance-related information that supervisors could provide to their subordinates became frequent in the 1960s and has continued to be a major use of ratings. Work measurement and employee development are coming closer together.

Performance Feedback and Appraisal

Herbert Meyer was the central figure in a program of empirical field research about performance appraisal at General Electric in the 1960s that was probably more productive than any other organization-based work. Perhaps the best known conclusion of Meyer and his colleagues was that separate sessions should be devoted to the two distinct purposes served by many organizations' performance appraisal system. One session should address the developmental needs and plans of the individual, whereas issues of salary adjustment should be covered in a separate meeting (Meyer, Kay, & French, 1965). Indeed, Meyer and his colleagues suggested that much more frequent developmental sessions would be useful, even though an annual salary adjustment session would generally be sufficient. Other interesting findings were that appraisal sessions were more effective when the manager was a skilled communicator about performance information (Meyer & Walker, 1961); participation in the appraisal session by the employee increased the appraisal's effectiveness (French, Kay, & Meyer, 1966); and self-ratings could serve effectively as a basis for appraisal interviews (Bassett & Meyer, 1968).

The ubiquitous nature of performance feedback in today's work organizations makes it difficult to realize that the term as applied to information about one's job or task performance appears to be only about 50 years old. The term *feedback* as used in industrial–organizational psychology is likely derived from Wiener's (1948) cybernetic theory that discussed how mechanical and electrical control systems could adapt their system parameters based on information received about the effects of their prior values.

Perhaps the most apt theory for describing performance appraisal feedback and how individuals react to and anticipate that feedback is control theory. The idea of a control system applicable to human behavior was derived from the mechanical control system as depicted by Wiener (1948), which emphasized the negative feedback loop. The negative feedback loop results from the comparison of performance feedback with some goal or standard. If people perceive a discrepancy between their goal/standard and their feedback, they are motivated to reduce that discrepancy in some way (Levy, 2003). Miller, Galanter, and Pribram (1960) presented this type of analysis via their TOTE sequence—Test, Operate, Test, Exit. In this framework, individuals compare their standard with the information or feedback that is available to them (Test) and one of two outcomes emerge. If the testing leads to a match, nothing further is required; if, however, the testing identifies a discrepancy between the standard and the current operational state (Operate), changes are made and further comparisons follow (Test). Once the discrepancy has been resolved, control is placed outside the system (Exit).

Although this approach has been applied to goals (Campion & Lord, 1982), self-assessments (Levy, 1993; Levy & Foti, 1990), desired outcomes (Edwards, 1992), and general models of motivation (Klein, 1989; Lord & Hanges, 1987), its application to performance appraisal has been most carefully described by Taylor, Fisher, and Ilgen (1984). These scholars suggested that a control theory orientation applied to performance appraisal is useful in explaining (a) how work standards are developed, (b) how conflicting standards are resolved, (c) the frequency with which standards are compared to feedback, and (d) how individuals react to feedback in affective, cognitive, and behavioral ways (Taylor et al., 1984). Using control theory as a heuristic for the feedback process provides a nice foundation for the use of feedback within performance management systems. The general lack of interest before the 1960s from industrial psychologists in research on the use of ratings as information for the employee may have been related to the lack of useful psychological theory concerning feedback concepts.

THE 1980S TO PRESENT

In their seminal article on performance ratings, Landy and Farr (1980) argued that at best 4% to 8% of the variance in performance ratings could be accounted for by the appraisal format, and thus they called for a "moratorium" on performance appraisal format research. Although their suggested moratorium was observed in large part, recent work has provided a call to revisit the importance of format. For example, Borman and his colleagues (Borman et al., 2001) have developed what they label as Computerized Adaptive Rating Scales (CARS), which appear to have promise.

Landy and Farr (1980) also presented perhaps the first truly refined and coherent model of the performance appraisal process and argued, in particular, for more research targeted at gaining a better understanding of the cognitive processes involved in performance judgments. This model, along with a related article by Feldman (1981), proceeded to have a substantial effect on performance appraisal research for the next dozen or so years.

Austin and Villanova (1992) suggested that the work of Landy and Farr, as well as Feldman, led to the beginning of a paradigm shift toward the use of cognitive frameworks for understanding and depicting the performance appraisal process. Many models were developed, with the work of Feldman (1981, 1986), DeNisi, Cafferty, and Meglino (1984), and Wexley and Klimoski (1984) leading the way.

Ilgen, Barnes-Farrell, and McKellin (1993) reviewed the decade of appraisal process research that followed from the recommendations of Landy and Farr (1980). Their review argued that this research could be evaluated along two dimensions: how well it enhanced our understanding of the cognitive processing involved in performance appraisal and how well it suggested ways to improve performance appraisal in organizations. They concluded that the research conducted during this period had substantial effects on our understanding of the cognitive processes involved in performance appraisal, and, in particular, the role played by observation was much better understood as a result of this research. However, Ilgen et al.'s evaluation with respect to the contribution of this research to actual "appraisals in use" was much less favorable. They agreed with Banks and Murphy (1985) that the effect of this research on appraisal practices has been quite limited. Up to this point in the history of performance appraisal research, the majority of work was clearly concentrated on either issues of rating formats/scales (from about the 1910s to the 1960s) or cognitive errors (from the 1960s to 1990s). Ilgen et al. (1993) put it very succinctly:

> Many of the problems that have plagued these systems still remain. However, rather than attribute them to the failure of either the process approach or a focus on rating errors, it would be better to explore other domains where greater relative contributions may be made in the future. We feel that it is far more likely that the major problems facing performance appraisals at this time lie neither in the cognitive process domain nor in that of rating scale construction. (p. 361)

Along with Ilgen et al. (1983), Murphy and Cleveland (1991) argued for viewing performance appraisal as a social–psychological process or what is often referred to as the social context of performance appraisal. Identifying the organizational context in which appraisal takes place as integral to truly understanding and developing effective performance appraisals has been the framework driving the research of the end of the 20th century and the beginning of the 21st century. Whether it's discussed as the social–psychological process of performance appraisal (Murphy & Cleveland, 1991), the social context of performance appraisal (Ferris, Judge, Rowland, & Fitzgibbons, 1994), the social milieu of performance appraisal (Ilgen et al., 1993), performance appraisal from the organizational side (Levy & Steelman, 1997), the games that raters and ratees play (Kozlowski et al., 1998), or the due process approach to performance appraisal (Folger et al., 1992), the message has been very clear that performance appraisal takes place in a social context and that context plays a major role in the effectiveness of that process and how participants react to that process (Bretz, Milkovich, & Read, 1992).

In terms of the application of performance appraisal in work organizations, the interesting research questions and central controversies related to performance feedback and appraisal are related to the use of multisource rating and feedback systems (also frequently called 360-degree ratings). Although this is an already voluminous and still rapidly expanding literature that we cannot cover in any detail, a point of historical interest is that, unlike all of the other rating approaches that we have discussed, multisource rating and appraisal systems were developed initially for the primary (and often sole) purpose of providing feedback to individual employees (usually managers) for their use in the development of their work-related skills and behaviors. Pressure in many organizations has been strong to use the performance judgments that are gathered from several sources (e.g., supervisors, peers, subordinates, self) also for administrative purposes. Although Meyer and colleagues argued that separate appraisal sessions should be held for different purposes (Meyer et al., 1965), a new question has emerged regarding whether it is now reasonable to use the same set of judgments (such as 360-degree ratings) for two distinct purposes (developmental and administrative).

LESSONS LEARNED

Much has been learned about the performance appraisal process in these first 100 years. The period in time marked by World War I through the Great Depression was an important one for performance appraisal because, in part, it was really the beginning of any focused interest in this area. Some of the research and practice pioneers during this time took the trouble to present in codified ways their suggestions or rules for developing and using rating scales in performance appraisal and other domains. First, among the most active contributors to the development of rating systems was D. G. Paterson through his work with the Scott Company and the University of Minnesota. He proposed 12 principles of psychological ratings that are summarized in Table 13.1 (Paterson, 1923). Second, similar lists produced by Bingham, Freyd, and Poffenberger, to name a few, added things to Paterson's list like ensuring that every person rated was really observed with respect to that quality, keeping the rating of one ability free from the influence of others, and not being influenced by friendship. It's pretty clear that these pioneers identified many of the issues, warnings, suggestions, and recommendations that have become important in the more recent history of performance appraisal and continue to be relevant today. Their thinking foreshadowed the recent/current emphasis on using performance appraisals proactively rather than reactively, on the dimensionality issues of performance measurement, on the benefits of multiple raters and multiple measurement times, on the importance of measuring actual work behaviors and tying these behaviors to work outcomes, on the importance of rater training, on the importance of simplicity in the rating system, on avoiding halo error, on the importance of weighting the dimensions, and on a concern about errors/biases like leniency and severity. From the applied work and careful thinking of these pioneers, Paterson, Poffenberger, Bingham, and Freyd as well as others like Scott, Ruml, and Rugg, we learned a great deal that has propelled us into the next era of performance appraisal and beyond. Kingsbury (1926–1927) was active during this time as well and he wrote the following about rating methods and scales:

> Which of these methods is best? Certainly, until a good deal more scientific inquiry has been made into the relative reliability of ratings made by each of these methods, a final answer will not be

forthcoming. But there are certain a priori considerations that should not be overlooked. It is the purpose of this paper to point out some of these, and to defend the answer that *there is no one best method*. (p. 1)

Even after considerably more inquiries into the relative reliabilities and validities of various rating scales over the past 80 years, the conclusion of the research community is the same as Kingsbury's in 1926—there really isn't one best method (see Landy & Farr, 1980).

Although the 1930s was mostly a continuation of the previous period with its emphasis on rating format and measurement from a "test metaphor" perspective, there began to be an interest on the part of some practitioners in how performance appraisal processes and feedback could help employees identify their own strengths and weaknesses as well as allow managers to help in employee development. Practitioners like Hepner and Humke highlighted this possibility and even called for more research on this topic as well as arguing that organizations would be better served by this kind of focus. Although this voice was perhaps a lone one in the 1930s, it is a voice that became louder and on key with the 1950s emphasis on humanistic organizations, participation, and employee development. This trend has grown in recent years and stems, it appears, from some of the early writings in this area. Of course, much of the period from the 1930s to the 1950s was still devoted to the "test metaphor," and some of this work that came from Wherry was important for affecting how others viewed the performance rating process. For instance, the cognitive movement in performance appraisal that stemmed directly from the work and suggestions of Landy and Farr (1980), stemmed indirectly from Wherry's "theory of rating," which was developed in the 1950s. Thus, the cognitive research of the 1980s can be traced back through Landy and Farr (and others) to Wherry's early work.

The 1960s and 1970s were marked by a return to measurement issues with a new emphasis on behavioral measurement (e.g., BARS) as well as better articulation of the role of feedback in the development of employees. These two threads have been extremely important to the refinement of performance appraisal systems to include employee participation and empowerment, two qualities that continue to drive much of the use of performance appraisal systems or what organizations typically refer to as "performance management" systems. Even though BARS may not be the modal approach to performance appraisal today, the emphasis and concern for behavioral measurement are clearly a key element of most current performance appraisal systems, and this behavioral emphasis stems directly from Smith and Kendall's (1963) ideas that led to the development of BARS.

Since the 1980s, two additional threads have developed in the performance appraisal domain. First, as mentioned earlier, consistent with the cognitive movement in psychology in general came a focus on the cognitive processing involved in performance appraisal. Without this emphasis and the flood of research that worked within a cognitive framework, we would know very little about the process of performance appraisal. The second thread is equally important, and it is the focus on "the social context" in which performance appraisal operates. We are beginning to gain a better understanding of this context and all of its subcontexts with respect to performance appraisal, but we still have far to go. We know a great deal about the cognitive process of appraisal, but this does not suggest that we have very clear, easy-to-implement suggestions guaranteed to work for organizations (that science–practice gap is not an easy one to resolve!). On the other hand, we know less about the how the social context operates in affecting the appraisal process, but we do have a growing database along these lines that promises to help organizations with their "appraisals in use" (Ilgen et al., 1993). Perhaps, Folger et al. (1992) can provide the best conclusion to what we know and don't know about performance appraisal: "Appraising people is a matter of judging them, not simply measuring them as if they were to be fitted for new clothes" (p. 171). Indeed, even a reliable tape measure only works as well as the tailor using it and that depends on what kind of day he or she has had, the relationship he or she has with the customer and organization members, and so on. Measurement and context … we have learned a great deal in less than 100 years but still have much to learn and details of implementation to continue to refine.

REFERENCES

Austin, J. T., & Villanova, P. (1992). The criterion problem: 1917–1922. *Journal of Applied Psychology, 77,* 836–874.

Banks, C. G., & Murphy, K. R. (1985). Toward narrowing the research-practice gap in performance appraisal. *Personnel Psychology, 38,* 335–345.

Bartlett, F. C. (1932). *Remembering.* New York: Macmillan.

Bassett, G. A., & Meyer, H. H. (1968). Performance appraisal based on self-review. *Personnel Psychology, 21,* 421–430.

Bingham, W. V. D., & Freyd, M. (1926). *Procedures in employment psychology.* Chicago: Shaw.

Blanz, F., & Ghiselli, E. E. (1972). The mixed standard scale: A new rating system. *Personnel Psychology, 25,* 185–199.

Borman, W. C. (1979). Format and training effects on rating accuracy and rater errors. *Journal of Applied Psychology, 64,* 410–421.

Borman, W. C., Buck, D. E., Hanson, M. A., Motowidlo, S. J., Stark, S., & Drasgow, F. (2001). An examination of the comparative reliability, validity, and accuracy of performance ratings made using computerized adaptive rating scales. *Journal of Applied Psychology, 86,* 965–973.

Bretz, R. D., Milkovich, G. T., & Read, W. (1992). The current state of performance appraisal research and practice: Concerns, directions, and implications. *Journal of Management, 18,* 321–352.

Burtt, H. E. (1926). *Employment psychology.* Cambridge, MA: Houghton Mifflin.

Campion, M. A., & Lord, R. G.(1982). A control systems conceptualization of the goal setting and changing process. *Organizational Behavior and Human Performance, 30,* 265–287.

DeNisi, A. S., Cafferty, T., & Meglino, B. (1984). A cognitive view of the performance appraisal process: A model and research propositions. *Organizational Behavior and Human Performance, 33,* 360–396.

DeVries, D. L., Morrison, A. M., Shullman, S. L., & Gerlach, M. L. (1986). *Performance appraisal on the line.* New York: Wiley.

Edwards, J. R. (1992). A cybernetic theory of stress, coping, and well-being in organizations. *Academy of Management Review, 17,* 238–274.

Feldman, J. M. (1981). Beyond attribution theory: Cognitive processes in performance appraisal. *Journal of Applied Psychology, 66,* 127–148.

Feldman, J. M. (1986). Instrumentation and training for performance appraisal: A perceptual cognitive view. In K. M. Rowland & G. R. Ferris (Eds.), *Research in personnel and human resources management* (Vol. 4, pp. 45–99). Greenwich, CT: JAI.

Ferguson, L. W. (1962–1965). *The heritage of industrial psychology* [14 pamphlets]. Hartford, CT: Finlay Press.

Ferris, G. R., Judge, T. A., Rowland, K. M., & Fitzgibbons, D. E. (1994). Subordinate influence and the performance evaluation process: Test of a model. *Organizational Behavior and Human Decision Processes, 58,* 101–135.

Folger, R., Konovsky, M., & Cropanzano, R. (1992). A due process metaphor for performance appraisal. In B. Staw & L. Cummings (Eds.), *Research in organizational behavior* (Vol. 14, pp. 129–177). Greenwich, CT: JAI.

French, J. R., Kay, E., & Meyer, H. H. (1966). Participation and the appraisal system. *Human Relations, 19,* 3–20.

Guion, R. M. (1998). *Assessment, measurement, and prediction for personnel decisions.* Mahwah, NJ: Lawrence Erlbaum Associates.

Gulliksen, H. (1950). *Theory of mental tests.* New York: Wiley.

Helson, H. (1947). Adaptation level as a frame of reference for prediction of psychophysical data. *American Journal of Psychology, 60,* 1–30.

Hepner, H. W. (1930). *Psychology in modern business.* New York: Prentice-Hall.

Hull, C. L. (1928). *Aptitude testing.* Yonkers-on-Hudson, NY: World Book.

Humke, H. L. (1938–1939). Full use of employee ratings. *Personnel Journal, 17,* 292–295.

Ilgen, D. R., Barnes-Farrell, J. L., & McKellin, D. B. (1993). Performance appraisal process research in the 1980s: What has it contributed to appraisals in use? *Organizational Behavior and Human Decision Processes, 54,* 321–368.

Jenkins, J. G. (1935). *Psychology in business and industry: An introduction to psychotechnology.* New York: Wiley.

Kane, J. S., & Lawler, E. E. (1979). Performance appraisal effectiveness: Its assessment and determinants. In B. Staw (Ed.), *Research in organizational behavior* (Vol.1, pp. 425–478). Greenwich, CT: JAI.

Katzell, R. A., & Austin, J. T. (1992). From then to now: The development of industrial-organizational psychology in the United States. *Journal of Applied Psychology, 77,* 803–835.

Kingsbury, F. A. (1926-1927). Making rating-scales work. *Journal of Personnel Research, 4,* 1–6.

Klein, H. J. (1989). An integrated control theory model of work motivation. *Academy of Management Review, 14,* 150–172.

Koppes, L. L. (2003). Industrial–organizational psychology. In I. B. Weiner (General Ed.) & D. K. Freedheim (Vol. Ed.), *Comprehensive handbook of psychology: Vol. 1. History of psychology* (pp. 367–389). New York: Wiley.

Kozlowski, S. W. J., Chao, G. T., & Morrison, R. F. (1998). Games raters play: Politics, strategies, and impression management in performance appraisal. In J. W. Smither (Ed.), *Performance appraisal: State of the art in practice* (pp. 163–205).

Landy, F. J., & Farr, J. L. (1980). Performance rating. *Psychological Bulletin, 87,* 72–107.

Landy, F. J., & Farr, J. L. (1983). *The Measurement of Work Performance.* New York: Academic Press.

Latham, G. P., & Wexley, K. N. (1977). Behavioral observation scales. *Personnel Psychology, 30,* 255–268.

Levy, P. E. (1993). Self-appraisal and attributions: A test of a model. *Journal of Management, 19,* 51–62.

Levy, P. E. (2003). *Industrial/organizational psychology: Understanding the workplace.* Boston: Houghton Mifflin.

Levy, P. E., & Foti, R. J. (1990, November). *The effects of feedback sign, performance discrepancy, and attributional discrepancy on feedback reactions.* Paper presented at the Meetings of the Southern Management Association, Orlando, FL.

Levy, P. E., & Steelman, L. A. (1997). Performance appraisal for team-based organizations: A prototypical multiple rater system. In M. Beyerlein, D. Johnson, & S. Beyerlein (Eds.), *Advances in interdisciplinary studies of work teams: Team implementation issues* (Vol. 4, pp. 141–165). Greenwich, CT: JAI.

Likert, R. (1961). *New patterns of management.* New York: McGraw-Hill.

Longenecker, C. O., Sims, H. P., & Gioia, D. A. (1987). Behind the mask: The politics of employee appraisal. *Academy of Management Executive, 1,* 183–193.

Lord, R. G., & Hanges, P. J. (1987). A control systems model of organizational motivation: Theoretical development and applied implications. *Behavioral Science, 32,* 161–178.

McGregor, D. (1957). An uneasy look at performance appraisal. *Harvard Business Review, 35*(3), 89–94.

McGregor, D. (1960). *The human side of enterprise.* New York: McGraw-Hill.

Meyer, H. H., Kay, E., & French, J. R. (1965). Split roles in performance appraisal. *Harvard Business Review, 43*(1), 123–129.

Meyer, H. H., & Walker, W. B. (1961). A study of the factors relating to the effectiveness of a performance appraisal program. *Personnel Psychology, 14,* 291–298.

Moore, B. V., & Hartman, G. W. (1931). *Readings in industrial psychology.* New York: Appleton.

Moore, H. (1939). *Psychology for business and industry.* New York: McGraw-Hill.

Miller, G. A., Galanter, E., & Pribram, K. H. (1960). *Plans and the structure of behavior.* New York: Holt, Rinehart & Winston.

Moss, F. A. (1927). Eliminating guesswork in rating teachers. *Industrial Psychology, 2,* 301–304.

Murphy, K. R., & Cleveland, J. N. (1991). *Performance appraisal: An organizational perspective.* Boston: Allyn & Bacon.

Murphy, K. R., & Cleveland, J. N. (1995). *Understanding performance appraisal: Social, organizational, and goal-based perspectives.* Thousand Oaks, CA: Sage.

Paterson, D. G. (1922). The Scott Company Graphic Rating Scale. *Journal of Personnel Research, 1,* 361–376.

Paterson, D. G. (1923). Methods of rating human qualities. *Annals of the American Academy of Political and Social Science, 110,* 81–93.

Poffenberger, A. T. (1927). *Principles of applied psychology.* New York: Appleton.

Poffenberger, A. T. (1942). *Principles of applied psychology.* New York: Appleton-Century.

Rugg, H. O. (1921, November & December). Is the rating of human character practicable? *Journal of Educational Psychology, 12,* 425–438.

Scott, W. D., Clothier, R. C., & Spriegel, W. R. (1949). *Personnel management: Principles, practices, and point of view.* New York: McGraw-Hill.

Sisson, E. D. (1948). Forced choice: The new army rating. *Personnel Psychology, 1,* 365–381.

Smith, P. C., & Kendall, L. M. (1963). Retranslation of expectations: An approach to the construction of unambiguous anchors for rating scales. *Journal of Applied Psychology, 47,* 149–155.

Taylor, M. S., Fisher, C. D., & Ilgen, D. R. (1984). Individuals' reactions to performance feedback in organizations: Control theory perspective. In K. Rowland & G. Ferris (Eds.), *Research in personnel and human resource management* (pp. 81–124). Greenwich, CT: JAI.

Viteles, M. S. (1932). *Industrial psychology.* New York: Norton.

Viteles, M. S. (1934). *The science of work.* New York: Norton.

Wexley, K. N., & Klimoski, R. (1984). Performance appraisal: An update. In K. Rowland & G. Ferris (Eds.), *Research in personnel and human resources* (Vol. 2, pp. 35–79). Greenwich, CT: JAI.

Wherry, R. J. (1950). *Control of bias in rating. Review of the literature*. Final Report, Subproject 1. Department of the Army, Personnel Research Section, PRS Report No. 898.

Wherry, R. J. (1952). *Control of bias in rating. VII. A theory of rating*. Final report, Subproject 9. Department of the Army, Personnel Research Section, PRS Report No. 922.

Wherry, R. J. (1983). Appendix: Wherry's theory of rating. In F. J. Landy & J. L. Farr (Eds.), *The measurement of work performance* (pp. 283–303). New York: Academic Press.

Wherry, R. J., & Bartlett, C. J. (1982). The control of bias in ratings: A theory of rating. *Personnel Psychology, 35,* 521–551.

Wiener, N. (1948). *Cybernetics or control and communication in the animal and the machine*. New York: Wiley.

V

Later Topics

This section contains four chapters that provide historical perspectives on topics that emerged later in the evolution of I–O psychology. As apparent throughout the text, the 1930s was a turning point in the types of questions asked and problems addressed by psychologists in business. Several research studies, along with World War II, expanded awareness on other work-related and organizational issues, including job attitudes, motivation, leadership, and work teams.

Our natural inclination when investigating history is to focus on accomplishments to celebrate the past; however, historical scholarship also consists of critically examining past events, which may not always indicate an accomplishment but, possibly, a failure. We can learn from this perspective as well. Chapter 14 provides a critical analysis of five organizational applications of psychology: the Hawthorne studies, the Harwood Pajama Factory, the U.S. State Department reorganization, Non-Linear Systems, Inc., and the Gaines Dog Food Plant in Topeka, Kansas. By looking closely at these early applications, the author intends to provide a more accurate picture of how organizational psychology came into being and provoke some reflection over how much of the field's assumptions and prescriptions may be founded on myth and legend.

Employee motivation is currently a cornerstone of I–O psychology. When and how did the subject of employee motivation become so important in I-O psychology? To answer this question, chapter 15 reviews the scholarly literature over the past 100 years. In doing so, the authors follow a directionally chronological path. Thus, the chapter is organized loosely into four time periods: the first (1900–1925), second (1925–1950), third (1950–1975) and fourth quarters (1975–2000) of the 20th century.

The authors of chapter 16 chose to tell the story of leadership through a critical historical analysis. Specifically, they focus on the influence of traits and individual differences, trait theories, and trait thinking on the development of leadership research, theory, and practice over the course of the 20th century. In doing so, the authors trace the emergence of leadership as a topic of scientific study and applied practice in the field of I–O psychology.

Within the context of this book, the most "recent" topic in I–O psychology to be included is work teams in organizations. Chapter 17 illustrates repeated waves of team research, separated by relative periods of calm. To describe these waves, authors structured the chapter around the events, topics, and people who have markedly contributed to the science of teams. Although the information provided in this historical reflection is organized by decade and centered around key topics, a zeitgeist approach (i.e., the naturalistic theory of history) is also used.

14

Applications of Organizational Psychology: Learning Through Failure or Failure to Learn?

Scott Highhouse
Bowling Green State University

> *You never can say anything for sure about labor and management. You ought always to write history and never prophesy. Mankind has a distressful way of swinging from intoxication to the "day after."*
> (Turner, 1926, p. 135)

Although historical treatments of our early pioneers tend to romanticize their efforts at applying behavioral science to real-world organizational problems, many of the most celebrated interventions resulted in making things no better than before and sometimes resulted in making things worse. By looking closely at these early organizational applications of psychology, I set out to provide a more accurate picture of how organizational psychology came into being and provoke some reflection over how much of the field's assumptions and prescriptions may be founded on myth and legend. My approach in this chapter was to spotlight a handful of celebrated interventions. This allowed me to dig deeper into individual stories and to introduce the reader to some of the behind-the-scenes material. For a more traditional historical review of organizational psychology applications, the reader is directed to the chapter by Cardy and Selvarajan (2001) in the *Handbook of Industrial, Work and Organizational Psychology.*

Documenting the history of the "O" side of I–O psychology is made difficult by the fact that no one is really sure just what constitutes organizational psychology. Contemporary textbooks with this title bear little resemblance to one another (e.g., Beehr, 1996; Jex, 2002, Lawson & Shen, 1998). Moreover, subdisciplines with titles ranging from *organizational psychology* (Bass, 1965), *organization theory* (Pugh, 1966), *organizational behavior* (Lawrence, 1987), and *organization development* (French, 1982) all point to the same pioneers and events in recounting their histories. The first formal call for the recognition of organizational psychology as a new field was made by Harold J. Leavitt at the Walter Van Dyke Bingham Lectures at the Carnegie Institute of Technology in 1961. The field Leavitt imagined, however, looked curiously like what we know today as organizational behavior or organization theory taught in business schools. That is, Leavitt (1962) envisioned a basic field that was as much influenced by economics, sociology, and mathematics as it was by psychology. As Leavitt put it, this new field would be "mongrelized with psychology as only one of an untangleable mass of forebears" (1962, p. 23).

Modern organizational psychology, although its forebears certainly include economists and sociologists, was also shaped considerably by the work of clinical and social psychologists with a decidedly applied–industrial orientation. Today's organizational psychology evolved from *industrial social psychology*, a term used earlier by Mason Haire (1959) to describe a field that emphasized things such as group processes, motivation, and attitude assessment. Haire noted that, in contrast to traditional industrial psychology, industrial social psychology had an implicit humanistic core (see also Massarik, 1992; Stagner, 1982). As described previously in other chapters, when the American Psychological Association (APA) Division 14 (now known as the Society for Industrial and Organizational Psychology [SIOP]) changed its name from "Industrial Psychology" to "Industrial–Organizational Psychology," it was recognizing a combination of forces. APA Division 14 was acknowledging a broadening of interests among industrial psychologists to what Viteles (1944) described as "the growing concern of industrial psychologists with the sentiments, feelings, and attitudes of workers, supervisors, and managers, and with the interplay of people in the social organization of the industrial enterprise" (p. 182). Another force was the growing interest in taking a "systems view" of organizations (e.g., Katz & Kahn, 1966; Schein, 1965). The organization was more and more being viewed as an organism that changes and grows and whose parts are interrelated. At the same time, however, Division 14 was broadening the definition of what it meant to be an industrial psychologist. That is, the name change opened the doors of Division 14 to a more humanistic breed of psychologist, one with training in areas outside of industrial psychology. In announcing the proposed name change, the APA Division 14 Executive Committee noted: "It is hoped, of course, that the proposed change would encourage many psychologists now believing themselves excluded from our Division to apply for membership." ("Notification of Proposed Change of Name," 1970, p. 4).[1]

The entry of psychologists with a more humanistic orientation led to historic tensions with traditional industrial psychologists over the relative value of a "hard" versus "soft" approach to research and practice (see Rodgers & Hunter, 1996) and even tensions among those who labeled themselves organizational psychologists over whether the field should be theory and science driven versus practice and value driven (e.g., Alderfer, 1972). Consider the following quote by outgoing Division 14 President Robert Guion (1973) interviewed in the first issue of *The Industrial–Organizational Psychologist* following its name change from *The Industrial Psychologist*:

> I think that there is no real great difference between traditional industrial psychology and what has become called organizational psychology so far as the topics are concerned. I think the difference has been more in methods and I would like to see more rigor in the methods, regardless of what people call themselves. (p. 30)

Guion was reacting to the softer, less rigorous methods associated with the humanistic social psychologists and consultants moving into Division 14. Thus, it is clear that the recognition of organizational psychology was more than simply a reflection of the expanding interests of industrial psychologists to include organizational phenomena. It was also a recognition of a different kind of industrial psychologist and further complicated the question of just what is meant by the term *organizational psychology*.

---

[1] As Division 14 president William Owens remarked in the early 1970s, "The indications are, at present, that if we change our name somewhat, we should perhaps also change our game a bit ... few would doubt that we find ourselves in the midst of a social revolution with implications for our very existence" (quoted in Meltzer, 1982). Guion (1973) noted more cautiously, "I hope that we do not move in the direction of untested organizational intervention, yet I see us potentially moving in that direction" (p. 6).

This chapter does not aspire to settle the issue of what constitutes organizational psychology. Instead, it focuses on the application side of the field in telling the story of how attitude and behavior change methods have been applied in organizations during the 20th century. These tales range from the familiar (e.g., Hawthorne) to the now obscure (e.g., Non-Linear Systems), and each tells us a little something about how we have tried to understand and change behavior in organizations and what it means to be called an organizational psychologist. Other chapters in this book do a fine job of covering the history of research and theory in core organizational areas, so theory and research are not the focus of this chapter. Nevertheless, much of the hard-nosed theory in organizational psychology was either inspired by or directly developed by the people engaged in the interventions described herein. As such, separating the applied and theoretical history of organizational psychology would never be possible—even for those organizational scholars who would like to distance themselves from their past.

PSYCHOPATHOLOGY IN THE WORKPLACE: HAWTHORNE REVISITED (AGAIN)

No other behavioral intervention in an organizational setting has received as much attention as the studies conducted at the Hawthorne Works of the Bell System's Western Electric Company in Cicero, Illinois (see also chap. 15). This landmark program of research was stimulated by an earlier series of industrial illumination tests conducted from 1924 to 1927 by the Committee on Industrial Lighting, an independent organization of members of the gas and electric lighting industry.[2] The illumination studies were (financially) motivated by concerns over improved lamps that provided more light per watt of electricity (Wrege, 1976). The committee hoped that, by demonstrating the association between increased illumination and increased productivity, business owners would boost the lighting in their factories, thereby off-setting the reduced wattage consumption of the improved lamps. The committee was emboldened by claims of industrial psychologists such as Hugo Münsterberg, A. T. Poffenberger, and Walter Dill Scott that lighting would prove to be a key factor in the happiness and productivity of workers (e.g., Hollingworth & Poffenberger, 1917; Münsterberg, 1917; W. D. Scott, 1911). Students of management, sociology, and psychology are familiar with the fact that the studies failed to support such claims and that nearly every aspect of the experiment other than the lighting seemed to be causing changes in worker performance. The textbook accounts describe naïve researchers stumbling on the discovery that human relations do indeed have an important influence on productivity. This discovery was said to be the reason that the researchers continued on to conduct the now famous relay assembly room research. Unfortunately, much of this story is overstated. According to Gillespie (1991), "This narrative of scientific defeat transformed into victory by a leap of insight has played a major role in investing the Hawthorne experiments with their mythic power" (p. 47). Early accounts of the illumination studies were written years after the experiments were conducted by people who did not have access to any of the research participants or unpublished reports (Wrege, 1976). Indeed, the electrical industry representatives were not too eager to promulgate accounts of research that questioned the relation between lighting and productivity.

The truth about the link between the illumination studies and the famous Hawthorne studies is much more mundane. Although the Committee on Industrial Lighting was focusing on establishing the connection between illumination and productivity, Hawthorne managers George Pennock and Clarence Stoll began to think about how this experimental method could be used to scientifically analyze the effects of personnel management techniques on perfor-

---

[2]Although the illumination studies are often considered to be part of the Hawthorne studies, they were conducted before the famous studies had even been planned. In *Management and the Worker*, the authors discuss the illumination studies only because their results inspired later studies.

mance (Gillespie, 1991). In 1927, just before the completion of the final series of lighting tests, the Hawthorne managers gathered a small group of researchers to apply the experimental method for studying the impact of rest periods and other factors in the industrial environment on worker fatigue and attitudes. These were called the relay assembly test room experiments.

The first and most important of the Hawthorne Studies began in 1927 when Pennock transformed one of the rooms used for the illumination experiments into a miniature version of the relay assembly department. Although the study was expected to last only a few months, the test room was in operation for nearly 5 years. The original goal was not to make any breakthroughs in the science of fatigue and the impact of attitudes on production. The researchers were simply interested in understanding how production could be improved on a job that occupied an important position in the success of the Hawthorne plant. As for the interest in worker attitudes, this was not so unusual when you consider that the Hawthorne plant was extraordinarily progressive for its time. The company had a history of concerning itself with employee welfare, providing employees access to a gymnasium, tennis courts, a rifle range, social clubs, and financial and health services. This conception of Hawthorne stands in ironic contrast to the sweatshop one might envision after reading textbook accounts of the Hawthorne studies. The Hawthorne management and researchers did not serendipitously stumble on the idea that a happy worker is a productive worker. It was a part of the corporate culture (Landsberger, 1958).[3]

Six women were chosen for the relay assembly test room (five assemblers and one layout person) ranging from 15 to 28 years of age. Approximately 3 months after moving the women into the test room, rest periods were introduced. All conceivable variations on rest periods were implemented, ranging from two 10-minute breaks to six 5-minute breaks, and the company provided free tea and food to the women. A shorter workday and a compressed workweek were also tried. The women had frequent visits to a physician as part of the research and were interviewed about their sleep patterns, eating habits, and general states of mind. Parties with cake and ice cream were even thrown to make the doctor visits more palatable (Gillespie, 1991). Reminiscent of the illumination studies, average hourly output steadily increased throughout the study, regardless of the change in work circumstances. The standard interpretation of these findings, propagated by Harvard's Elton Mayo (1923), was that the workers in this unusual situation came to know one another and that it was this group dynamic, along with attention from supervisors, that explained this increase in productivity. In reflecting on the experiments, Mayo's protégé, Fritz Roethlisberger, remarked, "I suppose that what has come to be called 'the Hawthorne effect,' from a scientific point of view, is the most important result of these experiments—that is, the big difference that the little difference of listening to and paying attention to the employees made to them" ("Conversation: An Interview with Fritz J. Roethlisberger" 1972, p. 32). One problem with this conclusion is that many alternative explanations were equally plausible. For example, the women in the test room were working under an incentive system that gave them considerably more control over their income than the system in place on the shop floor. In addition, working in the test room was highly desirable, as it protected the women from the mass layoffs that were going on at that time. The threat of removal from the test room was very palpable to the women, considering that two of the original six were removed for being "uncooperative."[4]

In fairness, Roethlisberger and Dickson (1939) acknowledged all of these alternative explanations in their highly detailed treatment of the experiments. Only the human relations mes-

---

[3]The notion that a happy worker is less likely to unionize was also likely to be a partial motivator. However, Hawthorne's progressive personnel policies predated the postwar union movement in the United States.

[4]One of the women removed, Irene Rybacki, pointed out the irony in this when she exclaimed, "For the love of Mike! They tell you to work how you feel, and when you do it, it isn't good enough.... I work like I feel and I don't feel like working any different" (quoted in Gillespie, 1991, p. 62).

sage survived, however, in the oral history of the Hawthorne experiments. Regardless of the explanation one favors for the rise in productivity in the test room, there is no getting away from the fact that performance increased dramatically without changing the job itself. This is a notable finding considering that it was not so long ago that Taylorism (i.e., scientific management) was the dominant school of thought (see chap. 10 in this text).

Eight months after the relay assembly test room studies had begun, researchers initiated an interviewing program to identify unfavorable working conditions for correction, provide a record of representative employee comments to management, and collect ideas for use in supervisory training. Elton Mayo, however, convinced Hawthorne management to modify the interview so that it would focus more on the personality of each worker. Mayo saw the primary function of the interview to be an increase in the employee's psychological self-awareness, not to provide accurate information about the conditions of work (Hsueh, 2002). Mayo viewed workers as suffering from a preoccupation with pessimistic thoughts which he labeled as "reveries," symptoms of a psychopathology (e.g., Mayo, 1923). Counseling based on the techniques of Jean Piaget[5] and Pierre Janet was seen by Mayo as the necessary remedy for this widespread malady in the industrial civilization (Griffin, Landy, & Mayocchi, 2002). Fritz Roethlisberger, who also believed that the worker's psychological well-being was just as responsible for job satisfaction as were the conditions of the job itself (Roethlisberger & Dickson, 1939), was charged with implementing the psychiatric components of the interviewing program.

The interviewing program was discontinued after 2 years in 1931 due to the Great Depression, and the Bank Wiring Test Room study was begun to concentrate their limited resources on a smaller group of workers. The wiring room study is notable primarily for bringing to light the development of worker "soldiering," or peer pressures to slow down production to levels commensurate with the rest of the group. The study, begun in 1931, contained no experimental manipulations but involved the observation of nine male workers set up in a test room. The focus was on examining how workers adjusted to the naturally occurring work situation. Under Mayo's direction, workers were interviewed regularly to uncover sources of psychological maladjustment. Despite the discontinuation of the larger interviewing program, Mayo claimed that the psychiatric benefits of the interviews raised production 30% to 40% and suggested that implementation of a plant-wide counseling program would raise efficiency by as much (cited in Trahair, 1984). Noted industrial psychologist Arthur Kornhauser was one critic of the interviewing approach, suggesting that the use of structured questionnaires would provide more reliable information (Trahair, 1984; Zickar, 2003).

The last chapter of *Management and the Worker* (1939), the classic account of the Hawthorne experiments by Roethlisberger and Dickson, is entitled "Implications for Personnel Practice." The entire chapter is devoted to what was seen as the primary practical outcome of the Hawthorne research—personnel counseling. In 1936, a personnel counseling program was established at Hawthorne to create a kind of "positive Hawthorne effect" wherein counselor concern would defuse worker dissatisfactions and increase productivity (Dickson & Roethlisberger, 1966). According to Dickson and Roethlisberger, "Once this kind of concern is established, other things in the external environment may not make so much difference" (p. 24). The scope of the counseling program expanded every year to a peak of 55 counselors covering 21,000 workers in 1941. Employees would be taken, during company time, to separate interviewing rooms containing chairs with sloping seats and backs so that the employee could lean back and relax. Counselors were prohibited from giving employees advice. Their function

---

[5]Although Piaget is not usually considered to be associated with psychotherapy, Mayo was intrigued by his approach to interviewing children using progressive counseling techniques (see Hsueh, 2002).

was simply to passively listen to work and nonwork problems. This nondirective approach resulted from Mayo's belief that counselors should deal with attitudes toward problems, rather than the problems themselves. Interestingly, this nondirective counseling approach was remarkably similar to an approach developed simultaneously and independently by Carl Rogers (Mahoney & Baker, 2002).

The counseling program lasted for 20 years, officially ending in 1956. By the end, the program was only a shadow of its former self. Many reasons can be given for the demise of personnel counseling at Hawthorne and the many other companies that followed Western Electric's lead (see Highhouse, 1999). Dickson and Roethlisberger (1966) blamed it on the failure to involve management and the dropping of the research function when moving from interviewing to counseling. Another likely reason for the failure of personnel counseling is that it was built on the assumption that talking about problems made them go away. Blum and Naylor (1968) referred to the counseling program at Hawthorne as "naïve" and "merely a substitute for a real need of employees to organize" (p. 326). As unions grew in power in the United States, workers had an increasingly powerful mechanism for resolving their unhappiness. Counselors were also often conflicted by playing both therapist and consultant to management. Many counselors resolved this conflict by identifying themselves more with the employees than with the company (Wilensky & Wilensky, 1951). As a result, management came to associate the counselors with the workers, dismissing their reports as biased. Higher management questioned the efficacy of a program that cost more than $350,000 in 1949 (Dickson & Roethlisberger, 1966), and the program lost many of its advocates as members of management were replaced over the years. The major practical outcome of the Hawthorne research, therefore, had resulted in a failed exercise in managerial paternalism.

THE BIRTH OF ACTION RESEARCH: HARWOOD PAJAMA FACTORY

Harwood Manufacturing Company was a pajama factory in rural Virginia that was at one time as well known in psychology as the Hawthorne plant in Chicago (Hilgard, 1987).[6] For nearly 30 years, beginning in 1939, the Harwood plant had been a proving ground for interventions designed to enhance employee productivity and reduce absenteeism and turnover. *Fortune* magazine touted the results of employee concern at Harwood to be "spectacular" ("Pajamas and the Ego," 1946), and the *New York Times* in 1948 ran the headline "Human Relations Raises Sales 300%." Harwood was being billed as a modern miracle, and psychology was clearly being taken seriously as a method for improving productivity as well as for staving off unionization efforts.

Harwood's vice-president, Alfred J. Marrow, held a PhD in psychology, an unusual characteristic for any manufacturing executive and certainly unusual in 1939. Marrow was deeply influenced as a graduate student by the psychologist Kurt Lewin and developed and maintained a friendship with Lewin that lasted until Lewin's death (Marrow, 1969). Although Lewin is most known for his influence on social psychology and group dynamics (see also chap. 17), his interest in industrial psychology is evident in some of his earliest writings on the need to humanize work (see Papanek, 1973). Marrow invited Lewin to Harwood in 1939 to consult on an employee performance issue. It seems that their employees, mostly women from the Virginia mountains, could not meet the high performance standards of employees in similar jobs in the North (Marrow, Bowers, & Seashore, 1967). Turnover in this job was also extremely high,

---

[6]Even though the Broadway musical *The Pajama Game* (later a movie starring Doris Day) is said to be loosely based on activities in the Harwood Plant (Gabor, 2000; Kleiner, 1996), I have seen no evidence for this. It seems more likely that it is based on the experiences of Richard Bissell, the author of *7-1/2 cents,* on which the musical was based, in his family's garment factory in Iowa.

probably because of the intense supervisory pressure to raise performance standards. Lewin emphasized the need to stop pressuring individual employees and to give them the feeling that the performance standard was realistic and attainable. He believed that the production and turnover problems could be explained by a general feeling of failure on the part of the worker (Marrow, 1948). Lewin's ideas about the need to consider the attainability and value of a performance standard were adapted from his earlier field theory (Lewin, 1936) and laid the foundation for later expected value theories, such as Vroom's (1964) expectancy theory. Curiously, management interpreted Lewin's advice as a license to hire, with considerable resistance from the local community, approximately 60 highly skilled workers laid off from a plant in a neighboring town. Marrow (Marrow et al., 1967) reported that the performance of the current employees began to rise after the addition of these new employees, presumably because the current employees now realized that the difficult performance goal was attainable. It seems that management failed to consider the possibility that performance of the locals increased in response to their fear of being replaced by additional outsiders.

Lewin encouraged Harwood management to hire Alex Bavelas, his graduate student at the University of Iowa, in a research and development role. Bavelas instituted a number of programs that were precursors to many later management innovations. For example, he gathered a small group of high-producing operators who met several times a week for approximately 30 minutes to discuss problems in the work area. These groups looked very much like what many years later came to be known as quality circles. Bavelas, and later J. R. P. French, who succeeded him at Harwood, instituted psychodrama and role-playing activities for training foremen. The idea was that, by playing the part of both the supervisor and the subordinate, the foremen gained greater insight into the perspective of the line worker. Although Harwood is credited with being the first organization to implement role playing (Baritz, 1960), the ideas originated with psychologist J. L. Moreno, whom Marrow introduced to Lewin some years earlier. Moreno made his proprietorship clear in a savage commentary accusing Lewin and his proteges of engaging in "astute and Machiavellian practices" by borrowing his concepts for use in industry (Moreno, 1953, p. 103). Much of the data collected by Bavelas and French on worker production following changes in the workplace were used by Lewin in formulating his ideas of quasi-stationary equilibrium and force fields (Lewin, 1947).

Although the early research at Harwood was recounted as well planned and methodical (e.g., Kelly & Ware, 1947; Marrow, 1948), the correspondence between Lewin and French and between French and Marrow reveals a much more scattershot approach to research design (J. R. P. French Papers, 1940–1945). French brainstormed studying the effects of things like music and "pep" talks on performance. Many of his proposals foreshadowed ideas that are reflected in major theories, and continue to occupy organizational psychologists. Table 14.1 shows some of French's proposals for future Harwood studies.

In a 1944 letter to French, Lewin advocated the following method of conducting field research (note that Lewin's parenthetical remark about Likert appeared in the original memo):

> I have thought over once more the chances for research. It appears to me that the best chance is a number of studies—each of which should not take longer than four weeks (That is the way Likert works, I guess). If a certain change is planned, one should measure the situation before and after and write it up. I think that, in a practical situation which changes so much, such short range studies could be very important theoretically and practically. (J. R. P. French Papers, February 16, 1944)

This appears to be the time when Lewin was beginning to formulate his ideas about what later came to be known as "action research" (see Peters & Robinson, 1984), and it is interesting that he credits Likert for originating the now famous "Lewinian" approach. Marrow, however, was

TABLE 14.1

Example Ideas for Areas of Action Research at Harwood in 1944

- Are good leaders born, and is it impossible to retrain to be good leaders?
- Is morale something intangible that cannot be measured?
- Is the total wage a worker receives more important to him than the wages of others?
- If group workers are allowed to set their own team goals, would they be inclined to set them lower than if they were set by the foremen?
- Is it possible to get a real change in attitude by threats of punishment?
- Are workers' interests confined to improvement in wages, hours, and physical surroundings?

Note. From J. R. P. French Papers, 1940–1945.

becoming impatient with the mini-experiment approach, calling for large-scale interventions. In a memo to French in July 1944, Marrow called for more immediate action. He favored a procedure whereby propaganda messages would be played over the loudspeaker, and group meetings would be held encouraging workers to avoid absenteeism and to stay committed to the company. Marrow expressed clear frustration over the continued inability of past research to solve any major problems (J. R. P. French Papers, 1940–1945).

Understanding just what happened at Harwood is made difficult by the favorability bias that seems to pervade written accounts of the activities (e.g., Kelly & Ware, 1947; Marrow, 1948, 1957; Marrow et al., 1967; Parker & Kleemeier, 1951). For example, a 1946 article in *Fortune* describes Harwood as an "industrial heaven" oozing with personal consideration, encouragement, and employee involvement, where "labor unions seem unable to make headway" ("Pajamas and the Ego," p. 140). However, various bits of evidence seem to belie such sentimental accounts. In the same year that the *Fortune* article was published, 400 of the plant's 800 employees became members of the garment workers union, I.L.G.W.U. (Career Management Association, circa 1948). In his 1957 book *Making Management Human*, Marrow espoused the benefits of democratic leadership, the importance of "togetherness," and the central role of communication for reducing misunderstandings. Throughout, he used his experiences at Harwood to demonstrate these principles in action. In 1958, however, interviews with a small sample of employees suggested that the typical worker at Harwood did not receive any special training, did not participate in the determination of management policies, did not believe that suggestions were welcome or would do much good, and had never met Dr. Marrow but might recognize him by sight ("Results of Interviews of Employees," 1958). It seems that Marrow's lectures and writings may have reflected his utopian vision of how organizations should run rather than what was actually happening in Marion, Virginia.

Harwood was making psychological headlines again when it merged with Weldon Manufacturing Company in 1962. Harwood financed a large-scale field study conducted by the University of Michigan's Institute for Social Research, which was under the direction of Rensis Likert. Although most of the work was done by Stanley Seashore and David Bowers, Likert's ideas about participative management (Likert, 1961) pervaded much of the execution and interpretation of the research. The idea was to examine what happens when a traditional, centralized company with an authoritarian philosophy (i.e., Weldon) merges with a "progressive" company that engages in participative management (Marrow et al., 1967). In addition to studying the situation, a major organizational change effort was instituted that involved a large number of psychological consultants charged with changing management attitudes and employee morale. The results of the change effort were assessed in 1964, after the consultants had pulled out. Positive effects were found on production, attitudes, and absenteeism. The assessed changes in employee participation, however, were not statistically significant. Hilgard (1987) suggested that the movement toward a union shop in 1964 may have been responsible for many of the observed gains, but this was not investigated in the research. It is notable though that a follow-up study in 1969 showed that many of the positive outcomes were still in place (Seashore & Bowers, 1970). In Seashore's APA Division 14 (Industrial Psychology) presidential address on the durability of change at Harwood, he expressed surprise that the company had continued along in such a positive direction. Seashore speculated that this sustained change effort may reflect the "inherent merit of the participative organizational model" (Seashore & Bowers, 1970, p. 233). Again, it is difficult to disentangle the effects of unionization from the effects of the interventions. Whatever the merits, however, Harwood closed the Marion plant in 1992, moving all operations to Honduras and Costa Rica, where labor is cheaper.[7]

SENSITIVITY AT STATE: REORGANIZATION OF THE U.S. STATE DEPARTMENT

Alfred Marrow leveraged his fame as an industrial psychologist/executive pioneer, and his friendship with dignitaries like Vice President Hubert Humphrey, to become involved in a major intervention aimed at changing the organizational culture at the Department of State. The State Department was renowned for its dysfunctional bureaucracy that Humphrey (1974) described as being "afflicted with dry rot" (p. xiii). John F. Kennedy is said to have once asked U.S. Ambassador Charles Bohlen, "What's wrong with that goddamned Department of yours, Chip?" (Schlesinger, 1965, p. 431). Kennedy reportedly set up his own White House foreign affairs operation because he could not find an effective use for the State Department (A. M. Scott, 1969). In 1964, the deputy undersecretary, William Crockett, initiated a major reform program. Crockett was inspired by Douglas McGregor's (1960) book, *The Human Side of Enterprise*, and believed that the modern innovations of business and psychology could turn the department around. Crockett solicited the advice of major industrial leaders including the vice-president of Union Carbide, the president of Esso Research and Engineering, and Marrow, who was considered to be the "midwife" of the project (Tannenbaum, 1996).

In June 1965, Crockett announced major reforms designed to increase openness and participation, decentralize responsibility, and encourage self-management and goal setting (Marrow, 1974). He began by eliminating six supervisory layers between himself and the operating managers. Ironically, many perceived this as an arbitrary order and not consistent with the espoused principles of participatory management. Several months after the reorganization had begun, Crockett's advisory group suggested he enlist the aid of a team of psychologists from the National Training Laboratories (NTL) to conduct a series of small-group conferences known as *t-groups*. At this point, I will back up and provide some background on the t-group movement.

Carl Rogers (1970) called the t-group the most important social invention of the 20th century. Although as many people disdained the t-group as admired it ("Is Sensitivity Training a Valuable Tool or a Risk?" 1970, p. 15), the movement was unquestionably a significant part of the history of I–O psychology (Highhouse, 2002). Indeed, Campbell and Dunnette's (1968) review of research on the t-group, published in *Psychological Bulletin,* is among the 10 most-cited articles in the history of industrial psychology (Sackett, 1994). The origins of the t-group date back to the period following the Second World War, when Kurt Lewin, Leland Bradford, Ronald Lippitt, and Kenneth Benne assembled a workshop to train businesspersons, labor leaders, and schoolteachers how to better deal with intergroup (including racial) tensions. The

---

[7]Harwood is now a division of the Sara Lee Corporation.

workshop included group discussions and role plays which, as Lewin had learned from the Harwood experience, were useful methods for getting people to see how their own behavior affected others (see also chap. 17). After the daytime classes, the researchers would meet at night to discuss their experiences during the day. By happy accident, three of the students invited themselves to attend one evening session. Although the researchers initially found this situation awkward and embarrassing (Bradford, 1967), they soon realized that both the students and researchers were benefiting from sharing different points of view. Eventually all students attended the sessions, which often continued well into the night. The training staff realized that it had "somewhat inadvertently" hit on a powerful method of attitude change (Benne, 1964).

Although Lewin died shortly after the Connecticut workshop, Bradford, Lippitt, and Benne continued with the idea of using groups as a method for expressing feelings and attitudes using what they now referred to as *feedback*. The group established the National Training Laboratory for Group Development, in Bethel, Maine, in 1947. The NTL workshop was described in its literature as a place to learn change-agent skills and concepts and to understand and help with group growth and development (Benne, 1964). Bradford and his colleagues soon concluded that the training objectives of the early workshops were overly ambitious. The trainers set out to teach diagnostic and action skills of the change agent, to provide an understanding of behavior in small groups, and to enhance understanding of democratic values. This was all to be done in addition to helping people internalize more effective processes of solving human problems by examining and analyzing ongoing interactions in the groups. According to Benne (1964), there was an early tension between discussion of here-and-now happenings and discussion of outside case materials. This tension was typically resolved by rejecting the outside problems as "less involving and fascinating" (p. 56). Thus evolved the t-group, a method aimed at gaining personal insight by focusing on the immediate behavior of the group members.

For the State Department project, Crockett called on the services of Bradford, Benne, and Chris Argyris of Yale University to conduct a series of t-group sessions with more than 200 foreign service officers and administrators. Also involved in the project were Floyd Mann, Herb Shepard, Charlie Seashore, and Bob Tannenbaum, all active in the NTL movement at the time. The project got off on the wrong foot, with many of the officers resenting being "coerced" into attending (Marrow, 1974). Nevertheless, many of the participants got quite involved in the small-group processes, which involved communicating candidly and emotionally, while always staying firmly in the here-and-now. The results of this major t-group intervention were published in a report titled "Some Causes of Organizational Ineffectiveness Within the State Department" by Chris Argyris (1967). The report included unedited details of the group interactions and became a bestseller among government agencies in Washington. Although Argyris repeatedly stressed in the report that the comments made by State Department staff were highly reflective of the kinds of comments made by members of any industrial organization, the report succeeded in airing a lot of the Department's dirty laundry. One officer, for example, was quoted in the report:

> If I were to be very honest, I think that one reason I have succeeded is that I have learned *not* to be open; *not* to be candid. Do the powers that be realize what you fellows (turning to the staff) are implying—that we should strive to be more open? That's like asking us to commit organizational suicide. (Argyris, 1967, p. 5)

The Argyris report painted a picture of a department that had little interpersonal openness and trust and where norms dictated withdrawal from conflict and low risk taking. The report ended with recommendations to engage in a major organizational development effort that would result in a situation where "the living system will permit [organizational members] to shed the social, normal, everyday defenses and masks" (p. 46). The Argyris report elicited considerable reaction, as evidenced by the multitude of letters to the editor of the *Foreign Services Journal.* Congressman John Rooney, chairman of the House committee in charge of appropriations to the State Department, was especially displeased by the report, questioning the expenditure of $3,000 to Chris Argyris to write it and of $1,500 to print it (see Marrow, 1974).

Secretary of State Dean Rusk was concerned that Crockett had moved too far in reducing the layers of management and that Crockett's own span of control was excessive. Rensis Likert's University of Michigan team, who had been contracted to evaluate the effectiveness of the reorganization, found that people were experiencing considerable uncertainty about their responsibilities and a lack of direction from the top. Indeed, some managers complained of longer delays in communication under this flatter organizational structure. This could be largely explained by the fact that Crockett was frequently away for months at a time, accompanying President Lyndon Johnson on overseas trips. Rumors had begun to circulate that Crockett would soon resign his position as undersecretary. Many members of the State Department were reluctant to institute changes, given that things would likely return to the normal routine after Crockett's departure. Attacks on Crockett by his superiors and subordinates were growing more intense, the progress of his reform was sluggish, and morale was poor. Crockett resigned in 1967, accepting a position with IBM. Crockett's replacement, Idar Rimestad, cut $25,000 from the contract with Likert's Michigan group and canceled the department's contract with NTL. In reflecting on the experience at State, Crockett regretted relying too much "on the diagnoses of outside experts, task forces, study groups, advisory bodies, and so on" (Marrow, 1974, p. 73). Presidential hopeful Richard M. Nixon vowed in 1968 to find a secretary of state who would join him in "cleaning house" at the State Department.

THEORY Y REORGANIZATION: NON-LINEAR SYSTEMS, INC.

Although Douglas McGregor often receives a nod or two in the histories of organizational psychology, his impact on thinking in the field does not usually receive proper treatment (see numerous other chapters in this text, however). One reason for this is that, aside from his seminal 1960 book *The Human Side of Enterprise,* he published very little (cf. McGregor, 1967). Nevertheless, many of the important figures in the history of organizational psychology, including Argyris, Haire, Herzberg, Likert, Scanlon, Schein, and many others, were profoundly influenced by McGregor's ideas. McGregor recruited Lewin to MIT and helped found the Research Center for Group Dynamics. He is credited, along with Richard Beckhard, with coining the term *organization development* to describe the application of behavioral science to major organizational change (Weisbord, 1987). In discussing McGregor's influence and legacy, Warren Bennis commented, "Just as every economist, knowingly or not, pays his dues to Keynes, we are all, one way or another, McGregorian" (Bennis, 1972, p. 140).

Inspired by the work of the humanistic psychologist Abraham Maslow and determined to reject his own strict religious upbringing that presented man as inherently evil, McGregor presented the now famous prototypes of theory X and theory Y managers in a speech delivered at the Fifth Anniversary Convocation of MIT's Alfred P. Sloan School of Management in 1957. According to McGregor, the theory X manager believes that people are by nature indolent, prefer to be led, are resistant to change, and are readily duped by charlatans and demagogues. The theory Y manager, on the other hand, believes that people are not, by nature, passive or resistant to organizational needs but are often brought to this state by their experiences with theory X managers. Although he was not the first to come up with the idea of different styles of leadership (e.g., Lewin, Lippitt, & White, 1939; Sherif & Sherif, 1954), he translated ideas from small group laboratories into a language that could be understood by everyone, manager and scientist alike. Indeed, Americans were ready for McGregor's ideas during this postwar period. The victory in World War II of democracy over authoritarianism appeared to suggest that a theory X management style was inferior to one that allowed the worker to pursue happiness and realize his or her true potential (see also chap. 15).

One disciple of McGregor was Andrew F. Kay, president of Non-Linear Systems, Inc., a small manufacturer of digital electrical measuring instruments. Kay was a scientist by training whose early career experiences led him to value experimentation and innovation, not only in work products but in work procedures as well. In 1942, Kay joined the Cleveland-based engineering firm Jack and Heintz Company. The cofounder of the firm, William Jack, was a strong believer that workers should police themselves. By supplying free lunches and $50 bonuses, Jack had instilled an atmosphere in which employees would criticize their peers for coming in late to work or for slacking off during work hours (Hoffman, 1999). After relocating to California following the war, Kay and Jack's paths crossed again, and Kay accepted a job with his former mentor as vice-president of the Bill Jack Scientific Instrument Company. During this time, Kay fervently consumed nearly everything written in the field of management, preparing to start his own company some 3 years later. Non-Linear Systems was established by Kay in Del Mar, California, in 1952 to manufacture instruments tailored to specific requirements of customers. The company grew from an initial five employees in 1952 to a high of 340 employees in the 1960s.

In 1960, even though business was booming, Kay decided that his employees "seemed unhappy." According to Kay, "everybody wanted to be at the tail end where it [the product] was finished" (Kay quoted in Hoffman, 1999, p. 249). Kay thus dismantled the assembly lines and replaced them with production teams of six or seven employees. He put in place an "executive council," composed of the president and seven vice-presidents, which functioned primarily as a planning and policy-making body. The department managers reported to the whole council rather than to individual members and were given complete authority for operational matters (Gray, 1978). The work teams dictated their own pace, worked on their own internal problems (tardiness, absenteeism, grievances, etc.), made their own rules, and did not keep records (Malone, 1975). Indeed, Kay was putting into place his own theory Y organization, borrowing ideas and elements from the writings of the psychologists and management scholars of the day. Six basic principles guided the organizational change efforts at Non-Linear Systems. These principles or beliefs included the notion that (a) work comes as natural as play and, under the right conditions, will be performed willingly; (b) workers require little direction or control when they are given clear goals to which they are committed; (c) rewards for meeting goals should be directed toward physiological, safety, social, ego, and self-actualization needs; (d) people are not only ready to accept responsibility, they seek to shoulder it; (e) imagination, ingenuity, and creativity are more widespread in the workforce than many executive choose to admit; and (f) a person's intellectual potentialities are only partially realized in modern industrial life. One can certainly see McGregor's optimistic notions about workers' desire and capabilities for self-management and Maslow's ideas about a human's basic needs and creative capabilities. As Gray (1978) noted, "The elements of autonomy, ambiguity, and job enrichment were designed into the system for the purpose of providing the opportunity for higher-level need satisfaction" (p. 34). The focus on goals and commitment was consistent with Peter F. Drucker's (1954) management by objectives concept.[8] Kay was also intrigued by Drucker's "eight objectives of business" (each of the eight members of the Non-Linear's executive committee was responsible for one of Drucker's eight objectives), which included market standing, innovation, productivity, physical and financial resources, profitability, manager performance and development, worker performance and attitude, and public responsibility. Drucker

---

[8]McGregor (1960) had a similar concept called "management by integration and self-control."

believed that profit should not be the sole objective of a firm, because it tends to direct efforts toward the short run at the expense of the long run.

The Non-Linear Systems reorganization received considerable fanfare. Gray (1978) called it "one of the most celebrated and ambitious 'field experiments' in a business firm since the famous Hawthorne Studies performed by the Western Electric Company between 1927 and 1932" (p. 31). The company received visits from management consultants like James V. Clark, Richard E. Farson, and Robert Tannenbaum. Celebrated psychologists like Carl Rogers and Abe Maslow, and even pop sociologist Vance Packard, had speaking engagements before the Executive Council. Maslow, however, became a sort of "resident guru" for Kay (Tannenbaum, 1996). In 1961, Kay invited Maslow to spend the summer observing operations at Non-Linear Systems. Maslow was given a lucrative stipend and was only required to visit the plant one afternoon per week. For Maslow, industrial psychology offered a whole new way of looking at and understanding human potential. Maslow was given the opportunity to experiment in what he viewed as a "new kind of life laboratory" (Hoffman, 1999). Each week that summer, Maslow dictated hours of thoughts in reaction to his visits to the plant and his readings in this previously undiscovered area of psychology. This resulted in the widely read book *Eupsychian Management* (1965), later to become known as *Maslow on Management.* Maslow admired Kay as a great business leader and a living example of a self-actualized man. His fascination with Kay and Non-Linear Systems was not strong enough, however, for him to accept a full-time permanent position with the firm. Maslow even confessed in his journal that he was a little worried about Kay and his advisors' too-ready acceptance of his ideas; "They're being taken as gospel truth, without any real examination of their reliability, validity … they're going ahead enthusiastically and optimistically, like Andy Kay, as if all the facts were in, and it was proven scientifically" (Maslow, quoted in Hoffman, 1999, p. 259).

Just 3 years into Kay's grand experiment in theory Y management, employee layoffs began and continued into 1965. By this time, Non-Linear Systems introduced modifications to its organizational operations amounting to, according to Malone (1975), the end of the experiment in progressive management. These modifications included a return to a traditional, hierarchical organizational structure, more direct supervision, centralization of authority, a return to record keeping, and performance-based pay. Sales volume was not living up to expectations, and administrative costs were heavy. The company had found itself less profitable under the new style of participative management, raising the question of whether it could ever afford the luxury of this enlightened approach to running an organization (Malone, 1975). In reflecting on the company's turn of fortunes, Kay confessed, "I must have lost sight of the purpose of business, which is not to develop new theories of management" ("Where Being Nice to Workers Didn't Work," 1973, p. 99). Certainly, it would be unfair to blame the organizational problems entirely on Kay's organizational changes. Indeed, the aerospace industry, among Non-Linear's primary customers, was coming apart at this time and, by 1970, orders from aerospace companies dropped by 50%. However, as Kay admitted in 1973, "The company was not set up to respond to that kind of event" ("Where Being Nice to Workers Didn't Work," 1973, p. 100). The organizational innovations being so widely praised in the media and academic community did not allow for cutting back during difficult economic times. The wage increases had cost the company dearly and had become increasingly burdensome (Malone, 1975). This is despite the fact that articles were commonly (mis)reporting that production time had been cut in half (e.g., "No-Assembly-Line Plan Gets Nothing But Results," 1964; Packard, 1963), and that productivity had risen by 30% to 50% (Kuriloff, 1963; "Non-Conformity at Non-Linear" 1964).

The changes that occurred to the structure of the company, away from a participative approach toward a more centralized approach, had a lot to do with the fact that the members of the Executive Council felt as though they had been rendered useless (Malone, 1975). The vice-presidents had previously been very active in daily problems and had a high degree of expertise in their specialties. As more and more power was given to managers at the lower levels, these vice-presidents no longer knew what their place was in the company. Their attempts to influence major policy in the company were also stymied by the highly charismatic Kay, who often steamrolled them with his quick mind and big ideas. Richard Farson, a management consultant who worked closely with the company, cautioned, "We should pay much closer attention to the style of the top guy of the company. That is a fact we must accept. We are working against considerable odds in democratizing management" ("Where Being Nice to Workers Didn't Work," 1973, p. 100).[9] The lower level managers who were delegated more authority were finding it difficult to operate without the previously close relationship with vice-presidents and were hamstrung by the need to deal with the Executive Council as a whole. These managers were also frustrated by the policy that none of their technical problems could be put into writing to be taken up at future council meetings (Malone, 1975). Kay had simply lost touch with what was happening to his company and engaged in considerable wishful thinking, whereas those surrounding him were highly skeptical of the major changes he introduced (Gray, 1978). Non-Linear Systems lost revenue and workforce steadily throughout the 1970s. The name was changed to Kaypro in 1983, as the company moved into the personal computer arena. Kaypro declared bankruptcy in 1990.

JOB ENRICHMENT: QUALITY OF WORK LIFE IN A DOG FOOD PLANT

Worker *alienation* was the buzzword of the 1970s and early 1980s, signaling concerns with the effects of the modern workplace on worker mental health. Sociologists had long been interested in discontent among American workers (e.g., Blumberg, 1968), and social psychologists, too, were becoming increasingly interested in remedies for "blue-collar blues" (see Kanungo, 1979). Even the federal government, by way of the Department of Health, Education, and Welfare under Presidents Nixon and Carter, was shifting its focus from community development and civil rights toward workplace reform (Kleiner, 1996). Moreover, substantial manufacturing costs were being linked to worker alienation, in light of increased international competition. I–O psychology itself was becoming increasingly interested in worker well-being. One example of this was a joint Division 13 and Division 14 symposium entitled "Humanizing Organizational Psychology," which ran at consecutive APA conferences in the early 1970s. Commenting on the symposia, Wickert (1974) noted, "Nothing is escaping humanizing pressures these days" (p. 32). Although a number of names were given to this movement, including humanization of work, sociotechnics, and job enrichment, the most common label was *quality of work life* (QWL). The emphasis was on work structure as the key to employee engagement, and its early pioneers included such figures as Frederick Herzberg and Eric Trist.

Frederick Herzberg, considered one of the fathers of job enrichment, broke from the employee participation–centered approaches of Lewin, McGregor, and others. He believed that simply advocating positive social interactions was not enough to enhance employee morale and productivity. A student of John Flanagan—who later founded the American Institutes for Research (AIR)—Herzberg adapted Flanagan's critical incident approach to the assessment of worker satisfaction. What emerged was the motivator/hygiene theory of job satisfaction, which suggests that workers have two basic desires, to grow and to avoid pain. According to Herzberg, satisfaction is a function of challenging and stimulating work. Dissatisfaction, on the other hand, is a function of the general job context (i.e., supervisor, pay, coworkers).

---

[9]Kay had invested nearly a million dollars in a "vocabulary-building" machine to enhance the verbal communication skills of his employees. Many privately referred to this as a folly that exacerbated the financial situation at Non-Linear Systems.

Herzberg believed that employers couldn't enhance growth by having people be nicer to each other; instead the redesign of jobs was the secret to real change (Dent, 2001). The publication of Herzberg, Mausner, and Snyderman's monograph in 1959 (Herzberg, Mausner, & Snyderman, 1959) thus signaled the beginning of a new focus on the work itself, something that had been ignored in earlier approaches to enhancing worker satisfaction (Locke, 1976; see, however, De Man, 1929; see also chap. 15).

Another important predecessor to the QWL movement was Eric Trist, a member of the Tavistock group in England. Following World War II, the Tavistock Institute of Human Relations was formed to combine psychoanalysis with psychosocial studies. The emergent focus on group dynamics made it sort of a British counterpart to the NTL in the United States. The Tavistock Institute was responsible for a number of studies on the factory as a social system (see chaps. 4 and 17). As one example of how technological change can disrupt the social system, Trist studied the introduction of a new technology in the British coal industry following World War II. The new technology required the substitution of small, cohesive work groups with large groups of specialized workers. Trist observed that the economic benefits of this new "long-wall" method resulted in emotional disturbances for the workers, low productivity, and an increasing sense of disorder (Wren, 1979). Trist was one of the earliest advocates of autonomous or self-managed work groups, believing that organizations were living systems that created order from the bottom up. Technological redesign cannot be effectively implemented, according to Trist, unless there is corresponding redesign in the system of social relationships (Trist & Bamforth, 1951). This idea came to be known as the sociotechnical systems approach.

The biggest story to come out of the QWL movement was the start-up of an innovative dog food plant in Topeka, Kansas, in January 1971. The Gaines dog food plant, maker of Gaines-burgers and Gravy Train, belonged to the consumer products conglomerate General Foods. The 1971 plant was a "greenfield" or start-up plant, conceived by Lyman Ketchum. Ketchum, a t-group veteran, spent 6 months studying how the best run high-performance plants were structured. NTL trainer and Harvard professor Richard Walton assisted Ketchum in this endeavor. An important objective was to find methods that would avoid the problems of employee alienation that were thought to be causing plant shutdowns, product waste, absenteeism, and sabotage at existing operations. The resulting "Topeka system" featured self-managing teams who assumed responsibility for most of the production process. The start-up of the plant involved extensive education, recruitment, and team building. The goal was to have a single job classification for all operators, such that every set of tasks included functions requiring planning, diagnosis, and teamwork (Walton, 1972). Pay was geared toward the mastery of new jobs, and support functions were integrated into the work teams (i.e., there was no separate quality assurance, custodial, or maintenance department). People frequently rotated among jobs, and status symbols were minimized. The idea was that no one innovation was expected to make a huge difference, but many changes together would result in "holistic" or "synergistic" effects. Following a widely read *Harvard Business Review* article by Walton (1972) on the Topeka experiment, claiming reductions in manufacturing costs and increases in job involvement, the plant became widely written about and discussed throughout the world. This little dog food plant was the topic of numerous newspaper and magazine articles and was the subject of a lengthy report on a popular NBC television news magazine (see Kleiner, 1996). Topeka was being held up as the prototype of what future humanized workplaces would be like, and it became a model forerunner of the total quality management (TQM) movement. It continues to this day to be held up as the prototype of a high-performance organization (e.g., Neal, Tromley, Lopez, & Russell, 1995).

The only problem with the Topeka story, according to Whitsett and Yorks (1983), is that it was "distorted" and "highly misleading" (p. 93). In fact, problems began almost immediately in Topeka. Accounts from former employees suggested that management hostility and power struggles between functions caused considerable turbulence to the new system ("Stonewalling Plant Democracy," 1977). The personnel people resented the fact that workers made hiring decisions, and engineers resented workers doing engineering work. People were having trouble with their new roles in this team-based environment, and many were reverting to traditional supervisor–subordinate roles (Walton, 1977). Walton also noted in his 1977 follow-up article that the unusual pay system became a source of tension. Although pay was closely related to learning and skill development, it was much less closely tied to participation, openness, and trust. Feelings of pay inequities were rampant, and many felt that the level of involvement required by the Topeka system was not justified by the pay. Topeka managers were beginning to see that being associated with this unusual plant spelled career obscurity. Between 1973 and 1976, five top managers left the Topeka plant. Ketchum himself, merely 9 months after the Topeka start-up began, moved from his position in operations to become a part of corporate organization development for General Foods. Ketchum's rapid rise up the corporate ladder drew considerable criticism from General Foods insiders against him and the Topeka system. Ketchum left General Foods in 1975 after trying unsuccessfully to duplicate the Topeka system in other parts of the corporation (Whitsett & Yorks, 1983). After General Foods was taken over by Phillip Morris, the Topeka plant was spun out to Quaker Foods. Quaker Foods sold the plant to Heinz in 1995, after which Heinz shut down half the plant and laid off 150 people.

CONCLUSIONS

In this chapter, I set out to understand the development of organizational psychology by focusing on some of the most well-known historical applications of behavioral science to the workplace. I have tried to show that many of the core theoretical areas of the field either inspired or grew out of the organizational applications discussed in this chapter. For example, Lewin's action research model grew out of his experiences in the Harwood pajama factory, and the field of group dynamics grew out of the work of the early NTL pioneers. Attempts to institute theory Y management at Harwood, the State Department, and Non-Linear helped to refine much contemporary theory in motivation and leadership. Job design and self-managed work teams were concepts that emerged from the work of people involved in Non-Linear and the Topeka project. Given that the success of these organizational innovations seems limited at best, one may wonder whether the underlying principles on which they were based are themselves flawed. That is, the espoused virtues of participative decision making, although well intentioned, may be wrong (Sewell, 2001). A reviewer of this chapter recounted the story of one early scholar who advocated participative management yet confessed to exercising benign dictatorship at home. One thing these stories show us is that many of the progressive principles and convictions were quickly forsaken by the companies when they hit difficult financial circumstances. Is it possible that applying organizational psychology (often referred to as organization development) is simply a pastime of wealthy companies? Does it have anything to offer companies decimated by foreign competition with cheap labor costs?

Although it is possible that the early theorizing was fundamentally flawed, it is also possible that the problem in these cases was misapplication of early behavioral principles (Bedeian, 2004). In discussing the legacy of the Hawthorne research, Lorsch (1975) suggested that it is not the theories that are flawed but their application in organizations. Lorsch suggested that scientists and practitioners take greater care in reading and interpreting the work of others. Similarly, Schein (1975) argued that McGregor's theory Y has been misinterpreted as much or more than anybody's work. He noted that theory Y is a theory of motivation, not a theory of how to run a corporation. According to Schein (1975, pp. 78–79):

Theory Y does not imply participative management or any other kind of management—it is only a statement about what people are fundamentally like, and what kind of organizational behavior they are capable of, if the conditions within the organization are appropriate.

McGregor (1967) himself noted that theory X and theory Y are not managerial strategies but are beliefs that guide leaders' actions. McGregor adopted a more contingency-based view of how to manage rather than advocating one best way (i.e., the issue may not be either theory X or theory Y).

It would be premature for readers to dismiss early theoretical work as failed and irrelevant. This would only exacerbate the problem of fads and fashions that has plagued management thinking (Abrahamson, 1996; Bedeian, 2004; Jackson, 2001) and, I would suggest, has retarded the development of organizational psychology. Instead, we should revisit and reconsider the ideas of these early humanists. A recent survey of organizational researchers showed that a majority viewed the work of people like Maslow, McGregor, Likert, Herzberg, and others to be of questionable scientific and practical usefulness (Miner, 2003). The current movement throughout psychology toward a more positive psychology, however, demands that we take a fresh look at the ideas of these early pioneers. Indeed, a recent book argues for a reconsideration of McGregor's ideas (Heil, Bennis, & Stephens, 2000). Recent research showing that positive and negative affect are not opposite ends of the same continuum calls for a reconsideration of Herzberg's two-factor theory (see Brief, 1998), as does Higgins' research on approach–avoidance conflicts (Brockner & Higgins, 2001). The early idea of internal versus external motivation is getting renewed attention as well (e.g., Sheldon, Elliot, Kim, & Kasser, 2001). Kluger and Tikochinsky (2001) argued that the rejection of theories, like Maslow's hierarchy of needs, represents a case of prematurely accepting the "theoretical null."

Even if we do separate the value of the theories from their applications, what are we to make of the fact the none of the organizational applications discussed in this chapter could be considered a success? The experiment in employee counseling—the direct implication of the Hawthorne research program—not only failed at Hawthorne but failed in the multitude of top corporations that implemented a personnel counseling program in the 1940s and 1950s (Highhouse, 1999). T-group-based reorganization was not only disastrous for the State Department but garnered considerable infamy throughout the world (Back, 1972; Highhouse, 2002). Participative management proved unprofitable at Harwood and Non-Linear Systems, and self-managed work teams just did not live up to grandiose expectations for Topeka. Certainly, we do not see much in the way of counseling and t-groups these days, but we seem undaunted in advocating for flatter organizations, management by participation, self-managed work teams, and so forth. In fact, many would have us believe that there are no traditional, hierarchical organizations left (e.g., Howard, 1995; Jackson & Ruderman, 1995; Wilson, 2003). The data, however, do not support the pervasiveness of such nontraditional practices. A 1993 survey of 7,000 organizations by the U.S. Bureau of Labor Statistics showed that only 14% of organizations used "worker teams" (Gittleman, Horrigan, & Joyce, 1998; see also chap. 17 in this text). With regard to participative management practices, Lawler, Mohrman, and Ledford (1998) found that only 38% of Fortune 1000 companies adopted employee participation groups. As for high-performance work organizations, instituting a holistic combination of recruitment, selection, participation, and innovative reward opportunities (see Becker & Huselid, 1998), these seem to be a "negligible phenomenon" including only about 1% of organizations in the United States (Blasi & Kruse, 2002, p. 2). Meta-analytic research on the effectiveness of participation (Wagner, 1994) and teams (Mullen & Copper, 1994) on productivity shows that the effect sizes, although positive in direction, are so small as to raise concerns about practical significance.

We seem to have built up a mythology in organizational psychology concerning the degree to which nontraditional organizational practices are pervasive and the degree to which they have been effective. The uncritical recounting of stories such as Hawthorne, Harwood, and Topeka is likely to have contributed to this situation. The humanistic roots of organizational psychology need to be reexamined, and the failed applications inspired by them need to be dealt with more critically. Walking the tightrope between science and advocacy has historically been difficult for organizational researchers (Yorks & Whitsett, 1985), and this situation seems to have changed little over the years.

FINAL NOTE

Earlier drafts of this chapter prompted some reviewers to comment that this history of applications of organizational psychology is unduly cynical and pessimistic. The argument is that I–O psychologists have historically been their own worst critics—and that this has only perpetuated our professional identity problems and our overall low professional self-esteem. I must confess some guilt to the allegation that I reported the glass as half empty and that I could have focused more on the positive, using a "lessons-learned" kind of approach to writing this chapter. I am sure that I could have looked harder to find examples of successes. I think it is typical of historians (and scientists too) to pursue more provocative theses, attending only to confirmatory evidence. My only defense is to point out what the stories in this chapter have in common: (a) They were marked by the involvement of many of organizational psychology's most important historical figures, (b) three of the five (i.e., Hawthorne, Harwood, Topeka) are stories about arguably the three most well-known (industrial) organizational interventions in history, and (c) with the possible exception of the State Department project, these stories are almost universally presented as successes. Although this chapter poses more questions than it answers, I hope that it succeeds in prodding us to revisit our assumptions about the history of organizational psychology, to consider whether this history needs to be relearned, and to consider how this alternative view of our history may change how we interpret our present.

ACKNOWLEDGMENTS

I am grateful to Michael Doherty, Steve Jex, Avi Kluger, Frank Landy, Gary Latham, Paul Muchinsky, and Ryan Tweney for their thoughtful comments on earlier drafts of this chapter. This research was supported with funds from an Academic Challenge Grant awarded to the BGSU Industrial–Organizational Psychology area by the Ohio Board of Regents.

REFERENCES

Abrahamson, E. (1996). Management fashion. *Academy of Management Review, 21,* 254–285.

Alderfer, C. P. (1972). Conflict resolution among behavioral scientists. *Professional Psychology, 3,* 41–47.

Argyris, C. (1967). Some causes of organizational ineffectiveness within the Department of State. *Occasional papers, Department of State.* Washington, DC: U.S. Government Printing Office.

Back, K. W. (1972). *Beyond words: The story of sensitivity training and the encounter movement.* New York: Russell Sage Foundation.

Baritz, L. (1960). *The servants of power: A history of the use of social science in American industry.* Middletown, CT: Wesleyan University Press.

Bass, B. M. (1965). *Organizational psychology.* Boston: Allyn & Bacon.

Becker, B., & Huselid, M. A. (1998). High performance work systems and firm performance: A synthesis of research and managerial implications. In G. R. Ferris (Ed.), *Research in personnel and human resources management* (Vol. 16, pp. 53–102). Greenwich, CT: JAI.

Bedeian, A. G. (2004). The gift of professional maturity. *Academy of Management Learning and Education, 3,* 92–98.

Beehr, T. A. (1996). *Basic organizational psychology.* Boston: Allyn & Bacon.

Benne, K. D. (1964). History of the t group in the laboratory setting. In L. P. Bradford, J. R. Gibb, & K. D. Benne (Eds.), *T-group theory and laboratory method* (pp. 80–135). New York: Wiley.

Bennis, W. G. (1972). Chairman Mac in perspective. *Harvard Business Review, 50,* 140.

Blasi, J. R., & Kruse, D. L. (2002, July). *High performance work practices at century's end: Incidence, diffusion, industry group differences and the economic environment.* Paper presented at the International Association for the economics of participation conference, Brussels, Belgium.

Blum, M. L., & Naylor, J. C. (1968). *Industrial psychology: Its theoretical and social foundations.* New York: Harper & Row.

Blumberg, P. (1968). *Industrial democracy: The sociology of participation.* London: Constable.

Bradford, L. P. (1967). Biography of an institution. *Journal of Applied Behavioral Science, 3,* 127–143.

Brief, A. P. (1998). *Attitudes in and around organizations.* Thousand Oaks, CA: Sage.

Brockner, J., & Higgins, E. T. (2001). Regulatory focus theory: Implications for the study of emotions at work. *Organizational Behavior & Human Decision Processes, 86,* 35–66.

Campbell, J. P., & Dunnette, M. D. (1968). Effectiveness of T-group experiences in managerial training and development. *Psychological Bulletin, 70,* 73–104.

Cardy, R. L., & Selvarajan, T. T. (2001). Management interventions. In N. Anderson, D. S. Ones, H. K. Sinangil, & C. Viswesvaran (Eds.), *Handbook of industrial, work and organizational psychology* (pp. 346–376). Thousands Oaks, CA: Sage.

Career Management Association. (circa 1948). "Harwood Studies" (box 1940, folder 3) Alfred Marrow Papers, Archives of the History of American Psychology, University of Akron, Ohio.

Conversation: An interview with Fritz J. Roethlisberger. (1972, Autumn). *Organizational Dynamics,* pp. 31–46.

De Man, H. (1929). *Joy in work.* New York: Holt.

Dent, E. B. (2001). *The messy history of OB&D: How three strands came to be seen as one rope.* Unpublished manuscript, George Washington University, Washington, DC.

Dickson, W. J., & Roethlisberger, F. J. (1966). *Counseling in an organization: A sequel to the Hawthorne researches.* Boston: Harvard University.

Drucker, P. F. (1954). *The practice of management.* New York: Harper.

French, W. L. (1982). The emergence and early history of organization development: With reference to influences on and interaction among some of the key actors. *Group and Organization Studies, 7,* 261–278.

Gabor, A. (2000). *The capitalist philosophers.* New York: Times Business.

Gillespie, R. (1991). *Manufacturing knowledge: A history of the Hawthorne experiments.* Cambridge, England: Cambridge University Press.

Gittleman, M., Horrigan, M., & Joyce, M. (1998). "Flexible" workplace practices: Evidence from a nationally representative survey. *Industrial and Labor Relations Review, 52,* 98–115.

Gray, E. R. (1978, February). The Non-Linear Systems experience: A requiem. *Business Horizons, 21,* 31–37.

Griffin, M. A., Landy, F. J., & Mayocchi, L. (2002). Australian influences on Elton Mayo: The construct of revery in industrial society. *History of Psychology, 5,* 356–375.

Guion, R. (1973). TIP talks to Bob Guion. *The Industrial–Organizational Psychologist, 11,* 6, 30–31.

Haire, M. (1959). Psychological problems relevant to business and industry. *Psychological Bulletin, 56,* 169–194.

Heil, G., Bennis, W., & Stephens, D. C. (2000). *Douglas McGregor, revisited.* New York: Wiley.

Herzberg, F., Mausner, B., & Snyderman, B. (1959). *The motivation to work.* New York: Wiley.

Highhouse, S. (1999). The brief history of personnel counseling in industrial-organizational psychology. *Journal of Vocational Behavior, 55,* 318–336.

Highhouse, S. (2002). A history of the t-group and its early applications in management development. *Group Dynamics: Theory, Research, and Practice, 6,* 277–290.

Hilgard, E. R. (1987). *Psychology in America: A historical survey.* San Diego, CA: Harcourt Brace Jovanovich.

Hoffman, E. (1999). *The right to be human.* New York: McGraw-Hill.

Hollingworth, H. L., & Poffenberger, A. T. (1917). *Applied psychology.* New York: Appleton.

Howard, A. (1995). *The changing nature of work.* New York: Jossey-Bass.

Hsueh, Y. (2002). The Hawthorne experiments and the introduction of Jean Piaget in American industrial psychology, 1929–1932. *History of Psychology, 5,* 163–189.

Humphrey, H. H. (1974). Foreword. In A. J. Marrow (Author), *Making waves in Foggy Bottom.* Washington, DC: NTL Institute.

Human relations raises sales 300%. (1948, February 16). *The New York Times,* p. 1.

Is sensitivity training a valuable tool or a risk? (1970, April). *Modern Management,* p. 15.

Jackson, B. (2001). *Management gurus and management fashions.* New York: Routledge.

Jackson, S. E., & Ruderman, M. N. (1995). *Diversity in work teams, research paradigms for a changing workplace.* Washington, DC: American Psychological Association.

Jex, S. M. (2002). *Organizational psychology: A scientist-practitioner approach.* New York: Wiley.

J. R. P. French Papers. (1940–1945). Correspondence. Archives of the History of American Psychology, University of Akron, Ohio.

Kanungo, R. N. (1979). The concepts of alienation and involvement revisited. *Psychological Bulletin, 86,* 119–138.

Katz, D., & Kahn, R. L. (1966). *The social psychology of organizations.* New York: Wiley.

Kelly, R. W., & Ware, H. F. (1947). An experiment in group dynamics. *Advanced Management Journal, 12,* 116–119.

Kleiner, A. (1996). *The age of heretics: Heroes, outlaws, and the forerunners of corporate change.* New York: Doubleday.

Kluger, A. N., & Tikochinsky, J. (2001). The error of accepting the "theoretical" null hypothesis: The rise, fall and resurrection of common sense hypotheses in psychology. *Psychological Bulletin, 127,* 408–423.

Kuriloff, A. H. (1963, November–December). An experiment in management—Putting theory Y to the test. *Personnel,* p. 14.

Landsberger, H. A. (1958). *Hawthorne revisited.* Ithaca, NY: Cornell University Press.

Lawler, E., Mohrman, S. A., & Ledford, G. E. (1998). *Strategies for high performance organizations: Employee involvement, TQM, and reengineering programs in Fortune 1000 corporations.* San Francisco, CA: Jossey-Bass.

Lawrence, P. R. (1987). Historical development of organizational behavior. In J. W. Lorsch (Ed.), *Handbook of organizational behavior* (pp. 1–9). Englewood Cliffs, NJ: Prentice-Hall.

Lawson, R. B., & Shen, Z. (1998). *Organizational psychology: Foundations and applications.* New York: Oxford University Press.

Leavitt, H. J. (1962). Toward organizational psychology. In B. von Haller Gilmer (Ed.), *Walter Van Dyke Bingham memorial program, March 23, 1961.* Pittsburgh, PA: Department of Psychology, Carnegie Institute of Technology.

Lewin, K. (1936). *Principles of topological psychology.* New York: McGraw-Hill.

Lewin, K. (1947). Frontiers in group dynamics. I. Concept, method and reality in social science: Social equilibria and social change. *Human Relations, 1,* 5–40.

Lewin, K., Lippitt, R., & White, R. K. (1939). Patterns of aggressive behavior in experimentally created social climates. *Journal of Social Psychology, 10,* 271–279.

Likert, R. (1961). *New patterns of management.* New York: McGraw-Hill.

Locke, E. A. (1976). The nature and causes of job satisfaction. In M. D. Dunnette (Ed.), *Handbook of industrial and organizational psychology* (pp. 1297–1350). Chicago: Rand McNally College.

Lorsch, J. W. (1975). Managers, behavioral scientists, and the Tower of Babel. In E. L. Cass & F. G. Zimmer (Eds.), *Man and work in society.* New York: Van Nostrand Reinhold.

Mahoney, K. T., & Baker, D. B. (2002). Elton Mayo and Carl Rogers: A tale of two techniques. *Journal of Vocational Behavior, 60,* 437–450.

Malone, E. L. (1975, January). The Non-Linear Systems experiment in participative management. *Journal of Business, 48,* 52–64.

Marrow, A. (1948). Group dynamics in industry—Implications for guidance and personnel workers. *Occupations, 26,* 472–476.

Marrow, A. J. (1957). *Making management human.* New York: Harper & Row.

Marrow, A. J. (1969). *The practical theorist: The life and work of Kurt Lewin.* New York: Basic Books.

Marrow, A. J. (1974). *Making waves in Foggy Bottom.* Washington DC: NTL Institute.

Marrow, A. J., Bowers, D. G., & Seashore, S. E. (1967). *Management by participation.* New York: Harper & Row.

Maslow, A. H. (1965). *Eupsychian management.* Homewood, IL: Richard D. Irwin.

Massarik, F. (1992). The humanistic core of industrial/organizational psychology. *Humanistic Psychologist, 20,* 389–396.

Mayo, E. (1923). The irrational factor in human behavior. *Annals of the American Academy of Political and Social Sciences, 110,* 117–121.

McGregor, D. (1960). *The human side of enterprise.* New York: McGraw-Hill.

McGregor, D. (1967). *The professional manager.* New York: McGraw-Hill.

Meltzer, H. (1982). The status and outlook for humanizing organizational behavior. *Academic Psychology Bulletin, 4,* 535–550.

Miner, J. B. (2003). The rated importance, scientific validity, and practical usefulness of organizational behavior theories: A quantitative review. *Academy of Management Learning & Education, 2,* 250–268.

Moreno, J. L. (1953). How Kurt Lewin's "Research Center for Group Dynamics" started. *Sociometry, 16,* 101–104.

Mullen, B., & Copper, C. (1994). The relation between group cohesiveness and performance: An integration. *Psychological Bulletin, 115,* 210–227.

Münsterberg, H. (1917). *Business psychology.* Chicago: LaSalle Extension University.

Neal, J. A., Tromley, C. L., Lopez, E., & Russell, J. (1995). From incremental change to retrofit: Creating high performance. *Academy of Management Executive, 9,* 42–54.

No-assembly-line plan gets nothing but results. (1964, May 25). *Steel,* p. 90.

Non-conformity at Non-Linear. (1964, August). *Quality Assurance,* p. 28.

Notification of proposed change of name. (1970, April). *The Industrial Psychologist, 4,* 4.

Packard, V. (1963, November). A chance for everyone to grow. *Reader's Digest,* p. 115.

Pajamas and the ego. (1946, August). *Fortune,* p. 140.

Papanek, M. L. (1973). Kurt Lewin and his contributions to modern management theory. *Academy of Management Proceedings,* 317–322.

Parker, W. E., & Kleemeier, R. W. (1951). *Human relations in supervision.* New York: McGraw-Hill.

Peters, M., & Robinson, V. (1984). The origins and status of action research. *The Journal of Applied Behavioral Science, 20,* 113–124.

Pugh, D. S. (1966). Modern organization theory: A psychological and sociological study. *Psychological Bulletin, 66,* 235–251.

Results of interviews of employees of Harwood Manufacturing Corporation, Marion, Virginia. (1958). "Harwood Studies" (box 1940, folder 2) Alfred Marrow Papers, Archives of the History of American Psychology, University of Akron, Ohio.

Rodgers, R., & Hunter, J. E. (1996). The methodological war of the "Hardheads" versus the "Softheads." *Journal of Applied Behavioral Science, 32,* 189–208.

Roethlisberger, F. J., & Dickson, W. J. (1939). *Management and the worker: An account of a research program conducted by the Western Electric Company, Hawthorne Works, Chicago.* Cambridge, MA: Harvard University Press.

Rogers, C. R. (1970). *On encounter groups.* New York: Harper & Row.

Sackett, P. R. (1994, April). *The content and process of the research enterprise within industrial and organizational psychology.* Presidential address, Society for Industrial and Organizational Psychology, Nashville, TN.

Schein, E. H. (1965). *Organizational psychology.* Englewood Cliffs, NJ: Prentice-Hall.

Schein, E. H. (1975). The Hawthorne group studies revisited: A defense of theory Y. In E. L. Cass & F. G. Zimmer (Eds.), *Man and work in society.* New York: Van Nostrand Reinhold.

Schlesinger, A. M. (1965). *A thousand days: John F. Kennedy in the White House.* Boston: Houghton Mifflin.

Scott, A. M. (1969). The Department of State: Formal organization and informal culture. *International Studies Quarterly, 13,* 1–18.

Scott, W. D. (1911). *Increasing human efficiency in business.* New York: Macmillan.

Seashore, S. E., & Bowers, D. G. (1970). Durability of organizational change. *American Psychologist, 25,* 227–233.

Sewell, G. (2001). What goes around, comes around: Inventing a mythology of teamwork and empowerment. *Journal of Applied Behavioral Science, 37,* 70–89.

Sheldon, K. M., Elliot, A. J., Kim, Y., & Kasser, T. (2001). What is satisfying about satisfying events? Testing 10 candidate psychological needs. *Journal of Personality and Social Psychology, 80,* 325–339.

Sherif, M., & Sherif, C. W. (1954). *Groups in harmony and tension.* New York: Harper & Row.

Stagner, R. (1982). Past and future of industrial/organizational psychology. *Professional Psychology: Research & Practice, 13,* 892–903.

Stonewalling plant democracy. (1977, March 28). *Business Week,* pp. 78–82.

Tannenbaum, R. (1996). *Bob Tannenbaum: An unfolding life.* Bethel, MN: National Training Laboratories.

Trahair, R. C. S. (1984). *The humanist temper: The life and work of Elton Mayo.* New Brunswick, NJ: Transaction Books.

Trist, E. L., & Bamforth, K. W. (1951). Some social and technical consequences of the longwall method of coal-getting. *Human Relations, 4,* 6–38.

Turner, J. M. (1926). Profit sharing that failed. In J. R. Commons (Ed.), *Industrial government* (pp. 135–157). New York: Macmillan.

Viteles, M. S. (1944). Postlude to the application of psychology in industry. *Journal of Consulting Psychology, 8,* 182–186.

Vroom, V. H. (1964). *Work and Motivation.* New York: Wiley.

Wagner, J. A. (1994). Participation's effects on performance and satisfaction: A reconsideration of research evidence. *Academy of Management Review, 19,* 312–330.

Walton, R. E. (1972). How to counter alienation in the plant. *Harvard Business Review, 50,* 70–81.

Walton, R. E. (1977). Work innovation at Topeka: After six years. *Journal of Applied Behavioral Science, 13,* 422–447.

Weisbord, M. R. (1987). *Productive workplaces.* San Francisco, CA: Jossey-Bass.

Where being nice to workers didn't work. (1973, January 20). *Business Week,* pp. 99–100.

Whitsett, D. A., & Yorks, L. (1983). Looking back at Topeka: General Foods and the quality-of-work-life experiment. *California Management Review, 25,* 93–109.

Wickert, F. R. (1974). Comments on an A.P.A. (Montreal) symposium "Humanizing Organizational Psychology." *The Industrial–Organizational Psychologist, 11,* 32–35.

Wilensky, J. L., & Wilensky, H. L. (1951). Personnel counseling: The Hawthorne case. *American Journal of Sociology, 57,* 265–280.

Wilson, T. B. (2003). *Innovative reward systems for the changing workplace.* New York: McGraw-Hill.

Wrege, C. D. (1976, August). *Solving Mayo's mystery: The first complete account of the origin of the Hawthorne Studies—The forgotten contributions of C. E. Snow and H. Hibarger.* Proceedings of the Eastern Academy of Management, Kansas City, MO.

Wren, D. A. (1979). *The evolution of management thought.* New York: Wiley.

Yorks, L., & Whitsett, D. A. (1985). Hawthorne, Topeka, and the issue of science versus advocacy in organizational behavior. *Academy of Management Review, 10,* 21–30.

Zickar, M. J. (2003). Remembering Arthur Kornhauser: Industrial–organizational psychology's advocate for worker well being. *Journal of Applied Psychology, 88,* 363–369.

15

The Study of Work Motivation in the 20th Century

Gary P. Latham
University of Toronto

Marie-Hélène Budworth
York University

Employee motivation is currently a cornerstone of industrial and organizational (I–O) psychology. By the late 20th century, motivation research dominated I–O psychology journal space, accounting for one third of the published articles (Cooper & Robertson, 1986). In the final decade, motivation became the "most frequently researched topic in micro organizational behavior" (O'Reilly, 1991, p. 431). Yet this was not true in the early part of that century. Then the focus was on employee selection, and the topic of motivation was left to studies of laboratory animals by experimental psychologists or to studies of tasks in the workplace conducted by engineers. As late as 1959, Cofer lamented that motivation was not one of the categories used by *Psychological Abstracts*.

When and how did the subject of employee motivation become so important in I–O psychology? To answer this question, this chapter reviews the scholarly literature over the past 100 years. In doing so, we try to follow a directionally chronological path. Thus, the chapter is organized loosely into four time periods: the first (1900–1925), second (1925–1950), third (1950–1975) and fourth quarters (1975–2000) of the 20th century. In the first time period, with the birth of behaviorism, experimental psychologists focused on observable behavior and the stimuli that elicited it. Inner motivational states were not studied. Engineers argued that money is the critical incentive for work and that employees should be assigned a specific difficult task or goal to be attained. The assumption was that a worker would choose to exert effort, to persist until the task goal was attained in order to obtain money. Choice, effort, and persistence are the three pillars defining motivation. In the second time period, I–O psychologists focused on employee attitudes and attitude measurement. The belief in this time period was that the pathway to discovering sources of employee motivation was to identify the attitudes of the workforce. Numerous surveys revealed that money was only one of multiple variables that people report as having an effect on their motivation. The Hawthorne studies and studies on participation in decision making supported this conclusion. Studies in this time period were for the most part atheoretical.

The third quartile of the 20th century witnessed the development of theories as frameworks for predicting, explaining, and influencing employee motivation. These theories focused on employee needs, cognition, and characteristics of the job itself. In the final quarter, three scientific theories dominated the scholarly literature on motivation in the workplace.

1900–1925

As described in other chapters in this text, Hugo Münsterberg, frequently referred to as the father of I–O psychology, engaged in systematic observations as well as interviews of factory workers (Münsterberg, 1913). This work is a precursor to the study of employee motivation in that it pointed to the need for overcoming "dreadful monotony" and "mental starvation" in the workplace (p. 196). His call went largely unheeded for nearly 2 decades. Münsterberg himself was far more interested in the issue of employee selection than he was in motivation.

Experimental Psychology

Behaviorism, articulated cogently by its founder, John B. Watson, advocated epiphenomenalism, namely that consciousness has no causal efficacy: "The time seems to have come when psychology must discard all reference to consciousness; when it needs no longer to delude itself into thinking that it is making mental states the object of observation" (Watson, 1913, p. 158). Behavior was viewed as automatic or reflexive to a stimulus rather than cognitive or intentional; the focus of the behaviorists was on learning rather than motivation (see also chap. 11).

E. Thorndike found that by presenting a reward (e.g., food) immediately after a behavior targeted by the experimenter occurred, the behavior increases. Thorndike (1911) labeled this discovery the law of effect. He also conducted an empirical study on satisfaction with work (Thorndike, 1917) that was published in the first volume of the *Journal of Applied Psychology*. Specifically, he examined the productivity and satisfaction of 29 adults who graded 10 printed compositions for 2 hours on 2 days. Speed of work, quality of work, and satisfaction were measured every 20 minutes. The results indicated that the quality and quantity of work remained the same during the 2-hour period but "satisfyingness" decreased steadily. Thorndike concluded that lack of rest affected a person's interest, willingness, or tolerance rather than the quality and quantity of the product produced. The seeds were now planted for what was to become a major controversy in I–O psychology throughout the 20th century, namely, the relation between job satisfaction and performance.

With minor exceptions, little or no attention was given by psychologists in this time period to the subject of motivation in the workplace. Widespread application of the methodology of behaviorism to motivation in organizational settings was ignored until the 1970s, some 50 years later. The emphasis of psychologists in this time period was on selection (see chaps. 1, 3, and 8). Burtt's (1926) comprehensive textbook on industrial psychology contained no mention of motivation. The implicit study of motivation, as defined by efficient/effective behavior, was left to engineers.

Scientific Management

As described in previous chapters, Frederick Winslow Taylor developed what he called scientific management (Taylor, 1911). Foreshadowing goal-setting theory, he advocated that each employee be given a task, that is, a specific difficult amount of work, of a certain quality. A task (or goal) was assigned on the basis of time and motion study. This technique, he said, identifies ways to maximize a person's productivity. The primary incentive for work in organization settings was presumed to be money. Taylor believed that employees should be paid from 30% to 100% of their wages for goal/task attainment (see also chap. 10 in this text).

1925–1950

As noted in previous chapters, in 1932, at the age of 34, Morris Viteles published *Industrial Psychology*. Unlike Burtt (1926), Viteles included a chapter titled "Motives in Industry." He argued that despite the use of financial incentive programs advocated by Taylor (1911), "analyses of restriction of output reveal not only an unhealthy economic condition, but a serious situation in workers' attitudes toward management" (p. 564). He stressed the need for "a detailed analysis of motives-in-work to determine the factors that underlie attitudes and activities which promote or interfere with economic efficiency and individual satisfaction at work" (p. 565). Viteles recommended a focus on "worker feelings and experiences rather than his logic or reasons as a factor in all his viewpoints and attitudes" (p. 581). The prime element "is the wish to enjoy the feeling of worth—recognition and respect on the part of others" (p. 582).

The research emphasis in this time period was primarily on ways of measuring employee attitudes to identify sources of motivation. The implicit theory was that positive attitudes toward or satisfaction with one's work has a positive effect on one's job performance.

Attitude Surveys

Thurstone (1929) defined attitude as affect or overall degree of favorability regarding a psychological objective. The anonymous employee attitude survey as a method for data collection in organizational settings by I–O psychologists became popular in the 1930s. Uhrbrock (1934) was among the first I–O psychologists to use the Thurstone (1929) scale. He assessed the attitudes of 3,934 factory workers, 96 clerical workers, and 400 foremen toward the company. Rensis Likert's (1932) doctoral dissertation at Columbia University revealed that a straightforward method of assessing attitudes, subsequently known as the Likert scale, eliminated the need for judges in scaling the statements, as well as the inclusion of negative statements. It correlated highly with complex methods of survey construction such as Thurstone's scales. Likert scales require nothing more than the respondent indicating on a 5-point scale the extent of agreement with, or approval of, a survey item.

The results of these attitude surveys immediately brought into question the validity of a core principle of scientific management, namely, that employees are uniformly motivated by a desire for money, and the assumption that other motives are of little consequence. Houser (1938) found that nonselling employees, including unskilled labor, of a large merchandizing company ranked money as 21st in importance. Of far greater importance were chances to show initiative (11.5), safety (3), steady employment (2), and fair adjustment of grievances (1).

In a study that focused explicitly on job satisfaction, Hoppock (1935) reported that satisfaction is affected by many factors other than money, including relative status of the person within the social and economic group with which he or she identifies himself or herself, relationships with superiors and associates on the job, the nature of the work, opportunities for advancement, variety, freedom from close supervision, visible results, appreciation, and security. These two studies foreshadowed theories subsequently put forth by Maslow (1943) and Herzberg (Herzberg, Mausner, & Snyderman, 1959).

Laboratory Experiments

Few laboratory experiments on motivation were conducted in this time period. An exception is a series of experiments conducted by Mace (1935) in Great Britain. He found that the standard that was set affected a person's performance, but only when the person's skill had developed to the point where there was a reasonable expectation by the individual that the standard could be reached. Otherwise, urging people to do their best led to the highest performance. This latter finding was replicated in the United States by Kanfer and Ackerman (1989) more than 50 years later in their goal-setting study involving Air Force cadets in an air-traffic control simulation. Setting a standard (goal) for the performance of the worker, Mace concluded, will be most effective if it is adjusted to his or her level of skill and ability. This finding is the bedrock of the field studies on goal setting by Latham and his colleagues 40 years later.

Field Experiments

By the late 1920s, the widespread use of time and motion studies by engineers led to highly repetitive work. Each employee was in effect "standardized." As Dunnette and Kirchner (1965) noted, employees were viewed by engineers as identical elements in the production process to be studied and manipulated as any other cog in the machinery of production.

Research in Great Britain by Wyatt, Fraser, and Stock (1929) was a precursor to job enlargement. They found that changing jobs at specific intervals reduces monotony. With light repetitive work, employees produce their best output if their task is changed every 1.5 to 2 hours. More frequent changes interfere with the "swing" of work. In addition, they found that piece rate resulted in fewer symptoms of boredom than hourly pay. This finding predates Lawler's (1965) findings and supports Taylor's (1911) earlier conclusion that money can indeed be an incentive for performance if job performance is the criterion for determining the person's pay.

A subsequent study by Wyatt, Frost, and Stock (1934) foreshadowed field research on goal setting. Factory workers reduced their boredom by creating "definite aims" to complete a certain number of units in a given period of time.

The application of scientific management principles in a Philadelphia textile mill in the 1920s increased employee antagonism toward management as well as labor grievances and turnover. Elton Mayo, a sociologist at Harvard, concluded, on the basis of observation, that these difficulties were due to the monotony of the work. His solution was to allow the workers to take rest periods according to their own agreed-on schedules. The result was a large decrease in turnover and an increase in productivity. Mayo's solution was based on his reasoning that money is only an effective incentive when it is used in conjunction with, rather than in opposition to, people's other needs.

Hawthorne Studies.   Mayo and his colleagues were subsequently asked to become involved with a series of studies of employee productivity (Mayo, 1933) for the Committee on Work in Industry of the National Research Council. Field experiments were conducted in the Hawthorne (Chicago) plant of the Western Electric Company, a manufacturer of equipment for the telephone industry. These experiments led to the "realization that the productivity, satisfaction, and motivation of workers were all interrelated" (Roethlisberger, 1977, p. 46).

The Hawthorne studies were attacked vigorously by Argyle (1953) for their lack of methodological rigor. In a reanalysis of the data, Franke and Kaul (1978) showed that two key reasons for relay performance improvement were the replacement of two low-producing workers as well as the introduction of an incentive system. By modern standards, these and other methodological confounds render the conclusions of the Hawthorne studies highly suspect. Where the advocates of scientific management simplistically assumed that person's most basic motive is economic, Mayo and his colleagues made an "equally oversimplified assumption that group membership and affiliation are the most fundamental and essentially the only human needs of any consequence" (Dunnette & Kirchner, 1965, p. 133).

Nevertheless, these studies were said to be seminal because they showed that when people are given the opportunity to express their preferences and opinions, are free of overly strict supervision, and are given standards, that is, goals that take into account their ability, they work effectively (Ryan & Smith, 1954). Years later Blum and Naylor (1968) concluded that just as Münsterberg's work is considered the birth of industrial psychology, the Hawthorne studies can be considered its "coming of age." (See chap. 14 for additional information and perspective on these studies.)

World War II

In response to the war with repressive fascist regimes in Europe, and in light of the findings of Mayo and his colleagues, the importance of employee participation in the decision making process (pdm) was becoming an implicit if not an explicit hypothesis of I–O psychologists, as well as union leaders. Harold Ruttenberg (1941), research director of the Steel Workers Organizing Committee, stated that the urge for self-expression is present in every individual in an industrial plant and that each person constantly seeks some way to express himself or herself.

Fifteen years of economic depression and war led Maier (1946) to conclude that the most undeveloped aspect of industrial progress is management of labor power.[1] He cited an unpublished field experiment by Alex Bavelas, a former student of Kurt Lewin's, as an example of how to motivate workers. By securing group participation, management found that previously unattainable goals were reached by those workers. Two years later Ghiselli and Brown (1948) argued that the new emphasis of industrial psychology should be to maximize productivity consistent with the abilities, energies, interests, and motives of the worker.

French, also a former student of Lewin's, showed that employee participation in decision making can overcome resistance to change (Coch & French, 1948). Similar findings were obtained 40 years later in terms of "voice," a concept central to organizational justice theory (Greenberg, 1987). Empirical research conducted by the University of Michigan's Survey Research Center (1948) in an insurance company also corroborated the importance of pdm:

> People are more effectively motivated when they are given some degree of freedom in the way in which they do their work than when every action is prescribed in advance. They do better when some degree of decision making about their jobs is possible than when all decisions are made for them. They respond more adequately when they are treated as personalities than as cogs in a machine. In short, if the ego motivations of self determination, of self expression, of a sense of personal worth can be tapped, the individual can be more effectively energized. The use of external sanctions, of pressuring for production, may work to some degree, but not to the extent that more internalized motives do.[2] (p. 10)

By the end of the second quarter of the 20th century and at the beginning of the third, I–O psychologists were showing contempt for scientific management. For example, Ryan (1947) concluded that time and motion study was inadequate because it relies on extremely crude estimates of effort by engineers. Moreover, it is based on the erroneous assumption that effort remains constant throughout comparisons of different work methods. Foreshadowing the research on job enrichment, he argued that wages are of secondary consideration because workers want a certain degree of independence and initiative plus recognition for their work and value to the organization. In addition, people want a superior who guides and directs rather than commands.

---

[1] It was Maier (1955) who proposed that job performance = motivation × ability.

[2] Erez (1997) reported that pdm is now used across cultures as a motivational technique. However, a meta-analysis by Wagner (1994) showed that the effect of pdm on an employee's performance has statistical but lacks practical significance.

Similar to Ryan, Harrell (1949), as did Mayo, argued that motivation does not occur through the application of money alone. Harrell called the erroneous assumption that money is the only important incentive the "rabble hypothesis" because workers are treated as a group of unorganized rabble insensitive to the social motives of approval and self-respect. Similarly, Stagner (1950) stated that the problem of industrial harmony would not be solved until there is realization that both executives and workers want democratic self-assertion. He took strong issue with what he called the dollar fallacy, the erroneous belief that employers and employees are motivated only by dollars and cents.

Tiffin (1952) took umbrage with reference to workers as "hired hands" because it too reflects a mistaken viewpoint by management. A person's hands alone are never hired. The factors he cited that affect a worker's morale were similar to those identified in the Hawthorne studies. It is not so much the job as how the person feels about it and how the boss regards the employee that determines morale. In addition, Tiffin advised the necessity of taking into account social factors and working conditions.

The concept of motivation was now being explicitly discussed in the I–O literature, so much so that Harrell (1949) concluded that as recently as 1930, we assumed that the importance of psychology in industry was largely confined to the use of tests; today we view its function as the analysis of human relations in industry. Ryan (1947) stated that motive refers to factors that raise or lower the level of effort an individual puts into the task. Shortly thereafter, with his former doctoral student, Patricia Cain Smith (Ryan & Smith, 1954), he stated that motivation is the central problem of industrial psychology.

Harrell (1949), after reviewing the literature, concluded that motives are based on physiological drives (i.e., food, water, rest, sleep, and sex activity) that act in combination with a learned response to gratify this drive. His conclusion was based on the ongoing research of the behaviorists in experimental psychology (e.g., Hull, 1943). The most important motives in industry are the activity or the work itself, hunger, sex, social approval, and self-respect. Sex as a motive for work, he said, operates indirectly by making a person work harder and steadier in order to get married or to support his wife and family. In addition, he emphasized: "Whether or not motivation will be effective depends in part on the internal state of the organism—his level of aspiration—what a man expects of himself" (p. 269). In general, American employees in either the professions or management, concluded Harrell, are highly motivated; this is not true, he said, of the factory worker.

As the first half of the 20th century came to a close, the near exclusive emphasis of I–O psychologists on employee selection had shifted to include the topic of motivation and satisfaction. With one exception, however, research up to this point in time was atheoretical. The exception was an essay written by Abraham Maslow, a clinical psychologist. In that essay he specified needs, and the cues that arouse them, that energize and direct behavior.

Need Hierarchy Theory

Maslow's (1943) theory of human motivation was based on his observations of individuals who came to him for assistance in coping with difficulties in their personal lives. The theory was written during the Great Depression. From the outset of his paper, Maslow acknowledged that

> The present theory then must be considered to be a suggested program or framework for future research and must stand or fall, not so much on facts available or evidence presented, as upon researches yet to be done, researches suggested perhaps, by the questions raised in this paper. (p. 371)

Rather than focus on attitudes, Maslow posited that there is a hierarchy of five sets of goals for which people strive in seeking satisfaction of their basic needs, namely physiological goals, safety, love, esteem, and self-actualization. Systematic research based on Maslow's theory did not occur in organizational settings for another 2 decades. Nevertheless, it had a tremendous influence in the very next decade on McGregor's (1957) formulation of "theory X" and "theory Y."

1950–1975

Research in the early part of the 1950s did not differ appreciably from the 4 decades of research that preceded it. Attitude surveys continued to be the primary method of data collection for I–O psychologists in their study of motivation. Behaviorism was at its zenith in experimental psychology with B. F. Skinner (1953) as its articulate champion.

Ryan and Smith (1954) argued against I–O psychology adopting the prevailing motivational paradigms of experimental and clinical psychology. To translate worker goals into Watson's terms of stimuli and responses, they said, was not only useless but misleading because it implies that the laws governing these stimuli and responses in experimental laboratory paradigms are the same as those which hold for all other stimuli and responses in everyday situations. The authors took issue with Hull's research on primary drives because to postulate some simple mechanism by which new activities come to be attractive to the organism makes it difficult, if not impossible, they said, to demonstrate that a particular activity in the work setting arises through biological determinism. As for Freud, Ryan and Smith noted wryly that his evidence that the individual is unaware of his or her real wish is likely due only to the fact that the individual does not wish to admit or explain it to the listener. Finally, they dismissed the relevance of behaviorism and psychoanalysis because of the deemphasis of the importance of consciousness in regulating behavior. Consequently, Ryan and Smith called for general theories of motivation by industrial psychologists that take into account the wants, wishes, desires, and experiences of the individual.[3] They argued the importance of intentions to anticipate future obligations or to avoid them.

> Whether a means activity is initiated, and the degree of effort which is devoted to it, are functions of (a) the attractiveness of the goal, (b) the attractiveness of the means activity itself and of its surrounding conditions, (c) the uniqueness of the goal (as perceived by the individual), (d) the directness of relationship between the means and the end result, also as perceived or understood by the subject, and (e) the individual's estimates of his ability to perform the means activity well enough to achieve the goal. (Ryan & Smith, 1954, pp. 387–388)[4]

Job Satisfaction and Job Performance

Viteles (1953) equated motivation with employee performance and morale. The conclusion emanating from attitude surveys as well as from the Hawthorne studies was that the worker who is highly productive is a worker who has positive attitudes toward the job. Thus, a primary variable of interest to I–O psychologists was employee morale or satisfaction.[5]

A major breakthrough in knowledge occurred with an enumerative review of the literature by Brayfield and Crockett (1955) that forcibly and thoughtfully challenged that belief. They showed that there was little or no relation between these two variables. Shortly thereafter, a

---

[3]Although people in the workplace were still referred to as men or girls, the use of the word *worker* was shifting to that of *employee* and the neutrally descriptive term *individual*.

[4]The seeds were now planted for their future doctoral student to sow a decade later, Edwin Locke.

[5]The terms *job satisfaction* and *morale* were used interchangeably until Guion (1958) and Stagner (1958) argued for differentiation. The former refers to the individual's attitudes toward the job; the latter refers to the perception that, through cooperation with the group, one's motives or needs will be met.

subsequent review by Vroom (1964) showed that the median correlation between a person's satisfaction and performance was only .14. Nevertheless, these two variables remained interdependent in the eyes of employers and I–O researchers.

Motivation Theory

As noted in previous chapters, in 1953, Viteles published his book *Motivation and Morale*. This became the definitive textbook on this subject for 3 decades. In his review of theories in both experimental and social psychology, he commented favorably on Lewin's "insistence that without a good 'theoretical' foundation applied research follows a path of trial and error, and becomes misdirected and inefficient" (p. 121). One-shot, one-context attitude surveys in the 1930s had mitigated the development of motivation theory in the workplace.

In the opening sentence of his *Annual Review of Psychology* chapter, Heron (1954), a psychologist in the United Kingdom, observed that

> it may well be that in the last five years we have experienced the end of an era in the history of industrial psychology. No startling development took place, no text appeared to establish a landmark, no new theory provoked widespread discussion and opened fresh vistas; but perhaps something less sensational may be detected. Discontent can sometimes be divine, provided it results in thinking which ultimately issues in more appropriate activity. (p. 203)

Heron's observation proved to be remarkably prescient. Innovation and knowledge in I–O psychology were about to blossom in the form of myriad theories of work motivation. These theories provided a framework for planning, conducting, and interpreting research. McGregor argued for the applicability of Maslow's theory to industry.

Theory X and Theory Y.   Douglas McGregor received his PhD from Harvard University, where he was influenced by Gordon Allport. However, McGregor did not see himself as an experimentalist (McGregor, 1960). Rather, he was, in the words of Warren Bennis (1985), a champion of the application of behavioral sciences with a flair for the right metaphor that generated and established a new idea. Of all behavioral scientists, he was in this time period the best known by managers until his death in 1964 (Boone & Bowen, 1987). (See also chap. 14 in this text.)

McGregor (1957) argued that the time had come to apply the social sciences to make human organizations truly effective: "To a degree the social sciences today are in a position like that of the physical sciences with respect to atomic energy in the thirties. We know that the past assumptions of man are in dispute and in many ways, incorrect" (McGregor, 1957, p. 22). The subject of motivation is the best way, he said, of indicating the inappropriateness of the conventional view of employees, which he called "theory X." The assumption underlying theory X is that without active intervention by management, people are passive—even resistant—to organizational needs. This is because the average person is by nature indolent, lacks ambition, is inherently self-centered, and is not very bright. This behavior is not a consequence of people's inherent nature, argued McGregor; rather, it is the outcome of management philosophy and practice. He then explained Maslow's theory in detail to show why theory X is an inadequate approach to motivation: "Unless there are opportunities *at work* to satisfy these higher level needs, people will be deprived" (p. 28). He further noted, "People will make insistent demands for more money under these conditions. It becomes more important than ever to buy the material goods and services which can provide limited satisfaction to the thwarted needs" (p. 28).

Thus McGregor concluded that a different theory of human motivation was needed in the workplace, a theory based on the correct assumptions about human nature, a theory that makes explicit "the human side of an enterprise." McGregor called this "theory Y." Theory Y differs from theory X in that the latter places exclusive reliance on external control of behavior, whereas theory Y emphasizes self-control and self-direction. McGregor stated that

> the motivation, the potential for development, the capacity for assuming responsibility, the readiness to direct behavior toward organizational goals are all present in people. Management does not put them there. A responsibility of management is to make it possible for people to recognize and develop these human characteristics for themselves. (McGregor, 1957, p. 6)

As was the presentation by Maslow (1943), McGregor's (1957) paper and subsequent book (McGregor, 1960) were void of data to support either theory Y or Maslow's theory on which it was directly based. It was not until the 1960s that theory-driven research was conducted.

Porter used Maslow's theory to frame issues of managerial motivation. Consistent with Maslow's theory, Porter (1961) showed that the highest order need, self-actualization, is the most critical in terms of both perceived deficiency in fulfillment and perceived importance to both bottom and middle management.

"A good theory is one that holds together long enough to get you to a better theory" (Hebb, 1961, p. 21). In the next decade, with the publication of Wahba and Bridwell's (1976) critique, Maslow's need hierarchy theory was largely abandoned by I–O psychologists. None of the factor analytic studies showed clear support for Maslow's classification of needs.

Alderfer (1972) reformulated Maslow's theory based on three related needs in an organizational setting, namely existence (e.g., pay, fringe benefits), relatedness (e.g., social interactions), and growth (e.g., esteem and self-actualization). Alderfer argued that, unlike Maslow's proposed hierarchy, these three needs can act simultaneously. Much of the research on this theory, conducted by Alderfer himself, yielded mixed results.

Job Characteristics.   McGregor (1960) argued for a shift from research on employee selection to an emphasis on satisfying the employee's needs:

> The reason is that we have not learned enough about the utilization of talent, about the creation of an organizational climate conducive to human growth. The blunt fact is that we are a long way from realizing the potential represented by the human resources we now recruit into industry. We have much to accomplish with respect to utilization before further improvements in selection will become important. (Preface, p. x)

McGregor (1960) cited approvingly a comprehensive study published in a book a year earlier that described how to design jobs that are conducive to satisfying needs for human growth:

> A recent, highly significant study of the sources of job satisfaction and dissatisfaction among managerial and professional people suggests that these opportunities for "self-actualization" are the essential requirements of both job satisfaction and high performance. The researchers find that "the wants of employees divide into two groups. One group revolves around the need to develop in one's occupation as a source of personal growth. The second group operates as an essential base to the first and is associated with fair treatment in compensation, supervision, working conditions, and administrative practices. *The fulfillment of the needs of the second group does not motivate the individual to high levels of job satisfaction and ... extra performance on the job.* All we can expect from satisfying [the second group of needs] is the prevention of dissatisfaction and poor job performance." (p. 55)

This book was written by Frederick Herzberg (Herzberg et al., 1959). It was the basis for what was to become known alternatively as the two-factor theory, motivation-hygiene theory, or job enrichment. People have two basic sets of needs, namely, survival and growth. Characteristics of the job facilitate or hinder satisfaction of the "growth needs" of self-esteem and self-satisfaction.

Herzberg obtained his PhD under the supervision of John Flanagan at the University of Pittsburgh. Herzberg's peers as a doctoral student included George Albee, who was to become a clinical psychologist, and William W. Ronan, who would become an I–O psychologist. Herzberg, torn between choosing a career in clinical or I–O psychology, decided to study the mental health of people in industry. In a doctoral seminar, he informed Flanagan that he wanted to use the critical incident technique (Flanagan, 1954) to collect data. Flanagan responded dryly as to the inappropriateness of doing so because of the likelihood that people would attribute satisfying incidents to their own behavior and incidents that were dissatisfying to them to factors outside their control (Ronan, personal communication, November 16, 1968). The warning was ignored.[6]

Similar to Maslow and McGregor, Herzberg (1966) believed that "the primary function of any organization, whether religious, political or industrial, should be to implement the needs for man to enjoy a meaningful existence" (Foreword, p. x). He and his colleagues analyzed the content of the critical incidents they collected from engineers and accountants regarding when these people felt exceptionally good or exceptionally bad about their jobs in order to determine ways to increase productivity, decrease turnover and absenteeism, and smooth labor relations. Just as Flanagan had predicted, the results showed that job content factors were a primary source of motivation or satisfaction whereas context or hygiene factors were the source of dissatisfaction, hence the label two-factor or motivation-hygiene theory. Herzberg's most controversial conclusion was that job satisfaction and job dissatisfaction, rather than being on one continuum, are two continua. That is, the opposite of dissatisfaction is not satisfaction, but no dissatisfaction; similarly, the opposite of job satisfaction is not dissatisfaction, but no job satisfaction. Herzberg (1966) argued that to enrich a job, attention should be given to the work itself (job content), recognition, responsibility, achievement, and opportunities for advancement. Contextual or hygiene factors such as working conditions, company policy, supervision (technical as well as interpersonal), and pay should be focused on only as ways to minimize job dissatisfaction. Focusing on the latter will have little or no effect on a person's effort or performance.

The two-factor aspect of the theory was subsequently explained by Vroom (1964) in his book, and again (Vroom, 1967) to a standing-room-only symposium at APA where Herzberg was a presenter, to be a methodological artifact. Herzberg's results were replicated only when the critical incident technique was used, a technique that had been originally designed by his mentor, Flanagan, for job analysis. Other psychologists agreed with Vroom's criticism (e.g., King, 1970). The same events caused both satisfaction and dissatisfaction, but different agents were perceived by employees as responsible—the self for satisfying events, and variables other than the self for dissatisfying events (Locke, 1976).

Herzberg (1966) responded in vain to this attack:

> The supposition that people would prefer to blame hygiene factors rather than the motivators for their job unhappiness in order to make themselves look good is naïve. It does not take too much experience with job-attitude data to find that the opposite is more often true. Employees who wish to make themselves look good are much more prone to say they are unhappy because they do not have responsibility, are not getting ahead, have uninteresting work, see no possibility for growth. (pp. 130–131)

A later version of job enrichment theory was formulated by Richard Hackman and his former doctoral student, Gregory Oldham (Hackman & Oldham, 1975, 1976). This theory took into account individual differences. In brief, they developed a job diagnostic survey to assess the motivating potential of a job and the employee's growth needs or readiness to perform in an

---

[6]Ronan was Gary Latham's master's thesis advisor.

enriched job. People who are high in achievement or growth needs are more satisfied and perform better than those who are lower when placed in an enriched job. An enriched job is one that scores high on skill variety, task identity, task significance, autonomy, and task feedback.

Subsequent studies showed that moderating effects of individual differences on task or job design were not significant. "Enriched jobs seem to exert positive affective and behavior effects regardless of an incumbent's desire for higher order need satisfaction, need for achievement, need for autonomy, etc." (Cummings, 1982, p. 546). Yankelovich's (1974) surveys of job-related attitudes among American youth revealed a strong preference for careers involving self-control over one's job activities and a desire for interesting work as well as material rewards, regardless of education level. He also found that people in general define success in terms of self-fulfillment. Moreover, consistent with what Maslow would have predicted in that time period, the survey showed that these respondents had little or no fear of economic hardship.

Equity Theory.   Herzberg's theory of job enrichment states that money can be a major source of dissatisfaction. The theory says little about what the person will do as a result of this dissatisfaction. Equity theory, developed by Jean "Stacy" Adams, filled in the blank. Adams, born in Belgium, received his PhD at the University of North Carolina, Chapel Hill. His theory was developed as a result of his association at Stanford University with Leon Festinger as well as his work at the General Electric Company.

Adams was influenced by Festinger's (1957) cognitive dissonance theory which states that to the extent that a discrepancy exists within the individual, the person is motivated to reduce it; the greater the discrepancy the greater the motivation. Equity theory deals primarily with money. In brief, the theory (Adams, 1963) states that people examine the ratio of their "outcomes" (denominator) relative to their "inputs" (numerator) relative to those of a comparison other.[7] Inputs include the person's effort, education, and experience. Outcomes include money, recognition, and working conditions. Equity theory states that unequal ratios produce tension within the person. This tension can be alleviated by cognitively distorting one's inputs or outcomes, leaving/quitting the situation, changing the inputs (e.g., increase/decrease effort) or outcomes, or changing one's comparison other. The solution most likely to be used to reduce inequity is the one with the least perceived cost.

The theory was attacked for lack of precision. Campbell, Dunnette, Lawler and Weick (1970) concluded that

> predictions from equity theory are made very difficult by the complexity making up the input–output package and the multitude of ways in which inequity can be resolved. However, the theory presents a clear warning to organizations that they must learn a great deal more about the nature of the input-output comparisons and the way they develop and change. (p. 382)[8]

---

[7]In 1958, Newell, Shaw, and Simon presented their theory of human problem solving that emphasized an information-processing model. Shortly thereafter, the study of motivation in the workplace went cognitive; the employee was immersed in thought.

[8]Adams' (1968) cogent response was, "The contrast between equity theory and 'expectancy' theory implies that performance in work situations must be accounted for by either one or the other. Multiple motivation states may determine behavior, though one state may be dominant in an individual and in a group of individuals at a particular point in time. Under particular conditions the motivation to achieve equity may dominate, under others maximizing gain (expectancy) may be salient and under some conditions the two may be pitted each against the other.... I doubt that anyone seriously questions the fact that desire to manage outcomes is a powerful determinant of behavior, and there is now ample evidence that desire to achieve justice has considerable influence on behavior. The question of importance is not whether equity or 'expectancy' theory accounts for such behavior as work productivity or quality, but under what conditions equity motives and gain maximizing motives account for certain proportions of observed performance variance" (p. 316). In a subsequent review of the literature, Mowday (1991) concluded that there is general support for equity theory's predictions, particularly regarding piece-rate and hourly overpayment. People who believe they are overpaid perform higher than those who perceive that they are equitably paid.

Because of these criticisms, and because another theory, expectancy theory, was viewed by influential psychologists, particularly Lawler (1970), as having greater predictive and explanatory power regarding performance in paid work settings than equity theory, the attention of I–O psychologists shifted to this theory.[9]

Expectancy Theory.   Victor Vroom, a Canadian from Montreal, earned his undergraduate and master's degree from McGill and his PhD from the University of Michigan, where he studied with N. R. F. Maier. Rather than focus on factors in a job that energize and sustain behavior, Vroom (1964, p. 6) used "the term motivation to refer to processes governing choices made by persons or lower organisms among alternative forms of voluntary activity." Influenced by the research of Tolman, an experimental psychologist, as well as Lewin, a social psychologist, Vroom developed a cognitive theory based on a person's expectancies, valences, choices, and instrumentalities. Central to the theory are two propositions (Vroom 1964).

> *Proposition 1.* The valence of an outcome is a monotonically increasing function of the algebraic sum of the products of the valences for all other outcomes and his conceptions of its instrumentality for the attainment of these other outcomes.

> *Proposition 2.* The force on a person to perform an act is a monotonically increasing function of the algebraic sum of the products of the valences of all outcomes and the strength of his experiences that the act will be followed by the attainment of these outcomes. (pp. 17–18)

That is, the effort that people exert is a function of their expectation or subjective probability estimate that certain outcomes will occur as a result of their performance and the valence for them of those outcomes. The greater the valence of any outcome, the more likely the person is to choose to exert effort to take action. The valence of an outcome is in turn a function of its instrumentality for obtaining other outcomes and the valence of those other outcomes.

Similar to equity theory, this theory states that people base their actions on their perceptions and beliefs. Unlike equity theory, which focuses solely on the outcomes of one's perceptions of fairness, expectancy theory was developed to explain virtually all work-related behavior ranging from occupational choice to performance on the job. Thus, expectancy theory was the first cognitive, broad-range theory of motivation developed by an I–O psychologist. The theory focuses on choice, effort, and persistence. Vroom's contribution was principally to show how expectancy type theories could be applied to work behavior. These processes included the factors affecting people's choice of their occupation and of the organizations in which to practice them, their satisfaction with their choices, and the effectiveness of their performance. It is the last of these dependent variables that has received the greatest attention. People make choices that determine the amount of effort they devote to performing their jobs effectively. The amount of such effort is hypothesized to be a function of four classes of variables: (a) the valence of rewards and sanctions potentially linked by the organization to effective performance, (b) the perceived instrumentality of effective performance for the attainment of these rewards and/or the avoidance of sanctions, (c) the intrinsic valence of high performance itself, and (d) the expectancy that higher effort will result in higher performance. The first two variables are frequently thought necessary for extrinsic motivation, whereas the last two are components of intrinsic motivation.

In the previous decade, the belief that job satisfaction affects job performance had been shattered by Brayfield and Crockett (1955). On the basis of expectancy theory, Lawler, to-

---

[9]Lawler's first doctoral student was Martin Evans. Evans developed the theory of path-goal leadership for his doctoral dissertation.

gether with his mentor, Porter (Lawler & Porter, 1967), argued that it is nevertheless important to measure the satisfaction level that exists in organizations because it influences both employee attendance and turnover. They then proposed the radical notion that rather than being a cause of performance, satisfaction is caused by it. They concluded that organizations should find ways of maximizing the relation between performance and satisfaction rather than satisfaction itself.

Platt (1964) argued that a theory that cannot be mortally endangered cannot be alive. That expectancy theory was very much alive is evident by voluminous research conducted to test it. In less than a decade there were two comprehensive reviews of this literature published in the prestigious *Psychological Bulletin* (Heneman & Schwab, 1972; Mitchell & Biglan, 1971). But by the mid-1970s, Miner and Dachler (1973, p. 381) concluded that "a closer examination of the literature reveals a number of inconsistent findings" and that it "is remarkably weak and contradictory in other respects" (p. 382). Locke (1975, p. 458) noted that "there are no consistent findings regarding which components are the best predictors of performance." Moreover, the results were suspect, he said, in that the theory predicts self-ratings of effort, attitude, and performance better than supervisory evaluations. Furthermore, he argued that the theory was incorrect in assuming (a) that people choose to maximize outcomes and (b) that they usually perform complex evaluations in making choices that will enable them to maximize outcomes. Finally, Schmidt (1973) pointed out that the formulas involved in the theory assume a ratio scale when there is no known way of measuring valences on this scale. In an enumerative review of 31 studies testing the theory, House, Shapiro, and Wahba (1974) reached similar conclusions. A meta-analysis (Van Eerde & Thierry, 1996) indicated that there is modest support for the individual components of Vroom's theory but that the model itself is not valid.

Behavior Modification. With Vroom's success in building a heuristic theory based in part on theory and research in experimental psychology, I–O psychologists ignored the concerns voiced by Ryan and Smith 2 decades earlier and began to examine behaviorism as studied and implemented by Skinner and his followers. In an influential essay, Nord (1969) argued the similarities between McGregor's basic arguments and Skinner's emphasis on the environment in shaping a person's behavior. In Skinner's (1953) view, behavior is said to be a function of reinforcers.

> Remove the gratuitous physiologizing, and the point is made that motives and purposes are in people while contingences of reinforcement are in the environment, but motives and purposes are at best the effect of reinforcements. The change wrought by reinforcements is often spoken of as the "acquisition of purpose or intention," and we are said to "give a person a purpose," by reinforcing him in a given way. These are convenient expressions, but the basic fact is that when a person is "aware of his purpose" he is feeling or observing introspectively a condition produced by reinforcement. (Skinner, 1974, p. 58)

Well trained in experimental methods, I–O psychologists in this time period increasingly turned to both laboratory and field experiments to provide rigorous tests of phenomena that were identified in correlational and case studies in the field. For example, Yukl, Wexley, and Seymore (1972), in a laboratory experiment, obtained results that were contrary to what might be predicted by instrumentality beliefs as posited by expectancy theory. Their results were consistent with Skinner's research with rats and pigeons. Performance was higher when people were paid on a variable ratio schedule of reinforcement than on a continuous one. Latham and Dossett (1978) showed that consistent with Skinner's findings, unionized mountain beaver trappers at the Weyerhaeuser Company who were inexperienced had higher productivity when paid on a continuous reinforcement schedule whereas their experienced counterparts had higher productivity on a variable ratio schedule.

In less than a decade following Nord's essay, Luthans and Kreitner (1975) published a book on ways of using behavior modification methodology in organizational settings. Dunnette (1976) referred to this methodology as one of seven milestones in I–O psychology because it makes explicit the operations that must be followed to increase the probability that the interventions will bring about a relatively permanent change in behavior. The methodology makes explicit the types of data that should be collected and the operations that should be followed in collecting these data. A *Handbook of Organizational Behavior Management* was published (Frederiksen, 1982).

With few exceptions (e.g., Komaki, 1998), the interest of most I–O psychologists in behaviorism quickly waned in the final quarter of the 20th century. Experimental psychologists such as Dulaney (1968) had demonstrated the effect of cognitive influences on these procedures as did Kaufman, Baron and Kopp (1966) regarding reinforcement schedules. I–O psychologists were troubled by the philosophy of behaviorism, especially determinism and epiphenomenalism. In addition, Locke (1977, 1978) showed how behavior modification researchers in I–O psychology implicitly include cognitive processes. He (Locke, 1980) argued that the effect of feedback on performance cannot be interpreted as supporting behaviorism, because feedback is mediated by goal setting.

With the decline of behaviorism in I–O psychology, two theories were about to dominate the literature on motivation for the remainder of the century, namely goal setting and social learning, later to be relabeled social cognitive theory.

Goal-Setting Theory.   Edwin Locke was educated at Harvard University, the bastion of behaviorism in that time period. He did his PhD at Cornell under the supervision of T. A. Ryan and Patricia Cain Smith. There he became an ardent critic of behaviorism.

Ryan (Ryan, 1947, 1970; Ryan & Smith, 1954) argued that people strive to behave intentionally. Needs, beliefs, and attitudes affect behavior through intentions. Thus, once they are formed, intentions are the immediate antecedents for predicting and explaining behavior. Neither equity nor expectancy theory explicitly addresses intentions.

Locke's doctoral dissertation at Cornell was based on a series of laboratory experiments to test Ryan's hypothesis regarding the effect of intentions. The culmination of these experiments (Locke, 1968) led to three propositions that are the core of goal-setting theory: (a) specific high goals lead to higher performance than no goals or even an abstract goal such as "do your best"; (b) given goal commitment, the higher the goal the higher the performance; and (c) variables such as monetary incentives, participation in decision making, feedback, or knowledge of results affect performance only to the extent that they lead to the setting of and commitment to specific high goals. In short, goals have the effect of directing attention and action (choice), mobilizing energy expenditure (effort), prolonging effort over time (persistence), and motivating the individual to develop relevant strategies (cognition) for goal attainment (Locke, Shaw, Saari, & Latham, 1981). Given goal commitment, job performance improves because the goal provides a regulatory mechanism that allows the employee to observe, monitor, subjectively evaluate, and adjust job behavior toward effective goal attainment. Goal setting taps a fundamental attribute of human behavior, namely, goal directedness (Lee, Locke, & Latham, 1989). In their reviews of the literature, both Austin and Vancouver (1996) and Mitchell and Daniels (2003) concluded that the one overriding common theme among almost all psychological approaches to motivation is goals.

As noted by Pervin (1989), the concept of goal as a motivational construct has a number of advantages over needs and external reinforcers. By emphasizing the cognitive representation or image of a goal, the employee is freed from the immediacy of a current stimulus. The employee is oriented toward the future as far as cognitive capacity permits.

The results regarding goal difficulty seemingly contradict those of Atkinson (1953), a social psychologist who had been a student of McClelland. Atkinson's theory of need for achievement states that task difficulty, measured as probability of task success, was related to performance in a curvilinear, inverse function. The highest level of effort is expended on tasks that are moderately difficult. Atkinson, however, did not measure personal preference goals or goal difficulty. His findings have not been replicated when task performance goals were measured.[10]

Similar to Lawler and Porter (1967), Locke (1970) too viewed satisfaction as resulting from performance. However, he argued that it is the result of goal-directed behavior and value attainment as a result of reaching one's goals. Goal specificity delineates the conditional requirements for positive self-evaluation. An abstract goal such as "do your best" is at best a placebo. It provides little or no basis for regulating one's efforts let alone for evaluating how one is doing.

In reviewing Locke's laboratory experiments, Hinrichs (1970, p. 525) questioned whether similar results "will carry through in the complex behaviors required in organizations." Similarly, in their review of expectancy theory, Heneman and Schwab (1972) stated,

> A noteworthy aspect of research on expectancy theory is the emphasis on investigating employees in their natural work environments, thus providing a high degree of external validity. In the case of motivation ... this is in direct contrast to research on ... goal setting theory (Locke, 1968) which has usually entailed student subjects working on laboratory tasks in experimental settings. The cost of external validity has been of course, a general inability to make causal inferences. (p. 8)

This was about to change with Latham's work at the American Pulpwood Association (e.g., Ronan, Latham, & Kinne, 1973), followed by his research conducted at the Weyerhaeuser Company (e.g. Latham & Yukl, 1975).

1975–2000

By the final quarter of the 20th century, dust bowl empiricism, or atheoretical, data-driven research, was dead. In their *Annual Review of Psychology* chapter on attitudes and motivation, Miner and Dachler (1973) were able to restrict their focus to theory and theory-oriented research. Although one theory of motivation that had appeared in the previous quarter continued to thrive in terms of theoretical and practical significance, interest in other theories waned as two others took their place.[11]

In his *Annual Review of Psychology* chapter, Mitchell (1979, p. 252) reported that Maslow's theory, Alderfer's ERG model, and Herzberg's theory of job enrichment "have simply been absent from current research." The same was true of equity theory. "While most people believe that a sense of justice is important in effecting [*sic*] work motivation, we still do not know much about how it is defined or its actual impact on performance"(Mitchell, 1979, p. 259). The answers would not be forthcoming until nearly a decade later when Greenberg and his colleagues would publish their research on organizational justice.

---

[10]Matsui, Okada, and Kukuyama (1982) found that achievement motivation has no effect on performance independently of goals that are set. Goals people set predict their performance and level of satisfaction better than do personality measures of achievement (Yukl & Latham, 1978). However, Kanfer and Heggestad (1997) developed a 48-item scale that assesses a person's general motivation. Using this scale, they found that people who have high achievement and low anxiety traits excel in self-regulation.

[11]A cynic might argue that researchers abandoned one theory for another because of fad, fashion, or folderol (Dunnette, 1966). History, however, suggests that identification of methodological weaknesses of the predictive or explanatory power of a theory by respected scholars led to the development of and subsequent attention to a new theory. As Philips (1987) noted, "Any position can be supported by positive reasons ... but what really counts is how well the position can stand up to vigorous assault" (pp. vii–ix). Pinder (1998) argued that a theory should be parsimonious; if one theory can legitimately subsume another, it should do so.

Roberts and Glick's (1981) highly critical review of Hackman and Oldham's job characteristics theory resulted in essentially no new work on it being published subsequent to 1983 (Schneider, 1985). Lack of reliability in measurement, lack of discriminant validity with other attitudinal measures of jobs, and halo error among perceived job characteristics were among the problems cited.

Goal-Setting Theory

At the beginning of the fourth quarter of the 20th century, there were a sufficient number of empirical studies on goal setting to warrant two literature reviews (Latham & Yukl, 1975; Steers & Porter, 1974). By the mid-1980s, "One topic that replaced expectancy theory for researchers was goal setting theory, a work motivation theory unconcerned with individual differences in needs, desires, or instrumentality perceptions" (Schneider, 1985, p. 577). Miner (1984), in his review of organizational behavior theories, concluded that goal-setting theory was among the most valid and practical. Pinder (1984, p. 169) stated that "goal setting theory has demonstrated more scientific validity to date than any other theory or approach to work motivation presented in this book."

In a field experiment involving research scientists and engineers at Weyerhaeuser, Latham, Mitchell, and Dossett (1978) showed that consistent with the theory, praise and public recognition had no effect on behavior unless a specific difficult goal was set. Employee participation in setting goals led to higher performance than an assigned goal, not because of goal commitment but because higher goals were set. Consistent with the theory, high goals led to high performance. Subsequent studies (e.g., Latham & Saari, 1979a; Latham & Steele, 1983) showed that when goal difficulty is held constant, assigned goals that are accompanied by a rationale (Latham, Erez & Locke, 1988) are as effective as participatively set goals in increasing an individual's performance.

Latham, Winters, and Locke (1994) found that the effect of pdm on performance is primarily cognitive rather than motivational; that is, the effect is mediated by self-efficacy and task strategy. A subsequent study by Seijts and Latham (2001) showed that people with high self-efficacy are more likely than those with low self-efficacy to discover and implement task-relevant strategies that in turn affect performance positively. Mediation analyses showed that strategies had both a direct effect on the person's self-efficacy and an indirect effect on performance. Thus, participation in decision making is effective, as its advocates in the 1940s proclaimed, but only when it leads to the discovery of an effective task strategy and increases the employee's self-efficacy. Later goal-setting research showed that on tasks that are complex for people, a specific, difficult learning goal rather than an outcome goal should be set (Winters & Latham, 1996).

By the close of the 20th century, research had shown that setting specific, difficult goals increases performance on more than 100 different tasks, involving more than 40,000 participants in at least eight countries (Locke & Latham, 1990, 2002). In short, goal setting was shown to be among the most valid and practical theories of employee motivation in organizational psychology (Lee & Earley, 1992).

Action theory, developed by German psychologists (e.g., Frese & Zapf, 1994), is simpatico with goal setting. The theory stresses the importance of implementation intentions in addition to goal intentions (Gollwitzer, 1993). The theory posits ways that people turn their intentions to actions, particularly in overcoming obstacles to goal attainment.

Control theory, as formulated by Carver and Scheier (1981), also emphasizes goal setting. As did Ryan (1970), Carver and Scheier stressed that when people pay attention to what they are doing, they usually do what they intend to do, relatively accurately and thoroughly. The theory asserts that the source of motivation is a negative feedback loop, such as characterizes a thermostat that eliminates goal-performance discrepancies. Perceived discrepancy between performance and the reference standard automatically triggers action to reduce the incongruence.

In disagreement with this position, both Bandura (1989) and Locke and Latham (2002) argued that goal setting is a discrepancy-creating process. Motivation requires feed-forward control in addition to feedback. After people attain their goal, they often set an even higher goal. The subsequent setting of a high goal creates rather than reduces motivation discrepancies to be mastered. "Self-motivation thus involves a dual cyclic process of disequilibratory discrepancy production followed by equilibratory reduction" (Bandura, 1989, p. 38). A regulatory process in which matching a standard begets inertness, argued Bandura, does not characterize self-motivation. Such a feedback control system produces circular action that leads nowhere. People can increase their level of motivation by setting goals before any feedback is provided regarding performance.

Farr and his colleagues (Farr, Hofman, & Ringenbach, 1993) were among the first to draw the attention of the I–O community to Dweck's work in educational psychology on goal orientation. Dweck argued that

> the study of motivation deals with the causes of goal-oriented activity.... Adaptive motivational patterns are those that promote the establishment, maintenance, and attainment of personally challenging and personally valued achievement goals. Maladaptive patterns, then, are associated with a failure to establish reasonable, valued goals, to maintain effective striving toward those goals or, ultimately, to attain valued goals that are potentially within one's reach. (Dweck, 1986, p. 1040)

VandeWalle and Cummings (1997) found that this individual difference variable affects a person's performance in organizational settings. Those with a learning goal orientation focus on mastery (learning) of complex tasks while those with a performance goal orientation choose tasks on which they believe they can excel. Subsequent research suggests that on complex tasks, the effect of this trait is masked by the setting of specific high learning goals (Seijts, Latham, Tasa, & Latham, 2004). As is the case with a performance outcome goal, a learning goal is a strong variable (Adler & Weiss, 1988).

Social Cognitive Theory

Still another theory that emphasizes the importance of goal setting on motivation is Bandura's social cognitive theory. Albert Bandura, a social psychologist, was born and raised in Alberta, earned his undergraduate degree in psychology at the University of British Columbia, and received his PhD under the supervision of Kenneth Spence, the highly respected behaviorist at the University of Iowa.

Bandura repudiated behaviorism, because it embodies, he said, an erroneously "mechanistic" view of behavior. Reinforcing events change behavior through the intervening influence of thought (Bandura, 1974). Similarly, Mischel (1973) suggested that people regulate their behavior through goal setting and self-produced consequences to goal attainment: "Even in the absence of external constraints and social monitors, persons set performance goals for themselves and react with self-criticism or self-satisfaction to their behavior depending on how well it matches their expectations and criteria" (Mischel, 1973, pp. 273–274).

The year 1977 was a watershed year for psychology with the publication of Bandura's theory in the *Psychological Review* (Bandura, 1977a), described more fully in a book (Bandura,

1977b). Originally calling it social learning, Bandura relabeled it social cognitive theory (Bandura, 1986) to avoid confusion with similarly named theories. In brief, the theory states that behavior is a continuous reciprocal interaction among cognitive, behavioral, and environmental variables. Explicit in this view is the argument that behavior both is determined by and affects environmental consequences, which in turn affect the person's conscious intentions or goals, and vice versa (Bandura, 2001). Thus, social cognitive theory provides a theoretical framework that encompasses the primary variables in both the cognitive and the behaviorist camps.

Whereas behavioristic doctrine states that learning can occur only through performing responses and experiencing their effects, social cognitive theory enlarges this view by emphasizing vicarious, symbolic, and self-regulating processes in acquiring and maintaining behavior. The theory states that people can learn vicariously by observing the behavior of others and its consequences for them. Through the use of symbols, people are able to foresee probable consequences, set goals, and act accordingly. Consequently, as a result of self-regulatory processes, people learn to function as agents in their own self-motivation, through rewards for progress toward goal attainment.

The impact of this theory on I–O psychologists was immediate (e.g., Latham & Saari, 1979b) for at least two reasons. The behaviorists advocated a "black box" approach to psychology. The sole focus on observable stimuli, responses, and consequences of responses removed the necessity of peering inside an organism (the "black box"); individual differences were dismissed as merely differences among organisms in their histories of reinforcement. Social cognitive theory identified two cognitive variables that play a mediating role among the stimulus, the response, the consequence, and the subsequent behavior. These two cognitive variables are outcome expectancies (one's belief that the given outcome will occur if one engages in the behavior) and self-efficacy (one's belief that one can execute a given behavior in a given setting). "In regulating their behavior by outcome expectations, people adopt courses of action that are likely to produce positive outcomes and generally discard those that bring unrewarding or punishing outcomes" (Bandura, 2001, p. 7).

> The likelihood that people will act on the outcomes they expect prospective performances to produce depends on their beliefs about whether or not they can produce those performances. A strong sense of coping efficacy reduces vulnerability to stress and depression in taxing situations and strengthens resiliency to adversity. (Bandura, 2001, p. 10)

Low self-efficacy can thus nullify the motivating potential of positive outcome expectancies.

Goals, argued Bandura, give direction to pursuits. They invest activities with meaning and purpose. The common factors conducive to enduring motivation, he argued, are setting goals in accordance with one's perceived capabilities (self-efficacy) and having informative feedback of progress.

Wood and Bandura (1989) as well as Gist and Mitchell (1992) explained in detail the applicability of the theory to organizational settings. Two separate meta-analyses of empirical research in work-related settings showed the strong link between self-efficacy and a person's performance (Sadri & Robertson, 1993; Stajkovic & Luthans, 1998). Perceived self-efficacy contributes independently to subsequent performance after controlling for prior performance and indexes of ability (Bandura, 1997). A strong belief in one's performance efficacy is essential to mobilize and sustain the effort necessary to succeed. After people attain their goals, people with high self-efficacy set higher goals. These higher goals create new motivating discrepancies to be mastered (Bandura & Locke, 2003). As Locke (1965, p. 84) had shown years earlier, "getting closer to a 'standard' is both a source of satisfaction and an impetus to continued effort."[12] Latham (2001) showed the importance of changing employee outcome expectancies to gain commitment to an organizational goal.

The theory differs from Vroom's expectancy theory in that it argues that people exclude entire classes of options rapidly on the basis of their perceived efficacy. There is an important difference, Bandura and Locke (2003) argued, between belief in the utility of effort and belief that one can mobilize oneself to sustain effort in the face of perceived impediments and setbacks. Expectancy theory's emphasis on effort, argued Bandura, limits it to routine activities.

Goal-setting theory and social cognitive theory are similar in that both emphasize the importance of conscious goals for predicting, explaining, and regulating performance as well as the importance of feedback as a moderator of the goal–performance relation (Erez, 1977). Goal setting and feedback in relation to the goal provide the framework for self-management (Latham & Locke, 1991). The effect of self-management on self-efficacy and job attendance of unionized employees was shown by Frayne and Latham (1987).[13]

The two theories differ primarily in their relative emphasis on the variables that constitute them. The emphasis in goal-setting theory is on the core properties of an effective goal, namely specificity and difficulty level, as well as the mediators, direction, effort, persistence, and strategy. Moreover, goal-setting research, relative to research on social cognitive theory, has focused on goal content (performance vs. learning) as well as on the method of setting goals (assigned, self, or participatively set). Goal-setting theory is not limited to but focuses primarily on motivation in work settings. In contrast to goal-setting theory, social cognitive theory and the research that underlies it have emphasized the importance of self-efficacy as well as outcome expectancy, two different motivational systems that enhance goal commitment and persistence in the face of difficulties. Social cognitive theory, unlike goal setting, specifies the ways that self-efficacy can be enhanced. There are no points of disagreement between the two theories in the assumptions that underlie them. In fact, the concept of self-efficacy has been integrated with goal-setting theory. People with high self-efficacy set higher goals, are more committed to assigned goals, find and use better task strategies to attain the goals, and respond more positively to negative feedback than do those with low self-efficacy (Locke & Latham, 2002).

Organizational Justice Theory

Toward the end of the 20th century, O'Reilly (1991, p. 432) found that "the bulk of organizational behavior continues to focus on two dominant theories: goal setting and equity." The issue of equity, specifically organizational justice, was addressed in a theory developed by Jerald Greenberg (1987), who received his PhD under the supervision of Gerald Leventhal at Wayne State. This theory filled a void noted earlier by Mitchell (1979) in that it provided a new framework that addresses fairness and trust in the workplace. It answered the question in the title of Leventhal's (1980) article, "What Should Be Done With Equity Theory?" Greenberg's theory supplanted Adam's equity theory as a central role in promoting organizational well-being.

Few things kill an individual's motivation faster than the perception that someone else is getting a better deal. Organizational justice theory states that in addition to being fair, the people who make decisions must be perceived as fair. Thus, the theory is arguably as much, if not more, about leadership than it is employee motivation. Distributive justice concerns what was

---

[12]Goal attainment, however, on tasks where there is no corresponding increase in the employee's growth or competence does not increase satisfaction (Latham & Yukl, 1976).

[13]Frayne's doctoral dissertation, summarized in that paper, was the first and only dissertation to this date to win the award for best dissertation of the year from both the Academy of Management and the Society for Industrial and Organizational Psychology.

distributed to whom and who got what. Procedural justice is concerned with such questions as, Are there procedures, processes, or systems in place for determining what was distributed to whom? The theory was adapted from the sociolegal literature on conflict resolution. The theory, and the empirical data that support it, further stated that the more employees perceive that the procedures are fair, the more they evaluate positively their boss and trust management. They are also less inclined to leave their jobs (Lind & Tyler, 1988).

Two key factors that affect perceptions of procedural justice are a priori criteria for making decisions and "voice." Voice advances the concept of pdm in that people must believe that their viewpoint was taken into account before the final decision was made. To the extent that their voice is heard, people are likely to support decisions that are not congruent with their earlier viewpoint.

The effectiveness of following these principles was demonstrated by Cole and Latham (1997). Canadian supervisors were trained to follow procedural justice principles in taking disciplinary action. Human resource managers and labor lawyers, "blind" to both the hypotheses and the experimental conditions, observed these supervisors in role plays with actual unionized employees. Those who followed the principles were judged to be more fair than those in the control group. Skarlicki and Latham (1996) found that the organizational citizenship behavior of union members in Canada increased significantly when their union leaders adhered to principles of procedural justice.

Job Characteristics Revisited

Interest in the effect of the job itself on performance and satisfaction is ongoing. Hackman and Oldham's (1976) theory provided a mediational framework, particularly with regard to the effects of job autonomy and skill variety on an employee's job performance and satisfaction (Fried & Farris, 1987). Campion and Thayer (1985), in a survey of 121 jobs in five plants, found that jobs that score high in enrichment had employees who are more satisfied, had higher rated job performance, and had less absenteeism. The level of the job was a moderator variable. A study in Germany showed that autonomous and complex/enriched work increased one's personal initiative (Frese, Kring, Soose, & Zempel, 1996).

A meta-analysis by Judge, Thoresen, Bono, and Patton (2001) revealed a correlation of .30 between job satisfaction and performance. The moderator was job complexity; the correlation was stronger in enriched than in simplified jobs. Parker (2003) found that unenriched simplified jobs increased an employee's level of job depression. Such work designs, she argued, are not likely to be conducive to an employee's self-efficacy. Her findings from a UK-based company are consistent with those of Theorell and Karasek (1996), which showed that lack of job autonomy can increase the risk of cardiovascular disease. It would appear that Herzberg was correct in his hypothesis that the job can affect a person's mental health; it can affect one's long-term physical health as well.

Comprehensive Theories

Theories of motivation in the 20th century were, with few exceptions, middle range rather than grand. They focused on the person (e.g., expectancy theory), behavior (e.g., behavior modification), or the environment (e.g., job enrichment).

An initial step toward developing a complete theory was made by Locke and Henne (1986). They stated that the fundamental motivational concept is that of need, physiological as well as psychological. A need leads to action after the person has identified it and discovers how to satisfy it. People have different values with regard to what is satisfying for them. Values are what the person takes action to acquire or keep. Whereas needs are inborn, values are acquired through cognition and experience. Many theories of motivation focus on the influence of one or more values such as fairness (organizational justice theory). Value theories are a step closer to action than need theories, argued Locke and Henne, but they are still incomplete because the acquisition and maintenance of values can occur in multiple ways. To predict what a particular person will do in a particular setting requires knowledge of how values are translated into specific goals. "Goals are a means of actualizing values. They are the mechanism by which values are translated into action" (Locke & Henne, 1986, p. 3). Thus, goals are the immediate precursor of action. Emotions are the experiences derived from value/goal appraisals. Positive emotion is a function of the extent to which the goal is attained.

At the end of the 20th century, Locke and Latham (1990) developed a theory of the high-performance cycle (HPC) that explains how to increase a person's performance as well as job satisfaction. It is an inductive theory based on the accumulated findings of empirical research on goal setting, performance, satisfaction, and organizational commitment. The theory states that

> specific difficult goals plus high self-efficacy for attaining them are the impetus for high performance. Goals and self-efficacy affect the direction of action, the effort exerted as well as persistence to attain the goal. In addition, the goals and self-efficacy motivate the discovery of strategies for effectively doing so. The effect of goals on performance is moderated by ability, the complexity of the tasks, situational constraints, the feedback provided in relation to the goal, and commitment to the goal.

> High performance on tasks that are perceived as meaningful and growth facilitating, plus high external and internal rewards, lead to high job satisfaction. The consequence is a willingness to stay with the organization and accept future challenges, hence the high performance cycle.

> The theoretical significance of the HPC is that it provides a comprehensive sequence of causal relationships that is consistent with research findings. The practical significance of the HPC is that it provides a model or blueprint for creating a high performing workforce that is also highly satisfied. (Latham, Locke, & Fassina, 2002, p. 203)

SEISMIC EVENTS: SUMMARY AND OVERVIEW

The seismic events that influenced research on and theories of employee motivation in the 20th century are at least 10-fold. The first two occurred as a result of research in experimental psychology as well as the methodology of engineers rather than the discoveries of I–O psychologists. Thorndike's law of effect is, in the words of Vroom (1964), among the most substantiated findings of experimental psychology and is at the same time among the most useful findings for applied psychology concerned with control of human behavior. Time and motion studies by engineers resulted in the routinization and simplification of tasks. Monetary incentives were tied to task completion, and performance increased significantly. The implicit theory in the first quarter of that century was that money is the primary, if not sole, motive of the worker.

I–O psychology's contribution to knowledge of motivation in the workplace occurred in the second quarter. "Restriction of output" by workers had become widespread despite the fact that bonuses were paid contingent on performance. Attitudes toward management were hostile as people during the Great Depression feared losing their jobs. The third seismic event was Rensis Likert's publication of findings from his doctoral dissertation. His methodology demonstrates the ease with which employee attitudes can be surveyed. Drawing on countless employee surveys, Viteles was able to argue forcefully that money is only one of many motives that influence choice, effort, and persistence to perform well. His argument was supported by a fourth seismic event, the Hawthorne studies. These studies were interpreted as supporting the conclusion that low morale and negative attitudes toward one's job were the result of routinizing work through time and motion studies. In addition, they suggested the interrelations among motivation, satisfaction, and performance as well as the myriad ways that they can be increased.

The end of the second quarter and the beginning of the third witnessed the formal development and use of theory to guide research on employee motivation. The fifth seismic event that influenced understanding of motivation was Maslow's need hierarchy theory. Not only was it the bedrock for McGregor's theory Y, but it was the basis for the first series of empirical studies on employee motivation based on theory, namely the early research by Porter; in addition, it spawned subsequent theory, Alderfer's ERG. Finally, need hierarchy theory focused the attention of researchers such as Herzberg on the job itself as an enabler or frustrator of the attainment of a person's higher order growth needs.

The sixth seismic event was the conclusion that rather than being simplified, jobs should be enriched. Herzberg argued that to form job attitudes that motivate employees motivators must be built into jobs that facilitate the attainment of growth needs. This is a seismic event because it shifted the attention of I–O psychologists to the importance of job design. It is a practical theory in that it stimulated practitioners to view the world of work, and to take courses of action, in ways they might not have done otherwise.

The development of theory in the latter half of the 20th century was an ongoing progressive process. In the third quarter, the emphasis shifted away from needs that people may or may not be aware of that influence their choice, effort, and persistence. Emphasis instead was on cognitive/perceptual theories. The seventh seismic event was Vroom's expectancy theory that viewed the employee as an information processor. Vroom showed that it is not only the presence or absence of characteristics of the job that is important to motivation in the workplace; it is the employee's perception of those characteristics that causes him or her to form beliefs and attitudes about choices to be made. Choice is determined by the person taking into account anticipated valences, expectations, and instrumentalities. These cognitive variables, argued Vroom, instigate and direct an employee's behavior. People attempt to maximize their overall best interest on the basis of their evaluation of this information.

Ryan, Locke's mentor, argued that needs, beliefs, and values determine behavior through an intervening variable, conscious intentions, and that people strive to act intentionally. Ryan's work was the precursor to the eighth seismic event in advancing knowledge of employee motivation, namely goal-setting theory. Whereas intention is a representation of a planned action, a goal is the object or aim of such an act, the target of one's intentional act. It is the standard by which one evaluates one's performance.

Similar to expectancy theory, goal setting is a cognitive theory. Unlike expectancy theory, it is more easily operationalized, measured, and tested, thereby making it easier to demonstrate its validity (Pinder, 1998). Mitchell and Daniels (2003) stated that at the close of the 20th century, Locke and Latham's (1990) goal-setting theory was "quite easily the single most dominant theory in the field, with over a thousand articles and reviews published on the topic in a little over 30 years" (p. 231).

Although vehemently disagreeing on the philosophy of science, the behaviorists and the cognitivists have relative points of agreement. Both camps agree that a reward should be a valued outcome and that these outcomes should be tied to desired behavior, as well as the effect of context on behavior. Job characteristics are important in that they influence perceptions regarding expectancy and instrumentality; they are antecedent stimuli for behavior as well as factors that affect the consequences of the behavior. The points of view between the two camps are also arguably complementary. Goals influence intentions. Expectancies influence choice.

Consequences or outcomes influence the probability that the behavior will reoccur. These similarities led to the ninth seismic event, Bandura's social cognitive theory. The theory postulates reciprocal determinism among the person's cognitions, behavior, and the environment. "External events may create the reason for doing something, but except in simple reflexive acts, they are not the originators of affect and action. External stimuli give rise to course of action through personal agency" (Bandura, 1986, p. 12).

This theory too emphasizes the importance of goal setting. Whereas Vroom had argued the importance of expectancy theory, namely one's subjective probability that effort will lead to performance, Bandura, working without knowledge of Vroom's theory, formulated the concept of self-efficacy, a similar yet broader concept that has generative properties. Self-efficacy can stimulate the behavior in question. To the extent that proximal subgoals promote and authenticate self-efficacy, they increase motivation through enhancement of perceived personal causation. In agreement with expectancy theory, this theory states that the person's perceptions and thought processes mediate the impact of the job environment (Wood & Bandura, 1989). In agreement with Porter and Lawler's contention that high performance leads to high job satisfaction, the theory states that people develop enduring interest in activities at which they feel self-efficacious. When people master valued levels of performance, they experience a sense of satisfaction.

Ford (1992) argued that three sets of variables are necessary for a complete theory of motivation, namely, goals, emotions, and agency. The tenth seismic event of the 20th century that advanced understanding of motivation focused on the second of these three variables, namely feelings of trust and fairness. Greenberg's theory of organizational justice focuses on a person's perceptions and attitudes, specifically evaluations of those perceptions. As an outgrowth of Adam's equity theory, the theory states that perceptions of inequitable treatment generate motivational forces that instigate behavior to reduce these feelings. The distribution of outcomes as well as the procedures for determining what is distributed to whom determines perceptions of fairness and feelings of trust.

So, in closing, at least one question remains: What is work motivation? A comprehensive definition that reflects the history of research and theory on this subject is Pinder's (1998, p. 71): Motivation in the workplace is a hypothetical construct defined as "a set of energetic forces that originate both within as well as beyond an individual's being, to initiate work related behavior, and to determine its form, direction, intensity, and duration." This definition takes into account psychological processes in the direction, energization, and regulation of behavior. The definition acknowledges motive states that are not in awareness as well as those that are conscious. It acknowledges that features of the environment such as job characteristics trigger motivational forces. The concept of force, Pinder stated, is central to this definition. Energetic forces suggest the multiplicity of both needs and external factors. The definition suggests that motivation will manifest itself through effort. The notion of improvement also emphasizes the importance of internal as well as external origins. Thus, Pinder's definition takes into account the importance of the environment in arousing as well as shaping behavior without downplaying the importance of the employee's needs, values, attitudes, or the belief that effort will lead to a desired outcome. Importantly, the direction of the motivated forces is also inherent in this definition. To predict and understand work motivation, one must know the specific goal toward which motivated energy is directed. Motivated arousal occurs to the extent that the goal is difficult. Duration or persistence occurs to the extent that the goal is perceived to be attainable (self-efficacy).

At the dawn of this new millennium, it would appear that cognitive theories of motivation will likely be integrated with affective processes as well as personality. This is evident in the review by Brief and Weiss (2002) on moods and emotions. A review by Eccles and Wigfield

(2002) underscored the advice by Seijts and B. Latham (2003) to continue to integrate social and I–O psychology theories because the former already provide frameworks for examining affective processes more fully. I–O theories of motivation will likely also benefit from integration with those in clinical psychology including those that deal with the unconscious (Latham & Heslin, 2003; Locke & Latham, 2004). A meta-analysis by Judge and Ilies (2002) showed that there is a relation between personality variables, namely conscientiousness (high) and neuroticism (low) with an employee's motivation (e.g., setting high goals). With the closing of the 20th century, I–O psychologists have done what William James (1892) suggested at the end of the previous millennium. They have taken conscious motivation seriously.

ACKNOWLEDGMENTS

We are grateful to Edwin Locke, Craig Pinder, Paul Thayer, and Victor Vroom for their critical review of an earlier draft of this chapter. Preparation of this chapter was funded in part by a grant to Gary P. Latham from the Social Sciences and Humanities Research Council, Canada.

REFERENCES

Adams, J. S. (1963). Toward an understanding of inequity. *Journal of Abnormal and Social Psychology, 67*, 422–436.

Adams, J. S. (1968). Effects of overpayment: Two comments to Lawler's paper. *Journal of Personality and Social Psychology, 10*, 315–316.

Adler, S., & Weiss, H. M. (1988). Recent developments in the study of personality and organizational behavior. In C. L. Cooper & I. T. Robertson (Eds.), *International review of industrial and organizational psychology* (pp. 307–330). Oxford, England: Wiley.

Alderfer, C. P. (1972). *Existence, relatedness, and growth: Human needs in organizational settings*. New York: Free Press.

Argyle, M. (1953). The relay test room in retrospect. *Occupational Psychology, 27*, 98–103.

Atkinson, J. W. (1953). The achievement motive and recall of interrupted and completed tasks. *Journal of Experiment Psychology, 46*, 381–390.

Austin, J. T., & Vancouver, J. B. (1996). Goal constructs in psychology: Structure, process, and content. *Psychological Bulletin, 120*, 338–375.

Bandura, A. (1974). Behavior theory and the models of man. *American Psychologist, 29*, 859–869.

Bandura, A. (1977a). Self-efficacy: Toward a unifying theory of behavioral change. *Psychological Review, 84*, 191–215.

Bandura, A. (1977b). *Social learning theory*. Englewood Cliffs, NJ: Prentice-Hall.

Bandura, A. (1986). *Social foundations of thought and action: A social cognitive theory*. Englewood Cliffs: Prentice-Hall.

Bandura, A. (1989). Self-regulation of motivation and action through internal standards and external goal systems. In L. A. Pervin (Ed.), *Goal concepts in personality and social psychology* (pp. 19–85). Hillsdale, NJ: Lawrence Erlbaum Associates.

Bandura, A. (1997). *Self-efficacy: The exercise of control*. Stanford, CT: Freeman & Co.

Bandura, A. (2001). Social cognitive theory: An agentic perspective. *Annual Review of Psychology, 52*, 1–26.

Bandura, A., & Locke, E. A. (2003). Negative self-efficacy and goal effects revisited. *Journal of Applied Psychology, 88*, 87–99.

Bennis, W. (1985). Foreword. *The human side of the enterprise: 25th anniversary printing*. New York: McGraw-Hill.

Blum, M. L., & Naylor, J. C. (1968). *Industrial Psychology: Its theoretical and social foundations*. New York: Harper & Row.

Boone, J., & Bowen, W. (1987). *The great writings in management and organizational behavior* (2nd ed.). New York: Random House.

Brayfield, A. H., & Crockett, W. H. (1955). Employee attitudes and employee performance. *Psychological Bulletin, 52*, 396–424.

Brief, A. P., & Weiss, H. M. (2002). Organizational behavior: Affect in the workplace. *Annual Review of Psychology, 53*, 279–307.

Burtt, H. E. (1926). *Principles of employment psychology*. Boston: Houghton Mifflin.

Campbell, J. P., Dunnette, M. D., Lawler, E. E. & Weick, K. E. (1970). *Managerial behavior, performance, and effectiveness*. New York: McGraw-Hill.

Campion, M. A., & Thayer, P. W. (1985). Development and field evaluation of an interdisciplinary measure of job design. *Journal of Applied Psychology, 70,* 29–43.

Carver, C. S., & Scheier, M. F. (1981). *Attention and self-regulation: A control-theory approach to human behavior.* New York: Springer-Verlag.

Coch, L., & French, J. R. P. (1948). Overcoming resistance to change. *Human Relations, 1,* 512–532.

Cofer, C. N. (1959). Motivation. *Annual Review of Psychology, 60,* 3–10.

Cole, N., & Latham, G. P. (1997). The effects of training in procedural justice on perceptions of disciplinary fairness by unionized employees and disciplinary subject matter experts. *Journal of Applied Psychology, 82,* 699–705.

Cooper, C. L., & Robertson, I. T. (1986). Editorial foreword. In *International review of industrial and organizational psychology* (pp. ix–xi), Chichester, England: Wiley.

Cummings, L. L. (1982). Organizational behavior. *Annual Review of Psychology, 33,* 541–579.

Dulany, D. E. (1968). Awareness, rules and propositional control: A confrontation with S-R behavior theory. In D. Horton & T. Dixon (Eds.), *Verbal behavior and S-R behavior theory* (pp. 340–387). New York: Prentice-Hall.

Dunnette, M. D. (1966). Fads, fashions and folderol in psychology. *American Psychologist, 21,* 343–352.

Dunnette, M. D. (1976). Mishmash, mush and milestones in organizational psychology: 1974. In H. Meltzer & R. F. Wickert (Eds.), *Humanizing organizational behavior* (pp. 86–102). Springfield: Thomas.

Dunnette, M. D., & Kirchner, W. R. (1965). *Psychology applied to industry.* Oxford, England: Appleton-Century-Crofts.

Dweck, C. S. (1986). Motivational processes affecting learning. *American Psychologist, 41,* 1040–1048.

Eccles, J. S., & Wigfield, A. (2002). Motivational beliefs, values, and goals. *Annual Review of Psychology, 53,* 109–132.

Erez, M. (1977). Feedback: A necessary condition for the goal setting-performance relationship. *Journal of Applied Psychology, 62,* 624–627.

Erez, M. (1997). A culture-based model of work motivation. In C. P. Earley & M. Erez (Eds.), *New perspectives on international industrial/organizational psychology* (pp. 193–242). San Francisco: Jossey-Bass Inc.

Farr, J. L., Hofman, D. A., & Rigenbach, K. L. (1993). *Goal orientation and action control theory: Implications for industrial and organizational psychology.* New York: Wiley.

Festinger, L. (1957). *A theory of cognitive dissonance.* Oxford, England: Row, Peterson.

Flanagan, J. C. (1954). The critical incident technique. *Psychological Bulletin, 51,* 327–358.

Ford, M. E. (1992). *Motivating humans.* Newbury Park, CA: Sage.

Franke, R. H., & Kaul, J. D. (1978). The Hawthorne experiments: First statistical interpretation. *American Sociological Review, 43,* 623–643.

Frayne, C. A., & Latham, G. P. (1987). The application of social learning theory to employee self-management of attendance. *Journal of Applied Psychology, 72,* 387–392.

Frese, M., Kring, W., Soose, A., & Zempel, J. (1996). Personal initiative at work: Differences between East and West Germany. *Academy of Management Journal, 39,* 37–63.

Frese, M., & Zapf, D. (1994). Action as the core of work psychology: A German approach. In H. C. Triandis & M. D. Dunnette (Eds.), *Handbook of industrial and organizational psychology* (pp. 271–340). Palo Alto, CA: Consulting Psychologists Press.

Frederiksen, L. W. (1982). *Organizational behavior management.* New York: Wiley.

Fried, Y., & Ferris, G. R. (1987). The validity of job characteristics model: A review and meta-analysis. *Personnel Psychology, 40,* 287–332.

Ghiselli, E. E., & Brown, C. W. (1948). *Personnel and industrial psychology.* New York: McGraw-Hill.

Gist, M. E., & Mitchell, T. R. (1992). Self-efficacy: A theoretical analysis of its determinants and malleability. *Academy of Management Review, 17,* 183–211.

Gollwitzer, P. M. (1993). Goal achievement: The role of intentions. In W. Stroebe & M. Hewstone (Eds.), *European review of social psychology* (pp.141–185). Chichester, England: Wiley.

Greenberg, J. (1987). A taxonomy of organizational justice theories. *Academy of Management Review, 12,* 9–22.

Guion, R. M. (1958). Industrial morale: The problem of terminology. *Personnel Psychology, 11,* 59–64.

Hackman, J. R., & Oldman, G. R. (1975). Development of the job diagnostic survey. *Journal of Applied Psychology, 60,* 159–170.

Hackman, J. R., & Oldman, G. R. (1976). Motivation through the design of work: Test of a theory. *Organizational Behavior and Human Performance, 16,* 250–279.

Harrell, T. W. (1949). *Industrial psychology.* Oxford, England: Rinehart.

Hebb, D. O. (1961). *The organization of behavior: A neuropsychological theory.* Oxford, England: Basic Books.

Heneman, H. G., & Schwab, D. P. (1972). Evaluation of research on expectancy theory predictions of employee performance. *Psychological Bulletin, 78,* 1–9.

Heron, A. (1954). Industrial psychology. *Annual Review of Psychology, 5,* 203–228.

Herzberg, F. (1966). *Work and the nature of man.* Oxford, England: World.

Herzberg, F., Mausner, B., & Snyderman, B. B. (1959). *The motivation to work.* New York: Wiley.

Hinrichs, J. R. (1970). Psychology of men at work. *Annual Review of Psychology, 21,* 519–554.

Hoppock, R. (1935). *Job satisfaction.* Oxford, England: Harper.

House, R.J., Shapiro, H. J. & Wahba, M. A. (1974). Expectancy theory as a predictor of work behavior and attitude: A re-evaluation of empirical evidence. *Decision Sciences, 5,* 481–506.

Houser, J. D. (1938). Measurement of the vital products of business. *Journal of Marketing, 2,* 181–189.

Hull, C. L. (1943). *Principles of behavior.* New York: Appleton-Century-Crofts.

James, W. (1892). *Psychology.* New York: Holt.

Judge, T. A., & Ilies, R. (2002). Relationship of personality to performance motivation: A meta-analytic review. *Journal of Applied Psychology, 87,* 797–807.

Judge, T. A., Thoresen, C. J., Bono, J. E. & Patton, G. K. (2001). The job satisfaction-job performance relationship: A qualitative and quantitative review. *Psychological Bulletin, 127,* 376–407.

Kanfer, R., & Ackerman, P. L. (1989). Motivation and cognitive abilities: An integrative/aptitude-treatment interaction approach to skill acquisition. *Journal of Applied Psychology, 74,* 657–690.

Kanfer, R., & Heggestad, E. D. (1997). Motivational traits and skills: A person-centered approach to work motivation. *Research in Organizational Behavior, 19,* 1–56.

Kaufman, A., Baron, A. & Kopp, R. E. (1966). Some effects of instructions on human operant behavior. *Psychonomic Monograph Supplements, 1,* 243–250.

King, N. (1970). Clarification and evaluation of the two-factor theory of job satisfaction. *Psychological Bulletin, 74,* 18–31.

Komaki, J. L. (1998). *Leadership from an operant perspective.* New York: Routledge.

Latham, G. P. (2001). The importance of understanding and changing employee outcome expectancies for gaining commitment to an organizational goal. *Personnel Psychology, 54,* 707–716.

Latham, G. P., & Dossett, D. L. (1978). Designing incentive plans for unionized employees: A comparison of continuous and variable ratio reinforcement schedules. *Personnel Psychology, 31,* 47–61.

Latham, G. P., Erez, M., & Locke, E. A. (1988). Resolving scientific disputes by the joint design of crucial experiments by the antagonists: Application of the Erez-Latham dispute regarding participation in goal setting. *Journal of Applied Psychology Monograph, 73,* 753–772.

Latham, G. P., & Heslin, P. A. (2003). Training the trainee as well as the trainer: Lessons to be learned from clinical psychology. *Canadian Psychology, 44,* 218–231.

Latham, G. P., & Locke, E. A. (1991). Self regulation through goal setting. *Organizational Behavior and Human Decision Processes, 50,* 212–247.

Latham, G. P., Locke, E. A., & Fassina, N. E. (2002). The high performance cycle: Standing the test of time. In S. Sonnentag (Ed.), *The psychological management of individual performance: A handbook in the psychology of management in organizations* (pp. 201–228). Chichester, England: Wiley.

Latham, G. P., Mitchell, T. R., & Dossett, D. L. (1978). The importance of participative goal setting and anticipated rewards on goal difficulty and job performance. *Journal of Applied Psychology, 63,* 163–171.

Latham, G. P., & Saari, L. M. (1979a). The effects of holding goal difficulty constant on assigned and participatively set goals. *Academy of Management Journal, 22,* 163–168.

Latham, G. P., & Saari, L. M. (1979b). The application of social learning theory to training supervisors through behavioral modeling. *Journal of Applied Psychology, 64,* 239–246.

Latham, G. P., & Steele, T. P. (1983). The motivational effects of participation versus goal setting on performance. *Academy of Management Journal, 26,* 406–417.

Latham, G. P., Winters, D. C., & Locke, E. A. (1994). Cognitive and motivational effects of participation: A mediator study. *Journal of Organizational Behavior, 15,* 49–63.

Latham, G. P., & Yukl, G. A. (1975). A review of research on the application of goal setting in organizations. *Academy of Management Journal, 18,* 824–845.

Latham, G. P., & Yukl, G. A. (1976). Effects of assigned and participative goal setting on performance and job satisfaction. *Journal of Applied Psychology, 61,* 166–171.

Lawler, E. E. (1965). Managers' perceptions of their subordinates' pay and their superiors' pay. *Personnel Psychology, 18,* 413–422.

Lawler, E. E. (1970). *Pay and organizational effectiveness: A psychological view.* New York: McGraw-Hill.

Lawler, E. E., & Porter, L. W. (1967). The effect of performance on job satisfaction. *Industrial Relations, 7,* 20–28.

Lee, C., & Earley, P. C. (1992). Comparative peer evaluations of organizational behavior theories. *Organization Development Journal, 10,* 37–42.

Lee, T. W., Locke, E. A., & Latham, G. P. (1989). Goal setting theory and job performance. In L. A. Pervin (Ed.), *Goal concepts in personality and social psychology* (pp. 291–328). Hillsdale, NJ: Lawrence Erlbaum Associates.

Leventhal, G. S. (1980). What should be done with equity theory? In K. J. Gergen, M. S. Greenberg, & R. H. Willis (Eds.), *Social exchange: Advances in theory and research* (pp. 27–55). New York: Plenum.

Likert, R. (1932). A technique for the measurement of attitudes. *Archives of Psychology, 140,* 55.

Lind, E. A., & Tyler, T. R. (1988). *The social psychology of procedural justice.* New York: Plenum.

Locke, E. A. (1965). The relationship of task success to task liking and satisfaction. *Journal of Applied Psychology, 49,* 379–385.

Locke, E. A. (1968). Toward a theory of task motivation and incentives. *Organizational Behavior & Human Decision Processes, 3,* 157–189.

Locke, E. A. (1970). Job satisfaction and job performance: A theoretical analysis. *Organizational Behavior and Human Decision Processes, 5,* 484–500.

Locke, E. A. (1975). Personnel attitudes and motivation. *Annual Review of Psychology, 26,* 457–480.

Locke, E. A. (1976). The nature and causes of job satisfaction. In M. D. Dunnette (Ed.), *Handbook of industrial and organizational psychology* (pp. 1297–1350). Chicago: Rand McNally.

Locke, E. A. (1977). The myths of behavior mod in organizations. *Academy of Management Review, 2,* 543–553.

Locke, E. A. (1978). The ubiquity of the technique of goal setting in theories of and approaches to employee motivation. *Academy of Management Review, 3,* 594–601.

Locke, E. A. (1980). Latham versus Komaki: A tale of two paradigms. *Journal of Applied Psychology, 65,* 16–23.

Locke, E. A., & Henne, D. (1986). Work motivation theories. In C. L. Cooper & I. T. Robertson (Eds.), *International review of industrial and organizational psychology* (pp. 1–36). New York: Wiley.

Locke, E. A., & Latham, G. P. (1990). *A theory of goal setting and task performance.* Englewood Cliffs, NJ: Prentice-Hall.

Locke, E. A., & Latham, G. P. (2002). Building a practically useful theory of goal setting and task motivation: A 35-year odyssey. *American Psychologist, 57,* 705–717.

Locke, E. A., & Latham, G. P. (2004). What should we do about motivation theory? Six recommendations for the 21st century. *Academy of Management Review, 29,* 388–403.

Locke, E. A., Shaw, K. M., Saari, L. M., & Latham, G. P. (1981). Goal setting and task performance: 1969–1980. *Psychological Bulletin, 90,* 125–152.

Luthans, F., & Kreitner, R. (1975). *Organizational behavior modification.* Glenview, IL: Scott, Foresman.

Mace, C. A. (1935). *Incentives: Some experimental studies* (Industrial Health Research Board [Great Britain], Rep. No. 72).

Maier, N. R. F. (1946). *Psychology in industry.* Boston: Houghton Mifflin.

Maier, N. R. F. (1955). *Psychology in industry* (2nd ed.). Boston: Houghton Mifflin.

Maslow, A. H. (1943). A theory of human motivation. *Psychological Review, 50,* 370–396.

Matsui, T., Okada, A., & Kakuyama, T. (1982). Influence of achievement need on goal setting, performance, and feedback effectiveness. *Journal of Applied Psychology, 67,* 645–648.

Mayo, E. (1933). *The human problems of an industrialized civilization.* Glenview, IL: Scott, Foresman.

McGregor, D. M. (1957). The human side of the enterprise. *Management Review, 46,* 22–28.

McGregor, D. M. (1960). *The human side of the enterprise.* New York: McGraw-Hill.

Miner, J. B. (1984). The validity and usefulness of theories in emerging organizational science. *Academy of Management Review, 9,* 296–306.

Miner, J. B, & Dachler, H. P. (1973). Personnel attitudes and motivation. *Annual Review of Psychology,* 379–402.

Mischel, W. (1973). Toward a cognitive social learning reconceptualization of personality. *Psychological Review, 80,* 252–283.

Mitchell, T. R. (1979). Organizational behavior. *Annual Review of Psychology, 30,* 243–81.

Mitchell, T. R., & Biglan, A. (1971). Instrumentality theories: Current uses in psychology. *Psychological Bulletin, 76,* 432–454.

Mitchell, T. R., & Daniels, D. (2003). In W. C. Borman, D. R. Ilgen, & R. J. Klimoski (Eds.), *Comprehensive handbook of psychology: Vol. 12. Industrial organizational psychology* (pp. 225–254). New York: Wiley.

Mowday, R. T. (1991). Equity theory predictions of behavior in organizations. In R. M. Steers & L. W. Porter (Eds.), *Motivation and work behavior* (5th ed., pp. 111–131). New York: McGraw-Hill.

Münsterberg, H. (1913). *Psychology and industrial efficiency.* Boston: Houghton Mifflin.

Nord, W. R. (1969). Beyond the teaching machine: The neglected area of operant conditioning in the theory and practice of management. *Organizational Behavior & Human Performance, 4,* 375–401.

Newell, A., Shaw, J., & Simon, H. (1958). Elements of a theory of human problem solving. *Psychological Review, 65,* 151–166.

O'Reilly, C. A. (1991). Organizational behavior: Where we've been, where we're going. *Annual Review of Psychology, 42,* 427–458.

Parker, S. K. (2003). Longitudinal effects of lean production on employee outcomes and mediating role of work characteristics. *Journal of Applied Psychology, 88,* 620–634.

Pervin, L. A. (1989). Goal concepts in personality and social psychology: A historical introduction. In L.A. Pervin, (Ed.), *Goal concepts in personality and social psychology* (pp. 1–17). Hillsdale, NJ: Lawrence Erlbaum Associates.

Philips, D. C. (1987). *Philosophy, science, and social inquiry: Contemporary methodological controversies in social science and related fields of research.* New York: Pergamon.

Pinder, C. C. (1984). *Work motivation: Theory, issues, and applications.* Glenview, IL: Scott, Foresman.

Pinder, C. C. (1998). *Work motivation: Theory, issues, and applications.* Glenview, IL: Scott, Foresman.

Platt, J. R. (1964). Strong inference. *Science, 146,* 347–353.

Porter, L. W. (1961). A study of perceived need satisfaction in bottom and middle management jobs. *Journal of Applied Psychology, 45,* 1–10.

Roberts, K. H., & Glick, W. (1981). The job characteristics approach to task design: A critical review. *Journal of Applied Psychology, 66,* 193–217.

Roethlisberger, F. J. (1977). *The elusive phenomena.* Oxford, England: Harvard University Press.

Ronan, W. W., Latham, G. P., & Kinne, S. B. (1973). The effects of goal setting and supervision on worker behavior in an industrial situation. *Journal of Applied Psychology, 58,* 302–307.

Ruttenberg, H. (1941). Self-expression and labor unions. In National Research Council, *Fatigue of workers.* New York: Reinhold.

Ryan, T. A. (1947). *Work and effort: The psychology of production.* Oxford, England: Ronald Press.

Ryan, T. A. (1970). *Intentional behavior.* New York: Ronald Press.

Ryan, T. A., & Smith, P. C. (1954). *Principles of industrial psychology.* New York: Ronald Press.

Sadri, G., & Robertson, I. T. (1993). Self-efficacy and work-related behavior: A review and meta-analysis. *Applied Psychology: An International Review, 42,* 139–152.

Schmidt, F. L. (1973). Implications of a measurement problem for expectancy theory research. *Organizational Behavior & Human Performance, 10,* 243–251.

Schneider, B. (1985). Organizational behavior. *Annual Review of Psychology, 36,* 573–611.

Seijts, G. H., & Latham, G. P. (2001). The effect of learning, outcome, and proximal goals on a moderately complex task. *Journal of Organizational Behaviour, 22,* 291–307.

Seijts, G. H, & Latham, B. W. (2003). Creativity through applying ideas from fields other than one's own: Transferring knowledge from social psychology to industrial/organizational psychology. *Canadian Psychology, 44,* 232–239.

Seijts, G. H., Latham, G. P., Tasa, K., & Latham, B. W. (2004). Goal setting and goal orientation: An integration of two different yet related literatures. *Academy of Management Journal, 47,* 227–239.

Skarlicki, D. P., & Latham, G. P. (1996). Increasing citizenship behavior within a labor union: A test of organizational justice theory. *Journal of Applied Psychology, 81,* 161–169.

Skinner, B. F. (1953). *Science and human behavior.* New York: Macmillan.

Skinner, B. F. (1974). *About behaviorism.* Oxford, England: Knopf.

Stagner, R. (1950). Psychological aspects of industrial conflict. II. Motivation. *Personnel Psychology, 3,* 1–15.

Stagner, R. (1958). Industrial morale: II. Motivational aspects of industrial morale. *Personnel Psychology, 11,* 64–70.

Stajkovic, A. D. & Luthans, F. (1998). Self-efficacy and work-related performance: A meta-analysis. *Psychological Bulletin, 124,* 240–261.

Steers, R. M., & Porter, L. W. (1974). The role of task-goal attributes in employee performance. *Psychological Bulletin, 81,* 434–452.

Survey Research Center, University of Michigan. (1948). *Selected findings from a study of clerical workers in the Prudential Insurance Company of America.* Survey Research Center Study 6. Ann Arbor: University of Michigan.

Taylor, F. W. (1911). *Principles of scientific management.* New York: Harper.

Theorell, T., & Karasek, R. A. (1996). Current issues to the psychosocial job strain and cardiovascular disease research. *Journal of Occupational Health Psychology, 1,* 9–26.

Thorndike, E. L. (1911). *Animal intelligence.* New York: Macmillan.

Thorndike, E. L. (1917). The curve of work and the curve of satisfyingness. *Journal of Applied Psychology, 1,* 265–267.

Thurstone, L. L. (1929). Theory of attitude measurement. *Psychological Review, 36,* 222–241.

Tiffin, J. (1952). *Industrial psychology.* Englewood Cliffs, NJ: Prentice-Hall.

Uhrbrock, R. S. (1934). Attitudes of 4430 employees. *Journal of Social Psychology, 5,* 365–377.

VandeWalle, D., & Cummings, L. L. (1997). A test of the influence of goal orientation on the feedback seeking process. *Journal of Applied Psychology, 82,* 390–400.

Van Eerde, W., & Thierry, H. (1996). Vroom's expectancy models and work-related criteria: A meta-analysis. *Journal of Applied Psychology, 81,* 575–586.

Viteles, M. S. (1932). *Industrial Psychology.* New York: Norton.

Viteles, M. S. (1953). *Motivation and morale in industry.* New York: Norton.

Vroom, V. H. (1964). *Work motivation.* New York: Wiley.

Vroom, V. H. (1967, September). *Some observations on Herzberg's two-factor theory.* Paper presented at the meeting of American Psychological Association, Washington, DC.

Wagner, J. A., III. (1994). Participation's effect on performance and satisfaction: A reconsideration of research evidence. *Academy of Management Journal, 19,* 312–330.

Wahba, M. A., & Bridwell, L. G. (1976). Maslow reconsidered: A review of research on the need hierarchy theory. *Organizational Behavior and Performance, 15,* 212–240.

Watson, J. B. (1913). Psychology as the behaviorist views it. *Psychological Review, 20,* 158–177.

Winters, D., & Latham, G. P. (1996). The effect of learning versus outcome goals on a simple versus a complex task. *Group and Organization Management, 21,* 236–250.

Wood, R. E., & Bandura, A. (1989). Social-cognitive theory of organizational management. *Academy of Management Review, 14,* 361–384.

Wyatt, S., Fraser, J. A., & Stock, F. G. L. (1929). The effects of monotony in work. A preliminary inquiry. *Industrial Health Research Board Report, 56,* 47.

Wyatt, S., Frost, L., & Stock, F. G. L. (1934). *Incentives in repetitive work.* (Industrial Health Research Board [Great Britain], Rep. No. 69).

Yankelovich, D. (1974). Turbulence in the working world: Angry workers, happy grads. *Psychology Today, 8,* 80–87.

Yukl, G. A., & Latham, G. P. (1978). Interrelationships among employee participation, individual differences, goal difficulty, goal acceptance, goal instrumentality and performance. *Personnel Psychology, 31,* 305–324.

Yukl, G., Wexley, K. N., & Seymore, J. D. (1972). Effectiveness of pay incentives under variable ratio and continuous reinforcement schedules. *Journal of Applied Psychology, 56,* 13–23.

16

Leadership: A Critical Historical Analysis of the Influence of Leader Traits

David V. Day
Pennsylvania State University

Stephen J. Zaccaro
George Mason University

Much of the history of leadership as a scientific topic of investigation has centered on the pivotal role of power (e.g., Follett, 1927; French & Raven, 1959; Hollander, 1985; Kleiser, 1923; Pfeffer, 1981). Clearly, the acquisition and use of power are important to the study and understanding of formal leadership; however, we argue that traits and individual differences have been at least as equally important in the evolution of leadership, especially informal leadership, as a scientific construct. One reason for this apparent underappreciation is that there are many possible ways to define the concept of trait and even more possible ways to study it. As a result, the perspective that during the approximate 40-year period between 1948 and 1986, traits were supposedly "dead" in leadership research and theory, is, we assert, overly simplistic, misguided, and in many ways just plain wrong.

In this chapter we take a critical historical approach to examining the influence of traits and individual differences, trait theories, and trait thinking on the development of leadership research, theory, and practice over the course of the 20th century through to the late-1980s. In addition to examining early writings on the topic of leadership by industrial psychologists (and a few sociologists and management scholars as well), we focus on the rise of the so-called "leader behavior" approach beginning in the late 1940s, which developed into the Ohio State studies under the guidance of Ralph Stogdill, Carroll Shartle, John Hemphill, and Edwin Fleishman. Specifically, we will examine how this contribution ultimately led to a split in the field. The more prominent group followed a situational or contingency approach to leadership (e.g., Fiedler, 1964; Hersey & Blanchard, 1969; House, 1971). The other, less traveled path focused on the role of follower perceptions in leadership (e.g., Calder, 1977; Hollander & Julian, 1969; Lord, Foti, & Phillips, 1982; Meindl, Ehrlich, & Dukerich, 1985). More recently, apparent rapprochements have occurred between these two divergent paths in the guise of charismatic leadership and well as the GLOBE (Globe Leadership and Organizational Behavior Effectiveness) project (House et al., 1999; House, Hanges, Javidan, Dorfman, & Gupta, 2004) in studying the cultural foundations of leadership. Leadership traits—broadly defined—are central to the presumed rapprochement; however, both the assumed nature of traits and the nature of leadership have evolved into more complex constructs than originally conceptualized.

We first provide a brief, general overview on the concepts of traits and leadership. Next we trace the emergence of leadership as a topic of scientific study and applied practice in the field of industrial–organizational (I–O) psychology. Although the trait approach to leadership is typically portrayed in many introductory I–O textbooks as the first systematic leadership theory in I–O, a critical reading of this early published literature revealed a variety of theoretical approaches to leadership. From the earliest beginnings of industrial psychology, trait theories were just one of myriad theoretical approaches to leadership. The final section of this chapter provides a detailed review of the two main leadership paths taken since the 1950s: leader behaviors and leadership perceptions.

GENERAL BACKGROUND ON TRAITS AND LEADERSHIP

There is longstanding confusion and disagreement on the meaning of the term *trait*. Zaccaro, Kemp, and Bader (2004) defined leader traits as

> relatively stable and coherent integrations of personal characteristics that foster a consistent pattern of leadership performance across a variety of group and organizational situations. These characteristics reflect a range of stable individual differences, including personality, temperament, motives, cognitive abilities, skills, and expertise. (p. 104)

Note that traits are defined here broadly to include a range of individual attributes that promote cross-situational consistency in leadership behavior, performance, and effectiveness. Because of fundamental differences in assumptions and scientific orientations, there may be little agreement between those who see leadership traits primarily as dispositional forces and guides to leader behavior and those who believe that traits are used mainly in the sense-making processing of followers. There are also differences between those who view traits as mainly inherited personality characteristics and those who believe that traits include individual differences that can be intervened on even in adulthood. These differences in perspectives are endemic to the historical development of the leadership field. One of our major purposes is to demonstrate how such perspective differences have resulted in long-lasting confusion about the underlying nature–nurture conflict in leadership. But there is an opportunity to bring true integration to the topic of leadership by considering it as a dynamic process involving leaders, followers, and the social situation.

An immediate problem that is faced in attempting to review the history of leadership theory, research, and practice is that the term *leadership* has no universally agreed upon definition either—perhaps because leadership takes "protean forms" (J. A. Murphy, 1941, p. 674). As a result of the lack of definitional consensus and the many possible leadership forms, it was argued at one time that it would be best to abandon the concept completely (Miner, 1975). Others have argued that leadership is purely symbolic (Pfeffer, 1977) or an overly heroic, romanticized concept (Meindl et al., 1985). Given what we do know about leadership from a scientific perspective and its relation with personality, this is simply not a credible position if I–O psychologists hope to influence leadership practice in organizations (Hogan, Curphy, & Hogan, 1994).

The concept of leadership has been a theme throughout much of history. Leadership was central to Homer's *Iliad* and *Odyssey,* the Bible, Plato's *Republic,* and most great works of literature—fiction and nonfiction—throughout the course of history. Leadership is recognized as a potent force that has been used for incredible good and inconceivable evil, which is probably why it originally attracted the attention of social scientists and practitioners. If leadership could be studied scientifically, then perhaps its effects could be reliably predicted and controlled. The scientific study of leadership offered the promise of harnessing the power of a great force for improving the world.

LEADERSHIP IN INDUSTRIAL PSYCHOLOGY

A turning point in terms of both the science and the practice of leadership was World War II. Numerous examples of very effective political and military leaders emerged during this time (e.g., Churchill, Hitler, Mussolini, Roosevelt, Patton, Rommel) that helped bring a leader's impact to the forefront of world attention. Probably more important, many social scientists were working in the military to support the war effort. As noted by Edwin P. Hollander, "So many psychologists in the military, especially in WWII, began to work on leadership. And this usually meant measuring the personal qualities of leaders" (personal communication, May 23, 2003). The assessment center research that was conducted by the Office of Strategic Services to identify persons suitable for espionage activities, and the advent of more sophisticated measurement techniques such as the leaderless group discussion as a leadership evaluation instrument (Bass, 1954), provided a framework and important tools for scientific study as well as practice. Identifying leaders in military and corporate settings became an important practical endeavor, one that was directly the result of research that applied psychologists conducted during the war.

An interesting historical trend in the study of leadership has been a change in the organizational level of leaders being studied. Despite the dominance of the "great man" approach to leadership (Carlyle, 1849; Ellis, 1904)—or studying leadership through the historical analysis of the lives of great men— the early studies of the psychology of leadership tended to focus on relatively low-level leaders such as foremen (Moore & Hartman, 1931a; Rutledge, 1937; Viteles & Thompson, 1946), student leaders (Bowden, 1926; Cowley, 1931), incarcerated criminal leaders and followers (Cowley, 1931), and military leaders among the noncommissioned and junior officer corps (Gibb, 1947; Jenkins, 1947). Although there was some early interest in executive leadership (Barnard, 1938; Craig & Charters, 1925) and the development of executive ability (Gowin, 1919), the focus of psychological research primarily was on first-level leaders. Later on, researchers began to also consider executive leadership from a psychological perspective (Browne, 1951; Shartle, 1949). However, the real change in focus to examining middle and upper level leaders came about as a result of the AT&T studies of progression into middle management (Bray, Campbell, & Grant, 1974). To better appreciate the origins of leadership in general, and trait approaches to leadership more specifically, we provide a historical review of some of the earliest published discussions of leadership in the industrial psychological literature.

Leadership in Industrial Psychology Texts

A selected review of classic texts in industrial psychology revealed a wide range of approaches to the scientific study of leadership—not just trait theories. The earliest offerings in applied psychology (Hollingworth & Poffenberger, 1917; Münsterberg, 1913; Scott, 1911) contained no mention of leadership. This is not surprising given the emphasis on industrial efficiency in these books; however, it does provide evidence that the earliest applied psychologists did not consider leadership as a relevant scientific construct. One of the first books devoted to the specific topic of psychological problems in industry (Watts, 1921) also contained no reference to leadership, focusing on topics such as industrial fatigue and inefficiency, selection, scientific management, industrial unrest, and creativity. Burtt's (1929) book on psychology and industrial efficiency also eschewed any mention of leadership, as did the first handbook of industrial psychology (Smith, 1944). Even some industrial psychology texts published in the 1950s contained no references to leadership (e.g., Gray, 1952; Ryan & Smith, 1954).

The first explicit treatment of leadership issues in an I–O text was found in Viteles (1932) under the heading "The New Leadership in Industry." It was the final section in the book. In that section Viteles summarized a list of qualities (i.e., traits) first proposed by Craig and Charters (1925) that were thought to be most characteristic of successful leaders in industry (e.g., forcefulness, ability to command respect, impartiality, control of temper, self-confidence). He closed the text with an extended quote from a Mary Parker Follet essay (Follett, 1927) on the importance of solving human relations problems, what she termed "certainly the greatest task man has been given on this planet" (p. 628 in Viteles; p. 243 in Follet). Viteles also noted that there were few experimental (i.e., empirical) investigations in the field of leadership: "The psychology of supervision and management represents largely a rationalization of psychological principles and findings in terms of supervisory and management problems" (p. 616, footnote 12). The scholarly literature on leadership—especially empirically based research—within the field of industrial psychology was sparse, at least until the 1940s.

Blum (1949) was the first text in industrial psychology that we found with an entire chapter devoted to leadership (pp. 300-318). Notable was its role-based approach, emphasizing the functions of leadership as proposed by Barnard (1938), the use of role playing to train leaders, and McGregor's focus on the subordinate–superior relationship in understanding leadership issues (McGregor, 1944). Leadership traits were not discussed explicitly in either of these texts. In the only handbook of applied psychology that we uncovered, Link (1950) equated all personality traits to the overarching trait of social effectiveness, and proposed, "Leadership is an aspect of social effectiveness. Leaders are not merely born, they are persons who have acquired social effectiveness to an unusual degree" (p. 3). Another interesting aspect of this chapter was the assertion that "leaders must learn to be good followers before they can become leaders" (p. 8).

Ghiselli and Brown (1955) addressed the study of leadership traits, apparently dismissing the area by concluding that the findings of relevant investigations "throw considerable doubt on the notion that there is a consistent general trait of leadership" (p. 470). They also hypothesized based on extant literature that "the correlation between performance as a leader in different situations would be no greater than .35" (p. 470). Ghiselli and Brown interpreted this as a particularly low correlation, confirming that if a general leadership trait existed that it would not be of much importance. This is interesting given that Pearson (1904) compared siblings on various personality traits such as vivacity, self-assertiveness, and conscientiousness, and found the average correlation coefficient to be about .50. From these data he concluded that the effect of heredity on personality characteristics was about the same as the effect on physical characteristics (pretty substantial). From the pessimistic conclusions of Ghiselli and Brown, other researchers extrapolated that if no general leadership trait existed, and therefore leadership performance varied by situation, then situational (i.e., contingency) theories of leadership were needed.

Specialized Leadership Texts

Foreshadowing an ominous trend of popular-press books on the topic, the first specialized book on leadership was a self-help book (Kleiser, 1923). The book consists of 28 separate self-development lessons for enhancing characteristics such as achievement, business ambition, willpower, self-confidence, and personal magnetism. Tralle (1925) was the first to address the psychology of leadership and wrote in the introduction to his chapter on personality factors: "No one can be a leader unless he can 'sell' himself to others, and he can do this only through a developed personality. Such personality may be said to embody nine basic qualities, or factors, all of which may be cultivated and strengthened" (p. 50). There is a similar theme in many books and other writings on leadership—personal qualities (i.e., traits) are important and these qualities can be developed.

The first empirically based book to address issues related to personal leadership in industrial settings was published in 1925 (Craig & Charters, 1925). The authors proposed 15 qualities that were inductively derived from interviews with 110 successful executives. These qualities were summarized into the overarching factors of intelligence and skill, forcefulness, teaching ability, health and nervous strength, kindliness, fairness, and sensitivity to the reactions of subordinates. These qualities or "traits" (p. 10) could be developed according to the authors by using self-training methods included as a concluding chapter in the book.

Tead's (1935) leadership book is notable for its explicit grounding in industrial psychology. Indeed, one of the people to whom the book is dedicated is Walter Van Dyke Bingham, one of the "three students of leadership who have encouraged my continuance of its study." Tead listed 10 "ideally desirable" (p. 83) qualities, such as enthusiasm, integrity, decisiveness, intelligence, and faith. These qualities could be very easily construed as traits. Without any apparent paradox, the final chapter was devoted to how to train leadership, indicating a consistent theme from this time period: Leadership qualities (traits) could be developed in individuals. These studies also indicate a fluid conceptualization of traits, typically viewing them as personal qualities rather than dispositional—and immutable—characteristics.

The remainder of this chapter focuses more intently on the role that psychologists, and especially industrial and organizational psychologists, played in the evolution of trait-oriented leadership theories.

GREAT MAN THEORY: THE FOUNDATION

The so-called "great man" approach to leadership is probably best summarized by the historian Thomas Carlyle, who wrote that the world's history was recorded in the biographies of great men (Carlyle, 1849). It is from this approach that the notion of great leaders being "born not made" evolved. A number of early 20th-century approaches to the study of leadership focused on refining lists of the names of great world leaders (e.g., Cattell, 1903; Ellis, 1904). As mentioned in the previous section, one of the first books that focused on leadership in industry was based on an inductive (qualitative) study of 110 successful executives that proposed a list of specific qualities needed to be a successful industrial leader (Craig & Charters, 1925). This list was also included in one of the earliest collections of readings on industrial psychology (Moore & Hartman, 1931b). The Craig and Charters study represents some of the earliest research that attempted to identify the essential traits of leaders in industry.

The influence of a biographical great man approach to the study of leadership could still be seen into the 1930s. A sociological and social psychology perspective on leaders and leadership contained lists of the 100 greatest world leaders along with their respective accomplishments and recognitions (Bogardus, 1934). An interesting aspect of the Bogardus book is his claim that "every person not only has leadership traits but also has what may be called *followership* traits" (p. 3, italics in original), recognizing that all individuals are both leaders and followers. This is the first published mention of the term *followership,* which was not reintroduced until the 1950s (Hollander & Webb, 1955) and still was not widely considered until the early 1990s and even then mainly in more popular treatments of leadership (e.g., De Pree, 1990). Bogardus described leadership as "personality in action under group conditions" and elaborated that it is "interaction between specific traits of one person and other traits of the many" (p. 3). In short, Bogardus recognized that both leaders and followers are necessary for leadership to occur.

In some of the earliest published writings by an industrial psychologist on the topic of leadership, Walter Van Dyke Bingham (Bingham, 1927) raised the important concern of whether leadership can be developed or is an inborn trait (i.e., leaders born or made). In discussing the 15 qualities and abilities of personal leadership set forth by Craig and Charters (1925), Bingham commented,

> These are, undoubtedly, some of the important components of leadership ability. Can they be developed? Can they be taught? It has been contended that leaders can be discovered but not developed; that the only way to make a leader is to give him the opportunity to lead, to exercise the unique traits of leadership which he inherited. **The student of psychology holds precisely the opposite position.** He maintains that leadership ability can be developed, and that it can be taught much more effectively if the task is approached systematically and analytically, and with definite rather than haphazard purpose. (pp. 253–254, bold added for emphasis).

Reflecting the scientific management perspective of that time in which all tasks can be broken down into their essential elements, Bingham went on to propose that whereas leadership is complex, it is "entirely capable of analysis" (Bingham, 1927, p. 255). By conducting a leadership analysis to identify the kinds of behaviors that differentiate successful and unsuccessful leaders, "you discover that these components of leadership are capable of development through training" through the application of the laws of learning (p. 255). He summarized his perspective in this way: "My fundamental proposition is that leadership as a whole is a group of qualities which are subject to improvement through conscious, systematic, planned training and development through exercise" (p. 258). As far as we can tell, this is the first published discussion of leadership development by an industrial psychologist. Nonetheless, Bingham's thinking on the topic of leadership apparently had little influence on other industrial psychologists of the time given that leadership was overlooked in most of the early industrial psychology textbooks.

The qualities needed for personal leadership set forth by Craig and Charters, and reinforced by Bingham, are in many ways strikingly similar to the concept of traits. The primary difference appears to be that personal qualities were thought to be developable, whereas traits were commonly viewed as inherited attributes (Galton, 1869; Terman, 1904). Nonetheless, the kinds of leadership qualities that were proposed in the early literature were remarkably similar in content to what we would presently term leadership traits.

In an essay from the same collection (Metcalf, 1927), Mary Follett discussed leadership in terms of its reciprocal nature between a leader and a group and said that power can be thought of "as the combined capacity of the group" (Follett, 1927, p. 221). Her discussion of leadership is remarkable in its complexity and foresight, far surpassing simplistic notions that great men are born to lead and about 75 years ahead of the recent emergence of shared leadership as an important topic of research and theory (Pearce & Conger, 2003). Those who are aware of Follett's work know that she was considered a visionary in numerous areas. Trained in political science at the "Harvard Annex" (now Radcliffe College), Follett published her first book on the topic of the speaker of the House of Representatives (Follett, 1896). She was later involved in social work and community activism but found her most enthusiastic audience among members of the business community. She proposed ideas in her writings and speeches related to topics that would be considered state of the art today, such as reciprocal leadership processes, community-based solutions, and the strength of diversity. Although it is beyond the scope of this chapter to provide a more in-depth review of Follett's life and her many contributions to the fields of leadership and management, interested readers are referred to a recent biography (Tonn, 2003) and edited collections of her writings (Graham, 1996; Metcalf & Urwick, 1941; also see http://www.follettfoundation.org and chaps. 2 and 17 in this volume).

As described earlier, another individual who proposed forward-thinking notions of leadership was Bingham, who recognized that leadership and formal authority are distinct concepts (also see Cowley, 1928, for a distinction between a leader and a headman). This leads him to conclude, "Leadership is found, then, throughout the entire hierarchy of organization" (Bingham, 1927, p. 247). These are not the types of theories one would expect to find being espoused in the 1920s. It also suggests that even at its earliest points in history there were prominent industrial psychologists who conceptualized leadership in ways that differed strikingly from classical trait theory: (a) that it was based on the interactions of two or more individuals (and not a sole dispositional property of an individual), (b) that it could be found at all levels of an organization (not just at the top or with "great men"), and (c) that it could be developed (it was not inherited). Thus, the roots of leadership as a complex integration of traits and situations lie not, as commonly supposed, in the leadership research emerging in the 1950s and 60s but rather in the origins of industrial psychology.

LEADER BEHAVIOR APPROACH: THE CONTROVERSY

A significant turning point in leadership and leader trait research occurred in the late 1940s after the publication of several reviews of the extant literature at that time. These reviews, by Bird (1940), Jenkins (1947), Gibb (1947), and Stogdill (1948), surveyed the literature to identify primary candidates for leader attributes (traits). The empirical literature contained studies using a variety of methods, including behavioral observation, sociometric rankings, peer and observer leadership nominations, leader selections and appointments, analysis of biographical data, and interviews with organizational leaders (Stogdill, 1948). The samples for these studies ranged across different age groups from preschool children to adulthood, across different types of leaders from school leaders to historical figures, and across many types of organizations. These literature reviews focused on a wide number of individual differences—Bird listed 70 potential leader attributes, whereas Stogdill listed 32 attributes.

The conclusions from these reviews were interpreted as being extremely negative for leadership trait theories. Gibb (1947) summarized that leadership must be relative to the situation in that the particular set of circumstances existing at the moment determines which attributes of personality will confer leadership status. In a review of the military leadership literature, Jenkins (1947) observed, "no single trait or group of characteristics has been isolated which sets off the leader from the members of the group" (pp. 74–75). Stogdill (1948) concluded that persons who are leaders in one situation may not necessarily be leaders in other situations. Gibb (1954) noted that "numerous studies of the personalities of leaders have failed to find any consistent pattern of traits which characterize leaders" (p. 889). A subsequent review by Mann (1959) mirrored these conclusions. These reviews were cited in many leading textbooks as indicating the futility of pursuing trait-based explanations for leadership processes and influence.

These studies prompted a refocus in leadership research on the effective behaviors of leaders (rather than traits or other personal characteristics) and the situational dynamics that gave rise to the display of effective leadership. The research embodying this refocus occurred primarily at the Personnel Research Board at the Ohio State University. Key initial researchers in this program were John Hemphill, Carroll Shartle, and Ralph Stogdill. Later, Edwin Fleishman was instrumental in the development of leader behavior description questionnaires that became widely used in leadership research in the late 1950s and continue to be used today. A parallel leader behavior research program was carried out at the University Michigan, headed primarily by Daniel Katz (Katz & Kahn, 1952; Katz, Maccoby, Gurin, & Floor, 1951; Katz, Maccoby, & Morse, 1950). Collectively, this body of work sought to identify what leadership behaviors were likely to be most effective in different situations and in a broader sense identify the situational characteristics that demand particular patterns of leadership.

The Ohio State leadership research program, along with the Michigan program, had several profound influences on the direction and focus of subsequent leadership research. First, the research program led to the development of questionnaires and assessment instruments that became the main tools over a period of 30 to 40 years used to describe leadership behavior (e.g., Leader Behavior Description Questionnaire, Supervisory Behavior Description Questionnaire, Leader Opinion Questionnaire; Fleishman, 1953a; Stogdill, 1963; Stogdill & Coons, 1957). These tools facilitated the investigation of leadership behavior across a variety of situations and were the precursors of 360-degree feedback instruments that became widely used in the 1990s. In the 1970s and 1980s these instruments came under criticism as being prone to a number of response biases and errors (e.g., Luthans & Lockwood, 1984; Schriesheim & Kerr, 1977) and as reflecting the assumptions and expectations of followers rather than the actual behavior of the leader (Lord, Binning, Rush, & Thomas, 1978). Nonetheless, various forms of leader behavior questionnaires are still used today, most notably the Multifactor Leadership Questionnaire for measuring transformational, transactional, and laissez-faire leadership (Bass & Avolio, 1997).

A second influence of this line of research was to focus attention on the leadership episode and particularly on the role of followers in at least partly defining the requirements of effective leaders. This emphasis reflects the earlier mention by Bogardus (1934) of the importance of followers in effective leadership. Hemphill (1949) quoted Cowley (1928) in this regard, who stated that "a leader is an individual who is moving in a particular direction and who *succeeds in inducing others to follow after him*" (p. 145; Hemphill added the italics, p. 4). Thus, Hemphill noted that a consideration of the situation that poses leadership requirements includes the characteristics, needs, and demands of the individuals being led. This notion gave rise to subsequent situational theories that included follower characteristics as key moderators of leadership behavior (e.g., Fiedler, 1964, 1971; Hersey & Blanchard, 1969; Kerr & Jermier, 1978). It also contributed to the emergence of the followership theories of Hollander in the 1950s and 1960s (Hollander, 1958, 1960; Hollander & Julian, 1970, Hollander & Webb, 1955).

Perhaps the most significant influence of this line of research was the aforementioned sense that the classical trait approach was ineffective for understanding leadership. Subsequent textbooks and reviews in industrial and organizational psychology consistently cited Stogdill's (1948) article as supporting this viewpoint. We argue, however, that this reaction was a major overinterpretation (or perhaps misinterpretation) of the data summarized by Stogdill. Indeed, Stogdill did not intend for his review to result in such a negative indictment of the classical trait approach and believed that researchers overgeneralized his conclusions (Stogdill, 1974). In his original review, he wrote,

> [Evidence from 15 or more studies indicates that] the average person who occupies a position of leadership exceeds the average member of his group in the following respects: (1) intelligence, (2) scholarship, (3) dependability in exercising responsibility, (4) activity and social participation, and (5) socioeconomic status.

> [Evidence from 10 or more studies indicates that] the average person who occupies a position of leadership exceeds the average member of his group in the following respects: (1) sociability, (2) initiative, (3) persistence, (4) knowing how to get things done, (5) self-confidence, (6) alertness to, and insight into, situations, (7) cooperativeness, (8) popularity, (9) adaptability, and (10) verbal facility. (p. 63)

Fleishman (personal communication, June 14, 2005) affirmed that Stogdill did not intend for his 1948 article to be a repudiation of trait approaches. Indeed, the behavioral approaches advocated by these programs do not necessarily contradict individual difference approaches to leadership. Initiating structure and consideration were viewed as generalized styles that were relatively enduring across situations. For example, Harris and Fleishman (1955) measured leader initiating structure and consideration over time and reported stable patterns of leadership behavior. Later, Fleishman and Peters (1962) cited this earlier study in asserting the stability and consistency of these styles.

Another widely cited critical review (Mann, 1959) also suggested more support for leadership attributes than is typically attributed. Mann concluded on the basis of his review that "a number of relationships between personality variables and individual behavior and [leadership] status variables appear to be well established" (p. 262). The positive relations of intelligence, adjustment, and extroversion to leadership were consistently significant. In addition, dominance, masculinity, and interpersonal sensitivity are found to be positively related to leadership, whereas conservatism is found to be negatively related to leadership. Mann's review and that of Stogdill were perhaps the ones most cited as indicating a lack of significant relations between leader traits and leadership. Yet, as Mann concluded, "It is encouraging to note, however, that many clear and significant trends emerge when the body of research on these relationships is considered as a whole" (p. 266).

These statements bolster the argument that the conclusions of subsequent leadership researchers were not in line with the data from that time and were overly pessimistic about the conclusions drawn by Stogdill (1948) and Mann (1959). Evidence existed for clear differences between leaders and nonleaders, and these differences generalized across situations. As several reviews noted (e.g., Bass, 1990; Gibb, 1954; Lord, DeVader, & Alliger, 1986), weak observed associations between attributes and leadership could be attributed to a range of statistical, measurement, and methodological artifacts that could be corrected or examined in further research. Indeed several later studies did just that, reporting general support for trait-based explanations for leadership (e.g., Kenny & Zaccaro, 1983; Lord et al., 1986).

Nonetheless, the Ohio State research program, along with the program at the University of Michigan, represented perhaps the tipping point in the changing zeitgeist toward more situational models of leadership effectiveness. If not data driven (given the aforementioned conclusions from the Stogdill and Mann reviews), what accounts for this paradigm shift? We suggest that the apparent widespread rejection of the classical trait approach to leadership on the basis of "unconvincing evidence" indicates the influence of the growing number of social psychologists who were beginning to focus on the topic of leadership. The social psychological analysis of behavior reflects primarily a contextual or situational explanation for human action. This contextual perspective emerges from Kurt Lewin and his classic formulation that behavior is a function of the person and the situation. Such a perspective becomes embedded in assumptions that oriented the researcher toward more situational influences as key drivers of behavior.

We note that leadership research in the late 1930s and 1940s was increasingly dominated by individuals schooled in the social psychological perspective. This shift can be traced initially to Lewin, Lippit, and White's (1939) examination of the social climates created by different leadership patterns. Ed Fleishman described this study as a significant influence on his classic dissertation on climate and leadership behavior (Fleishman, personal communication, April 14, 2003; see also Fleishman, 1953b). John Hemphill, who in turn was mentored by Filmore Sanford (a social psychologist at the Univerisity of Maryland), suggested this focus to Fleishman as he began to work on his doctoral thesis (Fleishman, personal communication, April 14, 2003).

Lewin initiated his work on leadership training in the 1940s, forming the National Training Laboratories in 1946. We have already mentioned the contributions of Bogardus (1934) to this perspective. Bird (1940) and Britt (1943) each devoted an entire chapter to leadership in their social psychology textbooks, a full 8 or 9 years before the first industrial psychology text did the same (Blum, 1949). Whereas Bird took a more classical trait approach in his chapter, Britt noted,

> Leadership in any one activity requires a certain amount of skill in *that* activity as well as evidence of other skills. A person cannot lead in all spheres; he must at times be a follower. In other words, if you wish to analyze the social psychology of leadership so that the materials will be useful to you personally, you should choose some *particular* situation and then, by observational or experimental methods, make a careful study of leadership in that particular kind of situation. (p. 278, emphasis in original)

Britt's (1943) prescription for the study of leadership came almost a decade before the Ohio State research program and was reflected in other treatises on social psychology. For example, Sherif (1948) noted in his text, "It follows that the leader role is determined not by absolute traits and capacities, but by the demands of the situation at hand" (p. 101). L. B. Murphy and G. Murphy's (1935) chapter in the first handbook of social psychology contained a section on companionship and leadership in relation to situational factors that documented the change in leadership status of children as a function of changing situational parameters.

These contributions created a zeitgeist for the emergence of a contextual perspective at Ohio State. A similar perspective operated at the University of Michigan through the work of Katz and Kahn and through the efforts of the Institute of Survey Research, which acquired some of Lewin's students and research foci after his death. Researchers began to interpret early leadership research seeking to identify stable differences between leaders and nonleaders within this general push toward contextual perspectives on leadership, resulting in an overly harsh or dismissive interpretation of relevant findings. The result was an almost 40-year focus (until the late 1980s) primarily on situational leadership.

SITUATION AND CONTINGENCY MODELS: THE ROAD MORE TRAVELED

After the emergence of the Ohio State and University of Michigan leadership programs that placed a heavy emphasis on leadership behavior, leadership researchers began to offer situation-based models of leadership. Fiedler's contingency theory (1964, 1967, 1971) was the first and perhaps most dominant of these approaches. He actually integrated traitlike qualities of the individual with specified situational contingencies that determined the efficacy of different leadership styles. Individuals were defined as having dominant leader styles; situations were specified in terms of leader–member relationships, position power of the leader, and the degree of task structure in the group. High task-oriented or high interpersonally oriented leaders were likely to be more or less effective in different combinations of situational parameters. This perspective was useful in providing a framework for how particular situational characteristics demanded certain qualities of the leaders. More than other contingency models, Fiedler's model argued that an individual could not be effective if the situation did not match his or her stylistic approach to leadership. Other approaches presupposed that leaders could change their behaviors readily in response to changing environmental circumstances. For Fielder's model, an individual can truly be a leader in one situation but not in another.

Other approaches followed that stressed how the leader's behavior changed as a function of the situation without necessarily articulating that a different individual would assume the leader role as situational demands changed. For example, path goal theory noted that several situational moderators such as follower characteristics, task characteristics, and environmental parameters determined the utility of different leadership behaviors (e.g., directive, supportive, participative, achievement oriented; House, 1971; House & Mitchell, 1974). Hersey and Blanchard (1969) and Kerr and Jermier (1978), who described the situational contingencies that constrained leadership, offered similar models. Hersey and Blanchard described follower maturity and competencies as a key moderator of leadership action, whereas Kerr and Jermier defined categories of situational characteristics that could moderate, substitute for, or neutralize leadership influence. Vroom and Yetton (1973) argued for a number of decision-making parameters, related to the role of the group and the expertise of followers, which defined how the leader ought to make decisions within the group. Leader member exchange theory (Dansereau, Graen, & Haga, 1975; Graen & Cashman, 1975) advanced the perspective that leaders change their ways of interacting with subordinates, depending on the degree of trust and commitment established between the leader and the subordinate.

These theories dominated the discussion of leadership in the 1960s and 1970s. They were described and viewed as in contraposition to the classic trait models. However, these theories can be compatible with leader trait models if one considers a capability to recognize situational parameters and respond accordingly as an important individual difference linked to leader effectiveness. Kenny and Zaccaro (1983) offered this perspective, arguing that leaders differed from nonleaders in their ability to respond effectively across a variety of different social situations. Using data from a study that rotated individuals through a variety of group tasks and gathered measures of leadership nominations, they found that leader emergence was attributable to a stable quality of the individual and argued that this reflected an "ability to perceive needs and goals of a constituency and to adjust one's personal approach to group action accordingly" (p. 678). Zaccaro, Gilbert, Thor, and Mumford (1991) specified this as a quality of social intelligence (see also Zaccaro, 2002). Several subsequent empirical studies have linked social intelligence and its components to indexes of leadership (Connelly, et al., 2000; Gilbert & Zaccaro, 1995; Hooijberg, 1996; Ritchie, 1994; Zaccaro, Foti, & Kenny, 1991). Such attributes of the leader provide for the situational variability linked to leader effectiveness by the Ohio State leadership program and by situational leadership models. This approach also fits neatly within the view that leaders differ from nonleaders and that they can be effective across very different social contexts. Defining social competencies as key leader traits also fits the followership models that represent an alternate line of research in the 1950s–1980s time frame.

LEADERSHIP PERCEPTIONS: THE ROAD LESS TRAVELED

The classic trait-based approach to leadership focused on the personality characteristics that made a person a leader. As discussed, this perspective is the oldest in the leadership literature, going back to the early 20th century (Terman, 1904). Given the dispositional nature of personality traits, this perspective implicitly assumes that leaders are born, not made. Although this might seem appealing to some in that it reduces leadership to a selection issue in organizations, it is both a limited and limiting perspective. It denies any opportunity for leadership capabilities to be developed in individuals—you either have it (leadership aptitude) or you don't. In addition to the antidevelopmental aspect of the hardcore classic trait approach to leadership, another limiting factor is the passive role that followers are thought to play in leadership processes. Great leaders act on followers through their motivating, goal-oriented, or inspirational words and deeds, which are caused by underlying personality traits. This is a very "leader-centric" approach to leadership and one that was not given much apparent credence even by some of the earliest industrial psychologists and management scholars who wrote about leadership (Bingham, 1927; Follett, 1927). As discussed, contingency or situational models later broadened the scientific lens to include aspects of the situation and how matching leadership styles to the situation were thought to result in more effective leadership outcomes (e.g., individual or group performance).

A different path—and one much less traveled in the scientific literature or the practice arena—broadened the lens in a different way by focusing on the perceptions and attributions of followers. In this way, the approaches discussed in this section are more "follower-centric" in nature. These approaches more fully recognize that followers allow leaders to influence them (or not), and therefore followers play a pivotal role in leadership processes. Without followers, there can be no leadership. This was not a novel perspective given the early writings of Follett (1927) and Bogardus (1934), in particular. What made this perspective somewhat unique is that it proposed that much of leadership depends on socioperceptual processes—followers must first perceive someone as a leader before they follow (i.e., are influenced).

The origins of the socioperceptual approach can be traced to the reintroduction of the term *followership* in the psychological literature (Hollander & Webb, 1955), although the notion of leadership as a process rather than a single person had been in the sociological literature for some time (J. A. Murphy, 1941). Hollander and Julian (1969) summarized the follower-centric perspective in this way: "Personality characteristics which may fit a person to be a leader are determined by the perceptions of followers, in the sense of the particular role expectancies and satisfactions, rather than by the traits measured via personality scale scores" (p. 389). In this manner, Hollander and Julian illustrated the important notion that personality traits can have multiple meanings. Whereas traits can mean personality scale scores (typical), traits can also mean the semantic labels that followers use to make sense of a leader's behavior (atypical). Traits "exist" in the heads of followers as sensemaking heuristics and are used to ascribe or attribute leadership to persons who manifest important leadership traits.

Acknowledging the role of followers in leadership was a critical advance in the field but one that still receives much less attention than the study of leaders (and leader traits). In many ways there is continuing confusion in the field due to a fundamental failure to distinguish between leadership as a process and the leader as a person who occupies a central—but not sole—role in that process (Hollander & Julian, 1969). According to Hollander, "The term leadership still refers to much of the field as having a new person in that role—what we now call a regime change" (personal communication, May 23, 2003). Leadership is based on a social relationship between leaders and followers (i.e., individuals holding different roles) that is developed over time and is manifested in mutual influence toward achieving group or organizational goals. The leadership process is considerably more complex than having one person (leader) dominating or directing the actions of others (followers). "Leaders and followers live with a common bond. That bond is very important to maintain" (Hollander, personal communication, May 23, 2003).

Hollander and Julian (1969) first proposed the notion of leadership perceptions as a key component in the dynamic leadership process. It took nearly a decade for other scholars to pick up on this theme and to couch it in more formal, theoretical terms. Both Calder (1977) and Pfeffer (1977) adopted an attribution theory lens in explaining leadership perceptions. It is worth noting again the recurring social psychological influence on leadership theory that shifted the theoretical focus from the leader to aspects of the situation—in this case the attributional tendencies of followers. Instead of focusing on the role of traits in shaping follower's perceptions, these authors argued that observers attribute leadership to salient individuals in their social environment. As such, leadership is a social construction of observers (followers) that is used to understand causal relations in social systems (i.e., make sense of the events taking place in the world). It had been argued that that people developed attributions that give them a sense of control over their environments (Kelley, 1971); thus, an emphasis on lead-

ership might be at least be partially due to a "desire to believe in the effectiveness and importance of individual action, since individual action is more controllable than contextual
variables" (Pfeffer, 1977, p. 109). Calder took a more radical position: "Leadership *exists* only
as perception" (p. 202, emphasis in original). Calder argued that because of its phenomenological nature, leadership was not a viable scientific construct; however, it was extremely
important as naïve psychology.

In many ways, Calder (1977) and Pfeffer (1977), as well as subsequent researchers who
picked up on this theme (e.g., Meindl & Ehrlich, 1987; Meindl et al., 1985), viewed leadership
as a type of attributional error or perceptual bias due to observers' needs for control and feelings of personal effectiveness. Thus, organizational outcomes are more likely to be attributed
to individual actions rather than to more potent or plausible situational, contextual, or environmental causes. From this perspective leadership is mainly symbolic. Leadership is important
because people believe it is important. Research purportedly demonstrating that individual
leaders have relatively trivial effects on organizational outcomes as compared with environmental factors (Lieberson & O'Connor, 1972; Salancik & Pfeffer, 1977) was used as evidence
to support the attributional perspective on leadership (although see Day & Lord, 1988, for a
critical reanalysis and reinterpretation of those studies).

A less phenomenological approach was taken at about the same time as the Calder (1977)
and Pfeffer (1977) theoretical pieces appeared. This alternate, empirically based approach
conceptualized leadership as a process anchored in person perception (rather than attributional
analysis) and examined how leadership is defined by the joint perceptions of followers (Lord,
1977). This study marks the beginning of Lord's pioneering work in the area of leadership perceptions that is grounded in the social cognitive literature on impression formation, person perception, stereotyping, and cognitive categorization.

An overall finding from this early work suggests that in most novel situations, leadership perceptions are based on general categories (i.e., stereotypes) rather than situation-specific criteria.
A key finding from this research was that the greater the number of functional leadership behaviors that were demonstrated (i.e., relative participation), the stronger the leadership perception.
Lord's (1977) study was pioneering in directly examining the assumption that functional behavior can be provided by any group member and not just the formal group leader (Cartwright &
Zander, 1968). Indeed, Lord's results indicated that group members form distinct leadership impressions about everyone in the group and that these impressions are based heavily on the frequency of functional leadership behaviors contributed by various group members.

Another important aspect of these findings is in demonstrating that leadership perceptions
are formed based on relatively simple processes and that leadership is not solely an
attributional bias. The key word here is *solely* because other subsequent research demonstrated
that leadership perceptions are influenced by performance outcome information. In other
words, there may be multiple routes to constructing and shaping leadership perceptions. One
route is based on more of a bottom-up approach in which perceptions are driven by observed
behaviors. Another route is more of a top-down approach in which leadership is attributed as a
causal explanation for varying levels of group performance.

The Lord (1977) study demonstrated that observer impressions of leadership were linked
closely to the overall amount of functional leadership behavior demonstrated by group members. These findings support the assertion that leadership perceptions are largely veridical and
grounded in observable behavior. If true, this would be good news for those who have developed or promoted questionnaire measures of leadership in either practice or research. Based on
these particular results, it would appear that perceptions are tightly coupled with the relative
number of leadership behaviors exhibited by group members. However, a series of studies on
the performance cue effect would challenge this assumption.

Performance Cue Studies

Research beginning in the mid-1970s (Downey, Chacko, & McElroy, 1979; Staw, 1975) consistently found that group members who received bogus group performance feedback distorted their group process ratings in the direction of that feedback. Subsequent research demonstrated that this "performance cue effect" also occurred with impartial group observers (McElroy & Downey, 1982). A further extension of this basic paradigm examined the effects of implicit leadership theories (ILT) on ratings of leader behavior (Larson, 1982; Lord et al., 1978; Rush, Thomas, & Lord, 1977). ILTs were conceptualized originally as cognitive heuristics or schemas (J. S. Phillips & Lord, 1982) that integrated all of the various expectations and beliefs that people hold implicitly regarding leaders and leadership (Eden & Leviathan, 1975). It was argued that one of the strongest beliefs held in the ILTs of most laypersons was that good group performance was the result of effective leadership. Thus, if either actors (e.g., group members or other participants) or observers (e.g., assessment center raters or other nonparticipants in the group) were led to believe that a group was high (or low) performing, then the "cause" of that performance must be effective (or ineffective) leadership. Behaviorally based ratings completed subsequently about the group leader would reflect the particular performance prime because of the mediating role of ILTs (Larson, 1982).

A typical methodology for investigating performance cue effects and ILTs (e.g., Lord et al., 1978) involves showing a videotape of a group interaction to participants assigned to different performance conditions. One condition involved telling participants that the group on the tape was second best in their task performance of all the groups that were videotaped (high performance), whereas in a second condition participants were told that the group they would see was second worst in their performance (low performance). In both conditions participants watched the identical videotape and rated the identical leader using the Leader Behavior Description Questionnaire (Hemphill & Coons, 1957). If leadership perceptions (as measured by questionnaire ratings) were primarily shaped by the amount of functional behavior demonstrated by the group leader, then the resulting ratings would be nearly identical across conditions. The results demonstrated unequivocally that this was not the case. Observers attributed effective leadership to the group that was thought to be high performing—regardless of the actual performance level—because of the leadership–performance association held as a key ILT component.

An unresolved (or perhaps conveniently overlooked) issue stemming from the performance cue effect and ILT studies is that any ratings of leadership are likely to be biased by information contained in the rater's ILT. If there is information or even a belief that the leader is associated with a high-performing group, business unit, or organization, then any subsequent leadership ratings will at least partially reflect this performance cue rather than observed behaviors. Separating the "true score" of leadership from the "noise" associated with ILTs is difficult if not an impossible task (Rush et al., 1977). The implications of these findings are that researchers and practitioners need to be very careful when using questionnaire-based ratings of leadership because of the biasing effects of ILTs. Given the enduring popularity of trying to measure leadership by means of questionnaires, the implications from these ILT and performance cue studies apparently have been largely ignored by leadership researchers, even today.

LEADERSHIP CATEGORIZATION THEORY

How do these studies on performance cue effects pertain to traits? Traits appear to have completely faded into the research background in favor of leader behaviors. Although leader traits were rarely mentioned explicitly, they were later shown to be the building blocks of leadership perceptions and key components of followers' ILTs. Lord and associates proposed and tested the proposition that implicit theories reflect the structure and content of the cognitive categories used to distinguish leaders from nonleaders (Lord, Foti, & De Vader, 1984; Lord et al., 1982). This leadership categorization theory is based on one of the most basic and important tasks of all organisms—to partition the environment into classifications in which different stimuli can be treated as equivalent (Rosch, 1973, 1978). These classifications comprise categories. Categorization is important from an evolutionary perspective because it allows for (a) quickly making sense of the environment, (b) providing meaning in the form of semantic labels to objects and events, and (c) enhancing effective and efficient communication. Just as people construct and hold in memory categories for natural objects (Mervis & Rosch, 1981) and for various types of personalities (Cantor & Mischel, 1979), they also are thought to hold a category for leader. What purportedly differentiates leaders from nonleaders is the degree that an individual fits an implicitly held leadership prototype.

A prototype is defined as an abstract composite of the most representative attributes of category members (Rosch, 1975). According to the theory, people hold an implicit superordinate-level prototype of a leader and more highly differentiated basic-level prototypes for various leadership domains (e.g., business, military, education, and politics). Instead of requiring some critical set of features to be perceived as a leader, the greater the match to the perceiver's leadership prototype the more likely an individual will be seen as a leader. At the broadest, most inclusive categorization level (i.e., leader vs. nonleader), findings indicated the five most prototypical leader attributes were (a) dedicated, (b) goal oriented, (c) informed, (d) charismatic, and (e) decisive (Lord, Foti, & De Vader, 1984, Study 1). An individual who is seen as demonstrating these key traits is more likely to be perceived as a leader—regardless of the context—than an individual who is not seen as possessing any of these traits. In this way, the category of leader follows a graded structure much like other categories. Not all of the prototypical leadership traits need to be seen for the label of leader to be bestowed on an individual (Lord et al., 1984, provided prototypicality ratings for 59 leader and 26 nonleader trait attributes). Instead, demonstrating just a few of the more prototypical traits would likely lead to being quickly and automatically (or spontaneously) labeled as a leader.

Lord recently observed that by necessity many of the early leadership trait studies were limited to estimating bivariate relationships between traits and outcomes (i.e., leader emergence and leader effectiveness) due to limited knowledge of multivariate statistical techniques at that time (R. Lord, personal communication, May 27, 2003). However, the role of traits on leadership perceptions is inherently multivariate: No one critical trait defines whether someone is a leader. Instead, leadership perceptions are determined by how well someone fits with a pattern of representative (i.e., prototypical) leadership traits.

The leadership categorization research by Lord and associates (e.g., Foti, Fraser, & Lord, 1982; Lord et al., 1984; Lord et al., 1982) marked a major stride forward in the development of a scientific theory of followership. Followers play a critical role in the leadership process by allowing those individuals who are perceived as leaders to influence them. In this way, the leadership perceptions of followers, which were shown to adhere to basic principles of cognitive categorization, are instrumental in the development of a social influence process that has been argued is at the core of leadership (Hollander, 1964; Hollander & Julian, 1969). Especially relevant to this critical–historical review of the leadership literature is that leader traits provided the foundation to the theory, but from the follower's perspective. Cognitive schemas related to leadership (i.e., implicit leadership theories) comprised primarily of traits are important perceptual constructs that predict leadership perceptions and leader emergence. Instead of limiting the concept of leader traits to only those characteristics that are measured by personality inventories, leadership categorization theory demonstrated that traits are important semantic labels that perceivers apply to others in making sense of their social environments.

Much as the term *personality* has multiple meanings, so does the term *trait* (Hogan, 1991). Traits may be used to describe key constructs in motivating individual leader behavior; however, they may be even more important as sense-making heuristics for followers. Subsequent research in the social cognition literature has shown consistently that individuals form spontaneous trait inferences of others (Winter & Uleman, 1984) and that these traits form the backbone of person impression formation (see Wyer & Lambert, 1994, for a review of this literature). By extension, if leadership depends heavily on leadership perceptions being formed on the part of the followers, then traits are important components in that process.

LEADERSHIP TRAITS REDUX

It has been commonly assumed that two early reviews of the relationship between personality and leadership (Mann, 1959; Stogdill, 1948) were responsible for bringing a halt to trait-based leadership research, as well as much skepticism about the role that traits play in leadership. As the preceding section demonstrated, studies of personality and leadership were being conducted during the 1970s and 1980s but with a different trait focus (i.e., followers' trait-based perceptions of leaders). It was also pointed out by Lord et al. (1986) that the Mann and Stogdill reviews were widely misinterpreted by those claiming that traits did not matter in leadership. A primary misinterpretation concerned the nature of the leadership outcomes that were included in those reviews. Instead of examining leadership performance or leadership effectiveness (as Mann's titled explicitly stated), the early reviews dealt only with leadership emergence or leadership perceptions. A second misinterpretation was the claim that there were no consistent patterns in the data between personality and leadership. Apparently, others chose to emphasize the pessimistic conclusions of Mann and Stogdill without referring to the original data. Using meta-analytic techniques that were unavailable at the time of the original Mann and Stogdill reviews, Lord et al. (1986) reanalyzed those data and demonstrated robust relationships between intelligence and dominance with leadership perceptions. The findings unequivocally demonstrated that traits do matter in leadership, especially in terms of shaping leadership perceptions.

Another reanalysis study during this time period (Kenny & Zaccaro, 1983) challenged a long-standing assumption that leadership emergence varied across group situations. It had come to be widely accepted among leadership researchers and theorists that who tended to emerge as group leader would depend heavily on conditions of the task or the situation. A particular study of interest that was the focus of the reanalysis used a rotational design in which both the task and the group membership were varied over time (Barnlund, 1962). That is, participants worked in several groups over time, with each group having a unique member composition. In addition, the type of task was varied in each group. The outcome of interest was the rank ordering of members in terms of their leadership (i.e., leadership emergence) across groups and to what extent this ordering was stable. The Kenny and Zaccaro reanalysis suggested that between 49% and 82% of the variance in leadership emergence was attributable to some stable characteristic—quite a large effect. These results also suggest that leadership perceptions may not be contingent on the situation. Those who emerged in one type of task group tended to emerge in other groups as well, contrary to the claim that "persons who are leaders in one situation may not necessarily be leaders in other situations" (Stogdill & Shartle, 1948, p. 65). Subsequent studies have identified particular leader traits and attributes that were associated with emergence across group situations (Ferentinos, 1996; Zaccaro, Foti, & Kenny, 1991).

CONCLUSIONS

In retrospect, any assertion that traits are irrelevant to leadership seems naïve at best. After all, leadership is based on a social relationship and therefore depends on relational processes.

There is a long history in psychology examining how the behavioral tendencies of actors and the perceptions and labeling of those tendencies by others interact in shaping relationships and relational processes. The assertion that leadership does not reside in a person still rings true (J. A. Murphy, 1941). Without followers and without social interaction, leadership cannot occur. Followers are not passive recipients of leadership, although there are contemporary scholars who still seem to believe this (e.g., Judge, Bono, Ilies, & Gerhardt, 2002; Kirkpatrick & Locke, 1991). Rather, followers are active participants in leadership processes. Thus, it is inevitable that followers and their perceptions of others in a group are critically important to any leadership that occurs.

Much like leadership, traits take protean forms. One continuing approach of contemporary I–O psychologists is to research and discuss leadership traits as if they are mainly inherited, dispositional characteristics that differentiate leaders from everyone else. For example, recent research indicates robust relationships between the Big Five "traits" and the outcomes of leader emergence and effectiveness (e.g., Judge et al., 2002). But what should we do with those results? The answer would appear to be limited to using personality inventories for leader selection, given the assertion that personality traits are thought to be immutable once an individual reaches adulthood. However, other approaches emphasizing a broader approach to traits as meaning a range of attributes that promote leader effectiveness across situations (e.g., cognitive skills and abilities, social capabilities) suggest enduring leader attributes that are indeed malleable through carefully constructed developmental interventions (Connelly et al., 2000; Fleishman, Mumford, Zaccaro, Levin, & Hein, 1991; Mumford, Zaccaro, Harding, Jacobs, & Fleishman, 2000; Zaccaro, et al., 2004). Models such as these have evolved trait perspectives, and therefore leader change interventions, beyond the earlier great man (person) approaches that were prevalent early in leadership research.

These trait and individual difference models need to be integrated more thoroughly with leader perception models. Research has made it abundantly clear that the implicit leadership theories (ILTs) of followers play an important role in leadership processes. Put simply, ILTs shape who is seen as a leader, which allows social influence processes to occur. Nonetheless, we know relatively little about the content of those ILTs, how they develop, or how they might be changed. Creating a shared theory of leadership in an organization could be highly instrumental as an initial step in developing leaders across all levels. Leadership traits within a broad-based, contemporary, trait-based approach to leadership can help contribute to that important research and practice objective.

THE FUTURE OF LEADERSHIP TRAIT THEORY

We would be remiss in failing to mention a more recent rapprochement of the leader-centric approaches with those that also include follower processes. Leader–member exchange theory, which examines the role-making processes involved in leadership, is one good example of a contemporary leadership theory that is based on both leaders and followers (Dansereau et al., 1975; Graen, Novak, & Sommerkamp, 1982; Graen & Uhl-Bien, 1995). In particular, the quality of the exchange that is developed between a leader and a follower is of core interest, and the perceptions of this exchange quality are measured from both the leader and follower perspectives. Research has demonstrated that dispositional characteristics (i.e., traits) can influence exchange quality perceptions from both of these perspectives (e.g., Day & Crain, 1992; A. S. Phillips & Bedeian, 1994). Another area in which rapprochement has occurred is that of charismatic leadership. It was proposed that regardless of the situation, charismatic leaders were likely to display high levels of emotional expressiveness, self-confidence, and self-determination (House, 1977), which would enhance follower identification with the leader. The personality of a charismatic leader is thought to be an important consideration (House & Howell, 1992), but so are follower perceptions. It has been argued that certain behaviors enhance an attribution of charisma on the part of followers (Conger & Kanungo, 1987). This elevates follower perceptions to a key component of the identification process in charismatic leadership.

Also of note in the study of leadership perceptions is Project GLOBE (Global Leadership and Organizational Behavior Effectiveness) (House et al., 1999, 2004; House, Javidan, & Dorfman, 2001). The project is a very ambitious effort involving a network of 170 scientists from 62 cultures working in a coordinated long-term effort to examine the interrelationships among societal culture, organizational culture and practices, and organizational leadership. One aspect of this extensive project was to identify culturally endorsed implicit leadership theories (CLTs). It is beyond the scope of this chapter to review the GLOBE findings in any detail. However, results indicated both culturally universal leader attributes as well as culturally contingent attributes. This work extends the literature on follower perceptions to address the global context in which leadership is enacted.

Although this chapter is in a book on historical perspectives in I–O psychology, we believe a few words about the future are in order. The philosopher George Santayana wrote: "Those who cannot remember the past are condemned to repeat it" (Santayana, 1905–1906). In the present context, those who cannot remember how trait theory has evolved over the course of the 20th century may find themselves boxed into a conceptual and practical corner if the only way in which traits are considered is as motive forces of leaders. As noted by Hogan (1991), using personality traits as causal explanations for behavior is "unfortunate" (p. 875) because it confounds description with explanation. Even from a classical perspective, traits merely describe behavioral tendencies or "recurring regularities or trends in a person's behavior" (p. 875). They have no magical qualities other than as semantic labels we use to make sense of the behavior of others and ourselves. In this way, it is clear how traits have been and will always be a part of leadership research and practice, at least so long as we have language.

ACKNOWLEDGMENTS

We express our deep appreciation to Ed Fleishman, Ed Hollander, and Bob Lord for their time, their comments on this chapter, and especially their historical perspectives on the field of leadership.

REFERENCES

Barnard, C. I. (1938). *The functions of the executive*. Cambridge, MA: Harvard University.

Barnlund, D. C. (1962). Consistency of emergent leadership in groups with changing tasks and members. *Speech Monographs, 29,* 45–52.

Bass, B. M. (1954). The leaderless group discussion as a leadership evaluation instrument. *Personnel Psychology, 7,* 470–477.

Bass, B. M. (1990). *Bass & Stogdill's handbook of leadership: Theory, research and managerial applications* (3rd ed.). New York: Free Press.

Bass, B. M., & Avolio, B. J. (1997). *Manual for the Multifactor Leadership Questionnaire*. Palo Alto, CA: Mindgarden.

Bingham, W. V. (1927). Leadership. In H. C. Metcalf (Ed.), *The psychological foundations of management* (pp. 244–260). Chicago: Shaw.

Bird, C. (1940). *Social psychology*. New York: Appleton-Century.

Blum, M. L. (1949). *Industrial psychology and its social foundation*. New York: Harper.

Bogardus, E. S. (1934). *Leaders and leadership*. New York: Appleton-Century.

Bowden, A. O. (1926). A study of the personality of student leaders in the United States. *Journal of Abnormal and Social Psychology, 21,* 149–160.

Bray, D. W., Campbell, R. J., & Grant, D. L. (1974). *Formative years in business: A long-term AT&T study of managerial lives*. New York: Wiley.

Britt, S. H. (1943). *Social psychology of modern life.* New York: Farrar & Rinehart.

Browne, C. G. (1951). Study of executive leadership in business. *Journal of Applied Psychology, 35,* 36–37.

Burtt, H. E. (1929). *Psychology and industrial efficiency.* New York: Appleton.

Calder, B. J. (1977). An attribution theory of leadership. In B. M. Staw & G. R. Salancik (Eds.), *New directions in organizational behavior* (pp. 179–204). Chicago: St. Clair Press.

Cantor, N., & Mischel, W. (1979). Prototypes in person perception. *Advances in Experimental Social Psychology, 12,* 3–52.

Carlyle, T. (1849). *On heroes, hero-worship, and the heroic in history.* Boston: Houghlin Mifflin.

Cartwright, D., & Zander, A. (Eds.). (1968). *Group dynamics: Research and theory.* New York: Harper & Row.

Cattell, J. M. (1903). A statistical study of eminent men. *Popular Science Monthly, 62,* 359–377.

Conger, J. A., & Kanungo, R. N. (1987). Toward a behavioral theory of charismatic leadership in organizations. *Academy of Management Review, 12,* 637–647.

Connelly, M. S., Gilbert, J. A., Zaccaro, S. J., Threlfall, K. V., Marks, M. A., &, Mumford, M. D. (2000). Cognitive and temperament predictors of organizational leadership. *Leadership Quarterly, 11,* 65–86.

Cowley, W. H. (1928). Three distinctions in the study of leaders. *Journal of Abnormal Social Psychology, 23,* 144–157.

Cowley, W. H. (1931). The traits of face-to-face leaders. *Journal of Abnormal and Social Psychology, 26,* 304–313.

Craig, D. R., & Charters, W. W. (1925). *Personal leadership in industry.* New York: McGraw-Hill.

Dansereau, F., Jr., Graen, G., & Haga, W. J. (1975). A vertical dyad linkage approach to leadership within formal organizations: A longitudinal investigation of the role making process. *Organizational Behavior and Human Performance, 13,* 46–78.

Day, D. V., & Crain, E. C. (1992). The role of affect and ability in initial exchange quality perceptions. *Group & Organization Management, 17,* 380–397.

Day, D. V., & Lord, R. G. (1988). Executive leadership and organizational performance: Suggestions for a new theory and methodology. *Journal of Management, 14,* 453–464.

De Pree, M. (1990). *Leadership is an art.* New York: Dell.

Downey, H. K., Chacko, T., & McElroy, J. C. (1979). Attribution of the "causes" of performance: A constructive, quasi-longitudinal replication of the Staw study (1975). *Organizational Behavior and Human Performance, 24,* 287–299.

Eden, D., & Leviathan, U. (1975). Implicit leadership theory as a determinant of the factor structure underlying supervisory behavior scales. *Journal of Applied Psychology, 60,* 736–741.

Ellis, H. (1904). *A study of British genius.* London: Hurst & Blackett.

Ferentinos, C. H. (1996). Linking social intelligence and leadership: An investigation of leaders' situational responsiveness under conditions of changing group tasks and membership. *Dissertation Abstracts International: Section B: The Sciences and Engineering, 57* (UMI No. 9625606).

Fiedler, F. E. (1964). A contingency model of leadership effectiveness. *Advances in Experimental Social Psychology, 1,* 149–190.

Fiedler, F. E. (1967). *A theory of leadership effectiveness.* New York: McGraw-Hill.

Fiedler, F. E. (1971). Validation and extension of the contingency model of leadership effectiveness: A review of the empirical findings. *Psychological Bulletin, 76,* 128–148.

Fleishman, E. A. (1953a). The description of supervisory behavior. *Personnel Psychology, 37,* 1–6.

Fleishman, E. A. (1953b). Leadership climate, human relations training, and supervisory behavior. *Personnel Psychology, 6,* 205–222.

Fleishman, E. A., Mumford, M. D., Zaccaro, S. J., Levin, K. Y., & Hein, M. B. (1991). Theoretical efforts in the description of leader behavior: A synthesis and functional integration. *Leadership Quarterly, 2,* 245–287.

Fleishman, E. A., & Peters, D. R. (1962). Interpersonal values, leadership attitudes, and managerial success. *Personnel Psychology, 15,* 127–143.

Follett, M. P. (1896). *The speaker of the House of Representatives.* New York: Longmans, Green.

Follett, M. P. (1927). Leader and expert. In H. C. Metcalf (Ed.), *The psychological foundations of management* (pp. 220–243). Chicago: Shaw.

Foti, R. J., Fraser, S. L., & Lord, R. G. (1982). Effects of leadership labels and prototypes on perceptions of political leaders. *Journal of Applied Psychology, 67,* 326–333.

French, J. R., & Raven, B. H. (1959). The bases of social power. In D. Cartwright (Ed.), *Studies in social power* (pp. 150–167). Ann Arbor: University of Michigan, Institute for Social Research.

Galton, F. (1869). *Hereditary genius.* New York: Appleton.

Ghiselli, E. E., & Brown, C. W. (1955). *Personnel and industrial psychology.* New York: McGraw-Hill.

Gibb, C. A. (1947). The principles and traits of leadership. *Journal of Abnormal and Social Psychology, 42,* 267–284.

Gibb, C. A. (1954). Leadership. In G. Lindzey (Ed.), *Handbook of social psychology* (Vol. 2, pp. 877–920). Cambridge, MA: Addison-Wesley.

Gilbert, J. A., & Zaccaro, S. J. (1995, August). *Social intelligence and organizational leadership*. Presented at the 103th annual meeting of the American Psychological Association. New York.

Gowin, E. B. (1919). *Developing executive ability*. New York: Ronald Press.

Graen, G. B., & Cashman, J. F. (1975). A role making model in formal organizations. In J. G. Hunt & L. L. Larson (Eds.), *Leadership frontiers* (pp. 143–165). Kent, OH: Kent State University.

Graen, G. B., Novak, M., & Sommerkamp, P. (1982). The effects of leader-member exchange and job design on productivity and satisfaction: Testing a dual attachment model. *Organizational Behavior and Human Performance, 30,* 109–131.

Graen, G. B., & Uhl-Bien, M. (1995). Relationship-based approach to leadership: Development of leader-member exchange (LMX) theory of leadership over 25 years: Applying a multi-level multi-domain perspective. *Leadership Quarterly, 6,* 219–247.

Graham, P. (Ed.). (1996). *Mary Parker Follett—Prophet of management*. Boston: Harvard Business School.

Gray, J. S. (1952). *Psychology in industry*. New York: McGraw-Hill.

Harris, E. F., & Fleishman, E. A. (1955). Human relations training and the stability of leadership patterns. *Journal of Applied Psychology, 39,* 20–35.

Hemphill, J. K. (1949). Situational factors in leadership. *Bureau of Educational Research Monograph, 32,* 136.

Hemphill, J. K., & Coons, A. E. (1957). Development of the leader behavior description questionnaire. In R. M. Stogdill & A. E. Coons (Eds.), *Leader behavior: Its description and measurement* (pp. 6–38). Columbus, OH: Ohio State University, Bureau of Business Research.

Hersey, P., & Blanchard, K. H. (1969). *Management of organizational behavior*. Englewood Cliffs, NJ: Prentice-Hall.

Hogan, R. T. (1991). Personality and personality measurement. In M. D. Dunnette & L. M. Hough (Eds.), *Handbook of industrial and organizational psychology* (2nd ed., Vol. 2, pp. 873–919). Palo Alto, CA: Consulting Psychologists Press.

Hogan, R., Curphy, G. J., & Hogan, J. (1994). What we know about leadership: Effectiveness and personality. *American Psychologist, 49,* 493–504.

Hollander, E. P. (1958). Conformity, status, and idiosyncrasy credit. *Psychological Review, 65,* 117–127.

Hollander, E. P. (1960). Competence and conformity in the acceptance of influence. *Journal of Abnormal and Social Psychology, 61,* 361–365.

Hollander, E. P. (1964). *Leaders, groups, and influence*. New York: Oxford University Press.

Hollander, E. P. (1985). Leadership and power. In G. Lindzey & E. Aronson (Eds.), *Handbook of social psychology* (Vol. 2, pp. 485–537). New York: Random House.

Hollander, E. P., & Julian, J. W. (1969). Contemporary trends in the analysis of leadership processes. *Psychological Bulletin, 71,* 387–397.

Hollander, E. P., & Webb, W. B. (1955). Leadership, followership, and friendship: An analysis of peer nominations. *Journal of Abnormal and Social Psychology, 50,* 163–167.

Hollingworth, H. L., & Poffenberger, A. T. (1917). *Applied psychology*. New York: Appleton.

Hooijberg, R. (1996). A multidirectional approach toward leadership: An extension of the concept of behavioral complexity. *Human Relations, 49,* 917–946.

House, R. J. (1971). A path-goal theory of leader effectiveness. *Administrative Science Quarterly, 16,* 321–338.

House, R. J. (1977). A 1976 theory of charismatic leadership. In J. G. Hunt & L. L. Larson (Eds.), *Leadership: The cutting edge* (pp. 189–207). Carbondale: Southern Illinois University.

House, R. J., Hanges, P. J., Javidan, M., Dorfman, P. W., & Gupta, V. (Eds.). (2004). *Culture, leadership, and organizations: The GLOBE study of 62 societies*. Thousand Oaks, CA: Sage.

House, R., Hanges, P. J., Ruiz-Quintanilla, S. A., Dorfman, P. W., Javidan, M., Dickson, M., Gupta, V., & Associates. (1999). Cultural influences on leadership and organizations: Project GLOBE. *Advances in Global Leadership, 1,* 171–233.

House, R. J., & Howell, J. M. (1992). Personality and charismatic leadership. *Leadership Quarterly, 3,* 81–108.

House, R., Javidan, M., & Dorfman, P. (2001). Project GLOBE: An introduction. *Applied Psychology: An International Review, 50,* 489–505.

House, R. J., & Mitchell, T. R. (1974). Path-goal theory of leadership. *Journal of Contemporary Business, 4,* 81–97.

Jenkins, W. O. (1947). A review of leadership studies with particular reference to military problems. *Psychological Bulletin, 44,* 54–79.

Judge, T. A., Bono, J. E., Ilies, R., & Gerhardt, M. W. (2002). Personality and leadership: A qualitative and quantitative review. *Journal of Applied Psychology, 87,* 765–780.

Katz, D., & Kahn, R. (1952). Some recent findings in human relations research in industry. In G. W. Swanson, T. M. Newcomb, & E. L. Hartley (Eds.), *Readings in social psychology* (2nd ed., pp. 650–665). New York: Holt, Rinehart & Winston.

Katz, D., Maccoby, N., & Morse, N. (1950). *Productivity, supervision, and morale in an office situation.* Ann Arbor, MI: Institute for Social Research.

Katz, D., Maccoby, N., Gurin, G., & Floor, L. (1951). *Productivity, supervision, and morale among railroad workers.* Ann Arbor: Survey Research Center, University of Michigan.

Kelley, H. H. (1971). *Attribution in social interaction.* Morristown, NJ: General Learning Press.

Kenny, D. A., & Zaccaro, S. J. (1983). An estimate of variance due to traits in leadership. *Journal of Applied Psychology, 68,* 678–685.

Kerr, S., & Jermier, J. M. (1978). Substitutes for leadership: Their meaning and measurement. *Organizational Behavior and Human Performance, 22,* 375–403.

Kirkpatrick, S. A., & Locke, E. A. (1991). Leadership: Do traits matter? *Academy of Management Executive, 5,* 48–60.

Kleiser, G. (1923). *Training for power and leadership.* New York: Doran.

Larson, J. R., Jr. (1982). Cognitive mechanisms mediating the impact of implicit theories of leader behavior on leader behavior ratings. *Organizational Behavior and Human Performance, 29,* 129–140.

Lewin, K., Lippitt, R., & White, R. K. (1939). Patterns of aggressive behavior in experimentally created social climates. *Journal of Social Psychology, 10,* 271–299.

Lieberson, S., & O'Connor, J. F. (1972). Leadership and organizational performance: A study of large corporations. *American Sociological Review, 37,* 117–130.

Link, H. C. (1950). Social effectiveness and leadership. In D. H. Fryer & E. Henry, R. (Eds.), *Handbook of applied psychology* (Vol. 1, pp. 3–10). New York: Rinehart.

Lord, R. G. (1977). Functional leadership behavior: Measurement and relation to social power and leadership perceptions. *Administrative Science Quarterly, 22,* 114–133.

Lord, R. G., Binning, J. F., Rush, M. C., & Thomas, J. C. (1978). The effect of performance cues and leader behavior on questionnaire ratings of leadership behavior. *Organizational Behavior and Human Performance, 21,* 27–39.

Lord, R. G., De Vader, C. L., & Alliger, G. M. (1986). A meta-analysis of the relation between personality traits and leadership perceptions: An application of validity generalization procedures. *Journal of Applied Psychology, 71,* 402–409.

Lord, R., G., Foti, R. J., & De Vader, C. L. (1984). A test of leadership categorization theory: Internal structure, information processing, and leadership perceptions. *Organizational Behavior and Human Performance, 34,* 343–378.

Lord, R. G., Foti, R. J., & Phillips, J. S. (1982). A theory of leadership categorization. In J. G. Hunt, U. Sekaran, & C. Schriesheim (Eds.), *Leadership: Beyond establishment views* (pp. 104–121). Carbondale: Southern Illinois University.

Luthans, F., & Lockwood, D. L. (1984). Toward an observational system for measuring leadership behavior in natural settings. In J. G. Hunt, D. Hosking, C. A. Schriesheim, & R. Stewart (Eds.), *Leaders and managers: International perspectives on managerial behavior and leadership* (pp. 117–141). New York: Pergamon.

Mann, R. D. (1959). A review of the relationships between personality and performance in small groups. *Psychological Bulletin, 56,* 241–270.

McElroy, J. C., & Downey, H. K. (1982). Observation in organizational research: Panacea to the performance attribution effect? *Academy of Management Journal, 25,* 822–835.

McGregor, D. (1944). Conditions of effective leadership in the industrial organization. *Journal of Consulting Psychology, 8,* 55–63.

Meindl, J. R., & Ehrlich, S. B. (1987). The romance of leadership and the evaluation of organizational performance. *Academy of Management Journal, 30,* 90–109.

Meindl, J. R., Ehrlich, S. B., & Dukerich, J. M. (1985). The romance of leadership. *Administrative Science Quarterly, 30,* 78–102.

Mervis, C. B., & Rosch, E. (1981). Categorization of natural objects. *Annual Review of Psychology, 32,* 89–115.

Metcalf, H. C. (Ed.). (1927). *The psychological foundations of management.* Chicago: Shaw.

Metcalf, H. C., & Urwick, L. (Eds.). (1941). *Dynamic administration: The collected papers of Mary Parker Follett.* New York: Harper & Brothers.

Miner, J. B. (1975). The uncertain future of the leadership concept: An overview. In J. G. Hunt & L. L. Larson (Eds.), *Leadership frontiers* (pp. 197–208). Kent, OH: Kent State University.

Moore, B. V., & Hartman, G. W. (1931a). The key position of foreman. In B. V. Moore & G. W. Hartman (Eds.), *Readings in industrial psychology* (pp. 509–510). New York: Appleton.

Moore, B. V., & Hartman, G. W. (Eds.). (1931b). *Readings in industrial psychology.* New York: Appleton.

Mumford, M. D., Zaccaro, S. J., Harding, F. D., Jacobs, T. O., & Fleishman, E. A. (2000). Leadership skills for a changing world: Solving complex social problems. *Leadership Quarterly, 11,* 11–35.

Münsterberg, H. (1913). *Psychology and industrial efficiency.* Boston: Houghton Mifflin.

Murphy, J. A. (1941). A study of the leadership process. *American Sociological Review, 6,* 674–687.

Murphy, L. B., & Murphy, G. (1935). The influence of social situations upon the behavior of children. In C. A. Murchison (Ed.), *A handbook of social psychology* (pp. 1034–1096). Worcester, MA: Clark University.

Pearce, C. L., & Conger, J. A. (2003). All those years ago: The historical underpinnings of shared leadership. In C. L. Pearce & J. A. Conger (Eds.), *Shared leadership: Reframing the hows and whys of leadership* (pp. 1–18). Thousand Oaks, CA: Sage.

Pearson, K. (1904). On the laws of inheritance in man. *Biometrika, 3,* 131–190.

Pfeffer, J. (1977). The ambiguity of leadership. *Academy of Management Review, 2,* 104–112.

Pfeffer, J. (1981). *Power in organizations.* Marshfield, MA: Pitman.

Phillips, A. S., & Bedeian, A. G. (1994). Leader-follower exchange quality: The role of personal and interpersonal attributes. *Academy of Management Journal, 37,* 990–1001.

Phillips, J., S., & Lord, R. G. (1982). Schematic information processing and perceptions of leadership in problem-solving groups. *Journal of Applied Psychology, 67,* 486–492.

Ritchie, R. J. (1994). Using the assessment center method to predict senior management potential. *Consulting Psychology Journal Practice and Research, 46,* 16–23.

Rosch, E. (1973). On the internal structure of perceptual and semantic categories. In T. E. Moore (Ed.), *Cognitive development and the acquisition of language* (pp. 111–144). New York: Academic Press.

Rosch, E. (1975). Cognitive representations of semantic categories. *Journal of Experimental Psychology: General, 104,* 192–233.

Rosch, E. (1978). Principles of categorization. In E. Rosch & B. B. Lloyd (Eds.), *Cognition and categorization* (pp. 27–48). Hillsdale, NJ: Lawrence Erlbaum Associates.

Rush, M. C., Thomas, J. C., & Lord, R. G. (1977). Implicit leadership theory: A potential threat to the internal validity of leader behavior questionnaires. *Organizational Behavior and Human Performance, 20,* 756–765.

Rutledge, J. J. (1937). *Mine foremanship: Qualities which effect leadership.* Wilmington, DE: Hercules Powder.

Ryan, T. A., & Smith, P. C. (1954). *Principles of industrial psychology.* New York: Ronald Press.

Salancik, G. R., & Pfeffer, J. (1977). Constraints on administrator discretion: The limited influence of mayors on city budgets. *Urban Affairs Quarterly, 12,* 475–498.

Santayana, G. (1905–1906). *The life of reason: Vol. 1. Reason in Common Sense.* New York: Scribner.

Schriesheim, C. A., & Kerr, S. (1977). Theories and measures of leadership: A critical appraisal. In J. G. Hunt & L. L. Larson (Eds.), *Leadership: The cutting edge* (pp. 9–45). Carbondale: Southern Illinois University Press.

Scott, W. D. (1911). *Increasing human efficiency in business.* New York: Macmillan.

Shartle, C. L. (1949). Leadership and executive performance. *Personnel, 25,* 370–380.

Sherif, M. (1948). *An outline of social psychology.* New York: Harper.

Smith, M. (1944). *Handbook of industrial psychology.* New York: Philosophical Library.

Staw, B. M. (1975). Attribution of the "causes" of performance: A general alternative interpretation of non-sectional research on organizations. *Organizational Behavior and Human Performance, 13,* 414–432.

Stogdill, R. M. (1948). Personal factors associated with leadership: A survey of the literature. *Journal of Psychology, 25,* 35–71.

Stogdill, R. M. (1974). *Handbook of leadership: A survey of the literature.* New York: Free Press.

Stogdill, R. M. (1963). *Manual for the Leader Behavior Description Questionnaire Form-XII.* Columbus: Ohio State University, Bureau of Business Research.

Stogdill, R. M., & Coons, A. E. (1957). *Leader behavior: Its description and measurement.* Columbus: Bureau of Business Research, Ohio State University.

Stogdill, R. M., & Shartle, C. L. (1948). Methods for determining patterns of leadership behavior in relation to organization structure and objectives. *Journal of Applied Psychology, 32,* 286–291.

Tead, O. (1935). *The art of leadership.* New York: McGraw-Hill.

Terman, L. M. (1904). A preliminary study in the psychology and pedagogy of leadership. *Pedagogical Seminary, 11,* 413–451.

Tonn, J. C. (2003). *Mary P. Follett: Creating democracy, transforming management.* New Haven, CT: Yale University.

Tralle, H. E. (1925). *Psychology of leadership.* New York: Century.

Viteles, M. S. (1932). *Industrial psychology.* New York: Norton.

Viteles, M. S., & Thompson, C. E. (1946). *The role of leadership in supervisory management.* New Wilmington, PA: The Economic and Business Foundation.

Vroom, V. H., & Yetton, P. W. (1973). *Leadership and decision making.* Pittsburgh: University of Pittsburgh.

Watts, F. (1921). *An introduction to the psychological problems of industry.* London: Allen & Unwin.

Winter, L., & Uleman, J. S. (1984). When are social judgments made? Evidence for the spontaneousness of trait inferences. *Journal of Personality and Social Psychology, 47,* 237–252.

Wyer, R. S., Jr., & Lambert, A. J. (1994). The role of trait constructs in person perception: An historical perspective. In P. G. Devine, D. L. Hamilton, & T. M. Ostrom (Eds.), *Social cognition: Impact on social psychology* (pp. 109–141). San Diego, CA: Academic Press.

Zaccaro, S. J. (2002). Organizational leadership and social intelligence. In R. Riggio, S. Murphy, & F. J. Pirozzolo (Eds.), *Multiple intelligences and leadership* (pp. 29–54). Mahwah, NJ: Lawrence Erlbaum Associates.

Zaccaro, S. J., Foti, R. J., & Kenny, D. A. (1991). Self-monitoring and trait-based variance in leadership: An investigation of leader flexibility across multiple group situations. *Journal of Applied Psychology, 76,* 308–315.

Zaccaro, S. J., Gilbert, J. A., Thor, K. K., & Mumford, M. D. (1991). Leadership and social intelligence: Linking social perceptiveness and behavioral flexibility to leader effectiveness. *Leadership Quarterly, 2,* 317–331.

Zaccaro, S. J., Kemp, C., & Bader, P. (2004). Leader traits and attributes. In J. Antonakis, R. Sternberg, & A. Ciancola (Eds.), *The nature of leadership* (pp. 101–124). Thousand Oaks, CA: Sage.

17

Work Teams in Organizations:
A Historical Reflection and Lessons Learned

Eduardo Salas, Heather A. Priest, Kevin C. Stagl,
Dana E. Sims, and C. Shawn Burke
University of Central Florida

Historically speaking, the focus on organizational teams has ebbed and flowed in synchronicity with ongoing changes in our world. When needed by organizations or society in general, research on teams and the phenomena that surround them are the focus of frantic observation and exploration. However, when attention is once again redirected toward societies' latest pressing problems, concern for teams is minimal at best. This pattern has played itself out time and again over the last century as team research has been driven by highly publicized tragic events (e.g., World War II, Florida airlines crash into the Potomac River, the September 11 tragedy, Columbia Shuttle disaster), organizational changes (e.g., flattened hierarchies, distributed human resources, self-managing work teams), and technological innovations (e.g., computers, collaboration software, networks) but is, by comparison, relatively dormant the rest of the time.

This chapter illustrates these repeated waves of team research, separated by relative periods of calm. To illustrate these waves we have structured this chapter around the events, topics, and people who have markedly contributed to the science of teams. Although the information provided in this historical reflection is organized by decade and centered around key topics, we also use a zeitgeist approach (i.e., the naturalistic theory of history). The zeitgeist approach contends that discoveries and new ideas do not develop in a vacuum and therefore must be interpreted in light of the prevailing "spirit of the times" (Boring, 1950). With this approach in mind, we have organized this review of team research in the 20th century to more fully capture the essence of the key actors and events as they relate to teamwork.

We begin our discussion with the early 1900s. However, this was not the first time in history a "revolution" had generated interest in collectives. Previous marked advances in stone tool making had already led to a dependence on hunting parties, whereas agricultural innovations led to the widespread use of farming groups. In fact, in retrospect the opening act of the 20th century did not even turn out to be the most important period during which interest in collectives was spurred on by fundamental societal changes. Certainly, a strong argument could be advanced that the current technological revolution holds more promise for understanding the nature of teams, and for reaping the benefits of teamwork, than during any previous historical period.

We begin this chapter by reviewing team research that occurred during the first 30 years of the 20th century. We then proceed to structure our review around successive 20-year periods. Within these time frames, the events and people that exemplify team research and practice are presented and lessons learned follow each section. Reflected in our choice of content for inclusion is the belief that although the first 60 years of the 20th century were an important time for teams, an even stronger wave of studies addressing team phenomena has occurred during the last 4 decades, and especially during the last 25 years (see, e.g., Beyerlein, Johnson, & Beyerlein, 2003; Campbell & Kuncel, 2001; Campion, Medsker, & Higgs, 1993; Cohen & Bailey, 1997; Edmondson, 1999; Fleishman & Zaccaro, 1992; Guzzo & Dickson, 1996; Hackman, 1990; Ilgen, 1999; Kozlowski & Bell, 2003; Marks, Mathieu, & Zaccaro, 2001; McGrath, Arrow, & Berdahl, 2000; Salas, Stagl & Burke, 2004; Sundstrom, McIntyre, Halfhill, & Richards, 2000; Swezey & Salas, 1992; West, Tjosvold, & Smith, 2003; Zaccaro, Rittman, & Marks, 2001). Consequently, the majority of this chapter is dedicated to recent programmatic research initiatives investigating team phenomena undertaken within the last 40 years. Figure 17.1 provides a timeline of notable events to help frame the current chapter.

GROUPS OR TEAMS?

An important issue at the outset of this chapter concerns the differences between the terminologies used in the group and team literature at different times throughout history. While examining the historical evolution of work teams in organizations, we were faced with a dilemma about the appropriate breadth for this review. In other words, should we limit the scope of this chapter to cover only what is termed *work teams* or do we adopt a more inclusive stance by reviewing all group and team research over the last 100 years? This dilemma is indicative of the larger ongoing debate about the similarities and differences between groups and teams. This issue has been addressed in numerous other publications (see Fleishman & Zaccaro, 1992; Guzzo & Dickson, 1996; Guzzo & Shea, 1992; Katzenbach & Smith, 1993; Salas, Dickinson, Converse, & Tannenbaum, 1992), and forging an ultimate resolution is beyond the scope of this chapter. Instead, we define both terms to clarify their use within the present chapter.

Work groups are defined herein as a (a) social entity, (b) nested within a larger social and technical system, (c) consisting of members who may work interdependently to complete shared tasks, (d) whose outcomes affect others in the larger system, as well as each other (Guzzo & Dickson, 1996). *Teams* are conceptualized to be similar to but different from work groups. Specifically, work teams are defined herein as complex entities characterized by (a) two or more individuals (b) who interact socially, (c) dynamically, (d) recursively, (e) adaptively; (f) who have shared or common valued goals; (g) who hold meaningful and high levels of task, feedback, and goal interdependencies; (h) who are often hierarchically structured; (i) whose group has a limited life span; (j) whose expertise and roles are distributed and (k) who are embedded within an organizational/environmental context that influences and is influenced by enacted competencies and processes, emergent cognitive and affective states, performance outcomes, and stakeholder judgments of team member and team effectiveness (Salas, Stagl, Burke, & Goodwin, in press).

We believe that teams develop from groups based on shared commitment and "strive for synergy among members" (Guzzo & Dickson, 1996 p. 309). One key differentiation between groups and teams is that the former have individual accountability, whereas the latter have both individual and mutual member accountability (Katzenbach & Smith, 1993). This conceptualization of teams reflects the sentiment that simply putting individuals in a group does not mean that they constitute a team (Katzenbach & Smith, 1993; Salas, Bowers, & Cannon-Bowers, 1995).

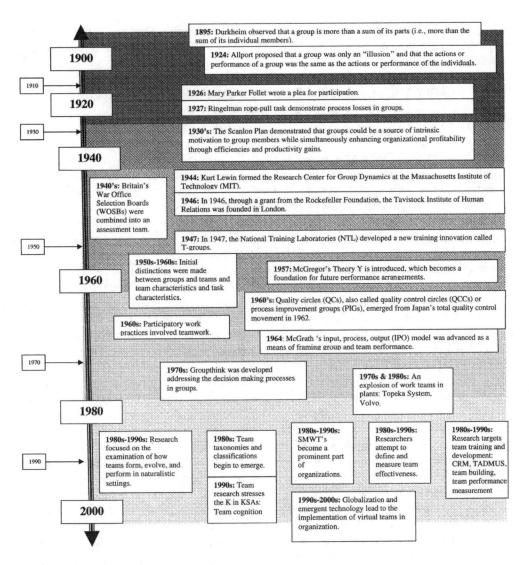

FIG. 17.1.   History of Teams Timeline.

In this chapter, the terms *teams* and *groups* are used interchangeably for a number of reasons. First, much of the earliest research investigating collectives was conducted by social psychologists, and this literature addresses groups (Levine & Moreland, 1991). In contrast to initial efforts to understand such collectives, more recent research has been undertaken from an organizational psychology perspective and predominantly emphasizes teams (Ilgen, 1999). Therefore, the term *groups* is more appropriate for most of the research and practice described at the beginning of this chapter, whereas the term *teams* is more appropriate for research described in the later time periods reviewed. In fact, team research grew out of group research, so there is a natural, temporal progression. We acknowledge that there may be degrees of difference between work teams and groups. However, we do not dwell in these distinctions; rather, throughout this review, as noted, we use the terms interchangeably. Our goal in this chapter is to provide a rich picture of the historical development of the theory, research, and practice centered on collectives.

EARLY THEORIES AND RESEARCH ON GROUPS: 1900–1920S

Enduring Themes

In the initial decades of the 1900s, researchers predominantly trained in psychology (e.g., social, clinical, experimental), engineering, and management began publishing their theories on group phenomena. This movement coincided with the burgeoning industrial revolution ongoing in the United States and worldwide, described in previous chapters.

The three decades from 1900 to 1930 are, however, a valuable resource for team researchers and practitioners. This 30-year period was the first time in history that group issues were addressed on a large scale using the scientific method. In their quest for efficiency (i.e., Efficiency = Outputs / Inputs), the supporters of scientific management had convinced key stakeholders of the necessity to govern their private and public sector institutions via the rational analysis of data in lieu of relying on intuition or rules of thumb (Shafritz & Ott, 2001). The resulting body of knowledge provided a necessary but insufficient set of circumstances to facilitate organizational administration. The missing ingredient was a set of frameworks from which to interpret the collected facts, and this key element was advanced by the great classical organizational theorists (e.g., Webber, Taylor, Barnard) at the dawn of the 20th century.

Admittedly, most of the classical theorists did not start out with the intention of directly addressing group or team issues per se. However, their theories ultimately had profound implications for individuals, groups, organizations, industries, and entire economies. In fact, the two most enduring themes of the classical period (i.e., coordination, cooperation) are both directly relevant to the core of teamwork. Coordination concerns the ongoing balancing act between horizontal differentiation (i.e. division of labor) and vertical integration (i.e., hierarchy). Cooperation is grounded in the mutual interests of subordinates and their supervisors for the greater good of the enterprise.

The classical thinkers were the first to espouse the essential role of the behavioral sciences in achieving coordination and cooperation by proactively managing organizational structure and subordinate attitudes, motivation, and actions (Shafritz & Ott, 2001). Despite the backlash against classical organizational theory by subsequent schools of thought, both coordination and cooperation remain enduring themes into the 21st century. In fact, coordination and cooperation are so prominent that they are repeatedly reflected in the team theory, research, and practice presented in this section, as well as throughout the remainder of this chapter. The contents of this retrospective examination support our belief that modern theorists, researchers, and practitioners would be well advised to ground their initiatives in the lessons learned over the 100 years of group and team history.

Early Group Theories

One example of late 19th- and early 20th-century research is found in the work of French sociologist and philosopher Emile Durkheim (1895). Durkheim's research took a gestalt approach in examining how divisions of labor affect how people work together. Specifically, Durkheim (1895) observed that a group is more than a sum of its parts (i.e., more than the sum of its individual members). This insightful finding and its wide-ranging implications helped propel a century of team research and led Durkheim (1895) to state, "It is a condition of the group repeated in individuals because it imposes itself upon them. It is in each part because it is in the whole, but far from being in the whole because it is in the parts" (p. 56).

Unfortunately, the years before the First World War yielded little in the way of unequivocal results regarding groups. However, with the onset of World War I, the world and its inhabitants changed dramatically. The United States, as well as its allies, engaged in an unprecedented united effort both on the war front and at the home front to meet the previously unimaginable challenges that surfaced almost daily. Although teams were undoubtedly central to this effort, little, if any, time could be spent on the systematic exploration and documentation of team issues.

In addition to the fundamental changes going on in the world, psychology itself was experiencing a paradigm shift. After John Watson's 1913 behaviorism manifesto *Psychology as the Behaviorist Views It* (Watson, 1913), psychologists focused on observable individual phenomena (see also chaps. 11 and 15). This widespread preoccupation with the observable aspects of individuals led to less interest in and acceptance of group studies often grounded in social psychology. In fact, Floyd Henry Allport, a prominent social psychologist, said the following about his reception at Harvard University after World War I

> I found Behaviorism ascendant and rampant. I found that though my Social Psychology had enjoyed before the war a much larger vogue than I had realized, it and I were now back-numbers, relics of a bygone and superseded age.... Another difficulty which I had not foreseen was that the numerous graduate students ... with very few exceptions ... had been taught some form of mechanistic psychology, with the consequence that they looked upon me and my outlandish theories with suspicion. (as cited by McDougall, 1930, p. 213)

Before his death in 1916, Hugo Münsterberg had successfully lobbied Allport to refocus his dissertation research on groups. Allport accepted the challenge and emerged as an influential group researcher who reported his theories as part of his widely acclaimed 1924 book *Social Psychology*. In contrast to Durkheim's research, Allport (1924) proposed that a group was only an "illusion" and that the actions or performance of a group was the same as the actions or performance of the individuals comprising the collective. Although this theory starkly opposed Durkheim's position advanced decades earlier, and much of what is accepted about teams today, it was nonetheless important research in its own right. It, after all, was one of the few initiatives that systematically investigated group issues in an environment not yet friendly to research.

Other research undertaken in the first 3 decades of the 20th century also produced evidence that group performance could hinder productivity. For example, the results from experiments such as the "Ringelman rope-pull" suggested that group force on a rope-pulling task was less than the sum of the force expected when group members pulled alone (Moede, 1927). Over the next 40 years, researchers replicated these results (Ingham, Levinger, Graves, & Peckham, 1974; Steiner, 1972). This later research revealed that "process losses," or what we call today "performance decrements," were largely due to a lack of member motivation and coordination. This interpretation is consistent with the fact that the groups assessed in Moede's studies consisted of members with little or no history or investment in the group. Moede's programmatic research, and others following it in the same vein, eventually led Steiner (1972) to conclude that actual group productivity equals potential group productivity minus processes losses plus process gains (i.e., $AP = PP - PL + PG$).

Key Contributors

F. W. Taylor. As noted previously, the first 3 decades of the 20th century were a relatively quiet time in team research. However, during these 30 years there was a building wave of support for the tenets of Taylorism (i.e., scientific management; see also chap. 10), which focused on achieving valued organizational objectives by maximizing the efficiency of the individual worker (Taylor, 1911). Taylor's approach to organizing industry did not emerge in isolation; in fact, it was heavily influenced by his friend and predecessor Henry Towne and by Adam Smith's seminal work on modern economic thought, *The Wealth of Nations* (see also chap. 1).

What is ironic is that scientific management, with its predominant focus on individuals, ultimately spawned the development of theories that influenced how groups work together. On closer inspection, however, perhaps this turn of events is not so surprising given that the fourth principle of scientific management centers on fostering teamwork. Specifically, Taylor suggested that the success of an organization hinges on a redivision of work responsibilities to create tighter interdependencies and thereby teamwork between management and workers. Taylor described this new arrangement as a "democracy" or "co-operation" (Taylor, 1911).

Mary Follett.   The principles of participation rest on the premise that leadership is granted by those who are governed. This same line of reasoning has been repeatedly articulated by the likes of John Locke, Jean Rousseau, and the authors of the Declaration of Independence (McCarthy, 2002). By the 1920s, however, the practice of participative management began for the first time in history to receive systematic scientific inquiry. Organizational scholars such as Mary Parker Follet (1926) wrote a plea for participation. Although Follett's research appeared in the same historical period as Taylorism, her ideas, and the assumptions underlying them, starkly differed from the classical thinkers. In fact, coupled with the research undertaken by the Mayo team in the Western Electric Co. Hawthorne studies (see Roethlisberger, 1941), Follett's ideas represent some of the original statements comprising the organizational behavior/human resource paradigm of organizational theory (see chaps. 2 and 16).

Follett's plea for participation focused on three core thrusts: collective responsibility, cross-functioning, and a system of committees whose purpose was integration (Beyerlein & Porter, 2000). Follett proclaimed that positive attitudes could be fostered if both employees and employers cooperated to discover the law of the situation. Once identified, the law could be dictated to either party by the other. This line of thinking emphasized a participatory approach to leadership and resonated with stakeholders at all echelons in the system. Furthermore, other ongoing research (see Lewin, 1939) paralleled Follet's ideas. This second stream of research suggested that leadership is a function of the situation and the organizational environment within which an individual is embedded, thus emphasizing the importance of context (Bavelas, 1960) and continuous feedback for enabling free will and self-direction (Argyris, 1970; Drucker, 1992).

However innovative Follett's ideas were, her views were largely ignored at the time. Perhaps this is not surprising given the subjugated status afforded to women in the early 20th century. Furthermore, the milieu of the times was characterized by an escalating effort to fuel an ever-expanding hedonistic society (i.e., the "Roaring Twenties"). Fortunately, a new breed of scholars (e.g., Follett, Roethlisberger, Janis), most closely aligned with the emerging organizational behavior/human resource paradigm of organizational theory, advanced innovative ideas and via their persistence reshaped the organizational landscape. The work of Follett as detailed here, as well as research described in forthcoming sections of this chapter, collectively shifted the accepted paradigm from a state of worker dependence on management to a state of codependence (Shafritz & Ott, 2001).

Some Early Lessons Learned

Lesson Learned 1: Emphasis on collective behavior has been driven by repeated waves of historical revolution including those made in farming, manufacturing, and technology.

Lesson Learned 2: Group issues can be studied scientifically (Roethlisberger, 1941).

Lesson Learned 3: Groups can be beneficial (Durkheim, 1895), but sometimes they are not and result in process losses (Allport, 1924; Moede, 1927; Steiner, 1972).

Lesson Learned 4: The "whole is more than the sum of its parts" in groups (Durkheim, 1895).

Lesson Learned 5: Context matters. That is, members of organizations, and by extension groups, are influenced by their operational environment (Lewin, 1939; Bavelas, 1960).

Lesson Learned 6: Optimizing human resources is equally important to achieving organizational objectives as making the most of material resources (Taylor, 1911).

IMPORTANT DEVELOPMENTS IN THE 1930s AND 1940s

The Scanlon Plan

During the economic chaos of the Great Depression, organizations became increasingly cognizant of the business necessity to maximize all of their available material and human resources. For example, CANCADE Ltd., a manufacturer of agricultural and construction equipment, describe on their Web site how they survived the Great Depression by staying lean and avoiding the expenses incurred by typical manufacturing bureaucracies at the time. Regardless of their industry, mission, or strategy, organizations were highly concerned with trying to make a dollar out of 15 cents.

In some cases, maximizing resources meant a single-minded focus on slashing costs that seems to parallel similar industry approaches more than 70 years later during the economic recession that marked the early 21st century. Some circles, however, slowly became aware of the need to simultaneously cut costs and increase productivity in order to grow revenue and meet other established objectives. Intertwined with this new emphasis on increasing productivity was a growing appreciation for the value of human resources to achieving growth and revenue targets. Furthermore, there was a greater appreciation for treating individuals with respect and dignity, not just as human capital.

It was during these tough times that Joe Scanlon devised a plan to steer through the fiscal crisis. Scanlon, a union leader in the steel industry, forged cost-saving/sharing plans for both workers and management. The success of the Scanlon plan led to the process being benchmarked and implemented across many other organizations and is largely credited with keeping many companies afloat during these turbulent economic circumstances (Frost, 1974). In fact, derivatives of this approach were found to be effective even after the Great Depression ended. Perhaps the most unique aspect of Scanlon's approach was its firm commitment to participative decision making. It demonstrated that groups could be a source of intrinsic motivation to group members while simultaneously enhancing organizational profitability through efficiencies and productivity gains (Frost, 1974).

Team-Based Selection Boards

"The war to end all wars" (i.e., World War II) changed the face of the political, economic, and social landscape of the 20th century and beyond. One result of this turning point is witnessed in the increasing number of research studies and industry interventions focusing on and including teams. An example of this shift is found in Britain's War Office Selection Boards (WOSBs). A given WOSB consisted of a president, a psychiatrist, a psychologist, and military testing officers. The psychiatrists and psychologists who set up and comprised the WOSBs were recruited heavily from the Tavistock Institute of Medical Psychology, which came to prominence during the 1940s.

Although initially each member of the WOSB council was responsible for a specific piece of the holistic assessment process, over time this fragmented approach "violated the sensibilities of the assessors who valued the rounded judgment based on observation of the total person" (Highhouse, 2002a, p. 368). Eventually, WOSB assessors were combined into an assessment team that worked together as an interdependent assessment unit to gauge candidate potential. Although the interdependencies of these teams were not as high as typically witnessed in military teams, such as action teams and command and control teams, assessors did regularly meet to exchange information and reach overall judgments about a candidate's effectiveness (see also chap. 4).

Benchmarking Britain's success with the WOSBs, the Office of Strategic Services (OSS) implemented assessment teams in the United States. The OSS used teams of assessors to interrogate, interview, and assess would-be spies and saboteurs. One goal of this process was to gauge how a candidate would respond to the intensive pressures and possible torture that would occur if one were captured behind enemy lines. Derivatives of this process still exist today and have been instituted by many other countries with advanced military and intelligence infrastructures (see also chaps. 7 and 8).

The use of assessor teams by the WOSB and OSS to meet the challenges posed by World War II is far from the only or even most important use of teams in the military. Indeed, teams have stood the test of time, and their use in the military to perform complex missions continues to increase today, perhaps largely so because teams are an intuitive work unit (Salas & Cannon-Bowers, 2000). In the decades following the World Wars, team research and practice began to accelerate, albeit slowly at first, and this movement is discussed in greater detail in the next section.

Tavistock Institute

The second World War also led to another global phenomenon, the large-scale exchange of resources across borders. This change is reflected in the programmatic research of Trist and Emory. Specifically, World War II brought together a number of talented psychologists, psychiatrists, and anthropologists through the British Army (Trist, Emory, Murray, & Trist, 1997). This group of scholars was known as the Tavistock Institute and is credited with generating many innovative social ideas. As previously described in chapters 4 and 14, in 1946, through a grant from the Rockefeller Foundation, the Tavistock Institute of Human Relations was founded in London. Its goals included understanding the health and well-being, conflict, and breakdown of individuals and organizations. Researchers at the Tavistock Institute viewed organizations as open, sociotechnical systems, in that "any system (biological or business organization) must continually interact across boundaries with its environment to obtain inputs and to discharge output" (Beyerlein & Porter, 2000, p. 9).

Tavistock researchers conducted studies on a myriad of topics including the "longwall method," which introduced some automation to the process of cutting and blasting coal in the 1950s in the form of conveyor belts. Although expected to improve efficiency, the method significantly altered the nature of the roles, interpersonal relationships, and social structure of the coal-mining teams and often led to a complete breakdown in production.

A hard lesson from the Tavistock coal-mining studies speaks to the implementation of technology from a purely engineering perspective. When organizations are primarily preoccupied with parts instead of people, the implementation of technology can backfire and ultimately damage the social relationships of team members to a degree that a machine can no longer be used efficiently. As organizations have grown increasingly dependent on technology, the lessons learned from the Tavistock Institute have generalized far beyond coal miners. In fact, the importance of fostering positive social relationships within teams continues to be an issue of concern well into the 21st century.

The Tavistock Institute also brought about the examination of groups by clinicians, for example, Bion's (1948) psychoanalytic theory of groups, which addressed group attitudes and beliefs. This theory proposed that any one work group consists of two belief systems: (a) the work group belief system (i.e., performance oriented and cognizant of the group's purpose) and (b) the basic assumption belief system (i.e., dysfunctional latent assumptions that interfere with group performance). The basic assumption belief system is further characterized by dependency and unconscious fears of inadequacy and incompetence, which undermine a group's ability to perform rationally. Although not prevalent in modern organizational thinking, training in Bion's theory is still available through the Tavistock Institute of London and at the A. K. Rice Institute in the United States.

Key Contributors

Kurt Lewin and the Research Center for Group Dynamics.   Kurt Lewin's research has profoundly affected the domains of leadership, experiential learning, action research, and group dynamics. In 1944, Lewin formed the Research Center for Group Dynamics at the Massachusetts Institute of Technology (MIT) (Beyerlein & Porter, 2000). The MIT center was chiefly concerned with group productivity, communication, social perception, intergroup relationships, group membership, and training group leaders. After 4 years at MIT, Lewin's research center relocated to the University of Michigan as a division of the Institute for Social Research. In conjunction with the Office of Naval Research, Lewin and colleagues also laid the groundwork for the National Training Laboratories, which are addressed in greater detail later in this chapter.

Lewin continues to be a powerful force who has affected many areas of scientific study (e.g., management theory, organizational behavior, organizational development) via a cadre of former students who carry on his message (Tedford & Baker, 2000) and applied research institutes that "bridge the gap between basic research and the practical problems for which society needed answers" (McKeachie & Brim, 1984, p. 1254). Furthermore, Lewin's theory, research, and findings helped encourage industry to adopt participative management and other similar humanistic practices (McCarthy, 2002).

Lewin's early concept of "social climate," derived from his work on emergent leadership in small groups (clubs) of adolescent boys (see Lewin, Lippitt, & White, 1939), is credited by Fleishman (personal communication, June 20, 2005) to have influenced the design of his earlier research on the effects of "leadership climate" at the International Harvester Company (Fleishman, 1953). This research was the first to show how leadership climate, emerging from the behavior and attitudes of plant managers, influenced the nature of lower level managers' interactions with their work groups and even overrode the effects of lower managers' leadership training.

John Hemphill's Situational Factors in Leadership.   Hemphill's historic (and classic) 1949 book, *Situational Factors in Leadership,* outlines his research on the identification, measurement, and evaluation of 15 group dimensions for the description and differentiation of numerous types of groups (see Table 17.1). This work was a marked departure in the study of groups and was based on considerable conceptual, empirical, and, at that time, innovative methodological applications using large samples and stringent methods of evaluation. Among

TABLE 17.1
Commonly Examined Characteristics of Groups (Hemphill, 1949)

Group Dimensions	Dimension Description
Group size	Number of members in the group
Viscidity	Group characteristics that differentiates a group from a collection of individuals
Homogeneity	Diversity in membership (e.g., age, gender)
Flexibility	Degree group adheres to a standard set of behaviors
Permeability	Restriction on those who are considered group members or able to join the group
Polarization	Orientation toward a single, specific goal
Stability	Pace change occurs within the group
Intimacy	Degree of association among members
Autonomy	Independence from other groups
Control	Amount of behavior regulation by other team members
Position	Role or status within the group
Potency	Individual member's need satisfaction by group membership
Hedonic tone	Feelings of satisfaction, pleasantness, or agreeableness associated with group membership
Participation	Amount of time/effort spent on group tasks
Dependence	Relationship between the team and its leader in ensuring group needs are met

the many groups described in his work, Hemphill (1949) attributed the differences in the 15 dimensions to variation in leadership behavior. It is also important to note his generation of diagnostic items within each of the 15 dimension scales and further refinement of a questionnaire (Hemphill & Westie, 1950). The questionnaire used 355 descriptive statements according to these dimensions, where each statement was accompanied by a scale for rating the applicability to the group described. The scales were applied to the description of bomber groups, university departments, fraternities, athletic groups, industrial groups, and others (see Shartle, 1956). The contribution of Hemphill's work lies in the illustration of groups with different functions in a variety of organizational settings, with groups profiled according to the 15 dimensions—many of which are still useful and the subject of research today.

Some Lessons Learned

Lessons Learned 7: Collectives are a source of sustained competitive advantage (Scanlon; Frost, 1974).

Lesson Learned 8: Work groups can be studied as open, sociotechnical systems (Trist et al., 1997).

Lesson Learned 9: To succeed, collectives must freely exchange resources across team members while maintaining their interpersonal relationships. This lesson is even more salient when teamwork is made increasingly complex by the introduction of technology or additional tasks (Tavistock coal studies; Trist et al., 1997).

Lesson Learned 10: Groups and teams are not the domain of any single discipline but rather should be the focus of an integrated multidisciplinary effort (Bion, 1948).

Lesson Learned 11: Leadership behaviors matter in groups (Hemphill, 1949).

A NEW MOMENTUM IN TEAM AND GROUP RESEARCH: 1950s–1960s

The Human Resource Paradigm and Teams

In the mid-20th century, momentum was building for the humanistic ideals espoused by a growing community of researchers (e.g., Follett, Roethlisberger, McGregor, Janis). At the heart of this movement was a historically unprecedented assumption that organizations exist to serve human needs (Shafritz & Ott, 2001). This new line of thinking changed the nature of the relationship between employers and employees from one of dependence to codependence. However, although the set of assumptions underlying the human resource/organizational behavior (OB) perspective stood in stark contrast to the assumptions underlying the classical school's assertions, the new mantra of codependence only reinforced the importance of the two enduring themes of coordination and cooperation previously advanced by the classical thinkers.

The distinguished scientists noted here, along with hundreds of others, created a wave of research activity that produced an enormous body of supporting literature and methods. Slowly, these tools, techniques, strategies, and methods began to permeate the practices of many organizations. One manifestation of this movement is witnessed in the wide range of motivation theories that shaped how organizations went about proactively influencing employee attitudes, perceptions, beliefs, and motivations (e.g., Maslow's need hierarchy [Maslow, 1943], Herzberg's [Herzberg, 1966] two-factor theory). Also, these initial theories such as Herzberg's two-factor theory served as a platform for future endeavors (see Hackman & Oldham's [1975] job characteristics theory) that would eventually illuminate the complexities of motivated behavior in groups and teams.

One example of how the OB paradigm is intertwined with teamwork is found in participatory work practices. Participatory work practices encourage the use of teams because collectives can draw from their diverse reservoir of resources to better accept responsibilities traditionally reserved for management. For organizations, this meant that layers of middle management could be unceremoniously stripped away as empowered teams began to delegate work, determine strategies for task accomplishment, and resolve interpersonal conflicts. Certainly, this new state of affairs made for leaner, more adaptive organizations. In fact, recent research suggests that including employees in decision making results in higher levels of cooperation, satisfaction, productivity, and quality and lower levels of absenteeism and turnover (Manz & Neck, 1995). (See also chap. 15 for a historical perspective on participative decision making.)

Group Interventions

T-Groups. Training groups (t-groups) also became prominent in the United States postwar era. In 1947, the National Training Laboratories (NTL) developed a new training innovation known as t-groups. T-groups were an early precipitation of team building. Based on theories of human behavior, t-groups facilitated interaction by enlightening members about options for their behavior in groups. In other words, group members were given training on how to look within themselves and their groups in an effort to gain a deeper level of insight and thereby appreciation. Core components of this process included self-observation, self-disclosure, vicarious learning, and catharsis (Rogers, 1970).

Over time, t-groups led to the use of sensitivity groups, implemented to explore and enhance group members' interpersonal sensitivity. T-groups also gave way to team building, which overcame some of the problems inherent to the process (Cranton, 1996). Although t-groups are still in use today, the 1970s brought about a backlash against touchy-feely training interventions that notably curtailed the formerly widespread use of this approach (see Highhouse, 2002b).

Quality Circles.   Quality circles (QCs) are another intervention with a long and storied history. The origination of QCs is often attributed to the United States in the 1950s. However, medieval European guilds also adopted a QC approach to guarantee the quality of their crafts (McCarthy, 2002). The modern form of QCs, also known as quality control circles (QCCs) or process improvement groups (PIGs), emerged from Japan's total quality control movement in the 1960s (Glassop, 2002). Today, QCs are most closely associated with Professor Kaoru Ishikawa, who became known as the pioneer of QCs after this approach was re-exported to the West in the 1960s. QCs were developed as a training mechanism for promoting departmental quality. The key to this approach is the use of statistical processes to eliminate problems caused by unwanted variations in the work system.

In the 1960s, QCs were conducted outside normal work hours but have since been intertwined with ongoing operations to better address a wider variety of problems in a shorter period of time. Typically, modern QCs consist of small groups of co-located workers who meet for a short amount of time each week to identify, analyze, and solve various work-related problems by making recommendations to management (Tang & Butler, 1997). By the mid-1980s, QCs had been Americanized and were one of the most promising team-related strategies implemented in industry (see Bettenhausen, 1991).

Delineating the Nature of Teams

In the mid-20th century, team theory building, research, and practice began to accelerate, albeit slowly at first. The 1950s and 1960s witnessed the proposal of the initial distinctions between groups and teams and team characteristics and task characteristics by team researchers. An important example is the research of Roby and Lanzetta (1957), who studied the negative impact of task overload on team communication and performance. Also, Briggs and Johnston (1967) examined the importance of team member backup behavior in reducing flight errors. This line of research is especially important to the history of teams, given that today it is generally believed that effectiveness criteria are contingent on the nature of the team under consideration (Cohen & Bailey, 1997).

A major organizational development during this period was the establishment of the Crew Consortium Research Laboratory, as a unit of the Air Force Personnel Research and Training Center (AFPRTC) in San Antonio, Texas (see chap. 7). This was a primary effort to conduct experimental studies of group formation and functionary, team performance, and team effectiveness. The staff included Robert French (director), Thornton Roby, John Lanzetta, Donald Forgays, Lemar Berkowitz, Bernard Lery, Seymour Rosenberg, and others. The research of Roby and Lanzetta (1957) provides only one example of many developed in this laboratory and published in scientific journals. The laboratory provided one of the early opportunities to study the formation, assembly, simulation, and performance of real teams in relevant operational settings. These individuals moved on to distinguished academic careers.

In time, the research of Roby and Lanzetta (1957) and Briggs and Johnston (1967) would serve as a platform for researchers attempting to build a science of teams. For example, distinctions would be made between taskwork and teamwork. Specifically, taskwork refers to the individual behaviors team members engage in while enacting their skills during team performance. Taskwork is "a team's interactions with tasks, tools, machines and systems" (Bowers, Braun, & Morgan, 1997, p. 90). Teamwork behaviors include backup behavior, coordination, collaborative problem solving, and dynamic reallocation of function. Moreover, the behaviors that comprise teamwork can have an individual or team-level referent. The findings from this research have been essential in designing, delivering, and evaluating team processes, structures, and training interventions.

Framing Group and Team Effectiveness

In the previous section, we noted how researchers began to address the nature of teams in the mid-20th century. As findings accumulated from these programmatic initiatives, it became apparent that a framework was necessary to house the myriad of constructs comprising and impinging on team effectiveness. Researchers such as McGrath (1964) analyzed group interactions through organizing frameworks in an effort to illuminate those illusive factors that make some groups effective (i.e., process gains), whereas others experienced process losses and failure. From these efforts, the input, process, output (IPO) model was advanced as a means of framing group and team effectiveness (McGrath, 1964).

An IPO approach to understanding team effectiveness shed new light on the moment-to-moment interteam and intrateam processes that comprise teamwork. Although the idea seems simple, it was revolutionary for those concerned with teamwork to have moved beyond the basic manipulation of inputs as a means of controlling outputs and toward understanding the "black box" of team process. This movement is reflected today in the growing number of conceptualizations of team performance and effectiveness, which show an appreciation for the importance of time and its relevance for dynamic processes and their interrelationships (e.g., Dickinson & McIntyre, 1997; Marks et al., 2001; Shiflett, Eisner, Price, & Schemmer, 1985). Specifically, an IPO approach is flexible enough to model the more dynamic aspects of effectiveness (e.g., feedback loops, recursive processes, linear time, reciprocal linkages).

The use of an organizing IPO framework was indeed a major advancement in the group and team domains (e.g., Ilgen, Hollenbeck, Johnson, & Jundt, 2005). In fact, the importance of the IPO model to the study of group effectiveness can not be understated, because this approach is widely used today as an organizing framework. Over time, findings have supported the basic model, which outlines how team performance is affected by system inputs (e.g., individual, group, environmental) acting through interaction processes. However, much debate remains about the nature of the construct relations modeled within an IPO approach. This particular issue concerns whether processes are best conceptualized as mediators or moderators in the IPO chain (Kozlowski & Bell, 2003).

Key Contributors

Douglas McGregor.   If Follett and the members of the Mayo team at Hawthorne can be considered the initial visionaries of the OB movement, then the defining statement of this paradigm was advanced by Douglas Murray McGregor in 1957. As described in several other chapters, McGregor's theory X and theory Y radically reframed thinking about the nature of workers and what they could be empowered to accomplish. McGregor (1957) proposed that the managerial assumptions about the nature of workers comprising both theory X (i.e., employees are unmotivated and require constant direction) and theory Y (i.e., employees are active participants that can be developed and trusted) would, over time, crystallize to form self-fulfilling prophecies and thereby effect worker behavior.

Whereas theory X owed its epistemological roots to classical organizational theory, theory Y was a revolution that suggested workers could be trusted to provide their own self-direction, would seek out responsibility, and should develop and grow while achieving financial objectives. These basic tenets became the bedrock on which future performance arrangements (e.g., self-managing work teams, distributed teams, shared team leadership) would be built.

Irving Janis. If McGregor's assertions were the flagship for the promise of OB, Janis' ideas were equally powerful in warning about the dangers of interdependent interaction. Although the treatment of Janis (1972) in this chapter technically belongs in the next period of time reviewed in this chapter (i.e., 1970s–1980s), his research on social conformity in groups so contrasts the optimism exuded by McGregor's research that we felt a discussion of these issues within this subsection offered the reader an appropriate amount of historical balance.

Janis' (1972) research addressed "groupthink," described as the train of thought that highly cohesive group members adopt when concurrence seeking takes precedence over reality. This line of research suggests that decision making in cohesive groups during crisis situations (e.g., Vietnam, Cuba invasion, Columbia shuttle) can create a pressure to conform at all costs. Furthermore, once a decision is collectively reached, entities suffering from groupthink act to suppress dissent, overestimate their probability of success, and establish mindguards. Janis suggested that fortunately, the groupthink phenomenon is relatively easy to identify and can be effectively dealt with (see Janis, 1972).

Some Lessons Learned

Lesson Learned 12: Groups can help foster quality products and processes in organizations.
Lesson Learned 13: It is essential to recognize the importance of actively promoting group interaction and collaboration (Briggs & Johnston, 1967; Cranton, 1996).
Lesson Learned 14: Work groups are an intuitive unit that can address and solve complex organizational problems (Tang & Butler, 1997).
Lesson Learned 15: Not all teams are created equal; they vary in the degree of task interdependence.
Lessons Learned 16: Group and team effectiveness can be framed as a series of inputs, processes, and outputs (IPO; McGrath, 1964).
Lesson Learned 17: Framing group and team effectiveness from an IPO perspective facilitates modeling the dynamic "black box" of team process (McGrath, 1964).

INFLUENCE OF TECHNOLOGY ON TEAMS AND GROUPS: 1970s–1980s

Technological Advancements

In the late 1940s, the first computer was designed and just a decade later the launch of Sputnik started a space race. However, it would take until the 1970s for technology to fully captivate the public's attention. Throughout the 1970s, technological innovations were made daily, spread widely, and began to affect our everyday lives. Video games, optical fiber, barcodes, the fleet of space shuttles, genetic engineering, and the artificial heart are just a few examples of how technology began to change the world. Once again, a revolution had put teams back in the spotlight and complex context had ensured they were here to stay.

A building wave of team research began to mount in part because from designers to end users, teams were intertwined with technology. Technological advancements changed the way jobs were performed and people communicated and made decisions. Advances in technology opened the door to address previously unapproachable problems (e.g., space travel, genetic sequencing, ocean floor mapping). However, the complex nature of these challenges required more than innovative technological solutions. Problems of this magnitude required teamwork. Furthermore, society's hopes rested on the shoulders of expert teams, not just teams of experts.

During this historical period, the world was becoming increasingly characterized by a freer and liberated spirit, and this change in attitudes inevitably influenced organizations to adopt humanistic values. One manifestation of the changing perspectives is found in the widely popularized belief that employees are not just interchangeable cogs in the organizational wheel (Weber, 1972). This belief reflects the humanistic ideals that were underlying a majority of the work conducted in the previous decades, as well as much of the research in vogue at the time.

The resurgence in team research also led to much theoretical and applied advancement. A wide range of research was undertaken to investigate everything from sociopsychological constructs to the deeper cognitions that permeate information processing in groups. The following subsections illustrate a representative sample of this theoretical work and illustrate applied examples for the reader in an effort to demonstrate the successful application of theory to industry.

Work Groups in Plants

General Foods.   An explosion of team implementations took place in the 1970s in response to new technologies used in manufacturing plants and warehouses. These technological innovations resulted in more complex workplaces and necessitated the need for teams to handle the operational complexity and to maximize the value of these new technologies. For example, the General Foods plant in Topeka, Kansas, is one of the most widely cited case studies of the implementation of a humanistic management approach. Specifically, "the plant has taken a position in many minds as a classic demonstration of the power of a system-wide organizational innovation, quality-of-work-life interventions, and sociotechnical systems approaches" (Whitsett & Yorks, 1983, p. 93).

As described in chapter 14, the planners of the Topeka plant aimed to create an organization that not only would be efficient but would also provide employees with jobs that would be rewarding, interesting, and challenging. Their most innovative vision was to have the plant evolve to a self-managing multiteam system. This vision, once taken to fruition, would largely alleviate the need for formal management, give all personnel an equal voice in the plant activities, and tear down barriers by removing differential status symbols common in most plants (i.e., reserved parking places). On implementation, this vision was known as the Topeka system.

The Topeka system consisted of several components addressing the work design, supervisory structure, social system, and reward system. The work design component of this process included the use of three types of teams that covered the entire phase of the plant's operation: processing, packaging/shipping, and office support. Each team, including approximately 14 members, was empowered to control how tasks would be completed. The teams also managed the process of interviewing new job applicants, redistributing work when members were absent, scheduling breaks, establishing and changing schedules, conducting performance evaluations, and counseling those not meeting established quality control standards. The supervisory structure under the Topeka system was also novel in that team leaders were chosen to be "managers of people rather than technical specialists" (Whitsett, & Yorks, 1983, p. 96).

The reward system is unquestionably the most innovative aspect of the Topeka system because it was designed to compensate employees for mastering both individual and team KSAs. Specifically, the compensation system consisted of four pay rates that varied on a sliding scale ascending as a function of employee knowledge and skill development. This compensation system was designed to encourage employees to proactively engage in self-development rather than reactively waiting for formally sponsored organizational training to be administered.

Each employee in the Topeka system started at the same rate. An employee could then be raised to the "single job rate" when it was determined by the team leader that he or she had mastered the initial job assignment. The next rate was the "team rate" and was earned when the employee mastered the jobs of all the team members. Finally, a "plant rate" could be earned when an employee learned all of the jobs in the entire plant. There was also an "add-on" rate if the employee had some special capability, such as electrical maintenance (Whitsett & Yorks, 1983).

Although the Topeka plant was intended to be innovative and was eventually modeled in other General Foods plants, the dream was never fully achieved as it had been envisioned (Whitsett, & Yorks, 1983; see chap. 14). However, it should be noted that team members in the Topeka system responded enthusiastically to this intervention. In fact, product quality was uniformly high (e.g., 10% to 40% greater than comparable organizations), absenteeism and turnover were significantly below industry standards, and theft was reported to be negligible ("The Plant," 1972).

Volvo.   Volvo has a long history of employee-centered innovation that is now in part credited for its status as a world-class automaker and organization. Pehr Gyllenhammer became Volvo's CEO in 1971 and believed that if Volvo was to remain a world-class competitor, the corporate culture had to change (Bernstein, 1988). Under Gyllenhammer's leadership, Volvo attempted to improve job satisfaction through job rotation, management–employee councils, small work groups, modern technology, and employee-oriented facilities (Gyllenhammer, 1973).

One example of Volvo's innovativeness took place in the upholstery division at the Torslanda plant (Bernstein, 1988). Incumbents of this division often complained of work-related muscle strains due to the repetitive nature of their work. To remedy this problem, the workers began experimenting with groups and found that through job rotation and cross-training, their muscle strains were largely eliminated. Furthermore, the implemented work changes resulted in secondary benefits such as improved group cohesion and a renewed emphasis on quality. The Lundby plant is a second example of teams implemented in Volvo (Bernstein, 1988). Managers of the Lundby plant empowered teams to be responsible for individual functions or parts of the car. The implementation of these "functional teams" resulted in higher productivity and quality by increasing employee involvement.

A third example of how Volvo used teams to achieve its organizational objectives is found in the Kalmar plant, built in 1974. The Kalmar plant relied heavily on teams. However, unlike the General Foods Topeka plant discussed earlier, this facility was specifically designed to facilitate teamwork. For example, the physical design of the plant encouraged greater employee productivity by providing work team collaboration areas, more windows and sunlight, and a less pressured work environment. Furthermore, the work itself was organized so that each group was responsible for a particular portion of the car. This method of automobile assembly provided the group with a sense of task identity (see Hackman & Oldham, 1975) via a product that they could craft from start to finish. Today, Kalmar exemplifies a successful team implementation that was due in large part to organizational support for teams, joint decision making, communication, flexible work schedules, and new production technologies (Bernstein, 1988).

Some Lessons Learned

Lesson Learned 18: People should be managed in teams and groups, not just the technology (Whitsett & Yorks, 1983).

Lesson Learned 19: Organizations that use teams can be efficient while providing employees with jobs that are rewarding, interesting, and challenging (General Foods).

Lesson Learned 20: Many aspects (e.g., work design, supervisory structure, social system, rewards) of the same system should be changed simultaneously to foster teamwork (Topeka system).

Lesson Learned 21: Employees should be compensated for mastering both individual and team-based KSAs (Topeka system).

Lesson Learned 22: Functional teamwork (e.g., empowering teams to be responsible for individual functions) increases involvement (Hackman & Lawler, 1971)

Lesson Learned 23: Teams share the load because team members can compensate for one another to ensure everyone remains healthy and productive (Bernstein, 1988).

Lesson Learned 24: Job/task characteristics can be manipulated to induce desired cognitive and affective states and thereby increase desired individual, as well as team, outcomes (Hackman & Oldham, 1975).

THE BOOMING AND EXPLOSIVE 1990S AND BEYOND

Team Maturation

The systematic study of group and team maturation has been ongoing for almost 4 decades. One of the first researchers to engage in this line of work was Tuckman (1965), who examined the maturation of t-groups, therapy groups, and laboratory groups. From his research findings Tuckman delineated and advanced a stage model of group development. This classic model illustrates how groups develop over time by transcending from one stage to the next (see Wheelan, 1994). Four stages are typically proposed in most maturation conceptualizations including forming, storming, norming, and performing. Occasionally, a fifth stage (i.e., adjourning) is also used to describe the process via which groups dissolve.

Although Tuckman's seminal work has served as a platform for current research initiatives, its primary focus on interpersonal conflict has limited its widespread applicability to understanding teamwork. As a result of this restricted focus, a stage approach usually fails to model many of the important aspects of context, tasks, and the often discontinuous configural compilation process via which team member inputs, dyadic role exchanges, and team level contributions emerge to form team performance (Kozlowski & Bell, 2003).

Fortunately, research is underway to examine how teams form, evolve, and perform in naturalistic settings (see Ancona & Chong, 1999; Edmondson, 1999; Gersick, 1989; Harrison, Mohammed, McGrath, Florey, & Vanderstoep, 2003; Ilgen, 1999; Kozlowski, Gully, Nason, & Smith, 1999; Morgan, Salas, & Glickman, 1993; Sheard & Kakabadse, 2002). This research has been undertaken to address some of the previously noted weaknesses of the classic stage models by approaching maturation and performance from a more integrative, contextualized perspective.

Some of the findings from this new breed of research suggest that team development may be driven as much by temporal entrainments as by interpersonal dynamics (Gersick, 1989). Furthermore, theoretical and empirical research suggests that maturation requires the development of both taskwork and teamwork KSAs (Glickman et al., 1987; Marks et al., 2001; Morgan et al., 1993). In addition, Kozlowski and colleagues (1999) advanced a team compilation model that includes aspects of both team development and performance.

Team Performance and Effectiveness

All of the research discussed in this historical review contributes to the collective understanding about team performance and stakeholder judgments about the effectiveness of team performance. However, a growing number of initiatives have directly addressed the complexities of team performance and effectiveness by advancing integrative theories on the issue (see Dickinson & McIntyre, 1997; Gersick, 1988; Gladstein, 1984; Hackman, 1987; Marks et al., 2001; Nieva, Fleishman, & Reick, 1978; Tannenbaum, Beard, & Salas, 1992). One comprehensive synthesis of this literature identified more than 800 empirical studies addressing some aspect of teamwork and 138 models and frameworks of team performance and effectiveness that have been advanced in just the last 25 years (Salas, Stagl, Burke, & Goodwin, in press). In fact, the results of this review suggest that there was a 257% increase in the number of models and frameworks of team performance and effectiveness advanced in the 1990s compared with the prior decade.

Although even a surface-level discussion of these 138 models and frameworks of team performance and effectiveness is beyond the scope of this chapter, one comprehensive initiative undertaken by Campion and colleagues is briefly reviewed as an illustrative example of this body of research. Campion et al. (1993) advanced a "meta" model that highlights the importance of five categories of variables (i.e., job design, interdependence, composition, context, process) that are proposed to directly affect team effectiveness. Each of these five categories includes a number of variables. For example, the job design category includes five specific variables: self-management, participation, task variety, task significance, and task identity. One of the greatest strengths of Campion and colleagues meta model is its empirical support accumulated from two diverse samples of teams (see Campion et al., 1993; Campion, Papper, & Medsker, 1996).

In addition to the previously noted models and frameworks, which attend to the nature of routine performance, a growing but sporadic body of theory and research has also highlighted the importance of adaptability, adaptive team performance, and team adaptation to fostering team effectiveness (Arrow, McGrath, & Berdahl, 2000; Chen & Ployhart, 2004; DeShon, Kozlowski, Schmidt, Milner, & Wiechmann, 2004; Entin & Serfaty, 1999; G. Klein & Pierce, 2001; Kozlowski et al., 2001; LePine, 2003; Marks, Zaccaro, & Mathieu, 2000; Pulakos, Arad, Donovan, & Plamondon, 2000; Pulakos et al., 2002; Waller, 1999). Despite the importance of team adaptation to team effectiveness, little is currently known about the nature of this construct or the proximal and distal constructs contributing to it (Campbell & Kuncel, 2001). In fact, to date team adaptation has not been the subject of systematic investigation in the behavioral sciences. Thus, this is one area that is ripe for theory building, laboratory research, and qualitative and quantitative field studies.

Team Types and Taxonomies

The current science of teams is the result of a century of effort by scientist practitioners from a wide range of disciplines and philosophies engaging in theory building, research, and practice. Unfortunately, however, the varying assumptions, approaches, and interpretations of these theoreticians, researchers, and practitioners have created a diverse and sometimes unconnected body of team research findings. In an effort to impose structure on this diffuse body of knowledge, researchers have undertaken taxonomic initiatives (e.g., Fleishman & Zaccaro, 1992). The purpose of these endeavors is to define and classify elements to infer general statements about property classes and class interrelations (Fleishman & Quaintance, 1984). Taxonomic initiatives are increasingly important for capturing and codifying accumulated findings because there is an accelerating storm of team research and application as we begin the new millennium. In fact, encoding what is currently known is a challenge for team researchers as well as the behavioral sciences in general (Campbell, 1990).

Fleishman (1975) and Fleishman and Quaintance (1984) described an extensive conceptual and empirical process to develop and assess taxonomies of human performance that would enhance predictions and generalizations about human performance. Primary considerations were the adoption of task definitions that permitted reliable task descriptions, the inclusion of categories that were neither specific nor too general, the development of measurement systems that correspond to taxonomic categories, and the establishment of criteria for psychometric assessment of these approaches.

Fleishman and his colleagues extended this work on individual performance taxonomies to the analysis and assessment of team performance (Cooper, Shiflett, Korotkin, & Fleishman, 1984; Fleishman & Zaccaro, 1992; Nieva et al., 1978; Shiflett et al., 1985). This multiyear effort, initially supported by the Army Research Institute and the Air Force Systems Command, involved considerable conceptual and methodological development and application of a measurement system to evaluate interactions among team descriptions, their reliability and independence, and their validity for predicting team performance (e.g., using Army construction units, command and control teams, etc.). It appears that a meaningful taxonomy and measurement system for describing and evaluating team performance functions, emphasizing requirements for coordinated actions of team members to produce synchronized output, can be developed. Table 17.2 provides a recent outline of this taxonomy (Fleishman & Zaccaro, 1992).

One area that has particularly benefited from the application of taxonomies is the study of team types. Over the last quarter of the 20th century, organizations began to increasingly use

TABLE 17.2
A Taxonomy of Team Functions

I. Orientation functions
 a. Information exchange regarding member resources and constraints
 b. Information exchange regarding team task and goals/mission
 c. Information exchange regarding environmental characteristics and constraints
 d. Priority assignment among tasks

II. Resource distribution functions
 a. Matching member resources to task requirements
 b. Load balancing

III. Timing functions (activity pacing)
 a. General activity pacing
 b. Individually oriented activity pacing

IV. Response coordination functions
 a. Response sequencing
 b. Time and position coordination of responses

V. Motivational functions
 a. Development of team performance norms
 b. Generating acceptance of team performance norms
 c. Establishing team-level performance–rewards linkages
 d. Reinforcement of task orientation
 e. Balancing team orientation with individual competition
 f. Resolution of performance-relevant conflicts

VI. Systems monitoring functions
 a. General activity monitoring
 b. Individual activity monitoring
 c. Adjustment of team and member activities in response to errors and omissions

VII. Procedure maintenance
 a. Monitoring of general procedural-based activities
 b. Monitoring of individual procedural-based activities
 c. Adjustments of nonstandard activities

Note. From Fleishman & Zacarro (1992).

teams for many different functions. In response, a building wave of research has been undertaken and theoretical advancements have been made by directing attention toward different "types" of teams (e.g., action teams, self-managing teams, management teams). In fact, over the past century, dozens of team types have been advanced.

In an effort to impose structure on the multiple labels that exist in the current literature base, several researchers have created team typologies (e.g., Argote & McGrath, 1993; Cohen & Bailey, 1997; Devine, 2002; Devine, Clayton, Philips, Dunford, & Melner, 1999; Hackman, 1990; Mohrman, Cohen, & Mohrman, 1995; Sundstrom, DeMeuse, & Futrell, 1990; Sundstrom et al., 2000). For example, one widely accepted team typology was presented by Sundstrom and colleagues (2000), who condensed a myriad of team labels into six main types of teams: management, project, product, service, action, and parallel. These researchers chose to classify and describe team types on the basis of differentiation, external integration, and work cycles (see Sundstrom et al., 2000). A similar initiative by Devine (2002) resulted in 14 team types. Devine's (2002) effort emphasizes teams performing day-to-day operations, teams engaged in intellectual work, and relevant contextual forces.

All of these types of teams serve different purposes. Furthermore, the organizational culture, team size and structure, and organizational support, to name a few, affect the success of each type of team within its own organization. This is critical because team effectiveness criteria vary with the team type under consideration (Cohen & Bailey, 1997). Thus, the efforts just reviewed and other similar initiatives are essential to understanding team effectiveness and to designing interventions to foster teamwork.

In addition to the general team typologies reviewed here, a number of specific types of teams have been investigated. One of the most important types of teams operating in dynamic environments is the self-managing work team (SMWT; Pearce & Ravlin, 1987). In response to modern, chaotic context, organizations are enabling and empowering team members to make real-time tactical decisions. A primary reason for the growing base of support behind this approach is that organizations are increasingly cognizant of the value gained from enabling team members to act in a proactive, adaptive manner to capitalize on opportunities while simultaneously reducing the losses incurred when it is necessary to react to events.

Self-managing work teams are empowered to manage themselves and therefore continually focus on improving their own work processes. As such, these teams are responsible for much of what would traditionally be accomplished by hierarchical leadership outside the team. Although there is some degree of variability, typical characteristics of SMWT include (a) a distinct set of tasks that workers can identify with, (b) members with a variety of skills that are related to the task, and (c) high levels of empowerment (i.e., discretion over how work is done; Hackman, 1987). Others have argued that these teams tend to have a flat structure and shared leadership and that they emphasize leader coaching and facilitation (Wellins, Byham, & Wilson, 1991). Although SMWT have high levels of empowerment, they are still subject to some external control. For example, self-managing work teams do not typically set strategic objectives or compensation policies (Stewart, Manz, & Sims, 1999).

We suspect that the importance of self-managing work teams to organizations will continue to grow in step with the accelerating rate of operational complexity. In fact, self-managing work teams are ubiquitous in large organizations as witnessed by a recent report indicating that 47% of Fortune 1000 companies are using them (Cohen, Ledford, & Spreitzer, 1996). It seems that despite arguments to the contrary (see Mullen & Cooper, 1994), organizations are actually "in search of excellence" (see Peters & Waterman, 1982). A major concern for such systems is the development of their members' capacities so that they can fully capitalize on their empowerment; this and other training issues are addressed in the next section.

Hierarchical Team Decision Making

Decision making is ubiquitous to teamwork and is one of the most frequently studied phenomena in the behavioral sciences. Unfortunately, however, the vast majority of research to date has applied the social decision scheme model and the social transition scheme model to understanding the consensus decisions of small groups (e.g., jury decisions; see Davis, 1992). Collectives such as juries can be characterized as a collection of largely independent members who are by nature equal in status and expertise. In contrast, teams are typically hierarchically structured, reflecting important differences in member status and expertise. Moreover, teams have much higher levels of goal, task, and feedback interdependencies than do juries and other groups. Therefore, the generalizability of the inferences that can be drawn from the accumulated findings of studies investigating consensus decisions in groups, to more highly interdependent collectives such as teams, remains an unanswered empirical question.

Fortunately, researchers have begun to move beyond the study of group decisions to systematically investigate and model the decisions of teams (see Ilgen, Major, Hollenbeck, & Sego, 1991). For example, recent research has advanced and tested multilevel theories of team decision making (see Hollenbeck, Ilgen, LePine, Colquitt, & Hedlund, 1998; Hollenbeck et al., 1995). Hollenbeck, Ilgen, and colleagues' theory of multilevel team decision making extends prior theories of group decision-making by (a) emphasizing the inputs into a decision rather than beginning with decision outcomes, (b) characterizing decision alternatives along a continuum rather than a dichotomy, and (c) modeling both individual team member and team-level decision processes. This seems to be a particularly promising approach to understanding and improving team decision making, as witnessed by research results suggesting that operationalizations of the constructs core to this theory can account for more than 50% of the variance in team performance.

Team Training and Development

Team Training.   Although a body of literature addressing training emerged in the 1920s (Ford, 1997), team training has just begun evolving into an integrated science during the past 2 decades (see Campbell & Kuncel, 2001; Kraiger, 2002; Salas & Cannon-Bowers, 2001; Tannenbaum & Yukl, 1992). One area that has received considerable attention concerns the design, development, and delivery of team-based instructional strategies. Throughout the late 1990s and into the 21st century, a number of strategies for team training began to be applied that emphasized teamwork competencies in aviation, health care, the military, and the nuclear power industry, to name a few. Team-based instructional strategies are forged from a set of methods, tools, team-based KSAs, and targeted learning outcomes. These components, when considered with organizational factors (e.g., resources, policy, size), help determine which strategy is appropriate for a given team or work group.

Another important development was the U.S. Navy's Tactical Decision Making Under Stress (TADMUS) project, which began in 1990 as an interdisciplinary research initiative undertaken to understand decision making under stress and provide instructional strategies for teams. It was the Navy's expectation that adopting a systematic approach to illuminating the complexities of decision making in high-pressure environments would lead to theoretical breakthroughs that could be translated into practical products for future use in team training and human factors technology. In retrospect, they were more than correct, because the science of team training has markedly benefited from the broad range of strategies developed through TADMUS research (see Cannon-Bowers & Salas, 1998; see also chap. 7).

The multiple, team-focused strategies available today are historically unprecedented. Organizations now have tools, techniques, and strategies that can train both team members and entire teams beyond simple task proficiency and toward skill generalization and adaptation (see chap. 12). A particular exemplar, successful in the aviation industry and more recently in health care, is discussed in greater detail next.

Crew Resource Management.   A major movement in team research took place in the skies. Cockpit or crew resource management (CRM) originated from a NASA workshop, *Resource Management on the Flightdeck,* in 1979 (Helmreich, Merritt, & Wilhelm, 1999). The program was held in response to the findings that a majority of aviation crashes could be linked to human error and specifically to failures of interpersonal communications, decision making, and leadership (Helmreich et al., 1999; Salas, Wilson, Burke, & Bowers, 2002). In fact, reports suggest that 60% to 80% of aviation crashes can be traced to pilot error, many of which are due to a lack of coordination in the cockpit (FAA, 1998). The FAA has proactively addressed this problem with CRM training as "a way to prevent aviation accidents by improving crew performance through better crew coordination" (FAA, 1998, p. 4). CRM was developed to improve and enhance the use of all resources available on the flightdeck, which includes teams, systems, interpersonal aspects of flight operations, information between team members, and information exchanged between systems and team members.

CRM has contributed to the science of team training by providing a systematic approach to optimizing team performance. In fact, CRM can be used to develop backup behavior, feedback, performance monitoring, and coordination, all processes now accepted as necessary for effective team performance. CRM remains a dynamic and encompassing training program for team effectiveness in the cockpit and can be beneficial to a variety of industries, such as natural resource refinement on oilrigs (Flin, 1995) and health care (Gaba, Howard, & Fish, 1994). For more organizational applications of CRM, see recent publications by Salas, Bowers, and Edens (2001) and Merritt and Helmreich (1995).

Team Building.   Team-building interventions were extremely popular in the 1980s but have received relatively less attention recently. Perhaps this is because the economic prosperity of the "me generation" of the 1980s led to corporate retreats and other "touchy-feely" interventions similar to t-groups. By nature, team building stresses the importance of an action research model of data collection, action planning, and feedback. Although a great deal of research on team building was conducted in the 1960s through the 1980s, more recent endeavors are characterized by a concentration on increasing role clarification and social aspects of teams. Although team building has been found to lead to many positive affective outcomes for team members, questions remain about the behavioral changes of teams following these interventions (Salas, Rozell, Mullen, & Driskell, 1999).

Team Performance Measurement

As teams began to be better understood through the 1990s, the complexity of teamwork led to a growing concern for how to measure team process and performance (see Brannick, Salas, & Prince, 1997; Day & Lance, 2004). By this time, researchers and practitioners had come to the realization that teams are different from both their constituent members and from each other. Previously, highly informal and thereby subjective measures were used to evaluate team effectiveness such as asking members for their impressions of the team's performance or by observing the quality or frequency of specific behaviors (Weingart, 1997).

Over time, however, it became apparent that observable behaviors are inadequate to understand team performance. A team's knowledge and attitudes are also important, requiring new and more formalized measurement techniques. Subsequently, there have been advancements in measurement ranging from event-based measurement (e.g., systematically creating opportunities to observe behaviors of interest), real-time assessments (e.g., automated data collection of team members inputs such as key strokes), and improvements in observation and coding schemes (e.g., use of behavioral rating scales). Researchers also learned that team performance measurement must be multilevel and dynamic to capture teamwork (Cannon-Bowers & Salas, 1997; Klein & Kozlowski, 2000). This suggests that not only the performance of the team but also the performance of every individual on the team must be evaluated (Tesluk, Mathieu, Zaccaro, & Marks, 1997). Measures must also be flexible enough to capture the dynamic, recursive nature of teamwork. However, even as performance measures have become the focus of research, there is still a considerable gap between what researchers have found and what practitioners typically use in their daily affairs.

Shared Cognition

Recent team studies are increasingly incorporating constructs, theory, and findings from cognitive psychology (e.g., transactive memory, shared mental models, metacognition; Austin, 2003; Griffith & Neale, 2001; Lewis, 2003; Moreland, 1999; Salas & Fiore, 2004; Wegner, 1987). The emphasis on the K (i.e., knowledge) in teamwork KSAs is indeed as important as teamwork skills. From this movement, new tools for knowledge elicitation and the measurement of knowledge structures (e.g., cognitive mapping, card sorts) have been advanced. These breakthroughs have made the study of team cognition accessible to a wider audience.

Many researchers beginning in the 1980s and continuing into the 21st century began to examine shared cognition, which refers to overlapping, accurate, flexible knowledge structures (e.g., Campbell & Kuncel, 2001; Cannon-Bowers, Salas, & Converse, 1993; Ensley & Pearce, 2001; Entin & Serfaty, 1999; Hinsz, Tindale, & Vollrath, 1997; Klimoski & Mohammad, 1994; Orasanu, 1990). Research in the late 1980s referred to constructs such as "team mind" (G. A. Klein, 1998) or "transactive memory" (Wegner, 1987). Early empirical work found support for the role of shared cognition in a team's ability to coordinate implicitly (Kleinman & Serfaty, 1989). Further evidence reinforced this idea, stressing the benefit of shared cognition in predicting what team members will do, given unexpected or novel events (Orasanu, 1990).

As research on shared cognition progressed, it came to be largely focused on shared mental models (SMM). Shared mental models are defined as "organized knowledge that is shared by team members" (Orasanu & Salas, 1993, p. 8). However, Cannon-Bowers and colleagues (1993) expanded that definition to specify that "in addition to shared knowledge team members must hold shared expectations that are generated from this knowledge" (p. 228). This line of research is founded on the premise that team synchronicity (i.e., process gains) can be achieved when team members develop clusters of shared and accurate instantiated knowledge structures (i.e., shared mental models). Essentially, team members operating from a shared mental model have a common conceptual framework that enables them to perceive, interpret, and respond to dynamic environments in a coordinated, adaptive fashion.

It has been repeatedly suggested that SMMs can ameliorate the negative effects of time pressure and stress by facilitating implicit coordination and communication (Kleinman & Serfaty, 1989). In fact, there is an accumulating body of evidence suggesting the sharedness and accuracy of SMMs facilitate team performance and effectiveness (Marks, Sabella, Burke, & Zaccaro, 2002; Mathieu, Heffner, & Goodwin, 1996; Stout, Cannon-Bowers, Salas, & Milanovich, 1999).

Distributed and Virtual Teams

Globalization and technological innovations have enabled organizations to seek out the best talent regardless of where it is located and organize that human capital via distributed performance arrangements (e.g., distributed teams, virtual teams). Virtual teams are defined as teams where "members' primary interaction is through some combination of electronic communication systems, such as telephone, fax machine, e-mail, and computer-based video conferencing" (Townsend, DeMarie, & Hendrickson, 1996. p. 122) in which team members "are mediated by time, distance, or technology" (Driskell, Radtke, & Salas, 2003, p. 3). Not surprisingly, organizations are implementing these types of teams without regard for the science behind their effectiveness. Despite the increased use of virtual teams, we do not have a good understanding of the impact that becoming "virtual" has on team member and team processes and performance. In fact, most of what is currently known has been generalized from research with colocated teams.

Given what is known about colocated teams and their coordination requirements, it has been argued that teams separated by time and or space have additional demands placed on them during distributed interaction. For example, team researchers have explored the absence of cues (e.g., facial expressions) for distributed teams. The lack of stimuli input taxes the working memory of distributed team members and prevents much of the scaffolding often used to reduce memory load in colocated teams (Fiore, Salas, Cuevas, & Bowers, 2003). This research led to the term *team opacity,* which refers to a special form of workload based on a lack of cues or lack of shared situational awareness.

An accumulating body of research has been undertaken to investigate a host of other distributed teamwork issues (see Bell & Kozlowski, 2002; Zaccaro, Ardison, & Orvis, 2004). For example, Aubert and Kesley (2003) found that trust was less prevalent in distributed teams. Fortunately, distributed teams with low levels of trust were still able to provide high-quality outputs. In addition, research has recently been undertaken to address a number of issues related to virtual team leadership (Cascio & Shurygailo, 2002; Zaccaro & Bader, 2003), communication (Jarvenpaa & Leidner, 1999), collaboration (Cohen & Mankin, 1999), conflict (Montoya-Wise, Massey & Song, 2001), and technology (Driskell et al., 2003; Kendall, 1999). Further illuminating the factors that comprise and impinge on distributed team performance and effectiveness is an agenda that warrants closer consideration in forthcoming research initiatives.

Team Member Individual Differences

To achieve and sustain team effectiveness, all organizations must be prepared to identify, import, and invest in human capital. Moreover, there is a growing imperative to proactively manage human resources at multiple levels (e.g., staffing, selection, training). In a team context, the process of securing and developing human capital often involves the assessment of team member characteristics or individual differences. Assessment is conducted to quantify the characteristics of individuals within a given population. In team member personnel selection systems, the emphasis is on assessing interindividual differences, or those characteristics that differentiate one team member from the next. By contrast, in team member training interventions, the concern shifts to the assessment and development of intraindividual differences, or those characteristics that can change within a team member over time.

Individual differences serve as both direct and indirect determinants of teamwork and team performance. In turn, the outcomes of teamwork and team performance are the basis for stakeholder judgments about team effectiveness. Direct determinants of team performance include job relevant knowledge, skill, and volitional choice behavior (Campbell & Kuncell, 2001). Direct determinants are a function of indirect determinants such as cognitive and psychomotor abilities, personality characteristics, perceptions, cognitive styles, cultural assumptions, and experience. In sum, the impact of indirect determinants on team performance is mediated and or moderated by the effort group members exert on a task, the knowledge and skills members can apply to a task, and the task performance strategies used to accomplish a task (Driskell, Hogan, & Salas, 1987).

There is a growing wave of theory building and empirical research concerned with team member individual differences that facilitate team process, performance, and effectiveness (see Barrick, Stewart, Neubert, & Mount, 1998; Barry & Stewart, 1997; LePine, 2003; Neuman & Wright, 1999). The preponderance of research to date has emphasized team member efficacy beliefs, abilities, personality characteristics, and cultural assumptions. By comparison, however, fewer initiatives have investigated the role of team member cognitive styles, attributions, mental models, and critical thinking skills. This state of affairs is unacceptable if organizations intend to truly leverage the synergies that are possible when a team of experts interdependently interacts as an expert team.

Some Lessons Learned

Lesson Learned 25: Teams evolve and mature over time (Morgan et al., 1993; Tuckman, 1965).

Lesson Learned 26: All teams are not created equal; different types of teams have varying functions, structures, processes, and work cycles (Devine, 2002; Sundstrom et al., 2000).

Lesson Learned 27: The complexities of routine and adaptive team performance and effectiveness can be meaningfully captured by integrative theories (Campion et al., 1993; Dickinson & McIntyre, 1997; Hackman, 1987; Pulakos et al., 2000).

Lesson Learned 28: A meaningful taxonomy can be developed for describing team performance and functions, emphasizing requirements for coordinated actions of team members to produce synchronized effort (Fleishman & Zaccaro, 1992; Nieva et al., 1978; Shiflett et al., 1985).

Lesson Learned 29: A reliable and valid measurement system for observers to evaluate the performance of teams on these performance functions can be developed (Brannick et al., 1997; Cooper et al., 1984; Fleishman & Zaccaro, 1992).

Lesson Learned 30: Organizations can navigate complex operations in dynamic environments by using self-managing work teams (Pearce & Ravlin, 1987)

Lesson Learned 31: Teamwork skills are different than taskwork skills (McIntyre & Salas, 1995).

Lesson Learned 32: Multilevel theories of team decision making offer beneficial insight into the process comprising teamwork (Hollenbeck et al., 1995; Ilgen, 1999).

Lesson Learned 33: CRM is an effective (when designed appropriately) and popular team training intervention in aviation, health care, and other industries (Helmreich, Weiner, & Kanki, 1993; Salas et al, 2001).

Lesson Learned 34: Cross-training, team self-correction, team coordination training, scenario-based training, team leadership training, and meta-cognition training are viable instructional strategies for training teams.

Lesson Learned 35: Team training works, helps to promote teamwork, and is vital for effective team performance.

Lesson Learned 36: Teams require measurement that is dynamic, process oriented, and multilevel (K. Klein & Kozlowski, 2000). Individual measurements of team members are not enough to capture team-level processes and emergent states.

Lesson Learned 37: Shared mental models provide a theoretically grounded platform for understanding team performance in complex environments (Cannon-Bowers et al., 1993; Rentsch & Hall, 1994).

Lesson Learned 38: Distribution in space–time changes aspects of team performance and effectiveness (Bell & Kozlowski, 2002; Fiore et al., 2003; Zaccaro et al., 2004).

Lesson Learned 39: A set of team-based competencies can be outlined and identified (Cannon-Bowers, Tannenbaum, Salas, & Volpe, 1995; Stevens & Campion, 1999).

Lesson Learned 40: Team member interindividual and intraindividual differences are important to team effectiveness and can be targeted via selection and training interventions (Barrick et al., 1998; LePine, 2003).

WITH THE BENEFIT OF HINDSIGHT …

From this historical account it is clear that teams are integral to the success of individuals, organizations, industries, and whole societies operating in an increasingly complex environment. To date, research has yielded a great deal of information about the utility of teams (see Gibson & Kirkman, 1999). However, much theory building, research, and practice remain to be done. It seems that after we compile all the lessons we have learned over the last century, one message is clear: Industries, governments, and organizations count on teams. Even when research is not focused on teams, factories, the military, the medical community, and the aviation industry rely on teams for operational excellence. Teams have proven to be beneficial and will continue to proliferate as the complexity of our work environments increases. Teams always have and always will exist.

Lesson Learned 41: Teams have stood the test of time.

Lesson Learned 42: Teams are here to stay.

ACKNOWLEDGMENTS

The views expressed in this work are ours and do not necessarily reflect official Army policy. This work was partially supported by funding from the Army Research Laboratory's Advanced Decision Architecture Collaborative Technology Alliance (Cooperative Agreement DAAD19-01-2-0009). This work was also partially supported by the DoD Multidisciplinary University Research Initiative (MURI) program administered by the Army Research Office under grant DAAD19-01-1-0621. We acknowledge Drs. Richard Guzzo, Scott Highhouse, Laura Koppes, Paul Thayer, and three anonymous historian reviewers for their editorial feedback and insightful comments. We are particularly thankful to Dr. Edwin A. Fleishman for providing numerous historical sources and information about teams.

REFERENCES

Allport, F. H. (1924). *Social psychology.* Boston: Houghton Mifflin.

Ancona, D., & Chong, C. L. (1999). Cycles and synchrony: The temporal role of context in team behavior. In R. Wageman (Ed.), *Research on managing groups and teams: Groups in context* (Vol. 2, pp. 33–48). Stamford, CT: JAI.

Argote, L., & McGrath, J. D. (1993). Group processes in organizations: Continuity and change. In C. L. Cooper & I. T. Robertson (Eds.), *International review of industrial and organisational psychology* (Vol. 8, pp. 333–389). New York: Wiley.

Argyris, C. (1970) *Intervention theory and method: A behavioral science view*, Reading, MA: Addison-Wesley.

Arrow, H., McGrath, J. E., & Berdahl, J. L. (2000). *Small groups as complex systems: Formation, coordination, development, and adaptation.* Newbury Park, CA: Sage.

Aubert, B. A., & Kelsey, B. L. (2003). Further understanding of trust and performance in virtual teams. *Small Group Research, 34,* 575–618.

Austin, J. R. (2003). Transactive memory systems in organizational groups: The effects of content, consensus, specialization, and accuracy on group performance. *Journal of Applied Psychology, 5,* 866–878.

Barrick, M. R., Stewart, G. L., Neubert, M. J., & Mount, M. K. (1998). Relating member ability and personality to work-team processes and team effectiveness. *Journal of Applied Psychology, 3,* 377–391.

Barry, B., & Stewart, G. L. (1997). Composition, process, and performance in self-managed groups: The role of personality. *Journal of Applied Psychology, 1,* 62–78.

Bavelas, A. (1960). Leadership: Man and function. *Administrative Science Quarterly, 4,* 491–498.

Bell, B. S., & Kozlowski, S. J. (2002). A typology of virtual teams: Implications for effective leadership. *Group & Organization Management, 27,* 14–49.

Bernstein, P. (1988). The learning curve at Volvo. *Columbia Journal of World Business, 23,* 87–95.

Bettenhausen, K. L. (1991). Five years of group research: What we have learned and what needs to be addressed. *Journal of Management, 17,* 345–381.

Beyerlein, M., Johnson, D., & Beyerlein, S. (2003), *Team based organizing: Advances in interdisciplinary studies of work teams* (Vol. 9). Oxford, England: Elsevier Science.

Beyerlein, M., & Porter, G. (2000). Historic roots of team theory and practice. In M. Beyerlein (Ed.), *Work teams: Past, present and future.* Dordrecht, The Netherlands: Kluwer.

Bion, W. R. (1948). Experiences in groups. *Human Relations, I–IV,* 1948–1951.

Boring, E. (1950). *A history of experimental psychology* (2nd ed.). New York: Appleton-Century-Crofts.

Bowers, C. A., Braun, C. C., & Morgan, B. B., Jr. (1997). Team workload: Its meaning and measurement. In M. T. Brannick, E. Salas, & C. Prince (Eds.), *Team performance and measurement: Theory, methods, and applications* (pp. 85–108). Mahwah, NJ: Lawrence Erlbaum Associates.

Brannick, M. T., Salas, E., & Prince, C. (Eds.). (1997). *Team performance assessment and measurement: Theory, methods, and applications.* Mahwah, NJ: Lawrence Erlbaum Associates.

Briggs, G. E., & Johnston, W. A. (1967). *Team training* (NAVRADEVCEN-1327-4, AD-660019). Orlando, FL: Naval Training Device Center.

Campbell, J. P. (1990). The role of theory in industrial and organizational psychology. In M. D. Dunnette & L. M. Hough (Eds.), *Handbook of industrial and organizational psychology* (pp. 39–74). Palo Alto, CA: Consulting Psychologists Press.

Campbell, J. P., & Kuncel, N. R. (2001). Individual and team training. In N. Anderson, D. S. Ones, Sinangil, H. K., & C. Viswesvaran (Eds.), *Handbook of industrial, work and organizational psychology: Personnel psychology* (Vol. 1, pp. 278–312). London: Sage.

Campion, M. A., Medsker, G. J., & Higgs, A. C. (1993). Relations between work group characteristics and effectiveness: Implications for designing effective work groups. *Personnel Psychology, 46,* 823–850.

Campion, M. A., Papper, E. M., & Medsker, G. J. (1996). Relations between work team characteristics and effectiveness: A replication and extension. *Personnel Psychology, 49,* 429–452.

Cannon-Bowers, J. A., & Salas, E. (1997). A framework for developing team performance measures in training. In M. T. Brannick, E. Salas, & C. Prince (Eds.), *Team performance assessment and measurement: Theory, research, and applications* (pp. 45–62). Mahwah, NJ: Lawrence Erlbaum Associates.

Cannon-Bowers, J. A., & Salas, E. (Eds.), (1998). *Decision making under stress: Implications for training and simulation.* Washington, DC: American Psychological Association.

Cannon-Bowers, J. A., Salas, E., & Converse, S. A. (1993). Shared mental models in expert team decision-making. In N. J. Castellan Jr. (Ed.), *Individual and group decision making* (pp. 221–246). Hillsdale, NJ: Lawrence Erlbaum Associates.

Cannon-Bowers, J. A., Tannenbaum, S. I., Salas, E., & Volpe, C. E. (1995). Defining competencies and establishing team training requirements. In R. A. Guzzo & E. Salas (Eds.), *Team effectiveness and decision making in organizations* (pp. 333–381). San Francisco: Jossey-Bass.

Cascio, W. F., & Shurygailo, S. (2002). E-leadership and virtual teams. *Organizational Dynamics, 31,* 362–376.

Chen, G., & Ployhart, R. E. (2004, April). *Time for a change: Towards a theory of performance change.* Paper presented at the 19th Conference of the Society for Industrial and Organizational Psychology, Chicago, IL.

Cohen, S. G., & Bailey, D. E. (1997). What makes teams work: Group effectiveness research from the shop floor to the executive suite. *Journal of Management, 23,* 239–290.

Cohen, S. G., & Mankin, D. (1999). Collaboration in the virtual organization. In C. L. Cooper & D. M. Rousseau (Eds.), *Trends in organizational behavior: Vol. 6. The virtual organization* (pp. 105–120). Chichester, England: Wiley.

Cohen, S., Ledford, G., & Spreitzer, G. (1996). A predictive model of self-managing work team effectiveness. *Human Relations, 49,* 643–676.

Cooper, M., Shiflett, S., Korotkin, A. L., & Fleishman, E. A. (1984). *Command and control teams: Techniques for assessing team performance* (AFHRL-TP-84-3). Brooks Air Force Base, TX: Air Force Human Resources Laboratory.

Cranton, P. (1996). Types of group learning. In S. Imel (Ed.), *Learning in groups: Exploring fundamental principles, new uses, and emerging opportunities. New directions for adult and continuing education* (pp. 25–32). San Francisco: Jossey-Bass.

Davis, J. H. (1992). Some compelling intuitions about group consensus decisions, theoretical and empirical research, and interpersonal aggregation phenomena: Selected examples, 1950–1990. *Organizational Behavior and Human Decision Processes, 52,* 3–38.

Day, D. V., & Lance, C. E. (2004). Modeling leader growth and development. In D. V. Day, S. J. Zaccaro, & S. M. Halpin (Eds.) *Leadership development for transforming organizations* (pp. 41–69). Mahwah, NJ: Lawrence Erlbaum Associates.

DeShon, R. P., Kozlowski, S. W. J., Schmidt, A. M., Milner, K. R., & Wiechmann, D. (2004). Multiple goal feedback effects on the regulation of individual and team performance in training. *Journal of Applied Psychology, 89,* 1035–1056.

Devine, D. J. (2002). A review and integration of classification systems relevant to teams in organizations. *Group Dynamics: Theory, Research, and Practice, 6,* 291–310.

Devine, D. J., Clayton, L. D., Philips, J. L., Dunford, B. B., & Melner, S. B. (1999). Teams in organizations: Prevalence, characteristics and effectiveness. *Small Group Research, 30,* 678–711.

Dickinson, T. L., & McIntyre, R. M. (1997). A conceptual framework for teamwork measurement. In M. T. Brannick, E. Salas, & C. Prince (Eds.), *Team performance assessment and measurement: Theory, methods, and applications* (pp. 19–43). Mahwah, NJ: Lawrence Erlbaum Associates.

Driskell, J. E., Hogan, R., & Salas, E. (1987). *Personality and group performance. Group processes and intergroup relations: Review of personality and social psychology* (pp. 91–112). Beverly Hills, CA: Sage.

Driskell, J. E., Radtke, P. H., & Salas, E. (2003). Virtual teams: Effects of technological mediation on team performance. *Group Dynamics, 7,* 297–323.

Drucker, P. (1992). *The age of discontinuity: Guidelines to our changing society.* Piscataway, NJ: Transaction.

Durkheim, E. (1895). *Rules of sociological method.* New York: Free Press.

Edmondson, A. (1999). Psychological safety and learning behavior in work teams. *Administrative Science Quarterly, 44,* 350–383.

Ensley, M. D., & Pearce, C. L. (2001). Shared cognition in top management teams: Implications for new venture performance. *Journal of Organizational Behavior, 22,* 145–160.

Entin, E. E., & Serfaty, D. (1999). Adaptive team coordination. *Human Factors, 41,* 312–325.

Federal Aviation Administration (FAA). (1998). *Crew resource management training* (Advisory Circle No: 120-51C). Retrieved December 18, 2003, from http://www.crm-devel.org/resources/ac/ac120_51c.html

Fiore, S. M., Salas, E., Cuevas, H. M., & Bowers, C. A. (2003). Distributed coordination space: Toward a theory of distributed team process and performance. *Theoretical Issues in Ergonomics Science, 4,* 340–364.

Fleishman, E. A. (1953). The description of supervisory behavior. *Personnel Psychology, 37,* 1–6.

Fleishman, E. A. (1975). Toward a taxonomy of human performance. *American Psychologist, 30,* 1127–1149.

Fleishman, E. A., & Quaintance, M. K. (1984). *Taxonomies of human performance: The description of human tasks.* Orlando, FL: Academic Press.

Fleishman, E. A., & Zaccaro, S. J. (1992). Toward a taxonomy of team performance functions. In R. W. Swezey & E. Salas (Eds.), *Teams: Their training & performance* (pp. 31–56). Norwood, NJ: Ablex.

Flin, R. (1995). Crew resource management for teams in the offshore oil industry. *Journal of European Industrial Training, 19,* 23–27.

Follett, M. P. (1926). The giving of orders. In H. C. Metcalf (Eds.), *Scientific foundations of business administration* (pp. 156–162). Baltimore: Williams & Wilkins.

Ford, J. K. (1997). Advances in training research and practice: An historical perspective. In J. K. Ford & Associates (Eds.), *Improving training effectiveness in work organizations* (pp. 1–18). Mahwah, NJ: Lawrence Erlbaum Associates.

Frost, C. F. (1974). *The Scanlon plan for organization development: Identity, participation, and equity.* Lansing: Michigan State University Press.

Gaba, D. M., Howard, S. K., & Fish, K. J. (1994). *Crisis management in anesthesiology.* New York: Churchill Livingstone.

Gersick, C. G. (1988). Time and transition in work teams: Toward a new model of group development. *Academy of Management Journal, 31,* 9–41.

Gersick, C. J. (1989). Marking time: Predictable transitions in task groups. *Academy of Management Journal, 32,* 274–309.

Gibson, C. B., & Kirkman, B. L. (1999). Our past, present, and future in teams: The role of human resources professionals in managing team performance. In A. I. Kraut & A. K. Korman (Eds.), *Evolving practices in human resources management: Responses to a changing world of work* (pp. 90–117). San Francisco: Jossey-Bass.

Gladstein, D. L. (1984). Groups in context: A model of task group effectiveness. *Administrative Science Quarterly, 29,* 499–517.

Glassop, L. I. (2002). The organizational benefits of teams. *Human Relations, 55,* 225–249.

Glickman, A. S., Zimmer, S., Montero, R. C., Guerette, P. J., Campbell, W. J., Morgan, B. B., Jr., et al. (1987). *The evolution of teamwork skills: An empirical assessment with implications for training* (NTSC Tech. Rep. No. 87-016). Orlando, FL: Naval Training Systems Center.

Griffith, T. L., & Neale, M.A. (2001). Information processing in traditional, hybrid, and virtual teams: From nascent knowledge to transactive memory. In B. Staw and R. Sutton (Eds.), *Research in organizational behavior* (Vol. 23, pp. 379–421). Stamford, CT: JAI.

Guzzo, R. A., & Dickson, M. W. (1996). Teams in organizations: Recent research on performance and effectiveness. *Annual Review of Psychology, 47,* 307–338.

Guzzo, R. A., & Shea, G. P. (1992). Group performance and intergroup relations in organizations. In M. D. Dunnette and L. M. Hough (Eds.), *Handbook of industrial and organizational psychology* (2nd ed., pp. 269–313). Palo Alto, CA: Consulting Psychologists Press.

Gyllenhammer, P. (1973). Volvo's solution to the blue-collar blues. *Business and Society/Innovation, 7,* 50–54.

Hackman, J. R. (1987). The design of work teams. In J. Lorsch (Ed.), *Handbook of organizational behavior* (pp. 315–342). New York: Prentice-Hall.

Hackman, J. R. (1990). *Groups that work (and those that don't).* San Francisco: Jossey-Bass.

Hackman, J. R., & Lawler, E. E. (1971). Employees' reactions to job characteristics. *Journal of Applied Psychology, 55,* 259–285.

Hackman, J. R., & Oldham, G. R. (1975). Development of the job diagnostic survey. *Journal of Applied Psychology, 60,* 159–170.

Harrison, D. A., Mohammed, S., McGrath, J. E., Florey, A. T., & Vanderstoep, S. W. (2003). Time matters in team performance: Effects of member familiarity, entrainment, and task discontinuity on speed and quality. *Personnel Psychology, 56,* 633–669.

Helmreich, R. L., Merritt, A. C., & Wilhelm, J. A. (1999). The evolution of crew resource management training in commercial aviation. *International Journal of Aviation Psychology, 9,* 19–32.

Helmreich, R. L., Wiener, E. L., & Kanki, B. G. (1993). The future of crew resource management in the cockpit and elsewhere. In E. L. Wiener, B. G. Kanki & R. L. Helmreich (Eds), *Cockpit resource management* (pp. 479–501). San Diego, CA: Academic Press.

Hemphill, J. K. (1949). *Situational factors in leadership.* Columbus: Ohio State Bureau of Educational Research.

Hemphill, J. K., & Westie, C. M. (1950). The measurement of group dimensions. *The Journal of Psychology, 29,* 325–342.

Herzberg, F. (1966). *Work and the nature of man.* Cleveland: World Publishing.

Highhouse, S. (2002a). Assessing the candidate as a whole: An historical and critical analysis of individual psychological assessment for personnel decision making. *Personnel Psychology, 55,* 363–396.

Highhouse, S. (2002b). A history of the T-group and its early applications in management development. *Group Dynamics, 6,* 277–290.

Hinsz, V. B., Tindale, R. S., & Vollrath, D. A. (1997). The emerging conceptualization of groups as information processors. *Psychological Bulletin, 121,* 43–64.

Hollenbeck, J. R., Ilgen, D. R., LePine, J. A., Colquitt, J. A., & Hedlund, J. (1998). Extending the multilevel theory of team decision making: Effects of feedback and experience in hierarchical teams. *Academy of Management Journal, 41,* 269–282.

Hollenbeck, J. R., Ilgen, D. R., Sego, D. J., Hedlund, J., Major, D. A., & Phillips, J. (1995). Multilevel theory of team decision making: Decision performance in teams incorporating distributed expertise. *Journal of Applied Psychology, 80,* 292–316.

Ilgen, D. R. (1999). Teams embedded in organizations: Some implications. *American Psychologist, 54,* 129–139.

Ilgen, D. R., Hollenbeck, J. R., Johnson, M., & Jundt, D. (2005). Teams in organizations: From input-process-output models to IMOI models. *Annual Review of Psychology, 56,* 517–543.

Ilgen, D. R., Major, D. A., Hollenbeck, J. R., & Sego, D. J. (1991). *Decision making in teams: Raising an individual model to the team level* (Tech. Rep. No. 91-92). East Lansing: Michigan State University.

Ingham, A. G., Levinger, G., Graves, J., & Peckham, V. (1974). The Ringelmann effect: Studies of group size and group performance. *Journal of Experimental Social Psychology, 10,* 371–384.

Janis, I. L. (1972). *Victims of groupthink: A psychological study of foreign-policy decisions and fiascoes.* Boston: Houghton Mifflin.

Jarvenpaa, S. L., & Leidner, D. E. (1999). Communication and trust in global virtual teams. *Organization Science, 10,* 791–815.

Katzenbach, J. R., & Smith, D. K. (1993). The discipline of teams. *Harvard Business Review, 7,* 111–120.

Kendall, K. E. (Ed.). (1999). *Emerging information technologies: Improving decisions, cooperation, and infrastructure.* Camden, NJ: Rutgers University.

Klein, G. A. (1998). *Sources of power: how people make decisions.* Cambridge, MA: MIT Press.

Klein, G., & Pierce, L. (2001). Adaptive teams (Draft report, purchase order H438556 [A] for Link Simulation and Training Division/Army Prim Contract No. DAAD17-00-A-5002). Fairborn, OH: Klein Associates.

Klein, K., & Kozlowski, S. W. J. (2000). A multilevel approach to theory and research in organizations: Contextual, temporal, and emergent processes. In K. J. Klein & S. W. J. Kozlowski (Eds.), *Multilevel theory, research, and methods in organizations: Foundations, extensions, and new directions* (pp. 3–90). San Francisco: Jossey-Bass.

Kleinman, D. L., & Serfaty, D. (1989). *Team performance assessment in distributed decision making*. Proceedings of the Symposium on Interactive Networked Simulation for Training (pp. 22–27), Orlando, FL.

Klimoski, R., & Mohammad, S. (1994). Team mental model: Construct or metaphor? *Journal of Management, 20,* 403–437.

Kozlowski, S. W. J., & Bell, B. S. (2002). Work groups and teams in organizations. In W. C. Borman, D. R. Ilgen, & R. J. Klimoski (Eds.), *Comprehensive handbook of psychology: Vol. 12. industrial and organizational psychology* (pp. 333–375). New York: Wiley.

Kozlowski, S. W. J., Gully, S. M., Brown, K. G., Salas, E., Smith, E. A., & Nason, E. R. (2001). Effects of training goals and goal orientation traits on multi-dimensional training outcomes and performance adaptability. *Organizational Behavior and Human Decision Processes, 85,* 1–31.

Kozlowski, S. W. J, Gully, S. M., Nason, E. R., & Smith, E. M. (1999). Developing adaptive teams: A theory of compilation and performance across levels and time. In D. R. Ilgen & E. D. Pulakos (Eds.), *The changing nature of work and performance: Implications for staffing, personnel actions, and development* (1st ed., pp. 240–292). San Francisco: Jossey-Bass.

Kraiger, K. (2002). Decision-based evaluation. In K. Kraiger (Ed.), *Creating, implementing, and managing effective training and development systems in organizations: State-of-the-art lessons for practice* (pp. 331–375). San Francisco: Jossey-Bass.

LePine, J. A. (2003). Team adaptation and postchange performance: Effects of team composition in terms of members' cognitive ability and personality. *Journal of Applied Psychology, 88,* 27–39.

Levine, J. M., & Moreland, R. L. (1991). Culture and socialization in work groups. In L. B. Resnick and J. M. Levine (Eds.), *Perspectives on socially shared cognition* (pp. 257–279). Washington, DC: American Psychological Association.

Lewin, K. (1939). Field theory and experiment in social psychology: Concepts and methods. *American Journal of Sociology, 44,* 868–896.

Lewin, K., Lippitt, R., & White, R. K. (1939). Patterns of aggressive behavior in experimentally created "social climates." *Journal of Social Psychology, SPSSI Bulletin, 10,* 271–299.

Lewis, K. (2003). Measuring transactive memory systems in the field: Scale development and validation. *Journal of Applied Psychology, 88,* 587–604.

Manz, C. C., & Neck, C. P. (1995). Teamthink: Beyond the group think syndrome in self-managing work teams. *Journal of Managerial Psychology, 10,* 7–15.

Marks, M. A., Mathieu, J. E., & Zaccaro, S. J. (2001). A temporally based framework and taxonomy of team process. *Academy of Management Review, 26,* 356–376.

Marks, M. A., Sabella, M. J., Burke, C. S., & Zaccaro, S. J. (2002). The impact of cross-training on team effectiveness. *Journal of Applied Psychology, 87,* 3–13.

Marks, M. A., Zaccaro, S. J., & Mathieu, J. E. (2000). Performance implications of leader briefings and team-interaction training for team adaptation to novel environments. *Journal of Applied Psychology, 6,* 971–986.

Maslow, A. H. (1943). A theory of human motivation. *Psychological Review, 50,* 370–396.

Mathieu, J. E., Heffner, T. S., & Goodwin, G. F. (1996). *Linking cognitive and behavioral components of aircrew coordination*. Orlando, FL: Naval Air Warfare Center.

McCarthy, P. (2002). *Brief outline of the history of I-O psychology*. Retrieved January 21, 2002, from http://www.mtsu.edu/~pmccarth/io_hist.htm

McDougall, W. (1930). William McDougall. In G. Lindzey (Ed.), *A history of psychology in autobiography* (Vol. 7, pp. 191–223). Worcester, MA: Clark University Press.

McGrath, J. (1964). *Social psychology: A brief introduction*. New York: Holt, Rinehart & Winston.

McGrath, J. E., Arrow, H., & Berdahl, J. L. (2000). The study of groups: Past, present, and future. *Personality and Social Psychological Review, 4,* 95–105.

McGregor, D. M. (1957). The human side of enterprise. *Management Review, 46,* 88–92.

McIntyre, R. M., & Salas, E. (1995). Measuring and managing for team performance: Emerging principles from complex environments. In R. A. Guzzo & E. Salas (Eds.), *Team effectiveness and decision making in organizations* (pp. 9–45). San Francisco: Jossey-Bass.

McKeachie, W. J., & Brim, O. G. (1984). Lessons to be learned from large behavioral research organizations. *American Psychologist, 11,* 1254–1255.

Merritt, A. C., & Helmreich, R. L. (1995). CRM in 1995: Where to from here? In B. J. Howard & A. R. Lowe (Eds.), *Applied aviation psychology: Achievement, change, and challenge. Proceedings of the 3rd Australian Aviation Psychology Symposium* (pp. 111–126). Aldershot, England: Avebury Aviation.

Moede, W. (1927). Die Richtlinien der Leistungs-Psychologie. *Industrielle Psychotechnik, 4,* 193–207.

Mohrman, S., Cohen, S., & Mohrman, A. (1995). *Designing team-based organizations: New forms for knowledge work*. San Francisco: Jossey-Bass.

Montoya-Weiss, M. M., Massey, A. P., & Song, M. (2001). Getting it together: Temporal coordination and conflict management in global virtual teams. *Academy of Management Journal, 44,* 1251–1262.

Moreland, R. L. (1999). Transactive memory: Learning who knows what in work groups and organizations. In L. L. Thompson & J. M. Levine (Eds.), *Shared cognition in organizations: The management of knowledge* (pp. 3–31). Mahwah, NJ: Lawrence Erlbaum Associates.

Morgan, B., Salas, E., & Glickman, A. S. (1993). An analysis of team evolution and maturation. *Journal of General Psychology, 120,* 277–291.

Mullen, B., & Cooper, C. (1994). The relation between group cohesiveness and performance: An integration. *Psychological Bulletin, 115,* 210–227.

Neuman, G. A., & Wright, J. (1999). Team effectiveness: Beyond skills and cognitive ability. *Journal of Applied Psychology, 84,* 376–389.

Nieva, V. F., Fleishman, E. A., & Rieck, A. M. (1978). *Team dimensions: Their identity, their measurement, and their relationships* (Tech. Rep.). Washington, DC: ARRO.

Orasanu, J. (1990, October). *Shared mental models and crew performance.* Paper presented at the 34th Annual Meeting of the Human Factors Society, Orlando, FL.

Orasanu, J., & Salas, E. (1993). Team decision making in complex environments. In G. A. Klein, J. Orasanu, R. Calderwood, & C. E. Zsambok (Eds.), *Decision making in action: Models and methods* (pp. 327–345). Stamford, CT: Ablex.

Pearce, J. A. I., & Ravlin, E. C. (1987). The design and activation of self regulating work groups. *Human Relations, 40,* 751–760.

Peters, T., & Waterman, J. (1982). *In search of excellence.* New York: Warner Books.

The plant that runs on individual initiative. (1972). *Management Review, 61,* 20–26.

Pulakos, E. D., Arad, S., Donovan, M. A., & Plamondon, K. E. (2000). Adaptation in the workplace: Development of a taxonomy of adaptive performance. *Journal of Applied Psychology, 85,* 612–624.

Pulakos, E. D., Schmitt, N., Dorsey, D. W., Arad, S., Hedge, J. W., & Borman, W. C. (2002). Predicting adaptive performance: Further tests of a model of adaptability. *Human Performance, 4,* 299–323.

Rentsch, J. R., & Hall, R. J. (1994). Members of great teams think alike: A model of team effectiveness and schema similarity among team members. In M. M. Beyerlein & D. A. Johnson (Eds.), *Advances in interdisciplinary studies of work teams: Theories of self-managing work teams* (Vol. 1, pp. 223–261). Greenwich, CT: Elsevier Science/JAI.

Roby, T. B., & Lanzetta, J. T. (1957). Conflicting principles in man–machine system design. *Journal of Applied Psychology, 41,* 170–178.

Roethlisberger, F. J. (1941). *Management and morale.* Cambridge, MA: Harvard University Press.

Rogers, C. R. (1970). *Carl Rogers on encounter groups.* New York: HarperCollins.

Salas, E., Bowers, C. A., & Cannon-Bowers, J. A. (1995). Military team research: Ten years of progress. *Military Psychology, 7,* 55–75.

Salas, E., Bowers, C. A., & Edens, E. (2001). An overview of resource management in organizations: Why now? In E. Salas, C. A. Bowers, & E. Edens (Eds.), *Improving teamwork in organizations: Applications of resource management training* (pp. 1–5). Mahwah, NJ: Lawrence Erlbaum Associates.

Salas, E., & Cannon-Bowers, J. A. (2000). Designing training systems systematically. In E. A. Locke (Ed.), *The Blackwell handbook of principles of organizational behavior* (pp. 43–59). Malden, MA: Blackwell.

Salas, E., & Cannon-Bowers, J. A. (2001). The science of training: A decade of progress. *Annual Review of Psychology, 52,* 471–499.

Salas, E., Dickinson, T. L., Converse, S. A., & Tannenbaum, S. I. (1992). Toward an understanding of team performance and training. In R. W. Swezey & E. Salas, (Eds.), *Teams: Their training and performance* (pp. 3–29). Stamford, CT: Ablex.

Salas, E., & Fiore, S. M. (Eds.) (2004). *Team cognition: Understanding the factors that drive process and performance.* Washington, DC: American Psychological Association.

Salas, E., Rozell, D., Mullen, B., & Driskell, J. E. (1999). The effect of team building on performance: An integration. *Small Group Research, 30,* 309–329.

Salas, E., Stagl, K. C., & Burke, C. S. (2004). 25 years of team effectiveness in organizations: Research themes and emerging needs. In C. L. Cooper & I. T. Robertson (Eds.), *International review of industrial and organizational psychology* (pp. 47–91). New York: Wiley.

Salas, E., Stagl, K. C., Burke, C. S., & Goodwin, G. F. (in press). Fostering team effectiveness in organizations: Toward an integrative theoretical framework of team performance. In J. W. Shuart, W. Spaulding, & J. Poland, (Eds.), *Modeling complex systems: Motivation, cognition and social processes, Nebraska Symposium on Motivation* (Vol. 51). Lincoln: University of Nebraska Press.

Salas, E., Wilson, K. A., Burke, C. S., & Bowers, C. A. (2002). Myths about crew resource management training. *Ergonomics in Design, 10*(4), 20–24.

Shafritz, J. M., & Ott, J. S. (Eds.). (2001). *Classics of organization theory* (5th ed.). San Diego: Harcourt.

Shartle, C. L. (1956). *Executive performance and leadership.* Englewood Cliffs, NJ: Prentice-Hall.

Sheard, A., & Kakabadse, A. (2002). From loose groups to effective teams: The nine key factors of the team development landscape. *Journal of Management Development, 2,* 131–151.

Shiflett, S., Eisner, E. J., Price, S. J., & Schemmer, F. M. (1985). *The definition and measurement of military small unit team functions*. (Res. Rep.). Bethesda, MD: ARI.

Steiner, I. (1972). *Group process and productivity*. New York: Academic Press.

Stevens, M. J., & Campion, M. A. (1999). Staffing work teams: Development and validation of a selection test for teamwork settings. *Journal of Management, 25,* 207–228.

Stewart, G., Manz, C., & Sims, H. (1999). *Team work and group dynamics*. New York: Wiley.

Stout, R. J., Cannon-Bowers, J. A., Salas, E., & Milanovich, D. M. (1999). Planning, shared mental models, and coordinated performance: An empirical link is established. *Human Factors, 41,* 61–71.

Sundstrom, E. D., De Meuse, K. P., & Futrell, D. (1990). Work teams: Applications and effectiveness. *American Psychologist, 45,* 120–133.

Sundstrom, E., McIntyre, M., Halfhill, T., & Richards, H. (2000). Work groups: From the Hawthorne studies to work teams of the 1990s and beyond. *Group Dynamics, 4,* 44–67.

Swezey, R. W., & Salas, E. (1992). Guidelines for use in team-training development. In R. W. Swezey & E. Salas (Eds.), *Teams: Their training and performance* (pp. 219–245). Westport, CT: Ablex.

Tang, T. L., & Butler, E. A. (1997). Attributions of quality circles' problem-solving failure: Differences among management, supporting staff, and quality circle members. *Public Personnel Management, 26,* 203–225.

Tannenbaum, S. I., Beard, R. L., & Salas, E. (1992). Team building and its influence on team effectiveness: An examination of conceptual and empirical developments. In K. Kelley (Ed.), *Issue, theory, and research in industrial/organizational psychology* (pp. 117–153). Amsterdam: Elsevier.

Tannenbaum, S. I., & Yukl, G. (1992). Training and development in work organizations. *Annual Review of Psychology, 43,* 399–441.

Taylor, F. W. (1911). *The principles of scientific management*. New York: Norton.

Tedford, K., & Baker, D. (2000). Kurt Lewin: Contributions to organizational development. In M. Beyerlein (Ed.) *Work teams: Past, present and future* (pp. 107–114). Dordrecht, The Netherlands: Klewer.

Tesluk, P., Mathieu, J. E., Zacarro, S. J., & Marks, M. (1997). Task and aggregation issues in the analysis and assessment of team performance. In M. T. Brannick, E. Salas, & C. Prince (Eds.), *Team performance assessment and measurement: Theory, methods, and applications* (pp. 197–224). Mahwah, NJ: Lawrence Erlbaum Associates.

Townsend, A. M., DeMarie, S. M., & Hendrickson, A. R. (1996, September). Are you ready for virtual teams? *HR Magazine, 41,* 122–128.

Trist, E. L., Emory, F., Murray, H., & Trist, B. (Eds.). (1997). *The social engagement of social science: A Tavistock anthology: The socio–ecological perspective*. Philadelphia: University of Pennsylvania Press.

Tuckman, B. W. (1965). Personality, structure, group composition, and group functioning. *Sociometry, 27,* 469–487.

Waller, M. (1999). The timing of adaptive group responses to nonroutine events. *Academy of Management Journal, 42,* 127–137.

Watson, J. B. (1913). Psychology as the behaviorist views it. *Psychological Review, 20,* 158–177.

Weber, M. (1972). Bureaucracy. In H. Gerth & C. W. Mills (Eds.), *Max Webber: Essays in sociology*. Oxford, England: Oxford University Press.

Wegner, D. (1987). Transactive memory: A contemporary analysis of the group mind. In B. Mullen & G. Goethals (Eds.), *Theories of group behavior* (pp. 185–208). New York: Springer-Verlag.

Weingart, L. R. (1997). How did they do that? The ways and means of studying group process. *Research in Organizational Behavior, 19,* 189–239.

West, M. A., Tjosvold, D., & Smith, K. G. (2003). *International handbook of organizational teamwork and cooperative working*. West Sussex, England: Wiley.

Wellins, R. S., Byham, W. C., & Wilson, J. M. (1991). *Empowered teams creating self-directed work groups that improve quality, productivity, and participation*. San Francisco: Jossey-Bass. Wheelan, S. A. (1994). *Group processes: A developmental perspective*. Needham Heights, MA: Allyn & Bacon,

Whitsett, D. A., & Yorks, L. (1983). Looking back at Topeka: General Foods and the quality-of-work-life experiment. *California Management Review, 25,* 93–109.

Zaccaro, S. J., Ardison, S. D., & Orvis, K. L. (2004). Leading virtual teams. In D. Day, S. J. Zaccaro, & S. M. Halpin (Eds.), *Leader development for transforming organizations* (pp. 267–292). Mahwah, NJ: Lawrence Erlbaum Associates, Inc.

Zaccaro, S. J., & Bader, P. (2003). E-Leadership and the challenges of leading E-teams: Minimizing the bad and maximizing the good. *Organizational Dynamics, 31,* 377–387.

Zaccaro, S. J., Rittman, A. L., & Marks, M. A. (2001). Team leadership. *Leadership Quarterly, 12,* 451–483.

VI

Reflections and Future

The book concludes with chapter 18, where the author asks certain questions of the historical record and, given the answers, infers how we might go about trying to maximize our contributions in the future. The previous chapters are used to identify the principal reasons the field came to be as it is. Trends in the kinds of issues the field has been addressing over the last century are discerned. Major contributions of I–O psychology to the body politic of psychological science and psychological practice are identified. And finally, structures and strategies that I–O psychology should promote are offered.

18

Profiting From History

John P. Campbell
University of Minnesota

This chapter is not a summary of, a review of, or a critical analysis of the previous chapters. They contain a wealth of information and can be judged on their merits by individual readers, given the objectives of each chapter's authors. Instead, the objective here is to ask certain questions of the historical record for this comparatively young field and, given the answers, attempt to infer how we might go about trying to maximize our contributions in the future. Depending on one's perspective (i.e., chronological age), industrial and organizational (I–O) psychology is only three or four generations old, and everyone can trace his or her genealogy back to one or more of the founders. Is this a long enough record, or sample size, to produce stable assessments? Perhaps not, but let's do it anyway.

This chapter will try to do four things briefly:

First, it will use the previous chapters to identify the principal reasons the field came to be. That is, why do we have such a field? What was its early nature? Did its developmental latent structure have few factors, many factors, or a lot of specific variance? Are the reasons it first emerged the same reasons that it persists, and will they be the same reasons for its existence in the future?

Second, are there discernable trends in the kinds of issues the field has been addressing over the last century? What seems to account for them, if anything?

Third, what have been the major contributions of I–O psychology to the body politic of psychological science and psychological practice? Or, is I–O psychology a totally derivative enterprise that uses theories, findings, and methods from other parts of the discipline and applies them to individual behavior in organizations?

Fourth, to maintain the health of our field and continually enhance its contributions to understanding, predicting, and improving individual functioning in organizations, what structures and strategies should I–O psychology promote? That is, what should we do to further our own improvement?

To be forewarned, those who do not examine the value judgments underlying the origins and development of this field, and actually engage them, are condemned to a professional and scientific decay, by fits and starts. One clear conclusion from reading these chapters is that we do not contemplate our values enough.

The principal theme here is an evolutionary one. Both science and practice must always adapt to changing problems, changing political/economic conditions, changing sources of resources, changes in the competition, changes in related disciplines, and so on. Effective adaptation to all these changing elements is facilitated by variability. That is, variability in the education and training backgrounds of I–O psychologists, variability in their work settings, variability in their occupational goals, variability in the sources of their research issues, variability in the applied versus basic nature of their research, variability in methods and approaches, and even variability in value orientations all provide a wider range of potential responses, and a higher probability of using effective ones, when significant changes occur. Consequently, whether it be in graduate training, the "set of most important research questions," methods of research and practice, the settings where research gets done, or the reasons for conducting research, uniformity is not adaptive. One specific implication of this view is that standardization, accreditation, and licensure are to be avoided, or at least drastically downplayed.

A contrarian view is to argue that it is the individual that must be broadly adaptable, not the discipline. The "ideal" graduate training program would produce uniformly adaptive scientists/practitioners. This requires much faith.

THE EARLY YEARS

As documented in a number of chapters, applications of psychological science to understanding and influencing individual behavior at work emerged in a number of industrializing countries at about the same time (i.e., 1890–1920) due primarily to the problems created by the beginnings of the industrial revolution; the rise of the bureaucratic organizational structure, with its critical distinctions among owners, managers, and workers; military human resource issues during World War I; and the increasing importance of the nation-state as a context for industrialization. That is, governments sought to increase economic growth by various means and that included supporting attempts to improve human capital. Moreover, the nature of the governmental support or intervention was, and is, very much a function of a specific nation's culture and political–economic system.

The emergence of applied psychology in many countries during this period was not the result of a direct diffusion of research and development (R&D) goals and expertise from a common source. Worldwide it seems to have been driven more by a common, but independent, recognition in a number of countries that industrialization generates issues regarding personnel selection, vocational guidance, skills training, and the effects of the workplace on the individual's physical and mental health that should be addressed. As noted by Warr and others (this volume), the professionals who first confronted these issues were not necessarily psychologists. In fact, the psychologist was in the minority. There was also involvement from psychiatrists, physicians, engineers, organizational managers, and even physicists. Of course, the meddling of economists can simply be taken for granted. Consequently, we cannot argue that applied psychology in general and I–O psychology, in particular, were born in Leipzig under Wundt and were spread by the students he trained in the 1880s and 1890s, who quickly began addressing applied problems (e.g., Münsterberg, Scott). In virtually every country, there were always key people (i.e., pioneers) involved who were not psychologists.

What Is and What Isn't I–O Psychology

The variety of disciplines involved highlights one of the major problems encountered in trying to write a history of this field. Virtually all of the chapters are vexed by it. The issue pertains to what are the most appropriate specifications for delineating I–O psychology from non-I–O psychology. One approach would be not to worry about it. Make it a nonissue and ignore it. Let everybody use whatever delineation, explicit or implicit, that they want. However, if the title of this volume refers to historical perspectives in I–O psychology and if we have a national organization currently designated as the Society of I–O Psychology (SIOP), then there must be common variance of some kind that is worthy of specification. A very encompassing specification would be to focus on the setting (i.e. individual adult behavior in "organizations"—broadly defined) and say that I–O psychology is the application of psychological theory and methods to understanding, predicting, and enhancing individual adult behavior in organizations.

This specification would say that although the Lewin, Lippitt, and White (1939) studies of participative versus directive leadership in children's play groups had important implications for the study of adult leadership in organizations, they were not doing I–O psychology. However, Lewin later became associated with the "experiments" at Harwood and took on considerable I–O coloring.

Again, before the turn of the century, and up until the 1920s, there were no I–O psychologists, as noted in chapters throughout this text. The field was in its prenatal stage, and the psychologists who addressed questions about individual behavior in organizations were trained in the classic "experimental psychology" theory and methods of the time with a dose here and there of William James and Edward Titchener. And, as noted previously, psychologists of any variety were in the minority among those trying to address what we now refer to as human resource issues in organizations.

With the advent of I–O graduate training programs, things changed. I–O psychology came more and more to refer to what the graduates of these programs do. The current SIOP membership is not entirely, but very largely, made up of such graduates, at least for those members under 50 years of age. This represents a significant narrowing of the specifications for what is and what isn't I–O psychology.

What Our Dependent Variables Tell Us About Our Early Selves

One way of defining a field is to take note of the dependent variables it tries to explain, predict, or influence, and it is instructional to itemize the array of dependent variables that were of concern during the early formative period (i.e., 1890–1920). The list is longer than we might have expected, given the substantive content of today's literature and conference programs, at least in my opinion.

Based on an aggregate look at the chapters in this volume, the following set of dependent variables is offered as the critical criteria that the field was trying to address in its early years. Again, the dependent variable is the variable of real interest. The independent variable exists only to explain, change, or predict the dependent variable. We would have no interest in personality, cognitive abilities, or instructional programs if they could not predict, change, or explain important criteria.

Job Performance.   Individual performance was a major concern in the beginning, as it is now. The almost universal concern for better selection and training was focused on achieving gains on this dependant variable. The word *almost* is necessary because individual differences in performance were not the primary concern in certain countries with pronounced socialist or collectivist political–economic systems. Also, in Great Britain, Europe, Eastern Europe, Russia, Asia, and even in the United States, individual performance was by no means the only criterion of concern.

Job Satisfaction.   Job satisfaction is still a major dependent variable for I–O psychology, and it was certainly there early on. However, the historical characterization is less as an indication of attitudes toward specific job rewards or outcomes (e.g., pay, supervision, working conditions) and more as a subjective judgment about one's overall well-being, or life satisfaction. Currently, although life satisfaction and job satisfaction are addressed concomitantly by some researchers (e.g., Judge, Erez, & Bono, 1998), the bulk of current research on self-judgments of individual well-being has been ceded to social psychology (e.g. Diener, 1984; Diener & Oishi, 2000).

Productivity.   In the conventional economic sense, productivity is a macrovariable indexed by the ratio of group, firm, or industry output to the costs of the resources used for producing that output. Productivity can be increased by reducing costs, increasing output, or both, and there are subfacets of productivity that might be labeled as the productivity of labor, capital, or technology. At the individual level, productivity is sometimes labeled as "efficiency" and individual efficiency (i.e., the ratio of individual output to the time or effort needed to achieve it), which was an important criterion during the first half of the 20th century. However, the investigators were generally not psychologists but engineers or management consultants (e.g., Gilbreth, 1917; Taylor, 1919). During the last 50 years, I–O psychology has not really focused on individual productivity as a dependent variable (i.e., criterion). Although we use the term *individual productivity* a lot, it virtually always means the same thing as performance (i.e., the numerator). Productivity in the traditional sense is still left to the nonpsychologists.

Fatigue.   Fatigue can be indexed in at least two major ways. Although not frequent, some early studies focused on physical measures such as hours of sleep deprivation, decrements in arm or hand steadiness, decreases in reaction time, or decreases in physical strength. Probably more attention was devoted to perceptions of fatigue or tiredness. Perceptions of fatigue can result from many things besides physical or mental exertion, such as coworker relationships or the lack of intrinsically interesting work. Regardless of how it is indexed, the study of fatigue has been predominantly investigated by medical specialists, engineers, human factors psychologists, sociologists, and even anthropologists. It has generally not been addressed by what we now think of as I–O psychology.

Illness and/or Injury.   Although illness and injury at work have been concerns ever since the beginnings of the industrial revolution, and given that such concerns might wax and wane with changes in political and economic conditions, these criteria have again been addressed primarily by the medical specialties and not applied psychologists. The attempts by the American Psychological Association (APA) to develop programs in occupational health psychology run counter to this trend and may yet develop into an important component of I–O psychology in the United States.

Perceived Stress.   Perceived stress was a dependent variable in the field in the beginning but has waxed and waned since. Currently, it seems to play more of a major role in the European I–O literature, but not in the United States (Hart & Cooper, 2001). One major difficulty, or fascination, with studying perceived stress is that individual differences in perceived stress, or stress reactions, in response to the same situation are considerable. That is, one person's stress is another person's excitement.

Performance Stability.   Historically this has referred to performance consistency within individuals. Why are some of us consistent performers and others not? Is the inconsistency simply measurement error in the index or real fluctuation in the true score? At the organizational level, variation in the productivity or performance indexes that are judged central to the goals of the firm is usually considered bad. To loosely paraphrase Deming (1981), and the productivity improvement programs that came after, stability around an improving trend line is good. Only a few I–O psychologists have worried about these issues (e.g., Kane & Lawler, 1979). More recently, there has been increasing interest in modeling performance growth using more sophisticated structural models of "change." However, although the quantitative models are relatively elegant, the substantive models of what performance growth or change means are not yet their equal. That is, which substantive determinants, conditions, and components of performance are held constant and which ones are free to vary when estimating performance "change"?

Person–Job and Person–Organization Fit. Vocational guidance and job placement were prominent features of psychology applied to work in the early years. Person–job fit and person–organization fit are not infrequent dependent variables in current research as well, but there is a major difference between then and now. Before World War II, the work on vocational guidance within applied psychology was primarily from the individual perspective. That is, the dependent variable was the degree of benefit to the individual, as judged by the individual. Current research on person–job or person–organization fit seems to reflect primarily the organization's (i.e., management's) perspective. That is, better fits are better because they enhance the organization's goal accomplishments. From then to now, with regard to this particular dependent variable, the value system within which the research questions are asked seems to have shifted. When reading these chapters, I was struck by the small amount of attention given to Donald G. Paterson, who has godlike status at Minnesota. The obvious reason is that most of his work on ability assessment, job placement, occupational success, and individual differences was done within the individual perspective. That is, he wasn't thinking about helping managements, he was thinking about helping individual persons (Paterson, 1957). Consequently, many might not regard him as an I–O psychologist (his students such as Marvin Dunnette, William Owens, and many others, notwithstanding). (See chaps. 2 and 13 for information about Paterson.)

Errors. Error analysis was a significant part of the early years. Münsterberg himself was interested in accident reduction, and it has always been a major activity in a number of engineering professions. Also, the frequency and magnitude of errors have always played a major criterion role in human factors psychology. As commented on in chapter 10, the study of aircraft operation has always held a dominant place in human factors because the errors are so critical.

Aside from human factors, the frequency and magnitude of errors, as criterion variables, have virtually disappeared from I–O psychology. If job satisfaction and job dissatisfaction have different antecedents (Herzberg, Mausner, & Snyderman, 1959) as some have suggested (Campbell & Pritchard, 1976; Dunnette, Campbell, & Hakel, 1967), perhaps particularly high and particularly low performance do as well. The continuous normal distribution may not be the optimal representation for all criterion variability.

Adaptability. Performance adaptability, as a specific component of performance, is a relatively recent development in I–O psychology (Pulakos, Arad, Donovan, & Plamondon, 2000), although it has been a buzzword for considerably longer. Nothing resembling performance adaptability is reflected in any of the descriptions of I–O psychology's origins included in this volume. Consequently, it represents an expansion, not a contraction, of the dependent variables of interest to the field. As such, one might wish for a more detailed and substantive specifications for what performance adaptability is and what it is not. It is not enough to say that adaptability is being able to adapt to changing requirements or to maintain a high level of performance when "conditions" change. What conditions, and under what circumstances? Is a changed condition the same thing as a new performance requirement? What are the determinants of high versus low adaptability? Are they motivational? Ability based? Skill based? Perhaps adaptability is really a personality trait or an ability and should be thought of as an independent and not a dependent variable. Adaptability as a construct still needs considerable explication and specification, but that is the way science progresses, by continual revision and refinement.

A Moral in the Dependent Variable Story?

In sum, the dependent variables of interest during the early years were many and varied, as were the backgrounds of researchers and practitioners seeking to predict and influence them. In my opinion, as our field has developed, both the specifications for what an I–O psychologist is and the diversity of criterion variables of interest have seemed to narrow. Until just recently the bulk of the attention was on performance and job satisfaction, with turnover/attrition as a distant third, at least as reflected in the major journals and SIOP programs. Although the increasing specialization and single-mindedness may be of some benefit, are they optimal for enhancing the future contributions of I–O psychology?

THE DEVELOPMENTAL YEARS

The 50-year developmental period of approximately 1920–1970 is well described across the chapters in this volume. It was a period of considerable growth, relatively speaking, in the application of psychology to behavior at work, although most of the expansion occurred during and after World War II, both in the United States as well as in Europe and Great Britain. In general, growth and expansion were pushed by the following:

• The two World Wars. In both instances, a large number of psychologists from mainly academic institutions volunteered or were conscripted into the war effort and turned their attention to applied human resource problems. The efforts and accomplishments of the Committee on the Psychological Examination of Recruits (Yerkes) and the Committee on the Classification of Personnel (Scott) in World War I are well known. World War II was a much more massive effort on the part of psychologists in many countries. Personnel selection, placement and classification, skills training, officer (aka management) training, leadership identification and training, ergonomics, human factors and systems design, and the determinants and consequences of morale all received much attention.

• Postwar economic expansion. What is not so often acknowledged is that such war efforts produce an economic expansion, at least for the winning side. Both after World War I and to a much, much greater degree after World War II, the psychologists who were, or became, interested in applied problems during the conflict were discharged into an expanding economy that could make good use of their skills.

• Government investment policies. To some degree, all governments invest in human resources. These investments may wax and wane to some degree, and there is variability in the proportions of such resources that are devoted to research and development versus operational programs. Also, there is variation in the degree to which different areas in the discipline participate in government-funded R&D efforts. However, in the aggregate, such R&D investments have significantly facilitated the expansion of I–O psychology. For example, the U.S. Department of Labor has supported considerable research on job/occupational analysis, and who can forget the U.S. Office of Personnel Management's support for the developments in meta-analysis and validity generalization?

• Investment in higher education. After World War II, and particularly between 1955 and 1975 in both the United States and United Kingdom, public investments in higher education were increased to meet the increased demand for college/university education. Graduate education also benefited from this investment, and the capacity to train I–O psychologists grew. The greater number of students and the greater number of faculty that resulted increased the volume of basic and applied research enormously.

• Private sector investment. For the most part, the private sector buys "practice" and not "research," although large organizations often do fund R&D to address their particular problems. During much of the post–World War II period, corporations such as Sears, General Motors, AT&T, Ford, and Proctor and Gamble maintained considerable in-house R&D resources in I–O psychology and contributed significantly to the research literature in management selection and development, skills training, job design, personnel selection and placement, employee attitudes, and organizational development. Sometimes, as with employment discrimination issues, the R&D investment is virtually mandated by public policy or the courts. More recently, the focus has tended to move from in-house R&D, as in the era of the Dearborn group (Meyer, chap. 6, this volume), to research that is contracted to external sources.

The primary reason for discussing the preceding influences is to argue that both the origins and early development of I–O psychology have resulted from multiple sources and that these different sources serve different goals. For example, a private employer funds R&D to enhance the bottom line, whereas a university supports R&D to enhance general knowledge and benefit the common good. Although they are not exclusive to I–O psychology, these multiple goals have produced a number of meta issues that always should be kept in mind.

THE META ISSUES

The origins of I–O psychology and the sources of its growth have produced a scientist/practitioner model that is somewhat different than the one represented by clinical and counseling psychology, which incorporates contributions to the "science" and service to the individual "client." Besides the science and the individual job holder (i.e., the client), we also explicitly deal with the interests of management or the ownership and with the public good (e.g., a more effective police force—or even a more effective national labor force). Different I–O researchers and practitioners address different interests, which is a good thing. We are not simply "servants of power" (Baritz, 1960). However, every one of us should always be clear about what interests we are attempting to address. We must not claim one goal while pursuing another.

Over much of the field's history, these multiple goals have highlighted several important choices. The most frequently discussed is probably the goal of contributing to science (being a productive researcher) versus the goal of helping the management (being an effective practitioner). Graduate programs agonize over how much each should be emphasized, and the SIOP program committee argues about how much program time to allocate to research and how much to allocate to describing and promoting effective professional practice. (See chap. 3 in this text for further discussion on the interplay between science and practice.)

Among those pursuing research goals, a second discussion often revolves around whether time and resources should be allocated to basic or applied research. For example, is it better to spend resources in investigating the basic covariance structures of personality, abilities, and components of occupational performance, or should our effort be spent on specific selection problems that specific organizations have (e.g., the St. Paul, Minnesota, Fire Department). A difficult feature of this discussion is that it is not always perfectly clear how to distinguish between basic and applied research.

Finally, we should never lose sight of the distinction between the individual and the institutional value systems, to use Cronbach and Gleser's (1965) terms. Again, this dichotomy is represented somewhat differently in clinical and counseling psychology than it is in I–O psychology, but for us, it is illustrated by the distinction between using research on individual differences in abilities, personality, interests, and performance to build better selection systems for the institution versus using this same research base to develop person–job fit procedures to serve the interests of individual job seekers. The latter was a major part of our field's history. Currently it has been swamped by the former and has been largely ceded to counseling psychology in its various forms. Again, it hurts a Minnesotan to realize that D. G. Paterson has been virtually defined out of I–O psychology's history.

Personal grief aside, the fundamental conclusion about all these choices is that none of them should be "resolved." They each highlight an important issue that the field must always think about; but as real choices, they are false. Science and practice are both critically important; basic and applied research are both valuable and necessary; and I–O psychology as a discipline should serve all of its masters—the science, the organization, the individual, and the public good.

ANOTHER KIND OF ISSUE: WHAT IS OURS?

Over the course of its development, from its origins to its current state, what has been the nature of the relation between I–O psychology and its mother discipline? One question to ask is whether the productive transport of theory, research, methodology, and the technology of professional practice from one part of the discipline to another has been a one-way or two-way street. That is, has I–O psychology developed theory and methods it can call its own, or have we simply borrowed everything from other parts of psychology? In considering this question we must keep in mind the difficulty of making the distinction between I–O psychology and other kinds of psychology. In the beginning, when the discipline was very small, they were one and the same. Currently, the membership is much more easily identified.

It would take a number of volumes to address this issue thoroughly and the distal reaction might be "so what," but the conclusion here is that I–O psychology has indeed made significant contributions to the broader discipline, and it has also borrowed a lot. However, the moral of the story is that it should do much more of both.

Realizing that the appropriate level of documentation is not possible in a brief chapter, areas of research, theory, and practice that have indeed had their core development within I–O psychology and should be transported elsewhere are noted subsequently. Many readers will disagree with the choices. Argument and discussion are invited.

Leadership

First and foremost I would argue that theory, research, and the practices associated with leadership identification and development are ours. Obviously, leadership has been of great interest to biographers and historians for centuries, but the scientific study of leadership really commenced during World War I with a concern for appraising leadership performance and conducting officer training under the guidance of the Committee on Classification chaired by Walter Dill Scott. The handbook of leadership research has always been compiled and edited by an I–O psychologist (e.g., Bass, 1990; Stogdill, 1974), and the theory and research efforts that finally broke away from the historical/literary "great man" model were conducted by I–O psychologists at Michigan and Ohio State (Yukl & Van Fleet, 1992). Virtually all subsequent theory developments have been the product of I–O efforts (Hughes, Ginnett, & Curphy, 1993; Yukl, 1998), and I am including the organizational behavior types located in schools of business and management under the I–O umbrella.

It is also true that the 20th century saw a long tradition of research on emergent leadership in social psychology (e.g., Mann, 1959), but the focus there was on the individual, situational, and task characteristics that correlated with emergence as a leader in originally leaderless small face-to-face groups. Although the lack of large trait correlations posed problems for the "great man" model, there was little concern in this research paradigm for leadership theory broadly construed or for going much beyond the operational definition of emerge/not emerge as a criterion of leader performance.

Leadership is a vitally important role in the human experience, and it plays a big part in the functioning of organizations. It also plays a critical role in the family, the classroom, and the social network. It is not simply in the eye of the beholder. To what extent have leadership theory, research findings, and leadership development practices been exported from I–O to these other venues? If the answer is not much, then the next question is why not?

Training Design

When Robert Gagné (1962) challenged the primacy of the contributions of basic theory and research in "learning" to the design of instruction, he shifted the focus from the conditions of learning (e.g., types of practice) to the more fundamental questions of what should be learned and how the optimal instructional content should be specified. This paradigm shift occurred in the context of military skills training and thus is an I–O psychology development, even though Gagne was trained in educational psychology. Also, the closest historical precursor is not in educational psychology, or learning theory, but in the work of Walter Dill Scott and Walter Van Dyke Bingham at the Carnegie Institute of Applied Psychology (Gilmer, 1961). Their early work focused on insurance sales training and had a very modern look to it. In sum, there is simply much more to training design than considerations of learning principles (i.e., practice, feedback, part vs. whole, etc.) or choices among what media bells-and-whistles to use (e.g., distance learning or virtual classrooms); I–O psychology offers the most comprehensive account of the instructional/training design process (Campbell & Kuncel, 2001).

Performance Theory

It was a long time in coming, but I–O psychology has at last produced comprehensive models of complex individual performance, as it is found in occupational settings (Borman & Motowidlo, 1993; Campbell, Gasser, & Oswald, 1996; Murphy, 1989). These models are specifications for what the content of performance is; for how it is related to other variables such as productivity, unit effectiveness, and the "bottom line"; and for how the determinants of individual differences in performance should be conceptualized and structured. Not to know this literature at a very expert level is to be prevented from thinking clearly about a fundamental part of the field. Unfortunately, the developments in performance theory in I–O psychology seem not to have made any significant inroads into other parts of the discipline that use the term *human performance* as a label for a dependent variable. By and large, outside of I–O psychology the meaning of performance is either unexamined or tied directly to whatever specific measure happens to wind up on the dependent variable side. Possible exceptions are performance in specific sports or artistic expression, but even in these domains the contextual factors of performance may be ignored.

Human Motivation (i.e., to Expend Effort in a Certain Direction, at a Certain Intensity, and for a Specific Length of Time)

We could argue at some length about whether I–O psychology "owns" motivation, and many would disagree that it does. For example, the original proponents of social learning theory (Bandura, 1997) and action control (Kuhl, 1986) were not I–O psychologists, and they were not trying to offer explanations for individual differences in choice behaviors that are similar to the choices of effort direction, level, and duration that we worry about in the work context. Similar things could be said about operant models, behavior modification, and the behaviorist tradition. Although I–O psychology has used all of these to address workplace issues, they originated elsewhere (e.g., see Kanfer, 1990). On another dimension, the traditional experimental psychology concern with physiological markers of arousal level as an indicator of motivation has been of little relevance for understanding work motivation.

However, two major pillars of theory and research in human motivation that are I–O psychology based are cognitive-expectancy theory as formulated by Vroom (1964) and the work on goal setting and its effects by Locke and his colleagues (Locke & Latham, 1990). These contributions were developed by I–O psychologists for I–O psychology, but they appear to have had very little application outside of I–O psychology (Latham & Budworth, this volume). The vexing question is why we often make quite good use of theory and research developed in other parts of the discipline but the reverse seems not to be true, particularly for things such as leadership, performance modeling, and motivation.

The High-Performance Work Team

The study of inter- and intragroup relationships has been a mainstay of social psychology for decades (e.g., Cartwright & Zander, 1968; McGrath, 1966). It includes the literature on emergent leadership mentioned earlier as well as a myriad of independent variables ranging from group member personalities, abilities, and attitudes to group interaction formats (e.g., nominal groups vs. face to face), to variation in group member roles (e.g., task vs. maintenance), to reward contingencies, to the manipulation of interpersonal perceptions. The dependent variables have been equally diverse (e.g., group problem-solving achievement, inter- or intragroup conflict, degree of social loafing, expressions of subgroup bias, communication effectiveness, satisfaction with other group members, etc.).

The concern of I–O psychology with the work group also has a long, but perhaps not as diverse, tradition. It began in earnest with the concern for within-group social norms and their effects on group member productivity and satisfaction at Hawthorne. It intensified during and after World War II with the increased attention devoted to participation in decision making and modeling the role of an effective work-group leader. Research on work-group leader training (e.g., Maier 1963; Maier & Shaskin, 1971; Vroom & Yetton 1973) is almost exclusively an I–O enterprise. Currently, concern for work-group phenomena seems to center on the "high performance team" (Salas, Priest, Stagl, Sims, & Burke, chap. 17, this volume), which is characterized by cross-training of group members, making every group member responsible for certain supervisory/management functions (e.g., cost control, performance monitoring, work scheduling, problem solving, supporting other group members, etc.) and team as well as individual reward systems.

Research and theory on the high-performance team are a valuable contribution to our understanding of a very important kind of group, and they can be credited to I–O psychology. However, perhaps the most striking characteristic of this general area is the relatively small degree to which the theory and research in social psychology have seemed to influence the work on high-performance teams in I–O psychology and vice versa. If the research and theory in one domain were common knowledge in the other, both would be enriched.

Assessment Methods

Because so much of our existence is based on reliable and valid measurement of critical dimensions of individual differences, can I–O psychology lay claim to the development of important assessment techniques? It's a mixed record. Certainly, Binet, Cattell, and Thurstone were not trained I–O psychologists. However, the developers of the Army Alpha, the precursor of all group measures of general mental ability, had very strong tendencies toward applied occupational psychology. Bruce Moore and Thomas Freyd had a lot to do with interest measurement, and one might even call E. K. Strong an I–O psychologist. Also, between 1930 and 1960 a large number of psychomotor and cognitive ability tests were developed to assess specific ability factors. (See Tiffen and McCormick, 1965, and Fleishman and Reilly, 1992, for comprehensive discussions.) These assessment tools had wide use in vocational counseling and guidance as well as personnel selection and job placement and were developed by I–O psychologists. Personal background information (i.e., "bio-data") is used in research in many areas of psychology, but I–O psychology has done the bulk of the research on its utility and latent structure (Mumford & Owens, 1987). We have had much to offer here.

A major assessment technique that was developed within I–O psychology is the assessment center, and its origins go back to its role in officer selection in the German military and its use in selecting intelligence operatives for the U.S. Office of Strategic Services in World War II. The AT&T Management Progress Study (Bray, Campbell, & Grant, 1974; Bray & Grant, 1966) made the assessment center method part of our body and soul. One question we might ask is whether I–O psychology has "exported" the assessment center to the same extent that we have imported personality assessment via self-description inventories. For example, are assessment centers used to select students for professional schools, for professional certification, for determining student's developmental needs, for data collection in social psychology, and so on? I think the answer is that the assessment center is not one of our major exports. Why is that? Should it be?

The Nature of Human Judgments of Performance

The nature of one individual's judgments about the characteristics of another is studied by researchers in behavioral decision theory, cognitive psychology, social psychology, clinical psychology, economics, and probably many other disciplines as well. However, the contributions of our large body of literature on performance ratings seem relatively unique and can be set apart from behavioral decision theory and social cognition. No one else has had the same concerns with reliability, validity, and the full modeling of the variance components in such judgments. The comprehensive decomposition of rating variance into its discriminable and potentially estimable components by Robert Wherry (Wherry & Bartlett, 1982) is a tour de force and can subsume all known I–O research on performance judgments. Although we may despair over our inability to make large improvements in the reliability, accuracy, and decontamination of performance judgments, we have made major gains in our understanding of such judgments, going far beyond considerations of interrater reliability and the classic rating errors (e.g., McCloy & Putka, 2004; Murphy & Cleveland, 1995).

If performance judgments encompass so many critical questions in many fields, not just ours, and if I–O psychology has been a substantial contributor to theory and research on these issues, what has been our impact on other parts of the discipline? Again it would be difficult to document, but my own judgment is that "we" have used more from "them" than "they" have from "us," even though one person's judgment about another's performance is as important for understanding social interactions, educational processes, and clinical interventions as it is for assessing of individual job performance. Also, even though we have made profitable use of work in social cognition (e.g., stereotypes as measurement contaminants) and cognitive information processing models, there is much more that could be imported. I have a growing conviction that when we consider issues of individual behavior in organizations, I–O psychology still does not fully use the resources that the parent discipline has to offer.

Attitude (Job Satisfaction) Assessment

I–O psychology seems not to have contributed to basic attitude theory and measurement, and we have borrowed heavily from social psychology, personality measurement, and scaling technology. Nevertheless, theory and research on job satisfaction are perhaps our largest single body of literature, and although the measurement methods came from elsewhere, the body of reliable findings is extensive, sometimes counterintuitive (e.g., are people actually more "satisfied" than they should be?), and has important implications for our society. What's again surprising is that although we tend to frequently cite work from other areas on issues pertaining to life satisfaction, happiness, or self-estimates of well-being, the reverse tends not to be true. Researchers of "happiness" (Lykken, 1999) and "well being" (Diener, 1984; Diener & Oishi, 2000) do not cite the job satisfaction literature. More recently, Diener and Seligman (2004) have given at least some recognition to I–O research.

Quantitative Modeling

Although I–O psychology has made many important embellishments to factor analysis, reliability estimation, utility models, and item response theory (see Zickar & Gibby, chap. 3, this volume), in general the statistical models used to describe or estimate the latent structure of psychological data did not come from within I–O psychology. However, there are three major exceptions, all of which are critical.

The first is the development of personnel classification models that permit the evaluation of the complex parameters that characterize any real-world selection and classification context. That is, what are the effects on the potential gains from selection and classification of the predictor validities, the latent structure of the predictor set, the selection ratio, the number of jobs, the assignment quotas, and the degree of differential prediction? Classification models have broad applicability across clinical, counseling, and vocational psychology, as well as for personnel decision making from the institutional perspective (Cronbach & Gleser, 1965).

The second is the modeling of "bias" and "fairness" in personnel decision making (Hough, Oswald, & Ployhart, 2001). The models that portray the complex interplay of statistical estimates, measurement considerations, and the value judgments that cannot be avoided come from I–O psychology. One can make different choices about what bias and fairness mean, but the necessity for making the choices cannot be escaped (Campbell, 1996). These models deserve greater export than they have achieved. The lack of export is perhaps because they illuminate choices that people do not want to make.

The third, of course, is meta-analysis and validity generalization. Hunter and Schmidt's (2004) contributions are one of I–O psychology's most significant exports. If there is one prime example where the trade balance favors exports over imports, this is it. Although the contributions of Eugene Glass (1977) must be acknowledged, and the models that deal only with the sampling error artifact when describing study-to-study variation are the same in psychology as they are in physics (Hedges, 1987), the Schmidt and Hunter contribution is a major innovation. Hunter and Schmidt were formally recognized by the American Psychological Association for their contributions to psychological science in general. Courses in meta-analysis taught by I–O psychologists are attended by students from many different disciplines, and methodological articles on meta-analysis are published in journals with more general audiences than I–O journals.

Summary

The bottom line here is that I–O psychology has produced a number of valuable innovations that have enriched our theory and practice. To a certain extent they have also influenced research and practice in other areas of psychology, but not to the extent that they should. We import more than we export and most certainly should do much more of both.

Although individual readers may disagree with some of the named innovations or think that there are serious errors of omission, the topics represent a broad sample ranging from basic to applied contributions and represent both research and practice. This is as it should be if I–O psychology is characterized as the application of psychology to the measurement, understanding, prediction, and change of individual behavior in organizations. We are obligated to use the science in its entirety.

THE FUTURE: ADAPTATION AND GROWTH

So far, this chapter has considered (a) the multivariate nature of our origins, particularly if we resist a U.S. myopia and fully include other countries in the historical account; (b) the diversity of the dependent variables that characterized the field, at least early on; (c) the multiple forces that seemed to promote our historical growth; (d) the critical value judgments with which we must deal; and (e) the varied number of innovations the field has produced.

If we now look toward the future and ask how we can profit from the past and continue to improve our contributions, it brings us back, I think, to the adaptability of variability. To be less esoteric, what specific policies, practices, and structures would help us on our way, if history is a guide? How can we profit from history? The following points are offered.

What to Study

I am, let's face it, elderly, and I participated in a SIOP (then APA Division 14)-sponsored conference on innovations in I–O research in 1980. The conference produced four books, one of which was titled *What to Study* (Campbell, Hulin, & Daft, 1982). Looking back on it, I think the volume paid too much attention to the independent variable side and not enough to the dependent variable side. That is, there was an almost exclusive concern with performance and job satisfaction, and the innovative action was on the independent variable side.

In my opinion, I–O psychology has regressed from the early dependent variable (i.e., criterion) diversity chronicled in several of the chapters in this book to a much narrower focus. There are many other dependent variables that have current or potential importance for the viability of the occupational system (e.g., physical and mental health, fatigue, stress, occupational choice, critical errors, etc.), and we should not lose sight of them. For example, if future economic or political events so influence the occupational choices that people make that critical positions go begging for talent, will we be prepared as a field to address this issue? To be even more specific, we currently have a professional volunteer Army. A relevant set of research questions concerns the conditions under which the number of people willing to enlist will go up or down, and why.

I–O psychology could diversify its criterion array even more if it were not fixated quite so much on modeling criterion variation as a continuous normal distribution. Human factors psychology, as well as various engineering specialties, sometimes focuses on the determinants of serious "errors," or discrete outcomes of critical importance. In human factors psychology, an outstanding success story in this regard is the analysis of airline accidents that led to the development of cockpit resource management (CRM) training (Foushee, 1984; Helmreich & Foushee, 1993). Another example is the study of what determines the achievement of particularly high expertise (Ericsson & Charness, 1994). Both error analysis and the analysis of expertise could be much more widely used in I–O psychology. Sensing our weakness in these areas (they say so explicitly), cognitive/human factors psychologists have intruded into job analysis itself, our traditional heartland (Schraagen, Chipman, & Shalin, 2000).

The overall assertion here is that the number of critical dependent variables our field pursues has become smaller over our short history. Also, although the normal bivariate model is a very useful one for examining the possible determinants of variation in the dependent variable, it is not the only way to model criterion variation and its determinants. We should be more eclectic.

The Influence of Other Specialties

In the beginning, there were no I–O psychologists, only physicians, engineers, managers, and other kinds of psychologists who addressed applied problems dealing with individual behavior at work. From then to now, researchers from a variety of disciplines and subspecialties have continued to contribute theory and knowledge and enrich our field. Many of the chapters in this volume speak to these contributions. We ourselves have borrowed heavily from social, cognitive, clinical, and counseling psychology; personality and individual differences; and even behavior genetics. All of this is a good thing. It promotes new questions, new models, and new methods and contributes to our ability to adapt to changing conditions. We should do even more of it. The more each of us knows about theory and research in other areas, the higher the probability that we can avoid mistakes already committed elsewhere and the greater the likelihood of finding innovative procedures and models.

By contrast, the innovations in I–O psychology tend not to influence other subspecialties as much as they influence us. Why is that? There may be two major reasons. First, we tend to publish in journals that are not generally read by people in other specialties, and second, we tend not to invade others' turf (e.g., education, mental health, economics, higher order cognition), although they freely invade ours. It is as if we don't have any particular need or desire to exert a broader influence. Everyone can probably think of exceptions to these assertions (e.g. meta-analysis, cognitive ability models, personality theory), but it is surprising to see how untouched other subspecialties are by I–O developments in leadership theory and research, motivation, and instructional design. Wider exposure would help our field develop its future. We should adopt it as a goal. What seems to prevent us from doing that? Are the reasons motivational, knowledge and skill based, or structural (i.e., constraints that function independently of individual motivation and skill)? Unfortunately, the answer may be all of the above.

It is probably the case that a smaller and smaller percentage of I–O psychologists are in work settings that reward research on general problems with broad implications. The consequences are that there are fewer role models and fewer students whose socialization points them toward a broader perspective. Also, the greater the extent to which our work is intended to serve the interests of organization management, the less is the attention given to serving the science and the public good, which in turn results in further insulation from the broader discipline. As many graduate training programs take on a narrower perspective, so do the breadth of knowledge and skill of both faculty and students. We may be quite methodologically and substantively sophisticated about in-house issues but not in ways that better connect us to the discipline.

Science, Practice, and Values

Our history shows that we have benefited immensely from the scientist–practitioner model, even before it was given a name at the Boulder Conference in 1949. We are a discipline that is trying to make a difference in a set of dependent variables that are critical for the functioning of the economy and society. Basic research, applied research, and the experiences of practice all contribute to this goal, and it is difficult to forecast when the contributions of one versus the other will be the most beneficial. They inform each other and all must be nurtured. There must be institutional support for each.

Such support has come from a variety of settings: colleges and universities, research centers affiliated with universities, the military services, private corporations, federal agencies, nonprofit research organizations, and for-profit research and consulting firms. This variety is golden and vitally necessary for our future. I worry that the spectrum is shrinking, especially with regard to the support and protection of basic research and also with regard to the support for organizations that conduct cutting-edge R&D on specific new practices.

Part of this overall issue is the preservation of differing value systems. Research and practice can serve the interests of the individual, the employing organization, or the "common good," as in federally supported human resource programs that benefit both individual job seekers and employers. We might ask whether we have become too focused on just one of these. Serving the management is an important goal, but it should not be the only goal. Researchers and practitioners who focus on the needs of individuals and on a common good that benefits everyone should be supported as well. At the very least we should all recognize our own value system, be it explicit or implicit, with which we go about our own work.

Education and Training in I–O Psychology

If this history argues for anything it is that education and training in I–O psychology must incorporate a great deal of variability. One training model should not fit all. It can't possibly anticipate all the changes in disciplinary expertise that will be needed. Universal accreditation of graduate programs would be even worse. Both accreditation and only one training model would, at worst, virtually guarantee our extinction and at best severely limit our adaptability to a changing world.

Another implication of the need for variability is that "ranking" programs in terms of their overall excellence is sheer folly and really benefits no one. Graduate programs are not unidimensional. What dominating general factor is implied when programs are ranked on a single dimension? Competition for rankings has an even more deleterious effect on our future viability as a field. We should cherish multidimensionality in programs, not try to stamp it out.

A FINAL WORD

As reflected in the chapters in this volume, the history of I–O psychology worldwide is characterized by diversity in its participants, dependent variables, sources of support, settings for research and practice, relative emphasis on research (basic and applied) and practice, and the goals that it serves. As the field developed over the 20th century, some critical elements of this diversity seemed to contract due to a variety of factors and not because anyone was at fault.

However, variability promotes adaptability, and if we wish to grow in aggregate "value," then uniformity in membership, goals, questions addressed, potential users, work settings, and training strategies should be avoided.

REFERENCES

Bandura, A. (1997). *Self-efficacy: The exercise of control.* Stanford, CT: Freeman.

Baritz, L. (1960). *The servants of power: A history of the use of social science in American industry.* Middletown, CT: Wesleyan University Press.

Bass, B. M. (1990). *Bass and Stogdill's handbook of leadership: Theory, research and managerial applications* (3rd ed.). New York: Free Press.

Borman, W. C., & Motowidlo, S. J. (1993). Expanding the criterion domain to include elements of contextual performance. In N. Schmitt & W. C. Borman (Eds.), *Personnel selection in organizations* (pp. 71–98). San Francisco: Jossey-Bass.

Bray, D. W., Campbell, R. J., & Grant, D. L. (1974). *Formative years in business: A long-term AT&T study of managerial lives.* New York: Wiley.

Bray, D. W., & Grant, D. L. (1966). The assessment center in the measurement of potential for business management. *Psychological Monographs: General and Applied, 80.*

Campbell, J. P. (1996). Group differences and personnel decisions: Validity, fairness, and affirmative action. *Journal of Vocational Behavior, 49,* 122–158.

Campbell, J. P., Gasser, M. B., & Oswald, F. L. (1996). The substantive nature of job performance variability. In K. R. Murphy (Ed.), *Individual differences and behavior in organizations* (pp. 258–299). San Francisco: Jossey-Bass.

Campbell, J. P., Hulin, C. L. & Daft, R. L. (1982). *Generating and developing research questions in applied psychology.* Beverly Hills, CA: Sage.

Campbell, J. P., & Kuncel, N. R. (2001). Individual and team training. In N. Anderson, D. S. Ones, H. K. Sinangil, & C. Viswesvaran (Eds.), *Handbook of work and organizational psychology* (Vol. 1, pp. 278–312). London: Blackwell.

Campbell, J. P., & Pritchard, R. D. (1976). Motivation theory. In M. D. Dunnette (Ed.), *Handbook of industrial and organizational psychology* (pp. 63–130). Chicago: Rand McNally.

Cartwright, D., & Zander, A. (Eds.). (1968). *Group dynamics. Research and theory.* New York: Harper & Row.

Cronbach, L. J., & Gleser, G. C. (1965). *Psychological tests and personnel decisions* (2nd ed.). Urbana: University of Illinois Press.

Diener, E. (1984). Subjective well-being. *Psychological Bulletin, 95,* 542–575.

Diener, E., & Oishi, S. (2000). Money and happiness: Income and subjective well-being across nations. In E. Diener & E. M. Suh (Eds.), *Culture and subjective well-being* (pp. 185–218). Cambridge, MA: MIT Press.

Diener, E., & Seligman, M. E. P. (2004). Beyond money: Toward an economy of well-being. *Psychological Science in the Public Interest, 5,* 1–31.

Deming, W. E. (1981). Improvement of quality and productivity through action by management. *National Productivity Review, 1,* 12–22.

Dunnette, M. D., Campbell, J. P., & Hakel, M. D. (1967). Factors contributing to job satisfaction and job dissatisfaction in six occupational groups. *Organizational Behavior and Human Performance, 2,* 143–174.

Ericsson, K. A., & Charness, N. (1994). Expert performance: Its structure and acquisition. *American Psychologist, 49,* 725–747.

Fleishman, E. A., & Reilly, M. E. (1992). *Handbook of human abilities: Definitions, measurements, and job task requirements.* Palo Alto, CA: Consulting Psychologists Press.

Foushee, H. C. (1984). Dyads and triads at 35,000 feet: Factors affecting group processes and aircrew performance. *American Psychologist, 39,* 885–893.

Gagné, R. M. (1962). Military training and principles of learning. *American Psychologist, 17,* 83–91.

Gilbreth, L. (1917). *Applied motion study.* New York: Sturgis & Walton.

Gilmer, B. V. H. (1961). *Industrial psychology.* New York: McGraw-Hill.

Glass, G. V. (1997). Integrating findings: The meta analysis of research. *Review of Research in Education, 5,* 351–379.

Hart, P. M., & Cooper, G. L. (2001). Occupational stress: Toward a more integrated framework. In N. Anderson, D. S. Owens, H. K. Sinangil, & C. V. Viswesvaran (Eds.), *Handbook of work and organizational psychology* (Vol. 2, pp. 93–114). London: Sage.

Hedges, L. (1987). How hard is hard science, how soft is soft science: The empirical cumulativeness of research. *American Psychologist, 42,* 443–455.

Helmreich, R. L., & Foushee, H. C. (1993). Why crew resource management? Empirical and theoretical bases of human factors training in aviation. In E. L. Wiener, B. G., Kanki & R. L. Helmreich (Eds.), *Cockpit resource management* (pp. 3–45). New York: Academic Press.

Herzberg, F., Mausner, B., & Snyderman, B. (1959). *The motivation to work.* New York: Wiley.

Hough, L. E., Oswald, F. L. & Ployhart, R. E. (2001). Determinants, detection, and amelioration of adverse impact in personnel selection procedures; Issues, evidence, and lessons learned. *International Journal of Selection and Placement, 9,* 152–194.

Hughes, R. L., Ginnett, R. C., & Curphy, G. J. (1993). *Leadership: Enhancing the lessons of experience.* Boston: Irwin.

Hunter, J. E., & Schmidt, F. L. (2004). *Methods of meta-analysis: Correcting error and bias in research findings* (2nd ed.). Thousand Oaks, CA: Sage.

Judge, T. A., Erez, A., & Bono, J. E. (1998). The power of being positive: The relationship between positive self-concept and job performance. *Human Performance, 11,* 167–187.

Kane, J. S., & Lawler, E. E. (1979). Performance appraisal effectiveness: Its assessment and determinants. In B. Staw (Ed.), *Research in organizational behavior* (Vol.1, pp. 425–478). Greenwich, CT: JAI.

Kanfer, R. (1990). Motivation theory and industrial/organizational psychology. In M. D. Dunnette & L. Hough (Eds.), *Handbook of industrial and organizational psychology: Vol. I. Theory in industrial and organizational psychology* (pp. 75–170). Palo Alto, CA: Consulting Psychologists Press.

Kuhl, J. (1986). Integrating cognitive and dynamic approaches: A prospectus for a unified motivational psychology. In J. Kuhl & J. W. Atkinson (Eds.), *Motivation, thought, and action* (pp. 307–336). New York: Praeger.

Lewin, K., Lippitt, R., & White, R. K. (1939). Patterns of aggressive behavior in experimentally created social climates. *Journal of Social Psychology, 10,* 271–279.

Locke, E. A., & Latham, G. P. (1990). *A theory of goal setting and task performance.* Englewood Cliffs, NJ: Prentice-Hall.

Lykken, D. T. (1999). *Happiness: What studies on twins show us about nature, nurture, and the happiness set point.* New York: Golden Books.

Maier, N. R. F. (1963). *Problem solving discussions and conferences.* New York: McGraw-Hill.

Maier, N. R. F., & Sashkin, M. (1971). Specific leadership behaviors that promote problem solving. *Personnel Psychology, 24,* 34–44.

Mann, R. D. (1959). A review of the relationships between personality and performance in small groups. *Psychological Bulletin, 56,* 241–270.

McCloy, R. A., & Putka, D. J. (2004, April). *Estimating interrater reliability: Conquering the messiness of real-world data.* Master tutorial. Society for I–O Psychology annual conference, Chicago.

McGrath, J. E. (1966). *Small group research.* New York: Holt, Rinehart & Winston.

Mumford, M. D., & Owens, W. A. (1987). Methodology review: Principles, procedures, and findings in the application and background data measures. *Applied Psychological Measurement 11,* 1–31.

Murphy, K. R. (1989). Dimensions of job performance. In R. Dillon & J. Pelligrino (Eds.), *Testing: Applied and theoretical perspectives* (pp. 218–247). New York: Praeger.

Murphy, K. R. & Cleveland, J. N. (1995). *Understanding performance appraisal: Social, organizational, and goal-based perspectives.* Thousand Oaks, CA: Sage.

Paterson, D. G. (1957). The conservation of human talent. *American Psychologist, 12,* 134–144.

Pulakos, E. D., Arad, S., Donovan, M. A., & Plamondon, K. E. (2000). Adaptability in the work place: Development of a taxonomy of adaptive performance. *Journal of Applied Psychology, 85,* 612–624.

Schraagen, J. M., Chipman, S. F., & Shalin, V. J. (Eds.). (2000). *Cognitive task analysis.* Mahwah, NJ: Lawrence Erlbaum Associates.

Stogdill, R. M. (1974). *Handbook of leadership.* New York: Free Press.

Taylor, F. W. (1919). *Principles of scientific management.* New York: Harper.

Tiffin, J., & McCormick, E. J. (1965). *Industrial Psychology* (5th ed.). Englewood Cliffs, NJ: Prentice-Hall.

Vroom, V. H. (1964). *Work motivation.* New York: Wiley.

Vroom, V. H., & Yetton, P. W. (1973). *Leadership and decision making.* Pittsburgh: University of Pittsburgh Press.

Wherry, R. J., & Bartlett, C. J. (1982). The control of bias in ratings: A theory of rating. *Personnel Psychology, 35,* 521–551.

Yukl, G. (1998). *Leadership in organizations* (4th ed.). Englewood Cliffs, NJ: Prentice-Hall.

Yukl, G., & Van Fleet, D. D. (1992). Theory and research on leadership in organizations. In M. Dunnette & L. Hough (Eds.), *Handbook of industrial and organizational psychology* (2nd ed., Vol. 3, pp. 147–198). Palo Alto, CA: Consulting Psychologists Press.

VII

Appendix

Appendix One

Some Historical Resources
for Psychology and I–O Psychology

This appendix contains a list of historical resources for the scholar, teacher, practitioner, or student whose curiosity has been inspired to learn more about I–O history and/or psychology history. An attempt was made to not replicate resources/references presented elsewhere in the book, although some repetition is possible. This is not an all-inclusive or complete listing of every resource available; of course, there is a considerably wider range of resources available than shown here. The Web addresses are correct at the time of going to press; however, given the nature of the Internet, these addresses may have changed. The information presented here was derived from the editor's research, and input from others. The idea for the structure was guided by L. T. Benjamin's research sources (see note a the end of Appendix One).

1. Obituaries and death dates of specific individuals

Necrologies formulated by Edwin G. Boring in the journal *Psychological Bulletin* (1928, *25*, 302–305 and 621–625, for years 1903–1927), (1954, *51*, 75–81, for years 1928–1952), (1966, *65*, 193–198, for years 1953–1964)

New York Times Obituary Index (1857–1968)

Monthly listings of the *American Psychologist*, beginning in 1946 for death dates, and beginning in 1978 for obituaries

American Journal of Psychology, beginning in 1887

Benjamin, L. T., Jr., & Schossman, W. (1983). Biographical sketches of eminent psychologists: A selected bibliography. *Psychological Documents, 31,* 1.

The Industrial–Organizational Psychologist, official publication of SIOP, www.siop.org

Obituaries may also be located in various journals related to the psychologist's expertise.

2. Manuscript collections for individuals and papers for professional organizations

For I–O psychology:

Bingham, W. V. D.: Carnegie Mellon Libraries: Research: University Archives

Bregman, E. O: Archives of the History of American Psychology (AHAP), University of Akron, Akron, Ohio 44325, www.uakron.edu/ahap/

461

Ferguson, L.: Carnegie Mellon Libraries: Research: University Archives
Gilbreth, F., & L. M.: Purdue University
Hayes, M. H. S.: U.S. National Archives, Washington, DC
Moore, B. V.: AHAP
Münsterberg, H.: Boston Public Library; Harvard University
Paterson, D. G.: University of Minnesota; AHAP
Scott, W. D.: Northwestern University
Stagner, R.: AHAP
Taylor, F.: F. W. Taylor Collection at the Stevens Institute of Technology, http://attila.stevens-tech.edu/~rdowns/
Viteles, M.: Penn State University; AHAP
Yerkes, R.: Yale University
Information on psychologists employed in universities can often be found in the archives of the universities where they were employed.
Society for Industrial and Organizational Psychology (APA Division 14): AHAP; APA Archives at the Library of Congress

For psychology, in general:

Sokal, M., & Rafail, P. (1982). *A guide to manuscript collections in the history of psychology and related areas.* New York: Kraus.
National Union Catalog of Manuscript Collections, The Library of Congress, http://www.loc.gov/coll/nucmc/
Locator file of the Archives of the History of American Psychology (AHAP), University of Akron, Akron, Ohio 44325, www.uakron.edu/ahap/
U.S. National Archives, http://www.archives.gov/
Locator files of the American Psychological Association (APA), Library of Congress (http://lcweb.loc.gov/) and the Archives of APA (www.apa.org)

3. Other sources of biographical material available on psychologists

For I–O psychology:

Clifford, G. J. (1984). *Edward L. Thorndike: The sane positivist.* Middletown, CT: Wesleyan Press.
Gilbreth, L. M. (1998). *As I remember: An autobiography.* Norcross, GA: Engineering and Management Press.
Graham, L. (1998). *Managing on her own: Dr. Lillian Gilbreth and women's work in the interwar era.* Norcross, GA: Engineering and Management Press.
Kraus, M. P. (1986). *Walter Van Dyke Bingham and the Bureau of Personnel Research.* New York: Garland.
SIOP Past–President Autobiographies, www.siop.org
Thayer, P. W. (1992). Autobiographies of past presidents of SIOP. *The Industrial–Organizational Psychologist, 29*(4), 42–50.

For psychology, in general:

American Psychological Association Directories (beginning in 1948)
Benjamin, L. T., Jr. (1980). Women in psychology: Biography and autobiography. *Psychology of Women Quarterly, 5,* 140–144.

enjamin, L. T., Jr., & Heider, K. L. (1976). History of psychology in biography: A bibliography. *JSAS Catalog of Selected Documents in Psychology, 6,* 61.

ography Index: A Cumulative Index to Biographical Material in Books and Magazines (a quarterly journal that began in 1947)

oring, E. G. (1980). *A history of experimental psychology* (22 ed.). NY: Appleton-Century-Crofts.

attell, J. M. (beginning in 1905), *American Men of Science*

orsini, R. J. (Ed.). (1994). *Encyclopedia of psychology* (Vol. 4). New York: Wiley.

eedheim, D. K. (Vol. Ed.). (2003). *History of psychology.* In I. B. Weiner (General Ed.), *Comprehensive handbook of psychology* (Vol. 1). New York: Wiley.

arraty, J. A. (Ed.). (1999). *American National Biography.* New York: Oxford University Press.

uthrie, R. V. (1998). *Even the rat was white: A historical view of psychology* (2nd ed.). Boston: Allyn & Bacon.

azdin, A. (Ed.). (2000). *Encyclopedia of psychology* (8 volumes). Washington, DC, and New York: American Psychological Association and Oxford University Press.

Connell, A., & Russo, N. F. (Eds.). (1983, 1988). *Models of achievement: Reflections of eminent women in psychology* (Vols. 1 and 2). New York: Columbia University Press and Hillsdale, NJ: Lawrence Erlbaum Associates.

Connell, A., & Russo, N. F. (Eds.). (1990). *Women in psychology: A bio–bibliographic sourcebook.* Westport, CT: Greenwood.

arborough, E., & Furumoto, L. (1988). *Untold lives: The first generation of American women psychologists.* New York: Columbia University Press.

evens, G., & Gardner, S. (1982). *The women in psychology* (Vols. 1 and 2). Cambridge, MA: Schenkman.

asne, L. (1975). *Names in the history of psychology: A biographical sourcebook.* New York: Halsted.

ree series containing monograph-length autobiographies:

History of Psychology in Autobiography

Vol. 1, 1930, C. Murchison (Ed.), Clark University Press
Vol. 2, 1932, C. Murchison (Ed.), Clark University Press
Vol. 3, 1936, C. Murchison (Ed.), Clark University Press
Vol. 4, 1952, E. G. Boring, et al. (Eds.), Clark University Press
Vol. 5, 1967, E. G. Boring & G. Lindzey (Eds.), Irvington
Vol. 6, 1974, G. Lindzey (Ed.), Prentice Hall
Vol. 7, 1980, G. Lindzey (Ed.), Freeman
Vol. 8, 1989, G. Lindzey (Ed.), Stanford University Press
Vol. 9, 1994, G. Lindzey (Ed.), Stanford University Press

e Psychologists

Vol. 1, 1972, T. S. Krawiec (Ed.), Oxford University Press
Vol. 2, 1974, T. S. Krawiec (Ed.), Oxford University Press

ortraits of Pioneers in Psychology

Vol. 1, 1991, Kimble/Wertheimer, APA

Vol. 2, 1996, Kimble/Wertheimer, APA
Vol. 3, 1998, Kimble/Wertheimer, APA
Vol. 4, 2000, Kimble/Wertheimer, APA
Vol. 5, 2003, Kimble/Wertheimer, APA
Vol. 6, in press, APA

4. Photographs of psychologists or other illustrations

Bergman, L. V., & Dallenbach, K. M. (1933). Portraits useful to the psychologist. *Americ* *Journal of Psychology, 45,* 165–171.
Bringmann, W. G., Luck, H. E., Miller, R., & Early, C. D. (Eds.). (1997). *A pictorial history psychology.* Carol Stream, IL: Quintessence.
Luck, H. E., & Miller, R. (Eds.). (1993). *Illustrierte geschichte der psychologie.* Munic Quintessence.
Popplestone, J. A., & McPherson, M. W. (1994). *An illustrated history of American psyche ogy.* Madison, WI: Brown & Benchmark.
Roback, A. A., & Kiernan, T. (1969). *Pictorial history of psychology and psychiatry.* Ne York: Philosophical Library.
The Psychologists series
A History of Psychology in Autobiography series
Portraits of Pioneers series

5. Information about a particular topic

Baldwin, J. M. (1904). *Dictionary of psychology and philosophy* (Vols. 1–3). New Yor Macmillan.
Bibliographical Index: A Cumulative Bibliography of bibliographies (1938 through today
Hall, G. K. (1966). *Cumulative subject index to psychological abstracts (1927–1960)* (Vols and 2). Boston.
Index of American Journal of Psychology (Vols. 1–30, 1920).
ISIS Cumulative Bibliography of the History of Science (Vols. 1 and 2, 1971).
London: Mansell. (Note: these two volumes covers the years 1913 to 1965. Subsequent vc umes are complete through 1985. Annual bibliographies are published by ISIS.)
Kimble, G. A., & Schlesginer, K. (Eds.). (1985). *Topics in the history of psychology.* Hillsda NJ: Lawrence Erlbaum Associates.
Lawry, J. D. (1990). *Guide to the history of psychology.* Lanham, MD: University Press America.
Louttit, C. (1928). *Bibliography of bibliographies on psychology, 1920–1927.* Washingtc DC: National Research Council.
Popplestone, J. A., & McPherson, M. W. (1988). *Dictionary of concepts in general psyche ogy.* New York: Greenwood.
Watson, R. I. (1978). *The history of psychology and the behavioral sciences: A bibliograph guide.* New York: Springer.
Watson, R. I., Sr., & Evans, R. B. (1991). *The great psychologists: A history of psychologic thought.* New York: HarperCollins.
Viney, W., Wertheimer, M., & Wertheimer, M. (1979). *History of psychology: A guide to infc mation sources.* Detroit: Gale.
History of Psychology journal (1998–present)
Journal of the History of the Behavioral Sciences (1965–present)

Information about published works

Annual Reviews of Psychology. Palo Alto, CA: Stanford University Press.

Psychological Abstracts. Washington, DC: American Psychological Association.

Fleishman, E. A. (1961). *Studies in personnel and industrial psychology.* Homewood, IL: Dorsey Press.

Hall, G. K. (1960). *Cumulative author index to psychological index (1894–1935) and psychological abstracts (1927–1963),* 6 volumes.

Hepner, H. W., & Gilmer, B. V. H. (1952). *Readings in industrial and business psychology.* New York: McGraw-Hill.

Moore, B. V., & Hartman, G. W. (Eds.). (1931b). *Readings in industrial psychology.* New York: Appleton.

Murchison, C. (1929 and 1932). *The psychological register* (Vols. 2 and 3). Worcester, MA: Clark University Press.

Watson, R. I. (1974, 1976). *Eminent contributors to psychology* (Vols. 1 and 2). New York: Springer.

Other information on psychologists and psychology

For I–O psychology

Society for Industrial and Organizational Psychology (SIOP), www.siop.org

Andy's Family Tree in *TIP*, www.siop.org

SIOP Surveys, www.siop.org

TIP historical series (1991–1993) (E. Levine, project editor) and other *TIP* issues

Lawrence Erlbaum Associates Series in Applied Psychology

SIOP: Organizational Frontiers Series

SIOP: Professional Practice Series

Bernreuter. R. G., Maxfield, F. N., Paterson, D. G., Reymert, M. L., & Fryer, D. H. (1937). The proposed American association of applied and professional psychology. *Journal of Applied Psychology, 21,* 320–341.

Civil Service Assembly of the United States and Canada. (1939). *Men at work: A progress report on the civil service assembly's survey of public personnel policies and practices.* Chicago: Civil Service Assembly.

Drenth, P. J. D., Thierry, H., Willems, P. J., & de Wolff, C. J. (Eds.). (1984). *Handbook of work and organizational psychology.* New York: Wiley.

Hedelyi, M., & Grossman, F. (1939). *Dictionary of terms and expressions of industrial psychology ("Psychotechnics").* New York: Pitman.

Fleishman, E. A. (1961). *Studies in personnel and industrial psychology.* Homewood, IL: Dorsey Press.

Louttit, C. M. (1943). *Directory of applied psychologists* (2nd ed.). New York: American Association for Applied Psychology.

Meltzer, H. (1960). Industrial psychology in *Psychological Abstracts* 1927–1959. *Journal of Applied Psychology, 44,* 111–114.

Smith, M. (1944). *Handbook of industrial psychology.* New York: Philosophical Library.

For psychology, in general:

Baxter, P. M. (1993). *Psychology: A guide to reference and information sources.* Englewood, CO: Libraries Unlimited.

Benjamin, L. T., Jr., Pratt, R., Watlington, D., Aaron, L., Bonar, T., Fitzgerald, S., et al. (198? *A history of American psychology in notes and news, 1883–1945: An index to journ sources.* New York: Kraus.

Bruner, J. S., & Allport, G. W. (1940). Fifty years of change in American psychology. *Psych logical Bulletin, 37,* 757–776.

Camfield, T. (1973). The professionalization of American psychology, 1870–1917. *Journal the History of Behavioral Sciences, 9,* 66–75.

Evans, R. B., Sexton, V. S., & Cadwallader, T. S. (Eds.). (1992). *The American Psychological A sociation: A historical perspective.* Washington, DC: American Psychological Association

Furumoto, L. (1987). On the margins: Women and the professionalization of psychology in t United States, 1890–1940. In M. G. Ash & W. R. Woodward (Eds.), *Psychology in twen eth-century thought and society* (pp. 93–113). Cambridge, England: Cambridge Universi Press.

Hillner, K. P. (1984). *History and systems of modern psychology: A conceptual approach.* Ne York: Gardner.

Osier, D. V., & Wozniak, R. H. (1984). *A century of serial publication in psycholog 1850–1950.* New York: Kraus.

Street, W. R. (1994). *A chronology of noteworthy events in American psychology.* Washingto DC: American Psychological Association.

Zusne, L. (1987). *Eponyms in psychology: A dictionary and biographical sourcebo* Westport, CT: Greenwood.

Society for the History of Psychology (APA Division 26), http://shp.yorku.ca/
Psychological Index, 1894–1935

8. Web sites (please note that these Web addresses are subject to change)

For psychology, in general:

http://elvers.stjoe.udayton.edu/history/history.htm (a web site that serves as a gateway to mo than 1,000 www resources related to the history of psychology)

History and philosophy of psychology Web resources:
  http://www.psych.yorku.ca/orgs/resource.htm

Professional societies and university programs:
  http://www.psych.yorku.ca/orgs/profsocs.htm

Individuals: http://www.psych.yorku.ca/orgs/individ.htm

General archives, collections, and individual links:
  http://www.psych.yorku.ca/orgs/archcoll.htm

Online books, journals, and other texts:
  http://www.psych.yorku.ca/orgs/onlinebj.htm

Cheiron: The International Society for the History of Behavioral and Social Scienc
  http://people.stu.ca/%7Echeiron.staff/#

Other:

The History of Phrenology on the Web, John van Wyhe. http://pages.britishlibrary.n phrenology/

Business History at Ohio State, www.history.ohio-state.edu/bus.htm

Economic History Services, http:/cs.muohio.edu/other/

University of Maryland Libraries Guide to Business History Resources, http://www.lib.umd.e UMCP/MCK?GUIDES/business_history.html

The World Wide Web Virtual Library: Labour and Business History, http://www.iisg.nl/~w3vl/

The Business History Conference, http://eh/net/bhc/

The Academy of Management Management History Division, http://www.fitapg.org/mhd/mdh.html

European Business History Association (EBHA), http://www.rdg.ac.uk/EBHA/home.html

The Society for the History of Technology, http://shot.press.jhu.edu/associations/shot/index2.htm

Centre for International Business History, University of Reading, http://www.rdg.ac.uk/CIBH/

Journal of Management History, http://www.mcb.co.uk/cgi-bin/journal1/jmh

Business History, http://www.frankcass.com/jnls/bh.htm

Business History Review, http://www.hbs.edu/bhr/

9. Other references containing historical information

Annals of the American Academy of Political & Social Science (Crennan & Kingsbury, 1923, Psychology in business [special issue], *110,* 2–232.

Journal of Applied Psychology (since 1917)

Journal of Personnel Research, now *Personnel Journal* (since 1922)

Journal of Consulting Psychology (Viteles, 1944)

Personnel Psychology (since 1948)

Boring, E. G. (1950). History of experimental psychology (2nd ed.). NY: Appleton Century-Crofts.

Fleishman, E. A. (1999). Applied psychology: An international journey. *American Psychologist, 54,* 1008–1016.

Meltzer, H., & Shulman, A.D. (Eds.). (1982). Special section on industrial–organizational psychology. *Professional Psychology, 13,* 889–953.

Meltzer, H., & Stagner, R. (Eds.). (1980). Industrial–organizational psychology: 1980 overview [Special issue]. *Professional Psychology, 11,* 347–546.

Viteles, M. S. (Ed.). (1944). Industrial psychology [Special issue]. *Journal of Consulting Psychology, 8,* 1–185.

The Thoemmes Encyclopedia of the History of Ideas features biographies (e.g., A. Maslow, E. Mayo, F. Taylor), www. Thoemmes.com/encyclo.htm

The Thoemmes Encyclopedia of the History of Ideas, Biographical Dictionary of Management also features biographies (e.g., F. Fiedler, R. Likert), www.thoemmes.com/dictionaries/ entries.htm

Note: In addition to the editor's research, the following sources were used to generate this Appendix:

Austin, J. T. (n.d.). *Book prospectus.* Unpublished manuscript.

Benjamin, L. T., Jr. (n.d.). *Research sources in the history of psychology.* Unpublished manuscript.

Benjamin, L. T., Jr. (1999, October 11). *Books on business and industrial psychology in the library of Ludy T. Benjamin, Jr.* Unpublished manuscript.

Katzell, R. A., & Austin, J. T. (1992). From then to now: The development of industrial–organizational psychology in the United States. *Journal of Applied Psychology, 77,* 803–835.

Zedeck, S. (n.d.) *Listing of classic I–O books.* Unpublished manuscript.

Appendix Two

Timeline of Events and Developments
in Industrial and Organizational Psychology
in the United States

Following is a timeline highlighting contextual influences and developments. This timeline was generated from the chapters in this book and several other sources. It is not an all-inclusive and exhaustive list. The events and developments were selected at the sole discretion of this book's editor to be representative.

PRIOR TO 1900

Societal, Cultural, Economic, and Legal Environment: Relevant Aspects

Scientific naturalism became the worldview.
Adam Smith's and Karl Marx's economics.
Darwin's evolutionary theory.
Galton's research on individual differences.
Angelo Mosso's laboratory experimentation on fatigue.
The flowering of science.
Industrial Revolution; rise of capitalism.
Americans and Europeans are captivated by phrenology, a pseudoscience of the brain; emphasizes importance of function and is a form of measurement.

Psychological Environment

Psychology taught within traditional philosophy departments.
Wilhelm Wundt founds the psychological laboratory at Leipzig University in Germany to distinguish psychology from philosophy; trains James McKeen Cattell, Hugo Münsterberg, and Walter Dill Scott.
First American psychology laboratories: Amherst, Brown, Bryn Mawr, California, Catholic, Chicago, City University of New York, Clark, Columbia, Cornell, Denison, Harvard, Indiana, Iowa, John Hopkins, Kansas, Michigan, Minnesota, Nebraska, Ohio State, Pennsylvania, Pennsylvania State, Princeton, Randolph Macon, Smith, Stanford, Texas, Trenton State, Wellesley, Wesleyan, Western Reserve, Wisconsin, Yale.

- Structuralism flourished under Titchener at Cornell University.
- Beginnings of American functionalism and its conflict with structuralism.
- Founding of new journals: *Pedagogical Seminary* (1891), *Psychological Review* (189 *Psychological Monographs* (1894), and *Psychological Index* (1894)
- Formation of the American Psychological Association in 1892 by G. Stanley Hall and othe
- Clinical psychology emerges as an applied psychology to solve societal problems.
- Publication of William James' *Principles of Psychology* (1890).
- Coining of the term "mental test" by James McKeen Cattell and development of anth pometric mental testing (1890).
- Hugo Münsterberg moves from Germany to Harvard University to run the Experimen Psychology Laboratory.
- Galton coins the term "co-relation" (1888).
- Edgeworth introduces coefficient of correlation (1892).
- Karl Pearson discovers mathematics behind calculating the correlation coefficient a discovered the chi-square distribution.
- James McKeen Cattell establishes psychological laboratory at the University of Pennsyl nia and co-founds the journal, *Psychological Review*, 1894.

Industrial Psychology

- Roots of industrial psychology are formed, including experimental psychology, individ differences or differential psychology, and psychometrics/measurement.
- Kraepelin's studies on physical and mental fatigue and work performance.
- Formation of psychotechnics first in Germany then the United States: a scientific meth for capturing individual differences in fatigue, efficient, and performance

- *Selection*
  - ➤ Thomas Peters, a businessman in the Washington Life Insurance Co, Atlanta, int duces the personal history inventory (1894).
  - ➤ Bryan and Harter investigate how professional telegraphers develop skills in sendi and receiving Morse code (1897).

- *Advertising*
  - ➤ Mentalistic approach to studying psychology and advertising

- *Leadership*
  - ➤ Great man theory first introduced by Carlyle (1849).

- *Work Teams*
  - ➤ A group is more than a sum of its parts, observed by Durkheim (1895).

1900–1909

Societal, Cultural, Economic, and Legal Environment: Relevant Aspects

- Rapid changes in American society: industrialization, immigration, high birth rate, edu tion reform, urban growth, technology changes (telephone, telegraph, typewriter); expa sion of railways.
- Business objectives: improve efficiency, increase productivity, decrease costs, all throu standardization and simplification.

- Progressive era in America society; Americans want to make America a better and safer place to live.

Psychological Environment

- Publication of the four volumes of Titchener's *Experimental Psychology* ("The Manuals") (1901–1905).
- E. L. Thorndike's *Theory of Mental Measurement* (1904).
- Formalization of American functional psychology (functionalism) at the University of Chicago and Columbia University.
- The Eugenics movement (the improvement of races through breeding) captivates several psychologists, including James McKeen Cattell; first eugenic sterilization law in Indiana (1907).
- Binet scale translated in America by Henry Herbert Goddard working at the Vineland Training School (1908).
- Thorndike's law of effect introduced.
- Methodological developments and statistical techniques, such as mental tents, regression, simple correlation, partial correlation, factor analysis.
- Early roots of test validation proposed by Binet and Simon (1905).

Industrial Psychology

- Period of establishment.
- Formation of scientific management to study work; time and motion studies become popular.
- *On the Witness Stand* (H. Münsterberg, 1908).

- *Selection*
  - ➤ Early selection studies by Pizzoli, Lahy, Meriam.
  - ➤ Study on the acquisition of typing skills (Book, 1980)

- *Advertising*
  - ➤ Gale first uses the order of merit technique for advertising (1900).
  - ➤ W. D. Scott advertising talk to Agate Club in Chicago (1901).
  - ➤ *The Theory of Advertising* (W. D. Scott, 1903).
  - ➤ *Psychology of Advertising* (W. D. Scott, 1908).

- *Training*
  - ➤ Vestibule training in large businesses (1900).

1910–1919

Societal, Cultural, Economic, and Legal Environment: Relevant Aspects

- Continuation of the Progressive Era and Industrial Revolution.
- World War I provides a significant impetus to applied psychology, particularly mental testing and abnormal psychology.

Psychological Environment

- Psychologists stationed at 40 Army hospitals during the war.

- Watson publishes his behaviorist manifesto, *Psychology as the Behaviorist Views It* (1913).
- Methodological developments, measurement methods, and statistical techniques, such as observations of workers, case studies, laboratory experiments, and quasi-experiments.
- Society for Applied Psychology formed (1915).
- Economic Psychology Association established (1915).
- Lewis Terman's version of Binet scale, the Stanford–Binet (1917).

Industrial Psychology

- Continued period of establishment; rapid growth.
- *Increasing Human Efficiency in Business* (W. D. Scott, 1911).
- *Influencing Men in Business* (W. D. Scott, 1911).
- *The Principles of Scientific Management* (W. D. Scott, 1911).
- *Psychology and Industrial Efficiency* (H. Münsterberg, 1913).
- Early roots of test validation proposed by Münsterberg (1913), and Scott (1917).
- L. M. Gilbreth finishes first dissertation related to industrial psychology (1915).
- Division of Applied Psychology, Carnegie Institute of Technology, the first major university-based consulting organization to collaborate with businesses; development of: application blanks (biodata), interviewing ratings, tests (1915).
- W. D. Scott appointed professor of applied psychology, Carnegie Institute of Technology; develops *Aids in the Selection of Salesman* (1916).
- First full-time PhD psychologist in industry, Henry Link, Director of training and psychological research, Winchester Repeating Arms Co. (1917).
- *Journal of Applied Psychology*, founded by G. Stanley Hall (1917).
- *Applied Psychology* (Hollingworth & Poffenberger, 1917).
- W. D. Scott develops four methods to estimate the diagnostic and prognostic value of a test (1917).
- Studies of work methods and job design with efficiency as the dependent variable (Gilbreth & Gilbreth, 1916, 1917).
- Approximately 17 members of the American Psychological Association are working primarily in various applications of psychology (1917).
- Geissler (1918, *Journal of Applied Psychology*) discusses training for consulting psychologists.
- The Industrial Fatigue Research Board (1918) established in Great Britain, later to be renamed the Industrial Health Research Board in 1927.
- The Scott Company, the first private consulting firm formed (1919); it develops and uses techniques, job standards, performance ratings, interviewer's guide; hires female psychologist, Mary Holmes Stevens Hayes, as a professional consultant.
- *Employment Psychology* (H. C. Link) (1919).
- R.H. Macy and Company in New York hires female psychologist Elsie Oschrin Bregman (1919).
- The founding of LISRB (Life Insurance Sales Research Bureau) (1919).

- *Selection*
  - ➤ Development of an aptitude test for streetcar operators by Münsterberg (1910).
  - ➤ Psychology Committee of the National Research Council and Committee on Classification of Personnel formed for psychologists to assist the Army during World War I on selection and classification problems (1917).
  - ➤ Development of group tests: Army Alpha and Army Beta (1918).

➤ Use of Stanford–Binet intelligence test in organizations (1918).
➤ Woodworth introduces the Personal Data Sheet (1919).
➤ Trade tests to evaluate specific occupational skills (Chapman & Toops, 1919; Robinson, 1919).
➤ Numerous early selection studies by Link, Oschrin (Bregman), McComas, Jones, Rogers.

Job Analysis

➤ First recording of job analysis, Dennison Manufacturing Company (1914).
➤ Development of Army Trade Specifications, early job analyses (1919).
➤ Elemental molecuralist school of thought in job analysis.

Human Factors

➤ Use of anthropometry for World War I.
➤ Dodge's research on vision, including visual fixation and eye movement.

Advertising

➤ *Advertising: Its Principles, Practice, and Technique* (Starch, 1914).
➤ *Advertising and Its Mental Laws* (Adams, 1916).
➤ Dynamic perspective of psychology and advertising.

Training

➤ Four-step method of job instruction (show-tell-do-check).

Performance Appraisal

➤ Man-to-Man Scale for rating performance (Scott, 1917).

1920–1929

Societal, Cultural, Economic, and Legal Environment: Relevant Aspects

After World War I, euphoria and prosperity sweep the United States.
Significant increase in gross national product.
Growth in employment; U.S. companies creates personnel departments.
Emphasis on capitalism and efficiency.
Executives hired psychologists as consultants or employees.
Employment management as a discipline grows.

Psychological Environment

Gestalt psychology ideas cross the Atlantic.
Structuralism disappears after the death of Titchener in 1927.
Debates over nature–nurture.
APA establishes a certification program for consulting psychologists.
Behaviorism becomes dominant system of psychology.
Decade of greatest popularity of psychology with the public.
First popular psychology magazines published, one on industrial psychology.
Social Psychology (G. Allport, 1924).

Industrial Psychology

- Rapid growth in early 1920s, with a decline in later 1920s.
- Extension of Army techniques and program into private industry; opportunities for p chologists proliferate.
- The International Congress of Psychotechnology (1920).
- First I–O PhD graduate, Bruce Moore, Carnegie Institute of Technology (1921).
- Personnel Research Federation established (1921).
- The Psychological Corporation formed to advance and promote applied psychology (1921
- New York State Association of Consulting Psychologists formed (1921).
- The National Institute of Industrial Psychology in Great Britain established (1921).
- *The Psychology of Industry* (J. Drever, 1921).
- *Journal of Personnel Research* first published (1922).
- *Industrial Psychology and the Production of Wealth* (H. D. Harrison, 1925).
- *Principles of Employment Psychology* (H. E. Burtt, 1926).
- Analysis of variance developed (1926).
- Implementation of a wage incentive system, job classification method, and job evaluati program at Aetna Life Insurance by Marion Bills, early female psychologist (1926).
- *Industrial Psychology Monthly* published.
- *Applied Psychology: Its Principles and Methods* (A. T. Poffenberger, 1928).
- Mid-1920s, beginning of the Hawthorne studies at the Western Electric Corp.
- Emphasis on quantification and experimentation.
- Primary tool: testing.
- Research Bureau of Retail Training, Carnegie Institute of Technology.
- L. L. Thurstone revises scaling techniques (1927).
- Psychologists hired by private organizations, such as Harry Hepner at Kaufman Depa ment Store, Ruml at Macy's, Marion Bills at Aetna, H. G. Kenagy at Procter & Gamb Sadie Myers Shellow at Milwaukee Electric Railway and Light Company.
- Psychologist with I–O interests hired at universities, including Viteles at the University Pennsylvania, Kingsbury at the University of Chicago, Paterson at the University of M nesota, Mayo at Harvard University, and Fryer at New York University.
- Universities that prepare industrially oriented psychology doctorates include Ohio Sta University, University of Minnesota, and Stanford University.
- By the end of the 1920s, approximately 50 full-time psychologists in industry.

- *Selection*
  - ➤ *Psychological Tests in Business* (Kingsbury & Kornhauser, 1924).
  - ➤ Bingham defines criterion as a measuring stick; Burtt uses the term *criterion* as a j proficiency index (1926).
  - ➤ *Vocational Interest Inventory* developed (1927).
  - ➤ Millicent Pond publishes a study (dissertation) on the selection and placement of a prentice metal-workers at Scoville Manufacturing Co. (1927).
  - ➤ Use of the term *validity*.

- *Job Analysis*
  - ➤ Viteles introduces the job psychograph, as a job analysis method (1923).
  - ➤ Task analytic molecularists, job analysis school of thought.

- *Human Factors*
  - ➤ Automotive industry research at Ohio State University.

➤ Miles conducts research on eye movements, night and color vision, and dark adaptation at Yale University.

- *Advertising*
  - ➤ *The Mind of the Buyer* (Kitson, 1921).
  - ➤ *Psychology of Selling and Advertising* (Strong, 1925).
  - ➤ *Psychology in Advertising* (Poffenberger, 1925).

- *Performance Appraisal*
  - ➤ Graphic rating scale is introduced (1922).
  - ➤ Paterson provides 12 principles of psychological ratings (1923).
  - ➤ Kornhuaser reports three empirical studies of ratings and discusses the reliability of ratings, rater comparisons, and comparisons of ratings on different traits (1926–1927).

- *Motivation*
  - ➤ Motivation research: focus on money as the motivator.

- *Leadership*
  - ➤ Self-help book on leadership (Kleiser, 1923).
  - ➤ Mary Parker Follett's essay on leadership and participation (1927).
  - ➤ Early leadership studies (see Bowden, 1926; Moore & Hartman, 1931).
  - ➤ Leader qualities proposed by Craig & Charters (1925).

- *Work Teams*
  - ➤ Ringelman role-pull task study (Moede, 1927).

1930–1939

Societal, Cultural, Economic, and Legal Environment: Relevant Aspects

- Major economic depression influences employment; heightens concerns for the humanization of work.
- President Roosevelt's New Deal program.
- Federal legislation during this period generates funding for public training in handicrafts such as leatherwork, weaving, and chair caning.
- The National Labor Relations Act (Wagner Act); labor unions become more powerful (1935).
- The Fair Labor Standards Act (1938).
- Personnel management on the rise.

Psychological Environment

- Social psychology, child psychology, and behaviorism are prevalent.
- Attitudes measurement is further refined by R. Likert.
- Decade for grand theories of personality (Allport, Murray).
- Beginning of neobehaviorism (Tolman, Hull, Guthrie, Skinner).
- Large influx of émigré psychologists from Europe, especially Germany and Austria.
- Psychology's public popularity at a low point.
- Psychometric Society formed (1935).
- Society for the Psychological Study of Social Issues formed (1936).

- *Journal of Consulting Psychology* first published (1937).
- Establishment of the American Association for Applied Psychology (AAAP) (1937).
- Metropolitan New York Association for Applied Psychology formed (1939).

Industrial Psychology

- Period of refinement.
- Doctorate in I–O psychology offered by Pennsylvania State College (now university) (1930).
- Minnesota Employment Stabilization Research Institute; develops theory of work adjustment and occupational aptitude patterns (1931).
- *Industrial Psychology* (M. Viteles, 1932).
- *The human problems of an industrialized civilization* (Elton Mayo, 1933).
- *Psychology in Business and Industry* (J. G. Jenkins, 1935).
- Academy of Management established (1936).
- AAAP includes Section D, Industrial and Business Psychology, with Harold E. Burtt as the first president (1937).
- The Occupational Research Center formed (first established as the Division of Educational and Applied Psychology, Purdue University) (1937).
- Kuder–Richardson, KR-20 introduced (1937).
- Emphasis on operationism and operational definitions.
- Emergence of industrial social psychology.
- Thurstone introduces factor analysis.
- Several additional universities offer I–O oriented degrees, such as Purdue University, Columbia University, and University of Pennsylvania.
- Approximately 100 psychologists identified as I–O psychologists (1939).

- *Selection*
  - ➤ U.S. Employment Service conducts research to validate aptitude tests.
  - ➤ General Aptitude Test Battery is developed by the U.S. Employment Service.

- *Job Analysis*
  - ➤ *Dictionary of Occupational Titles,* the first large-scale job analysis, published (1939).

- *Human Factors*
  - ➤ National Research Council, Committee on Aviation Psychology formed (1939).

- *Training*
  - ➤ Beginning of humanistic approach to training.

- *Performance Appraisal*
  - ➤ Discussion of performance ratings in article by Hepner (1930).

- *Organizational Psychology*
  - ➤ Studies of employee attitudes and morale.
  - ➤ Attitude survey distributed at Kimberly-Clark Corporation.
  - ➤ Attitude studies at Procter & Gamble (Uhrbrock, 1935).
  - ➤ Hoppock studies on job satisfaction (1935).
  - ➤ Counseling program established in a private corporation as an intervention.

➤ The Hawthorne studies completed and published; increased awareness of employees' attitudes and group interactions; beginning of human relation movement. (1933, R. Rothlisberger & W. Dickson, *Management and the Worker.*)

➤ Harwood Pajama Factory research, beginning of organizational interventions.

➤ Kurt Lewin conducts research on psychological aspects of work

- *Motivation*
  - ➤ Motivation research focuses on attitudes.

- *Leadership*
  - ➤ *The Art of Leadership*, 10 desirable qualities of a leader (O. Tead, 1935).
  - ➤ Leadership studies on foremen, student leaders, incarcerated criminal leaders.

- *Teams*
  - ➤ The Scanlon Plan introduced.

1940–1949

Societal, Cultural, Economic, and Legal Environment: Relevant Aspects

- World War II begins and ends.
- Passage of Servicemen's Readjustment Act of 1944 (GI Bill) results in rapid expansion of American higher education system.
- Educational Testing Service formed (1947).
- General Agreement on Trade and Tariffs (1947).
- Postwar affluence and prosperity.

Psychological Environment

- Psychologists perform admirably in contributions to World War II in selection of personnel, training, design of military equipment, psychological warfare, therapy for victims, etc.
- Tremendous growth of psychology—new doctoral programs, new job opportunities for graduates.
- National Council of Women Psychologists established (1941).
- *MMPI* developed (1942).
- New APA formed by merger of several groups (particularly AAAP). Central Office established in Washington, DC (1945).
- *American Psychologist* journal first published (1946).
- Boulder Conference establishes scientist/practitioner model of training for clinical psychologists (1949).
- Increased interest in physiological psychology.

Industrial Psychology

- Establishment of consulting firms, university research centers, military research centers, and research groups in private corporations.
- For the war effort, various techniques and programs developed for evaluating performance, training, developing teams, designing equipment, and changing attitudes and morale.
- Programs and techniques for the war extended to business and industry.
- *Strong Vocational Interest Blank* published (1943).

- AAAP Section D merges with APA to form Division 14, Industrial and Business Psychology (130 members) (1945).
- Early work on utility analysis by H. Brogden (1946).
- Personnel Research Section (PRS), Army Adjutant General's Office—Forerunner of Army Research Institute formed (1945).
- American Institutes for Research (AIR) formed (1946).
- Life Insurance Agency Management Association (LIAMA) established (1946), a merging of Association of Life Agency Offices from 1916, and the Life Insurance Sales Research Bureau from 1919.
- Psychologists Full-Time in Industry, an informal group began meeting (1947–1948).
- Ghiselli and Brown's seminal book *Personnel and Industrial Psychology* published (1948).
- Office of Naval Research.

- *Selection*
  - ➤ The Office of Strategic Services develops "assessment centers" to select spies.
  - ➤ Development of the Army General Classification Test (AGCT).
  - ➤ Applied Psychology Panel established to address selection and classification problems for the military (1942).
  - ➤ Development of the Aircrew Classification Test Battery (Flanagan, 1946).
  - ➤ Robert Thorndike's book, *Personnel Selection* (1947).
  - ➤ Air Force Human Resources Research Center established in San Antonio, TX (1948).

- *Human Factors*
  - ➤ Air Force Psychology Branch established, Wright Field (1945).
  - ➤ Naval Electronic Laboratory, San Diego (1946).
  - ➤ Biomechanics division of the Psychological Corporation formed (1946).
  - ➤ Establishment of the Aviation Psychology Program, by J. Flanagan; work is summarized in a 19-volume series (1947).
  - ➤ As a result of military applications and research, Human Factors emerges as a distinct entity.
  - ➤ *Work and Effort: The Psychology of Production* (T. A. Ryan, 1947).
  - ➤ *Applied Experimental Psychology* (Chapanis, Garner, & Morgan, 1949).
  - ➤ Renshaw Recognition System developed at the Ohio State University.
  - ➤ Fitts' law developed.
  - ➤ Johns Hopkins University, Systems Research Laboratory, use of systems theory for examining personnel working in simulated combat information centers; Communications Research Laboratory researches and develops the current telephone keyboard configuration.

- *Training*
  - ➤ Job rotation as a training method.
  - ➤ American Society of Training Directors established (later known as American Society of Training and Development) (1945).
  - ➤ *Multiple Role Playing Training for Managers* (N. R. F. Maier & A. Baveles, 1947).
  - ➤ "Sensitivity Training," T Groups (L. Bradford, 1947).

- *Performance Appraisal*
  - ➤ Forced choice rating procedures introduced (D. Sisson, 1947).

➤ Critical Incident Approach (J. Flanagan, 1949).

Organizational Psychology

➤ Tavistock Institute of Human Relations was established (1946–1947).
➤ *Human Relations* journal first published (1947).
➤ *Group Dynamics in Industry* (A. Marrow, 1947).
➤ *Studies on Resistance to Change and Participation* (L. Coch & J. French, 1948).

Motivation

➤ Maslow's need hierarchy theory introduced.
➤ Alderfer's ERG theory appears

Leadership

➤ Research and applications on leadership become prevalent.
➤ Ohio State Leadership Studies, Personnel Research Board, established by C. L. Shartle at The Ohio State University, and leadership studies at the University of Michigan Institute for Social Research (A. Campbell, R. Likert, D. Katz, 1945).
➤ M. Blum includes an entire chapter devoted to leadership in his industrial psychology text (1949).

Work Teams

➤ Lewin establishes the Research Center for Group Dynamics at Massachusetts Institute of Technology (MIT) (1944).
➤ National Training Laboratory formed, development of t-groups (1946–1947).
➤ Research Center for Group Dynamics relocates from MIT to University of Michigan to join the Institute for Social Research (1948).
➤ 15 group dimensions, and their measurement scales, for the description and differentiation of numerous types of groups, *Situational Factors in Leadership* (J. Hemphill, 1949).

1950–1959

cietal, Cultural, Economic, and Legal Environment: Relevant Aspects

Beginnings of a civil rights movement in American society, with the *Brown v. Topeka Board of Education*, in 1954.
National Science Foundation formed (1950).
Computers used in military shifted to use in business.
Post–World War II prosperity; greater concern for the good life.
Late 1950s, shift from a manufacturing-based economy to a service-based economy.

ychological Environment

Interest in groups, teams, and attitudes increases among social psychologists.
Social psychology gains in prominence.
Modern cognitive psychology surfaces as behaviorism declines.
APA forms a committee to create technical and scientific standards for testing.
First professional school of psychology, Adelphi University.
Publication of first APA code of ethics (1953).
Increased attention to licensing of psychologists.

- Emphases on human factors, physiological psychology, development across the lifesp scientific method, statistics.
- New fields: space psychology, psychopharmacology, use of computers.

Industrial Psychology

- Continues to extend war programs and techniques to business and industry.
- *Handbook of Applied Psychology* (D. Fryer & E. Henry, 1950).
- International Harvester Studies established at Ohio State University, Personnel Resea Board (1950).
- Human Resources Research Organization (HumRRO) formed (1951).
- The Dearborn Conference Group began meeting (1951).
- Cronbach's coefficient alpha introduced (1951).
- Item response theory introduced (F. Lord, 1952).
- *Motivation and Morale* (Viteles, 1953).
- Patricia Cain Smith publishes her studies on the measurements of monotony and bored in the workplace (1953, 1955).
- The No-Name Group was established (1954).
- First large scale factor analyses identifying abilities in the psychomotor performance main; relation of different attributes of learning (E. Fleishman & W. Hempel, 1954).
- *Administrative Science Quarterly* journal first published (1955).
- Increased interest in decision making.
- Some attention to labor unions (A. Kornhaush, R. Stagner).
- Development of graduate programs in I–O psychology, including terminal master's degi programs.
- Military develops research centers: Army Research Institute for the Behavioral and Soc Sciences (ARI), Navy Personnel Research and Development Center (NPRDC), Air Fo Human Resources Laboratory (AFHRL).
- At least 1,000 psychologists employed full-time in industry (1959).
- *Psychology and human performance: An introduction to psychology* (R. Gagné & Fleishman, 1959), first introductory psychology textbook to include chapters in selecti training, leadership, and other I–O topics.

- *Selection*
  - ➤ Synthetic validity introduced by C. Lawshe (1952).

- *Job Analysis*
  - ➤ Critical incident technique by J. Flanagan.
  - ➤ Functionalists, job analysis school of thought.

- *Human Factors*
  - ➤ Rise in engineering psychology.
  - ➤ APA Division 21, Society of Engineering Psychology created (1956).
  - ➤ Seminal article published: *The Magical Number Seven, Plus or Minus Two: So Limits on Our Capacity to Process Information* (Miller, 1956).
  - ➤ Human Factors Society formed.
  - ➤ *Human Factors* journal first published (1958).

- *Performance Appraisal*
  - ➤ The Dollar Criterion (H. Brogden & E. K. Taylor, 1950).

➤ Theory of ratings (Wherry, 1950, 1952).
➤ Simulators (L. J. Briggs, 1955).

- *Organizational Psychology*
  ➤ A. Brayford & W. Crockett, seminal *Psychological Bulletin* article on relations between employee attitudes and performance (1955).
  ➤ Cornell University studies of work satisfaction led by Patricia C. Smith.
  ➤ Human relations concerns becomes prevalent.
  ➤ McGregor gives seminal speech on theory X and theory Y.

- *Motivation*
  ➤ Viteles equated motivation with job satisfaction and job performance (1953).
  ➤ Theory X and theory Y (McGregor, 1957).
  ➤ *Motivation to Work*, Two factor theory (Herzberg, 1959).

- *Leadership*
  ➤ Identification and measurement of "consideration" and "initiating structure" (J. Hemphill, R. Stogdill, E. Fleishman, 1950–1956).
  ➤ Shift in leadership research from traits to a focus on behaviors.
  ➤ Introduction of "followership" in leadership research;peer nominations (E. Hollander).
  ➤ Beginning of AT&T longitudinal research program (D. Bray & D. Grant).
  ➤ Beginning of contingency theories of leadership (F. Fiedler).
  ➤ Leaderless Group Discussion (LGD) (B. Bass).

- *Training*
  ➤ First evaluation of effects of formal leadership training programs, *Leadership and supervision in industry* (E. Fleishman, E. Harris, & H. Burtt, 1955).

- *Work Teams*
  ➤ Quality circles introduced.
  ➤ Early distinction between groups, teams, team characteristics, and task characteristics.

1960–1969

Societal, Cultural, Economic, and Legal Environment: Relevant Aspects

- Unrest in American society; civil rights movement strengthens.
- New generation of employees who question the authority of organizations.
- Flagging productivity.
- Shift in organizations from highly bureaucratic to open systems, using methods such as total quality management, teamwork, and employee participation.
- John and Robert Kennedy, Martin Luther King, and Malcolm X are assassinated.
- Vietnam War.
- Equal Pay Act (1963).
- Civil Rights Act, Title VI, prohibits employment discrimination (1964).
- Age Discrimination in Employment Act (1967).
- Occupational Safety and Health Administration established.

Psychological Environment

- American Association of State Psychology Board formed (1961).
- American discovery of Piagetian ideas, especially in education
- History of psychology becomes a specialty field; Archives of the History of American Psychology founded at University of Akron by John Poppelstone (1965).
- Major growth of cognitive psychology.
- Concerns over the social relevance of psychological research and theory.
- Humanistic psychology begins.
- Majority of states pass laws for licensure of psychologists, a process completed in the 1970s.
- First edition of *Standards for Educational and Psychological Tests and Manuals* (1966).
- *Professional Psychology* journal first published (1969).
- Association of Black Psychologists (1968).

Industrial Psychology

- Baritz's highly critical book of industrial psychology, *Servants of Power.*
- "Business" dropped from APA Division 14 label, to become APA Division 14 Industrial Psychology (1962).
- L. Ferguson publishes 14 pamphlets: *The Heritage of Industrial Psychology* (1962–1965).
- *The Structure and Measurement of Physical Fitness* (Fleishman, 1964) describes first large scale factor analyses identifying abilities and measures in the physical performance domain.
- SIOP guidelines for I–O doctoral training issued (1965).
- Personnel Decisions Research Institutes, Inc. (PDRI) formed (1967).
- Academic psychology flourishes with excellent financial support from business and government; more doctoral programs in I–O implemented.

- *Selection*
  - ➤ Interviews become standard for screening and selecting employees.
  - ➤ It is generally accepted that a test must be validated for the job in which it is used.

- *Job Analysis*
  - ➤ Functional Job Analysis introduced (S. Fine).
  - ➤ Ability Requirements Analysis (E. Fleishman).
  - ➤ Position Analysis Questionnaire (E. McCormick).

- *Human Factors*
  - ➤ Research on human computer interactions.

- *Advertising*
  - ➤ APA Division of Consumer Psychology born (1960).

- *Training*
  - ➤ *Training in Business and Industry,* which introduced three-step training needs assessment process (W. McGehee & P. Thayer, 1961).
  - ➤ R. M. Gagné's *Conditions of Learning* published (1962).
  - ➤ Beginning of participative approach to training.
  - ➤ Increasing use of human relations training.

- *Performance Appraisal*
  - ➤ Behavioral Anchored Rating Scale (BARS) developed (Smith & Kendall).
  - ➤ Performance appraisal research at General Electric (Herb Meyer).

- *Organizational Psychology*
  - ➤ *The Human Side of Enterprise* (D. McGregor, 1960).
  - ➤ Organizational Psychology (B. Bass, 1965).
  - ➤ Organizational Psychology (E. Schein, 1965).
  - ➤ Research on communication, conflict management, socialization, organizational climate and culture, and group/team development and maturation.
  - ➤ Organizational development and change interventions (e.g., sensitivity training, team development, survey feedback).

- *Motivation*
  - ➤ Equity theory (S. Adams, 1963).
  - ➤ *Work & Motivation* expectancy theory (V. Vroom, 1964).
  - ➤ Goal-setting propositions (E. Locke, 1968).

- *Leadership*
  - ➤ R. Likert's *New Patterns of Management*, based on research of the University of Michigan's Institute for Social Research (1961).
  - ➤ Situation-based models of leadership introduced.
  - ➤ Notion of leadership perceptions first introduced (1969).

- *Teams*
  - ➤ Input, process, output (IPO) model advanced as a means of framing group and team effectiveness (McGrath, 1964).
  - ➤ Four stages of group development (Tuckman).
  - ➤ Quality circles emerge.

1970–1979

Societal, Cultural, Economic, and Legal Environment: Relevant Aspects

- The federal government establishes EEOC and subsequently issues administrative guidelines for defining discrimination, adverse impact (*Uniform Guidelines on Employee Selection Procedures*).
- Several U.S. Supreme Court decisions confirm the importance of validation and job analysis (e.g., *Griggs v. Duke Power Company,* 1971).
- Three Mile Island nuclear accident heightens awareness about workplace safety.
- Vietnam War.
- Watergate scandal.

Psychological Environment

- Debate over professional training models lead to Vail Conference (1974) and development of the Doctorate of Psychology (PsyD); subsequent growth of professional schools.
- *Cognitive Psychology* journal first published (1970).

- Herbert Simon, Nobel Prize (1978).
- Organizational issues achieve prominence in forming I–O psychology.

Industrial and Organizational Psychology

- LIAMA changes name to LIMRA, Life Insurance Marketing and Research Association.
- Development Dimensions International established (1970).
- Center for Creative Leadership formed (1970).
- The Mayflower Group begins meeting (1971).
- APA Division 14 renamed as *Industrial and Organizational Psychology* due to increased attention on organizational issues (1973).
- *Journal of Occupational Psychology* was created (1975), later renamed as *Journal of Occupational and Organizational Psychology*.
- *Handbook of Industrial and Organizational Psychology* published (M. Dunnette, 1976).
- Advanced Research Resources Organization (ARRO) established (1976).
- Navy Personnel Research and Development Center (NPRDC) based in San Diego.
- Influence of Skinnerian neobehaviorism: organizational behavior modification.
- Increased attention to cognitive theory in leadership, job design, motivation, and performance appraisal.
- Emphasis on theory development and theory-related research.
- Greater use of laboratory experimentation.
- Topeka System is implemented in General Foods Plans in Topeka, Kansas.
- Further refinement of job satisfaction measurement.

- *Selection*
  - ➤ Validity generalization and meta-analyses are further refined as means to generalize validity results (F. Schmidt & W. Hunter, 1977).
  - ➤ Increased attention to ethnic and gender differences in the validity and fairness of employment tests.

- *Job Analysis*
  - ➤ Publication of the *Position Analysis Questionnaire* (1972).
  - ➤ Comprehensive Occupational Data Analysis Program (CODAP) developed (R. Christal, 1974).
  - ➤ First comprehensive book on job analysis (E. McCormick, 1979).

- *Performance Appraisal*
  - ➤ New techniques of performance ratings appear.

- *Motivation*
  - ➤ Behavior modification movement.
  - ➤ Goal-setting theory (Latham et al.).
  - ➤ *Pay and Organizational Effectiveness* (E. Lawler, 1970).
  - ➤ Job characteristics introduced (Hackman & Oldham, 1976).
  - ➤ Social learning theory (Bandura, 1977).
  - ➤ Cognitive perspective on motivation.

- *Leadership*
  - ➤ Path-goal theory of leadership (R. Hause, 1971).

➤ Vroom–Yetton's theory of leadership (1973).
➤ *Current Developments in the Study of Leadership* (Fleishman & Hunt, 1973), initial publication of a series of biannual conferences initiated by J. G. Hunt at Southern Illinois University.
➤ Leader member exchange theory.
➤ Implicit leadership theories (R. Lord).
➤ Leadership categorization theory.

• *Work Teams*
  ➤ Group think (I. Janis).

1980–1989

Societal, Cultural, Economic, and Legal Environment: Relevant Aspects

• Sluggish productivity.
• Threats to economic well-being.
• Increased global competition.
• Fall of Communism and collapse of Soviet Union.
• Global and diverse workforce.
• Restructuring of organizations, including mergers and acquisitions.
• Advancements in computer technology, personal computers become a standard; computer technology installed throughout technology.
• National Science Foundation supports 3 volumes on *Human Performance and Productivity: Human Capabilities* (M. Dunnette & E. Fleishman), *Information Processing* (W. Howell & E. Fleishman), *Stress* (E. Alluisi & E. Fleishman), 1982.

Psychological Environment

• Lillian Gilbreth becomes the only American psychologist ever to appear on a U.S. postage stamp (1984).
• American Psychology Association of Graduate Students is formed (1988).
• American Psychological Society is established by many scientists who leave APA (1988).

Industrial Psychology

• *Journal of Occupational Behavior* (now known as *Journal of Organizational Behavior*) first published (1980).
• APA Division 14 incorporated as the Society for Industrial and Organizational Psychology (SIOP) (1982).
• Attention to utility analysis.
• Item response theory.

• *Selection*
  ➤ Computerized Adaptive Testing introduced.
  ➤ SIOP publishes *Principles for the Validation and Use of Personnel Selection Procedures.*
  ➤ Revival of personality testing in industry; five-factor model of personality receives increased attention.
  ➤ Army Project A, development of ASVAB.

- *Job Analysis*
  - ➤ Occupational Analysis Inventory, Generalized Work Inventory (J. W. Cunningham, 1983).
  - ➤ NASA Task Load Index developed.
  - ➤ *Taxonomies of Human Performance: The Description of Human Tasks* (E. Fleishman & M. Quaintance, 1984).
  - ➤ *The Job Analyses Handbook for Business, Industry, and Government* (S. Gael, 1988).

- *Human Factors*
  - ➤ APA Division renamed as Division of Applied Experimental and Engineering Psychology (1983).
  - ➤ Emergence of macroergonomics.

- *Training*
  - ➤ Transfer of training.

- *Performance Appraisal*
  - ➤ Call for a moratorium on performance appraisal research; importance of cognitive processes (F. Landy & J. Farr).

- *Motivation*
  - ➤ Social cognitive theory (A. Bandura).
  - ➤ Organizational justice theory (J. Greenberg).

- *Work Teams*
  - ➤ Research on how teams form, evolve, and perform.
  - ➤ Team taxonomies and classifications.
  - ➤ Self-managed work teams.
  - ➤ Team effectiveness definitions and measurements.
  - ➤ Team training and development; team building; team performance measurement.

1990–present

Societal, Cultural, Economic, and Legal Environment: Relevant Aspects

- Americans with Disabilities Act (1990).
- Civil Rights Act of 1964 is amended to prohibit quota hiring (1991).
- Downsizings, acquisitions, and mergers become commonplace.
- Sophistication in statistical software.
- Global and diverse workplace.
- European Union is formed.
- Terrorists destroy the World Trade Center in New York; heightened awareness of workplace violence, security.
- Ubiquitous computing: Internet, laptop computers, etc.
- Knowledge-based economy; importance of knowledge management.
- Virtual organization structure.
- Formation of the U.S. Department of Homeland Security.

Psychological Environment

- Positive psychology.
- Increased specialization.

Industrial Psychology

- *Journal of Occupational and Organizational Psychology* (formerly known as *Occupational Psychology* and *Journal of Occupational Psychology*) first published (1992).
- *International Journal of Selection and Assessment* first published (1993).
- SIO Guidelines for I–O master's training issued.
- Second edition, four-volume, *Handbook of I–O Psychology* (Dunnette & Hough) published.
- Continued interest in validation strategies and validity generalization.
- Interests in nontraditional I–O areas: work and family balance, worker health and well-being, careers.
- SIOP membership: 3,627 professional members (fellows, members, associates, international affiliates), and 2,901 student members (2005, July 6).
- Performance adabtability introduced.
- Performance theory developed.

- *Selection*
  - ➢ Publication of Project A.
  - ➢ Internet use of recruitment, application, and assessment.

- *Job Analysis*
  - ➢ The Common Metric Questionnaire (CMQ) (R. J. Harvey, 1991).
  - ➢ Fleishman Job Analysis Survey (F-JAS) (1992)
  - ➢ O*Net developed to replace the *DOT.*
  - ➢ Ergometricians, job analysis school of thought.
  - ➢ *Ergometrika*, a new electronic journal, founded by J. Mitchell & J. Cunningham (2000).

- *Human Factors*
  - ➢ Board of Certification in Professional Ergonomics initiated certification (1992).
  - ➢ APA Division 21 published *Journal of Experimental Psychology: Applied* (1995).

- *Training*
  - ➢ *International Journal of Training and Development* first published (1997).
  - ➢ Strategic approach to training.

- *Performance Appraisal*
  - ➢ Criteria of performance.
  - ➢ Importance of cognition.

- *Organizational Psychology*
  - ➢ Research on work and family conflicts and balance.

- *Motivation*
  - ➢ High-performance cycle (Locke & Latham).

- *Leadership*
  - ➤ *Handbook of Leadership: Theory, Research, and Managerial Applications* (Bass & Stogdell, 1990).
  - ➤ GLOBE project.
  - ➤ Importance of cognition.
  - ➤ Transformational leadership (B. Bass).
  - ➤ *Leadership Quarterly*, three special issues on Individual Differences and Leadership (2001).
  - ➤ Metanalysis of Validity and Independence of "consideration" and "initiating structure" measures over a 50 year period, (published in *Journal of Applied Psychology* by T. Judge et al., 2004).

- *Work Teams*
  - ➤ U.S. Navy's Tactical Decision Making Under Stress (TADMUS) project.
  - ➤ Hierarchical team decision making.
  - ➤ Self-managed work teams.
  - ➤ Taxonomy of team functions (Fleishman & Zacarro).
  - ➤ Team cognition.
  - ➤ Team effectiveness definitions and measurements.
  - ➤ Team training and development; crew resource management (CRM); team building; team performance measurement; team member individual differences.
  - ➤ Virtual teams.

Additional Sources for the Timeline

Benjamin, L. T., Jr. (n.d.). *The first century of psychological science and practice in America.* Unpublished manuscript.

Katzell, R. A., & Austin, J. T. (1992). From then to now: The development of industrial–organizational psychology in the United States. *Journal of Applied Psychology, 77,* 803–835.

Koppes, L. L. (2003). Industrial–organizational psychology. In I. B. Weiner (General Ed.) & D. K. Freedheim (Vol. Ed.), *Comprehensive handbook of psychology: Vol. 1. History of psychology* (pp. 367–389). New York: Wiley.

Landy, F. J., & Conte, J. M. (2004). *Work in the 21st century: An introduction to industrial and organizational psychology.* New York: McGraw-Hill.

Muchinsky, P. (2003). *Psychology applied to work* (7th ed.). Belmont, CA: Wadsworth/Thomson Learning.

Appendix Three

Additional Information

TABLE A.1
Presidents of the International Association of Applied Psychology (IAAP)

Year of Presidency	Name	Country
1920–1941	E. Claparede	Switzerland
1947–1953	H. Pieron	France
1953–1958	C. B. Frisby	United Kingdom
1958–1968	M. S. Viteles	United States
1968–1974	G. Westerlund	Sweden
1974–1982	E. A. Fleishman	United States
1982–1990	C. Levy–Leboyer	France
1990–1994	H. C. Triandis	United States
1994–1998	B. Wilpert	Germany
1998–2002	C. D. Spielberger	United States
2002–2006	Michael Frese	Germany

TABLE A.2
Editors of the *Journal of Applied Psychology* (1917–2008)

1917–1920	G. Stanley Hall
1920–1942	James P. Porter
1943–1954	Donald G. Paterson
1955–1960	John G. Darley
1961–1970	Kenneth E. Clarke
1971–1976	Edwin A. Fleishman
1977–1982	John P. Campbell
1983–1988	Robert M. Guion
1989–1994	Neal Schmitt
1995–1996	Philip Bobko
1997–2002	Kevin R. Murphy
2003–2008	Sheldon Zedeck

TABLE A.3

Heads of Personnel Research at the U.S. Office of Personnel Management (OPM) and Its Predecessor, the U.S. Civil Service Commission (USCSC)

Year	Name	Title and Department
1922–1943	L. J. O'Rourke, PhD	Director of Personnel Research, USCSC
1944–1947	Thomas L. Bransford, PhD	Chief, Test Development, USCSC
1948–1949	Dorothy G. Adkins, PhD	Chief, Test Development, USCSC
1950–1962	John F. Scott, JD	Chief, Test Development and Occupational Research Section, USCSC
1962–1971	Albert P. Maslow, PhD	Chief, Personnel Measurement Research and Development Center, USCSC
1972–1974	John S. Howland, PhD	Chief, Personnel Research and Development Center, USCSC
1974–1979	William A. Gorham PhD	Director, Personnel Research and Development Center, USCSC
1980–1989	Helen J. Christrup, MA	Director, Personnel Research and Development Center, OPM
1989–2000	Marilyn K. Gowing, PhD	Director, Personnel Research and Development Center, OPM
2000–2003	Donna J. Gregory, MA	Associate Director, Personnel Resources and Development Center, OPM
2003	Brian S. O'Leary, PhD	Acting Supervisor, Personnel Resources and Development Center, OPM
2003, March 1	Brian S. O'Leary, PhD	Director, Assessment and Training Assistance Services Group, Division for Human Resources Products and Services, OPM

Note. The content for this table was provided by Lorraine Eyde.

Name Index

Subject Index